From Mediation to Nation Building

From Mediation to Nation Building

Third Parties and the Management of Communal Conflict

Edited by Joseph R. Rudolph, Jr. and William J. Lahneman

LEXINGTON BOOKS
Lanham • Boulder • New York • Toronto • Plymouth, UK

Published by Lexington Books
A wholly owned subsidiary of The Rowman & Littlefield Publishing Group, Inc.
4501 Forbes Boulevard, Suite 200, Lanham, Maryland 20706
www.rowman.com

10 Thornbury Road, Plymouth PL6 7PP, United Kingdom

Chapter 14 "Somalia: Intervention in Internal Conflict" by David D. Laitin from *Military Intervention Cases in Context for the Twenty-First Century*, Rowman & Littlefield, 2004.

Chapter 15 "Intervention in Internal Conflict: The Case of Bosnia" by Steven L. Burg from *Military Intervention Cases in Context for the Twenty-First Century*, Rowman & Littlefield, 2004.

British Library Cataloguing in Publication Information Available

Library of Congress Cataloging-in-Publication Data Available

ISBN 978-0-7391-7694-8 (cloth : alk. paper)
ISBN 978-0-7391-7695-5 (electronic)
ISBN 978-1-4985-5655-2(pbk:alk, paper)

™ The paper used in this publication meets the minimum requirements of American National Standard for Information Sciences—Permanence of Paper for Printed Library Materials, ANSI/NISO Z39.48-1992.

Printed in the United States of America

Dedication

In memory of the lost opportunities in life as in peacemaking, I dedicate this book to GG, AR, and W. Marvin Will (1937-2006), who in a kinder world would have been an important contributor.

Joseph R. Rudolph, Jr.

I dedicate this book in loving memory to my parents, Bill and Kay Lahneman.

William J. Lahneman

Contents

Dedication v
Acknowledgments xi

1 Introduction: Communal Conflict and Third Party Intervention in a "Responsibility to Protect" World 1
Joseph R. Rudolph, Jr.

Part 1. Diplomacy

2 "Peace Without Victory:" The Promise and Constraints of Third-Party Mediation in Civil Wars 19
Paul T. McCartney

3 Ending the "Troubles": Brokering Peace in Northern Ireland 33
Elham Atashi

4 Implementing the Liberal Peace: Observations from the Field 55
Linda S. Bishai

5 Election Observers, Democratization, and Preventive Diplomacy 69
Joseph R. Rudolph, Jr.

Part 2. Legal Approaches

6 International Law and Internal Conflicts 83
I.M. Lobo de Souza

7 Turbulent Transition: From the UN Human Rights Commission to the Council 99
David P. Forsythe

8 Transitional Justice in Divided Societies: Using Hybrid Courts to Manage Conflict 127
James DeShaw Rae

Part 3. Economic Measures

9 Economic Instruments of Internal Conflict Resolution 145
Stephen D. Collins

10 Externally Mandated Economic Liberalization and the Onset of Civil Conflict 171
Matthew Hoddie and Caroline Hartzell

11 Conditional Conditionality: The European Union, International Justice, and the Democratic Transition in Serbia 189
Victor Peskin and Mieczysław P. Boduszyński

12 The EU and Roma Rights 211
Neil Cruickshank

Part 4. Military Operations and Communal Conflict

13 Military Intervention as a Tool of Conflict Resolution and Institution Building 235
William J. Lahneman

14 Somalia: Intervention in Internal Conflict 257
David D. Laitin

15 Intervention in Internal Conflict: Lessons from Bosnia and Kosovo 273
Steven L. Burg

16 The Bosnian Intervention: Stabilization Without Guidelines 303
Brigid Myers Pavilonis

17 Rebuilding a Democratic Iraqi Police Force: The Effects of the Militia on the Rebuilding Process 317
DiJon Jones

18 Security Without Weapons: Nonviolent Peaceforce in Sri Lanka 333
M.S. Wallace

Part 5. Mentoring, Political Tutelage, and Nation-building as Tools of Conflict Prevention and Management

19 Third Party Nation-Building Today: Fifth Time Charmed? 355
Joseph R. Rudolph, Jr.

20 "Nation Building" and Democratization in Afghanistan: The Need to Rethink the "Democratic Reconstruction Model" 369
Mohammad Ashraf

21 International Intervention and Ethnic Tolerance in Bosnia-Herzegovina: Evidence from Public Opinion 389
Sam Whitt

22 Whither Sovereignty? The Limits of Building States through International Administrations 419
Mateja Peter

23 Bosnia-Herzegovina and the Development of Democratic Policing 439
Donald R. Zoufal

24 NGOs, Peace Support Activity, and the UNPREDEP Mission in Macedonia 463
Daniela Irrera

Part 6. Conclusion

25 Conclusions: Third Parties and the Management of Communal Conflict 481
William J. Lahneman

Bibliography 491
Index 523
About the Contributors 531

Acknowledgments

No book writes itself, and certainly not an edited volume, which always depends more on its contributors than its architect-editors. So, we begin at the obvious point, with deep thanks to the contributors to this volume, many of whom have been with us virtually from the book's inception and early organizing panels at the meeting of the Central and Eastern European International Studies Association (CEEISA) in Wroclaw in 2008, the Global International Studies Conference in Ljubljana in 2009, and the New Orleans meeting of the International Studies Association in 2010, or participated in the final panel leading to the book at the CEEISA's 2011 meeting in Istanbul. To those who served as commentators on those panels, we also remain grateful.

As the book developed, and the need to include specific additional chapters from practitioners as well as academics became clear, it gradually filled out as others graciously consented to join in the project. And if the final product seems unduly weighted towards the harder forms of third party efforts to manage ethnic and national conflict, and to the Balkans in location, it is primarily because it has been the military and state-reconstruction efforts that have dominated in the recent past, and the Balkans where the greatest concentration of challenges initially appeared.

With two exceptions, the chapters that follow were written for this volume, some based on previously unpublished data. In the former case, we wish to express our appreciation to Rowman and Littlefield for permitting the re-publication of Professor Laitin's chapter on Somalia, and Oxford University Press, Inc. for allowing the amended reprint of Professor Forsythe's chapter, which initially appeared in its *Encyclopedia of Human Rights* (copyright 2009). As to the latter, we are particularly grateful to the United States Department of State for making available for publication the data contained in Professor Whitt's chapter on Bosnia-Herzegovina, and the United States Institute of Peace for allowing one of its senior analysts, Linda Bishai, to publish her reflections on its work in Sudan.

Beyond our contributors we also owe our sincere thanks to those in the wider academic community whose advice we have sought and who have given it freely during the development of this volume, as well as to our home university for its direct (sabbatical leave) and indirect (convention travel grants) support of this project. Even closer to home we wish to express our most sincere gratitude to our department's graduate assistant, Anneliese Johnson, without whose invaluable aid in the final editing of this volume it might well still be in preparation. Finally, collective thanks to our editors at Lexington Press for their encouragement, assistance, and patience during the past year. Whatever mistakes may exist are solely ours.

Finally, and more individually, I would like to express my appreciation to the Fulbright Association, the United States Department of State, and the Organization for Security and Cooperation for the opportunities that they have given me to conduct research and participate to a very limited degree in democratization projects in the Balkans, and to Chris Hall, President, and Brian Bowen, Provost, for their hospitality and encouragement while at the American University of Kosovo on a Fulbright appointment during the fall of 2011.

On behalf of my co-editor and co-contributor, William J. Lahneman, and myself,

Joseph R. Rudolph, Jr.
Baltimore, October, 2012

Chapter 1

Introduction: Communal Conflict and Third Party Intervention in a "Responsibility to Protect" World

Joseph R. Rudolph, Jr.

The eruption of highly visible humanitarian crises and exceedingly bloody civil wars during the early 1990s in the Horn of Africa, imploding Yugoslavia, and Rwanda set in motion a trend toward third party intervention in communal conflicts in areas as far apart as the Balkans and East Timor. Haltingly and selectively, that trend is still discernible, motivated as it was during the 1990s by the inability of in-house accommodation methods to resolve ethno-political conflicts peacefully and the danger of such conflicts spilling into the international system in the form of massive refugee flows, regional instability, and failed states hosting criminal and terrorist elements. In its various forms, third party intervention has become a fixed part of today's international system. This chapter explores that development. The remainder of this volume focuses on the roles that third parties have played and the tasks that they have undertaken over the past two decades in their efforts to reduce conflict and, sometimes, to reshape parts of the political world.

The Changing Character of Conflict and Conflict Management

Humanitarian military intervention in civil wars, as well as less costly and less intrusive third party efforts to manage communal conflicts, have some of their deeper roots in the changing nature of warfare after World War II. Prior to 1940, the majority of wars were waged across international boundaries by rival states. A shift away from such interstate warfare to intrastate conflicts embodying varying degrees of violence, however, occurred almost immediately after World War II, even as the major rivalry in global affairs became the Cold War between the United States and Russia, backed by their respective allies. Hence, of the 225 armed conflicts identified as occurring between 1946 and 2001, according to one major study nearly three quarters (163) were intrastate in nature and only 42 conformed to the earlier pattern of interstate conflict.[1] That percentage has remained relatively constant throughout the first decade of the 21st century. As the *Conflict Barometer* report for 2010 noted, of the 363 crises, wars, and other conflicts that it chronicled for that year, 269 (74.13%) were intrastate and only 94 were interstate.[2]

A variety of explanations have been offered to explain this shift, including the dawn of the nuclear age. Given the danger of violent interstate conflicts escalating into global thermonuclear war, the argument runs, states began searching for less dangerous modes of warfare. Thus was born the international civil war in which countries fight one another inside a particular country—for example, Israel and Syria dueling in Lebanon—rather than across international frontiers. Iran's arming of religious paramilitaries in Iraq as a means of attacking the United States through make-shift proxy armies would fit into this mode. Nonetheless, a greater explanation for the changing nature of warfare lies in the changing nature of international actors after 1945. With decolonization, which significantly began with the partition of the Indian sub-continent into India and Pakistan, the character of the countries composing the world took a sharp turn away from the prototypical nation-state of the western world toward a world of multinational states whose citizens not only vary significantly in culture, but often have long standing histories of animosity towards one another. Walker Connor summarized the consequences of this trend in his landmark essay on "The Politics of Ethnonationalism," noting that by the 1970's less than a third of the states composing the world could be fairly labeled nation-states composed of a single political community whose members identified with one another as a nation and with the government as their government. In the remainder, multiple, politically self differentiating peoples co-exist, their separate sense of self kept alive by differences in language, religion, history, ethnicity, and perhaps physical appearance.[3] Twenty years later, this trend continued when the partition of Czechoslovakia, the violent breakup of Yugoslavia, and the implosion of the Soviet Union combined to produce slightly under 25 new states, most of which contain at least one significant national or ethnic minority.[4]

Furthermore, although not all intrastate conflicts are necessarily violent, the evidence is strong that most of the violent conflicts tend to be intra-state. Heidelberg's Institute for International Conflict Research's 2008 report was particularly telling. In addition to noting that of the cases it logged overall, 254 were intrastate and only 91 were interstate, it emphasized that "intrastate conflicts accounted for the vast majority of violent, and especially highly violent conflicts. . . . Eight of the nine wars as well as all of the 30 severe crises were conducted within a state."[5] The latter is not surprising. On an average, 40% of the most violent intrastate conflicts reportedly involved a struggle for control of territory; that is, secession-born, intrastate wars involving territorialized national minorities seeking self-determination. In states where the center is too weak to suppress the rebellion and the separatists are too weak to succeed, these wars often become very prolonged in nature.

The Intractability of Communal Conflict

Managing conflict in the volatile world of multiethnic and multinational politics is a challenging undertaking at the outset. Relatively few multinational states, especially in the developing world, are blessed with an excess, or even an adequacy of wealth that can be used to co-opt minority leadership or accommodate groups feeling alienated from or discriminated against by the political process. Where it does exist—for example, Nigeria's oil resources—ugly conflicts can ensue over its control or distribution. Even after more than a half century of independence, trust in authority, the rule of law, and domestic institutions of conflict resolution remain weak in many states. Where it has been established, it has often been shattered in ethnic conflicts that have tribalized bureaucracies, police services, courts, and military services, or destroyed them during ethnic civil wars.

There is also the problem of communal conflict itself. Ethnic and nationalistic demands are frequently expressed in zero-sum terms even in the developed western world, whose states enjoy high levels of literacy and affluence, whose societies are organized around such communally cross-cutting cleavages as class, gender, and age structures, and whose peoples are normally heirs to a history of political accommodation. Thus, between 1970 and 2000 five western democracies (Canada, Belgium, Spain, Switzerland, and Britain) found it necessary or useful to revise their constitutions in order to accommodate ethnoterritorial communities composing them.[6]

The probability of intractable ethnic or national conflict substantially increases where experience with political tolerance is low, cross-cutting ties are weak, ethnic, religious, economic, and regional cleavages reinforce one another, and economic prosperity and the stabilizing influence of a large middle class is a rarity. In such an environment, the wedding of ethno-communal grudges to nationalistic aspirations can produce a destructive offspring of considerable longevity. Indeed, it is the emotional nature of the demands raised by conflicting communal groups which often places communal conflict outside the normal channels of cost-benefit analysis, accommodative politics, and conflict resolution. In international as in domestic politics, disputes are most likely to be settled when conflicting interests can be objectively addressed and resolved or at least managed by redressing the grievances of the "injured" party without jeopardizing the security of others. Yet, in instances of communal conflict it is sometimes difficult to find a genuine interest in negotiating issues on the basis of objective criteria. Those feeling wronged—or their leaders who have achieved influence by exploiting that sense of injury—may demand compensation for previous injustices as well as responses to present issues. Meanwhile, dominant groups may fear that should they concede any ground they will only whet the appetites of those whom they have mistreated during the past.

Even where good will exists, the mechanics for finding a mutually satisfying solution can be difficult, especially where minority and majority communities are so intermingled as to preclude a viable territorial approach to conflict management by granting local autonomy to aggrieved groups or federally reorganizing the state along ethnoterritorial lines. The odds against resolving the conflict peacefully become longer still when there is a deep sense of insecurity in both camps because each can envision itself in a minority condition within a slightly broader context. Efforts to resolve the United Kingdom's "Irish Question" were thus historically frustrated by not just the fact that Ulster's Protestants were separated from its Catholics by ethnic origin, religion, and political preference (Unionists versus Nationalists), but also by the fact that although the Protestants long constituted a solid majority in Ulster they would represent less than a quarter of the population in a united Ireland. A more recent manifestation of the same mathematical conundrum can be found in Kosovo, which is celebrated by its Serbs as the ancient birthplace of the Serbian nation, and by its Albanians as the birthplace of Greater Albanian nationalism (in Prizren during the mid-19th century). United with Serbia, the province's Serbs would be the majority community; in Kosovo, whose independence has now been recognized by most western states, they constitute less than 5% of the population and would be only a fraction of that were the country's more radical Pan-Albanian party ever to succeed in linking Kosovo to Albania and the heavily Albanian areas of western Macedonia.

Finally, the mediation of communal conflicts too often is handicapped by the degenerative dynamics of inter-communal warfare. Once the threshold of political violence is crossed, communal conflicts tend to escalate rapidly, often being conducted by paramilitary irregulars with little regard for the established rules of warfare and capable of committing great atrocities, as occurred during the wars in Croatia, Bosnia-Herzegovina, and Kosovo during the 1990s. Because the domestic forces for conflict resolution (e.g., the political class, the local police, the military) often have already been tainted or overwhelmed by communal politics by that point, the nature of the situation becomes a problem in its own right. Such conflicts may even, as noted at the outset, quickly become international in nature or implications, with refugees spilling over interstate boundaries into neighboring states, the contending groups reaching outside their borders to find sponsors, and/or the rival groups being encouraged or manipulated by outside forces.

The Drift toward Extra-Systemic Options

For the reasons already noted, to a large extent the demands of ethnic and national groups in the established democratic world have been subject to accommodation by a series of in-house responses. Often, the groups have essentially sought a greater or different set of governmental *outputs*; for example, affirmative action programs or the right to teach in their minority languages. On other occasions they have focused on achieving a greater share of decision-making *authority*; for example, by an adherence to the principle of proportionality or equality in Cabinet membership and in the upper rungs of bureaucratic and military leadership. Whether satisfied legally or by convention, management devices of this nature exact a higher cost on the establishment than reallocating the outputs of government; however, they have usually, if reluctantly, been conceded because they are less costly than contending with continuing minority grievances or the escalating demands of frustrated minorities.

Still more costly to accommodate have been those demands centering on the structure of the *regime*. Usually raised by territorialized political (if not numerical) minorities seeking more control over their affairs, these demands focus on shifting the state's structure in the direction of ever more peripheral forms of federalism; that is, from a centralized unitary state to one devolving authority to regional structures, from the latter to a federal system, and within an existing federation to enhancing the federal unit's autonomy.[7] To be sure, even in the developed world there have also been, and still remain, protracted conflicts over the very definition of the *political community* and groups focused on separatism that have rarely been initially susceptible to accommodation. But conflicts of this nature—most notably involving Basque separatism in Spain during the latter years of the last century—have been the rare exception in the established democracies of the economically and politically developed western world.

By contrast, since decolonization and the later emergence of the newer multinational states in the former communist world, ethnonational conflicts have often been precisely about what constitutes *the* political community, and the right of nationally self-differentiating communities to choose in what state they want to reside, including a new state of their own. The dominance of such community-centered politics in these areas, the continuing presence of protracted conflicts elsewhere, including conflicts such as that between Greek and Turkish Cypriots over the future of that island have gradually shifted ethnic and national conflict-management processes toward a growing number of unconventional and/or extra-systemic approaches and outcomes.

Table 1 enumerates the principal systemic and extra-systemic "options" that states, international organizations, and discontented minorities have pursued over the last two decades in dealing with ethno-political conflicts. Included as well are outcomes that can hardly be called "management devices" and that have been thoroughly condemned and sometimes prosecuted by the international community. Some of this activity involves decisions voluntarily and more or less amicably reached by the parties to the dispute in an effort to resolve or manage it in a controlled if sometimes unconventional manner; for example, the decision to split Czechoslovakia into two states.[8] Other examples would include the Indian-Sri Lankan Accord and the Good Friday Agreement in Ulster, both of which involved bringing outsiders into the management process, with unsuccessful results in the first case but a more positive outcome in the latter. Also falling into this loose category would be the willingness of many states in the European Union prior to the September 11, 2001 terrorist attack on the United States to "upload" decisions involving the immigration of non-EU citizens and their rights in EU member states to the EU's decision-making bodies in Brussels. These options, however, have also been of an imposed and coercive nature; for example, when outside force has been used to restore order where governments have been unable to accommodate or repress successfully the demands of a militant ethno-political community and the dispute has escalated towards civil warfare. (See Table 1)

Table 1. Systemic and Extra-Systemic Responses to Communal Conflict

Mode of Response	Examples
A. Systemic Responses	
1. Ignore or Challenge the legitimacy of ethnonationalists	Policy of governments in Spain, Britain, France, and Belgium prior to 1970
2. Accommodation of Demands	
a. Output concessions	Increased economic assistance for Wallonia; Welsh-language television programming for Wales
b. Authority concessions	Adoption of linguistic parity as basis for Belgium's Cabinet in the 1970's; appointing a black Justice to U.S. Supreme Court
c. Regime modification	Regionalization of policy-making in Belgium during 1980s; federalization in post-Franco-Spain
B. Extra-Systemic Responses/Outcomes	
1. Separation	
a. Negotiated Division	Creation of two states from Czechoslovakia
b. Successful secession	Separation of Baltic Republics from former Soviet Union

2. Unrestrained Civil War	Yugoslavia-Serbia-Croatia-Bosnia-Herzegovina conflict
3. Unrestrained Border Conflicts	Armenia-Azerbaijan conflict over Nargono-Karabakh
4. Peacekeeping Coping Mechanisms	Northern Ireland; Cyprus; Kosovo forces
5. Treaty Arrangements providing outside Guarantors of minority rights	British Treaty with Ireland concerning Ulster's Catholic minority
6. Non-codified International Pressure	EU, UN, and US pressure on post-communist states to alleviate anti-Romany discrimination
7. International Tutelage and Community Building activity	Post civil war Bosnia-Herzegovina and Kosovo
8. Bribery	France offering foreign workers cash to return to their home states in the 1970s
9. Forced Expulsion	Uganda's expulsion of Asians under Amin
10. Genocide	Rwanda, 1994

Third Party Involvement in Communal Conflict: a Growth Industry

The involvement of third parties as stabilizing forces in the politics of other states is hardly new.[9] As an essay in this volume notes, the Concert of Europe deployed election observers more than a century and a half ago to validate voting outcomes, and the deployment of troops during colonial times to quell riots and restore order was not limited to the British *Raj* in India and Britain's mandate in Palestine. Similarly, after World War II the United States was instrumental in helping the Italian Christian Democratic Party secure control of Italian politics, and during the 1950s and 1960s former colonial powers not infrequently deployed forces to shore up the successor regimes in their former holdings. Likewise, on the multinational front the United Nations sent peacekeeping forces to deal (unsuccessfully) with tribal warfare in the Congo in 1960, and its essentially successful peacekeeping mission in Cyprus has been in place since 1964.[10] What *has* changed is the widening scope and altered nature of third party efforts to manage communal conflict.

The most common extra-systemic devices, as well as the fastest growing area of extra-systemic conflict management, are our focus here: those involving the diplomatic, legal, economic, and military-political efforts of third parties to manage intra-state conflicts that Article II (7) of the United Nations Charter once was interpreted to put off limits because they fell "essentially within the domestic jurisdiction" of the state.[11] Civil wars, in particular, prior to the 1990s were routinely viewed as falling under this provision, and a state's treatment of its minorities short of genocide was rarely considered a fit subject for diplomatic commentary. Indeed, as David Forsythe summarized in the midst of the Cold War, "The main intent of traditional international law of civil war was to urge restraint and nonintervention by third parties."[12] Today, however, in a truly significant shift in interpretation in a short period of time during the 1990s, international law does not just permit intervention in civil wars when the conflict becomes "internationalized" as a result of human rights violations. It also threatens those committing such acts with prosecution and imprisonment for war crimes by the International Criminal Court in the Hague, itself an outgrowth of the first court of this nature, which emerged as a result of the carnage in Rwanda and provided the precedent for creating a similar international tribunal following the atrocities committed during the wars in the former Yugoslavia.[13] Likewise, the rights of internal minorities have been often internationalized by treaties like the European Convention on Human Rights, Hungary had no second thoughts when it threatened to hold up Slovakia's admission to the Council of Europe because of the manner in which the Slovak Republic was treating its Hungarian minority, and both NATO and the EU during the 1990s threatened to withhold the admission of Central European states because of their discrimination against their Romany minorities.

The Lure of Humanitarian Intervention

Perhaps above all, contemporary third party efforts to manage conflict represent a significant departure from those of the past in terms of procedure and justification. When the British sent troops to Jordan to bolster that country's shaky regime in the mid-1950s, and India sent 80,000 of its troops to Sri Lanka to quell what Prime Minister Gandhi termed the "inter-mestic" civil war there in the late 1980s, it was at the request of the regimes, and heed was still paid to the diplomatic protocols involved in deploying troops on the territory of a sovereign state. Likewise, UN peacekeeping forces in the Sinai (1956) had to be approved by Egypt before they could be deployed on its soil, and could be invited out at any moment by that state, as occurred in 1967 when President Nasser demanded their removal. By contrast, UN actions in the former Yugoslavia and the 1999 NATO operation involving Kosovo did not involve such requests but rather rested on the grounds that because of ongoing human rights violations contrary to international law, military intervention on humanitarian grounds was justified in a world where the powerful bear a responsibility to protect the weak.[14] Moreover, these military actions have usually been coupled with post-conflict democratization and state- and community-building efforts. Collectively these peace*making* and "peacebuilding" operations now constitute by far the most ambitious of the extra-system conflict management devices involving outside parties.[15]

This shift in focus—or at least in justification—to humanitarian grounds as the basis for hard power intervention in ethnic and national conflicts has, in turn, opened two doors: one to non-state actors becoming an increasingly common part of the scene; and the other to the need for often prolonged, post-conflict peace-building efforts designed to protect minorities by erecting genuine democratic institutions in a frequently grudge-filled, unstable postwar environment.

The presence of humanitarian non-government actors in theaters of war as well as postwar settings is hardly new, of course. The International Red Cross began its operations in 1863 and won its first Nobel Peace Prize for tendering aid to the battlefield wounded in World War I. But in the contemporary world it is not unusual to find scores of NGO's present in the initial rebuilding operations of war ravaged areas like Kosovo, Iraq, and Afghanistan, with many lingering for years in semi-peaceful zones like the Palestinian areas occupied by Israel. And, as the essays in this volume by Daniela Irrera and Molly Wallace attest, the range of their activities has steadily widened.

Meanwhile, the shift in mandate from just ending hostilities to providing for a safe postwar environment respectful of human rights and the rule of law has necessitated a variety of tasks more reminiscent of United States efforts to rebuild and restructure post-World War II Germany and Japan than prior, multinational peacekeeping or—in the case of the UN's enforcement action in the Gulf War—military efforts. Economies have had to be salvaged, necessitating grants and loans from such international bodies as the EU and the IMF, and the luring of corporate actors. Constitutions have had to be written and political parties formed under the guiding hand, or at least with the heavy advice of states, NGOs, and international organizations with frequently differing objectives and competing ideas. Paramilitaries have had to be disarmed, streets made safe, refugees returned to their homes wherever possible, and local court systems and police forces constituted, often from the ground up. Meanwhile, the tools themselves, from soft to hard options have to be scrutinized in the hope of finding the best option for a particular task. In the process, troops, diplomats, construction companies, and humanitarian organizations invariably co-mingle and sometimes collide in the resultant environment to the point that coordinating their activities on the ground has become an issue in its own right. Moreover, the differing parties have often chosen different strategies in attempting to do so.[16] On occasion, considerable, systematic efforts have been made to organize things by delegating specific tasks to the different entities, most notably in Bosnia-Herzegovina (BiH) and Kosovo. There, overall political control was assigned to UN personnel (the Office of the High Representative [OHR] in Bosnia-Herzegovina and the UN Mission in Kosovo [UNMIK]), security was placed essentially in the hands of NATO (IFOR and later SFOR in BiH and KFOR which is still present in Kosovo), democratization fell to the Organization for Security and Cooperation in Europe (OSCE) in both countries, the EU and its member countries were to assume primary responsibility for economic reconstruction, and humanitarian relief was heavily left to the NGOs. Often, however, the flaws in the design have readily become apparent, as Mateja Peters notes in her study of OHR. Even more often, coordinating plans have been absent or flawed from the outset, with a resultant jumble of actors operating on different planes in what Muhammad Ashraf's essay on Afghanistan suggests are doomed "nation-building" efforts.

The expansion itself of third party activity beyond the older, preventive diplomacy mode of peacekeeping activity reflects the already noted fact that in most post civil war areas communal warfare has destroyed the legitimacy of the pre-existing institutions for conflict control, if not those institutions themselves. Thus, while the reconstruction processes are underway, these duties—enforcing the peace, instituting court proceedings, *etc.*—often fall on the intervening parties, especially where delicate tasks must be performed as part of a peace settlement agreement; for example, the repatriation of internally displaced peoples and refugees to their former homes in zones which have been ethnically cleansed. In Bosnia-Herzegovina and Kosovo, the UN has additionally undertaken tasks of political tutelage akin to those previously farmed out to individual states under its (and its predecessor League of Nations') mandate system. Indeed, in the case of Bosnia-Herzegovina, at this writing, the OHR still exercises control over the process of democratization, complete with the right to dismiss elected officials.[17]

As for the increasing frequency and costly nature of such intervention, the changing nature of United Nations' peacekeeping operations during the past twenty years paints a clear picture. Prior to 1990, with the notable exception of the Congo and Cyprus operations, UN peacekeeping activities were primarily of a preventive diplomacy nature; that is, they focused on preventing conflicts from rekindling by placing a thin line of peacekeeping forces between belligerents along established cease-fire lines or in demilitarized zones. They have often been of long duration (UN peacekeepers, for example, have been in Kashmir since 1947, Korea since 1950, and Cyprus since 1964); however, because prior to 1989 UN peacekeepers were normally deployed to maintain an *existing peace*, the missions rarely utilized more than a few hundred troops. In fact, of the twenty-six peacekeeping missions that the UN undertook between 1947 and 1992, only the 1960-1964 Congo operation required more than six thousand troops, and the twenty thousand troops deployed there were not enough for success because the UN found no peace to keep in that civil-war torn, former Belgian colony.

By contrast, Congo-like environments were frequently a common characteristic of UN missions during the 1990s, when—flush with success from its enforcement activity against Iraq in the 1991 Gulf War—beginning with the ill-fated mission in Somalia the United Nations launched more "peacekeeping" ventures than it had during its first forty-seven years of existence. In truth, many were peacemaking outings, and the deployment of insufficient numbers of, and/or inadequately armed peace-makers to accomplish their missions quickly led to embarrassment in the former Yugoslavia, where a detachment from the

Indian sub-continent was taken prisoner by one of the warring parties. Consequently, mission size increased substantially during the 1990s along with the danger of the mission. Many—most notably the UN Operation in Somalia, the protection and stabilization forces in Croatia and Bosnia-Herzegovina, and NATO's still functioning stabilization force in Kosovo—involved the initial or eventual deployment of twenty thousand or more troops into highly dangerous theaters of war. There, in seeking to enforce status quo cease-fire lines or curfews in dynamic situations where the status quo was often *the* issue, the peacekeepers themselves frequently became part of the conflict, causing some donor states to reconsider committing their forces to such risky undertakings.[18] Moreover, although often justified as humanitarian intervention, these deployments increasingly came to support the principle of minority self-determination, in stark contrast to the western world's earlier, anti-separatist stance in favor of a state's territorial integrity.[19]

Managing Ethnic Conflict in Today's World: A Continuum of Intrusiveness

Our intent here is to explore these changing developments affecting outsider responses to communal conflict and efforts to manage it in the contemporary world. Essays are organized around the broad categories of available options, explored in terms of—generally speaking—the costliness and intrusiveness of third party activities to donor and recipient states alike. The costliness of any form of third party intervention to the third party and its intrusiveness in the political process of the recipient state and the affairs of its political communities are obvious. Soft power options such as student exchanges[20] and diplomatic initiatives, for example, impinge less on the budget of third parties and are less politically invasive in the domestic affairs of a recipient state than formidable economic assistance and the strings likely to be attached to it. Similarly, the step from economic to military involvement constitutes a major escalation in costliness in terms of money, manpower, and human risk for the outside party and often signals or acknowledges a loss of political control by the recipient state.

In turn, that loss or qualification of political control can be costly in the long term as well as the short term to local political actors. At this writing nearly a dozen years have passed since Serbia was forced to allow UN and OSCE personnel, and a NATO-dominated military force admission to its Kosovo region, and nearly five years have passed since the region was permitted to declare its independence. Yet it would be political suicide for any Serbian politician to recognize Kosovo's independence, however sincerely the EU might offer membership in return for such a move. Meanwhile, the more heavily a third party invests in restoring order and democratizing an area like Kosovo, the more that involvement can become politically intrusive into the third party's political system. The fear of the region succumbing again to communal warfare if peacekeeping forces are removed can clash with the need to establish the timetables for withdrawal that are politically popular and perhaps electorally necessary on the home front. And no incumbent wants to admit to having made an error in making such a major commitment to begin with, given the risks attendant to admitting to costly mistakes if they want to stay in office.

As a framework for discussion, we have thus organized the collected essays on the advantages and limits of various tools for managing communal conflicts on the basis of the increasing costs and levels of intrusiveness involved in moving from diplomatic to legal options, and from legal options (excluding the ICC) to economic involvement, and from the carrots and stick options of economic tools to the overtly hard power options of military and all-out political involvement in the conflicts troubling a foreign state. (See Table 2). Before moving to those essays, though, we would offer three qualifying observations with respect to our approach.

Table 2. Common Instances of Third Party Intervention

Diplomacy	Legal Instruments	Economic Tools	Military Intervention	Political Tutelage
Mediation Election Monitoring	Rules of Warfare Treaties; ICC Prosecution	IMF Loans Strings on EU membership	Peacekeeping Peacemaking Side-taking	Institution-building Democratization Veto on activity
Low <		Cost and Degree of Intrusiveness		> High

First, obviously not all third parties who operate in and perhaps significantly affect policy in foreign countries are public actors or NGO's any more than all third party public actors that do so are concerned with managing ethnic conflict. Multinational corporations, in particular, have a long history of backing political parties and otherwise involving themselves in domestic politics and/or playing states off against one another in order to get their best deal in investing abroad and protecting their business operations once established. In fact, the need to attract private capital can lead states to alter profoundly their policies, as the government of Georgia found it useful to do during the last decade. There, not only have corporate profits been capped at a low 20% tax rate and export and practically all import duties removed, but the labor market has been "liberalized" back to turn of the last century in America, with the repeal of minimum wage laws and a marked absence of regulations governing hiring, layoffs, and firings. Policies of this nature have little to do with reducing communal violence. Indeed, to the extent that they disproportionately benefit or handicap one community over another, a multinational corporation's arrival on the scene may actually aggravate conflict.

Secondly, the lines between the diplomatic, legal, economic, military, and political tools of conflict management pursued by states, international organizations, and NGO's are anything but hard and fast. Often they reinforce one another to the point where it becomes hard to say whether, for example, the EU's threat to withhold the economic benefits of membership to states unwilling to address discrimination against the Romany was an economic or diplomatic tool of statecraft. Likewise, the use of military power—for example, NATO's bombing of Serbian artillery during the summer of 1995—has historically opened the door to the diplomatic "settlement" of disputes, and to the entry of outside overseers of those settlements, as in the case of Bosnia-Herzegovina in the negotiation and execution of the Dayton Peace Accord discussed by Steven L. Burg in this volume.

Finally, because the management of ethnic conflict is not necessarily a geographically uniform undertaking inside a country, not only is it possible to find multiple actors executing related tasks in a given area at the same time, but it is not unusual to find that the focus is on different tasks in different areas at the same time. Economic restructuring under World Bank directives and overall UN supervisions in a secure climate maintained by peacekeeping forces, for example, may be simultaneously occurring in one zone while military units are still combating paramilitaries in an attempt to pacify another part of the state. Or, as was the case in Kosovo following NATO's 1999 bombing campaign against Serbia and the return of hundreds of thousands of Kosovar Albanians from Macedonia and Albania, NGO's may be immediately busy coordinating the return of one component of an area's multinational population while others languish in impoverished refugee locales abroad.

Notes

1. Nils Petter Gleditsch, Peter Wallensteen, Mikael Eriksson, Margareta Sollenberg, and Havard Strand, "Armed Conflict 1965-2011: A New Dataset," *Journal of Peace Research,* 39, no. 5, (2002): 615-637, 620. See also Monty G. Marshall and Ted Gurr, *Peace and Conflict, 2005: A Global Survey of Armed Conflicts, Self Determination Movements and Democracy* (College Park, Md.: University of Maryland Center for International Development, 2005), and Kristine Eck, "A Beginner's Guide to Conflict Data: Finding and Using the Right Dataset." Uppsala Conflict Data Program Paper # 1 (December, 2005), at http://pcr.uu.se/digitalAssets/18/18128_UCDP_paper1.pdf.

2. Heidelberg Institute for International Conflict Research, *Conflict Barometer 2010: Crises, Wars, Coups d'Etats, Negotiations , Mediations. Peace Settlements, 19th Annual Conflict Analysis*: 1-2, last accessed 6 December 2011 at http://hiik.de/en/konfliktbarometer/.

3. Walker Connor, "The Politics of Ethnonationalism," *Journal of International Affairs*, 27, number 1 (1973): 1-22.

4. The exact number of these new states is intentionally left vague. The peaceful partition of Czechoslovakia into two countries, each with a significant Roma minority

and one (Slovakia) with a large Hungarian minority, added one new country to that list. The case of Yugoslavia is more muddled. Slovenia may be considered a nation-state given the departure of most of its Serbs; however, Montenegro and Serbia are at least multiethnic, and Croatia, Bosnia-Herzegovina, and Macedonia are multinational in nature and troubled by that factor. So, too, is Kosovo, but some might argue that the fact it has thus far been recognized by only a minority of the countries in the world requires at least an asterisk in listing it among the states composing the contemporary multination world.

5. Heidelberg Institute for International Conflict Research, *Conflict Barometer 2008: Crises – Wars – Coups d'Etats – Negotiations – Mediations – Peace Settlements, 17th Annual Conflict Analysis*: 2, last accessed December 6, 2011 at http://hiik.de/en-/konfliktbarometer/pdf/ConflictBarometer_2008.pdf.

6. Canada revised its federal structure to give greater power to Quebec province than that enjoyed by other units in the Canadian federation, Belgium began dismantling perhaps Europe's most centralized unitary state in a federalist direction in which Brussels, Flanders, and Wallonia would eventually enjoy far-reaching autonomy, Spain found it necessary to create a federal system to accommodate its Basque and Catalonia regions as it democratized following Franco's death, Switzerland split its predominantly German-speaking canton of Bern in two in order to placate the French-speaking majority in its Jura region, and – in the late 1990s – Britain's Labour government honored its pledge to create assemblies in Wales and Scotland. For details concerning the developments in Belgium, Spain, Switzerland, and Canada during the 1970-1990 period, as well as an examination of the devolution issue in Britain at that time, see Joseph R. Rudolph, Jr. and Robert J. Thompson (eds.), *Ethnoterritorial Politics, Policy, and the Western World* (Boulder, Co: Lynne Rienner, 1989).

7. See Joseph R. Rudolph,, Jr. and Robert J. Thompson, "Ethnonational Movements and the Policy Process: Accommodating Nationalist Demands in the Developed World," *Comparative Politics*, XVII (April, 1985):291- 311.

8. On the unique set of circumstances which explain the willingness of Czech and Slovak leaders to divide their state peacefully into two republics ("the Velvet Divorce"), see this author's treatment of Czecho-Slovak politics in Joseph Rudolph, *Politics and Ethnicity: A Comparative Study* (New York: Macmillan/Palgrave Press, 2006): Chapter 7.

9. For a broader and quantitatively supported discussion of this topic in the post-World War II setting, see Renata Carbetta, "Determinants of Third Parties' Intervention and Alignment Choices in Ongoing Conflicts, 1945-2001," *Foreign Policy Analysis*, VIII (January 2010):61-85.

10. For an overview of 20th century UN peacekeeping operations, see Barbara Benton (editor), *Soldiers for Peace: Fifty Years of United Nations Peacekeeping* (New York: Facts on File, 1996).

11. The key text of Article 2(7) stipulates that outside of Security Council enforcement action "Nothing contained in the present Charter shall authorize the United Nations to intervene in matters which are essentially within the domestic jurisdiction of any state."

12. David P. Forsythe, "UN Peacekeeping and Domestic Instability." *Orbis*, XV (Winter, 1972):1064-1084, 1064.

13. On this shift in the nature of international law, see especially Josh Delbruck, "A Fresh Look at Humanitarian Intervention Under the Authority of the United Nations," *Indiana Law Journal*, LXVII (1992):887-901, and Ruth Gordon, "United Nations Intervention in Internal Conflicts: Iraq, Somalia, and Beyond," *Michigan Journal of International Law*, XV (Winter, 1994).:519-546. Concerning the long struggle to

prosecute war crimes, see Kingsley Moghalu, *Global Justice: the Politics of War Crimes Trials* (Stanford, CA: Stanford University Press, 2008). On the ICC, see Kate Mackintosh, "The Development of the International Criminal Court," *Humanitarian Exchange Magazine*, Issue 32 (December, 2005) at http://www.odihpn.org/report.asp?id =2767.

14. For follow-up reading on the link between humanitarian action and the growing number of peacekeeping missions written at the time, see Jan Eilasson, "Humanitarian Action and Peacekeeping," in Olara A. Otunnu and Michael W. Doyle (eds), *Peacemaking and Peacekeeping for the New Century* (Lanham, MD: Rowman & Littlefield, 1998): 203-213.

15. For a European perspective on the growth of humanitarian intervention in the 1990s, and "parallel concepts like responsibility to protect and obligation to interfere," see Ander Gutierrez-Solana, "From Kuwait to Myanmar: New Challenges for Humanitarian Intervention," a paper presented at the 2009 Convention of the International Studies Association, available on-line in the Archives of the International Studies Association. The quotation is on page 26. For a discussion of the need to keep humanitarian intervention in its proper place as a "minor but honorable" piece of foreign policy that "must be gauged on the balance of values and interests, ideals and reality, what is right and what is prudent," see Alexander M. Haig, Jr., "The Question of Humanitarian Intervention," *Foreign Policy Research Institute Wire* 9, no.3 (2001), at http://www.fpri.org/fpriwire0902.haig.humanitarianintervention.html.

16. See, for example, Gorm Rae Olsen, "Civil-military cooperation in Crisis Management in Africa: American and European Union Policies Compared," *Journal of International Relations and Development*, v.14, 5 (July, 2011): 333-353. For a broader discussion of EU activities in the field, see Eva Gross and Ana Juncos (editors), *EU Conflict Prevention and Crisis Management: Roles, Institutions and Policies* (London: Routledge, 2011).

17. This power to dismiss elected officials deemed uncooperative was used not infrequently during the early period of establishing Bosnia-Herzegovina's governing bodies under the terms of the 1995 Dayton Accord,; however, it has been ever less frequently invoked since that time. The influence of the United Nations' overseer of the Dayton Accord is well treated by Mateja Peter in this volume.

18. On peacekeepers becoming a part of the conflict, see this author's "Intervention in Communal Conflict," *Orbis*, XXXIX, 2, (1995):259-273. To UN and NATO missions can also be added OAU intervention in civil wars in Africa, and the Russian-led, Commonwealth of Independent States (CIS) peacekeeping activity in Georgia's breakaway regions and the separatist Transnistria area of Moldova. Awareness of the costliness of these ventures in terms of money, time, and sometimes lives curtailed the launching of new ventures of this type even before the United States and its allies invested their military assets in the wars in Afghanistan and Iraq. In the 1990s, however, there was considerable optimism about what international organizations and other third parties could do to remold President George H.W. Bush's post-soviet, "new world order." See, for example, Larry Diamond, *et al* (eds.), *Consolidating the Third Wave Democracies* (Baltimore, Md.: The Johns Hopkins University Press, 1997), Carnegie Commission on Preventing Deadly Conflicts, *Preventing Deadly Conflict: Final Report with Executive Summary* (New York, NY,: Carnegie Corporation, 1997), Elizabeth M. Cousens, *et al*, *Peacebuilding as Politics: Cultivating Peace in Fragile Societies* (Boulder, CO.: Lynne Rienner, 2000), Jocelyn Coulon, (Phyllis Aronoff and Howard Scott, translators), *Soldiers of Diplomacy: the United Nations Peacekeeping and the New World Order* (Toronto: University of Toronto Press, 1998), and Robert I. Rotberg (ed.),

Vigilance and Vengeance: NGOs Preventing Ethnic Conflict in Divided Societies (Washington: Brookings Institution Press, 1996).. For less glowing critiques of UN activity and a less optimistic assessment of the potential of peacekeeping forces to resolve ethnonational conflict, see, respectively, Ted Galen Carpenter, *Delusions of Grandeur: the United Nations and Global Intervention* (Washington, DC: the CATO Institute,1997), and Gidon Gottlieb, "Nations Without States," *Foreign Affairs*, LXXIII, (1994):100-112.

19. For a discussion of the argument that "The evidence that democracy almost never works in societies that are highly divided along linguistic and cultural lines is overwhelming," see Michael Lind, "In Defense of Liberal Nationalism," *Foreign Affairs*, LXXIII, (May-June, 1994) 87-99 @ 95. For a broad analysis of the (then) unfolding trend towards supporting secession in the name of self-determination, see Morton H. Halperin, David J. Scheffer, and Patricia L. Small, *Self-Determination in the New World Order* (Washington, DC: Brookings Institute Press, 1992).

20. See Carol Atkinson, "Does Soft Power Matter? A Comparative Analysis of Student Exchange Programs 1980-2006," *Foreign Policy Analysis*, VI (January 2010):1-22.

Part One

Diplomacy

Chapter 2

"Peace without Victory:" The Promise and Constraints of Third-Party Mediation in Civil Wars

Paul T. McCartney

Among the many redolent phrases bequeathed by Woodrow Wilson to posterity, "peace without victory" has acquired, along with "a war to end all wars," a naïve ring to modern ears. Wilson coined the term during his speech to the Senate on January 22, 1917, in which he articulated the liberal principles of his envisioned postwar international system. Arguing that a peace imposed through force of arms would be "accepted in humiliation, under duress, at an intolerable sacrifice, and would leave a sting, a resentment, a bitter memory upon which terms of peace would rest," he concluded that "only a peace between equals can last."[1] As we all know, Britain and France did not share Wilson's understanding of how wars should be settled, and they imposed on Germany onerous terms that indicated that World War I did indeed have victors. It is not surprising that France and Britain pursued victory in the war, nor that they sought to punish their conquered foe. After a war ends, one expects its winners to take advantage of their position by dictating the terms of the new reality created by their triumph. And yet, when supporters of diplomatic solutions propose to end civil conflicts through outside mediation, they are hoping that the conflicting parties will forgo their chance to fashion their state's postwar politics and accept instead the Wilsonian offer of a peace without victory.

For reasons that will be explained, Wilson's offer only produces its intended result under limited conditions, many of which are beyond the mediating actor's capacity to change. Most importantly, unless the parties engaged in a civil conflict are prepared to make peace, they will not try to do so. Political scientists analyzing third-party diplomatic interventions into civil conflicts have found the following variables to be related to a successful mediation. First, the timing must be ripe. If the actors believe they have a chance to win, they pursue victory rather than peace. Second, the mediator must have the "right" identity in order to move a peace process forward, although different identities are useful in different contexts. Third, the strategies and goals pursued in the course of mediation efforts can increase the likelihood of success in some cases. Outside parties can rarely help alleviate the deeper underlying issues that prompted the hostilities, but they can foster negotiating conditions that make a peaceful resolution more likely. By focusing their efforts on facilitating dialogue rather than "fixing" structural causes, third party mediators can help civil war participants to approach peace if they are ready to do so. Whether those efforts are likely to yield a lasting peace or a mere respite from the violence is another question.

This chapter will focus on the diplomatic efforts of third-party actors to help broker peace agreements between civil war participants, with some attention given to ethnic conflicts, whose characteristics magnify the challenges endemic to all civil conflict resolutions. In addition to examining the role of third party states in mediation, this chapter will briefly consider the efforts of non-state actors, who have become increasingly important players in this field. Given the nature of civil wars (if one is taking place, then we are dealing with a situation of maximum dysfunction) any lasting solution must ultimately reflect a fundamental change in both the broader situation and in the attitudes of the actors. Despite the long odds of success and the relative modesty of that success which is immediately attainable due to third-party diplomacy, those efforts are worth engaging. Easing or ending the horrific violence of ethnic conflicts justifies any effort that has a chance of working.

Baseline Conditions for Ameliorating Ethnic Violence

No matter who ultimately intervenes in a civil conflict and what strategies they employ, peace will not result unless the conditions are ripe for a mediatory resolution. Indeed, offers of mediation are unlikely even to be considered in the absence of the necessary baseline conditions, which include the sense that a prolonged and costly stalemate is likelier than a victory (usually due to a rough balance of power between the combatants), a willingness of both sides to make concessions, the absence of secessionist aspirations, and a willingness to work with the prospective mediator, among others. Typically, these conditions require that a certain amount of time has already elapsed in the conflict before outside offers of mediation will even be entertained, although powerful states can sometimes exert sufficient influence through military intervention to "persuade" actors to come to the negotiating table.[2] This section surveys the factors contributing to the sense that a civil conflict is "ripe" for mediation.

Civil wars differ from interstate conflicts in ways that present special challenges to all aspects of conflict resolution, including getting the process started.

In the absence of outright conquest and annexation, which is an increasingly rare occurrence in international politics, any interstate conflict will end as it began, with two actors that regard each other with more or less mutual hostility occupying their own states. By contrast, in the case of civil conflicts and excepting successful secessionist wars, which are the hardest to resolve, the combatants will have to learn to co-exist within the same polity upon the conclusion of hostilities, a prospect that shapes how they approach the peace process. Interstate wars can end in a stalemate, with the combatants retreating behind internationally recognized juridical boundaries, but this luxury is unavailable in intrastate wars.[3] Instead, civil conflicts that are stalemated are almost certain to resume in some guise as long as the underlying grievances are unresolved, since groups who have begun the process of "othering" and then killing each other are unlikely to move forward as if nothing had happened. This situation creates sensitivities that are absent in interstate conflicts.

In particular, there is often a heightened atmosphere of distrust and guardedness, as a unilateral initiation of the mediation process would potentially leave the initiating group vulnerable to the other by signaling weakness; a combatant with a reasonable prospect of victory is not ordinarily disposed to seek a compromise solution.[4] Prematurely inviting mediation can thus inspire increased aggression from the other side and make the situation worse. This pervasive fear of exploitation means that both sides must be willing to seek mediation simultaneously.[5] Even when the parties agree to accept mediation, ongoing fears of exploitation complicate the peace process, because a failed negotiation leaves each party vulnerable to the other in future iterations of the conflict due to the fact that both sides can gain information about the other's weaknesses during negotiations.[6] This situation typically requires that an outside party provide security guarantees before negotiations can proceed.[7] Consequently, third party states offering a diplomatic intervention in a civil war must often be prepared to provide more extensive management of the conflict zone than would typically be expected with interstate wars. Third parties with little or no stake in the conflict state are thus less likely to offer their services to the combatants, and even those with reason to get involved will be more cautious in choosing to do so.

Other challenges to initiating conflict resolution relate to the reasons why the war started. One major cause of civil conflicts is "distributional deprivation," which is often structured around ethnic differences. In these cases the government privileges one or more segments of society over others. Another cause is a rebel group taking advantage of weak governance to assert economic independence around a particular region or resource.[8] As long as rebels continue to profit from their control of extractable resources, which can in turn be funneled into additional arms purchases, they are likely to forgo negotiations.[9] Whether the issue is distributional deprivation or rebel profiteering, the solution to the conflict will build around resource distribution. These conflicts are susceptible to mediated outcomes that can be presented as more profitable than continued fighting.[10] Conversely, one side or the other will resist peace efforts as long as war serves its economic interests.

Simple cost-benefit analysis, therefore, will often determine whether a mediation offer will be solicited or accepted. Sometimes, the costs of continued fighting no longer feel justified, and the parties feel compelled to seek resolution. Since the government party in the conflict usually has the most to lose in a negotiated settlement because it will lose its putatively preexistent monopoly on power under any circumstances short of victory, mediation becomes more attractive only in proportion to the government's sense that its prospects for victory are in irreversible decline.[11] Under almost any circumstances, in fact, governments will be inclined to reject dispute resolution, since any process involving outside actors tacitly legitimates the rebels simply by giving them a seat at a negotiating table that also includes members of the world community. Belligerency's formal status under international law is not one that state actors are interested in conferring on their own citizens. The state actor in a civil conflict, therefore, will resist outside diplomatic overtures for as long as possible.[12] For the nongovernmental forces in cases of distributional deprivation, meanwhile, acceptance of outside diplomatic efforts towards peace implies a willingness to continue living in a state whose regime has already demonstrated a willingness to forcibly and systematically deny its economic interests. Rebel profiteers similarly see little incentive to transfer their wealth-generating enterprises within the state. For all actors, in short, acceptance of mediation signals resignation that a jointly defined, hence suboptimal, change in conditions presents the best possible outcome. Participants who have made the plunge into civil war do not arrive easily at this point.[13] It is its own form of surrender. But sometimes, all sides will conclude that the benefits of continued fighting are just not worth it anymore. That is when mediation first becomes possible and, as discussed below, the duration of the war factors into this assessment.

Once ethnic identity is incorporated into a conflict dynamic, resolution becomes much more difficult, as at least one axis of difference becomes inherently fixed. According to Jacob Bercovitch and Karl DeRouen, Jr.,

> For a conflict to be described as ethnic, the parties involved would have a sense of collective and separate identity, common ancestry, a shared culture and history, and an attachment to a specific piece of territory. An ethnic conflict is thus a conflict that involves two or more groups who inhabit a common region, have many features in common, yet each perceives itself to be different, is seen by others as different, and where one or more of the groups has a strong sense of grievance (about cultural, political, or economic resources).[14]

Unlike narrowly economic disputes, those rooted in identity are not readily amenable to compromise. As a result, ethnic conflicts last longer than others.[15] Post-conflict coexistence is least tolerable in these types of wars, especially for minorities, but the alternative of a secession is the outcome least likely to be accepted by state parties. It is therefore unsurprising that the word used most often in the literature to describe ethnic conflict is, "intractable."[16] Neither side is likely to find the motivation to seek peace or agree to the conditions on which such a peace might be built. Moreover, because ethnicities commonly spill across borders, such conflicts frequently become internationalized. As a result, the imperative to find a solution to them is typically greater than in other civil conflicts.

The time eventually arrives when mediation becomes a viable option. When this moment arrives, all three parties (the two in conflict as well as the potential mediator) must recognize it and be ready to act.[17] Upon arriving at this juncture, each side in the conflict must not only be prepared to make concessions to the other, but also be willing to signal to its foe that it has arrived at this point; as already indicated, a combatant who is open to making concessions communicates potential weakness, so this can be a delicate moment.[18] It means that rough power parity (and its recognition) between the two sides is typically one precondition for negotiations.[19] Another precondition is that the conflict has gone on long enough that both sides have lost their illusions that a quick and easy victory is possible,[20] but not so long that the sunk costs are too high.[21] Finding the sweet spot in a civil war's duration thus seems critical when evaluating its prospects for successful diplomatic resolution. Unfortunately, that time can often be recognized only retrospectively.

Much also depends on the mediator as well. At a minimum, actors hoping to facilitate a peaceful solution to a civil conflict must recognize the unique features of the situation they are addressing. The complexity of civil conflicts, involving as they do all layers of a given society, typically means that outside actors will face serious challenges in understanding all facets of the conflict.[22] The particularities of a given conflict (for example, whether it is driven primarily by ethnicity or by rebel greed) will determine the best strategies for managing it, and third parties must be willing to adapt their goals and strategies accordingly.[23] Sometimes, the outside actor will conjoin mediation strategies with economic or military intervention in order to create the power parity required to coerce acceptance of a bargaining offer. As discussed below, third parties act from a variety of motives, and they represent the full spectrum of international actors. Their identities help shape the strategies pursued in the peace process, and, if properly tailored to the circumstances of the case, can influence the prospects for peace.

Third Parties: Who Are They?

All civil conflicts, but ethnic conflicts in particular, include structural characteristics that make it almost impossible for the actors involved to deal with each other diplomatically without the assistance of a third party. Among the outside actors who engage in third-party mediation are states, IGOs, and NGOs, some of which (e.g., the Carter Center) exist primarily to perform this function on the world stage, and others of which have broader portfolios. Intergovernmental organizations such as the United Nations can intervene diplomatically without the taint of ulterior motive that sometimes attaches to states. Similarly, nongovernmental organizations, including religious groups, can bring an aura of neutrality and a sense of purpose that established political actors have difficulty emulating. Nevertheless, states remain the most important actors in this field, and a majority of this analysis will concern both the contributions they can make to civil war resolution and constraints they face in their efforts to do so.

States are self-interested actors, so any state that is willing to intervene diplomatically in another state's civil conflict can be expected to have an interest of some sort in resolving the situation. Mediation is different than traditional diplomacy, which Hans Morgenthau describes as "nothing but a symptom of the struggle for power among sovereign nations."[24] This description does not always describe the kinds of motivations that inspire states to mediate the internal conflicts of others, which can include humanitarianism or altruism, reputation building, geography, historical ties, or a vested interest in one side's victory.[25] States in the geographic vicinity of a civil war are likely being harmed by spillover effects of the war. States in such a position, as well as states with formal ties to the conflict state (usually via an alliance relationship), have the strongest incentives to intervene for purely self-interested reasons. They frequently serve as mediators. Historical linkages that inspire mediation offers include religious affiliation, shared membership in past or present empires (such as the United Kingdom or the Soviet Union), and former colonial relationships. These kinds of ties can enhance trust and communication, although conflict states are apt to reject a mediation offer from a former colonizer.[26] When states have historical ties with one another, they become more inclined to offer, accept, or solicit mediation. The self-interest of the outside party in this case may not be material, but rooted in domestic politics, regional interests, or the sense that the state's reputation might be implicated by inaction. The self-interested basis of states' offers to mediate, however, has the effect of reducing the chance that peripheral states will gain much outside attention, especially from great powers.

In general, though, great powers regularly participate in third party diplomacy. Several possibilities might account for their involvement, including the increased chance that they will have an interest in the conflict, whether for trade, alliance, or other reasons; the superior leverage that they have available for pressuring the two sides to make concessions; their ability to coerce participation in a peace process, either by creating power parity by assisting the weaker (usually rebel) side or by threatening to do so; and their desire to preserve a reputation for shaping international politics. Their track record is mixed. On the one hand, the ability of great powers to extract concessions and provide credible security guarantees is sometimes the only thing that will bring parties to the table, as in the case of the ongoing involvement of the United States in the Israeli-Palestinian conflict, where Arab and Palestinian negotiators recognize that no one else could possibly induce Israel to make any sacrifices.[27] Great powers are also uniquely capable of providing the kinds of security guarantees that are needed for mediation to begin. On the other hand, the coercive methods they occasionally use can lead to superficial peace agreements that do not hold.[28]

Even when they achieve their goal of stopping the killing without resort to coercive methods, great powers often produce a superficial, hence temporary, peace. Sometimes, though, states, including great powers, gain a reputation for effectiveness in helping settle intrastate conflicts. When these states offer to mediate conflicts, their invitation is likely to be accepted if the right conditions are in place.

The critique that great powers produce only temporary solutions to conflicts applies as well to those states whose primary motivation is reputational. For these intermediating states, as long as hostilities cease, they can mark another notch in their belt. This leads to the paradoxical situation in which biased mediators, who are motivated by self-interest and are more supportive of one side in the conflict than the other, often produce deeper and more lasting solutions to civil conflicts than neutral mediators (including non-state actors), who seek instead to develop a name as peacemakers. States can be biased in favor of either the rebels or the government; in either case, they have credibility when negotiating as a result of their ability to speak for "their side" during times when they cannot or will not speak for themselves. The interest of biased mediators in creating a lasting peace (since a mere cessation of active hostilities does nothing to help their long-term stake in the situation) often leads them to participate in institution-building processes and other actions reflecting a more than passing involvement in the issue.[29]

Non-state actors offer a different set of qualities than states; some are conducive to generating lasting solutions to a conflict, others limit their ability to alter the underlying dynamics. Track 2 practitioners, as non-state participants in conflict resolution are called, do not act on behalf of states, although they often cooperate with them. (Track 1 actors represent states and speak for their interests.) In cases of Track 1 and Track 2 coaction, state representatives will typically engage the leaders of the conflicting parties, while non-state actors will seek to influence mass opinion in order to cultivate confidence in the prospect of sharing a state upon conclusion of hostilities.[30] When multiple actors work together to settle a conflict, it is vital that they have a unified message even if their efforts are targeted at different constituencies and their motivations differ.[31] In addition to working side-by-side with states, Track 2 negotiators will sometimes act independently. Those who engage in mediation include (in addition to IGOs and NGOs): private citizens, religious organizations, government workers acting in a private capacity, business groups, media outlets, and educational institutions.[32] The most active and effective practitioners of Track 2 diplomacy, however, are the United Nations, the Catholic Church, and the Organization for African Unity (OAU). The OAU has a regional mandate to intervene diplomatically throughout a continent where the opportunities to do so are unfortunately plentiful, the Catholic Church has a formal religious bond with many actors engaged in civil conflicts, and the UN can bring unique capabilities to bear in any conflict situation.[33] It merits additional comment.

The United Nations is seen both as impartial and as representing the aspirations of all peoples. As such, it can carry unusual influence in negotiations, particularly in ethnic conflicts.[34] Unlike the situation with neutral state actors, the UN's lack of bias is not seen as encouraging stopgap solutions crafted to enhance its reputation. Instead, the United Nations is often welcomed as a third-party diplomatic intervener because it is a world organization dedicated to a stable global peace, with additional foci on development and other strategies designed to address the underlying causes of conflict. Its assets are several. For example, the UN is well suited to deter outside parties from intervening in a conflict who might destabilize or otherwise worsen the situation. In addition, it has the tools not only for peacekeeping operations, but also for mediating or arbitrating conflicts, facilitating communication between the parties, providing humanitarian assistance (which can reduce tensions in addition to serving as an end in itself), and assisting in post-conflict peace-building.[35] It can also coordinate other actors willing and able to contribute to a lasting settlement, including states, regional IGOs, NGOs, and other private actors, such as religious organizations.

Religious organizations provide another distinctive approach to mediation. While their strategies overlap with those employed by other mediating agents, their moral authority can prove unusually compelling in the right circumstances. Edward Luttwak summarizes their ability to contribute to peacemaking as follows:

> The conflict-resolution efforts of religiously motivated third parties can do more than merely offering a negotiating mechanism, a method of communication, or any such procedural assistance. By introducing the authority of religion into the negotiating equation, they enable the parties, if they so desire, to concede assets or claims to that authority itself. . . . Concessions previously regarded as intolerable evidence of a lack of fortitude, may become politically acceptable if they can be presented as acts of deference to religion. . . . By thus reducing the vulnerability of rulers and governments on each side to accusations of weakness, the range of politically feasible negotiating positions is expanded, more options for solution become available, and the chances for reaching a settlement are increased accordingly.[36]

As is the case with other third party negotiators, the qualities that allow religious organizations to mediate effectively are not restricted to intrastate conflict, but they can prove especially valuable in such localized conflicts when considerable religious overlap among the parties exists. Such has often been the case in Latin American civil conflicts. Even where religious diversity not only exists but exacerbates a conflict, as in Nigeria or Southeast Asia, neutral religious bodies can still command considerable moral authority.

Non-state actors depend for their success on this moral authority, but aside from the United Nations and major regional organizations like the OAU, they lack the material resources that conflict resolution can require. States, meanwhile, are often most effective when they are seen as biased, although examples of successful nonbiased mediation by states also exist. States, especially great powers, also have sufficient power and will to alter the dynamics on the ground.

Unlike most non-state actors, they can offer security guarantees, thus creating the space needed to engage in negotiations. The wide range of actors, as well as the diverse reasons underlying their motivations and effectiveness, attests to the complexity of civil conflicts, and especially ethnic conflicts. Context-sensitive approaches are therefore essential to any successful mediation effort. In addition, the role of third parties as mere facilitators of the effort to create enduring structures of peace (a task that must be primarily undertaken by the war's participants themselves) limits the range of strategies that can ordinarily be expected to contribute to a conflict resolution. Nevertheless, if third parties are not a sufficient cause of peace, they often prove to be necessary.

Strategies for Successful Third Party Interventions

The primary contribution that mediators can make to ending a civil war is to generate communication where it was previously absent. The mere presence of mediators signals that a war is entering a new phase, because it means that the combatants have arrived at the point of thinking that ending hostilities has become conceivable and possibly even desirable.[37] But direct talks between the two sides is sometimes impossible for a variety of reasons. In these cases, third parties serve as go-betweens. And where direct talks are possible, they still require an outside presence to set the terms of the discussion and keep the talks on track. Third parties who intervene diplomatically in a civil war, then, do not typically bring civil wars to an end as much as they create the conditions in which the combatants themselves can end them.

Mediation is a nonbinding, noncoercive, and nonviolent form of intervention.[38] Jacob Bercovitch and Karl DeRouen define it as, "a process of conflict management where the disputants seek the assistance of, or accept an offer of help from, an individual, group, state, or organization to settle their conflict or resolve their differences without resorting to physical violence or invoking the authority of law."[39] Mediators can mitigate the anger of the combatants by helping to clear up misconceptions about intentions and other sources of anxiety. The nonbinding nature of their proposals allows dialogue to take place in an atmosphere of decreased tension. This lowering of the perceived stakes in turn can foster creativity and a willingness to entertain options, at least in the abstract, that might have been suppressed in an arbitrated or adjudicatory setting.[40] Mediation can in this way alter the combatants' understanding of the range of possibilities before them.

In the absence of mediation, the goal of combatants is to misrepresent every aspect of their intentions and capabilities in order to enhance their prospects for victory. With the shift in goals from victory to peace that occurs at the mediating moment, the requirements of dialogue must adjust accordingly, and third parties serve an indispensable function in allowing this transformation to occur.[41] As

Patrick M. Regan and Aysegul Aydin write, "Absent an outside intervention. . . neither side has a unilateral incentive to honestly convey its military capabilities, expectations of victory or defeat, or the value of a settlement that it would accept for fear of exploitation by its adversary."[42] Over time, the diplomatic dance that mediators conduct can build trust, without which no settlement would be possible in the first place. As noted, unlike with interstate conflicts, civil wars require combatants to live and work together at their conclusion, so the peace process must begin the process of recreating the trust that lies at the heart of community. Mediators' ability to foster open communication where it was previously impossible thus represents a crucial contribution to moving war-torn societies back to normalcy.

Conflict situations typically proceed in stages, and third parties (especially Track 2 actors) can intervene at any one of them. Before conflicts get "hot," third parties can assist in "provention," or inhibiting the development of conditions that accelerate the outbreak of active violence, and prevention, which takes place during the period when hostilities have started to turn violent but are still short of full-blown war. Provention can include diplomacy, but its emphasis is more on development; prevention, meanwhile, features more intensive diplomatic efforts. Interventions, when outside parties provide economic or military inducements to stop fighting, can follow if earlier efforts have failed; these can be accompanied with diplomatic campaigns aimed at creating either a peace settlement or a conflict resolution. Peace settlements, which are also called conflict suspensions, are temporary and are typically marked by a formal cease fire; conflict resolution requires a more comprehensive approach to the crisis and aims at recreating conditions within the state that will allow for a lasting peace. Finally, outside parties can assist in post-conflict reconstruction, which involves stabilizing social cohesion and building durable institutions to deter a future outbreak of violence. This stage often overlaps with provention in societies suffering through recurrent cycles of violence.[43] Quite often, the best a third party can hope to achieve is a peace settlement. If the parties are not ready for a more comprehensive agreement, then they cannot be forced to accept one. In addition, unless an outside party has developed a strong interest in the conflict state, the level of commitment required to advance from conflict suspension to resolution might exceed its endurance.

If the goal of the diplomatic intervention is conflict resolution, then societal reconstruction becomes necessary. Non-state actors can prove especially useful in these contexts. Some debate surrounds whether retributive or restorative justice better serves the prospects of peace; retributive justice involves holding accountable those who have committed atrocities, while restorative justice programs aim to move the state beyond its dark days of conflict by providing amnesty for the transgressors. That debate, however, is beyond the purview of this analysis. Of note for present purposes is that third parties are usually required to help implement whichever system of post-conflict justice the state seeks, in addition to the comprehensive social rebuilding that accompanies it.[44] Diplomacy during the conflict stages helps the combatants to recognize the prospects for realizing either justice program, thus enabling an end to the active violence. Ending the violence, in other words, becomes intertwined with other, broader issues during many diplomatic interventions.

Fostering fruitful rather than perfunctory communication between the combatants can serve many important goals, and third parties can help achieve it in various ways. For example, simply providing a neutral setting for the parties to meet can remove an important obstacle to negotiations.[45] Mediators can also encourage combatants explicitly to embrace cooperation as a goal, share information about compromises they might be willing to consider for their shared post-conflict society, and communicate the limits of their willingness to deal with the other side without necessarily escalating the conflict.[46] They can therefore create turning points in the negotiating process. Track 2 mediators, meanwhile, can lay the groundwork in the broader society to accept compromises made at the elite level that might have been hitherto framed as fundamentally unacceptable. They can also help to communicate the desire to compromise up the line, from the grassroots level to the negotiators' table. Third parties can thus generate a transitional social reality for a conflict society that bridges the existing state of mutual hostility and violence to a future postwar order that has prospects of being more stable and peaceful.

Track 2 diplomats employ many strategies to achieve their goals. In addition to sponsoring dialogues, meetings, and roundtables (i.e., formal communication), they sponsor joint projects, such as school building and other grassroots activities; engage in research and assessment; draft resolutions and occasionally small-bore statements of agreement; offer advising, consultation, and confidence-building services; train members of both sides for cooperative coexistence; and assist in post-trauma healing processes.[47] In conjunction with other activities, such as humanitarian assistance and reconstruction, these services can buttress formal diplomatic efforts and deepen ties between the combatants. Both Track 1 and Track 2 actors can also engage in diplomatic functions such as fact-finding or conciliation, which create factual and normative baselines upon which peace initiatives can build. Even where these diplomatic efforts fail to generate peace in the short term, they can plant seeds that future actors can nurture under more suitable conditions.

Conclusions

Ultimately, only the combatants can end their wars. If they believe they can win, they will likely fight on. Even if they do not necessarily believe they can win but refuse to compromise with the other side, they will fight on. If and when they become willing to sacrifice their larger goals in an effort to end the bloodshed, however, combatants can begin to grope towards peace. Third party diplomatic initiatives can play a significant role in facilitating their efforts. Especially where conflict resolution rather than conflict suspension is the goal, outside actors can only offer supplemental services. But these services can prove critical in allowing recalcitrant actors to transition from implacable mutual hostility to a more accommodating posture. States, and to a lesser degree the United Nations, can offer security guarantees that give actors the confidence to engage in sensitive negotiations, while non-state actors can assist both elites and mass publics in the difficult transition back to (semi-)normalcy. Third party diplomacy cannot bring lasting peace by itself, and it may offer only modest or temporary improvements in the situation on the ground, but without it, peace of any sort is frequently impossible. Combatants in a civil war will prefer victory to peace as long as they think the former is attainable, but once they begin to have their doubts, outside actors can bring about the needed transformation in social and political conditions to favor peaceful engagement. Typically, outside diplomatic interventions are only possible after considerable damage has already been done, but mediators have proven capable of not only helping to bring violence to a halt, but also helping the societies to heal in a war's aftermath. These efforts are to be commended and encouraged.

Notes

1. Thomas J. Knock, *To End All Wars: Woodrow Wilson and the Quest for a New World Order* (Princeton: Princeton University Press, 1992), 111-115.

2. J. Michael Greig and Patrick M. Regan, "When Do They Say Yes? An Analysis of the Willingness to Offer and Accept Mediation in Civil Wars," *International Studies Quarterly* 52 (2008): 759-81.

3. Mehmet Gurses, Nicolas Rost, and Patrick McLeod, "Mediating Civil War Settlements and the Duration of Peace," *International Transactions* 34 (2008): 132-33.

4. Greig and Regan, "When Do They Say Yes?," 762.

5. Greig and Regan, "When Do They Say Yes?," 766.

6. Isak Svensson, "Who Brings Peace?: Neutral versus Biased Mediation and Institutional Peace Arrangements in Civil Wars," *Journal of Conflict Resolution* 53 (2009): 451.

7. Gurses *et al.*, "Mediating Civil War Settlements," 135.

8. Jacob Bercovitch and Karl DeRouen, Jr., "Managing Ethnic Civil Wars: Assessing the Determinants of Successful Mediation," *Civil Wars* 7, no.1 (Spring 2005): 99; Gurses *et al.*, "Mediating Civil War Settlements," 139.

9. Patrick M. Regan and Aysegul Aydin, "Diplomacy and Other Forms of Intervention in Civil Wars," *Journal of Conflict Resolution* 50 (2006): 751.

10. Greig and Regan, "When Do They Say Yes?," 760.

11. Grieg and Regan, "When Do They Say Yes?," 760; Bercovitch and DeRouen, "Managing Ethnic Civil Wars," 100.

12. Raymond C. Taras and Rajat Ganguly, *Understanding Ethnic Conflict: The International Dimension* (New York: Longman, 2002), 98-99.

13. Greig and Regan, "When Do They Say Yes?," 765-66.

14. Bercovitch and DeRouen, "Managing Ethnic Civil Wars," 99.

15. Regan and Aydin, "Diplomacy and Other Forms of Intervention in Civil Wars," 751.

16. See Benedikt C. Harzl, "Conflicting Perceptions: Russia, the West and Kosovo," *Review of Central and East European Law* 33 (2008): 491-518; Bercovitch and DeRouen, "Managing Ethnic Civil Wars," 111; and Taras and Ganguly, *Understanding Ethnic Conflict.*

17. Gurses *et al.*, "Mediating Civil War Settlements," 135.

18. Greig and Regan, "When Do They Say Yes?," 760; Bercovitch and DeRouen, "Managing Ethnic Civil Wars," 104.

19. Greig and Regan, "When Do They Say Yes?," 761.

20. Regan and Aydin, "Diplomacy and Other Forms of Intervention in Civil Wars," 749, 751, and 753-54.

21. Greig and Regan, "When Do They Say Yes?," 777.

22. Bjorn Hettne and Frederik Soderbaum, "Intervening in Complex Humanitarian Emergencies: The Role of regional Cooperation," *The European Journal of Development Research* 7, no.3 (2005): 452.

23. Susan Allen Nan, Daniel Druckman, and Jana El Horr, "Unofficial International Conflict Resolution: Is There a Track 1½? Are There Best Practices?," *Conflict Resolution Quarterly* 27, no.1 (2009): 77.

24. Hans J. Morgenthau, *Politics among Nations: The Struggle for Power and Peace*, brief edition, revised by Kenneth W. Thompson (New York: McGraw-Hill, 1993), 373.

25. Svensson, "Who Brings Peace?," 447-48; Grieg and Regan, "When Do They Say Yes?," 763-64.

26. Greig and Regan, "When Do They Say Yes?," 778.

27. Harzl, "Conflicting Perceptions," 517-518; Svensson, "Who Brings Peace?," 449.

28. Svensson, "Who Brings Peace?," 448; Gurses *et al.*, "Mediating Civil War Settlements," 148; Bercovitch and DeRouen, "Managing Ethnic Civil Wars," 104; Greig and Regan, "When Do They Say Yes?," 761.

29. See Svensson, "Who Brings Peace?"

30. Nan *et al.*, "Unofficial International Conflict Resolution," 65-66.

31. Harzl, "Conflicting Perceptions," 502.

32. Nan *et al.*, "Unofficial International Conflict Resolution," 66; Amira Schiff, "'Quasi Track-One' Diplomacy: An Analysis of the Geneva Process in the Israeli-Palestinian Conflict," *International Studies Perspectives* 11 (2010): 97.

33. Greig and Regan, "When Do They Say Yes?," 770.

34. Bercovitch and DeRouen, "Managing Ethnic Civil Wars," 104.

35. Taras and Ganguly, *Understanding Ethnic Conflict*, 97.

36. Edward Luttwak, "Religion and International Affairs," in *Religion, the Missing Dimension of Statecraft*, eds. Douglas Johnston and Cynthia Sampson (New York: Oxford University Press, 1994), 17-18.

37. Gurses *et al.*, "Mediating Civil War Settlements," 136.

38. Regan and Aydin, "Diplomacy and Other Forms of Intervention in Civil Wars," 745.

39. Bercovitch and DeRouen, "Managing Ethnic Civil Wars," 101-102.

40. Gurses *et al.*, "Mediating Civil War Settlements," 131; Schiff, "'Quasi Track-One' Diplomacy," 95.

41. Svensson, "Who Brings Peace?," 463.

42. Regan and Aydin, "Diplomacy and Other Forms of Intervention in Civil Wars," 740.

43. Hettne and Soderbaum, "Intervening in Complex Humanitarian Emergencies," 453-55.

44. Svensson, "Who Brings Peace?," 452-53; Hettne and Soderbaum, "Intervening in Complex Humanitarian Emergencies," 451.

45. Bercovitch and DeRouen, "Managing Ethnic Civil Wars," 101.

46. Regan and Aydin, "Diplomacy and Other Forms of Intervention in Civil Wars," 738-742.

47. Nan *et al.*, "Unofficial International Conflict Resolution," 67-70.

Chapter 3

Ending the "Troubles": Brokering Peace in Northern Ireland

Elham Atashi

While the years following the Cold War have been marked with an increase in what has been regarded as intrastate violence, there has also been a significant number of conflict terminations. Conflicts have ended often as a result of diplomatic efforts and third party interventions in what has become known as a "peace process." Darby defines "a peace process as the cycle of activities necessary to produce a just and lasting agreement stretching from the actual period of negotiations and steps involved extending beyond the actual signing of an agreement."[1] This definition goes beyond traditional diplomatic methods to manage or terminate conflicts and focuses on efforts by all sectors of society to address the root causes. In general, a peace process can follow different phases including pre-negotiation, negotiation, ceasefire, agreement, post agreement, and peace-building.[2] Peace processes can be formal or informal, private or public, elite or grass roots, inclusive or exclusive, supported by international mediators or handled domestically. They can be enduring lasting years to generations or unstable and fragile faced with fierce opposition from spoilers leading to re-escalation of violence.[3]

Northern Ireland is often considered as an example of a successful peace process. The peace agreement ended what has been known as the "Troubles," referring to the outbreak of violent conflict since 1969. As soon as the Agreement was signed, literature began to circulate as to why, after so many years, the political conflict was finally over. Some argued that the Agreement came about because of the increasing level of intervention and influence by external actors, mainly the United States, Irish, and British Governments. Others argued that, similar to other intractable and long drawn out conflicts, the conflict in Northern Ireland had reached a stalemate and political parties lost trust in a successful outcome of their cause through violence. Thus, they attempted to reach their goals by negotiating with the other side. Some considered the significant role of the British Government and a shift in its policy due to changes in global trends that no longer deemed Northern Ireland a significant national security concern, particularly given the exhausting resources dedicated to dealing with the increasing security needs of the Island.[4]

This chapter assesses third party and mediation strategies, mainly by the United States, Britain, and Ireland, that successfully brokered a peace agreement in Northern Ireland. It traces the history of the conflict as well as previous peace initiatives that lay the foundation of what eventually became known as the "Good Friday Agreement." I argue that the Agreement was a historic political achievement bringing about an end to political violence. It came about as a result of several factors including the willingness of parties to accept third party intervention. The ceasefire and the peace process have ended the bombings, overt sectarian violence, and the way political conflict had been dealt with in the past. The example of Northern Ireland provides much insight in other contexts on the role of third parties in ending conflicts as well as the transformation of militant groups to political parties as in the case of the IRA.

A History of Divisions

The conflict in Northern Ireland is often defined in terms of its religious and sectarian nature. However, similar to other intrastate conflicts its cause is multilayered, deeply engulfed in a contested history and hostility between two distinct groups. While the conflict is rooted in identity, culture, and religious differences, this is somewhat misleading as competing aspirations of native and settlers, economic inequality, historical experiences, and political dynamics also play a role. The conflict is also embedded in collective memory as each group considers the other as the cause of the conflict and itself as a victim of violence.[5]

The terms Unionist and Loyalist refer to Protestants in Northern Ireland that support union with the United Kingdom.[6] Their history dates back to Anglo British control following King Henry's conquest of Ireland in 1171. A British policy in Ireland, known as the plantation of Ulster in the 16th century involved giving away lands that had been seized from the Irish people. The lure of free land encouraged the arrival of migrant Scottish and British settlers to the north of Ireland, Ulster. The Plantation plan was very successful in Ulster but had a negative impact on the lives of native Irish Catholics, causing deep resentment. By the 17th century the British had imposed a series of harsh penal laws aimed at diminishing the native Irish's social freedom and political power. These included denying them the right to vote, participate in parliament, own land, and teach or attain education. Some of the penal codes were eventually eased but by 1778, Catholics only owned about 5 percent of the land in Ireland. Deprived of their right to land, a series of rebellions ensued, eventually ending with their defeat at the Battle of Boyne in 1690. This victory is glorified among the

Protestants as their legitimate right to settlement and to this day is celebrated every year by the contentious Orange parades, where Unionists march through Catholic neighborhoods.

Economically, the linen factories, booming labor market, and industrial investment played a role in the British reliance on the region.[7] For the Catholics, the arrival of the settlers marks the beginning period of systematic occupation, deprivation, and intrusion into their culture, language, and religion.[8] By the 18th century the Protestants were a majority in the north of Ireland and wealthy landowners. But this did not ease their fears. The Unionists, though a majority in Northern Ireland, perceived themselves as a minority surrounded with a hostile Catholic majority in the south of Ireland opposed to their religion, heritage, and way of life.

The Nationalists and Republicans are Catholics who support self rule or union with the Irish Republic.[9] From their perspective, the conflict is rooted in the deliberate policy of discrimination and displacement of the natives. They justify their struggle against British colonization based on the history of collective political and economic deprivation.[10] The Catholics, the majority population in Ireland, soon found themselves as a minority marginalized from social and political power. A series of revolts for freedom from British rule and independence for the whole of Ireland led to the formation of the Irish Republican Army (IRA) with its political wing Sinn Fein (SF). The Irish Nationalists continued to claim their right to self determination and demand some form of self rule from the British government. By 1912, with the December 1910 election of the Liberal Party in Britain, the Irish Nationalists had hoped to secure a vote for some level of autonomy, known as Home Rule and the right to a parliament, but their hopes were dashed.

The Unionists rejected Home Rule and vowed to fight with armed resistance if independence was granted to Ireland. The Ulster Volunteer Force (UVF), the paramilitary faction of the Unionists, also made it known that they would oppose any attempt to introduce Home Rule, which they perceived as autonomy for Catholics in the form of an Irish Parliament separate from the United Kingdom.[11] The Nationalist movement for freedom was perceived as a plot to bring about a united Ireland that would leave the Ulster Unionists as a minority fearful of the millions of Catholics living south of their border.

Intense political revolt and escalation of violence on both sides eventually led to the partition of Ireland endorsed by the Government of Ireland Act in 1920. The island would be part of the United Kingdom but divided into a predominantly Catholic Irish Free State in the South, and Northern Ireland consisting of six of the nine counties in Ulster, with its Protestant majority. The creation of Northern Ireland was consistent with establishing a secure political homeland with a Unionist majority. Subsequent negotiations between the British government and Nationalists led to the first of many treaties known as the Anglo Irish Treaty. It established the Irish Free State as a self-governing territory and also provided Northern Ireland with an option to opt out of the Irish Free State, which it exercised. Later the south would gain its independence and become known as the Republic of Ireland in 1954. Northern Ireland, although remaining part of the UK was given its own parliament, the Stormont, with limited autonomy and ruled by the British parliament in areas of defense, income tax, and foreign policy. The Nationalists, now stripped of any political power, considered the partition of Ireland as illegitimate and this for many became the cause of reactionary violence by paramilitary forces.[12]

The newly created Northern Ireland consisted of a 60 percent Protestant population, leaving the Catholics as a minority. Their status as the majority meant that the Protestants had control of the Stormont parliament, whose seats were dominated essentially by a single party, the Ulster Unionists Party (UUP). The UUP remained the dominant political party for most of Northern Ireland's history, effectively ruling the Stormont for fifty years. With an electoral majority, support of the British government, and a largely Protestant police force—the Royal Ulster Constabulary (RUC)—the Unionists had guaranteed their identity and political ties to the United Kingdom. British government policies also favored the Unionists in housing, education, and employment.[13] Northern Ireland's status under British control and as part of the United Kingdom territory remained a contested issue.

"The Troubles"

Frustration with lack of political power, high unemployment, economic degradation, and inequality among the Nationalists led to a period known as the "Troubles." The "Troubles" does not necessarily refer to a specific time period or an event but a steady escalation of strategies by both sides to achieve their goals. It also marks an increase in the use of violence by paramilitary groups. By the 1960s hostility, fear, and intimidation had led to a widespread segregation of the two communities.[14]

To date, demographic segregation impacts all aspects of life from housing, employment, health, transport, recreation, and freedom of movement. Fear contributes significantly to the most basic choices, such as education and employment.[15] The systemic nature of segregation has historically led to the perception that the two communities are not able to coexist. Hence, segregation has been a means of conflict management, to keep the two communities separated. Despite the peace process, segregation remains a significant obstacle to peace and reconciliation on the ground.[16] Historically Unionist neighborhoods had received more government investment and housing assistance. This left Nationalists as an underdog class with communities in decline, overcrowded, and with little opportunity for employment.[17] The state controlled, predominantly Protestant educational system reinforced religious divisions, with Catholic children attending schools maintained by the Catholic Church and limited access to university education.

The system of segregation was further encouraged by the use of the so called "peace walls" that separate communities and minimize interaction. These are long cement or steel barrier walls used to ease tensions, protect neighborhoods from offenses from each other, and de-escalate violence. The first was built in 1969 as a buffer zone and a six months temporary measure, but due to their effective nature they became permanent structures. There are currently around eighty peace walls in Northern Ireland.[18] Markers such as displays of flags, paintings, and murals also cause intimidation and distinguish each community based on identity differences.

In the late 1960s, inspired by the freedom movements, particularly in the US, a new civil rights movement arose among the Nationalists with a focus on non-violent methods to end discrimination.[19] However, the pursuit of civil rights turned violent as riots and confrontation between Unionists and Nationalists turned Northern Ireland into turmoil. Soon thereafter the British army intervened to restore order and protect the Nationalist minority against attacks by the Unionists. Although this move was initially welcomed by the Catholics, who did not trust the Royal Ulster Constabulary (RUC), the local police force, the reaction soon turned negative as thousands felt themselves the victim of discrimination and unfair treatment by the British troops. The British army implemented curfews, raided homes, and imprisoned many Nationalists without trials. The last straw came with the violent intervention at a civil right protest in 1972 in which thirteen Catholic protesters were shot by British soldiers in a confrontation known as "Bloody Sunday." The soldiers claimed to have come under sustained attack by gunfire from the protesters, a claim that the Catholics deny. A follow up inquiry cleared British soldiers of blame on the grounds that those killed were in possession of arms. The escalation of violence and unrest that followed, led to increased activity by paramilitary groups on both sides. The RUC's inability to cope with what was increasingly shaping up to be a civil war ultimately led to the deployment of British troops.

This marked a significant date in Northern Ireland as it led to the suspension of parliament in Stormont and the introduction of Direct Rule by the British government. Thereafter, the "Troubles" dominated the history of Northern Ireland for thirty years and led to the death of 3,700 people and another 35,000 injured, a majority of which were civilians. During the Troubles, relations between the two communities became increasingly polarized. Escalation of paramilitary violence and membership in various militant groups on both sides also expanded rapidly. The IRA divided into factions, the more militant group of which was the Provisional IRA (PIRA), which emerged as a response to state violence against the Nationalists and with a more aggressive use of force and ideology than the IRA.[20] In presenting themselves as the direct heirs of Republicanism, the PIRA stressed the necessity of violence and a rejection of any sort of compromise with the British government.[21]

At the same time, Loyalist paramilitary groups also escalated their violent tactics, leading to the resurgence of the Ulster Volunteer Force (UVF) and formation of the Ulster Defense Association (UDA). In the period of 1968-1994,

Northern Ireland witnessed sectarian bloodshed and atrocities committed by both sides against each other. The conflict affected mainly people from deprived and poor working class backgrounds with most of the violence resulting in death occurring during the early and mid-1970s.[22] Given the small size of the population in Northern Ireland, one and a half million people, it has been estimated that the number of people closely associated to those who were killed or injured was about half the population.

Peace Initiatives

Northern Ireland's peace process was a culmination of years of secret talks, political negotiations, and third party intervention by the British, Irish, and US governments as well as the European Union. It was also the result of compromise by political parties and paramilitary organizations on both sides. Some attribute the success in ending the conflict to timing and the conflict's "ripeness" for intervention by third parties.[23] The concept of a "ripe moment" centers on the perception of a "mutually hurting stalemate" associated with the history of conflict or a recently avoided catastrophe.[24] From this perspective, parties resolve their conflict only when they are ready to do so and when they perceive that they are mutually hurting from continuing with the conflict. At this stage, they are often ready to begin negotiations.

Efforts to de-escalate the violence began in 1973 with the British government attempting to defuse the violence with the Sunningdale Agreement. Even though it did not lead to an end of violence, it opened up the road to future possibilities for the British government, a stakeholder in the conflict, to act as a peace broker. Beyond the optimism of producing some sort of an agreement, the post Sunningdale period can be characterized as disastrous. The Unionists then led by the dominant political party, the UUP, experienced a shift in power with the 1971 formation of the Democratic Unionist Party (DUP) headed by Ian Paisley. A charismatic figure, Paisley soon attracted majority support based on his working class image and focus on protecting the union with Britain.[25] Paisley and the DUP's popularity increased as they became known as the "No Party" advocating resistance against any attempt for power-sharing or political favors to the Nationalists. Paramilitaries on the Unionist side also demonstrated their resistance with a massive bomb explosion leaving thirty two dead and bringing Northern Ireland back into Direct Rule. The Nationalists also rejected the Agreement as it did not meet their goal of British withdrawal. Many Republicans believed that a military strategy would lead to their ultimate goal of British withdrawal from Northern Ireland. Since the British government was considered as illegitimate, the IRA continued their refusal to participate in negotiations.[26]

A political stalemate followed as various attempts for peace ultimately failed to bring about results. In 1985, after seven years of negotiations, the

Anglo-Irish Agreement was signed by the Prime Ministers of the United Kingdom and the Irish Republic. It was considered as the most radical effort by both governments to end the political conflict in Northern Ireland.[27] Some consider the approach taken as a sign of a shift in the British government's interests as well as the result of growing international focus and sympathy for the Nationalists. Harvey Cox argues that the death of ten Nationalists and their leader Bobby Sands in prison as a result of prolonged hunger strike brought immense international support for their cause.[28] This marked a significant shift in the Northern Ireland conflict as the hunger strikes became symbolic of the suffering of Nationalists.

The Agreement confirmed that Northern Ireland would remain independent of the Republic as long as it was the will of the majority in Northern Ireland. It was also considered as paving the way for the Unionists to achieve some form of power-sharing government with the Nationalists. The Agreement did not last but it was a significant achievement in other ways. For the first time, the Republic of Ireland had a political and interventionist role in representing the Catholics, one that would eventually be instrumental in bringing about an end to the conflict. It was also an acknowledgement by the British government that ending the conflict in Northern Ireland and future political negotiations would have to include the Republic of Ireland. Feargal Cochrane considers the Agreement as the biggest threat to Unionist identity, leading to a significant shift in their political leadership and an escalation in militant behavior.[29] The Republicans and primarily Sinn Fein rejected the Agreement, arguing that it did not meet their goals of ending British control and a united Ireland. The Unionists, left out of the negotiations responded with rallies, strikes, and the resignation of all members of the Unionist party. For them, the Agreement was perceived as the first step towards a united Ireland and, more importantly, a loss of political interest by the British government. It also posed a threat to the constitutional standing of Northern Ireland as an integral part of the UK. The response was a massive demonstration, known as the "No Campaign" rejecting the Agreement. Opposition eventually led to increased violent attacks by paramilitary groups on both sides. Such attacks were not always directed against the members of the opposing groups but also within communities particularly those accused of being supporters, sympathizers, and collaborators with the other side. Rachel Monaghan confirms a relationship between paramilitary forces, community violence, and the wider political context. She notes that punishment beatings in Loyalist areas saw a 300 percent rise in 1986 immediately after the signing of the Anglo Irish Agreement.[30]

Despite its failure to end the violence, the Agreement led to a significant acknowledgment that further negotiations would have to be inclusive of paramilitary groups on both sides. However, conditions were placed on the inclusion of such groups, the most significant being the promise of a ceasefire. The political environment in Northern Ireland was changing and it required both sides to reconsider their strategies. First, the success of the hunger strikes had proved to the Nationalists that a more successful strategy beyond the use of violence was needed.[31] The Republicans had to shift away from the armed struggle which had brought them little success and into mobilizing support politically. In 1983, Sinn Fein had experienced some success in electing its president, Gerry Adams, to the British House of Commons. Adams' leadership had transformed Sinn Fein into a stronger and more influential political party. As a result McAllister argues that IRA strategy was transformed into a hybrid electoral and military campaign of "a ballot paper on one hand and Armalite in the other."[32]

Fatigued by the use of violence, the British and Irish governments looked at further opportunities to start negotiation talks. It was time for a compromise and Gerry Adams, president of Sinn Fein, took this chance. Secret talks were initiated with the British and Irish governments as well as the more moderate Nationalist party which had formed during the civil rights campaign, the Social Democratic and Labor Party (SDLP). These secret talks provided the foundation to the Joint Framework Document known as the "Downing Street Declaration." It committed both governments to developing a political solution and including parties on both sides, provided that they lay down their arms and give up violence. The most significant contribution was the pledge to include Sinn Fein in negotiations for a political settlement in return for a ceasefire by the IRA. Although the ceasefire did not last it was later renewed, but this time with the help of third parties, mainly the United States.

Peace Making by the United States

Throughout much of the "Troubles" the United States' status as a third party mediator had been mainly limited to diplomatic efforts in the Middle East conflict. Therefore, its active involvement in Northern Ireland was a shift in strategy despite Northern Ireland being significant to many Irish Americans. The United States had always been supportive of finding a solution but considered the conflict as an internal affair for the United Kingdom, one of its major allies. The refreshed engagement was the result of several factors. First, the end of the Cold War brought about fresh opportunities for the United States' foreign policy agenda.[33] Under the Clinton presidency the US was pursuing an engagement role to emphasize its leadership in Europe, as evident by its military intervention to end the conflict in the Balkans.

President Clinton was the first to pursue a risky but sustained involvement in the Irish conflict. Previous Presidents such as Carter had made some effort by encouraging private investment and financial aid to address the conflict, but with no sustainable political impact. Later, although refusing to get directly involved in the conflict, President Reagan had also supported financial assistance and urged Prime Minister Margaret Thatcher to enter negotiations with the Republic of Ireland.[34] Throughout that period, US policy had a double role, one to secure domestic support and votes from US citizens with Irish backgrounds and the other to protect its special security cooperation and relationship with the British Government. Cochrane considers the role of the US and Irish Americans as the most significant in bringing an end to IRA's campaign of violence.[35] A strong Irish American lobby, economic ties to Ireland, and support from members of Congress were also responsible.[36] In the first of many confidence building measures, in February 1994, after eight denied entries, the United States granted a visa to Gerry Adams. The granting of the visa constituted a break in relations with the UK over Northern Ireland as well as a clear message that the US was taking a central role in the conflict.[37] Over time, American support for Sinn Fein would grow, with Gerry Adams being invited to the White House for St Patrick's Day. The visit was a huge success for Adams, where he received positive media attention as well as an enthusiastic welcome.

In a clear breakthrough after many years of seeking a settlement to the conflict, the IRA, urged by Bill Clinton, announced a complete cessation of military operations. This was followed by announcements from the main Unionist paramilitary organizations, the UVF and UDA of a ceasefire. This was the first time that the IRA had hinted a policy shift by its willingness to engage in negotiation talks. As a confidence building measure and a reward, the British government removed some of its troops, army patrols, and security installation in Belfast. This was astonishing and something that Northern Ireland had not seen in three decades. The people of Northern Ireland were experiencing a new sense of calm, security, and normalcy in the streets. Hopes for the promise of permanent ceasefires were high with celebrations throughout Northern Ireland. The road appeared clear with promises of a ceasefire by both sides, which should have paved the way for their inclusion in negotiation talks. However, confusion soon formed over the terms of the ceasefire, mainly on its temporary or permanent status.

Although the peace talks resumed by 1995, neither Sinn Fein nor the Loyalists were approved to enter negotiations. The main reason was the UK Prime Minister, John Major's announcement that Sinn Fein could only join talks after promises of a permanent ceasefire and decommissioning of weapons by the IRA.[38] Sinn Fein was furious and claimed that decommissioning was not an agreed condition when the IRA had called its ceasefire. After all, they would not know what the negotiations would yield and could not promise any prior concessions. In 1995, the stalled peace process received a much needed break with Clinton's historic visit to Northern Ireland, demonstrating support for the peace process. For Clinton, playing mediator in Northern Ireland was considered low risk/high gain, for if he succeeded not only would he win praise among the Irish American community, but he would also be renowned as a peacemaker.[39] The visit was received with a warm welcome by both sides, especially from the people of Northern Ireland, where tens of thousands lined the street. The first visit by a US president was hailed as a catalyst in pushing the peace process beyond the stalemate.[40] In his speech Clinton asked the people of Northern Ireland to "stand firm against terror" and set aside "old habits and hard grudges" in order to build a new era of peace and prosperity.[41]

Third Party Intervention

George Mitchell, a former US senator, became President Clinton's Secretary of State on Economic Initiatives in Ireland. Mitchell's first step and testing ground was to organize a conference focusing primarily on trade and investment as a way to boost up a shattered economy. In his memoir he notes that his arrival in Northern Ireland was received with much hope and welcome by the people of Northern Ireland. He considered the conference a success with attendance by hundreds of US businesses as well as political parties on both sides, who as a gesture were later invited to the White House by Clinton.[42] A year later, Mitchell was asked by the British and Irish governments to break the impasse and act as a third party to chair an international group charged with devising a plan for decommissioning. Along with General John de Chastelain, a former Canadian Ambassador, and Harri Holkeri, previous Prime Minister of Norway, he would form the International Body on Decommissioning of Weapons. They would make recommendations on dealing with the issues of disarmament, a difficult area that had stalled the talks. Senator Mitchell presented his report based on six principles that had to be accepted by both sides before they could enter negotiations. The report, known as the "Mitchell principles", sought to guarantee that the end of the conflict would be handled in a democratic manner.

To assure that these guidelines were being followed, Mitchell developed six ideas that had to be accepted before each party could be allowed into the talks. A compromise was made that decommissioning of weapons could take place parallel to multi-party negotiations. A few days later, the fragile ceasefire ended when a massive IRA bomb exploded in London's financial district, killing two and causing considerable damage. The UK government announced that it would not hold any talks or contact with Sinn Fein until they disarmed.[43] Despite this setback, the Mitchell principles had established the groundwork for future talks. The UK government led by John Major had battled with changing definitions and multiple attempts to define the conditions for Sinn Fein's entry into the negotiations.[44]

The surge in paramilitary violence and the stalemate received a boost with the election of the Labour Party in the UK. The British leadership change brought much needed optimism to the stalled process and played an important role in shaping the events that ultimately led to the peace process.[45] Tony Blair, the new Prime Minister, was determined to renew the talks. Blair sought to secure a ceasefire even if this had to involve risky secret meetings with the IRA.[46] He also announced that he would allow Sinn Fein to join multi-party talks in exchange for an IRA declaration of a new cease fire. In 1997, Sinn Fein agreed to cooperate with the Mitchell principles and as a result won a seat at the multi-party talks. The inclusion of Gerry Adams was a significant factor in gaining support among the Nationalists, particularly the IRA, for the peace process.[47] The IRA announced a ceasefire, agreeing to disarm during the all-party talks. For the first time in twenty five years all parties in the conflict had agreed to sit together for talks in the Stormont. Much of the credit for the IRA ceasefire and renewed talks was given to third party intervention by Mitchell and Clinton as well as Blair, who targeted a May 1998 deadline for the resolution of the conflict.[48]

External Aid: Peace Dividends

Research dealing with violent conflicts has been responsive to the need to consolidate a peace agreement by political and economic means after a ceasefire has been reached. External economic aid has often been used as an integral dynamic in the post-agreement stage as a peacebuilding strategy. Various literatures in the study of peace processes argue that economic aid can provide a positive role in peace building efforts.[49] Aside from its benefits at the political level, peace dividends can create incentives and convince people that they are stakeholders, thereby increasing public support at different stages of the peace process.[50] The conflict in Northern Ireland benefited from third party intervention by the United States. President Clinton had managed to link pursuing foreign policy in Northern Ireland with maintaining domestic economic interests and jobs.[51] Since 1969 and later in 1986, the United States had provided aid to the region through the Irish Northern Aid Committee (NORAID) and the International Fund for Ireland (IFI).[52] The IFI had supported economic investment, cross-community engagement, and development projects in Northern Ireland as well as the Republic of Ireland. After the announcement of the IRA ceasefire in 1994, the Clinton administration looked for ways to support the peace process with economic incentives. As the first step, the US initiated its intervention role by focusing on economic dividends as a road to political settlement by organizing an investment conference to bolster the private sector. Private sector growth supported by the US was a significant factor in creating employment, direct investment, and improving economic disparity.[53] Economic assistance and development presented much needed tangible improvements in the daily lives of people. Wilson argues that Clinton's strategy was linked to the idea that economic prosperity is a significant component of peace and stability.[54]

The European Union was not directly involved in the political negotiation and mediation efforts. It limited its role to supporting economic development in the post-ceasefire period by providing external aid. British and Irish cooperation on Northern Ireland began with their entry into the European Union.[55] One of the major aspects of EU policies in Northern Ireland has been to revitalize and improve the work of civil society with economic aid.[56] In an attempt to transform conflict from the ground up, some policy initiatives in Northern Ireland attempted to reduce segregation and inequality and improve community relations by increasing cross community contact. EU funding in the form of the "Peace and Reconciliation" package, commonly referred to as "Peace Money," became available through a three phased program. The aim of financial aid was to move both communities towards a peaceful and stable society by getting involved in inclusive projects to promote cross community contact and dialogue, reconciliation, business development, employment, and development of cross border communication.[57]

The first peace money was delivered in 1995-98 and provided around $500 million followed by Peace II (2000-2006) and the ongoing Peace III (2007-2013). The decision by the EU can be seen as a significant step to reward the decision by the paramilitary organizations to end the violence. For its part, funding was to be directed towards social inclusion, employment, and economic development.[58] The objective was mainly regeneration with a goal to target those, particularly the working class, that had been marginalized throughout the conflict. This was considered as an integral component of bottom up peacebuilding to encourage an inclusive approach from all sectors of society to move towards a better and peaceful future. It was hoped that external economic assistance and benefits would play a positive role in decreasing the deep communal divisions that cause violence. The strategy is to provide incentives for people to support the peace process in return for dividends of peace.[59] Racioppi and O'Sullivan argue that external funds by the EU promoted participation by civil society and, as a result, complemented peacemaking efforts by various third parties.[60]

A general evaluation of the role of "peace dividends" in Northern Ireland reveals that external assistance did significantly assist the struggling economy and contributed to the progress of the peace process. While it is unlikely that external aid can exclusively solve a conflict, it can be used as a tool in combination with other efforts. Third party intervention by the US and indirectly by the EU thus played a crucial role in involving the private sector, promoting peace dividends on the ground, and encouraging the peace process.

The Good Friday Agreement

"We rise from this table knowing that the Union is stronger than it was when we first sat down." David Trimble[61]

"We have resisted attempts to force us out, to marginalize us, to silence and intimidate us. We remain absolutely committed to our Irish Republican objectives." Gerry Adams[62]

These quotes from the two opposing party leaders following the Agreement set an important precedent. They point to the diverging interpretations of the Agreement in 1998, a year of momentous change in the history of Northern

Ireland. Following years of informal and two years of formal negotiations, the peace process in Northern Ireland began to move towards a final negotiated settlement, the "Good Friday" Agreement. For the first time in the history of Northern Ireland, the Catholic minority were guaranteed a share of decision making in their political and local affairs in an inclusive Assembly alongside their previous enemy, the Protestants. The Agreement was successful in establishing many new political structures. The first was an inclusive power-sharing Assembly involving the main parties, with 108 seats, presided over by a cross community Executive and headed by a First Minister and a Deputy Minister. Constitutional change in the Republic of Ireland resulted in the ending of its territorial claim to Northern Ireland, and cross-border bodies with executive powers set up by the two governments. A newly established north and south Ministerial Council was to oversee cooperation between the new Assembly and the Irish parliament as a way to encourage political cooperation between Northern Ireland and the Republic of Ireland. Another new institution was the Irish-British council, consisting of British, Irish, Scottish, and Welsh Assemblies to oversee cooperation among all related communities.

Apart from these historic political developments, one of the most important aspects of the Agreement was the constitutional future of the island. The right to self determination was for once left in the hands of the people in the north and south and to their consent through a general referendum. This was a historic democratic step, as it was the first time that the future of the island was left to the will of its people rather than political leaders. Other aspects of the Agreement were also "people" driven, attempting to make a difference in the life of people and their concerns on the ground. Under the terms of the Agreement, paramilitary prisoners were to benefit from an early release program. The number of British troops on the island was to be decreased and check points removed to convey a sense of security and normalcy. A newly established Northern Ireland Human Rights Commission would promote social, cultural, and economic equality and inclusion. The European Convention on Human Rights would be incorporated into Northern Ireland law. Establishment of a Civic Forum would allow representation from a wide range of civil society and grass root organizations. New economic initiatives included in the Agreement would also promote inclusive economic development strategies. Various independent commissions were set up to review legal and justice codes, as well as make structural changes to the tarnished image of the police service, which historically had consisted almost entirely of Protestants. Viewed by the Catholics as a brutal structure of the British government, the dismantling of the RUC can be considered as one of the most radical transformations since the signing of the Agreement. In 2001, the RUC, in effect since 1921, was to be overseen by the new Policing Board and renamed the Police Service of Northern Ireland (PSNI). As an effort to make the police service more representative of the whole community, the first class of recruits were under a new quota system drawn equally from both sides.

From the onset the Agreement appeared comprehensive, addressing approaches that would promote political inclusiveness as well as the institutions that would address people's needs on the ground. However, one very important issue was left vague. Looking through the history of events and previous attempts at political negotiations, it becomes clear that decommissioning remained a stumbling block. The language in the Agreement dealing with decommissioning was ambiguous and lacked clarity and detail. The section dealing with decommissioning only states that all participants "reaffirm their commitment to the disarmament of all paramilitary organizations and political parties will use influence to achieve decommissioning of all weapons within two years of the Agreement."[63] One thing should have been clear from lessons learned in the past negotiation efforts. If you leave this issue vague and not address it in detail, it is likely to be the main spoiler in the peace process. And that is exactly what happened. Decommissioning would prove to be the bedrock for "Troubles phase two" as it created major problems in the post agreement stage. Perhaps overcome by euphoria that negotiations were finally over, by the lack of alternatives, or pressure by third parties to produce an Agreement and oversee its problems later, the initial reaction by political parties was satisfaction. The Agreement was considered as the best thing they could come up with, given the circumstances. A member of the Sinn Fein commented:

> We knew there were going to be problems, but initially the happiness was so thick, you could not believe it was happening. So we thought let's do this and make people have something to rejoice about and worry about the details later; well the details turned out to cause a lot of problems and we had undermined them.[64]

The Agreement: Win-Win or Winners and Losers

At least at the official level, leaders had obtained some of what they wanted, enough to come up with the Agreement. The Nationalists had been promised an inclusive government with a powersharing Executive and mandated north and south bodies. Unionists wanted an elected Assembly and they were promised exactly that. A bonus point for Unionists was that the Government of Ireland would abolish Articles 2 and 3 of the Irish Constitution, claiming territorial rights to the Island.[65] This provided the Unionists with some security, for at least they would not be forced to be part of Ireland, unless the majority consented to it. Remaining pessimistic on the issue of decommissioning, they stressed a strict timeline on the complete decommissioning of all paramilitary weapons with a date set for two years from the time of the referendum. The Agreement also compromised in reaffirming the principle of consent. This meant that there would be no change to the constitutional situation of Northern Ireland without the consent of the majority of people in Northern Ireland. In 1998 David

Trimble and John Hume celebrated the successful negotiation and an end to the conflict by sharing the Nobel Peace Prize.

David Trimble's acceptance of the Good Friday Agreement was endorsed by a meeting of his Ulster Unionist Party (UUP) and within days following the Agreement, Gerry Adams of Sinn Fein meeting with his party. Elections for the new Assembly were held in 1998 and the biggest winners were the UUP with twenty eight seats, the SDLP with twenty four, and Sinn Fein with eighteen seats. The subsequent violent events in 1998 were shocking to people on the ground and a catalyst for political support of the peace process despite reservations on both sides. In the backdrop of the elections, the Orange Order's parade in Drumcree spread violence and tension throughout Northern Ireland and the Omagh bombing killed twenty nine civilians. Public outrage pushed political leaders to go beyond their differences and lend their support to continuing with the peace process. Interestingly, in this instance, violence pushed political leaders and the public at large to strive for peace. By November 1998, the issue of decommissioning kept the process lagging behind and Unionists became increasingly dissatisfied. Many were becoming frustrated with what they strongly believed was a win-lose situation, in which the Nationalists were politically benefiting. The Good Friday Agreement was running into problems as its implementation was interpreted differently by the parties.

By 1999, intervention once again by President Clinton produced the Hillsborough Declaration, which stressed paramilitary decommissioning verified by an independent commission, followed by establishing the institutions guaranteed by the Good Friday Agreement. Determined to push the Agreement ahead, Prime Minister Tony Blair insisted on June 1999 as the deadline for the implementation of the Agreement and the establishment of the Assembly. Some argued that this was naive, considering that there were so many issues that remained unclear as far as the details of how and when the IRA would dismantle its arms. Trimble, facing increasing internal pressure, decided to stay away from participation in the Assembly, and once again the implementation of the Agreement was faced with a political obstacle. Something had to be done. President Clinton and the British and Irish Governments all turned to Senator Mitchell to help resuscitate the Agreement. Senator George Mitchell got straight to work and in 1999 produced "The Mitchell Review," a report suggesting decommissioning and reform measures for the police force. After much turmoil, the Agreement was once again back on track. Yet Unionists remained dissatisfied. The police reforms were considered as "too much too fast" by Unionists and "too little too slow" by Nationalists. Furthermore, another conflict over the issue of policing was brewing. The dilemma was not whether there should be reforms in the police force, but different expectations on what these changes would entail.

Nationalists wanted to see a complete structural change of the police force. They wanted the name and symbols to change and Catholic recruitment to the force increase. In other words, they did not want reform, but a total dismantling of the existing force. Unionists were cautious of radically changing the RUC and were conscious of negative public reactions to changes. They feared that changes would be considered as an insult to the Unionists and the families of those killed during the "Troubles." The Pat Finucane Center summarized Catholic perceptions of the police reforms as:

> People cannot be expected to join the new police force, while key human rights questions remain unresolved. As the situation stands at present, the institutional factors that have led to human rights abuses in the past have not been adequately dealt with.[66]

Meanwhile, continuing prisoner release and reform in the police service was making many within the Unionist party uncomfortable. Convincing paramilitaries to uphold the ceasefire, in the light of what was regarded as very few concessions from Nationalists and slow progress in decommissioning, became challenging.

The View from the Ground

Although public opinion remained cautious on whether the Agreement would bring about a lasting peace, the majority remained optimistic. In the referendum of 22 May 1998, by a majority vote of 71 percent, the people of Northern Ireland voted "YES" in favor of a peace agreement, providing the Agreement with a substantial mandate. Popular support for the Agreement highlighted public support for peace. Yet questions remained. How would this Agreement differ from past efforts to negotiate peace and why did it have so much public support?

Two significant strands set this Agreement apart from previous efforts. First, the Agreement was constructed on the basis of inclusivity, designed to bring all parties into a political process, including three parties linked to paramilitary organizations. Second, it had a ground level or people's dimension. Voters on both sides of the border endorsed it, acknowledging the will and consent of the majority of Irish people. This was more than a symbolic gesture in that the electorate throughout all of Ireland was taking part in a simultaneous vote for the first time since 1918. But it was also an exercise that was emblematic of the practice of some form of self determination, even if falling short of the full self determination demanded by Republicans. Furthermore, by voting to support the Agreement, the people of Ireland for the first time had in effect voted by 94.4 percent to accept partition of their country. The people thought that voting "yes" was enough to safeguard a future of peace. There were few public protests against the Agreement and since the major paramilitary organizations were included in the negotiations, this reaffirmed public support for a new era and the principle that violence was to be a thing of the past.

Decommissioning of Arms

By 1999, the political atmosphere once again looked promising. For the first time in over twenty years, the Northern Ireland Assembly was working, with a locally accountable government making decisions on local issues. General de Chastelain was appointed as the chairman of the Independent International Decommissioning Commission. The IRA declared that it was willing to put down its arms and be inspected by third parties. This brought a new enthusiasm that the Agreement was back on track. Despite three IRA arms dumps inspected by third parties, Unionists regarded the issue of decommissioning as unfinished and remained increasingly dissatisfied. Of the paramilitary organizations whose political surrogates signed the Agreement (IRA, UVF, UDA) none of them had performed any arms decommissioning that was satisfactory under the terms of the Agreement.[67]

The implementation of the peace agreement faced difficult challenges in both the areas of IRA decommissioning and the Unionist request for support and recognition of the police and justice system. By 2002, lack of progress and increasing distrust had led to repeated suspension of the power-sharing Assembly. The issues of decommissioning and demilitarization remained the main obstacle to future political negotiations between the Unionist and the Nationalist parties. While the collapse of the Assembly did not necessarily mean that the peace process had failed, it provided many challenges. As for decommissioning, the surrender of weapons by the IRA to what it regarded as the enemy was considered as the equivalent of a total surrender. Secondly, although the British Government had removed many security installations from urban areas in its pledge to return to normality, these measures had not provided enough assurances for many Republicans. The Republicans argued that the UK Government still retained an armed police force and continued to hold legal arms. Hence, the IRA could potentially only put their weapons away when the state demilitarized as a whole.

Conclusions

In 2005, the IRA formally declared an end to its campaign of violence and vowed to dump its weapons in a historic declaration. General de Chastelain confirmed the completion of IRA decommissioning, a significant step in reviving the peace process. The UK and Irish Governments called for renewed negotiations with the "St. Andrews Agreement," intended to break the political stalemate. The new proposal recommended that the DUP, now the largest Unionist party, form a government with Sinn Fein. It also demanded recognition from Sinn Fein of two previously contested sectors, police and justice services. By 2007 the British army and troops no longer played a significant role in policing of Northern Ireland. As the last hurdle to the implementation of the power sharing Assembly, Sinn Fein supported the reformed Police Service of Northern Ireland (PSNI). Almost a third of PSNI officers now come from the Catholic community. The last key element in the Northern Ireland peace process was accepted in 2010 after a long period of political negotiations, and justice and police powers were restored locally to the Stormont after decades of external British control.

The Good Friday Agreement has been the most significant and comprehensive step towards peace since the partition of the island in 1921. Third party intervention and mediation efforts played a significant role in bringing it about. While vulnerable at times, it has moved Northern Ireland into a post-conflict society.

Northern Ireland provides many lessons for other intractable conflicts and their termination. One is the use of successful mediation with flexibility, continuous commitment, and long term development assistance from external third parties. Perhaps the biggest achievement so far has been its bottom up approach and democratic pledge that the future of Northern Ireland will depend on the consent and will of its people. Hopes for the sustainability of the Agreement remain high as despite many setbacks both sides have successfully formed a power-sharing government. The journey of the peace process has been bumpy yet unbroken, and it is likely that after decades of conflict future tensions between the Protestants and Catholics is unavoidable. At the same time the peace process has remained in place, proving that the violence of the "Troubles" is a thing of the past.

Notes

1. John Darby, *The Effects of Violence on Peace Processes* (Washington, DC: The United States Institute of Peace Press, 2001), 11-12.

2. Harold, H. Saunders, *Public Peace Process: Sustained Dialogue to Transform Racial and Ethnic Conflicts* (New York: St. Martin's Press, 1999), 13-20.

3. Stephen J. Stedman, "Spoiler Problems in Peace Processes," *International Security* 22, no. 2 (1997), 5-53.

4. Michael Cox, "Bringing in the International: The IRA Ceasefire and the End of the Cold War," *International Affairs, Royal Institute of International Affairs* 73, no. 4 (October 1997): 671-693.

5. For the impact of violence on civilians see Marie Smyth, "Putting the Past in its Place: Issues of Victimhood and Reconciliation in Northern Ireland," in *Burying the Past and Doing Justice after Civil Conflict*, ed. Nigel Biggar (Washington, DC: Georgetown University Press, 2001).

6. It is important to point out that not all Protestants fall directly into these two categories. Most but not all are descendants of British-Scottish settlers. The term Loyalist is often used to refer to a more militant faction of Unionists.

7. Anthony C. Hepburn, *A Past Apart: Studies in the History of Catholic Belfast 1850-1950* (Belfast: Ulster Historical Foundation, 1996), 3-5.

8. Joseph Ruane and Jennifer Todd, *The Dynamics of Conflict in Northern Ireland: Power, Conflict and Emancipation* (Cambridge: Cambridge University Press, 1996), 25-26.

9. Not all Catholics fall into the two categories. The Republicans support unification with Ireland and are considered as more militant in pursuing this goal.

10. John D. Brewer, "Sectarianism and Racism and their Parallels and Differences," *Ethnic and Racial Studies* 15, no. 3 (1992): 352-364.

11. Tim P. Coogan, *The Troubles: Ireland's Ordeal 1966-1996 and the Search for Peace* (Boulder, CO: Roberts Rinehart, 1996), 25-26.

12. Jonathon Tonge, *Northern Ireland* (Cambridge: Polity Press, 2006), 42-43.

13. Michael Farrell, *The Orange State* (London: Pluto Press, 1976), 256-257.

14. Paul Doherty and Michael A. Poole, "Ethnic Residential Segregation in Belfast, Northern Ireland, 1971-1991," *Geographical Review* 87, no. 4 (October 1997): 520-536.

15. Neil Ferguson and Ed Cairns, "Political Violence and Moral Maturity in Northern Ireland," *Political Psychology* 17, no. 4, (December 1996): 713-725.

16. Austin Smith, "The Implications of Segregation for Transport within Northern Ireland," *Community Relations Council for Northern Ireland Report*, Issue 2 (June 2000), 3-6.

17. For discrimination practices see John Whyte, "How Much Discrimination was there under the Unionist Regime, 1921-68" in *Contemporary Irish Studies*, ed. Tom Gallagher and James O'Connell (Manchester: Manchester University Press, 1983), 1-35, Alan O'Day, *Political Violence in Northern Ireland, Conflict and Conflict Resolution* (Westport, CT: Praeger, 1997), 8-9.

18. Henry McDonald, "Belfast's Peace Walls Treble After Ceasefires," *The Guardian*, 28 July, 2009, (14).

19. For more on the shift in strategy to non-violence see Roger Mac Ginty and John Darby, *Guns and Government, the Management of the Northern Ireland Peace Process* (NY: Palgrave, 2002), 1-16.

20. Robert White, "From Peaceful Protest to Guerrilla War: Micro-mobilization of the Provisional Irish Republican Army," *The American Journal of Sociology* 94, no. 6 (May 1989): 1277-1302.

21. Joanne Wright, "PIRA Propaganda: The Construction of Legitimacy," *Conflict Quarterly* 10, no. 3 (Summer 1990): 24-41.

22. While society as a whole was affected by the conflict, the impact has been more severe in certain areas. For a discussion on this see Fay M. Therese, Mike Morrissey, and Marie Smyth, *Northern Ireland's Troubles: The Human Costs* (London: Pluto Press, 1999). Marie Smyth and Mike Morrissey, *Northern Ireland After the Good Friday Agreement: Victims, Grievance and Blame* (London: Pluto Press, 2002).

23. Sean J. Byrne, "The Roles of External Ethnoguarantors and Primary Mediators in Cyprus and Northern Ireland," *Conflict Resolution Quarterly* 24, no. 2 (Winter 2006): 149-172.

24. William Zartman and Maureen Berman, *The Practical Negotiator* (New Haven: Yale University Press, 1982), 66-78. Sadia Touval and William Zartman, eds, *International Mediation in Theory and Practice* (Boulder, CO: Westview Press, 1985), 258-60.

25. Brian Graham, "The Past in the Present: The Shaping of Identity in Loyalist Ulster," *Terrorism and Political Violence* 16, no. 3 (2004): 483-500.

26. Montgomery Sapone, "Ceasefire: The Impact of Republican Political Culture in the Ceasefire Process in Northern Ireland," *Peace and Conflict Studies* 7, no. 1 (May 2000): 21-47.

27. Michael Connolly and John Loughlin, "Reflections on the Anglo-Irish Agreement," *Government and Opposition* 21, no. 2 (April 1986): 146-160.

28. Harvey Cox, "Managing Northern Ireland Intergovernmentally: An Appraisal of the Anglo Irish Agreement," *Parliamentary Affairs* 40, no. 1 (*1987*)*:* 80-97.

29. Feargal Cochrane, *Unionist Politics and the Politics of Unionism Since the Anglo Irish Agreement* (Ireland: Cork University Press, 2001), 1-35.

30. Rachel Monaghan, "The Return of Captain Moonlight: Informal Justice in Northern Ireland," *Studies in Conflict and Terrorism* 25, no. 1 (2002): 41-56.

31. Ian McAllister, "The Armalite and the Ballot Box: Sinn Fein's Electoral Strategy in Northern Ireland," *Electoral Studies* 3, no. 1 (March 2004): 123-142.

32. Ibid, 128.

33. Adrian Guelke, "The United States, Irish Americans and the Northern Ireland Peace Process," *International Affairs* 72, no. 3 (July 1996): 521-536.

34. Andrew J. Wilson, "From the Beltway to Belfast: The Clinton Administration, Sinn Fein, and the Northern Ireland Peace Process," *New Hibernia Review* 1, no. 3 (Autumn 1997): 23-39.

35. Feargal Cochrane, "Irish-America, the End of the IRA's Armed Struggle and the Utility of Soft Power," *Journal of Peace Research* 44. *no. 2 (*March 2007): 215-231.

36. Joseph O'Grady, "An Irish Policy Born in the U.S.A.: Clinton's Break with the Past," *Journal of Foreign Affairs* 75, no. 3 (May-June 1996): 2-7.

37.Timothy Lynch, "The Gerry Adams Visa in Anglo-American Relations," *Irish Studies in International Affairs* 14 (2003): 33-44.

38. Colin Brown and David Mckittrick, "Peace Process Will Not be Derailed," *The Independent*, February 29, 1996, http://www.independent.co.uk/news/peace-process-will-not-be-derailed-1321558.html (accessed January 2005).

39. Timothy Lynch, *Turf War: The Clinton Administration and Northern Ireland* (Aldershot: Ashgate, 2004), 37-38.

40. David McKittrick, "From the Shankill to the Falls, Clinton Kindles Hope," *The Independent,* December 1, 1995, http://www.independent.co.uk/news/from-the-shankill-to-the-falls-clinton-kindles-hope-1523394.html. (accessed Janurary 2005).

41. Terence Hunt, "Clinton Sees Both Sides of Belfast," *Associated Press*, December 1, 1995, http://www.independent.co.uk/news/from-the-shankill-to-the-falls-clinton-kindles-hope-1523394.html. (accessed January 2005).

42. George Mitchell, *Making Peace*, (New York: Alfred Knopf, 1999), 22-39.

43. Steven J. Brams and Jeffrey M. Togman, "Cooperation through Threats: The Northern Ireland Case," *Political Science and Politics* 31, no. 1 (March 1998): 32-39.

44. Nick Randall, "New labor and Northern Ireland," in *New Labor in Power*, ed. David Coates and Peter Lawler (Manchester: Manchester University Press, 2000), 94-101.

45. David Brown, *The Development of British Defense Policy, Blair, Brown and Beyond,* (Surrey: Ashgate, 2010), 108-109.

46. Nicholas Watt, "Revealed: Blair's Offer to Meet Masked IRA leaders," *The Guardian*, March 17, 2008, (1),

47. Gregory M. Maney, Ibtisam Ibrahim, Gareth I. Higgins, and Hanna Herzog, "The Past's Promise: Lessons from Peace Processes in Northern Ireland and the Middle East," *Journal of Peace Research* 43, no. 2 (March 2006): 181-200.

48. Eoin McKiernan, "IRA Deserves Credit for Progress in Talks," *National Catholic Reporter*, December 12, 1997, (1).

49. On private sector see Allan Gerson, "Peacebuilding: the Private Sector's Role," *American Journal of International Law* 95, no. 1 (January 2001): 102-119. For external

aid in peacebuilding see Elham Atashi "Peace Dividends: the Role of External Aid in Peace Building", in *Peace Building in Northern Ireland*, ed. Maria Power (Liverpool, UK: University of Liverpool Press, 2011), 209-228.

50. Elham Atashi, "Challenges to Conflict Transformation from the Streets," in *Conflict Transformation and Peacebuilding: Moving from Violence to Sustainable Peace*, ed. Bruce W. Dayton and Louis Kreisberg (New York, NY: Routledge, 2009), 45-60.

51. Roger Mac Ginty, "American Influences on the Northern Ireland Peace Process," *The Journal of Conflict Studies* 17, no. 2 (Fall 1997): 31-43.

52. Mari Fitzduff, *Beyond Violence: Conflict Resolution Process in Northern Ireland*, (Tokyo: United Nations University Press, 2002), 136.

53. "Economics in Peacemaking: Lessons from Northern Ireland," *The Portland Trust*, (London: UK, May 2007), 23-34.

54. Andrew J. Wilson, "Doing the Business: Aspects of the Clinton Administration's Economic Support for the Northern Ireland Peace Process, 1994-2000," *Journal of Conflict Studies* 23, no. 1 (2003), 155-176.

55. Jonathan Stevenson, "Peace in Northern Ireland: Why Now?" *Foreign Policy* no. 112 (Autumn 1998): 41-54.

56. Arthur Williamson, Scott Duncan, and Peter Halfpenny, "Rebuilding Civil Society in Northern Ireland: the Community and Voluntary Sector's Contribution to the European Union's Peace and Reconciliation District Partnership Program," *Policy & Politics* 28, no. 1, (January 2000): 49-66.

57. Sean Byrne, Chuck Thiessen, and Eyob Fissuh, "Economic Assistance and Peacebuilding in Northern Ireland," *The Canadian Journal of Peace and Conflict Studies* 39, no. 1-2 (2007): 7-22, Sean Byrne and Michael J. Ayulo, "External Economic Aid in Ethno-Political Conflict: AView From Northern Ireland," *Security Dialogue* 29, no. 4 (1998), 421-434.

58. *The Special Support Programme for Peace and Reconciliation in Northern Ireland and the Border Counties of Ireland (1995-1999)* Brussels: Commission of the European Communities Communication, 26.11.1997. COM, 97-642.

59. Atashi, "Challenges to Conflict Transformation from the Streets." 46-47.

60. Linda Racioppi and Katherine O'Sullivan, "Grassroots Peacebuilding and Third-party Intervention: The European Union's Special Support Programme for Peace and Reconciliation in Northern Ireland," *Peace and Change* 23, no. 3 (July 2007): 361-390.

61. *Irish Times,* April, 11, 1998, (1).

62. *Irish Times,* April, 11, 1998, (1).

63. Text of Good Friday Agreement, *The Agreement* (Belfast: The Northern Ireland Office, HM Government: HMSO, 1998).

64. Author interview with an anonymous Sinn Fein party member, Belfast, February 12, 2003.

65. This term refers to articles in the 1937 Constitution of Ireland. The original Articles 2 and 3 laid claim to the whole of the island of Ireland but recognized the border in so far as the laws of the Irish parliament would only apply to the Republic of Ireland.

66. Reaction to Police Reforms, The Pat Finucane Center (Derry-Londonderry, Press release, 21 August 2001). The Pat Finucane Center is an organization dedicated to bringing about justice for Pat Finucane a Catholic lawyer killed by the RUC, and to defending other Catholic victims of conflict.

67. Good Friday Agreement, Section 7, Appendix One.

Chapter 4

Implementing the Liberal Peace: Observations from the Field

Linda S. Bishai

Critiques of Liberal theory and its grand plan to reformat the developing world in its own image have recently become abundant. One such critique characterizes Liberal internationalism in terms of efforts to establish and perpetuate a "Liberal Peace." Perspectives differ as to whether the Liberal Peace is misguided, mis-implemented, unnecessary, or pragmatically counterproductive. Many of these critiques are based on theoretical differences and thus confront Liberalism's underlying commitments. A few critiques (those taking issue with the implementation and/or the unintended consequences) provide a closer look at specific cases of Liberal Peace efforts engendering neither liberalism nor peace in the target country. This chapter falls into a slightly different category. Drawing on personal experience in peacebuilding work in Sudan, I wish to offer a critique of these Post-Liberal critiques of Liberalism. This is not going to be a defense of Liberalism but rather a questioning of the Post-Liberal theorists who offer improvements to the Liberal Peace. The perspective offered here stems from the sense that the critics have crafted an image of the Liberal Peace that has never quite existed as they describe and that does not actually operate on the ground in the manner they suggest. In practice, the idealist theory of the Liberal Peace has had to yield to the pragmatism of the "others" encountered in the field. To some extent, the Liberal Peace is a straw man—easy to knock down and only a rough sketchy shape of the entity it claims to represent. Thus Post-Liberal efforts to reform the Liberal Peace do not offer significant improvements on the original. Not only is the Liberal Peace far less likely to be implemented as advertised, but current efforts at peacebuilding are already far more likely to resemble the suggested modifications in practice.

The Liberal Peace is often portrayed as a monolithic grand narrative, a global master plan, with specific goals and coordinated international efforts. The international community appears as a singular actor with a specific blueprint of statehood and the stipulated requirements of peaceful transition. In particular here, I refer to the arguments from *Liberal Peace Transitions: Between Statebuilding and Peacebuilding* by Oliver Richmond and Jason Franks,[1] and several articles by Richmond as prominent critics of the Liberal Peace. Specifically, I will address the charges made by Richmond and Franks that Liberal Peace models fail to respond to the every day needs of ordinary citizens and to local conditions such as cultural differences and capacity needs. Second, I will provide descriptions from my work with local partners in Sudan (and what is now South Sudan) to illustrate the extent to which the Liberal Peace framework has already been modified in practice by significant engagement with the sub-elite and grass roots levels. To use Richmond's terminology, peacebuilding programs on the ground have already created multiple forms of hybridity, or mutually responsive international/local approaches, in adapting to local and cultural conditions. It is critically important to note here that I present my own experiences as only an example of many similarly engaged approaches. Doing peacebuilding work for the last seven years, I have encountered numerous internationals from government and nonprofits whose work reflects deep commitments to grass roots outreach, localized understanding, and long-term outcomes. Sustainability and local capacity rather than imported models and development handouts have become accepted themes throughout the world of global peacebuilding institutions. In the conclusion, I suggest not a whole new approach to peacebuilding, since whole approaches are part of the problem, but an alternative way of envisioning the relationships between international and local actors engaged in the cause of peaceful social transformation.

The Liberal Peace and its Post-Liberal Critics

Despite Liberalism's broad parameters, when it comes to modes of Liberal international intervention there is significant consensus among scholars. Liberal states regard intervention as a key means of dealing with conflict, and in particular of spreading the Liberal recipe for internal peace and stability to the rest of the world. Much has been written about the truth or falsehood of the assumption of inherent peacefulness in liberal democratic societies (see "Democratic Peace Theory") but both supporters and critics agree on the key components of the model that has been designed specifically for export in cases dealing with armed conflict and peacebuilding. Richmond and Franks list five key elements of the Liberal Peace with the caveat that concerns for security during the transitional period provide the overall backdrop.[2] These elements consist of efforts to create or strengthen democratization, human rights, civil society, the rule of law, and economic reform (with an emphasis on a free market).[3] The same elements are confirmed, though with considerably more detail, in *The Guiding Principles for Peace Operations*.[4] The United States Institute of Peace and the U.S. Army

Peacekeeping and Stability Operations Institute developed this manual jointly with the intent to provide guidance for civilian actors that would complement military manuals on peacekeeping operations. According to *Guiding Principles*, the framework for conflict transformation should consist of the rule of law, a secure environment, a sustainable economy, stable governance, and social well-being.[5] The manual describes these five categories with particular concern for local participation and "ownership" of the process.

What various conceptualizations of the Liberal Peace have in common is a description of goals for political and social life in the target country that resemble the principles of liberal democracies (although existing liberal democracies all have noticeable and significant degrees of variation from the ideal). From its very inception then, the Liberal Peace project can be critiqued as the imposition of a "foreign" or ideal model on societies that have different commitments and their own "authentic" practices for governance that should not be coerced into an unsuitable or unrealistic blueprint. This is a fair point, especially given the unsuccessful track record of many so-called humanitarian interventions that have been oblivious to local practices and attempted to graft foreign models wholesale onto societies emerging from conflict.[6] But it neglects the complex power dynamics that have arisen between developed and less-developed nations in the international system whereby the rules of the global economy and international law favor free market democracies. States that cannot function well within these global legal and economic frameworks play the game of international politics with a serious handicap.

Developing states that do not fit the Liberal Peace profile at least in part suffer from limited foreign investment, less equal or unfair trade patterns, and from a range of possible legal sanctions because of human rights violations. Leaders of poorer states can then argue that they require aid (technology transfers, weaker carbon restrictions, loan forgiveness, military/police training and equipment) in order to have the tools to fully participate in the global system, while at the same time cautioning against the imposition of Western values in cases of intervention to manage conflict. This could be described as the *colonial conundrum*. It looks like colonialism when Western states impose their social model through humanitarian intervention, but the same Western states can also be accused of a kind of colonialist economic exploitation if they maintain isolationism, refuse to intervene, and merely reap the advantages of a global economy that is stacked in their favor. To be sure, there is violence baked into the very assumptions of any model that makes claims of moral superiority since force can always be justified to promote it.[7] So, is the Liberal Peace a failed project?

Oliver Richmond argues that it is a failure, insofar as it has failed to create liberal states and positive peace after so many significant efforts at intervention. This is a commonplace observation but Richmond attributes the failure to a lack of concern for the local, the everyday, and the emergence of a social contract in post-conflict societies.[8] Liberal peacebuilders place too much emphasis, Richmond argues, on security and market reform (changes that benefit and entrench elites) while failing to address the core issues of conflict in its particular context, especially regarding internal patterns of exploitation, and to meet the basic needs of the population. While there is much truth to this critique, Richmond seems to attribute these failures to a monolithic international liberal *project* that proceeds with deliberation, coordination, and reflexive self-awareness. Although there are certain agreed elements of what a liberal peace should look like, the actual implementation has been nothing like a coherent effort.

In that sense, the Liberal Peace is a failed project because its premise—that the liberal internationalist states can and should collectively and uniformly spread their successful socio-economic model to the conflict-prone failed states of the world—was based on profound cultural provincialism, not to mention administrative overreach, and thus impossible from the start. Rather than stop there, Richmond assumes that a genuine and coordinated project to implement the Liberal Peace has been ongoing. But he fails to examine the multitude of actors, both national and international, that are inevitably involved in any instance of humanitarian intervention or peacebuilding project. Not only are multiple states and international organizations involved, but multiple sectors and agencies within, each with its own bureaucracy, approach, funding levels, deadlines, and limitations. Richmond's particular lapse is not distinguishing the critical role played by the use of military force—or not—in such cases and how it can set the stage for the civilian activities that follow. Further, Richmond too lightly dismisses the real adaptations that have occurred (and continue to evolve) during various interventions as both military and civilian actors realize what works and does not work in practice for their respective missions, and attempt to draw lessons from their failures. For example, a working group of representatives of the U.S. Armed Forces, civilian agencies, and non-governmental humanitarian organizations have developed a set of generally accepted guidelines for more smooth coordination of working relationships in conflict zones or "potentially hostile environments."[9] These guidelines required several years of contentious discussion and a difficult process of consensus building. Their mere existence points to the seriousness these actors bring to the ongoing effort to improve their activities in conflicted areas.

Ultimately, Richmond's writings on the Liberal Peace display his Liberal credentials. Despite his own harsh criticism of the Liberal Peace, calling it "an insidious form of conversion and riot control. . . [and] profoundly anti-democratic in many ways," Richmond's prescription is not to jettison the project.[10] In order to mindfully address conflict, we "need not abandon the humanitarian project, its internationalism or transnationalism, and its transformative commitment to human rights."[11] Though, he notes, these features are highly characteristic of the liberal perspective. Instead, Richmond suggests, it might be enough to adopt a better model of the Liberal Peace—"a model that is designed from the ground up in each case in locally resonant ways, respecting autonomous agency, capacity, custom, identity, religion, and alternative models of politics, society, and economics."[12] Such a model, drawing on his concept of hybridity, would then be post-liberal. After examining five case studies of the failures of the Liberal Peace, and the dangerous confusion between peacebuilding and statebuilding, Richmond and Frank offer four steps that post-liberal peacebuilders should follow if they are to succeed in transcending the failed Liberal Peace.

First, according to Richmond and Frank, they must act as if there is a social contract requiring care and empathy between local actors and internationals in post-conflict societies.[13] Thus peacebuilders must remain aware of their impacts on local everyday life and take care that their actions are based on welfare for the least powerful. Second, they must develop their plans separately in each case after consultation with local partners and representation from the broadest possible reaches of society. Peacebuilders should adopt the role of mediator between international and local norms and should resist privileging the application of the former. Third, post-liberal peacebuilders should apply the norms of democracy, equality, justice, and others to their own actions in the process as well as to the societies they are trying to transform. This step addresses the tendency of internationals to operate in separate bubble worlds that seem far removed from the people they are supposedly working to help. Finally, Richmond and Frank insist that peacebuilders must shift the priorities of their projects to give primacy to human needs instead of wealth and property. This would also require more reliance on customary patterns of governance in order to reach the broader population beyond the capital city elites who are usually involved in facilitating (and corrupting) the liberal project.

This chapter argues that Richmond and Frank's model of post-liberal peacebuilding is in fact already taking place within the collection of broader Liberal Peace efforts, and makes the point that the Liberal Peace really amounts to multiple liberal pieces of response to international conflict. Further, it is a necessary and inevitable part of Liberal Peace that it has been disaggregated and uncoordinated. To truly consolidate and synchronize peace efforts by multiple international actors into a global project would have the effect of creating a frightening (and illiberal) peace—the peace of absolute compliance. Rather, the goal should be to promote a general understanding of the consequences of intervention such that intervening actors make responsible long-term efforts to build local capacity and sow the seeds of internally driven transformation. This is hardly new.[14] There have always been international actors operating within the Liberal Peace who have followed an ethic of care and empathy and who have worked within the four steps described above to create more interactive and sustainable forms of institutions in the name of peacebuilding. Although the amount of waste, corruption, and counter-productive insistence on non-contextual norms has been staggering, the Liberal Peace has also included many individuals and programs that have understood the importance of making their efforts more locally informed and population oriented. These post-liberal pockets are a predictable outcome of the diversity of actors participating in the disaggregated Liberal Peace paradigm. In other words, the Liberal Peace has always had post-liberal peacebuilding practices within it.

The reason, perhaps, that critics are so determined to present alternate theories of peacebuilding is that the concept of peace itself proves to be a vacuum that can be filled in a limitless number of ways. Because peace is so under-theorized, especially as opposed to war, there is a tendency for scholars to fill the void with their own political self-image. Peace can therefore be anything, but it must not be messy or corrupt or wasteful—those are the characteristics associated with conflicted or failed states. But in fact peace must include politics—contestation and negotiation, as well as all the messiness of imperfect social relations. Human societies, even when not in a state of war, contain multiple instances of confusion, waste, power imbalances, injustice, and other failures. They are not—they cannot be—perfect. So, yes the Liberal Peace is a failure. Its goals are mis-conceptualized from the beginning. Liberal societies do not attain their own standards and societies emerging from conflict cannot be expected to do so in any meaningful way either. But Liberal Peace has also contained within it examples of productive post-liberal practice by virtue of its own necessary "imperfection."

Images from Sudan

Beginning

Sudan in many ways does not fit the classical model for humanitarian intervention. Although it has been struggling with successive civil wars since its independence in 1956, it has never been subjected to externally imposed regime change or to major international statebuilding efforts such as those Richmond and Franks examine. While UN peacekeeping forces have been present since 2005, and UN and multinational humanitarian efforts much longer, the international response has been thus far sensitive to the sovereign claims of the existing government—even when the current head of state was indicted for war crimes and crimes against humanity for events in Darfur. The result is a country where billions of dollars are spent on humanitarian and development aid each year, where violent conflict has long been endemic, where the UN Security Council has referred the government's extreme efforts to squelch rebellion to the International Criminal Court, where there has been an intense glare of publicity from millions of activists on the issue of Darfur, and yet where there is minimal political will to put "boots on the ground" to do anything other than the challenging mission of keeping a peace that has not yet had a chance to develop.

My work in Sudan started in 2006. Six years and many hundreds of thousands of dollars later, I continue to be amazed at the many contradictions one finds in this conflict-ridden country of vast potential. I am also constantly impressed by the commitment and capacity of so many dedicated citizens of this society with whom I have been privileged to work. Because The United States Institute of Peace (USIP) does not generally maintain offices abroad, the standard practice is to locate trustworthy local partners who can help us design and implement effective programs for the particular needs of Sudan. On its face this procedure looks vulnerable to Richmond's accusation that blueprints are generated in Western capitals for blind application in the field. In practice, program officers at the Institute make serious efforts to assess the situation on the ground and to canvas opinions from a mix of local actors, including government officials, academics, members of the diaspora, and political experts before shaping a plan for the best use of limited funds. Without this triangulation of experience, it would be easy to fly to Khartoum for two weeks and choose the first civil society organization that could articulate a sympathetic message. True, the target issues of focus are developed in Washington, but they are chosen on the basis of extensive efforts to assess local needs and are often interpreted loosely in response to difficulties or resistance presented from the ground conditions. Additionally, Richmond's charge that Liberal Peace actors work nearly exclusively with the elites at the expense of the grass roots comes true all too often, but this does not necessarily stem from lack of awareness of the problems with this approach. Rather, in conflict zones such as Sudan, it takes tremendous patience to develop the capacities of those in local communities to be able to use funds broadly aimed at sustainable peacebuilding (as opposed to humanitarian aid aimed at keeping people alive). In other words, effective approaches to long-term peace really do require elite buy-in, though conscientious international actors must be vigilant about the conflicts of elite interests with those of the general population in the sectors where they work.

Finding a Credible Local Partner

For us, part of the solution was to develop close ties with a civil society organization committed to reaching all levels of society from village youth to government officials. We were particularly fortunate because since the start of our partnership, the organization has demonstrated an unflagging energy and commitment to the cause of peaceful social transformation for the country. In order to avoid harassment from government officials, the organization walks a delicate tightrope in its activities, and maintains a determined political neutrality. In Sudan's heavily politicized atmosphere, this last characteristic is especially rare. Because of its social and ethnic connections, it would be tempting for this organization to take the easy path and join the ranks of the government-co-opted by making a few chosen remarks about the role of the ruling party in working for peace in Sudan. Despite the watchfulness and discretion required to work within these parameters, the benefits of partnering with such an organization as this one have been many, not least that it is credible, respected, and well placed to provide a beneficial link between a peacebuilding organization such as USIP and local communities across Sudan.

The Challenges of Having a Credible Local Partner

There have, however, also been challenges. The current regime in Sudan governs by punishing, co-opting, or mimicking its critics. Those who attempt to change the status quo will face numerous temptations to become less effective, not least of which is the appearance of pseudo NGOs that are encouraged by the government to become successful at appearing to be well-organized (and thus competing for international funds) while not expending much effort in the follow up activities that make social change possible. Having thus corrupted the field with its own organizations the government saps support for many local NGOs by charging that they are politically affiliated and generally motivated by profit. Our program experienced this personally when one of the Sudanese NGOs that had promised to co-train and facilitate travel to a workshop in El Geneina, Darfur, suddenly became evasive and uncooperative. We were later informed by two other separate sources that this particular NGO was known to be close to the government. In the end, we managed to find an alternative source of help for travel permission and local logistical support and were able to travel to and work in Darfur. Negotiating a social contract in this environment, as Richmond urges, is extremely unlikely. The web of domestic actors and their conflicting (often compromised) interests, as well as deeply entrenched political power centers, makes it difficult to foster a process that could lead to genuinely just and fair commitments. Being aware of these problems is important to working effectively in the country, but it does little to broaden your choices as an international attempting to promote peacebuilding practices. In this murky environment, it is essential to have a local partner whose judgment can be trusted to be ultimately grounded in long-term best outcomes for the country. Because of this remarkable relationship, it goes without saying that my program plans have been developed uniquely for Sudan and in consultation with this local partner.

How Being an Outsider Helps

Despite these challenges, my experience has been surprisingly positive in terms of being an American in Sudan. Rather than prompting prejudice and suspicion, our presence has often provided an opportunity to bring groups together that have been isolated by mutual hostility and violent histories. Of course it helps that my colleagues and I have made every effort to design our programs with the particulars of Sudan in mind and to be respectful of general social customs. An outside third party perceived as trustworthy and disinterested can provide a safe environment for a healthy exchange of views. Because USIP does not represent or implement U.S. government policy in Sudan, and because its mission is so strictly focused on peacebuilding and not economic development, it can earn the trust of local parties quickly. On several occasions, it was apparent that outsider status was actually useful in bringing parties together. One example of this was in the conflict prone region of the Nuba Mountains in South Kordofan. Working through local partners, USIP sponsored back-to-back programs in electoral violence prevention and in peace consultations to resolve local problems in this heavily politicized region. The fact that we had traveled the long (and sometimes rough) road from Khartoum to Dilling to stand under a tent in the blistering heat was not lost on the participants and they responded to this display of fortitude with a commitment to the problem solving process and the training. At the end of the five-day program two tribal leaders who had not been speaking took advantage of the opportunity to reach out to each other. It was not miraculous, but the first step of a long slow process that had been facilitated by the presence of third parties who were not allied with local politics. It is also important to note that, in the Sudanese context, disenchantment with the government runs so deep that outsiders (even or maybe especially those associated with the international critique of that government) can be seen as a reassuring presence just by showing up. Concern with the local, as Richmond notes, is a key element of peacebuilding that is often missed by those more focused on events in the capital. In the case of the program in the Nuba Mountains, paying attention to the local was as simple as making the effort to get out of Khartoum to a troubled region. But also, there are times when not being too closely identified with particular local actors provides a peacebuilding benefit. Unfortunately, this region of Sudan has fallen prey to violence connected to state elections and the new international border between Sudan and South Sudan. It is currently too dangerous for international third parties to do locally based work.

Another opportunity to bring alienated groups together occurred in Khartoum when I worked with my local partner to sponsor a joint workshop on electoral violence prevention for the police and civil society activists. This program was daring in its aim to train these antagonist groups together but it was also the logical outcome of dynamics we observed during several electoral violence prevention training programs that involved presentations by invited guest police speakers. The participants—generally a mix of civil society sectors including media, lawyers, activists, students, and teachers—were polite but insistently critical and clearly skeptical that the police were not acting in support of the ruling party. The police, for their part, continued to insist that their primary concern was professionalism and maintaining order. When we brought the two sectors together it seemed at times that little progress was being made in mutual understanding. But it was also clear that the government itself could not have provided a platform that civil society activists would have considered genuine, and conversely, local civil society could not have initiated a process by itself that the police would have considered worthy of their time. The context of elections, however, provided a great opportunity, as there has been a scramble of interest for knowledge about the electoral process and concern about the risk of violence. Since CSOs have had a history of harassment and arrest in their association with the police, there would normally have been great reluctance to attend a joint program with them (especially as it was held on the premises of the police academy). But in the context of the elections and a trusted outside party in USIP, a number of representatives from youth and women's groups participated. The outcome was again less than revolutionary, but it was clear from the brief interaction during a three day program that the two groups had strong negative stereotypes about each other and also that both could see the benefit of learning more about each other. That insight led USIP to sponsor a series of police/community dialogues aimed at providing an ongoing process for key representatives of these constituencies to interact in a comfortable and trust-building manner.

Modeling Democratic and Human Rights Values

In addition to being able to sometimes provide a neutral or trusted presence for various Sudanese groups to come together, programming by international actors can also provide the impetus for progressive social change or for modeling the behavior that we seek to encourage. For example, my co-trainers for most of my Sudan programs have been women, and the fact that we travel so far from home as professionals sets an example that is not lost on our participants. We rarely attempt to raise the issue of women's rights directly, but we do take advantage of any opportunities to use examples involving strong, politically empowered women in the public sector when we can.[15] Our participant groups always include women, and in some cases they make up fifty percent of the group. As western women who are offering non-gender oriented training that men also desire, our role is doubly beneficial. We are accorded a kind of complimentary masculine status because we are foreign, but we also refrain from making judgments on Sudanese society, merely offering a model of what educated empowered women can do and offering training in the skills of negotiation, communication, and decision making that can help the society handle the inevitable social friction that comes with the transformation of gender roles. One of the best things we can offer to our participants is the gift of patience and understanding. Gender roles are still being defined in western countries, decades after the universal declaration on human rights, and we should not expect rapid transformation in other parts of the world, especially if it is externally driven.

Because a significant component of the electoral violence prevention program involved an understanding of democratic norms and the rights and duties of citizenship, we also drew attention to the need to create fair, respectful spaces within the workshop and among the participants. Although every group has its share of extra-vocal and shy participants, we made an effort to vary the activities so that everyone found a level of comfort in which they could begin to express their opinions and participate. One of the more interesting features of Sudanese participants—especially in urban settings where many rely on poor public transportation options—is the tendency to be significantly late at the start of any program. It has also become customary to keep cell phones on and to accept calls while walking out of the room for further discussion. These practices can grate on a professional western sensibility. And, notably, the behaviors occur after repeated expressions by the participants that they should be banned and punished as violations of the rules of any workshop. Rather than simply expressing displeasure or withholding a much-treasured certificate, our approach has been to point out the social subtext of this constant rule-violation. When told that their inattentiveness to time and their lax use of cell phones is actually a sign of disrespect to their colleagues, most participants change their behavior. When the connection is made between simple social rule observance and a stable and functioning democratic society their attention sharpens. Of course these points must be made in the context of a program where the trainers, as Richmond argues, model the democratic and accountable manners they seek to spread. In our case, we made sure to be ready on time and present our full attention to participants in a similarly appropriate manner, but such modeling goes farther than hectoring in convincing participants that their behavior is deeply implicated in the future peace (or not) of their country.

Different Versions of the Local

One of the difficulties of Richmond's prescription to maintain empathy and awareness for local everyday life is that this life is multiple, contradictory, and complex. It cannot be condensed or simplified, even—as Richmond suggests—by economic factors, and any effort to benefit some sectors over others comes fraught with unintended consequences. A recent program brought together a group from the northern capital of Khartoum with a group from several southern states in a training-of-trainers workshop. It was designed to further the sustainability as well as geographic reach of our election violence prevention materials and methods and to join trainers from the north and the south in a cooperative network that would extend beyond the election period and regardless of South Sudan's subsequent vote for independence. Notably, most members of the Khartoum group had never been to the less-developed South, which was primarily why we chose the southern capital, Juba, as the site of the joint workshop. Few international organizations have brought a group of civil society actors from the generally better developed Arab-identified north to the generally impoverished African-identified south. Our aim was two-fold. First, we very much wanted to open the eyes of the privileged northerners to the conditions that their fellow citizens were enduring, and the challenges they faced. Secondly, we wanted the group to confront their own respective stereotypes of each other and realize that they could work with each other on common peacebuilding goals regardless of their geographical and social differences. The program was conducted in both Arabic and English, though some members of each group spoke both. The lesson learned turned out to be quite different from what we expected. Despite differences in education, language, religion, and heritage, the two groups cooperated remarkably well, even sharing folk songs and dances during a group dinner.

One key difficulty during that program came from a female participant. Her behavior offended a number of her northern colleagues (who were apparently anxious that the lapse not be apparent to their southern counterparts). The difficulty lay in the vastly different stories told to us about the nature of her offense. The first version of the tale was quite serious and involved inappropriate behavior in mixed company. In this version, her roommate was said to have locked the door in order to keep her from going out at 2:00am and damaging her own and everyone else's reputations. Subsequent versions of the story were more restrained and focused on the public drunkenness and attitude. Our concerns as organizers and sponsors of the program were to make sure that everyone returned home safely and that the reputations of the local partner and participants were not damaged. As the international, I refrained from interacting directly with the participants on this issue but in my discussions with my partner we concluded that while the offending woman had an international human right to make her own decisions, in this context, where bedrooms were shared, she also had an obligation to her roommate and to the general reputation of her colleagues. Interestingly, the concept of an individual woman's rights did not seem to matter to the women's rights activists in the group, who were more concerned with social norms and political rivalries than in upholding principles they normally championed. In the end, my partner had a stern talk with the woman about being careful when she was in a strange city and about her obligations to be polite to her roommate. She modified her behavior the next day and the tempest seemed to blow over. For us, though, it was a stressful exposure to the unpredictable nature both of the coercive social norms of Sudanese society and the commitment of activists for women's rights to make their own decisions.

Hybridity and the Valorization of the Local

Ultimately, the problem with the critique of the Liberal Peace is that it sets up a straw man and then knocks it down with oversimplified prescriptions for an extremely complicated environment. There are certainly plenty of mistakes and hypocrisies to western peacebuilding efforts. But the suggestions offered by Richmond and Franks are premised on a reading of these mistakes as a function of the wrong perspective adopted by a uniform set of actors at a planning meeting. In fact the mistakes are the result of many actors with many conflicting aims and procedures working in a complex and bewildering environment and failing to coordinate enough to learn from each other's mistakes (thereby condemned to repeat them).

One risk embedded in Richmond's attempt to remedy the mistakes is that the local will become its own illusion of a monolithic and valorized presence. Shahrbanou Tadjbakhsh puts it well when she notes that "the main problem with the functional search for hybridity and exoticizing 'indigenous' and 'traditional' practices is that it relies on essentializing culture. The international community swings from one extreme of trying to redo every institution to uncritically embracing all that is 'traditional.'"[16] In the case of Sudan, which local practices are we to embrace? Those of the government itself when it claims that Sudan is an Islamic country following Shari'a law (despite the presence of Muslim citizens who believe in secular government)? Or the practice of a northern man who believes that a northern woman should be able to drink when she goes to the south? Or the practice of southern men who firmly believe that women should not inherit property because it is a male entitlement? While it is important to understand and—critically—to respect the local cultures where you work as an international, ultimately Richmond's prescriptions do not offer any guidance for navigating the complex terrain of cultures in the throes of social and political transformation.

The post liberal peace is messy, long and expensive. Perhaps we have been too hasty to assume that the multitudes of international actors working to make peace are not learning from their mistakes. Partnership and patience, not rescue, should provide the overall framework from which peacebuilding approaches are derived.

Notes

1. Oliver P. Richmond and Jason Franks, *Liberal Peace Transitions: Between Statebuilding and Peacebuilding* (Edinburgh, Scotland: Edinburgh University Press, 2011).

2. Richmond and Franks, *Liberal Peace Transitions*, 3.

3. Richmond and Franks, *Liberal Peace Transitions,* 3.

4. United States Institute of Peace and U.S. Army Peacekeeping and Stability Operations Institute, *Guiding Principles for Peace Operations,* November 2009, http://www.usip.org/resources/guiding-principles-stabilization-and-reconstruction (accessed October 7, 2012).

5. *Guiding Principles for Peace Operations.*

6. See Rajiv Chandrasekaran, *Imperial Life in the Emerald City: Inside Iraq's Green Zone* (New York: Alfred A. Knopf, 2006).

7. Linda Bishai, "Liberal Internationalism and the Law vs. Liberty Paradox," *Journal of International Relations and Development* 15 (April 2012): 201-223.

8. Oliver P. Richmond, "Becoming Liberal, Unbecoming Liberalism: Liberal-Local Hybridity via the Everyday as a Response to the Paradoxes of Liberal Peacebuilding," *Journal of Intervention and Statebuilding* 3, no. 3 (November 2009): 325-344, 338.

9. See United States Institute of Peace, *Guidelines for Relations Between U.S. Armed Forces and Non-Governmental Humanitarian Organizations in Hostile or Potentially Hostile Environments,* July 2007, http://www.usip.org/publications/guidelines-relations-between-us-armed-forces-and-nghos-hostile-or-potentially-hostile-envi (accessed October 7, 2012).

10. Oliver P. Richmond, "Liberal Peace Transitions Need Urgent Rethink," *openDemocracy*, 20 November 2009, http://opendemocracy.net/oliver-p-richmond/liberal-peace-transitions-rethink-is-urgent (accessed October 7, 2012).

11. Richmond, "Liberal Peace Transitions Need Urgent Rethink."

12. Richmond, "Liberal Peace Transitions Need Urgent Rethink."

13. Richmond and Franks, *Liberal Peace Transitions*, 213-214 (the following discussion is also taken from these pages).

14. See Mary Anderson, *Do No Harm: How Aid Can Support Peace—or War* (Boulder, CO: Lynne Rienner, 1999).

15. On the need to approach women's issues from a sensitive and incremental perspective, see Nicholas Kristoff and Sheryl WuDunn, *Half the Sky: Turning Oppression into Opportunity for Women Worldwide* (New York: Knopf, 2009).

16. Shahrbanou Tadjbakhsh, "Liberal Peace is Dead? Not so Fast," *openDemocracy*, 27 November 2009, http://www.opendemocracy.net/shahrbanou-tadjbakhsh/liberal-peace-is-dead-not-so-fast (accessed October 7, 2012).

Chapter 5

Election Observers, Democratization, and Preventive Diplomacy

Joseph R. Rudolph, Jr.

The preponderance of the literature on the rise and proliferation of international election monitors focuses on their headliner role in the process of democratization, and for good reason. It is not elections which are essential to the creation and maintenance of democratic institutions, but *legitimate* elections in which the people are given an opportunity to choose freely and fairly between competing candidates, and in which the will that they express at the ballot box is honored by those in government. In today's world, the corps of election observers regularly deployed by numerous, highly respected international organizations and non-governmental monitoring groups serve as the world's umpires in judging that legitimacy. Nor does their task always end there. In the highly charged settings following bloody civil wars and marking the birth of new countries, they often operate as street envoys exerting a calming influence by their presence in large numbers in potentially insecure situations, and by assuring those perhaps voting for the first time that their efforts will be taken seriously and that if fraud occurs there will be someone to speak on their behalf.

Election Monitors and Democratization

Given the hype that often accompanies the activities of election observers in elections seen as pivotal in the world of international politics, it is perhaps well to keep their role in perspective from the outset. In the world of democratizing and supposedly democratizing political processes, election monitors function as a piece of the overall process of third parties supporting democratization efforts. Thus, although elections are by definition necessary for representative democracy to exist, they are only a component of what Carl Friedrich labeled Constitutional Government more than half a century ago and what western diplomats seek to build abroad.[1] That system also embraces, at a minimum, a free media, free association and speech, competitive parties, protection of minority rights, and respect for the rule of law.[2]

Likewise, the monitoring of elections is only a part of the broad range of international electoral assistance being tendered by governmental and private organizations. Other areas cover everything from assisting in the design of ballots[3] to assistance in designing voting districts and making the choice between proportional representation and single member district systems, registering voters, providing advice on the layout of voting stations and administrative assistance in the overall conduct of elections, and supporting campaigns and voter education programs.[4] In short, election day is only a piece of an election process, and groups like USAID now fund "election capacity building" over two to three year periods during which the actual voting is only the center piece.

On the other hand, within this framework election monitoring is not just a widespread and still expanding endeavor, but the most important and best funded part of third party efforts to promote democratization abroad.[5]

Election Monitoring, a late 20th Century Growth Industry

Historically speaking, the monitoring of elections is not entirely a recent event. As early as 1857 a Commission operating under the authority of the Treaty of Paris monitored elections in Moldova and Wallachia, and in the twentieth century the Organization of American States (OAS) (established 1948) deployed election observers to oversee elections in the Western Hemisphere as early as 1962.[6] Still, as late as 1974 there were only thirty nine countries regularly holding multiparty national elections, and most of these were long established democracies in little need of outside monitors. Thirty-two years later, that number had more than tripled to 120. Most of those would fall under the rubric of Third Wave democratizing polities and most were newly recreated states or countries that had only recently begun to employ democratic elections as a means of choosing or legitimatizing their regimes.[7]

It was during the 1990s, often in conjunction with peacekeeping operations and the restoration of civilian government after ethnic civil wars, that the previously incremental growth in election observation soared, spear-headed by the growing activity of the Organization for Security and Cooperation in Europe (OSCE) in parts of the former Yugoslavia and the fallout states from the former Soviet Union. As a consequence, it is now estimated that 80 percent of all elections in even the developing world take place under the eyes of international election monitors sent by such international organizations as the OAS, the EU, the UN, the Organization of African Unity (OAU), and the most active of all, the OSCE and its Office for Democratic Institutions and Human Rights (ODIHR). Nor does the story end there. Interested states also dispatch monitoring representatives to elections important to their foreign policy objectives, and a wide range of private electoral assistance and election-monitoring organizations also exist, the best known of which is the Carter Center. Indeed, Jimmy Carter is widely seen as the person responsible for popularizing the practice of monitoring elections abroad.[8] The Carter Center, however, is not the only one enjoying widespread credibility. Other highly active, private agencies with solid reputations include Sweden's International Institute for Democracy and Electoral Assistance (International IDEA) and, since 1987, the United States based International Foundation for Elections Assistance.

The prevalence of election monitoring can be read in the raw numbers. Since the 1990s, the OSCE alone has sent observers–often hundreds at a time and with the United States normally accounting for the plurality–to cover more than a thousand elections abroad and ODIHR has had a presence in more than 230.[9] More importantly in terms of its credibility, not only has election monitoring grown vastly in reach during the recent decade, but the scope of the operations conducted by the more professional election monitoring organizations has also expanded dramatically to cover the pre-balloting, election day, and post-election activities related to the democratic election of public officials. Long term observers are deployed early in the pre-election period to monitor such areas as media coverage (especially of opposition candidates), the ability of groups to hold rallies, and the use of coercion by the existing regimes to intimidate candidates and voters. They then remain until after the official announcement of results to monitor possible fraud in the final calculation of votes and result stage of the election. Shortly before election day, their ranks are increased substantially by the arrival of perhaps hundreds of short term observers whose duties will include both visiting numerous polling stations on election day in order to check for such improprieties as ballot stuffing or instances of voter exclusion, and monitoring the tabulation of results in the regional polling centers.[10] And although the short term observers normally leave within a day or two of the vote, if protesters gather in the aftermath of the announcement of results, and especially where fraud appears to have taken place, the long term observers may linger even longer to monitor developments and sometimes issue commentaries that may shape events.

Democratization as a late 20th Century Growth Industry

Viewed from a slightly different perspective, the growth of election monitoring has been the by-product if not the direct result of the diffusion of, at the very least, the trappings of democratic government throughout once blatantly non-democratic areas during the past two decades. The externally—and internally—driven factors explaining this development have been varied but often interrelated.

As Steven Levitsky and Lucan Way have noted, the end of the Cold War and the collapse of the Soviet Union and communist systems in Central and Eastern Europe opened the window for pursuing new objectives and introducing new international norms into a world suddenly and significantly defined by the hegemony of western liberal democracies.[11] In turn, the sudden disintegration of the old, authoritarian order ushered in a concern with regional stability as well as humanitarian challenges, and a collective belief that regional stability could best be secured by spreading democracy in Eurasia and elsewhere.[12] Peacekeeping ventures were therefore tied to the promotion of democratic institutions, and with the revelations of ethnic cleansing and other war crimes in the former Yugoslavia and Rwanda, the protection of human rights also became a goal whose realization was tied to creating broadly democratic institutions of governance.

To this "push" for democratization from the western democracies, and under western direction and control in Bosnia-Herzegovina after the 1995 Dayton accords and in Kosovo after 1999, there was added a "pull" for countries shedding their old regimes and/or at least claiming to be democratizing. The economic and other benefits made available by western institutions to states choosing to democratize beckoned them, and these states, too, began to hold elections in increasing numbers. In turn, as the holding of elections under international observation became a litmus test for countries claiming to democratize, monitors had to be deployed in ever larger numbers and on an ever widening global stage.

Evaluating the Missions

In short, just as democracy, its pursuit, and its spread became something of a universal international norm during the past two decades along with the need to safeguard basic human rights, so the presence of international election monitors has been elevated to the status of a public good as a means of measuring compliance with those norms. But what, more specifically, can international elections observers do in abetting democratization processes?

What follows is a short list of the contributions normally ascribed to election observers, with the important caveat that here we are primarily referencing the most professional and respected monitoring organizations; that is, those who regularly use experienced observers and operate long term as well as extensive polling day missions. In other words, international organizations like the OSCE, ODIHR, and EU, and private bodies like the Carter Center. The list does not, of course, apply to all missions but neither is it an idealized list of what might happen. Rather it is based on what missions have accomplished, with the contributions listed in no particular order of importance.[13]

- Detect manipulations by the government or others in terms of falsifying data, excluding voters, violating confidentiality, etc. The OSCE criteria for elections are that they be freely conducted with high levels of transparency, fairly conducted in terms of impartiality and an equality attached to each person's vote, secretly conducted in terms of the confidentiality of a person's vote, and that those who depart from these standards be accountable for their actions;[14]

- Verify, conversely, that the governments holding the elections *are* playing by the rules;
- Publicize, reduce, and prevent fraud by their presence in the country and by the publication of reports deemed to influence the international allocation of funds;[15]
- Provide logistical assistance to local and national election officials;
- Monitor the media to insure its fairness in covering the campaign of incumbents and challengers alike;
- Stabilize, by their presence, "shaky electoral processes in transitional countries;"[16]
- "Keep an electoral process on track when an entrenched leader loses the election and then balks at giving up power;"[17]
- Underscore the idea that honest and regularly scheduled "elections are a political right rather than merely a political option that has gained considerable ground internationally;"[18] and
- Contribute cumulatively to incremental change in a democratic direction in regimes going through the transition from authoritarianism towards democracy, whatever the label placed on them.[19]

In each instance, the importance of having election observers present as well as their leverage absolutely depends on the individual organization's international credibility. Nonetheless, the evidence is seemingly strong that, overall, monitors have been successful in detecting enough fraud to force many states to look for less illegal ways of influencing election outcomes; for example, by manipulating the economy before elections in order to put the government in the most favorable light, a practice not uncommon among the consolidated democracies of the west.[20] There is also a significant amount of indirect evidence that, especially in the case of those transitioning governments close to the west in Latin America and Central Europe, their presence has been very helpful in more rapidly establishing democratic institutions of government. In fact, even outside those areas evidence suggests that they have been influential in shaping more honest elections.[21] Studies, for example, indicate that the presence of monitors has overall reduced incumbents' *share* of the vote even if it has not necessarily resulted in them losing their control over the state.[22]

To be sure, monitors are not magic talismans and the results of deploying legions of them are not all one sided. On the negative side of the ledger, to state the obvious first, observers now only *observe*. They do not have the direct authority to right any wrongs, unlike during the immediate aftermath of the wars in Yugoslavia in 1995, and the bombing campaign against Serbia over Kosovo in 1999. Then, the OSCE trained and deployed election *supervisors* essentially to run elections in each polling station in Bosnia-Herzegovina and Kosovo for several years before entrusting local election boards with full control over the process. OSCE workers also provided registration and voter identification services in these areas and oversaw the campaign activities in them, and in both areas international overseers (the UN's Office of the High Representative [OHR] in Bosnia and the United Nations Mission in Kosovo [UNMIK]) had the power to void elections and disqualify candidates not measuring up to established standards. The OHR still exists, but those powers are much less frequently used in Bosnia-Herzegovina. Likewise, since Kosovo declared its independence, the international hand is much less present in its elections. Indeed, because several OSCE member states do not recognize Kosovo's independence, the OSCE currently leaves its observation duties in that troubled state to other respected international monitoring organizations that follow its procedures.

Secondly, as Susan Hyde and Judith Kelley have noted, despite the frequent acceptance of their findings by the reporters who cover international elections, there is often a large number of "pseudo-monitors" present from interested states or gadfly organizations whose amateurish and/or biased instant announcements often deflect from the findings of the more professional organizations, whose own final evaluations of the fairness of elections may not appear for months.[23]

Thirdly, and closely related, the observers of even reputable professional monitoring organizations may be subject to cross pressures, or under so much pressure from their home governments to produce favorable or unfavorable findings in a given election that it can affect their objectivity. Here we are not just talking about monitors such as those sent by Russia to Ukraine in 2004 or Belarus (pick an election) with the expectation that they will sanction even openly fraudulent votes. Because OSCE observers now work in teams of two, instances can occur where observers within a team drawn from quite different countries with different political cultures and perspectives might look at the same election with different eyes, and in good faith disagree on its legitimacy or degree of illegitimacy. Similarly, Americans covering elections in a country to which the United States has committed considerable resources to advance the cause of democracy may be under self-pressure to see elections in a more favorable light than observers from other countries.[24]

Fourthly, authoritarian-leaning hybrid regimes that use repression to retain power and invite observers from a wide range of actors when holding elections in order to provide the semblance of legitimacy in justifying their continued hold on power have the luxury of picking and choosing among their reports those that support their "victory." Nor do the odds favor this happening only rarely. In a world in which few states refuse outright to admit election observers, only a minority of those now holding elections can be considered consolidated democracies where established rules of the game are routinely followed.[25]

Fifthly, the democratization process itself can produce considerable tension, especially in a post-war society. Elections held either too soon (when hatreds still run high) or too late (when frustration has set in) can themselves increase those tensions, whether election monitors are present or not.[26] More troubling, there is some evidence that in fraudulent elections the presence of monitors documenting that fraud encourages opposition groups to mount violent, and violence-begetting protests because the international finding of fraud can provide them with a "focal point."[27]

Finally, numerous analysts mention the broad problem of overcoming subjectivity in amassing an overall evaluation of the fairness of elections in hybrid regimes. Certainly there are times when it can be an imprecise judgment call. It is one thing to label a squeaky clean election free, fair, etc, and equally easy at the opposite end of the continuum to label as tainted those elections where the government refuses to admit or dismisses monitors, or flagrantly subverts all or most parts of the pre-election, voting day, and post-election processes. But most elections, especially in Africa and Asia, take place somewhere in the middle, where democratizing and not-so-democratizing countries may admit monitors to offer a veneer of legitimacy to their efforts to retain their hold on power.[28] Here, the problem can quickly become determining the *degree* of fairness or fraud, and this problem can become particularly acute when an organization is understaffed, arrives late in the game or only for election day, and must contend with a government that is neither fully cooperative nor especially hostile to its presence. [29]

On the other hand, a caveat is in order here, even if only one based on anecdotal evidence. It has been the experience of this author and the literally hundreds of OSCE observers with whom he has worked and talked over a decade and a half, that this criticism of election monitoring should not be elevated too highly. Governments that engage in fraud either before, after, or during election day have not usually drawn the line too finely between these periods, or even between fraud and outright intimidation to the point of harassing, beating, and even jailing opposition candidates if they believe that their hold on power is imperiled. Long term observers have abundant opportunity to observe and log these and lesser transgressions. Likewise, minor polling station transgressions on election day have not usually been that difficult to separate from outright fraud. It is one thing when the one literate son of an extended family in rural Kosovo arrives with his six illiterate relatives and, contrary to OSCE rules which specify that a specific person can only help one other vote, is allowed to accompany, in turn, all six to the voting booth to explain the ballot. It is another when someone enters a voting station in Azerbaijan with a wad of completed ballots in his hand and the local election committee's chair airily waves to him to put them in the already overstuffed ballot box.

Election Monitors and Preventive Diplomacy

As a form of preventive diplomacy, election monitoring lives somewhere along the line earmarked by Good Offices mediation/negotiations at one end and the deployment of lightly armed peacekeeping forces designed to keep a conflict from emerging or expanding. Within this narrow but important corridor, election monitors can be significant precisely because elections can themselves be important means of managing conflicts. As I. William Zartman notes, particularly in transitioning states, elections can

- Provide "cooling off" periods between the end of hostilities and election day. Organizing parties, selecting candidates, and conducting campaigns are all time consuming enterprises, and that time can be important in post-civil war locations;
- Provide a means of resolving issues through party politics and the ballot box rather than on a battle field or along a sniper's alley.
- Provide an *authoritative* means of demonstrating the relative strength of contending parties, sparing them and the political community the need for unruly protests, disruptive strikes, and bombastic statements which reveal little of their broad support in society. And, where appropriate
- Provide a means of resolving an issue once and for all through a referendum.[30]

There is, of course, no guarantee that elections will always function in these directions, and even less likelihood that they will always work to enhance the election of moderates. In fact, they are unlikely to do so in the immediate aftermath of an ethnic civil war, when the likelihood that electorates will be mobilized around raw wounds and ethno-national issues is high. Thus, the elections in Bosnia-Herzegovina approximately two years after the signing of the Dayton Accord ending the warfare there, which saw Serbian nationalists dominate elections in the Serb Republic (*Republika* Srpska, or RS) and Croatian nationalists win heavily in their parts of the (Muslim) Bosniak/Croat Federation, are frequently cited as an example of the risk of holding elections so close to the end of such hostilities. Yet even there the old adage that elections are subliminal civil wars seemed to hold. Simply stated, the 1997 local elections and the national elections the following year contained within the arena of party politics the violent conflict that had torn the region apart between 1992-1995 and introduced "ethnic cleansing" into our popular vocabulary. Furthermore, although Serb nationalists have continued to dominate the RS political scene and Croatian nationalists are now demanding that the Federation of Croats and Muslims be split so that they can have a state of their own in the country, the running of mostly fair elections within the framework of OSCE specifications and under the eyes of OSCE and other international observers has resulted in the replacement of the old Serbian guard through a turnover among the Serbian nationalists controlling the RS government. At least as importantly, secure in their control of the RS and able under the power-sharing arrangements of the Constitution to block the creation of a strong central government, Serbian nationalists have had little incentive to push the country back into bloodshed.[31]

As for the role of election observers, they do not *make* elections work in these ways, but they give them the chance to do so. Experienced monitors, even when conducting a whirlwind tour of a dozen stations in a single voting day, create an air of authority while still putting the local voters and election boards at ease when observing the identification and voting processes, checking the numbers voting against the number of ballots issued, and ensuring that the secrecy of the ballot is respected. And if the elections meet international standards, they can help head off post-election violence by attesting to the fact that they were fairly conducted and that all of it–the checking of identification, the spray marking of thumbs, the ultra-violet lights–were not just smoke and mirrors designed to deflect voter attention in one direction while the government stole the election in another. Or, as in Serbia in 2000, they can verify the victory of the opposition in the face of a leader's refusal to accept defeat, and thereby indirectly abet protesters in bringing an end to a regime and moving the state at least temporarily in a democratic direction.

Alternately, there have been those cases where governments have been caught impermissibly manipulating outcomes and where the fraud findings by election monitors have encouraged other forces in the state (courts, the media) to join civil society groups in calling for new elections, and in which relatively peaceful change has brought legitimately elected officials to office. Georgia's Rose Revolution and Ukraine's Orange Revolution are the most conspicuous and frequently cited examples of this happening; however, they are by no means the only ones.[32] As Philipp Kuntz and Mark Thompson have noted, fraudulent elections can be "revolutionary triggers." Even though the final outcome of a revolution is frequently unpredictable, there are moments when, bolstered by the presence of outside monitors whose findings support the opposition's claims of repression and fraud, the outcome can tumble a repressive regime.[33]

In all instances, of course, and even more so than in the case of the work of election monitors in general, to be effective agents of conflict prevention and/or relatively peaceful change, it is essential that the monitors be objective, discreet, transparent in their work, and otherwise pursue courses of action that maintain their credibility. And, again perhaps even more so than in the case of observing elections in general, in the often tense settings in which election monitors function in a preventive diplomacy capacity, utter objectivity can be consciously or subconsciously difficult to manage. This is particularly true where the monitor's home country or organization has a vested interest in seeing the election as a success, whether because it has so heavily invested in the country's democratization process or because it desires to use the election's outcome as a pretense to withdraw its peacekeeping force and/or discontinue other forms of international assistance "before there is political stability or actual peace on the ground."[34]

Conclusions

For at least the near future, international election observers are going to remain institutionalized parts of a global order in which democracy has become a goal that is being pursued or at least given lip service by all but a few, mostly pariah states. Yet the "industry" is still plagued by many of the problems identified by Thomas Carothers when it was just beginning to take off a decade and a half ago. Now, as then, elections draw too many monitors from the more amateurish observing entities for either governments to meet their demands for briefings and access, or for consistency and consensus to be the products of their evaluations of individual elections. Similarly, now more than then too many of these observers are not merely unprofessional in their demeanor, but less than neutral in their evaluations of, or willingness to avoid observing, questionable elections. Those organizations that refused the United States' request to monitor Afghanistan's 2004 elections on the grounds that they would only have access to certain areas of the country are to be applauded; however, too often this is not the case.[35] To the contrary, frequently country delegations and other monitoring groups forfeit through their behavior and pronouncements the credibility that they need to be effective election monitors. It is thus well repeating Carothers' first piece of advice in 1997. "Bluntly stated, the amateurs need to leave the field to the professionals."[36] To this a second word of advice can be added. There is little that can be done about the special teams deployed by governments whose reports are essentially written before they arrive in country, but those other groups currently lacking credibility also need to leave the field. Or they need to begin to work hard through cooperation with the more professional entities and adopt those standards and procedures in order to gain the reputation that they need to be effective promoters of democracy and precinct level envoys in the world of preventive diplomacy.

Whatever happens in their world, the roles exercised by election observers are now established. Moreover, the sweep of their operations is likely to continue to expand as popular revolutions and uprisings bring down autocratic and authoritarian-leaning regimes, and launch or revive democratization efforts, invariably a complex and often lengthy and uneven process, as the unfolding of the 2011 revolutions in North Africa and the Middle East once again confirm.

Notes

1. See Carl Friedrich, *Constitutional Government and Democracy: Theory and Practice in Europe and America* (Boston: Ginn, 1946).

2. Richard Soudriette and Andrew Ellis, "Electoral Systems Today: a Global Snapshot," *The Journal of Democracy* 17, no. 22 (2006): 78-88, 78.

3. Even little things like voter friendly ballot designs can be important in sustaining voter turnout over time. See, for example, Richard Soudriette, "Revisiting Florida 2000:

Promoting Democracy at Home," *The Journal of Democracy* 12, no. 2 (2001): 133-138, 135.

4. See Soudriette and Ellis, "Electoral Systems Today," 85-88. For more detail, see also Richard Soudriette and Juliana Geran Pilon, eds, "Editor's Introduction," *Every Vote Counts: the Role of Elections in Building Democracy* (Boulder, Colorado: University Press of America, 2007).

5. Thomas Carothers, "The Observers Observed," *Journal of Democracy* 8, no. 3 (1997): 17-31, 18.

6. Judith Kelley, "Assessing the Complex Evolution of Norms: The Rise of Election Monitoring," *International Organization* 62, (Spring, 2008): fn.1. For its part, the United Nations did not send its first observation missions until the late 1980s, when it deployed monitors to first Namibia and Nicaragua and then Cambodia and Angola between1989-1992. The European Union (EU) joined the growing crowd in 1993 when it sent observers to cover Russia's elections in that year and elections in South Africa the following year.

7. Soudriette and Ellis, "Electoral Systems Today," 78.

8. On this topic, see Eric Bjornlund, *Beyond Free and Fair: Monitoring Elections and Building Democracy* (Washington, DC: Woodrow Wilson Center Press, 2004).

9. See Soudriette and Pilon, *Every Vote Counts,* 26, and OSCE/ODIHR, *Election Observation Handbook* (6th Edition, 2011): 8.

10. See Ursula E. Daxecker, "International Election Monitoring, Fraud, and Post-Election Violence," a paper presented at the Annual Meeting of the International Studies Association, Montreal, Canada, March 16-19, 2011, 5f. The paper is available at the International Studies Association (ISA) Paper Archives website: http://www.isanet.org/pubs/paper-archive.html.

11. Steven Levitsky and Lucan A. Way, "Elections without Democracy: the Rise of Competitive Authoritarianism," *Journal of Democracy* 13, no. 2 (2002): 51-65, 62f.

12. For a broader discussion of these developments, see especially Judith Kelly, "Assessing the Complex Evolution of Norms: The Rise of Election Monitoring."

13. See, for example, Susan D. Hyde and Judith G. Kelley, "The Limits of Election Monitoring: What Independent Observation Can (and Can't) Do," *Foreign Affairs,* forthcoming but available at this writing at Professor Hyde's website.

14. See the OSCE/ODIHR, *Election Observation Handbook,* 5-18.

15. See especially Susan Hyde, "How International Election Observers Detect and Deter Fraud," in *Election Fraud: Detecting Fraud, Deterring Electoral Manipulation,* eds. Michael R. Alvarez, Thad E. Hall, and Susan D Hyde (Washington, DC: The Brookings Institution, 2008): 201-215.

16. Carothers, "The Observers Observed," 20.

17. Carothers, "The Observers Observed," 20.

18. Carothers, "The Observers Observed," 21.

19. The terms most frequently used to refer to regimes with both democratic and authoritarian features include: unconsolidated democracies, illiberal democracies, hybrid states, transitioning regimes, and competitive authoritarianism.

20. See Susan D. Hyde and Angela O'Mahoney, "International Scrutiny and Pre-Election Fiscal Manipulation in Developing Countries," *The Journal of Politics* 72, no. 3 (2010): 690-704.

21. Levitsky and Way, "Elections without Democracy: the Rise of Competitive Authoritarianism," 59f.

22. See Susan D. Hyde, "The Observer Effect in International Politics: Evidence from a Natural Experiment," *World Politics* 60, no. 1 (2007): 37-63.

23. Hyde and Kelley, "The Limits of Election Monitoring."

24. On the issue of objectivity, see especially Judith Kelley, "D- Elections: The Politics and Norms of Election Observation," *International Organization* 63, no. 4 (2009): 765-787.

25. See Emilie M. Hafner-Burton, Susan D. Hyde, and Ryan Jablonski, "Terrorizing Freedom: When Governments Use Repression to Manipulate Elections," page 4 in a paper presented at the Annual Convention of the International Studies Association, New Orleans, Louisiana, February 17, 2010, available on-line in the Paper Archives of the International Studies Association.

26. On this topic, see especially Ursula E. Daxecker, "Emerging Issues: Government, Democratization and Violent Conflict," Peacebuild: the Canadian Peacebuilding Network, http://www.colostate.edu/dept/PoliSci/faculty/daxecker.html (accessed December 12, 2011).

27. Ursula E. Daxecker, "International Election Monitoring, Fraud, and Post-Election Violence."

28. On this point, see especially Carothers, "The Observers Observed," 24f.

29. Hyde and Kelly, "The Limits of Election Monitoring," 2-3.

30 . I. William Zartman, "Conflict Resolution and Elections," *SAISPHERE* (2007):75-77, 75-76.

31. For a thorough discussion of power-sharing as a successful means of preventing conflicts from rekindling, see Caroline Hartzell and Matthew Hoddie, *Crafting Peace: Power-Sharing Arrangements and the Negotiated Settlement of Civil Wars* (University Park, PA: Pennsylvania State University Press, 2007).

32. For a discussion of the role of election observers in influencing the Rose Revolution, see Charles H. Fairbanks, "Georgia's Rose Revolution," *Journal of Democracy* 15, no. 2 (2004): 110-124. On their role in Ukraine's 2004 movement towards democracy, see Bohdan A. Futey, "Averting Civil Conflicts through Elections in Ukraine," in *Every Vote Counts,* ed. Soudriette and Pilon, 121-139.

33. Philipp Kuntz and Mark R. Thompson, "More than Just the Final Straw: Stolen Elections as Revolutionary Triggers," *Comparative Politics* 41, no. 3 (2009): 253-272.

34. Ruth Wedgwood, "Elections are No Cure-All," *SAISPHERE* (2007): 68-69, 69.

35. On the United States' search for monitors willing to cover Afghanistan's 2004 elections, see Susan D. Hyde and Judith G. Kelley, "The Limits of Election Monitoring," 3.

36. Thomas Carothers, "The Observers Observed," 28.

Part 2

Legal Approaches

Chapter 6

International Law and Internal Conflicts

I.M. Lobo de Souza

International law may be regarded as the law of the international society. In Hedley Bull's view, an international society, as distinct from the international system, can be identified when a group of states share common interests and values, participate in the functioning of common institutions, and consider themselves bound by a common set of rules in their interactions. Bull argues that, as that body of common rules that display the status of law, international law contributes to international order by fulfilling some specific functions that help attain and sustain the elementary or universal goals of the society of states.[1] A slightly different but related perspective characterizes international law as a product of the international society, serving general purposes similar to those of national legal systems; namely, to maintain order, protect the property and other interests of its subjects, and uphold their values.[2]

The fact that some of the international legal system's subjects are sovereign entities (states) does not detract from the binding nature or effectiveness of international law. There is a considerable body of opinion that founds international law's authority upon the reality that its subjects, notably states, recognize it as law and as binding upon them, taking it into account in the conduct of their international affairs.[3] States remain as the defining subjects of international law, holding the "totality of international rights and duties" under international law,[4] but the "purely inter-state dimension of international law" has changed significantly, owing to the addition of new recognized subjects, such as international organizations and individuals, and the progressive formation of a truly universalist conception of international law.[5]

International law's peculiar structure and processes reflect the anarchical condition of the international society, which lacks a set of centralized common governmental institutions. Thus, despite missing a centralized judicial system, international law offers an array of methods or techniques for the peaceful settlement of international disputes.[6] In the absence of a common international legislature, international law has developed two decentralized law-making procedures (or formal sources) designed to create, modify, or extinguish international norms and principles: international treaties and international customs.[7] The norms, principles, procedures, and institutions created by international law provide the normative foundations of the international society, and contribute to the achievement of its goals. This Chapter will examine the role played by international law in limiting intra-state violence, and more specifically in preventing, containing, halting, and terminating armed conflicts within states.

Internal armed conflict has been the predominant type of conflict in the international society since the end of World War II. While inter-state conflicts have also occurred, and may have attracted more public attention due to their potentially devastating effects, there is no question that intra-state conflict continues to be prevalent and pervasive, even in the post-Cold War world. A position paper presented by the Secretary-General of the United Nations in 1995 pointed out that many of the conflicts since the end of the Cold War were "within States rather than between States," adding that this trend was confirmed by the fact that of "the eleven operations established since January 1992 all but two (82 percent) relate to intra-state conflicts."[8] A recent study on the incidence and types of armed conflicts from 1989 to 2006 reached the same conclusion: of the 122 conflicts, only seven were the traditional, inter-state conflict; all the others (115) were either intra-state or internationalized intra-state conflicts.[9] Internal armed conflicts have long represented a major threat to international peace and security. Most important, they have been shown to deeply affect human security, as their occurrence has been associated with war crimes, genocide, crimes against humanity, and widespread violations of human rights. The international legal system has developed a particular set of norms, procedures, and structures to deal with this sort of conflict and its repercussions. Before those issues are examined, however, it is necessary to draw attention to the definition of internal armed conflict and how it can be differentiated from other types of conflict.

Typology of Armed Conflicts

International law distinguishes two broad categories of armed conflict: 1) international armed conflict and 2) internal armed conflict, there being a different legal regime for each.

An international or inter-state armed conflict has been defined as "any difference arising between two States and leading to the intervention of armed forces (or similar forces)."[10] According to the United Nations (UN) Charter and customary international law, states are under an obligation to settle their international disputes by peaceful means only and not to threaten or use armed force against other states, except in the case of individual or collective self-defense or when authorized by the competent organ of the United Nations (in the words of the Charter, when "collective measures" are taken under the UN collective security system).[11] Once an armed conflict involving two or more states breaks out, the law of armed conflict (or international humanitarian law) regulates the conduct of, and the relationship between the belligerents. This normative body, a branch of international law, comprises both treaty-based and customary norms, the former being exemplified by the 1907 Hague Conventions and the four Geneva Conventions of 1949,[12] together with their Additional Protocol I (1977).[13] International human rights law, as embodied in treaties, declarations, and international customs, also applies to international armed conflicts.

An internal conflict, also known as an armed conflict of a non-international character, is an armed conflict that occurs in the territory of one state only. This is the broad definition found in common Article 3 of the 1949 Geneva Conventions, which creates the minimum legal regime to be applied in this situation. Subsequently (1977), states adopted the Additional Protocol II to the Geneva Conventions, relating to the Protection of Victims of Non-International Armed Conflicts, designed to develop and complement the protections afforded by common Article 3. This Protocol defined internal armed conflict in a narrower way, as a conflict that takes place in the territory of a state "between its armed forces and dissident armed forces or other organized armed groups which, under responsible command, exercise such control over a part of its territory as to enable them to carry out sustained and concerted military operations and to implement this Protocol." The objective criteria laid down in the Protocol are narrower in two senses: 1) it applies only to an armed conflict which involves the government's armed forces; and 2) dissident armed forces or armed groups must display a minimum level of capability and organization (responsible command, control over a part of the territory, the ability to carry out sustained and concerted military operations, and the ability to implement the obligations of the Protocol). Material criteria such as these serve to determine, on a relatively non-discretionary basis, the field of application of the Protocol but, on the other hand, leave some situations of internal armed conflict out. For instance, although most internal conflicts involve governmental forces either directly or indirectly, one may consider a situation of armed conflict in which only armed groups will be engaged in hostilities against each other and the government is incapable of exercising any real control over the conflict.[14] To cover this possibility, the Rome Statute of the International Criminal Court defines internal armed conflicts as those that "take place in the territory of a State when there is protracted armed conflict between governmental authorities and organized armed groups *or between such groups*" (emphasis added).[15]

The occurrence of a protracted armed conflict is a fundamental, objective criterion by which international law makes a further distinction between internal armed conflicts and other situations of internal disturbances and tensions, as illustrated by riots, demonstrations, or isolated and infrequent acts of violence.[16]

A special situation arises when a people is, in the exercise of its right to self-determination,[17] engaged in an armed conflict against a "colonial domination," "alien occupation," or a "racist regime." A cursory examination of this type of armed conflict would promptly identify the marks of an internal armed conflict; after all, there is often one or more armed groups fighting against the forces of a government in a territory whose control and jurisdiction is claimed by both sides. Wars of national liberation have been, however, included in the distinct category of international armed conflicts by virtue of the Protocol I Additional to the 1949 Geneva Conventions. Aside from political pressure exerted by developing and socialist countries at the time of its negotiation, legal justifications were advanced for this apparently peculiar classification, including the argument that a people, as a recognized holder of a right to self-determination, is an international legal person deserving to be treated as a subject of international law alongside states.[18]

A clear-cut categorization of armed conflicts does not always reflect the every so often complex reality on the ground. International criminal tribunals have recognized that an internal armed conflict may well become international or display simultaneously both characteristics if "(i) another State intervenes in that conflict through its troops (direct intervention), or if (ii) some of the participants in the internal armed conflict act on behalf of that other State (indirect intervention)."[19] The crisis in Libya during 2011 affords a good illustration of how actual developments on the ground may alter the nature of the conflict within a reasonably short time span. The preliminary report of the International Commission of Inquiry, set up by the Human Rights Council to investigate alleged violations of international human rights law in Libya, concluded that, bearing in mind the chain of events, all three categories above described could be identified: at first, there were internal demonstrations against the Government ("internal disturbances"), followed by an internal armed conflict (as government and rebel forces clashed), and finally a "separate coexisting international armed conflict" (with the start of foreign military intervention).[20]

International Law and the Prevention of Internal Armed Conflicts

From time to time, social unrest, riots, and political instability take place within countries, pitting groups of citizens or ethnic communities against their government and/or each other. Occasionally, social disturbances within a state may threaten to escalate into an internal armed conflict, endangering international peace and security. International law is not oblivious to such situations, and has put in place a normative framework designed to facilitate the resolution of the internal dispute.

First of all, the conduct of that government towards its citizens will be constrained by international human rights law. As a prerogative of their sovereignty, states have the recognized right to exercise exclusive authority and jurisdiction over their territory and their citizens in order to accomplish their main public functions, including the maintenance of public order and safety. They may even employ legitimate violence to the extent that it is necessary to maintain or restore public order. Their actions, however, are always guided and limited by international human rights norms embodied in international customs and international legal instruments, both universal and regional in scope, such as the Universal Declaration of Human Rights (1948), the 1966 International Covenant on Civil and Political Rights (ICCPR), and the European Convention for the Protection of Human Rights and Fundamental Freedoms (1950).[21] It is true that the ICCPR allows states in situations that qualify as a "public emergency which threatens the life of a nation" to take measures derogating from some of their obligations under the Covenant (Article 4), with the resulting limitation on the level of protection given to individuals' rights and freedoms. But the same provision sets out conditions for the legitimate resort to this most exceptional action: 1) measures should be temporary and fully justified; 2) measures should be consistent with the state's other obligations under international law and not involve discrimination on any ground; and, most important, 3) measures should not derogate from some fundamental rights and freedoms protected by the Covenant, including the right to life and the prohibition of torture or cruel, inhuman, or degrading punishment.[22] To ensure that states will not abuse their sovereign prerogatives to the detriment of their citizens, bodies created by human rights treaties (e.g., the Human Rights Committee , ICCPR) or on the basis of the UN Charter (e.g., the Human Rights Council) will readily make use of special procedures (e.g., country mandates, thematic mandates, state reporting, Universal Periodic Review mechanism, and individual complaints) to monitor the fulfillment by states of the obligations assumed under the human rights treaties or the Charter and, in cases of violations, demand compliance and redress. The limitations thus imposed on the resort to violence by state officials are bound to play a major role in preventing the escalation of the social unrest into a civil war.

A situation of internal disturbance can be the object of consideration by the UN Security Council (UNSC) with a view to achieving a peaceful resolution and preventing its further escalation into an internal armed conflict. Chapter VI of the UN Charter authorizes the Security Council to investigate any situation which might lead to international friction or give rise to a dispute, in order to determine whether its continuance is likely to endanger the maintenance of international peace and security. With regard to such situations, the Security Council is authorized by Chapter VI of the Charter to recommend appropriate procedures or methods of peaceful adjustment (such as negotiation or inquiry), and to recommend such terms of settlement as it may consider appropriate.[23] The Secretary-General, in turn, is empowered by the Charter (Article 99) to refer a situation to the Security Council and, when endorsed or mandated by the UNSC or the UN General Assembly, may act as a peacemaker by providing his/her good offices or mediating the internal dispute, either personally or through a special representative or envoy. Organs of regional organizations (such as the Organization of American States or the African Union) may also intervene in the internal dispute as peacemakers, seeking to reconcile the parties, when the state belongs to their region and their powers are being exercised in accordance with their constitutive treaties.

International Law Applicable to Armed Conflicts

If social disturbances escalate into an internal armed conflict, a broader legal regime is brought to bear by international law upon the belligerent parties and third states.

When it comes to third states, their conduct is guided by the long-standing principle of non-intervention, whereby states have a duty not to intervene in matters within the domestic jurisdiction of any State. The broad scope of this principle was laid down by the International Court of Justice as follows:

> The principle forbids all States or groups of States to intervene directly or indirectly in internal or external affairs of other States. A prohibited intervention must accordingly be one bearing on matters in which each State is permitted, by the principle of State sovereignty to decide freely. One of these is the choice of a political, economic, social and cultural system, and the formulation of foreign policy. Intervention is wrongful when it uses methods of coercion in regard to such choices, which must remain free ones.[24]

One of the practical applications of this principle on matters of internal armed conflicts is that other states must not "organize, assist, foment, finance, incite or tolerate subversive, terrorist or armed activities directed towards the violent overthrow of the regime of another State, or interfere in civil strife in another State."[25] There is no question that an internal armed conflict can be fueled by foreign states, thus undermining the prospects of a peaceful resolution of the conflict, stabilization of the country, and an end to violence. The non-intervention principle, if respected and effective, would work as a protective shield against such undesirable foreign interferences.

However clearly formulated and construed, the practice of states shows that the non-intervention principle has been more breached than observed. Most instances of internal armed conflicts will witness interference by one or more states through the provision of direct or indirect assistance to one of the belligerent parties. This has been termed "proxy wars" or "indirect aggression,"[26] to denote how states can make use of non-state entities (armed groups) to pursue their particular foreign policy goals. On rare occasions, there will be a determination that a state has violated the non-intervention principle. In the *Nicaragua* case (1986), for example, the International Court of Justice ruled that the United States had contravened the principle of non-intervention by giving support to the military and paramilitary activities of the *contras* in Nicaragua, in the form of financial and logistic assistance, training, supply of weapons, and intelligence.[27]

It has been argued that situations of internal conflict are also subject to a particular expression of the non-intervention principle found in the UN Charter.

According to Article 2(7) "nothing contained in the present Charter shall authorize the United Nations to intervene in matters which are essentially within the domestic jurisdiction of any state…." This is the so-called reservation of the exclusive domain of states, a principle that has been invoked by some states with a view to precluding the United Nations from examining, debating, and adopting resolutions about their internal disputes. An important detail often overlooked by those who invoke this provision is that it ends with the statement that "this principle shall not prejudice the application of enforcement measures under Chapter VII." In other words, once there is a determination by the Security Council that a particular situation involves a threat to the peace, a breach of the peace, or an act of aggression, the Council is then fully authorized to exercise its functions and powers invested in Chapter VII in order to maintain or restore international peace and security.

As a matter of fact, the UN organs have developed in their practice an extensive interpretation of this provision, harmonizing it with other provisions of the Charter and the purposes of the organization.[28] Thus, faced with an internal armed conflict that is likely to endanger the maintenance of international peace and security, the Security Council has shown an inclination to exercise its full range of functions and powers envisaged also in Chapter VI of the Charter (Peaceful Settlement of Disputes), such as recommending procedures or methods of peaceful adjustment and terms of settlement. The General Assembly has also included in its agenda situations of internal armed conflicts. In particular, human rights issues arising in connection with intra-state conflicts, traditionally deemed to be within the reserved domain of states, have long been accepted as matters that fall under those organs' sphere of competence.[29]

More recently, the practice of states has crystallized a significant exception to the non-intervention principle: the responsibility to protect principle (R2P).[30] The R2P principle, as enunciated in the 2005 World Outcome Document,[31] while reaffirming the primary responsibility of the state to "protect its populations from genocide, war crimes, ethnic cleansing, and crimes against humanity," recognizes the concomitant responsibility of the international community to protect the same populations from the same crimes. When a humanitarian crisis looms, involving genocide, war crimes, ethnic cleansing, or crimes against humanity, the R2P principle authorizes two forms of intervention by the "international community," both under the UN collective security system.[32] First, the UN may use "diplomatic, humanitarian, and other peaceful means, in accordance with Chapters VI and VIII of the Charter" to help protect that particular population. At a second stage, if those peaceful means are shown to be inadequate and national authorities are "manifestly failing to protect their populations," the UN is authorized to take collective action under Chapter VII of the Charter (meaning the use of coercive means, including armed force), in which case it may co-operate with relevant regional organizations. Therefore, in a departure from the non-intervention principle, the R2P principle effectively legitimizes the intervention of third states in an internal armed conflict by peaceful and non-peaceful means, provided those stringent criteria are met. Libya's internal armed conflict in 2011 arguably illustrates a case of foreign intervention in the domestic affairs of a state that was sanctioned by the R2P principle.[33]

All parties to an internal armed conflict (government and armed factions) will be subject to a specific legal regime. First, the protections offered by human rights treaties continue to apply to and limit the actions of government officials and organs.[34] It has been observed that even if a government decides to declare a state of emergency, some rights and freedoms are so fundamental that they cannot be curtailed by national emergency laws or measures, lest the state is found to be in breach of its legal obligations under human rights treaties or customary international law.

Violations of human rights norms may also be committed by insurrectional armed groups during an internal armed conflict. In this hypothesis, according to a well-established principle of international law, the conduct of insurrectional groups cannot be attributed to the government of the state, provided the group is truly independent from the state and the state is not found to be negligent in suppressing or controlling the insurrection.[35] The said government, however, will still be expected to do what is possible to protect its civilian population, and to make sure that human rights violators will be held accountable and the victims assisted or redressed. Once the insurrectional movement controls part of the territory of the state, exercising *de facto* authority and administration, it will be expected to bear responsibility for respecting international human rights norms. This view has been endorsed by several authoritative sources. For instance, the report of the Commission of Inquiry on Libya (2011) called on the National Transitional Council to ensure the observance of applicable international human rights law, to undertake investigations into all allegations of international human rights law violations, and to provide reparations to the victims or their families.[36]

In addition to human rights norms, the conduct of governmental forces and armed groups in internal armed conflicts will be regulated by international humanitarian law, which applies for the duration of hostilities until the conclusion of a peaceful settlement.[37] Humanitarian law applicable to internal armed conflicts has been developed by states through treaties and customs with the purpose of "humanizing" the conflict. The normative framework created by treaties includes common Article 3 of the four Geneva Conventions (1949), and the 1977 Additional Protocols I and II. It lays down a minimum level of protection applicable to all internal armed conflicts, prescribing that those taking no active part in the hostilities, including civilians and members of armed forces, shall be treated humanely, without any adverse discrimination. States practice consolidated international customs that reflect these and other norms of behavior.

A comprehensive study on customary international humanitarian law, sponsored by the International Committee of the Red Cross, identified an extensive list of customary rules applicable to all parties to internal armed conflicts, including the principle of distinction (comprising distinction between civilians and combatants and between civilian objects and military objectives, as well as proportionality of and precautions in attacks); rules that afford special protections to certain persons (e.g., medical and religious personnel, humanitarian relief personnel), objects (medical and religious objects, humanitarian objects), zones (hospital and safety zones, demilitarized zones), cultural property, and the natural environment; rules that impose prohibitions regarding specific methods of warfare (denial of quarter, starvation, and access to humanitarian relief) and the use of certain weapons (weapons of a nature to cause superfluous injury or unnecessary suffering and weapons that are by nature indiscriminate); and rules that demand humane and nondiscriminatory treatment of civilians and persons *hors de combat*.[38]

Compliance with international human rights law and humanitarian law applicable to internal armed conflicts will be monitored by a wide range of actors, including human rights bodies, UN organs, regional organizations, NGOs, Protecting Powers, and the International Committee of the Red Cross.

An internal armed conflict will likely seize the Security Council's attention and be included in its agenda on a continuous basis until it is finally settled. In dealing with this matter, the Security Council will have in mind two goals: 1) restoring international or regional peace and security, and 2) ensuring the protection of civilians during the conflict. The first objective may be attained by a mix of measures, coercive and non-coercive, designed to bring a halt to hostilities and establish the conditions for a peaceful settlement of the dispute. On the internal armed conflict in Sudan (Darfur), for example, the Security Council adopted Resolution 1828 (2008), by which it imposed provisional measures under Article 40 of the UN Charter to try to contain the conflict. When needed, the Security Council has gone beyond provisional measures and imposed sanctions under Chapter VII against the government and/or armed groups and their leadership. Targeted sanctions, for instance, have been imposed against the National Union for the Total Independence of Angola (UNITA),[39] armed groups operating in Somalia,[40] and the Libyan government.[41] Lastly, the Council may decide to authorize states to, either in isolation or through regional arrangements, use force and intervene militarily in the conflict in order to restore peace and protect the civilian population.[42]

In discharging its primary responsibility for the maintenance of international peace and security, the Security Council considers the protection of civilians in (internal) armed conflicts a high priority. An inquiry into the practice of the Security Council confirms its readiness to demand that all parties to the conflict respect international human rights and humanitarian norms, and to put in place mechanisms for the protection of civilians. As evidence of a gradual evolution in the Security Council's policy options to deal with intrastate conflicts, the Council has included the protection of civilians in the mandate of peacekeeping operations and authorized the use of force not only in self-defense but, beyond that, to enforce that mandate. In Resolution 1894 (2009), the Security Council reaffirmed "its practice of ensuring that mandates of UN peacekeeping and other relevant missions include, where appropriate and on a case-by-case basis, provisions regarding the protection of civilians."[43]

The Security Council has been invested with those powers by the UN Charter because it is the organ with primary, though not exclusive, responsibility for the maintenance of international peace and security. To ensure the effectiveness of decisions taken by the Security Council, in particular those that fall under Chapter VII of the Charter, this treaty imposed on members of the United Nations the duty to "accept and carry out the decisions of the Security Council in accordance with the present Charter" (Article 25). Furthermore, the Charter acknowledges a role for the General Assembly (GA) in the maintenance of international peace and security, authorizing it to "recommend measures for the peaceful adjustment of any situation, regardless of origin, which it deems likely to impair the general welfare or friendly relations among nations" (Article 14). On the basis of this provision, the GA is authorized to discuss and adopt recommendations addressed to a specific internal armed conflict, a prerogative equal to that of the Security Council under Article 38, Chapter VI of the Charter.

International Law in the Final Phase of Internal Armed Conflicts

An internal armed conflict may end on its own, when one of the parties prevails in the struggle or they come to a peaceful settlement. Often, the conflict will settle as a result of a peacemaking initiative undertaken by third parties, who could be an envoy from a state or group of states, a representative from the UN Secretary General, or any entity or person authorized or endorsed by an organ of an international organization. Hostilities will come to a halt by a cease-fire agreement between the parties, which may be followed by a more complex disengagement of forces agreement that could contain provisions regarding the location of the forward lines of the forces, the creation of zones with limited armaments, etc. If only the government and armed groups sign those agreements, such instruments would not present prima facie the nature of an international treaty. On the other hand, should other states and/or international organizations be parties to any such agreement either as sponsors or guarantors, that condition might turn it into an international treaty, thus generating international legal obligations for the parties concerned.

The last stage to be reached in the termination of an internal armed conflict is the negotiation and signing of a comprehensive peace agreement, paving the way for a major effort towards nation (re)building. The United Nations and regional organizations have frequently co-operated in this effort, on the basis of Chapter VIII of the UN Charter, providing coordinated political, financial, and security assistance to the implementation of the peace deal arrived at by the parties.

Peacekeeping operations have been a useful tool deployed by the UN in the aftermath of a cease-fire or peace agreement. Beginning with the first types of peace missions initiated in 1948, a discussion took place regarding what would be the legal basis for the creation of such operations. There was no explicit provision in the Charter authorizing any of the principal organs to establish peacekeeping missions. Issues pertaining to the expenses incurred with two peacekeeping operations (United Nations Emergency Force, or UNEF, [1956] and United Nations Operation in the Congo, or ONUC, [1960]) led to an Advisory Opinion by the International Court of Justice in 1962, where the Court elaborated on possible legal grounds for the establishment of said operations. Both operations were organized and deployed by the Secretary General on the authority of General Assembly (UNEF) and Security Council (ONUC) resolutions, even though there was no explicit reference to a legal foundation. In determining the general competence of the UN to create peacekeeping missions, the International Court of Justice relied on judicial precedent that espoused the doctrine of implied powers, according to which those powers "not expressly provided in the Charter, are conferred upon it by necessary implication as being essential for the performance of its duties."[44] The reasoning of the Court was expressed as follows: "when the Organization takes action which warrants the assertion that it was appropriate for the fulfillment of one of the stated purposes of the United Nations, the presumption is that such action is not *ultra vires* the Organization."[45] It then suggested that UNEF could have been based on Article 14 of the Charter, as a legitimate measure recommended by the General Assembly. With respect to the UN peacekeeping operation in the Republic of the Congo (ONUC), the Court seemed to suggest that the Council could have created it as a subsidiary organ necessary for the performance of its functions (Article 29) or as a special function entrusted by the Council to the Secretary General under Article 98.[46] This legal uncertainty has been settled by a consolidated practice whereby the Security Council, after making a determination that a particular internal conflict constitutes a threat to international peace and security (Article 39), acts explicitly on the basis of Chapter VII of the Charter to set up a peacekeeping operation or to extend its mandate.

International law may also play a momentous role in the aftermath of an internal armed conflict by ending impunity. The effective application of justice mechanisms (both national and international) that will bring accountability for those individuals suspected of genocide, crimes against humanity, war crimes, or serious violations of human rights law during the conflict is arguably one of the most important factors in achieving national reconciliation and securing deterrence against future crimes. International criminal law, a branch of international law, does not provide for the criminal responsibility of states when crimes under international law are committed by state officials, following a general line of reasoning first advanced in the Nuremberg Judgment and later endorsed by the International Law Commission's Articles on the Responsibility of States for Internationally Wrongful Acts. The same development, however, has firmly established the principle of *individual* criminal responsibility for the commission of crimes under international law, and that such crimes can take place in an internal armed conflict.[47] Therefore, individuals who are state officials or members of armed groups may be criminally liable internationally for their violations of international humanitarian law and other crimes under international law.

Crimes under international law are defined in international treaties,[48] statutes of international criminal tribunals,[49] and in several other international instruments.[50] International criminal law holds that individuals responsible for the commission of said crimes are liable for prosecution and punishment. To that end, international law has set up *ad hoc* international criminal tribunals and, more recently, the permanent International Criminal Court (ICC). These tribunals have either concurrent jurisdiction with national courts[51] or, as with the ICC, complementary jurisdiction, in the sense that it will only be authorized to prosecute individuals if the state is "unwilling or unable genuinely to carry out the investigation or prosecution," or national courts' proceedings were "for the purpose of shielding the person concerned from criminal responsibility for crimes within the jurisdiction of the Court," or were "not conducted independently or impartially in accordance with the norms of due process recognized by international law."[52] The way that the system is structured places on states the primary responsibility to investigate, prosecute, and punish the perpetrators of crimes under international law.[53] In any event, the exercise of international criminal jurisdiction will be reserved only for the most serious crimes (genocide or crimes against humanity) or grave violations of international humanitarian law.

International law is not an end in itself, but a means to an end. It purports to work alongside complex political processes within the broader international society in order to bring peace, stability, and prosperity to nations that have been plagued by internal armed conflicts. Its effectiveness and limitations, which will be considered in subsequent chapters of this section, reflect the strengths and weaknesses of the international society from which it is derived.

Notes

1. See Hedley Bull, *The Anarchical Society: a Study of Order in World Politics* (New York: Columbia University Press, 2002), 13, 122, and 134-136.

2. See Louis Henkin, "International Law: Politics and Values," *Recueil des Cours* 216 (1989): 22. The *Restatement of the Law, Third, Foreign Relations Law of the United States* (§ 101) defines international law as a body of "rules and principles of general application dealing with the conduct of states and of international organizations and with their relations *inter se*, as well as with some of their relations with persons, whether natural or juridical."

3. See G. Fitzmaurice, "The Foundations of the Authority of International Law and the Problem of Enforcement," *Modern Law Review* 19 (1956): 8; Ian Brownlie, "The Reality and Efficacy of International Law," *The British Year Book of International Law* 52 (1981), 1-5.

4. See Reparation for Injuries Suffered in the Service of the United Nations, Advisory Opinion, *I.C.J. Reports* 1949, 10.

5. See Antonio Augusto Cancado Trindade, "International Law for Humankind: towards a new Jus Gentium," *Recueil des cours* 316 (2005): 34. The notions of *jus cogens* (or a peremptory norm of general international law, as defined by the Vienna Convention

on the Law of Treaties, Article 53) and obligations *erga omnes* (as obligations that are the concern of all states and all states have a legal interest in their protection, cf. *Barcelona Traction, Light and Power Company, Limited*, Judgment, I.C.J. Reports 1970, pars. 33–34; and *Legal Consequences of the Construction of a Wall in the Occupied Palestinian Territory, I.C.J. Reports* 2004, par. 155) are a product of this evolution.

6. An accurate, though incomplete list of means for the peaceful settlement of international disputes may be found in Article 33 of the UN Charter.

7. International custom is defined as "a general practice (of states) accepted as law" (cf. Article 38 of the Statute of the International Court of Justice), and international treaty is "an international agreement concluded between States in written form and governed by international law, whether embodied in a single instrument or in two or more related instruments and whatever its particular designation" (see Vienna Convention on the Law of Treaties, Article 2(1)(a)). International treaties may assume a variety of names, such as "Treaty," "Convention," "Charter," "Protocol," and "Agreement." On the operation of law-making procedures, see Louis Henkin, *How Nations Behave* (New York: Columbia University Press, 1979): 28-38.

8. See Supplement to an Agenda for Peace, UN Doc. A/50/60, S/1995/1, 3 January 1995, par. 10-11.

9. See Harbom Lotta and Peter Wallensteen, "Armed Conflict, 1989-2006," *Journal of Peace Research* 44, no. 5 (September 2007): 624. The authors define internationalized intrastate conflict as the conflict in which "the government, the opposition or both sides receive military support from other governments."

10. Jean Pictet, editor, *Commentary to the III Geneva Convention Relative to the Treatment of Prisoners of War* (Geneva: ICRC, 1960), 23.

11. See UN Charter, Articles 2(3)(4), 42, and 51. See also Stephen Schwebel, "Aggression, Intervention and Self-Defence," *Recueil des cours* 136 (1972- II): 473; and Humphrey Waldock, "The Regulation of the Use of Force by Individual States in International Law," *Recueil des cours* 106 (1952-II): 492.

12. Convention (I) for the Amelioration of the Condition of the Wounded and Sick in Armed Forces in the Field; Convention (II) for the Amelioration of the Condition of Wounded, Sick and Shipwrecked Members of Armed Forces at Sea; Convention (III) relative to the Treatment of Prisoners of War; and Convention (IV) relative to the Protection of Civilian Persons in Time of War.

13. Protocol Additional to the Geneva Conventions of 12 August 1949, and relating to the Protection of Victims of International Armed Conflicts.

14. See Yves Sandoz, *et al.*, editors, *Commentary on the Additional Protocols of 8 June 1977 to the Geneva Conventions of 12 August 1949* (Geneva: Martinus Nijhoff Publishers, 1987), 1351. As this hypothesis falls outside the field of application of Additional Protocol II, the internal armed conflict will be regulated by common Article 3 of the Geneva Conventions only.

15. See Article 8(2)(f)).

16. This distinction is confirmed by Article 1(2) of Protocol Additional to the Geneva Conventions of 12 August 1949, and relating to the Protection of Victims of Non-International Armed Conflicts (Protocol II). Valid points regarding the shortcomings of emphasizing the intensity and duration of the conflict as a criterion of differentiation have been made by several authors. See, for example, Rene Dupuy and A. Leonetti, "La Notion de Conflit Armé a Caractère non International," in *The New Humanitarian Law of Armed Conflict*, ed. Antonio Cassese (Napoli: Editoriale Scientifica, 1979), 260-261.

17. A right of a people to self-determination is recognized by a number of international instruments, including the International Covenant on Civil and Political Rights, which defines it (Article 1) as the right of a people to freely determine its political status and freely pursue its economic, social, and cultural development.

18. See Antonio Cassese, "Wars of national liberation and humanitarian law," in *Studies and essays on international humanitarian law and Red Cross principles in honour of Jean Pictet*, ed. Christophe Swinarski (Geneva: Martinus Nijhoff publishers, 1984), 314-315.

19. International Criminal Court, Pre-Trial Chamber I, Prosecutor v. Dyilo (2007), Decision on the Confirmation of Charges, ICC-01/04-01/06, par. 209; International Criminal Tribunal for the Former Yugoslavia, *The Prosecutor v. Dusko Tadic*, Case n. IT-94-1-A, Appeal Judgement, 15 July 1999, par. 84. In the case of indirect intervention, the foreign state that sponsors and exercises a degree of authority or control over an armed group may be held accountable for violations of humanitarian law committed by that armed group (cf. *Tadic* case, par.97).

20. See Report of the International Commission of Inquiry, A/HRC/17/44, 1 June 2011, 4.

21. In the Americas, the major instruments are the American Declaration of the Rights and Duties of Man (1948) and the American Convention on Human Rights (1969).

22. The following rights are non-derogable: Article 6 (right to life); Article 7 (prohibition of torture or cruel, inhuman, or degrading punishment, or of medical or scientific experimentation without consent); Article 8, pars. 1 and 2 (prohibition of slavery, slave trade, and servitude); Article 11 (prohibition of imprisonment because of inability to fulfil a contractual obligation); Article 15 (the principle of legality in the field of criminal law); Article 16 (the recognition of everyone as a person before the law); and Article 18 (freedom of thought, conscience, and religion). On the scope and interpretation of Article 4, see Human Rights Committee, General Comment no. 29 (2001), CCPR/C/21/Rev.1/Add.11.

23. See Articles 34, 36, and 37-38 of the UN Charter.

24. See Military and Paramilitary Activities in and against Nicaragua (*Nicaragua v. United States of America*). Merits, Judgment, *I.C.J. Reports* 1986, par. 205.

25. See the 1970 Declaration on Principles of International Law concerning Friendly Relations and Co-operation among States in accordance with the Charter of the United Nations, adopted by General Assembly resolution 2625 (XXV), of 24 October 1970.

26. See Article 3(3) of the Definition of Aggression, adopted by UN General Assembly Resolution 3314 (XXIX), on 14 December 1974.

27. See "Military and Paramilitary Activities" (note 24), par. 242. There are authors who argue that with the recognition of a state of belligerency, international law authorizes third states to lend support to armed factions. See, for instance, Ann Van Wynen Thomas and A. J.Thomas, *Non-Intervention: the Law and Its Import in the Americas* (Dallas: Southern Methodist University Press, 1956), 219-220.

28. See Jean-Pierre Cot and Alain Pellet, *La Charte des Nations Unies* (Paris: Economica, 1985), 156-158.

29. See Henry Steiner, Philip Alston, and Ryan Goodman, *International Human Rights in Context: Law, Politics, Morals*, 3rd ed. (Oxford: Oxford University Press, 2008), 700-703.

30. The precise stage of legal development of the responsibility to protect principle is still open to discussion. It is not certain whether this is an old norm with a new name, an emerging new norm, or merely an expression of soft law. For a discussion of this particular point, see Carsten Stahn, "Responsibility to Protect: Political Rhetoric or Emerg-

ing Legal Norm?," *The American Journal of International Law*, 101, no. 1 (2007): 99-120.

31. See *2005 World Summit Outcome*, UN Doc. A/RES/60/1, 2005, par. 139.

32. The Outcome Document explicitly states that the international community will discharge its own responsibility "through the United Nations," thus dismissing any doubts as to whether unilateral interventions (that is, outside of the UN collective security system) would be permissible.

33. The Security Council had prior to 2011 expressly recognized the R2P principle in Resolution 1674/2006, on the protection of civilians in armed conflict, but the situation in Libya was arguably the first case in which the Council associated that principle with a particular country. Resolutions 1970/2011 and 1973/2011 recognized "the Libyan authorities' responsibility to protect its population" and authorized Member States to take all necessary measures to protect civilians and civilian populated areas under threat of attack. A NATO-led military intervention under this UN mandate followed suit.

34. See "Legal Consequences of the Construction" (note 5), par. 106; Case Concerning Armed Activities on the Territory of the Congo (*Democratic Republic of the Congo v. Uganda*), Merits, I.C.J. Reports 2005, par. 216; Inter-American Court of Human Rights, Judgment of November 23, 2004 (Preliminary Objections), pars. 107–19; General Comment no. 31, Nature of the General Legal Obligation Imposed on States Parties to the Covenant, 2004, CCPR/C/21/Rev.1/Add.13, par. 11.

35. See Draft articles on Responsibility of States for Internationally Wrongful Acts, with commentaries. *Yearbook of the International Law Commission*, 2001, Vol. II, Part Two, 50. The matter of whether an armed group is or is not under the overall control of the government is to be determined according to a complex list of criteria examined by the International Court of Justice in the Case concerning the Application of the Convention on the Prevention and Punishment of the Crime of Genocide (*Bosnia and Herzegovina v. Serbia and Montenegro*), *I.C.J. Reports 2007*, par. 385-415.

36. See Report of the International Commission of Inquiry, A/HRC/17/44, 1 June 2011, 84. In agreement with this principle, see the Report of the Special Rapporteur on Extrajudicial, Summary or Arbitrary Executions, E/CN.4/2005/7, 2004, 2004, par. 76, and the Report of the United Nations Fact Finding Mission on the Gaza Conflict, A/HRC/12/48, 25 September 2009, par. 305.

37. See Appeals Chamber of the International Criminal Tribunal for Former Yugoslavia, *Prosecutor v. Dusko Tadic a/k/a "Dule,"* Decision on the Defense Motion for Interlocutory Appeal on Jurisdiction, par.70.

38. See Jean-Marie Henckaerts and Louise Doswald-Beck, eds., *Customary International Humanitarian Law*, Vol. 1, *Rules* (Cambridge, United Kingdom: Cambridge University Press, 2005), 3–494.

39. Resolutions 864 (1993), 1127 (1997), and 1173 (1998).

40. Resolution 1844 (2008).

41. Resolution 1970 (2011).

42. See Resolution 1464 (2003), on the situation in Côte d'Ivoire.

43. For instance, since 2000 the Security Council has been renewing a mandate to the peacekeeping operation in the Democratic Republic of the Congo (MONUC), which contains a Chapter VII authorization to ensure the protection of civilians, including humanitarian personnel, under imminent threat of physical violence (e.g., Resolution 1794 [2007]).

44. See "Reparation for Injuries" (note 4), 12. Rama-Montaldo examined the *Reparations* case and argued that implied powers should not be confused with inherent powers derived from the personality of the organization, and that implied powers are in fact cir-

cumscribed by the principle of functional limitation. See Manuel Rama-Montaldo, "International Legal Personality and Implied Powers of International Organizations," *The British Year Book of International Law* 44 (1970): 124-131, and 147-152.

45. See Certain Expenses of the United Nations (Article 17, paragraph 2, of the Charter), Advisory Opinion of 20 July 1962, *I.C. J. Reports* 1962, 21. For an interesting discussion of how the Court construed the UN Charter to justify the constitutional basis of UN peacekeeping missions, see Hilaire McCoubrey and Nigel White, *The Blue Helmets: Legal Regulations of United Nations Military Operations* (Aldershot: Dartmouth, 1996), 39-55.

46. See "Certain Expenses" (note 45), 25, 30.

47. See Gary Solis, *The Law of Armed Conflict: International Humanitarian Law in War* (Cambridge: Cambridge University Press, 2010), 99-101. It is noteworthy that all cases under consideration by the International Criminal Court refer to internal armed conflicts.

48. E.g., the 1948 Convention for the Prevention and Punishment of the Crime of Genocide; the 1949 Geneva Conventions; and the 1984 Convention against Torture and Other Cruel, Inhuman or Degrading Treatment or Punishment.

49. E.g., the 1945 Charter of the International Military Tribunal; the 2002 Rome Statute of the International Criminal Court; the 1993 Statute of the International Criminal Tribunal for the Former Yugoslavia; and the 1994 Statute of the International Criminal Tribunal for Rwanda.

50. E.g., the Principles of International Law Recognized in the Charter of the Nüremberg Tribunal and in the Judgment of the Tribunal, 1950; the Draft Code of Offenses against the Peace and Security of Mankind, 1954.

51. See, e.g., Article 9 of the Statute of the International Criminal Tribunal for the Former Yugoslavia.

52. See the Rome Statute, Articles 17, 20.

53. See Article 49 of the First Geneva Convention, Article 50 of the Second Geneva Convention, Article 129 of the Third Geneva Convention, and Article 146 of the Fourth Geneva Convention. See also Ingrid Detter, *The Law of War*, (Cambridge: Cambridge University Press, 2000), 425-427.

Chapter 7

Turbulent Transition: From the UN Human Rights Commission to the Council

David P. Forsythe[1]

Half way through 2006 the United Nations Commission on Human Rights gave way to a new Human Rights Council. The General Assembly vote regarding this change was 170 in favor, four against (United States, Israel, Marshall Islands, Palau) and three abstaining (Belarus, Iran, Venezuela). The Commission, after sixty years of existence, had become so widely and vociferously criticized, especially in the West, that its credibility was challenged by no less than Secretary-General Kofi Annan himself.[2] It was not at all clear, however, whether the new Council would *be* very different from, or *act* very differently from, the old Commission. This brief analysis provides an overview of the Commission and compares it to the early days of the Council.

It is remarkable that the Commission, the traditional center of UN diplomacy about human rights for six decades, has received so little scholarly attention, particularly on the question of effectiveness. Only three books have been written about the Commission, only two of which move very far beyond legal description, and only one of which is recent.[3] There are few empirical studies about the dynamics of its proceedings or its impact on policy and practice, compared to legal descriptions of debates and resolutions.[4]

Within the limits of a relatively short overview, first we examine the membership of the two bodies, the electoral process involved, and the basic mandate at issue. Secondly we analyze the record on standard setting. Thirdly we look at the targeting and "punishment" of particular countries. Fourthly we examine the role of "special procedures." Lastly we look at miscellaneous matters such as openness to non-state actors and programs of assistance and technical services to states. A principal concern in all our inquiries is to deal with the question of effectiveness, so often ignored—in part perhaps because of the difficulty of analysis, or maybe because of the anticipated depressing conclusions.

Our initial assumptions are as follows, which we then test. 1) The Commission or Council, being comprised of governments representing states, could never be an impartial promoter and protector of human rights. Being composed of governmental representatives, the Commission and Council were always "politicized." 2) The Commission, despite its membership, compiled a respectable record on standard setting and other promotional matters, while its actual record on attempted protection matters was more mixed than often presented. 3) The Commission had a very weak impact on the actual protection of human rights inside states, certainly in the short run. 4) The Council in its early days constitutes essentially old wine in a new bottle. 5) While the Council has promotional, educational, and symbolic importance, effective short term protection of human rights is more important, even if often unlikely, through the UN Security Council—which has the legal authority to issue binding decisions in human rights matters as related to international peace and security, including those pertaining to sanctions.

Membership, Election, Mandate

The Commission

From 1946 the United Nations Economic and Social Council (ECOSOC), the parent of the Commission, decided that individuals in the Commission on Human Rights (CHR) would be state representatives. Thus the pursuit of human rights through the CHR would be made subject to state judgments about compatibility with national interests and other "political" matters. Whereas key human rights bodies in the Council of Europe, Organization of American States, and African Union would be comprised of independent experts sitting in their personal capacity, political will within the UN did not permit this option.[5]

In fact, key players in the 1940s like the United States, the United Kingdom, and the Soviet Union were strongly committed to a CHR of states. Each was aware of embarrassing problems that might be emphasized by an active Human Rights Commission of independent persons—the United States had its race problem, the United Kingdom its colonies, and the Soviet Union its dictatorial totalitarianism. During the life of the Commission there was never a strong movement to replace state representatives with independent experts, although the Sub-Commission was created based on the latter. The Sub-Commission, however, reported to the Commission, which in turn reported to ECOSOC and the General Assembly—all made up of states. Most member states of the UN never wanted a fully independent and impartial CHR, including the United States—the latter being primarily responsible for the human rights language of the UN Charter and the primary mover and shaker for UN human rights action 1945-1953.[6]

It was said that a CHR of states would have power behind its pronouncements. This argument was considerably undermined by the fact that the Commission never had the authority to do more than discuss and recommend, and even this organizational right was developed haltingly over considerable time, as we will see. What became lacking, most importantly, was the perceived moral power, or soft power, that came from consistent truth telling based on an ethical imperative. It was the latter that was widely seen to be sacrificed, to significant degree, to the shifting notions of national interest and political double standards that followed in the wake of a Commission of states.

With decolonization came several expansions of CHR membership, with the total number finally reaching fifty-three. Actual election to the Commission came via regional caucuses. It became apparent over time that most regional caucuses gave priority to friendly relations and taking turns, not serious review of human rights performance, so that major rights violators were often seated on the Commission. The CHR was never a club of the clean. Helping to bring an end to the CHR was the fact that in the era of 2001-2006, the United States failed to win election in 2002, while major rights violators like Sudan and Zimbabwe did. China and Russia were already there, reflecting the unspoken rule that those states traditionally said to be Great Powers should have a de facto permanent place whatever their human rights record. Adding insult to injury, dictatorial and highly repressive Libya was elected to the CHR presidency in 2003. Such events contributed to stinging critiques of the Commission not only by certain democratic states, but also prominent human rights non-governmental organizations and important segments of the UN Secretariat. Key elements of the Western media gave coverage to these critiques.

During 1947-1967 the original Commission of eighteen members—even when dominated by Western and aligned states—concentrated on standard setting and denied to itself the role of supervising state practice on human rights. Tom Farer and Felice Gaer captured the situation nicely when they wrote that the CHR manifested a "fierce commitment to inoffensiveness."[7] From 1967-1979 the slightly expanded CHR struggled to define a supervising role for itself. Despite the East-West and North-South fissures, the CHR of fifty-three members tried to supervise policy and practice in several ways from 1979-1991. In the decade without a name after the Cold War, 1991-2001, the same trends continued with only slight variation. And 2001-2006, the so-called era of global terrorism, the Commission supposedly slid downhill to its final demise.

Whatever the various historical demarcations, which are necessarily somewhat subjective and debatable, the CHR always dealt only with words. It had the authority to discuss and recommend, eventually to name and shame. It might have the power to damage governmental reputations within certain circles of opinion. But it had no authority to move beyond words, which themselves were non-binding, to manipulate threats and use of military force and various other forms of sanctions—whether diplomatic or economic. It could criticize, but it could not impose sanctions on elite travel and banking, and it could not threaten or deploy military forces.

To be sure, words expressing "mere" ideas can be important. Discourse may matter over time. Words can lead to, and then reflect, solidly entrenched expectations—which many social scientists like to call the social structure of international relations.[8] After all, the state itself is an idea. The notion of state sovereignty is an idea. Non-interference in the domestic affairs of states is an idea. Human rights can be a powerful idea.[9] And UN statements requesting or demanding attention to internationally recognized human rights can theoretically be powerful statements—especially when repeated over time and if internalized by important actors.

But the CHR never had the authority to challenge gross violators of human rights with more than advisory or non-binding words. Where a repressive government depended on systematic violation of certain human rights to stay in power, or in fact was ideologically opposed to the implementation of certain human rights, semantic appeals to human rights norms could often be a weak reed on which to lean.[10] The Commission always had a weak mandate, because most states—including most liberal democratic states—wanted it so. The CHR was essentially a moral talk shop, and over time it was widely perceived—rightly or wrongly— to have lost much of its moral authority.[11]

The Council

For the projected new Council of Human Rights, there was never a strong effort to change from state representatives to independent experts. This option was noted in a Swiss position paper but never pushed by that government or any other. There was also never a strong effort to change the basic mandate of the body in major ways—although some smaller changes were achieved. The broad understanding in 2005 and 2006 was that the new Council would be made up of states and would have the authority to discuss and recommend. That left the central question of membership tied to elections—that is, which states should be elected and how. This proved highly important but beyond easy agreement.

The Secretary-General's Panel on High Level Threats (2004), made up of leading experts on international relations, recommended that the new Council be a committee of the whole—namely, having the same membership as the General Assembly. This proposal found few supporters, given the Assembly's past record of highly politicized and selective attention to human rights issues. Beyond the approval of human rights conventions, the Assembly record did not inspire broad confidence.[12] Kofi Annan then followed with a proposal for election of only those states comprising "a society of the committed" by two-thirds vote of the Assembly, on the assumption that such a procedure would weed out gross violators of human rights. The 2005 UN World Summit of states did not try to resolve the membership issue. Rather, in endorsing the general idea of a new Council, it left to others the details of the new body.

In subsequent debates the United States and most "Northern" democracies proposed essentially a "club of the clean," made up basically of twenty elected states that met the test of being "real democracies" and also free from Security Council sanctions for reasons of human rights violations.[13] This proved politically unacceptable.

Human Rights Watch proposed different versions of the "club of the clean" with the core notion being the election of states only from those that had ratified the seven major human rights conventions and had met their obligations under those treaties. This standard would have excluded the United States, which had not ratified, and would not in the near future ratify, the International Covenant on Economic, Social, and Cultural Rights. China had not yet ratified the International Covenant on Civil and Political Rights. Most Arab states would be excluded for having, inter alia, failed the requirement of providing equality to women. And so on. So this position also fell by the wayside as politically unrealistic.

These and other similar proposals for a rigorously qualified Council were opposed strongly by most of the G-77, the caucus of so-called developing countries, which included China, many of whom were authoritarian or semi-authoritarian—along with Russia which, according to Freedom House, was declining from the "free" category to the "partially free." They saw particularly in the U.S.-led proposal another form of neo-colonialism if not neo-imperialism, in which the West lectured the rest. Most states of the G-77 stressed a broad process of tolerance and dialogue over time rather than naming and shaming by a select few.[14]

The final compromise on membership and election, brokered by General Assembly President Jan Eliasson, and approved by that body in March 2006, specified: a Council of forty-seven states; elected by the General Assembly by majority vote (obtain ninety-seven votes); with individual states standing as candidates which were not part of any closed caucus list; regional designation of seats (Africa: thirteen, Asia: thirteen, East Europe: six, Latin America and Caribbean: eight, West Europe and others: seven); term limits of two consecutive terms; with pledges to uphold human rights. Membership could be suspended by two-thirds vote in the Assembly for those committing gross violations of human rights. These egregious violations are not precisely defined in international law as such. Council members will be the first to have their human rights record reviewed by the Council in a new procedure to be developed.

The Council's membership, compared to the Commission's, actually enhances the voting power of the African and Asian states, while reducing that of the Western European and Others group, along with the Western Hemispheric group.[15] The latter two groups will only be able to pass measures in so far as they can attract support from the African and Asian groups.

These debates and negotiations during 2005-2006 showed above all that there was no consistent and wide-spread consensus about human rights and the

United Nations based on events since the 1940s. Whatever "learning" had occurred on the part of states in this domain was highly differentiated.[16] Belying the widespread ratification of the seven core human rights treaties, there was no broad agreement on how to move from formal acceptance of the norms to a more rigorous and impartial supervision guaranteeing their implementation. For the most part, a North-South conflict continued to manifest itself, with former colonies and/or authoritarian governments of the South firmly resisting vigorous supervision by a largely Northern group. Russia aligned with the South.

The first elections to the Council in May 2006 produced a body not radically different from the old Commission. The United States did not stand for election, but the other P-5 members were elected to the Council, including China and Russia. China remained authoritarian, and Putin's Russia had adopted brutal policies in Chechnya while whittling down many civil and political rights such as freedom of the press, a fully independent civil society, etc. While some gross violators did not enter the contest, serious and systematic rights violators like Cuba, Pakistan, and Saudi Arabia were elected. It could be said in summary that there was marginal improvement in the composition of the early Council, compared to the latter days of the Commission.

In a subsequent election in 2007, certain actors were able to block the election of Belarus, getting Bosnia to run—and win—in its place.[17] But it was remarkable that on the East European slate a serious violator of rights like Belarus could advance as far as it did before a concerted blocking campaign took hold. The near-election of Belarus, as well as the election of certain highly authoritarian and highly repressive regimes, demonstrated once again that many states did not take the protection of human rights seriously. There had been no sea change in attitudes on this question—only marginal improvement.

While the mandate of the Council had not dramatically changed, there was some tinkering, with some matters left in abeyance. As was true of the CHR, the Council is to promote and protect human rights by means of recommendations.[18] Building on the somewhat tortured history of the Commission, the authorizing resolution clearly states that the Council "should address situations of violations of human rights." As a subsidiary organ of the General Assembly rather than of ECOSOC, it should meet "regularly" and no less than three times a year, compared to the Commission's one regular session of six weeks. Like the Commission, the Council can meet in emergency or special sessions. The rather long list of specific duties is mostly a codification of Commission practice—e.g., develops the international law of human rights, provide advisory services, and promote human rights education.

One new feature is the undertaking of "a universal periodic review, based on objective and reliable information, of the fulfillment of each State of its human rights obligations." This procedure is being negotiated at the time of writing. If the history of the annual U.S. State Department Human Rights Country Reports is any guide, the first challenge will be to establish a valid record, probably with some type of oversight and commentary by public and private (NGO) bodies. That is, in the U.S. annual process, any perceived biases in reporting are likely to be debated by certain congressional committees and human rights NGOs. The second, and even greater, challenge will be to find a way to make public policy conform to the standards of the periodic review. The U.S. annual human rights reports are widely regarded as mostly accurate as far as they go (mostly civil and political rights covered, with the United States excluded from review). Their major defect is that generally subsequent U.S. policy often pays little attention to the rights violations rather objectively documented.

The Assembly resolution creating the new Council for the most part contains all the right words. The Council is to be objective, fair, and transparent, and manifest members who will uphold the highest human rights standards. The preamble says that the Council should eliminate double standards and politicization. As we will see below, the early evidence is that such wording will not greatly affect state policy in the Council. On paper what we find regarding membership, election, and mandate is marginal improvement but not revolutionary progress.

It can be noted in passing that the old Sub-Commission of independent experts has become a smaller advisory body to the Council. As of the time of writing it is not clear what the future holds concerning this change.

Standard Setting

The Commission

Conventional wisdom holds that the major achievement of the old CHR was the development of various human rights instruments, a record shared principally with the General Assembly. According to the distinguished jurist Thomas Buergenthal, "the most important contribution of the United Nations to the protection of human rights consists of the many human rights instruments—resolutions, declarations, and conventions it has adopted since it came into being."[19] Many of these originated in the Commission. In some ways the CHR played the role of an International Law Commission for human rights, drafting texts that were then revised and usually adopted by the Assembly. Within this purview, THE major achievement was the drafting of the 1948 Universal Declaration of Human Rights, the story of which, and the importance of which, have been told elsewhere.[20]

The seven fundamental conventions which developed the 1948 Declaration's principles into binding treaty form, and still more human rights treaties, declarations, and resolutions, created such a plethora of global legal norms in the human rights field that some commentators called for a moratorium on normative developments until the record of implementation could be improved.[21]

It was true that some relevant standard setting occurred outside the Commission. Notable in this regard was the continued development of international humanitarian law (IHL), which some referred to as the law of human rights in armed conflict. Consistent with tradition, IHL was developed in diplomatic conferences convened by the Swiss government, in close cooperation with the International Committee of the Red Cross. The Convention on the Elimination of Discrimination against Women was also negotiated outside the Commission.

But IHL, and the other regional human rights developments that occurred in an extra-UN process, did nothing to take away from the achievements of the CHR regarding universal standard setting. This short review is not the place for an extended discussion of how certain states, NGOs, and secretariat officials interacted in complicated ways to produce the extensive and relatively specific international instruments on human rights that existed by 2007. While, as noted below, efforts continued for even further legal development, a reasonable argument could be made that the norms negotiated through the Commission during its existence did indeed establish, for the most part, what was required for a life with human dignity.[22] That is to say, in large part because of the drafting of the CHR, the major problem for guaranteeing a life with dignity was not the absence of guiding global norms but rather the lack of their full implementation.[23]

It is rather remarkable that states, which according to the realist perspective are supposed to be self-interested rational calculators driven by a quest for physical security which transcends traditional political morality, have clearly articulated a liberal and cosmopolitan framework that is supposed to guide and constrain state policy both at home and abroad.[24] States, even in an anarchic international relations characterized by absence of central government with a resulting core security dilemma, have pledged to protect human rights and humane values in peace and war. Of course these same states, while negotiating human rights and humanitarian standards, also tried to ensure that the majority of control measures would be mostly weak. This fact suggests that a considerable degree of hypocrisy is not unknown in international relations. Yet there is also evidence that the notion of human rights has powerful appeal, and states wish to be associated with it. Herein lies a fundamental contradiction: most states wish to be associated with UN human rights standards, but they are also sensitive to "sovereignty costs" that would restrict national freedom of policy making in this domain.[25]

The Council

The solid record of standard setting by the CHR notwithstanding, the first year of the Council saw the approval of a new Convention on Enforced Disappearances, which was also then approved by the General Assembly. This normative development was rather remarkable in that from early 2002 the United States adopted a policy of forced disappearance for "high value detainees" in its so-called "war on terrorism." This U.S. policy was supported in reality by a number of European and other governments. Not unlike similar developments on torture, normative opposition to the practice was accompanied by considerable practice of the practice. About one-third of UN member states had ratified this new Convention at the time of writing.

This was followed by Council approval of a new draft Declaration on the Rights of Indigenous Peoples. On this matter the General Assembly proved unable to follow through immediately with its own support, due in large measure to determined opposition by Australia, Canada, the United States, and a number of other influential states. These states, all with significant indigenous populations, saw the draft Convention, which over time had grown to sixty-four articles, as divisive and a barrier to national unity and stability. But in 2007 the Assembly did approve the Declaration, despite continued opposition from important states.

The Council also created a working group to pursue further new norms regarding private petitions under the International Covenant on Economic, Social, and Cultural Rights.

Protection of Human Rights in Specific States

The Commission

If standard setting is widely seen as the CHR's greatest achievement, the protection of human rights in specific states is widely seen as its greatest failure. To again quote Buergenthal, "It must be recognized. . . that the United Nations and its various human rights institutions are largely ineffectual in dealing with individual human rights violations."[26] David Kennedy reminds us that particularly international lawyers can become so fixated on procedure and process that they fail to acknowledge that many procedures and processes fail to affect policy and behavior in progressive ways.[27] Conventional wisdom holds that the CHR failed to address many situations that should have been tackled with vigor and commitment, while extensively debating lesser violations of human rights by the *betes noires* of the G-77—principally Israel and its policies in the territories taken during and after 1967, and South Africa during apartheid.

It is true that to considerable degree the Commission, particularly from the 1970s when it repeatedly addressed itself to supervision of specific rights situations under the 1235 procedure, was indeed politicized and manifested double standards.[28] In the early part of the era 1970-1991, the CHR did indeed devote far more attention to Israel, South Africa during Apartheid, and Chile under Pinochet than to other gross violators of human rights. For example, Idi Amin's Uganda and pre-Gorbachev Russia never were the subject of a resolution of criticism despite their systematic and major violations of important human rights. In this same era, the only African state besides South Africa to be the target of a critical resolution under 1235 was Equatorial Guinea, despite the broad repression of rights and even atrocities in parts of that region. Five Islamic states drew critical resolutions, but harsh measures in places like Egypt, Morocco, and Saudi Arabia escaped condemnation. The picture for the Western Hemisphere was more balanced, with seven states of varying political ideologies drawing formal criticism, but the Argentine junta, supported by the Reagan Administration, never did, despite its systematic political murder and torture during 1976-1982. (Various multi-national reviews in the Commission did touch upon the junta's violations.)

If we broaden the analysis, a different picture emerges. James LeBovic and Erik Voeten studied CHR action 1979-2001, looking at four possible CHR steps based on both 1235 and 1503 as well as other measures: 1) discussing a state but taking no action on a country or discontinuing a CHR review; 2) continuing a confidential process; 3) voting for an advisory service to improve the situation or having the Chair issue a critical statement (a practice which started in 1988); 4) publicly condemning a state.[29] They compared CHR action, with the first option being most favorable to a state and the last option being the most critical, with a country's score on the political terror scale that purports to measure governmental repression,[30] looking at both which governments voted for what, as well as which governments were the targets of CHR deliberations. Their central finding is that "the results reveal unambiguously that the repression record of a country has a large positive influence on the probability of its being targeted and punished by the commission."[31]

Lebovic and Voeten argue that CHR "targeting and punishment were driven to a considerable degree by the actual human rights records of potential targets."[32] They find that by the mid-1990s some 60 percent of the more egregious violators (those with a PTS score of five, the worst category) were being addressed in the Commission and 40 percent of those with a PTS score of four (second worst category).[33] So the cliché appears to be true that the CHR glass was half-full and half-empty. There were double standards and a degree of attention that did not "fit the crime," but at the same time also some serious and appropriate diplomacy for genuine human rights reasons.[34]

According to this study, about 70 percent of the worst offenders were slapped with a formal critical resolution, while lesser violators were hit with lesser "penalties" in proportion to the "crime."[35] The more one moved beyond the Cold War, the more one found that human rights performance mattered as compared to strategic alignment. In other words, "the end of the Cold War brought a tightened link between rights violations of countries and their punishment by the commission."[36] Moreover, "Governments with better records were significantly *more* likely to cast shaming votes."[37] States that appeared to be trying to be good UN citizens by contributing to UN peacekeeping missions and helping with other public goods were treated more leniently than others.[38]

None of this is to deny that states like Israel remained of special concern to the CHR majority of states, or that China was able to use its growing diplomatic and economic clout to avoid critical resolutions despite its repressive nature. But it seems clear that the widespread emphasis on the defects of the Commission caused a number of actors, including liberal democratic states and leading human rights NGOs based in the West, to under-appreciate somewhat the encouraging patterns that existed at the same time. It seems probable that the lack of timely scholarly study of the Commission contributed to these blind spots.

Now if we add to the Lebovic and Voeten study, and in particular when we look at the period 2002-2005, we find that adding four more years does not change the overall pattern significantly, and the post-Cold War pattern existed until 2005.[39]

First, there is no evidence that concerns about human rights were a greater determinant of targeting in the post-Cold War period than during the Cold War period. However, this is not the case for the determinants of punishment. In other words, the human rights records of countries were an insignificant determinant of punishment during the Cold War, but were a significant determinant of punishment in the post-Cold War period. States with a PTS score of one have a small predicted probability of being punished by a critical resolution (0.007), but states with PTS score of five have a higher predicted probability (0.19) in the post Cold War period. Here we see some changes in the predicted mean probability, that is, it drops from 0.65 to 0.19. This is because there were some changes in the period 2002-2005. Lebovic and Voeten indicate that roughly 70 percent of states with a PTS score of five were slapped with a critical public resolution during 1991-2001.[40] However, during 2002-2005, this dropped to 43.7 percent. This can be understood from the overall pattern in the period of 2002-2005 in actions taken by the CHR. During the period of 1991-2001, passing a critical public resolution in the context of all the actions taken by the CHR occurred 50.4 percent of the time. However, during 2002-2005, this dropped to 32.6 percent. During 1991-2001, an advisory/Chairperson's statement occurred 23.2 percent among all the actions taken by the CHR. In 2002-2005, this rose to 33.8 percent. In other words, we find that there was a decline in using critical resolutions as a punishment and an increase in using advisory/chairperson's statement in the period of 2002-2005. In sum, the CHR progressively leaned toward relatively less critical forms of action, compared to the "ultimate sanction" of a formal resolution of criticism.

Second, involvement in international institutions is more likely to reduce the chances that a country was targeted by the commission. When we hold other variables at their means and modes, we find that states that did not participate in peacekeeping missions in the prior year had higher mean predicted probabilities (0.15) of being targeted than did participating states (0.05). In particular, when the 2002-2005 period is added, peacekeeping participation is a significant determinant of punishing a country at the CHR. In this context, we also confirm Lebovic and Voeten's finding that in the period of 1977-2005, states that vote in the UNGA only half the time had a higher probability of being targeted than states that vote all the time (a predicted probability of 0.28 vs. 0.17).

Third, ratification of the ICCPR is not a significant determinant in targeting and punishing states by the CHR. In particular, in the period of 2002-2005, we find that 85.8 percent of targeted states had ratified the ICCPR. Since about 86 percent of states around the world had ratified the ICCPR, it seems that ratification of this particular treaty is indicative of not very much, at least in the CHR.

Fourth, as Lebovic and Voeten indicate, states having above average capabilities had higher probability of being targeted than states having average capabilities (0.15 vs. 0.10). However, the fact that strong states can be targeted by the CHR does not necessarily mean that they can be punished just like less powerful states. In the post-Cold War years, a state having average capabilities could avoid sanctions or to keep the charges against it confidential an estimated 12.5 percent of the time; a state having capabilities one standard deviation above the mean escaped more than confidential treatment by the commission 15.3 percent of the time. For example, during 2002-2005, several CHR member states criticized the United States for arbitrary detention at the Guantanamo naval base, but no resolution was adopted against it.

Fifth, we do not find evidence that countries that regularly vote with the U.S. in the UNGA were more severely punished by the CHR.

Sixth, as Lebovic and Voeten argue, we find no evidence that countries with right-wing regimes are more likely to be targeted by the CHR. In particular, during 2002-2005 only 22.8 percent of all states being targeted had right-wing government. Similarly, during the period of 2002-2005, we find no evidence that states will be targeted and punished within the CHR by members that have dissimilar ideological views or alignments. When we look at each fifty-three member states' voting records in 2002 -2005, only 8.3 percent of member states voted to condemn targeted states which have dissimilar ideological views or alignments.

Seventh, in any period, we do not find that members of the commission were less likely than nonmembers to be targeted by the CHR. We also do not find evidence that once members were targeted, they were not treated more leniently than nonmembers, either.

Finally, as Lebovic and Voeten argue, governments with better PTS scores were more likely to cast shaming votes. This is significant in both full period (1977-2005) and post-Cold War period (1991-2005) irrespective of the inclusion of Israel. However, in 2002-2005 this pattern should not be exaggerated because, as we mentioned above, the number of public resolution (the most severe punishment) decreased during the period. In a similar vein, Steven Seligman analyzed the commission and the Human Rights Council during 2004-2006[41] on the basis of "Principled Voting Index" and found that there is "only a weak and inconsistent relationship between democratic governance and principled voting."[42]

In sum, we thought that the 9/11 terrorist attacks, and/or the absence of the United States from the CHR, might have altered Commission proceedings in significant ways. This did not turn out to be true. In the period of 2002-2005 there was no significant change in the number of actions taken by the CHR. Even though the number of actions taken by the CHR is not as many as it had been during the mid and late 1990s, the post-Cold War pattern remains during 2002-2005. If we look more specifically at four actions taken by the CHR in 2002-2005, we find that 77 percent of states with a PTS score of five were targeted by the CHR and 35.9 percent of states with a PTS score of four were targeted by the CHR. Thus, we find that a central observation by Lebovic and Voeten holds for this later period: the worse the human rights record of a state, the greater are its chances of being targeted by the CHR.[43]

Finally, if we look carefully not just at decision-making in the Commission but at its impact beyond UN meetings, we find that the CHR manifested a weak impact on the actual human rights situation in the various "targeted/punished" states.

Table 1 provides us with a simple but important "shortcut" of the impact of CHR's targeting [See Appendix]. The table shows the human rights record of repression (civil and political rights violations) over time of the most often targeted states by the CHR. None of the four measures of CHR action led to dramatic change in states' performance. However, it would be rash if we reject the effectiveness of the CHR on the basis of this simple comparison. Thus, we examined more systematic evidence concerning the effectiveness of CHR's targeting by looking at states' human rights performance over a twenty-six year period, 1980 to 2005, on a sample of 173 countries. As we have discussed above, there existed some different trends between the periods of the Cold War and post-Cold War. In other words, after the Cold War, the CHR was more "successful" in targeting the worst human rights violators. Therefore, first, we looked at the impact of the CHR targeting through 1980 to 2005. Then, secondly, we looked at the impact after the post-Cold War period, that is, 1991-2005.

If we set the four types of CHR action discussed above as independent variable, and then if we look at statistical accounts of state human rights performance, we find that, over the period of 1980-2005 and even 1991-2005, there is no evidence that being targeted/punished in the CHR and an improved human rights performance are meaningfully associated. That is to say, if first we look at various forms of attention to states in the CHR, from discussion to formal resolutions of criticism, and then we look at either the Political Terror Scale measuring governmental repression or the Freedom House scale measuring civil and political rights, we find that the one factor of the CHR focus on certain states had virtually no impact on human rights conditions inside those states.[44] One can note that the CHR's "punishment" interacts with various factors such as presence or absence of (liberal) democracy, presence or absence of armed conflict, population size, etc.[45] However, our analysis suggests that it still remains true that being targeted in some way in the CHR has no "value added" regarding a state's human rights record.[46]

Compliance with international human rights norms can be a complicated affair. One can look in detail at how targeted states respond to criticism.[47] But at the end of the day what matters most is what happens to individuals residing in states. And both quantitative and qualitative analysis shows that, in general, for most states, the CHR had no perceptible impact on conditions for individuals in targeted states. States might care about debates and other decisions in Geneva concerning human rights, and they might struggle mightily to protect their images and reputations, but when criticized or otherwise "punished" by the Commission, they did not change their fundamental policies on human rights—certainly not in the short term. This generalization holds whether one speaks of China, Iraq under Saddam, Israel in the territories, or any other state targeted for CHR punishment. In fact China, while taking various steps after the Tiananmen Square massacre to offset international criticism, actually increased the degree of repression.[48] It was not unusual for states targeted in the CHR to say nice things about human rights, to make further commitments, and to make some positive gestures, all the while maintaining the structural repression of rights.

One may argue that debates in the CHR helped to delegitimize South Africa's apartheid, especially when combined with various actions outside the Commission.[49] Perhaps the Commission, in conjunction with many other actors, played some role in the eventual return to democratic governance in Chile.[50] Thus, while lacking evidence of any *particular* CHR impact in such cases, one may argue that the Commission was useful for long term education and socialization, and that its meetings provided a focal point for human rights NGOs and movements and other actors as they sought to mobilize opinion. Targeted governments seemed to fear that their rule *might* be delegitimized by CHR critical discourse.

Still, the data are very clear that CHR "punishment" did not lead to altered human rights conditions in the targeted states as long as the violating government retained power. The extended debate about the Commission may be out of proportion to its actual role in the protection of human rights in the short term, whatever its contribution to the advancement of human rights ideas in the long run.

The Council

Given that the Council has only existed since early summer 2006 and that much of its first year was spent in its own institution building, not a great deal can be said yet about its treatment of particular governments.

Israel remained a disproportionate focus, with three special sessions directed mostly to its policies. It was the only state to draw a resolution of criticism in the Council's first year, as some states from the Organization of the Islamic Conference, plus a number of other African states, pushed the Council into that posture. No doubt the plight of persons in Gaza and the West Bank merited some attention, but Council resolutions were unbalanced as well as numerous,[51] and some even-handed reports were rejected.[52] Since the composition of the Council was not all that different from the Commission, it is not surprising that the former's nascent record in dealing with particular countries was not all that different from the Commission era. Israel remained a pariah. The U.S. government, which continued to largely boycott the Council, focused on that fact. And the American media and American-based human rights NGOs like

Human Rights Watch filed critical reports noting the lack of balanced treatment of the Jewish state.

The Council failed to show a similar determination to take a firm stand on Sudan and its Darfur region, although some progress on that subject appeared to be transpiring at the time of writing, but hardly due to the Council. Other major violations of human rights in the Democratic Republic of the Congo (DRC), Burma/Myanmar, China, and so on, also failed to draw the pointed criticism of the Council.

In a compromise, special rapporteurs were dropped regarding both Belarus and Cuba, despite lack of dramatic improvement in human rights conditions, as the price for continuing other country-specific rapporteurs for Burma, Burundi, DRC, Haiti, Liberia, North Korea, Somalia, and Sudan (plus Israeli occupied territories). This kind of horse trading among states was hardly the mark of principled protection of human rights. While the continuation of the country (and thematic) procedures could be seen as a procedural victory for human rights advocates, regardless of the ability of the rapporteurs to produce major short-term protections, the process of policymaking remained highly politicized. Among major states, China, Russia, and the United States could all have been targeted on genuine human rights criteria. The reasons have been noted already. Among other states, numerous ones like Egypt, Iran, the Philippines, Saudi Arabia, etc. might have faced a special rapporteur on the merits, if not a resolution of censure.

While true that the Council continued the Commission practice of using special sessions in addition to regular sessions, one should recall the limits of the process. The CHR had dealt with the situation in the Balkans in the early 1990s not only by means of a special rapporteur but also by special sessions. This did not mean that state members were prepared to take decisive action to stop atrocities, and in that time frame no such action was taken—leading to the resignation of the special rapporteur in protest. Likewise, the Council's special session on Darfur during December 2006 did not lead to dramatic action to stop atrocities *sur place*, whatever diplomatic signal that meeting may have sent to authorities in Khartoum.

Special Procedures

Commission

It should already be clear that the practice of appointing rapporteurs (by whatever name) and working groups is not entirely separate from the targeting of specific countries because of their human rights record. As Lebovic and Voeten suggest, short of passing a resolution criticizing a particular country, the Commission could vote to appoint a person or group to focus on the human rights defects of a country—a measure which attempted to keep a diplomatic spotlight on targeted states. Even the so-called thematic procedures could be used to put some diplomatic pressure on a violating state. If at a given time the votes were not there to criticize Chile under Pinochet for various violations of human rights, one might get the approval for a rapporteur on, say, the theme of disappeared persons, who might then try to visit, or at least write about, the practice of forced disappearance in Chile as part of a more general report.

At the end of the Commission's life, there were forty-one special procedures in operation. Even politically astute citizens in a given country would be hard pressed to keep up with this process, or even to be sure whether a particular country or problem was currently being addressed. Even in open societies, the visit of a special rapporteur or working group might not draw much attention in the national press, whether print or electronic. There are some exceptions which prove the general rule otherwise. Even governments that agreed to receive a rapporteur or working group did not always indicate to the Commission what follow-on measures it had adopted in the wake of the visit or report.[53] The reports of the rapporteurs and working groups were not usually discussed by the parent Commission in any systematic way, and there was usually no public pressure by the Commission on a targeted country in the wake of a country-specific report.[54] At best there was some subsequent open debate about whether to continue or terminate a special procedure. This is a very weak form of public pressure, one that has had little demonstrable effect in improving *structural* human rights conditions.[55]

At times thematic procedures contributed to the development of new standards. For example, the working group on disappeared persons was followed eventually by Council approval of a Convention on the same subject, as noted above. At times special rapporteurs developed emergency procedures in order to inquire about specific persons supposedly in need of urgent attention. Sometimes some actual *particular* protection came out of this process, although an exact accounting of how often persons improved their conditions because of the actions of CHR personnel was difficult if not impossible to establish.

What was clear was that in most cases Commission rapporteurs and working groups acted in an impartial or non-politicized manner, compiling reports that commanded respect from human rights NGOs for their fair and judicious attention to the facts—against the background of internationally recognized human rights. As usual there were sometimes exceptions. The dominant pattern of integrity did not mean that all governments received all reports all of the time with unbounded enthusiasm.[56] It is true that the special procedures guaranteed that no state was immune from review via the CHR,[57] but this is a different matter from getting a state to change its violation of rights because of that review. The record of integrity associated with the special procedures caused the question of their continuation to be an early litmus test for the Council.

The Council

By the end of the Council's first year it had decided to retain the practice of the special procedures. Moreover, it had decided to retain most of the country-specific and thematic measures in existence, dropping those on Belarus and Cuba as already noted. The Council did adopt a code of conduct for the rapporteurs, which reflected mainly some African discontent about the special procedures in a very few cases.

Miscellaneous

Commission

As the U.S. retreated from open leadership on human rights at the UN in 1953, it proposed an Action Plan to cover that retreat.[58] This plan had three main components: annual country reports, advisory services, and global studies.[59] The annual country reports fell by the wayside after a few halting steps, being more ambitious than the political will of that era. Advisory services at governmental request achieved a kinder fate but never constituted a major Commission program. From 1953 until 1962 only Costa Rica and Haiti requested Commission help with domestic human rights issues, and no state did so in the 1970s. Three governments sought Commission help in the 1980s (Bolivia, Equatorial Guinea, and Uganda). After the Cold War, western governments providing the voluntary funding for advisory services were able to emphasize the theme of democratization, and in the 1990s Bulgaria, Mongolia, Paraguay, and Romania all received Commission support in drafting constitutions and holding elections.[60] Much of this kind of expert help was taken over by the Office of the UN High Commissioner for Human Rights (OHCHR) after its creation in 1993. The GA resolution creating the OHCHR mandated that it would be the UN office with "principle responsibility" for human rights activity but under the guidance of the Secretariat, the General Assembly, ECOSOC, and the Commission on Human Rights. Among other tasks, the OHCHR was charged with providing technical and advisory services, through the Centre for Human Rights of the Secretariat, at the request of the states themselves.[61]

The technical and advisory services of the OHCHR have focused to a considerable extent on the development of national action plans which seek to strengthen democratic institutions, encourage legal system reform, provide human rights training for lawyers, judges, and police officers, and develop broad-based human rights education programs.[62] The relationship between the Commission and the OHCHR in the area of technical and advisory services became one of partnership. For example OHCHR technical and advisory services often occur in tandem with the actions of special rapporteurs chosen by the Commission.[63]

The Commission on Human Rights also provided advisory services through the mechanism of organizing human rights seminars and providing fellowships/scholarships for the study of human rights. The number of seminars and grants slowly increased over time, funded by voluntary contributions from (mostly western) governments, and awarded by the office of the Secretary-General. Up until 1987 some forty seminars were held on various human rights subjects, mostly attended by government officials as well as human rights experts. This pattern largely continued until the demise of the CHR. As UN and Commission membership changed, so did the subject matter of these seminars—from a focus on civil and political rights to a focus on subjects of interest to newly independent states, subjects like right to development and apartheid. A 1978 seminar in Geneva advanced the notion of national human rights commissions, which led to some changes at the national level around the world. A 1979 seminar in Monrovia on regional human rights commissions contributed to the development of the African Charter on Human and Peoples Rights, with its attached commission.[64] Increasingly after 1993, the UN General Assembly might pass a resolution pertaining to human rights education or training, leaving it to the OHCHR to carry it out, with the CHR being bypassed.

Closely linked to the seminar series was the global studies series, usually on a given specific issue (like arbitrary arrest), and often linked to suggested reforms submitted to ECOSOC and/or the General Assembly. While the seminar series sought to draw governmental officials into a dialogue with human rights experts, the global studies series was compiled by independent experts. This Commission activity ended in 1981, with a handoff to the Subcommission. Thus the Subcommission became, in part, a think tank for the Commission, with expert studies on a wide range of subjects impinging on human rights such as the flow of light weapons into conflict areas, extreme poverty, and the special needs of the elderly.

From especially the 1960s on, the Commission was a focal point for much activity by many human rights advocacy groups, or NGOs. This was a natural development, given the growing number of human rights NGOs and given the CHR as the traditional center of UN specialized diplomacy on human rights. The battle for NGO consultative status, and thus the NGO right to attend and participate in UN meetings, was played out in another UN body under ECOSOC. But in the Commission on Human Rights there was often evident tension between the NGO tendency to be assertive and explicit about particular human rights violations, and the state tendency to want to carefully control the discussion about embarrassing facts. This tension could at times affect NGO consultative status. Because of statements made at Commission meetings, Christian Solidarity International, Transnational Radical Party, and Reporters Without Borders, among others, all had trouble being admitted to subsequent Commission meetings.

Despite this friction, the input of NGOs has been an important element in CHR proceedings, and many international NGOs attended Commission meetings throughout the life of that body where they monitored state diplomacy and often challenged governmental statements. To show how involved NGOs were toward the final years of the Commission, during the sixty-first session of the Commission there were 261 accredited NGOs that participated during the session creating 354 written statements, 476 individual oral statements, and sixty-one joint oral statements.[65] NGOs have arguably had the most access to the Commission by working with the Commission's special procedures. First, all NGOs or civil society actors can have access to the special procedures regardless of whether they have consultative status or not. Second, NGOs can work with special procedures in six different ways: 1) submitting individual cases, 2) providing information on specific human rights issues, 3) providing support for the special procedure's country visits, 4) working locally to facilitate the work of special procedures, 5) participating in the annual meeting of mandate-holders, and 6) inviting mandate-holders to participate in their own separate initiatives.[66] How much this NGO pressure actually changed state behavior is a matter of dispute. As shown elsewhere in this paper, all the NGO pressure did not make the CHR a powerful protector of human rights in the short term. It is likely, on the other hand, that NGO activity in the CHR was important for NGO morale, focus, and sense of purpose.

Council

The Council is too new to have developed a track record on advisory services and various studies. It is clear already that, like the Commission, the Council will be a magnet and focal point for many human rights advocacy groups.

Conclusions

Given all the attention to reform of the UN Human Rights Commission, one might have thought that the CHR was actually important for the short-term protection of human rights. Such was not the case, unfortunately. Whether one analyzes the 1235 procedure, the 1503 procedure, the use of special country-specific and thematic procedures, the use of special sessions, or the cumulative effects of all these and other measures, the facts are that none have proven to be effective in the short term structural protection of human rights in offending states. The 1503 procedure was especially weak.

With regret, this author notes that what he wrote in 1985 about the Commission and the other UN bodies dealing with human rights remained essentially correct up to the end of the CHR.[67] While there have always been strong critics of the UN and in particular of the Commission regarding protecting human rights, these critics mostly missed the central point. What the UN bodies including the Commission were doing primarily was engaging in the long-term education/socialization of states concerning the importance of human rights. The contribution of the UN and CHR was largely in the realm of indirect protection through inculcation of values *over time,* not in the direct protection of rights in the here and now.[68]

The main point to be added to this previous analysis concerns the UN Security Council and its willingness to stretch Charter Chapter VII, permitting binding and coercive responses to threats to international peace and security to cover certain human rights issues. Thus the Security Council after the Cold War responded to such human rights events as repression in Northern Iraq (1991), massive starvation in Somalia (1992-93), various atrocities in Bosnia (1994), Operation Turquoise in Rwanda (1994), deployment of force in DRC (changing mandates 1999-2007), etc. with at least the invocation in New York of Chapter VII—and sometimes with some attempted forceful action in the field. (The process actually started during the Cold War, with the Security Council invoking Chapter VII regarding mandatory economic sanctions against Rhodesia/Zimbabwe and a mandatory arms embargo against South Africa). While the official rationale for UN action used the Charter language of threat to or breach of international peace, an important concern was protection of human rights.[69] The analysis of the effectiveness of this process requires extended treatment elsewhere.

Whatever the future of the Security Council and human rights, given the composition and mandate of the subsequent UN Human Rights Council it is rather unlikely that there will be revolutionary changes in the record it compiles compared to the CHR. The Council's membership and authority are basically the same as the Commission's. The first year of the Council suggests that in general, *la plus ca change, la plus c'est la meme chose*, or, the more things change, the more they stay the same. All of this means that the energy expended on UN reform, at least as far as human rights is concerned, has not only failed to produce major change, but has also probably forestalled other major reform efforts for some years. It was the West, states and NGOs, that pushed for change away from the Commission, but they had no workable view of what would follow, and they certainly obtained no agreement in advance on the nature of the Council. This was not a brilliant diplomatic record. A traditional Dutch saying seems relevant: one should not throw away old shoes until one has new shoes.

Nevertheless, the Commission did have importance, and so does the Council. First there is the matter of standard setting. It seems that UN member states cannot help but develop human rights norms, even as they continue to violate many of them. Even states that engage in major and systematic violation of human rights, whether the Argentine junta or the George Bush Administration, continue to profess their long term interest in human rights despite the supposed temporary deviations made necessary by security dilemmas. The old notion of one step back for the sake of two steps forward is not limited to Leninists who strike temporary compromises in their pursuit of the proletarian revolution. The "good" state must be saved, even if this involves the violation of human rights.[70] And so the Council will retain importance as a primary drafter of global human rights norms, driven by state general attachment to the idea and language of human rights, regardless of many violations.[71]

In this regard it can be noted that UN drafting carries additional significance now that international criminal justice has been rejuvenated since 1993. UN language about genocide, crimes against humanity, and major war crimes (the latter rules mostly drafted outside the UN) now stand increased chance of being adjudicated in international or internationalized criminal courts, whatever may transpire in national courts and rarely the International Court of Justice. If anything, therefore, drafting in the Human Rights Council and General Assembly will prove more important—not less. Human rights and humanitarian language is being adjudicated more—not less.

Moreover, UN drafting on human rights can lead to soft law—standards that may or may not be law, and usually not adjudicated in court, but accepted as appropriate norms to guide policy. The Sub-Commission created, and the Commission approved, the standard minimum rules on the treatment of detainees, and this document—although not binding—was subsequently used by various states to inform their public policies on such questions.

Can the new Council improve on the Commission's record for serious, balanced, and fair treatment of various states? If, simplifying Lebovic and Voeten, the old CHR was about 60 percent "correct" in the states it targeted and the "punishments" meted out, can the new Council get that figure up to 70 or 80 percent? If one sets aside the case of Israel, which is important but does not always capture or replicate the dynamics of other situations, then some improvement may be possible in this regard. Given the new rules, and given continued advocacy by leading human rights NGOs and like minded states, some increased balance and equity may be forthcoming. We will have to wait to see the playing out of the UPR (universal periodic review). It has never been clear how the UPR should relate to the treaty monitoring bodies or the country-specific rapporteurs, since both logically overlap with the UPR. Given the role of the Islamic Conference and other groupings on issues like Darfur, and given a general African and Asian lack of enthusiasm for rigorous UN supervision of state practice, it will often prove difficult to get a majority of states in the Council to elevate the equitable protection of human rights, even in symbolic diplomatic fashion, over competing interests and values.

One importance to the special procedures, so far retained in considerable measure by the new Council, is that the expert reports emanating there from are usually non-politicized. They thus contribute to an appropriate understanding of rights in context, avoiding the distortions introduced by states' expedient and ideological concerns. While the reports usually do not change the facts on the ground in the short run, contributing to correct interpretation is a worthy outcome in the long run.

In the last analysis, one can tinker with the institutional machinery of the UN, but reducing the influence of nationalism (not to mention chauvinistic nationalism) and reasons of state (however misguided) in the interest of universal human rights is more difficult. If internationally recognized human rights are about unpacking the individual from the grip of the state,[72] many states are quite ambivalent about implementing human rights through the UN. As long as the UN Human Rights Council is made up of states, its proceedings will be far from smooth and impressive.

Notes

1. The author would like to thank his graduate assistant, Baekkwan Park, for his help in finalizing this manuscript. The author would like to thank Tom Weiss and Howard Tolley, Jr. for comments on earlier drafts. He would also like to thank the participants in a conference in Potsdam in the summer of 2007 for commentary that led to revisions.

2. For a succinct overview see Paul Gordon Lauren, "'To Preserve and Build on its Achievements and to Redress its Shortcomings': The Journey from the Commission on Human Rights to the Human Rights Council," *Human Rights Quarterly* 29, no. 2 (May 2007): 307-345.

3. Jean Bernard Marie, *La Commission des droits de l'homme de l'Onu* (Paris: Pedone, 1975); Howard Tolley, Jr., *The U.N. Commission on Human Rights* (Boulder: Westview, 1987); Miko Lempinen, *The United Nations Commission on Human Rights and the Different Treatment of Governments* (Abo, Finland: Abo Akademi University Press, 2005).

4. Notable exceptions are Tolley; Lempinen; Philip Alston, "Reconceiving The UN Human Rights Regime: Challenges Confronting the New UN Human Rights Council," *Melbourne Journal of International Law* 7, no. 2 (2006): 185-224; James H. Lebovic and Erik Voeten, "The Politics of Shame: The Condemnation of Country Human Rights Practices in the UNCHR," *International Studies Quarterly* 50, no. 4 (December 2006): 861-888; Jack Donnelly, "Human Rights at the United Nations 1955-1985: The Question of Bias," *International Studies Quarterly* 32, no. 4 (1988): 275-303; Philip Alston, "The Commission on Human Rights," in *The United Nations And Human Rights: A Critical Appraisal*, ed. Philip Alston (Oxford: Oxford University Press, 1992; 2nd ed. forthcoming); Tom J. Farer and Felice Gaer, "The UN and Human Rights: At the End of the Beginning," in *United Nations, Divided World,* eds. Adam Roberts and Benedict Kingsbury (Oxford: Oxford University Press, 2nd ed., 1993), 240-296; and David Forsythe, "The United Nations and Human Rights 1945-1985," *Political Science Quarterly* 100, no. 3 (Summer 1985): 249-269.

5. The CHR nuclear/planning group proposed a commission of independent experts, but this was rejected by ECOSOC. See Alston, "Reconceiving The UN Human Rights Regime," 189-190. The European Commission on Human Rights (when it existed), the European Court of Human Rights, the InterAmerican Commission on Human Rights, the InterAmerican Court of Human Rights, the African Commission on Human Rights, and the nascent African Court of Human Rights were all staffed by persons sitting in their individual capacity. The same is true for the prosecutor and judges in various international and internationalized criminal courts.

6. Tony Evans, *US Hegemony and the Project of Universal Human Rights* (London: Macmillan, 1996). See also Stephen C. Schlesinger, *Act of Creation: The Founding of the United Nations* (Boulder: Westview, 2003).

7. Farer and Gaer, "The UN and Human Rights," 273.

8. The school of thought referred to as constructivism argues that international social structure can affect how states construct their identities and national interests. See, for example, Michael Barnett and Martha Finnemore, *Rules for the World: International Organizations in Global Politics* (Ithaca: Cornell, 2004) where the central argument is that international organizations and the ideas and values they embody can cause state members to change their political views.

9. For the development of this point by social scientists, see especially Thomas Risse, Stephen C. Ropp, and Kathryn Sikkink, eds., *The Power of Human Rights: International Norms and Domestic Change* (Cambridge: Cambridge University Press, 1999).

10. These types of "structural" barriers to the implementation of international human rights norms are discussed in David Forsythe, *Human Rights in International Relations* (Cambridge: Cambridge University Press, 2nd ed., 2006); and Jack Donnelly, *Universal Human Rights in Theory and Practice* (Ithaca: Cornell University Press, 2nd ed., 2003), inter alia.

11. The analysis of moral authority is no easy matter, since it is a subjective quality that exists only as perceived by various actors. See further Kent Kille, ed., *The UN Secretaries-General and Moral Authority: Religion and Ethics in International Leadership* (Washington: Georgetown University Press, 2007).

12. M.J. Peterson, *The UN General Assembly* (New York: Routledge, 2006). And Peterson, "The UN General Assembly and Human Rights," in *The Encyclopedia of Human rights,* ed. David Forsythe (New York: Oxford University Press, 2010). The Panel on High Level Threats saw that there would be no easy agreement on a new Council of restricted membership. Not being able to see a solution, they abandoned that quest.

13. At the time of these debates, the United States had adopted a policy of forced disappearance of certain suspected violent opponents, and their abuse through mistreatment and/or torture. The United States also engaged in state kidnapping and a-legal transfer of suspects to abusive states. The so-called basically Northern "club of the clean" refers in part to Northern self-image and use of shorthand in analysis. Other liberal democracies too, like Britain in Northern Ireland, or Israel in dealing with its violent opponents, did not have "clean hands" when it came to some actual human rights practice. Highly relevant is Alison Brysk and Gershon Shafir, eds., *National Insecurity and Human Rights: Democracies Debate Counterterrorism* (Berkeley: University of California Press, 2007) in which the present author has a chapter on the United States.

14. Beyond this generalization there were a number of exceptions and complexities. Switzerland tended to align with the G-77, in part because it was not supportive of public condemnation as a general principle. Some democracies of the South like Kenya tended to align with the North, as did Chile and Argentina.

15. Yvonne Terlingen, "The Human Rights Council: A New Era in UN Human Rights Work?," *Ethics & International Affairs* 21, no. 2 (Summer 2007). http://www.ethicsandinternationalaffairs.org/2007/the-human-rights-council-a-new-era-in-un-human-rights-work-full-text/ (accessed October 15, 2012).

16. For a theory of learning and change on human rights at the UN, see Ernst B. Haas, *When Knowledge Is Power: Three Models of Change in International Organizations* (Berkeley: University of California Press, 1990).

17. Warren Hoge, "U.N. Rejects Belarus for Seat on Its Rights Panel," *New York Times*, May 18, 2007, A6.

18. A/RES/60/251, "Resolution adopted by the General Assembly," 3 April 2006, paragraphs 2 and 3. http://www2.ohchr.org/english/bodies/hrcouncil/docs/A.RES.60.251_En.pdf (accessed October 15, 2012).

19. Thomas Buergenthal, "The Evolving International Human Rights System," *American Journal of International Law* 100, no. 4 (October 2006): 791. http://www.jstor.org/stable/pdfplus/4126317.pdf?acceptTC=true (accessed October 15, 2012)

20. For example Johannes Morsink, *The Universal Declaration of Human Rights: Origins, Drafting & Intent* (Philadelphia: University of Pennsylvania Press, 1999); Mary Ann Glendon, *A World Made New: Eleanor Roosevelt and the Universal Declaration of Human Rights* (New York: Random House, 2001).

21. For a standard compendium of instruments see Ian Brownlie and Guy S. Goodwin-Gill, eds., *Basic Documents on Human Rights* (Oxford: Oxford University Press, 5th ed., 2006). For an example of a weighty legal tome trying to analyze and discuss this broad subject matter, see Henry J. Steiner and Philip Alston, *International Human Rights in Context: Law, Politics, Morals* (Oxford: Oxford University Press, 3rd ed., 2007), almost 1500 pages.

22. Donnelly, *Universal Human Rights*, referring principally to the international bill of rights.

23. This essay is also not the place to discuss the point that international human rights norms are not the only form of moral discourse. Ethical and religious discourses, rather than "rights talk," also purport to advance the human condition.

24. See further David Forsythe, "Human Rights and US Foreign Policy: Two Levels, Two Worlds," in *Politics and Human Rights*, ed. David Beetham (Oxford: Blackwell, 1995), reprinted from *Political Studies* 43, Special Issue (1995).

25. Even the Netherlands, a liberal democratic state generally supportive of internationally recognized human rights, showed concern for its sovereignty costs in regard to UN human rights standards; see Hilde Reiding, *The Netherlands and the Development of International Human Rights Instruments* (Antwerp: Intersentia, 2007).

26. Buergenthal, "The Evolving International Human Rights System," 791.

27. David Kennedy, *The Dark Sides of Virtue: Reassessing International Humanitarianism* (Princeton: Princeton University Press, 2004).

28. ECOSOC resolution 1235 of 1967 permitted the CHR to address specific violations of human rights in particular countries. ECOSOC resolution 1503 of 1970 authorized the CHR to respond to private petitions. The CHR then adopted a 1503 procedure emphasizing non-public review, with only the option of a public notice about recalcitrant states (vis., states not responding progressively to such complaints over time). Since the 1503 procedure allows states to try to avoid public criticism by arguing that the matter is being treated in a discrete process, some observers have urged the repeal of the 1503 procedure. Alston (1992), after careful review, regarded the benefits of the 1503 procedure as insignificant compared to its use to shield states from public criticism. Alston, "Commission on Human Rights," 154-55.

29. James H. Lebovic and Erik Voeten, "The Politics of Shame: The Condemnation of Country Human Rights Practices in the UNCHR," *International Studies Quarterly* 50, no. 4 (December 2006): 861-888. We acknowledge that this classification is not clear-cut. The first and third indicators consist of two separate actions each. Thus the first and third "independent variables" are not entirely "clean." Nevertheless, we tested and expanded their study.

30. The PTS is made up of two interpretive variables. One variable is based on the reading and coding of annual Amnesty International reports and the other is based on the reading and coding of the annual U.S. State Department Country Reports on Human Rights. The variables seek to measure the abuse of human rights on a scale of one to five, with one representing states with the least amount of abuse and five representing states

with the highest level of abuse. Mark Gibney, *Political Terror Scales Dataset 1980-2005* (Asheville: University of North Carolina, 2006).

31. Lebovic and Voeten, "The Politics of Shame," 876.

32. Lebovic and Voeten, "The Politics of Shame," 863. This study, like many Western studies, focuses on repression to mean violation of civil and political rights. A study of the CHR and socio-economic rights has yet to be done.

33. Lebovic and Voeten, "The Politics of Shame," 867.

34. This was also the conclusion of Donnelly in 1988.

35. Lebovic and Voeten, "The Politics of Shame," 33.

36. Lebovic and Voeten, "The Politics of Shame," 879.

37. Lebovic and Voeten, "The Politics of Shame," 881.

38. Lebovic and Voeten, "The Politics of Shame," 885.

39. In the limited space of this paper we cannot include the complete results of our analyses here. Supporting data and results are available upon request.

40. Lebovic and Voeten, "The Politics of Shame," 867.

41. Principled Voting Index is the basis of analysis of states' votes on three types of resolutions at the UNCHR and UNHRC, 1) country-specific resolutions addressing Israel, 2) country-specific resolutions addressing other states, 3) thematic resolutions addressing economic, cultural, and social rights. See Steven Seligman, "Human Rights Politics and Principle at the United Nations." Unpublished manuscript. (2007): 12.

42. Seligman, Human Rights Politics," 18.

43. Lebovic and Voeten, 870.

44. We use the PTS and the Freedom House indices. We believe that, by testing the impact of CHR across both the PTS and Freedom House, we increase the validity of our analysis and strengthen confidence in the inferences drawn.

45. See further David P. Forsythe, *Human Rights in International Relations* (Cambridge: Cambridge University Press, 2nd ed., 2006). Various factors correlate positively with "good" national human rights scores: liberal democracy, absence of armed conflict, small population size, national prosperity, large middle class, and perhaps being a former British colony.

46. In this limited space, we cannot discuss any of these issues comprehensively. Supporting data, methodology, and outcomes are available upon request.

47. Sonia Cardenas, *Conflict and Compliance: State Responses to International Human Rights Pressures* (Philadelphia: Penn Press, 2007).

48. Cardenas, *Conflict and Compliance.*

49. See for example Neta Crawford, *Argument and Change in World Politics: Ethics, Decolonization, and Humanitarian Intervention* (Cambridge: Cambridge University Press, 2002).

50. Cardenas finds a positive role in this regard for combined international actions in *Conflict and Compliance.*

51. Terlingen, "The Human Rights Council."

52. Four human rights rapporteurs compiled a balanced report on Hezbollah and Israel in south Lebanon during the summer of 2006. This was attacked by mostly Arab and African representatives on the Council. Council Monitor, "Human Rights Council, 2nd session preliminary overview," pp. 7-8.

53. Alston, "Reconceiving The UN Human Rights Regime," 220.

54. Farer and Gaer, "The UN and Human Rights," 288.

55. See further Miko Lempinen, *Challenges Facing the System of Special Procedures of the United Nations Commission on Human Rights* (Abo, Finland: Institute for Human Rights, Abo Akademi University, 2001).

56. In 2006 five Commission rapporteurs dealing with subject matter that touched upon detention conditions combined their talents to write a careful and compelling report about how U.S. policies at the Guantanamo Bay detention facility violated various international standards. The Bush Administration, having denied them access to detainees, then criticized the report in no uncertain terms. For the report see E/CN.4/2006/120, 15 February 2006, 52. A U.S. critique of a draft version is contained in Annex II of this report.

57. Lempinen, *The United Nations Commission on Human Rights*, 229.

58. We would like to thank Danny Braaten for research on this section. The newly elected Eisenhower Administration, to preserve its foreign affairs and treaty making authority in the face of domestic conservative and isolationist pressures, promised to downplay its commitment to human rights developments at the UN. Its Action Plan was the resulting effort to maintain international standing in the human rights field while placating its domestic critics. Its liberal critics called the Action Plan in reality an Inaction Plan.

59. Statements of fact in this section not otherwise attributed are drawn from Tolley, *The U.N. Commission on Human Rights.*

60. Joe W. Pitts III and David Weissbrodt, "Major developments at the UN Commission on Human Rights in 1992," *Human Rights Quarterly* 15, no. 1 (February 1993): 122-196.

61. A/RES/48/141, "High Commissioner for the Promotion and Protection of All Human Rights," 7 January 1994. http://www.unhchr.ch/huridocda/huridoca.nsf/(Symbol)/A.RES.48.141.En (accessed October 15, 2012).

62. Fact Sheet No. 3 (Rev.1) Advisory Services and Technical Cooperation in the Field of Human Rights. http://www.ohchr.org/Documents/Publications/FactSheet3Rev.1en.pdf (accessed October 15, 2012)

63. Fact Sheet No. 3.

64. Alston, "The Commission on Human Rights."

65. "Working with the Office of the United Nations High Commissioner for Human Rights: A Handbook for NGOs," Office of the United Nations High Commissioner for Human Rights, HR/PUB/06/10, 40. http://www.ohchr.org/Documents/Publications/NGO Handbooken.pdf (accessed October 15, 2012).

66. "Working with the Office,"42.

67. Forsythe, "The United Nations and Human Rights 1945-1985." Some might add that what the majority of states in the CHR and Council were trying to do to Israel was to delegitimize it over time, despite its relatively good scores on the PTS and Freedom House scales—good scores for Israel proper, but not such rights-protective policies in the territories.

68. Forsythe, "The United Nations and Human Rights 1945-1985," especially 264-265 quoting scholars such as John Ruggie, Louis Henkin, and others.

69. The pattern is explained in some detail in Weiss, Forsythe, Coate, and Pease, *The United Nations and Changing World Politics* (Boulder: Westview Press, 2007, 5th ed.), 165-175. The limits of this process were shown in 2007 when China and Russia vetoed a resolution in the Security Council dealing with human rights in Burma/Myanmar on the grounds that human rights violations in that state had nothing to do with international peace and security.

70. E.g., Michael Ignatieff, *The Lesser Evil: Political Ethics in an Age of Terror* (Princeton: Princeton University Press, 2004).

71. IHL will likely continue to be drafted in diplomatic conferences technically outside the UN framework. The Rome Statute for the ICC, with its important definition of crimes against humanity, was also drafted apart from the UN Human Rights Commission.

72. Farer and Gaer, "The UN and Human Rights," 243.

Appendix

	GTM	SLV	COL	TCD	ZAR	BDI	RWA	SOM	MMR	CHN	AFG	IRQ	ZAF	SDN	IRN	ISR
1980	5	5									5					
1981	5	5									5		3		4	2
1982	5	5									5		3		5	2
1983	5	5									5		3		5	2
1984	5	5			3						4		4		5	2
1985	5	4			3						5		3		5	3
1986	4	5			3						5		4		4	3
1987	4	5			3						4	5	5		5	3
1988	4	5			3			5	5		4	5	4		5	3
1989	4	4						5	4	5	4	4	4		4	3
1990	5	4		4	3			5	4	4	4	5	4	4	4	3
1991	4	4		3	4			5	4	4	4	5	4	4	4	2
1992	4	4		5	4		4	5	5	4	4	5	5	5	4	2
1993	4	4		5	5	5	4	4	5	3	4	5	5	5	3	9
1994	4	3	5	4	4	5	5	5	5	4	5	5	5	5	4	9
1995	4		4	4	4	5	5	5	4	3	5	5	5	4	5	4
1996	4		5	4	4	5	5	4	4	4	4	5		5	4	4
1997			5	4	5	5	5	4	5	4	5	5		4	4	4
1998			5	4	5	5	5	4	4	5	5	5		4	4	4
1999			5		5	5	5	4	4	4	5	5		5	4	4
2000			5		5	4		4	4	5	5	5		5	3	4
2001			5		4	5		4	3	4	5	4		5	3	4
2002			5		5	5		4	3	4	5	4		4	3	4
2003			5		5	4		4	4	4	4	5		5		5
2004			5		5	4		4	4	4	4			5		5
2005			5		5	4		4	4	4	5			5		5

Table 1. The UNCHR Targeting and States' Human Rights Practice (AI PTS)

Chapter 8

Transitional Justice in Divided Societies: Using Hybrid Courts to Manage Conflict

James DeShaw Rae

This chapter explores the ongoing development of transitional justice mechanisms to promote accountability for war crimes, crimes against humanity, and genocide that includes domestic trials, truth and reconciliation commissions (TRCs), the two *ad hoc* war crimes tribunals for the former Yugoslavia and Rwanda, and the International Criminal Court (ICC). The focus of this chapter is on the five hybrid tribunal experiments in Bosnia,[1] Cambodia,[2] East Timor,[3] Kosovo,[4] and Sierra Leone.[5] Two were primarily ethnic conflicts in nature (Bosnia and Kosovo), though the other three had an ethnic dimension as well. A sixth tribunal for Lebanon has also been formulated, but is proceeding slowly.[6] This chapter seeks to develop a comparative framework to decipher common practices and pitfalls among each of the cases where hybrid mechanisms were employed.

Accountability Mechanisms and the Quest for Justice

Post-conflict societies are often in desperate need of functioning judicial institutions to establish the legitimacy of the government and to promote domestic stability. Practitioners understand that reform of domestic courts is a major component of the long-term promotion of the rule of law and future viability of the state. At the same time, special attention may be paid toward addressing grievous human rights violations and atrocities (particularly of an ethnic nature) from the previous era in order to establish a new political environment of accountability.

Wholly domestic mechanisms would ordinarily be considered the method of first resort and further processes would be unnecessary. Likewise, the concept of complementarity grants national courts the authority to conduct investigations and trials prior to the ICC seeking jurisdiction. However, the fear of show trials, political whitewash, or judicial incompetence has rendered this approach unpopular in those high profile cases where the international community has taken an interest. Thus, domestic courts are generally disfavored by third parties due to the perception (usually accurately) that local court officials are too biased, subject to political influence, and overall grossly lack the independence that is a standard of justice and accountability. Furthermore, in most developing countries, inadequate resources, poor infrastructure, and limited legal training weaken the operation of the judicial process and make comprehensive investigations and full-scale trials very difficult to achieve. Nevertheless, local forums remain the standard, particularly in the "dirty wars" across Latin America and ethnic and civil conflicts of Africa. Of course, fairly investigating oneself is rare and owning up to egregious violations of human rights is uncommon. More frequently, the courts become a venue for retributive justice and removing the last vestiges of the *ancien regime*.

Seeking to overcome these limitations, the United Nations created international courts to seek accountability after the bloody ethnic wars of Yugoslavia and Rwanda. With far more robust resources and well-trained international judicial personnel, international tribunals seemed a perfect final resolution to ethnic cleansing and genocide upon their formation in 1994. Such courts offered the hope of impartial justice handed down expeditiously by competent legal professionals with the added value of shining a spotlight on notorious human rights abusers and moving more firmly toward a legitimate deterrent to future war criminals. The ICC represents the culmination of the desire for global accountability and offers a permanent forum to try the worst perpetrators that often escape the international limelight or where the political will to set up a full scale process is lacking. After functioning for over fifteen years, the *ad hoc* international war crimes tribunals for Yugoslavia and Rwanda have lost much of their luster. Aside from the expense and squandering of resources and painfully slow process of trying alleged perpetrators, international tribunals have also been criticized for being irrelevant to the domestic population, as international staff generally lack an understanding of the local culture, context, and language(s). Nevertheless, the ICC continues to expand its inquiries into major atrocities in Central African Republic (CAR), Congo, Kenya, Libya, Sudan, and Uganda. Although the ICC's membership is well over one hundred countries, it is quite selective in its investigations due to UN Security Council influence (all cases are currently from Africa). One can expect that the ICC will indict fewer persons in a given case than the *ad hoc* tribunals due to its global mandate, and presumably conduct shorter trials since it has a permanent staff.

After the expensive and lengthy trials at the International Criminal Tribunal for the former Yugoslavia (ICTY) and the International Criminal Tribunal for Rwanda (ICTR), the international community further established a new precedent with the formation of hybrid or mixed tribunals, which have generally been perceived as cheaper, with greater involvement of local personnel, and the potential to leave a more lasting imprint on the domestic legal system by instilling respect for the rule of law. Thus, it is hoped that hybrid courts will be more fair and independent than domestic courts while more legitimate and relevant than international tribunals, and better at capacity-building than both. This chapter ultimately seeks to create a framework to evaluate these tribunals across a range of standards and answer the following question: "Was the accountability process as formulated in hybrid tribunals just, efficient, and relevant?" Several criteria are used to examine these issues. First, was justice and accountability attained in determining an acceptable time period and subject matter jurisdiction for review, and were the primary culprits apprehended, tried, and punished or given some form of amnesty, or otherwise able to elude arrest? Second, was due process followed in the actual conduct of the trials, were resources and budgets sufficient, did the process build capacity, and were cases prosecuted in an efficient and timely manner? Finally, was the process relevant to its intended audience, the affected population? Thus, were the trials held in a location accessible to the public and/or with effective media coverage, was the process understandable, and did the process gain wide public support? Throughout, uncertain security environments were major obstacles to the implementation of accountability mechanisms in each locale, as were cultural constraints that challenged the imposition of outside justice.

Preparing Justice: Jurisdiction and Impunity

In wrestling with the mandate of tribunals, the time period and subject matter jurisdiction become contentious issues that often delay the implementation of mechanisms. Limiting time periods to a given era has the practical purpose of highlighting the juncture when the worst atrocities occurred, as well as the need to set parameters for the scope of investigation. However, limiting the temporal range has other motivations as well: to include or exclude an influential actor (often a neighboring power or major state), to avoid culpability by the current government for possible responsibility, and to introduce the context of a historical pattern such as a cycle of violence or a response to previous attacks. The government in power has a strong incentive to limit the time period to a range of time where it might be able to minimize its own actions. Likewise, international actors that may not have clean hands may seek to restrict the time period to exclude any former role in a different era, perhaps during the proxy battles of the Cold War. The exclusion of past atrocities can contribute to a sense of victor's justice and politicize the whole undertaking. Subject matter jurisdiction usually includes crimes against humanity, genocide, war crimes, forced labor, torture, and other violations of domestic law. Owing to the nature of criminal prosecution, the underlying sources of the conflict, including historical grievances that may tie former colonial powers to contemporary violence, are not easily written into criminal indictments.

Usually, Western European nations, Canada, the United States, Japan, and a handful of others fund the tribunals. With the power of the purse and the influence of the permanent members of the Security Council, major players are unlikely to support an investigatory process that undermines their own version of the past. Most of these cases exist where great powers had little influence, with the exception of Cambodia. The time period at the Extraordinary Chambers of the Cambodian Court (ECCC) severed the relationship between the violence of 1975-79 from the larger conflicts of the Second and Third Indochina Wars. The Cambodian government tried to expand the time period to include the secret bombings of Cambodia by the United States and the brutal killings by the Lon Nol regime of tens of thousands in this broader context. However, the U.S. position ultimately prevailed; thus, the United States was able to exclude its role in support of the Khmer Rouge coalition after their overthrow. China, however, which supported the Khmer Rouge throughout, was unable to avoid masking its influence at this level. The Cambodia tribunal was ultimately limited to several key Khmer Rouge officials for alleged crimes against humanity and genocide committed from April 17, 1975 to January 7, 1979, clearly the worst era, and thus avoided any scrutiny of international involvement. In Lebanon, separating the single act of Lebanese Prime Minister Rafiq Hariri's assassination from the astounding violence of two decades of civil war and sectarian conflict seems to lessen the importance of all other politically-motivated violence. National governments may also seek to shape the time period to lessen their own role, particularly in hybrid courts where bargaining between international actors and the state is instrumental to the final conditions.

The decision to hold alleged perpetrators accountable is easier when the target has been defeated and the regime removed from power. Indicting war criminals still in positions of power (as head of state generally) could risk alienating the domestic populace, inflame nationalist sentiments, and ultimately destabilize a regime. Moreover, indicting significant rebel groups could likewise undermine a peace process and push such forces toward becoming spoilers or launching an overt insurgency. Often, notorious figures are granted amnesty in order to engage them in a bargaining process or in prioritizing the need for security on the reasoning that only a leader can deliver the constituents needed to secure the peace. This quandary represents the all too familiar trade-off between peace and justice. A further dilemma is whether to indict moderates or peacemakers in order to be impartial or to ignore their crimes as they may pale in comparison to the greater atrocities that were the focus of the process, despite such actors' checkered past. The indictments of Issa Sesay and Sam Hinga Norman in Sierra Leone undermined popular support as they were considered moderate leaders who had worked for national unity, despite some link to atrocities during the civil war.[7] Subject states are profoundly reluctant to agree to trials that are directly targeted at the regime's own atrocities; yet even when the state was not the instigator of violence, or even was the victimized group, leaders are reluctant to support such mechanisms. States face a different dynamic of maintaining a tranquil domestic environment and pacifying internal opponents, and of course seek to avoid an indictment of the regime. Nevertheless, some degree of support or acquiescence from the government is still invaluable.

Prosecution risks upsetting nationalist and ethnic passions, as was apparent in several cases. Initially, the United States generally opted for a peace over justice approach in dealing with Yugoslav President Slobodan Milosevic, who was considered a necessary actor to bring along the Serb nationalists and exert influence over Bosnian Serb leaders. Despite the operation of the ICTY since 1994, NATO only made its first arrest in July 1997. In early 1998, a UN Security Council resolution authorized the ICTY to investigate war crimes in Kosovo; Milosevic, along with four senior Yugoslav officials, was extradited to The Hague in June 2001, marking the first international war crimes tribunal to indict a sitting head of state. A nationalist backlash quickly ensued, the new president Vojislav Kostunica fiercely opposed the tribunal, and moderate Serbian Prime Minister Zoran Dindic was assassinated in March 2003 by those who feared being turned over to the tribunal. By 2011, the lure of membership in the European Union persuaded Serbia to hand over remaining war criminals Radovan Karadzic and Ratko Mladic.

Democracies may be more sensitive to nationalist sensibilities than even authoritarian regimes as they are fearful of losing public support. International leadership in the Kosovo hybrid courts exacerbated mutual animosity as they became more effective. Indictments were handled by the hybrid courts, but in a period of high tension where the warring sides were living within a single sovereign territory (unlike the Serbia and Croatia cases) and no permanent settlement was evident. While the Kosovan Albanian community had been the chief victims, now that they were dominant in the society and courts, Kosovan Serbians felt discrimination and fear. Fearing their own safety from more hard-line elements within the Albanian community, Albanian Kosovan judges released suspects. In East Timor, the indictments of major Indonesian leaders (like General Wiranto) created diplomatic tensions, yet the near impossibility of extradition lessened the backlash.

Indictments are also contentious in a hybrid court because the trials are conducted in-country, unless the government has set limits beforehand as in Cambodia. Cambodia avoided bargaining altogether by waiting until the Khmer Rouge was a spent force and no longer posed a threat. During the peace negotiations of 1989-91, Cambodia lobbied for inclusion of the term genocide and an international tribunal, though "the idea of importing foreign judges as an interim measure was rejected as bearing the taint of colonialism."[8] Cambodia's National Assembly outlawed the Khmer Rouge as a criminal organization in 1994, and as they represented less of a threat, the government cautiously accepted a legal trial process while stalling the outcome. Long-time Prime Minister Hun Sen is a former Khmer Rouge himself and has no strong domestic incentive to conduct trials. Of the remaining Khmer Rouge, five prominent leaders (Khieu Samphan, Ieng Sary, Ieng Thirith, Kaing Guek Eav-a.k.a. Duch, and Nuon Chea) were arrested and face trial.

To promote stability, amnesties are sometimes offered (only to be rescinded later). Still, one must question the ethics of renouncing amnesties, particularly if such actions are against the will of the national government or local population. Numerous pardons were granted in Cambodia, while in Sierra Leone, the Lomé Peace Agreement granted a blanket amnesty to ex-combatants, including Foday Sankoh. But in June 2000, after the resurgence of hostilities, President Ahmad Tejan Kabbah asked the United Nations to help Sierra Leone establish a "special court" to try those who had committed atrocities during the war. The representative of the UN Secretary-General present at the signing of the Lomé Peace Accord appended to his signature a reservation to the effect that the amnesty provisions "shall not apply to international crimes of genocide, crimes against humanity, war crimes and other serious violations of international humanitarian law." Thus, previous amnesties were ignored. In its most prolific arrest, Charles Taylor had been offered sanctuary in nearby Nigeria, but was captured in 2006 fleeing Nigeria for Cameroon, and flown to Freetown, and ultimately to The Hague, where he stood trial. Since amnesties are not guaranteed, the preference for justice may supersede the goal of peace and potentially reduce combatants' willingness to negotiate.

Invariably, where truth and reconciliation commissions and tribunals operate side-by-side, the temporal mandate of the tribunal is far narrower than the commission. The division of labor in such instances is that the most serious crimes are tackled by the tribunal, while the lesser crimes are addressed by the reconciliation process. Truth commissions essentially have a much wider subject matter jurisdiction, as they allow for a broader inclusion of historical causes and motivations for violence that could not easily be proven in a court of law, particularly the colonial influence and long patterns of retaliatory atrocities. Adjudicating ethnic conflicts can inflame attitudes, whereas a truth and reconciliation commission can seek out social and psychological explanations for mutual animosities. In Sierra Leone, the truth and reconciliation commission was empowered to deal with all human rights violations occurring since the beginning of the conflict in 1991, whereas the hybrid Special Court for Sierra Leone (SCSL) was established to try "those bearing the greatest responsibility" for serious violations of international humanitarian law and certain provisions of Sierra Leonean domestic law since November 30, 1996. Likewise, in East Timor, the UN mandate was limited to genocide, war crimes, crimes against humanity, murder, sexual offenses, and torture committed between January 1 and October 25, 1999; however, the worst violence was in fact committed during Indonesia's 1975 invasion and subsequent twenty four-year occupation. Timor's own constitution identified the creation of national and international courts to judge crimes against humanity from 1974-99, but this broader time period was ignored.[9] Thus, the hybrid tribunal only examined the 1999 violence, and indirectly left to the truth and reconciliation commission the most heinous crimes that occurred throughout the 1974-99 period. In Bosnia, a truth commission was conceived for a broader period from November 19, 1990 to the conclusion of the Dayton

Agreement on December 14, 1995, though the hybrid court focused on the three years from 1992-95.

Locating Justice: Relevance for Society

The relevance of a justice process is heavily dependent on whether anyone observes the court or is made aware of the proceedings. Whereas the international tribunals were held in distant Netherlands, the courts for Bosnia, Cambodia, East Timor, Kosovo, and Sierra Leone were held in country, though the most recent tribunal for Lebanon is based at The Hague despite having Lebanese and international judges and staff.

With two countries involved in East Timor, location was a central issue. When the Indonesian trials failed to achieve accountability, a hybrid court was created, seated in the Timorese capital. Cambodia was able to gain some measure of autonomy over the hybrid process in its negotiations with the United Nations. As negotiations unfolded, the United Nations and Hun Sen disagreed about the type of trial (international or mixed versus domestic), whom to try (the twenty to thirty top cadres, or whomever Hun did not pardon), and whether to call these crimes against humanity or genocide.[10] At one point, Hun Sen argued that Americans should be tried in an international court like Pol Pot for the American *coup d'état* against Sihanouk that brought the Khmer Rouge to power.[11] By April 2000, a renewed agreement was reached, establishing that four out of five judges would be needed for conviction, and that three judges would be Cambodian with two appointed by the United Nations. The court will try about one or two dozen surviving individual Khmer Rouge "senior leaders," not foreign countries or middle-ranking members. In the Sierra Leone case, Taylor was charged with crimes against humanity and violations of Geneva conventions, though his trial was moved to The Hague, possibly undermining the impact of his arrest in either Sierra Leone or Liberia. Nevertheless, the trials seem to have been fairly well regarded by the domestic population. Locating justice is not only impacted by where, but also when trials occur. Trials held so long after the commission of crimes undermine the sense of justice. In Cambodia, trials were not held during the large-scale UN peacebuilding mission, but rather more than fifteen years after that operation had ceased and fully thirty years since the Khmer Rouge were expelled from Phnom Penh by Vietnamese forces.

The Kosovo trials reflect the potential antagonisms stirred by in-country exercises and the sometimes detrimental impact on post-conflict peace processes where simply having international personnel does not always relieve such problems. There, the source of law became controversial as judicial dominance shifted from Serbian Kosovans to Albanian Kosovans and the ongoing lack of impartiality had negative repercussions in the ethnic communities. Lacking enough international judges to form a majority vote, the judicial system continued to abandon cases against ethnic Albanians while simultaneously over-charging ethnic Serbs. The sense of discrimination toward ethnic Serb defendants and impunity for ethnic Albanian perpetrators (including frequent releases of suspected criminals) undermined early attempts to establish the rule of law, which became apparent in August and September 2000, as Serbian Kosovans attacked the court at Prizren and fourteen Serbs escaped from Mitrovica jail. Alleged Serbian war criminals launched a hunger strike to protest slow trials, long detentions, and ethnic discrimination and demanded international judicial personnel (IJP) be assigned to their cases, which was granted by UN Mission in Kosovo (UNMIK) Regulation 2000/34 that expanded IJP to all of Kosovo. With the success of the hybrid courts in northern Kosovo at Mitrovica, local feelings of resentment swung against the IJP, this time for being too favorably disposed toward the Serb population.

Similarly, the *ad hoc* tribunals spurred a nationalist backlash. For instance, indicted war criminal Vojislav Seselj (who had surrendered to The Hague) and the Serbian Radical Party won the highest vote total in the December 2003 elections.[12] Even the triumphant arrest of Milosevic in March 2001 was contested by state sovereignty, as he was held in Serb jail for corruption, not war crimes. Over time, the ICTY achieved a certain level of trust among Bosniaks in the Bosnian Federation, but was widely perceived as a biased, anti-Serb body in the Republika Srpska. Although the Srpska Parliament passed a law on cooperation with the ICTY in September 2001, in practice resistance remained strong among Serbians, and Srpska was very slow to hand over war crimes suspects to the ICTY. War crimes cases are transferred to the State Court of Bosnia and Herzegovina (BiH), which was established by law in November 2002 and has jurisdiction over both entities of Bosnia and Herzegovina, where the special War Crimes Chamber includes international judges and prosecutors. Although the Tutsi-led Rwandan government suffered as victims, they still were displeased by certain elements of the international trials, including not hosting them. Distrust toward France also manifested itself, with Rwanda's opposition to French judges at the ICTR, and grew after a French judge issued arrest warrants in November 2006 for nine of Kagame's associates regarding the 1994 plane crash of President Juvenal Habyarimana.[13]

Closely linked to the location of the trials is gaining public input and support for an often unfamiliar process of formal legal and impartial justice. Commonly, the choice of which languages in which to conduct the trials was a great source of tension. In Cambodia, the court did not have the capacity to translate all of the documents that were generated by the parties or referred to in submissions to the court into English, French, and Khmer. Language was a major barrier to effective proceedings in East Timor as well, where four languages (English, Portuguese, Indonesian, and Tetum) shared the communication role. Though indigenous languages abound, Sierra Leone's Creole approximates English and alleviated some of these pressures, and a key advantage in the Bosnian trials was that the court operated in the same language. Nevertheless, public outreach needs to be improved. Ownership of the process was clearly lacking in public reactions across Yugoslavia, though the ICTY provided cover for the ongoing failure in Bosnia (rather than the moral force that the human rights community saw it as). In Rwanda, outreach by the ICTR did not begin until 2000, and with trials so far away, the domestic audience was not the focus. Public interest in the trials was quite limited in East Timor and Bosnia. In Sierra Leone, the public had a difficult time in distinguishing between the trials and truth commission process, though some outreach initiatives mitigated this problem.[14] In Kosovo, trials were eagerly followed by both antagonistic communities, and the Cambodian trials have achieved fairly high attendance marks. Yet the local population still remains largely uninformed regarding the actual proceedings of formal court hearings.

Aside from choosing a method of accountability, the cultural relevance of a process itself is important. Human rights advocacy organizations and victims groups generally prefer international justice, yet the adversarial courtroom process frequently did not comport with the practices of society. Thus, trials were not always the most relevant process and sometimes customary justice was more meaningful as substitute or in parallel in traditional societies. Customary justice was applied in East Timor, Rwanda, and Sierra Leone. Negotiations between the families of victims and offenders were part of this process and most ordinary and local disputes are still resolved through these mediations rather than the formal legal system or any other mechanism. Traditional justice can be discriminating, strongly affected by family, clan, village, or ethnic connections; thus negotiations do not often accommodate the individual rights of victims and may be misplaced in a multicultural society. Customary processes were available in other cases, but rarely used. Traditional justice has long ago eroded in Cambodia, where historically the king or his magistrates had the authority to determine justice. Little consideration was paid to traditional forms of dispute resolution in Kosovo either. Albanian Kosovans had an informal system of Ottoman-based customary law known as the *Kanun of Leke Dukagjini* that was commonly practiced in rural areas when the court system was deemed as unreliable or unfair. Incorporating such an unfamiliar traditional system in collaboration with the formal legal system was also ignored, thus the focus of proponents of the rule of law was on capacity building and reform of the existing justice system.

In several cases, tribunals and truth commissions have operated side by side, though the proper mutually beneficial arrangement has yet to be fully grasped. Perpetrators may not testify at a truth commission if they risk prosecution at a tribunal (unless amnesty is offered). Likewise such testimony could potentially undermine criminal investigations. Tribunal and TRC may also compete for resources from the same donor pool and undercut transitional justice generally, while officials from either body may disagree about the goals of each institution. The East Timor TRC (known as the Commission on Truth, Reception, and Reconciliation, CAVR in Portuguese) was carefully modeled after traditional justice methods (*nahe biti boot*) used in Timorese villages, though a balance was struck between the collective harmony of the village and human rights norms. The reconciliation aspect promoted community reconciliation through small-scale village meetings where victim and perpetrator met with traditional leaders and

CAVR facilitators to restore relations and help to heal society. The Lomé Peace Accord also provided for a National Truth and Reconciliation Commission (TRC) and participation in the hearings was robust: many leading figures came before the TRC, including President Kabbah and Valentine Strasser, and those who appeared before the TRC included both victims and perpetrators. Justice Geoffrey Robertson denied the TRC the public testimony of Special Court detainees, though he considered the mandates of the TRC and the Special Court and sought to balance the interests of the two.[15] A Bosnian truth commission to deal with "lower ranking executioners," victim reparations, historical analysis, and "the work of undiluted memory" was considered, but some worried that the proposed TRC mandate was too similar to that of the ICTY, particularly in the area of investigative powers. In 2001 and 2006, major initiatives were launched to establish a national truth commission, but both failed. Ultimately, only an investigation of the massacres at Srebrenica (the Srebrenica Commission) operated in 2003-04. Though debated, no TRC process occurred in Cambodia.

Performing Justice: Process and Capacity

Owing in large measure to the horrific scale of the ethnic cleansing and war crimes of the former Yugoslavia and the genocide in Rwanda and the international shame felt by Western powers for doing too little too late in both cases, the two *ad hoc* war crimes tribunals were granted ample funding and significant international attention. As a result of the inefficient use of those resources in relation to the number of trials concluded, new experiments in more affordable hybrid tribunals with much smaller budgets were adopted, though the hybrid tribunals generally lacked the resources to effectively conduct cases.

The example of Kosovo generally holds true for the other cases as well, where the gap in status undermined legitimacy. There, the effectiveness of the rule of law was hamstrung by basic logistical issues in terms of lack of equipment and resources. Few if any cars, computers, generators, supplies, court buildings, law libraries, or forensic labs were available. Aside from the overall limited size of the budget, the gap in pay between domestic and international staff was also an issue. Simply put, locals were compensated far less than were internationals. Moreover, as the subject matter jurisdiction of the panels increased, not enough international judges were available to adjudicate cases. Likewise, international personnel had differing levels of competency, legal background, and English language skills.[16] East Timor's Special Panels operated with a budget of around $6 million, the Bosnian War Crimes Court amounted to a regular annual budget of $13 million, and Sierra Leone's budget was rather limited, initially around $104 million for four years. In Cambodia, the budget became quite politicized. Cambodia's revised total budget for the court, from the beginning of operations through the end of 2010, was $135 million. This represents a $79 million increase over the original three year operational budget of

$56 million.[17] After the UN announced its establishment, a number of Cambodian ECCC employees alleged that they were forced to pay kickbacks in order to secure or retain their jobs with the court. The UN's Office of Internal Oversight Services (OIOS) reviewed those claims and reportedly found them credible; however, the OIOS may purportedly only conduct a full investigation of international staff, not Cambodian staff.

Beyond budgetary issues, the fundamental question in the pursuit of legal accountability is whether or not the perpetrators were indicted, arrested, tried, and sentenced. In general, the greatest obstacle to accountability was arresting fugitives, though the other stages presented hurdles to overcome as well. Indictments can be a political act, weighed against the need to maintain compliance with a diplomatic process. Having gained an indictment, capturing at large war criminals is challenging, yet in some cases, the period from arrest to trial became an issue, as the aforementioned limited resources began to impact the judicial process and raised questions of fairness and the violation of due process rights to the alleged criminals who were held in pre-trial detention. Finally, the length of sentencing was often much less than expected and, of course, capital punishment was not a penalty in any of these hybrid or international tribunals.

Each of the five hybrid tribunals here operated in some capacity, and developed relatively similar formulas whereby the court would comprise a close balance of national and international judges and the necessary number of votes to decide a case. As of September 2010, dozens of trials were being held before the Bosnian War Crimes Chamber; the Human Rights Chamber was set up as part of the Human Rights Commission under the Dayton Agreement and included both national and international jurists. The Chamber's caseload involved human rights violations related to property, unresolved disappearances, unemployment discrimination, and violations of due process in local war crimes trials. Until 2008, each of the five trial panels and the appellate panel included two international members and one national member; the balance of composition was later reversed to include two nationals and one international.[18] In Kosovo, the court evolved to address lower-level ethnic violence and war crimes. As a result of the continuing release of alleged Albanian Kosovan perpetrators, Regulation 2000/64 of December 2000 altered the composition of the panels to a voting majority of three international judges and only two ethnic Albanian judges. At the same time, Albanian judges were reluctant to serve on high profile war crimes cases and antagonize their own constituents. These changes often soured ethnic Albanian judges, who no longer wanted to participate as a single judge in a losing vote. When multiple systems of justice are operating simultaneously, the risk of unfairness rises. With a functioning ICTY, the hybrid process in Kosovo and Bosnia did not seek out major criminals, who if indicted and apprehended, like President Milosevic, were transferred to The Hague. The division of labor in Rwanda created one gross inequity; high-level Hutus at the ICTR faced life in prison, whereas lower-level Hutus in domestic Rwandan courts faced execution.

In East Timor, major figures were not held accountable and Indonesia refused to extradite any perpetrators for trial, despite multiple processes. An international tribunal was also suggested for East Timor, but the international community never brought itself to challenge Indonesia to such a degree. In 2000, the Serious Crimes Unit identified ten priority cases to pursue more vigorously. At the conclusion of the trials in May 2005, ninety-five indictments were filed against 392 accused persons, of whom 303 remained at large in Indonesia; eighty four convictions for crimes against humanity and murder were handed down along with three acquittals, and thirteen indictments were dismissed or cases withdrawn.[19] Sentencing was rather short, with militia members receiving prison sentences of around ten years for committing crimes against humanity. General Wiranto, the chief of the Indonesian military, was indicted but never extradited. In Cambodia, trial chambers are composed of two international judges and three Cambodian judges, while the Supreme Court consists of three international judges and four Cambodian judges. Though long delayed, several prominent Khmer Rouge leaders were arrested and stood trial; the Duch case concluded with a guilty verdict in July 2010 and others are ongoing. Here, one may question whether a quarter century of impunity can be rectified, especially as the elderly Khmer Rouge may pass on before trials conclude. Since its inception in 2002, the three judges (two appointed by the United Nations and one by the Sierra Leone government) of the Sierra Leone Trial Chamber and the five judges of the Appeals Chamber (three appointed by the United Nations and two by the Sierra Leone government) were appointed along with U.S. Army lawyer David Crane as chief prosecutor. Major indictments include Liberian President Charles Taylor, Minister of Internal Affairs Chief Sam Hinga Norman, who had previously been deputy minister of defense and coordinator of the Civil Defense Forces (CDF) during the last years of the civil war, and militia leader Foday Sankoh. The Taylor trial stands out for its prosecution of a former head of state. Again, major figures have already passed on, though significant trials have occurred.

Aside from accountability, another major purpose of hybrid mechanisms is to establish a foundation for the rule of law and judicial reform. Thus, capacity building is a second standard upon which to judge performances. Several options to address serious crimes were available to the international community in Kosovo, each with its own merits. Yet the ICTY was not considered a long-term solution to implementing the rule of law and building judicial capacity in Kosovo, and both ethnic communities were concerned that the international tribunal might prosecute their own war crimes. Thus, the UN considered forming a hybrid Kosovo War and Ethnic Crimes Court (KWECC); ultimately, the hybrid mechanism adopted was relatively successful at capacity building with continued international oversight.[20]

Owing in part to the discrimination toward the ethnic Albanian community for the past decade or more, the initial attempt to educate and train Albanian Kosovans to fulfill positions as judges, prosecutors, and public defenders proved enormously challenging. Over time, the Organization for Security and Cooperation in Europe (OSCE) established or supported the Criminal Defence Resource Centre (CDRC) to support the defense, the Kosovo Chamber of Advocates (KCA) and the Kosovo Judicial Institute (KJI) to train local judges and prosecutors, and the Department of Human Rights and Rule of Law to provide assistance in legal reform. The OSCE also formed a range of programs and institutions to monitor the rule of law in Kosovo, such as the Legal System Monitoring Section (LSMS). However, in an environment of ethnic animosity, careers as arbiters of justice became potentially dangerous. If impartial, judges from either ethnic community feared being considered traitors to their constituents, and risked their own personal security. Likewise, local justice actors paid little attention toward sexual violence, lacked knowledge of human rights standards, and often acted in an ethnically biased manner in offering services like access to defense counsel. Nevertheless, significant capacity building did occur, though the 2006 report of the Secretary-General's Special Envoy on Kosovo concluded that "the Kosovo justice system is generally regarded as the weakest of the Kosovo institutions," citing problems of family and clan solidarity; intimidation of witnesses, law enforcement, and judicial officials; and the wide-ranging consequences of organized crime and corruption.[21]

Elsewhere, the Bosnian War Crimes Chamber (BWCC) is a unique example of a hybrid court, consisting of a special chamber in a national justice system where nationals, empowered from the start with significant authority, are to take full responsibility over five years. In the plans for the BWCC, six phases were defined, from Planning (Phase I), which ended in August 2004, to the Completion of the Transition (Phase VI), which ended in December 2009. The Office of the High Representative (OHR) and the presidency of BiH signed an agreement establishing a Transitional Council on September 26, 2006 to aid the transition to a fully national institution as nationals gradually replace internationals along the way.[22] Despite setbacks in Indonesia, slight progress toward *demokrasi*, *reformasi*, and even accountability offers hope: active generals and military officials were actually tried in a civil court for the first time, a new human rights division in the Attorney General's office was formed, and judges began to be given international law training. In 2004, Indonesia's *Komisi Nasional Hak Asasi Manusia* (National Commission on Human Rights, Komnas HAM) identified five other major cases of abuse to focus upon, signaling a beginning of accountability by officialdom. As a result, decision-makers strongly want to avoid accusations and indictment. These negative reinforcements may serve to deter future excesses by military and political leaders.[23] In Cambodia, little judicial reform was achieved following the 1991-93 UN peacebuilding process and the onset of the hybrid tribunal does not appear to have fostered greater independence and impartiality by the Cambodian judiciary. Limited evidence suggests little capacity-building occurred after the trials in Sierra Leone.[24]

Conclusions

International organizations, NGOs, and interested governments have invested in transitional justice over the past two decades as a way to promote long-term peace through accountability and judicial reform. This study suggests that hybrid tribunals remain viable and adaptable institutions to promote justice and reconciliation in deeply divided societies. They are no panacea; they themselves require reform and improvement and will not be appropriate in every ethnic or political conflict. What is striking about the multitude of these processes is the growing degree that perpetrators are being held accountable globally. Agreement to create transitional justice mechanisms at all is a serious accomplishment, as is the drafting of mandates and rules of operation. Arrests and trials still symbolically signal a break with the past and have merit for that reason alone. While impunity still reigns, major figures once thought untouchable have been brought to the docket, including heads of state like Slobodan Milosevic, Charles Taylor, Augusto Pinochet, Saddam Hussein, and many lesser persons. The gruesome killing of Libya's leader Col. Moammar Qaddafi led his son Saif al-Islam (indicted by the ICC) to offer to surrender to The Hague to avoid a similar fate before he was captured trying to escape to Niger. [25]

The conduct of the processes themselves can be judged according to their ability to hold perpetrators accountable in an efficient and understandable manner. Cultural factors affect the success or failure of transitional justice, particularly the use of the local language(s) and indigenous customs where appropriate. The local population must feel a certain ownership of the process, and the effective use of the media will greatly impact public sentiment toward these institutions and is integral to their acceptance in the community. In the cases emphasized here, Bosnia and Kosovo reached a fair degree of accountability with many mid-level officials prosecuted, as did Sierra Leone (though the deaths of key figures like Foday Sankoh and Johnny Paul Koroma prevented prominent trials until Taylor's capture). Timor exhibited a lack of accountability, since major perpetrators were generally not apprehended, while Cambodia presents a mixed record: the arrest and trial of the last living leaders of one of the worst episodes of mass murder in modern history, albeit as the aged and decrepit figures await the culmination of a long journey to justice.

Notes

1. The Dayton peace agreement created the Office of the High Representative (OHR) to implement the accord in Bosnia. In turn, the OHR drafted the Criminal Code and Criminal Procedure Code creating the War Crimes Chamber of the Court of Bosnia and Herzegovina to investigate and prosecute persons allegedly involved in serious violations of international law during the 1992–95 conflict, which began its work in March 2005. *Law on Court of Bosnia and Herzegovina*. 2002.

Available at: www.sudbih.gov.ba/files/docs/zakoni/en/Zakon_o_sudu_16_02_-_eng.pdf.

2. Cambodia and the United Nations agreed to finalize the hybrid tribunal on June 6, 2003 to prosecute those most responsible for genocide and crimes against humanity committed during the 1975-79 period (April 17, 1975 to January 7, 1979) under Democratic Kampuchea, i.e. the Khmer Rouge. *Agreement between the United Nations and the Royal Government of Cambodia Concerning the Prosecution Under Cambodian Law of Crimes Committed During the Period of Democratic Kampuchea.* 2003. Available at: www.eccc.gov.kh/english/cabinet/agreement/5/Agreement_between_UN_and_RGC.pdf.

3. For East Timor, UN Security Council Resolution 1272 of October 25, 1999 established a hybrid court, the Special Panels for Serious Crimes (SPSC), under the authority of the United Nations Transitional Administration for East Timor (UNTAET), exclusively for genocide, war crimes, crimes against humanity, murder, sexual offenses, and torture committed between January 1 and October 25, 1999. United Nations Transitional Administration in East Timor (UNTAET). 2000. "Regulation 2000/11: On the Organization of Courts in East Timor." Available at: www.unmit.org/legal/UNTAET-Law/Regulations%20English/Reg2000-11.pdf.

4. Kosovo's special panels grew out of the UN's rebuilding efforts of the judiciary there under United Nations Mission in Kosovo (UNMIK) Regulation 2000/6 of February 2000, giving international prosecutors and judges authority to conduct criminal proceedings from the previous conflict to current events. The special Regulation 64 panels prosecuted violence by both Serbian and Kosovar Albanian perpetrators. United Nations Mission in Kosovo (UNMIK). 2000. "Regulation 2000/64: On Assignment of International Judges/Prosecutors and/or Change of Venue." Available at: www.unmikonline.org/regulations/2000/re2000_64.htm.

5. Security Council Resolution 1315 authorized the UN Secretary-General to create the Special Court for Sierra Leone (SCSL) on January 16, 2002 in agreement with the government of Sierra Leone to prosecute crimes against humanity, war crimes, and other serious violations of international humanitarian law and domestic crimes committed within Sierra Leone since November 30, 1996. *Statute of the Special Court for Sierra Leone.* 2002. Available at: www.sc-sl.org.

6. The Special Tribunal for Lebanon (STL) was established pursuant to UN Security Council Resolution 1757 (2007) to try the alleged perpetrators of political assassinations beginning in 2004, with jurisdiction over later attacks only if it finds them to be connected to the attack of February 14, 2005 that killed former Prime Minister Rafiq Hariri and of a similar nature and gravity. The mandate of the tribunal is limited to the time period from October 1, 2004 to December 12, 2005, or a later date to be determined by the United Nations and Lebanon with the consent of the Security Council. It is important to note that the Tribunal will have jurisdiction over the later attacks only if it finds them to be connected to the attack of February 14, 2005, "in accordance with the principles of criminal justice" and of a similar nature and gravity. This designation includes the overt activities of Syria, which was suspected to be behind the assassination. As of December 2011, it had not begun its trials. See <http://www.stl-tsl.org>.

7. International Center for Transitional Justice, *The Special Court for Sierra Leone,* 5-6.

8. MacAlister Brown and Joseph J. Zasloff, *Cambodia Confounds the Peacemakers* (Ithaca, NY: Cornell University Press, 1998), 80-81, 118, quoting Findlay, 149.

9. Part VII (Transitional and Final Provisions), Draft Constitution, Section 148.

10. Stephen Heder, "Hun Sen and Genocide Trials in Cambodia: International Impacts, Impunity, and Justice," in *Cambodia Emerges from the Past: Eight Essays*, ed. Judy Ledgerwood (Dekalb, IL: Northern Illinois University Press, 2002), 176-77.

11. Brown and Zasloff, *Cambodia Confounds the Peacemakers*, 248.

12. In March 2004, Kostunica coalition PM Seselj and Zivkovic were out.

13. Victor Peskin, *International Justice in Rwanda and the Balkans*, 162.

14. Mohamed Gibril Sesay and Mohamed Suma, *Transitional Justice and DDR: The Case of Sierra Leone* (New York, NY: International Center for Transitional Justice, 2006), 18.

15. Elizabeth Evenson, " Truth and Justice in Sierra Leone: Coordination between Commission and Court," *Columbia Law Review* 104, no. 3 (April 2004): 758.

16. Tom Perriello and Marieke Wierda, *Lessons from the Deployment of International Judges and Prosecutors in Kosovo* (New York, NY: International Center for Transitional Justice, 2006).

17. Government of Cambodia, "An Introduction to the Khmer Rouge Trials," August 2004.

18. The cantonal courts (in the Bosnian Federation), district courts (in Republika Srpska), and the Basic Court of Brčko District also have some limited power to try war crimes.

19. Judicial System Monitoring Programme, Justice Update, May 12-20, 2005, www.jsmp.minihub.org.

20. Perriello and Wierda, *Lessons from the Deployment of International Judges and Prosecutors in Kosovo.*

21. Perriello and Wierda, *Lessons from the Deployment of International Judges and Prosecutors in Kosovo.*

22. Bogdan Ivanišević, *The War Crimes Chamber in Bosnia and Herzegovina: From Hybrid to Domestic Court* (New York NY: International Center for Transitional Justice, 2008).

23. Asmara Nababan discussed these views at a lecture at the East West Center, Honolulu, Hawai'i, April 21, 2003.

24. Beth K. Dougherty, "Right-Sizing International Criminal Justice: The Hybrid Experiment at the Special Court for Sierra Leone," *International Affairs* 80, no. 2 (March 2004): 311-28, 325.

25. Laura Caroe, "Gaddifi son Al-Saadi 'offers to surrender,'" *The Sun* (United Kingdom), September 1, 2011, on-line at http://www.thesun.co.uk/sol/homepage/news/3786669/Gaddafi-son-Al-Saadi-offers-to-surrender.html (accessed February 15, 2013).

Part 3

Economic Measures

Chapter 9

Economic Instruments of Internal Conflict Resolution

Stephen D. Collins

Military force and diplomatic mediation are instruments frequently considered for use by external actors to resolve or deescalate civil wars. These approaches have likewise attracted considerable attention by scholars of internal conflict. In certain cases, dialogue diplomacy may constitute the optimal approach, with more coercive approaches being unnecessary or counterproductive. In other episodes, robust coercion may be warranted and military force may represent the only effective strategy. An alternative, however, to the rather stark choice of words or warfare is represented by economic statecraft, the use of financial sanctions and/or incentives to influence the behavior of states and other actors abroad. Economic statecraft offers an intriguing alternate path to conflict resolution, apart from the polar extremes of military intervention or discursive diplomacy. External actors have indeed begun in recent years to leverage pecuniary sticks and carrots in cases of intrastate conflicts.

This chapter introduces economic statecraft as one available approach that external actors can employ to facilitate the resolution of intrastate conflicts, examining the theory and practice of economic statecraft. First, economic statecraft is discussed broadly as a practice of international politics. What does the literature suggest about the most effective strategies of economic statecraft? When states and international organizations wish to dissuade certain behaviors and incentivize others, what are the specific economic tools that may be deployed? Second, the chapter turns more directly to the use of economic statecraft to mitigate internal conflicts. Economic sanctions represent a well-known instrument of economic statecraft and sanctions regimes can be assembled using a variety of tools. This section will survey the panoply of sanctions tools and assess the potency of each with respect to dissuading conflict. Economic incentives will be explored in the final section. Incentive approaches offer perhaps a broader variety of instruments and greater opportunities for creative statecraft. Several of the leading incentive approaches to conflict resolution—including conditional aid, development assistance, election aid, and civil society support—will be examined and evaluated. A central objective of this chapter is to highlight those economic strategies which have demonstrated the greatest promise with respect to mitigating internal conflict, and posit what the theory and empirical data suggest are ways to further enhance the effectiveness of economic statecraft as a means to resolve conflict.

Economic Statecraft—Use & Usefulness as a Foreign Policy Tool

An observer may wonder if economic instruments are of any use in cases of violent and intractable communal conflict. Indeed, contemporary scholars of international relations have often displayed a dubiety about the usefulness of economic influence strategies in general. This skepticism abounds despite the lengthy empirical record of states relying upon economic statecraft as a staple instrument in their foreign policy toolbox. Athens' trade embargo of Megara in 432 B.C., detailed in Thucydides' *History of the Peloponnesian War*, represents perhaps the earliest documented use of economic statecraft.[1] Between these antiquity writings and the modern period, other influential scholars and statesmen—including Adam Smith, Thomas Jefferson, and Abbe de Saint-Pierre—have discussed, and largely supported, the use and usefulness of economic statecraft.[2] However, modern scholars of the twentieth century—including Johann Galtung (1967), Anna Schreiber (1973), and Donald Losman (1979)—employing new rigorous social-scientific approaches, largely came to the converse conclusion, that economic statecraft was of greatly limited effectiveness.[3] This sentiment was especially evident with respect to economic sanctions. Robert Gilpin and Henry Bienen provide an illustrative example of this skepticism, stating, "With very few exceptions and under highly unusual sets of circumstances, economic sanctions have historically proven to be an ineffective means to achieve foreign policy objectives."[4]

Although skepticism dominated the discourse on economic statecraft during the Cold War, the work that became the definitive tome on the subject, David Baldwin's *Economic Statecraft*, challenged this conventional wisdom, asserting that economic statecraft was dramatically underestimated in terms of its effectiveness as an instrument of foreign policy. Baldwin explains economic statecraft as "a situation in which one actor (A) is able to manipulate the cost benefit ratios of the alternatives perceived by another actor (B) so that the latter would be foolish to choose any alternative" other than the one presented by actor (A).[5] Baldwin suggested that the extant corpus on economic statecraft employed an ambiguous and incomplete conceptualization of the practice, and these weaknesses were largely responsible for the negative assessments of the practice.

Baldwin emphasized that economic statecraft involves more than just sanctions. States can utilize economic instruments to influence the behavior of foreign actors, according to Baldwin, "1) by threats of punishment; 2) by promised rewards; 3) by actual punishment; 4) by actual rewards; and 5) by conveying correct or incorrect information to (the actor) with respect to the cost/benefit ratio of his alternatives."[6] Baldwin offered a far more comprehensive catalog of economic instruments of statecraft than previous works. He also suggested that sanctions critics err by failing to consider that sanctions efforts can succeed by dint of their deterrent and signaling effects, even if they do not produce immediate behavioral changes in target actors. Finally, Baldwin maintains that critics neglect to gauge the efficacy of sanctions in comparison to other policy approaches such as military force, which also frequently is unsuccessful and tends to be far more costly.

Economic Instruments of Statecraft

Sanctions

Trade	Finance
- Trade Embargo	- Aid Suspension
- Trade Boycott	- Aid Reduction
- Tariff Increase	- Asset Freeze
- Extraterritorial Trade Sanction ("Blacklisting")	- Expropriation
- Withholding Credit	- Withholding Payments to International Organizations
- Preclusive Buying[7]	- Capital Controls
- Product Dumping	- Currency Manipulation/Attacks
- Aviation Embargoes	- Bond Ratings Restrictions

Incentives

Trade	Finance
- Tariff Reductions	- Financial Grants
- Preferential Trading Arrangements	- Loan Capital Disbursements
- Product Quotas	- Investment Guarantees
- Direct Purchase[8]	- Encouraging Private Investment
- Disbursements from International Financial Organizations	- Support for Aid and Loan Capital
	- Debt Relief

- List adapted from Baldwin (1985): 41, 42

Despite the Baldwin work, and a select but increasing number of empirical studies testifying to the efficacy of economic statecraft, the conventional wisdom on economic statecraft at the turn of the twenty-first century remained negative. Academics and popular pundits continued to characterize the use of sanctions and incentives as futile or counterproductive. This assessment continued to be influenced by the seminal empirical studies on the subject which showed that economic statecraft often failed. However, most of these critical analyses were written during the heart of the bipolar era of the Cold War; an international environment where superpower competition inhibited the ability of sanctions and incentives to induce policy change in the target states. The prevailing assessment was quickly becoming an anachronism due to the polar shift that occurred in the international system with the demise of the Soviet Union. Under the new post-bipolar system, the pain of sanctions, or the inducement effects of aid, was less frequently nullified by offsetting aid offers. Furthermore, the contemporary international system has displayed greater unity, permitting more multilateral sanctions regimes. Incentives approaches have also received more attention and use in the contemporary era.

Though economic statecraft critics remain a powerful voice, the more recent literature has begun to reflect the augmented utility of the practice. Kimberly Ann Elliott, co-author of the prominent dataset *Economic Sanctions Reconsidered*, which was critical of sanctions efficacy, subsequently has trumpeted the merits of economic statecraft.[9] In reference to U.S. influence attempts in the developing world she argued that: "Despite the popular wisdom that 'sanctions never work,' economic coercion has been both a popular and somewhat effective tool of U.S. intervention."[10] David Cortright, Daniel Drezner, George Lopez, and Elizabeth Rogers are among the collection of scholars who affirm the efficacy of economic tools of statecraft. Rogers, for example, maintains that sanctions are "underrated" and are "more effective than most analysts suggest."[11] According to Rogers, the prevailing skepticism on sanctions is due "in part because unlike other foreign policy instruments sanctions have no natural advocate or constituency. . . . As a result, their successes are widely unreported, while their failures are exaggerated by those with an interest in either avoiding their use, or in using other instruments."[12] As economic instruments of statecraft have attracted more credibility due to their rising efficacy in international politics, this chapter will now consider the use of economic instruments more specifically as tools to manage internal conflict.

Economic Statecraft & Intrastate Conflict

As with international relations more generally, the scholarly corpus on civil wars and communal conflict resolution tends to devote more attention to military force and diplomatic mediation than to economic statecraft. Still, a select set of the internal conflict scholarship does address the role that economic sanctions and incentives play in efforts by external actors to resolve episodes of internal conflict. Unlike during the Cold War, where external actors more often fueled intrastate conflicts by arming various groups as a means of fighting proxy wars, in recent years more of the efforts and energies of powerful external actors have been devoted to conflict de-escalation and resolution (albeit, with notable exceptions). States with influence and assets have acted independently to sanction aggression and reward peaceful, conciliatory behavior. Collective efforts have also increased, with regionally-based multilateral efforts, and broadly multilateral efforts through the United Nations. External actors can levy sanctions and offer incentives in a variety of ways to prevent and resolve conflicts. As identified by Michael Brown, economic sticks and carrots can be employed in numerous ways, including (*inter alia*) to: alleviate security concerns, redress political discrimination, foster economic development and justice, address cultural discrimination and misperceptions, establish safe havens, dissuade the intervention of troublesome neighboring states, co-opt nefarious leaders, and ossify long-term development and stability.[13]

Not only can economic instruments work to redress many proximate and underlying causes of conflict, the approach also possesses the merit of being a relatively low-cost policy instrument; therefore the barrier to the use of this instrument is relatively low. Economic statecraft is an especially thrifty instrument when compared with military force. Incentive approaches can carry high-dollar costs at times—consider the aid promised to Israel and Egypt as part of the Camp David Accords. Yet, in the great majority of cases, successful approaches involve expenditures in the thousands and millions, not in the billions. One may compare these modest sums to the cost of the relatively limited military intervention by NATO in Libya in 2011. The financial cost of the intervention to the United States alone exceeded $1 billion.[14] While economic incentives are typically low-cost measures, economic sanctions are even more economical for external actors to levy. Sanctions often involve cuts of financial aid, which actually result in a net financial gain to a sanctioning state. In fact, sanctions senders more often benefit economically from sanctions as opposed to experiencing a pecuniary loss.[15] The following section examines the use and utility of economic sanctions as tools of conflict resolution.

Economic Sanctions and Intrastate Conflict

Economic sanctions represent perhaps the most potent instrument of coercion in international politics short of military force. Sanctions aim to shape the behavior of target actors (e.g., states, militants, firms, groups, individuals) by influencing targets' intentions and/or their capabilities. The first role, altering intentions, is perhaps the most well-known function of sanctions. By inflicting economic pain on targets as a consequence for undesirable behavior, sanctions seek to change the cost/benefit calculus of their actions. All policy actions, and certainly armed conflict, have their intrinsic costs. Sanctions impose additional costs which may represent a tipping factor, causing the target to determine that the costs of the disputed actions exceed the perceived benefits. The target may, therefore, decide that the rational course of action is to discontinue the activity. The second function of sanctions, eroding capabilities, is less well known, but represents a highly important effect of sanctions. In episodes involving armed conflict, the capabilities-eroding potential of sanctions may indeed be more consequential than sanctions' potential to affect intentions. Economic sanctions can restrict the supply or money and material to combatants (i.e., regimes or rebel groups) and therefore limit their ability to wage war. Additionally, by eroding their kinetic capabilities, sanctions facilitate concurrent or future efforts to subdue these actors.

Finally, sanctions may work to ameliorate internal conflict by acting as a catalyst for regime change. The hardships produced by sanctions may erode support for regime leaders at the mass and/or elite levels. Rising discontent among the mass population with the economic privation produced by economic sanctions may inspire a popular revolution, with the result being the overthrow of the regime. Leaders of the regime may also be deposed by elite elements in the military and business sectors. Collaboration between these forces can be inspired by concerns about the impact of sanctions on military readiness and about costly setbacks to corporate or personal fortunes. Whether the revolt is mass or elite led, the regime's demise is likely to produce new leadership eager to escape from the yoke of sanctions and thus more amenable to policy concessions which would ameliorate the conflict.

Economic sanctions possess a solid track record with regard to suppressing internal conflicts, asserts sanctions scholar Elizabeth Rogers. Indeed, sanctions efficacy with respect to internal conflicts is especially strong she contends, if one considers only those cases where sanctions were applied "seriously and systematically."[16] In addition to ensuring that sanctions packages are comprehensive and robust, Rogers suggests that for maximum effectiveness the sanctions campaign should be broadly multilateral, and must involve the United States as a leader of the sanctioning coalition.[17] Abel Escriba-Folch, in a study of eighty-nine civil wars in sixty-three states between 1959 and 1999, finds "robust" evidence that sanctions shorten the length of civil wars.[18] Additionally, Escriba-Folch finds that the most effective sanctions involve total economic embargos, and those which are imposed by international institutions. The value of comprehensive versus selective sanctions is, however, a contested point in the sanctions literature. The scope of sanctions should be calibrated to the regime type of the target state, argues Risa Brooks.[19] Comprehensive sanctions tend to work best against democracies in which mass discontent with economic hardship can force political reform; whereas in authoritarian states, according to Brooks, targeted sanctions tend to work more effectively as this sanctions type negatively impacts elites who are aligned with the regime.

An additional factor that is contested in the literature is the value of coupling sanctions with threats of military force. Chantal du Jonge Oadraat asserts that the threat to use military force must accompany sanctions if they are to prevent internal conflict.[20] According to Daniel Drezner, however, a target state's anticipation of future conflict with the sender state increases its reluctance to capitulate to target demands.[21] He finds that this explains why sanctions are more successful when imposed upon allies. Sanctions scholars do largely concur that threats *alone* can be highly effective. That is, the mere threat of imposing economic sanctions can often convince targets to capitulate to demands, even before sanctions begin to impose actual material hardships. Several examples exist of target states conceding either immediately prior to the imposition of sanctions, or in the immediate wake of their imposition. In the sanctions episodes involving Haiti (1993) and Sierra Leone (1997), both governments complied quickly with international demands after sanctions were imposed, and agreements were reached to resolve violent internal conflicts.[22] In the case of El Salvador, U.S. threats in 1990 to cut aid compelled the Salvadoran governments to make concessions leading to a negotiated resolution of the civil war.[23]

Sanctions Approaches

Policymakers possess a wide variety of economic instruments from which to choose if sanctions become the preferred route. Each sanctions campaign is distinct. States opting to employ sanctions can finely calibrate their approach, applying a unique set of tools based upon the nature of the conflict, the parties involved, the complicity of individual actors, the severity of violence and/or repression, and the nature of the target's economy. Tools derive from several categories of sanctions, and may include trade sanctions, aid suspensions, financial sanctions, investment sanctions, commodity bans, and arms embargoes. Each form of sanctions works in a different way to attempt to weaken either the willingness of combatants to engage in violence and provocation, or their capacity to do so. The following two sections highlight the role of trade sanctions and aid sanctions in conflict resolution.

Trade Sanctions

Trade sanctions represent perhaps the most assertive and coercive economic statecraft approach. In the contemporary era of globalization, where states are increasingly reliant on trade with the global marketplace, trade sanctions can threaten to inflict enormous damage on a state's economy. Grave economic privation is especially likely if targeted states are threatened with trade sanctions that are comprehensive on both the vertical and horizontal dimensions. Vertically-comprehensive sanctions can be damaging to targeted states as these measures prohibit the export and import of nearly all categories of goods upon which states rely for sustenance and foreign capital. Horizontally-comprehensive sanctions can greatly intensify the economic hardships experienced by targets as these sanctions campaigns are broadly multilateral; that is, all or a large proportion of the target's major trading partners participate in the sanctions campaign.

Comprehensive trade sanctions have been employed in several internal conflicts. In nearly all of these cases the target is a central government directly engaged in mass killings and systematic human rights violations, or is considered an instigator of communal violence. Comprehensive trade sanctions are more appropriate when a national government is the target of a sanctions campaign, as the hardships created by omnibus trade sanctions threaten regime goals, and may even jeopardize the political survival of regime leaders.[24] South Africa represents perhaps the most well-known internal conflict episode where broad trade sanctions were applied in order to stimulate positive progress. The sanctions substantially raised the costs of adhering to the targeted apartheid system. The measures applied by the international community, including by South Africa's security ally the United States in the 1986 Comprehensive Anti-Apartheid Act, played a role in convincing the regime that the perceived social benefits of the policy were now eclipsed by the significant economic costs.[25]

The sanctions campaign involving South Africa represents a highly isolated success story from the bipolar era, and actually took effect as the Cold War was ending. Comprehensive, multilateral trade sanctions would be utilized more frequently in the post-bipolar era. Yugoslavia was subject to broad trade sanctions on three occasions in the Milosevic-era 1990s. Indeed, sanctions appeared to play a significant part in the resolution, abatement, or prevention of multiple conflicts in the Balkans. Sanctions imposed against Yugoslavia in 1992 by the United Nations for its role in inciting and supporting violence in Bosnia-Herzegovina, played a substantial role in convincing Belgrade to sign the Dayton Peace Accords in 1995; an accord which has brought—if not reconciliation—a lasting peace to Bosnia for nearly two decades.[26] When Milosevic attempted to annul opposition victories in Serbia's 1996 municipal elections, a Washington-engineered IMF suspension of normalization talks, and a threat by the U.S. and EU to push for the reintroduction of UN sanctions, forced Milosevic to retract the annulment and allow the opposition to take office.[27]

Sanctions imposed by the U.S. and Europe in 1998, had likely the most consequential effect on reducing conflict in the Balkans. In response to Serbia's use of violence against Kosovo's Muslim-majority population, the West imposed a series of trade, aid, and financial sanctions against Serbia, including an embargo on oil and a ban on air-travel. Sanctions were designed with outer and inner walls, with the outer walls imposing broad constraints on trade with, and aid to, Yugoslavia, and the inner walls cutting off specific firms and individuals from global trade and travel privileges and thereby eroding elite support for Milosevic.[28] These sanctions, along with a robust military bombing campaign, decimated Serbia's economy and caused GDP to drop by 20 percent in 1999, a broad measure of unemployment to reach 33 percent, and the country's living standard to decline by one-third.[29] The mass disillusionment with these conditions, and the provocative policies which invited the sanctions, motivated the Serbian public in September 2000 to turn Milosevic out of office. Sanctions contributed greatly to the sacking of the Milosevic regime, and its replacement with more moderate, progressive leaders, who discontinued Serbia's role as an instigator of conflict in the region.[30]

Coups d'état represent a form of intrastate armed conflict which often generate wider internal and communal conflicts and repression. External parties, therefore, often levy trade sanctions in order to reverse these violent plots. In several cases, the swift imposition or threat of broad trade sanctions worked to quickly reverse a coup and force a return to civilian rule. In the case of Guatemala, for example, President Jorge Serrano's 1993 power grab, in which he dissolved Congress, shuttered the judiciary, and launched autocratic rule, was met with a threat by a large coalition of regional states to impose withering trade sanctions on the country. The consequences of this pending sanction were perceived as grave enough by all sectors of Guatemalan society that any support Serrano enjoyed in the military and business community quickly evaporated. Within days the coup was overturned, as the military sacked Serrano and restored Guatemala's democratic institutions.[31]

Regional Trade Agreements and Conflict Resolution through Sanctions

As regional trade agreements have proliferated across the globe, and their importance to states' economies has increased, membership status in these associations represents a new trade sanction instrument which can be levied to manage internal conflicts. Trade blocs can threaten to revoke the membership of governments employing violence against civilian populations or engaged in other human rights violations which may stoke communal violence. Indeed, nearly all of the major regional trade agreements have established political conditions of membership. Political conditionality has been unevenly enforced by the regional trade groups; however, the threat of expulsion or the suspension of accession talks, remains a powerful lever which has been used on numerous occasions to end internal conflicts or force the end of practices and policies which can provoke internal conflict.

South America's Mercosur trade association employed the membership sanction to rapidly reverse a 1996 military coup in member-state Paraguay. After General Lino Oviedo deposed elected president Juan Carlos Wasmosy in April 1996, Mercosur quickly threatened to expel Paraguay from Mercosur unless democracy was restored. Facing severe economic isolation within South America, coup leaders were forced to step down and reinstate Wasmosy.[32] Political conditionality applied by the world's largest regional trade bloc, the European Union, has also played an ameliorative role in the communal conflicts extant in the Baltics. Reform legislation in the 1990s which improved the treatment of minority communities in the Baltic states of Estonia and Latvia can be credited in large measure to trade bloc pressure. The EU's insistence that minority ethnic groups receive citizenship and language rights in Estonia and Latvia, as a condition for progress on membership accession talks, acted as an essential catalyst for the passage of these reforms.[33] Political conditionality was also employed successfully to improve the treatment of minority communities in Slovakia, Hungary, and Romania. In these states, the desire to secure EU admission trumped nationalist and sectarian pressures. Reform measures were passed in these states in order improve their EU prospects, and the reforms helped to stave off acute communal conflict.[34]

The North American Free Trade Agreement (NAFTA) also had an impact on communal conflict in the region; however the record is more variegated as compared to that of the European Union. The formation of NAFTA was an important catalyst for the Zapatista armed rebellion in southern Mexico, which was launched, not coincidentally, on January 1, 1994, the day NAFTA was set to come into effect. The threat of NAFTA to peasant farmers was a main grievance of the Zapatistas, whose ranks were filled predominantly from the indigenous communities of rural Chiapas state. Still, though the regional trade agreement helped to incite an armed conflict, on balance it worked to diffuse internal violence and conflict in Mexico. The PRI regime in Mexico—which had labored assiduously for the passage of NAFTA—was tremendously concerned that the revolt would shake the international investment community's confidence in Mexico, and thus jeopardize the expected windfall of foreign investment as a result of NAFTA. As the primary grievance of the Zapatistas was the dearth of authentic democracy in Mexico, the government not only hastened an end to hostilities with the rebel forces, it also introduced a series of sweeping electoral reforms. These reforms facilitated the emergence of authentic political pluralism in Mexico, and the victories of the PAN opposition party in the 2000 presidential elections. The presence of NAFTA therefore produced (relative) restraint in the Mexican government's response to the Zapatista uprising, and also encouraged the government to agree to a transition to a political system which privileges nonviolent approaches to conflict resolution, including for Mexico's other marginalized communities.[35]

Aid Sanctions

While trade sanctions are occasionally employed by external actors in reaction to the outbreak of intrastate violence, wholesale trade boycotts are infrequently imposed, as they are highly blunt instruments whose impacts are felt broadly in the target society. Additionally, trade sanctions can carry boomerang effects; that is, they can impose costs on domestic constituencies in the sender state itself. Aid sanctions are actually more commonly used as a first response by the international community in cases of intrastate violence. Trade sanctions do often accompany the suspension of aid; however, these typically involve targeted sanctions—highly circumscribed sanctions regimes which target only firms owned by regime or rebel leaders. Aid sanctions, conversely, tend to be more robust and unambiguous, with nearly all non-humanitarian assistance suspended. Comprehensive trade sanctions, therefore, are increasingly less common, though the threat of omnibus trade bans is commonly used to amplify the effect of aid sanctions.

Governments infrequently acquiesce immediately when aid is terminated, and at times remain recalcitrant for many years or even indefinitely. However, the suspension of foreign assistance does impose high costs on aid-dependent states, and therefore the sanction has the potential to induce significant policy changes. Aid cut-offs have been employed effectively in several instances to resolve intrastate conflicts. Peruvian president Alberto Fujimori's 1992 *autogolpe*, in which he shuttered the legislature and high court and declared rule by presidential decree, was met with sharp international opprobrium. The United States, Europe, and other donors immediately suspended all non-humanitarian aid to Peru. Furthermore, U.S. pressure resulted in the revocation of $2 billion in loans from the Inter-American Development Bank and other multilateral institutions.[36] The political crisis ended relatively quickly, as Fujimori capitulated to the economic pressure within six weeks. New elections were scheduled and shuttered democratic institutions were soon opened. Although, Peru remained an executive dominated state for years, the reforms Fujimori introduced under the pressure of aid sanctions did create the sufficient political space for a successful opposition challenge and the victory of opposition presidential candidate Alejandro Toledo in 2001, and the emergence of a more genuine democratic political system for Peru.[37]

Malawi presents another successful example of the use of aid sanctions to stem internal conflict. Rising levels of violence and repression carried out by the Banda government in 1992 elicited the opprobrium of the international community. Aid donors severed all non-humanitarian aid to Malawi, and conditioned its return on the Banda regime's consent to a transition to democratic rule. Banda consented to the reform measures, which set the stage for the victory of the reformist opposition movement, which won control of the presidency and the legislature in elections the following year.[38]

El Salvador and Guinea provide two additional cases of aid sanctions supporting conflict resolution processes. In El Salvador, a U.S. threat to curtail military aid played an important role in convincing the government to negotiate in good faith during the peace process; a process which led to the end of a bloody civil war in the country.[39] Guinea represents one of the most compelling cases for the coercive power of aid sanctions. The Camara regime, which seized power in a 2008 coup, was subject to an abrupt aid cutoff by donors in 2010, after a particularly grisly September 2008 massacre of demonstrators. Within four months, the government—heavily reliant on foreign aid—capitulated, quickly scheduling elections and then turning over power to the elected opposition. Opposition forces acknowledged the role of aid sanctions in resolving the conflict as opposition leader Sudia Toure asserted, "The pressure from the international community, the pressure was very strong, and very fast. The horizon was closed very quickly."[40]

Though change occurred quickly in the episode involving Guinea, foreign aid is hardly an infallible instrument that external forces can wield whenever internal unrest materializes. Aid sanctions tend to work only in those situations in which a central government is the primary antagonist. The suspension of aid, furthermore, does not always motivate states to modify their behavior. Aid sanctions levied against Cameroon in 1992, in response to rising levels of government repression, failed to precipitate any political change.[41] China's repression of dissidents continued unabated after aid sanctions were applied in the wake of the 1989 Tiananmen Massacre.[42] Aid suspensions following coups in Mauritania (2008) and Madagascar (2009) have yet to restore democracy and ease political conflict. In Myanmar, sanctions imposed by donor states over the course of two decades appeared wholly futile in motivating the government to end repression and implement political reforms in order to resolve the intense political conflict. A rather dramatic political opening occurred in the spring of 2012, however, with a wave of opposition victories in parliamentary elections. Aung san Sui Kyi, opposition leader and Nobel Peace Prize laureate, gave credit to the helpful role of sanctions in spurring the reforms introduced by the military government. The Myanmar episode may suggest that aid suspensions can be a latent force for conflict resolution, even in cases where they initially appear to be ineffective.[43]

Concluding Thoughts on Sanctions as Instruments of Conflict Resolution

The empirical record illustrates that economic sanctions can play an important contributing role in the resolution of internal conflicts. Trade and aid are valuable assets that external actors can manipulate to influence the behavior of governments and sub-state actors. There exists a wide variety of sanctions instruments, and sanctions regimes can be finely calibrated to adapt to each conflict episode. Sanctions are certainly no panacea, as determined actors can endure the cost of sanctions for a significant length of time without capitulating. Nevertheless, the evidence suggests that sanctions frequently act as a catalyst for serious policy changes, and these measures can help to resolve or ameliorate internal conflicts. The research also suggests that sanctions which enjoy broad participation (international or regional), exhibit greater rates of success than unilateral measures.

While sanctions may have an ameliorative impact on communal conflicts, external actors must consider the fact that economic sanctions can produce substantial humanitarian suffering, including increased levels of malnutrition, disease, and mortality. One way to limit the humanitarian costs of sanctions is to design sanctions regimes which focus the economic pain on regime leaders, state agencies aligned with repressive activities, and businesses associated with the regime. Additionally, in nearly all cases, humanitarian exceptions to the sanctions regime can be agreed upon by participating states, ensuring that humanitarian assistance is not adversely impacted. Sanctions, therefore, can make a helpful impact when calibrated to the specific case, and when designed to protect the civilian population by focusing the most severe material costs on the actual antagonists.

Economic Incentives and Intrastate Conflict

Though sanctions can often be useful, the approach is laden with certain drawbacks. Economic sanctions, as discussed, can cause substantial humanitarian suffering among civilian populations. Sanctions also hold the potential to provoke hostile and violent responses from those targeted. The Peloponnesian War and the Japanese attack on Pearl Harbor were launched, in part, as responses to punitive economic sanctions. Additionally, sanctions disrupt trade, and though they rarely have a large impact on the aggregate national economy of the sanctioning state, they can have outsized impacts on certain industries and firms.

Economic incentives offer an alternative or supplemental economic statecraft approach to conflict resolution, an approach which can elude many of the downsides of sanctions. Incentives avoid the problems of humanitarian hazards and adverse impacts to firms in the sanctioning state(s). Furthermore, incentive approaches can reduce tensions and minimize the possibility of hostile responses toward either external states or internal groups. Incentives tend to be perceived more favorably, often viewed more as measures of persuasion than of forceful coercion as per sanctions. Robert Axelrod's seminal work on *positive reciprocity* is helpful in illustrating how actors respond more favorably to incentives. He asserted that, when actors respond to one another with positive gestures, stable and mutually-beneficial outcomes can more readily be reached.[44] An additional benefit of incentives approaches is that unilateral actions are more feasible. Whereas sanctions success is highly reliant on securing the broad participation of other states, incentives can be applied unilaterally by a concerned external actor and still have a substantial impact (though, collective active is more impactful for incentives as well).

As with sanctions regimes, incentives packages can be assembled in a myriad of ways, using a variety of instruments and approaches. Conventionally, incentives are viewed as conditional offers of material benefits. Conditionality indeed constitutes an important component of incentive packages. Development assistance or trade preferences, for example, can be made contingent upon the termination of conflict or the cessation of provocative behaviors. These *top-down* incentive measures seek to resolve conflict by changing the intentions and behaviors of leaders in the respective camps. Incentive packages also, however, involve many unconditional incentives. Financial assistance can be targeted, for example, toward the creation or improvement of institutions in order to promote legal due process, impartial justice, professionalism, and accountability. As opposed to conditional incentives, which tend to promote change from the top-down, these incentives attempt to promote peace by promoting change from *inside* the state. Internal conflict is less likely to occur when institutions emerge that can restrain government abuse, and which apply laws impartially without regard to ethnicity, religion, class, region, or other sectarian category. Finally, external actors can employ a set of incentives which act to promote change from the *bottom-up*. Bottom-up incentives consist of providing funding to those actors in civil society that promote political pluralism, civil rights and freedoms, government integrity, and social tolerance. Donor states and international organizations can therefore provide funds to civic-minded NGOs, independent media, and, in some cases, opposition groups.[45] This section of the chapter will examine the particular instruments that accompany top-down, inside-out, and bottom-up incentive approaches to managing intrastate conflict.

Development Aid and Conflict Resolution

Fostering economic development is one of the most important roles that the international community can play in mitigating and resolving internal conflicts. *Homo economicus* arguments are as incomplete in divining the origin of communal conflicts as in explaining other social phenomena. Nevertheless, the desperate levels of economic hardship that exist in developing countries, and the often highly unequal distribution of national wealth, have long been considered major causal factors in internal conflict. As noted by Michael Brown, "grim economic prospects intensify resentments, polarize societies, and make people more receptive to ethnic and nationalistic appeals."[46] It is not simply that conflict occurs more frequently in the wake of economic decline or crisis, underdevelopment by itself appears to be a risk factor for armed internal conflict. According to recent research, economic development and intrastate violence are inversely related. James Fearon and David Laitin's study examining internal conflicts between 1945-1999 reports that the poorest countries (at the tenth percentile in income) had a 72 percent chance of experiencing an internal conflict during this period; countries with a median income had a 44 percent chance of experiencing such violence; while the richest countries (in the ninetieth percentile) only faced a 2.7 percent chance of intrastate conflict occurring.[47] Development assistance that helps to foster broad economic growth in a country has the potential to reduce conflict propensity. A study conducted by Zeric Smith concludes that, as per-capita gross domestic product increases in a country, ethnic conflicts decrease.[48]

In addition to reducing conflict by boosting economic growth rates, development aid can reduce conflict by ameliorating inequality. By focusing aid on the poorest segments and addressing rampant inequality, aid may reduce the resentments and tensions caused by inequality. As stated by Francis Fukuyama, "From the days of Aristotle, thinkers have believed that. . . societies with extremes of wealth and poverty are susceptible either to oligarchic domination or populist revolution."[49] Inequality has played a major role in numerous internal conflicts, including in the many Marxist-based rebellions during the Cold War, the 1994 Zapatista rebellion in Mexico, and today in Latin America and South Asia where inequality is among the highest in the world, and where Marxist groups emerge out of, and tap into, class-based resentments.[50]

Efforts to redress extreme poverty and inequality are important measures toward peace-building in conflict environments. Development assistance can be especially effective as a *preventive* measure by reducing the prospects that acute communal violence will occur, and also in *post-conflict* periods, where aid can reduce resentments as communities sense that their material deficits are finally being addressed. For a development aid approach to be successful, however, external parties must be scrupulous about planning and execution, need to view their efforts as long-term endeavors, and should have realistic expectations for what aid can accomplish. Large disbursements of foreign aid may have little beneficial effect unless development programs are carefully designed and implemented. Research conducted by Eli Berman, Joseph H. Felter, and Jacob N. Shapiro examining the effect of aid on insurgencies showed that economic support only succeeded in reducing violence when locals were involved in the design of the projects and when local firms were hired to perform the construction work.[51]

Development aid clearly plays a positive role in conflict resolution. Still, modest expectations should be maintained regarding the peace-inducing effect of development aid. External assistance has an uneven record of success in supporting economic development, and significant progress in economic development is typically a generations-long process, even under ideal circumstances. In the midst of intense conflict, therefore, *conditional* economic incentive approaches may be the most appropriate and effective. The top-down approach of conditional incentives promises substantial disbursements of financial aid to conflicting parties, but only after the disputants/combatants agree to lay down arms and/or take other major steps toward peace. Conditional economic incentives played a valuable role in securing the Dayton Accords, which brought an end to the 1990s armed conflict in Bosnia. Economic sanctions and NATO airstrikes played large roles in forcing Serbian elements to the table. Still, the U.S. pledge of some $500 million in reconstruction aid represented a significant catalyst, helping to persuade all sides that signing the peace settlement was in their best interests.[52] Economic incentives in the form of business enterprise funds were offered by the U.S. to Latvia in the 1990s, in exchange for improved treatment and civil right protections for ethnic-Russians living in the country. Although a comprehensive resolution of the conflict was not accomplished, these incentives produced some positive movement toward reconciliation.[53]

Democracy Assistance

Civil wars often emerge out of desperation, as a last-ditch effort by frustrated groups seeking a measure of justice, equality, and respect for their communities. Resistance groups are frequently animated by a belief that the status quo arrangement of power is designed to benefit a single privileged family, faction, tribe, religious group, or ethnic group. Furthermore, they believe that the system works to marginalize other groups through the use of terror and violence. A means of mitigating conflict therefore, is to promote reforms in states with such patterns of personalistic, sectarian, and abusive rule. Democracy assistance funds constitute, therefore, a very important peace-building incentive measure. When individuals from all groups in society have faith that their government is accountable, and is an objective broker of "*who gets what, when, and how*," they are disinclined to view armed violence as a necessary means of protecting their safety and welfare. Democracy assistance can, therefore, support the emergence and consolidation of democratic political institutions to ensure the presence of both political rights and civil liberties as a bulwark against violent internal conflict.

Election Assistance

Election assistance—the provision of funds and technical assistance for elections—may be the single most important incentive the international community can offer to ameliorate internal conflicts. Elections can help to end conflicts by offering both sides a legitimate, non-violent mechanism for the resolution of conflict. When care is taken to adopt democratic formats which do not exacerbate ethnic rivalries, elections can increase the post-conflict stability of countries, as the political system that emerges tends to enjoy deeper and broader legitimacy.[54] The peace-inducing potential of elections can only be realized, though, if elections are deemed to be free and fair. Conducting free and fair elections, however, is clearly no simple matter. Many of the states emerging from conflicts are among the poorest in the world, and lack the financial and technical capacity to create election systems in which universal participation can be guaranteed, and where ample oversight and monitoring by independent agencies help to ensure that the election results actually reflect the will of the public.[55] This is precisely where the international donor community can play a supportive role, as donors can provide both the funds and the technical expertise to enable the conduct of free and fair elections in post-conflict environments.

Election assistance has helped to carry out successful and authentic elections in numerous post-conflict states, including in, *inter alia*, El Salvador, Nicaragua, Bosnia, Serbia, Kosovo, Albania, Liberia, Ethiopia, Mozambique, Angola, Cambodia, and Timor-Leste.[56] Much of the election aid provided by international donors is devoted to the formation of credible and capable electoral institutions. Election aid typically includes funds and technical assistance to establish mass registration systems, voting booths and equipment, and computer networks to aggregate and tabulate votes. External aid has also helped in the vital task of creating independent election agencies to craft election rules and to provide oversight and monitoring. These election boards are indispensable in ensuring that actors observe election laws both before the election and during the balloting.

Civil Society Aid

While the bulk of election aid has been devoted to institution building (incentives from the *inside-out*), incentive funds are also used to improve elections and to support democratization from the *bottom-up*. This work includes funding civic organizations to encourage mass participation, underwriting the efforts of independent elections monitors (both domestic and foreign), and supporting independent media to track the observance of election laws. In Mexico, for example, aid provided by the United States to the Civic Alliance and other civic NGOs helped to improve the quality of elections during Mexico's 1990s transition to democracy. Aid supported Civic Alliance's voter education campaigns, allowed it to train and pay a staff of election monitors, and conduct parallel vote tabulations to dissuade the government from reporting fabricated election results.[57] Democratization scholar Thomas Carothers asserts that, due in part to external financing, "In Latin America and Eastern Europe in particular, the quality of the average election has improved dramatically. . . to the point where reasonably free and fair elections are common."[58]

Beyond support for civic groups' election efforts, incentives funds from the international donor community can work to ameliorate conflict by strengthening civic society more broadly in order to promote democratization and democratic consolidation. Aid can support the efforts of reform activists; civic groups; independent print, broadcast, and web media; labor unions; and private enterprise. Democracy scholars have long held that, for a robust democracy to emerge, civil society must be strong enough to check and balance the state, to push for reforms, and to keep government leaders accountable for its actions. Civil society support from external sources played a significant role in the democratic revolutions witnessed in Chile, Mexico, Malawi, Ghana, Yugoslavia, Slovakia, Ukraine, Georgia, Kyrgyzstan, and Egypt.[59] At times this support is disbursed with the permission of the government—even if grudgingly. In other environments, where autocrats are entrenched and unyielding to pressures for democratic reforms, aid is more covert, purposely circumventing governments. In these instances, bottom-up incentive approaches can work by supporting "people power" revolutions, using non-violent civil resistance tactics to bring down dictators. External aid was of critical support, for example, in the so-called "color revolutions" in Yugoslavia, Ukraine, Kyrgyzstan, and Georgia.

Yugoslavia may present the strongest example of how aid to opposition movements can bolster peace. Donors provided over $100 million to opposition groups in the country in advance of the 2000 presidential elections in Yugoslavia (now reduced to the Federation of Serbia and Montenegro). These groups, including the powerful student group Otpor, were critical in the drive to unseat Slobodan Milosevic. As he was the architect of the numerous Serb-led wars in the Balkans during the 1990s, support for the movement to bring down Milosevic was a dramatic step forward to reduce violence in the region. Serbian commentator Veran Matic emphasized the key role played by U.S. and European Union donations to democracy groups in the defeat of Milosovic, stating, "We could not have done it without outside aid."[60]

Funding popular revolutions to bring down dictators is an approach not without its dangers. When external actors encourage and/or sponsor popular revolts, it can result in an increase in violence, even when the revolts adopt nonviolent resistance movements. Authoritarian regimes have frequently demonstrated a zeal for countering nonviolent protest with lethal repression, as seen in 1989 at Tiananmen Square in China, and in 2011 at Tahrir Square in Egypt. Additionally, though popular revolutions can bring down dictators responsible for repression and stoking sectarian divisions and violence, the collapse of these regimes may produce systemic instability and anarchy. Ethnic tensions and conflict can erupt or intensify in these environments.

The long-term potential for reducing violent communal and political conflict may justify the substantial risks involved in promoting popular revolution. Still, if external actors choose to financially support and encourage these efforts, donors assume certain responsibilities. If the approach is used, it would be prudent to counsel domestic groups on the dangers involved, and to prioritize tactics that have been demonstrated to reduce violent responses, including coopting the security forces, and working to strengthen those groups within the opposition who seek broad popular support, as opposed to narrow sectarian support. Additionally, in the wake of the fall of a polarizing authoritarian regime, external actors can follow up with aid to support economic revival, security, and public health. External actors can contribute significantly to sustaining the peace by providing financial support for institutional, economic, and social reconstruction in the post-conflict period. Aid can be employed to support capable and democratic institutions, to buy back weapons, to support employment, and to build schools, healthcare facilities, and infrastructure. All of these measures are important in creating an environment in which former combatants, and the general population, perceive the tangible benefits of peace, and therefore are more likely to want to sustain it.[61]

Trade Preferences: The Role of Regional Trade Agreements in Peacemaking

Suspending a state from a regional trade agreement (RTA) was previously discussed as a sanctions instrument that holds promise in ameliorating certain conflicts. Regional trade agreements can also, however, be employed as a conflict resolution *incentive.* Members of regional trade agreements can use the lure of membership in discussions with states that are instigating or exacerbating internal conflict. The European Union has very openly and effectively used the lure of accession to the world's largest trade bloc to sway the behavior of states in the region. In the Baltics and Southeastern Europe, the European Union has succeeded in compelling governments to enhance democratic protections, withdraw anti-minority laws, and improve their civil protections for minority communities.[62] A study by Frank Schimmelfennig, Stefan Engert, and Heiko Knobel found that leveraging the appeal of access into the EU was the most successful strategy of inducing reform measures of all attempted by the group; more effective than the concurrent diplomatic approaches or transnational mobilization strategies of aid for, and appeals to, civil society.[63]

In Slovakia, the EU inducement was enough to convince the government to permit minorities to communicate with local authorities using their native languages.[64] The lure of EU accession has also diminished popular support for polarizing nationalist politicians in Serbia; especially evident in the success of moderates in Serbia's 2008 presidential and legislative elections. In Turkey, little progress was seen on democratic reform and minority rights until 1999, when the European Union extended candidate status to the country and expressed that Ankara's success would be conditioned on improvements in democratic governance and civil rights. Measurable progress in Turkey followed, including the August 2002 decision permitting the use of the Kurdish language in schools and media.[65] The lure of EU membership was not enough to produce wholesale change throughout these states; problems with divisive, conflict-provoking laws and actions remain. However, conflict de-escalation was realized in each case, and such progress may not have occurred without the use of economic incentive strategies.

Concluding Thoughts on Economic Incentives and Conflict Resolution

Economic incentive approaches offer an alternative or complement to sanctions measures, and avert some of the costs of sanctions, including humanitarian suffering and hostile responses from targets. An incentives approach can also be assembled using a wide variety of tools, allowing it to adapt to different circumstances. Incentives, nonetheless, possess certain limitations. In cases with recalcitrant regimes or rebels who are highly confident of their prospects, and who are inclined toward violent tactics, incentives face long odds of persuading these parties to lay down arms. Incentives may also be unproductive in instances where central governments are so weak as to be incapable of implementing agreements.[66] Donald Rothchild notes that while incentives can be used at every stage of conflict, as the intensity of fighting increases, the costs of incentives will rise significantly if they are to be effective.[67] The alacrity of the response of external parties also matters in incentive approaches. Rapid disbursement of promised incentives increases the chances of positive reciprocity from targeted parties.[68] When applying incentive approaches, therefore, external parties must have measured expectations for what incentives can do, and must pay heed of the importance of incentive design, implementation, and expeditious delivery.

Conclusions

When conflict erupts within countries, leading actors in the international community often express the need for external parties to intervene in order to contain security and economic threats, and also to mitigate humanitarian suffering. Military intervention represents one clear option. The military approach, however, typically encounters considerable reluctance due to the potentially immense costs in lives and treasury, and also due to concerns that military intervention may actually intensify the violence. External actors can, instead, opt for diplomatic approaches; however, committed antagonists often fail to respond to actions that do not involve some material pressure. When military intervention is not a viable option, and when diplomatic measures appear futile, external actors do not have to resign themselves to the role of passive observers of conflict. Economic statecraft offers a third way; a conflict mitigation strategy which navigates a middle course between war and words.

There has long been skepticism about the value of economic statecraft among both scholars and practitioners. Sanctions are frequently cast as hopelessly futile endeavors, and economic incentives receive scant attention. While the efficacy rate of economic statecraft is mixed, the historical record from Classical Greece to the present is replete with examples of financial sticks and carrots being used successfully to motivate states, leaders, and other influential actors to adjust their behavior. Indeed, since the end of the bipolar era, sanctions and incentives have become more potent instruments with respect to managing various issues areas, including intrastate conflict resolution.

Economic sanctions work by impacting the will and capacity of combatants to engage in conflict. Trade sanctions have been employed with considerable success in several episodes including apartheid-era South Africa, Yugoslavia, and Guatemala. Revoking or suspending a state's membership in a regional trade agreement has represented one of the most effective trade sanctions. The approach has been levied effectively by the European Union in several post-communist states, and by Mercosur in South America. Foreign aid presents another lever that can be employed in certain conflict episodes. Aid sanctions proved critical to the resolution of conflict episodes in Peru, El Salvador, Malawi, and Guinea.

The sanctions instrument, however, possesses certain drawbacks. Economic sanctions can potentially exacerbate tensions with target actors, produce humanitarian suffering, and adversely impact exporting industries in sender states. In many cases, a better approach is to substitute economic incentives for sanctions, or to complement sanctions with incentives. Conditional incentives can persuade actors to eschew violence and provocative actions by offering substantial material assistance as a reward. Most conflict-mitigation incentives, however, involve *unconditional* incentives. Development assistance can play an important role in conflict reduction, as research has shown underdevelopment and inequality to be risk factors for internal conflict.

Funding elections is an indispensable role that donor states and organizations can play in conflict environments. Elections can serve the cause of peace by convincing warring factions that violence is not the only viable path to power. Elections provide rebel forces with a reasonable prospect of controlling or at least sharing power if free and fair elections are held. Conducting genuine and competent elections in post-conflict environments, though, typically requires the financial and technical help of external donors. Other forms of unconditional incentives address the problems of abusive or partisan governments by funding institutional improvements. These democracy assistance programs help to foster nonpartisan, rule-of-law governance and other democratic reforms which help dissuade armed challenges to the political system. External aid can also promote the emergence of more democratic and inclusive governments by funding progressive forces in civil society. In cases of intransigent, abusive, and/or polarizing authoritarian regimes, the only feasible approach may be to circumvent the government and instead fund opposition movements in their efforts to produce a change of power.

Regional actors can promote conflict resolution by employing the lure of membership in regional trade agreements. The European Union has successfully leveraged membership in the EU to ameliorate communal conflicts on the continent; including in the Baltics, Eastern Europe, the Balkans, and in Turkey. Incentive approaches, however, may not always be the optimal or even appropriate course in every situation. Incentives are difficult to apply, or even counterproductive, in environments where regimes or rebels are implacably committed to violence and repression. Furthermore, the successful use of incentives relies heavily on precise implementation. Poor execution of incentive strategies can doom incentives' capacity to produce positive change.

In most communal conflict episodes, a combination of sticks and carrots likely offers the greatest prospect of swaying parties toward peace. Offering incentives concurrent with sanctions can ease compliance with demands, as it reduces the perception of capitulation under pressure, and thus mitigates targets' concerns that compliance will signal weakness to domestic constituencies, domestic adversaries, and foreign rivals. Economic statecraft approaches, while infrequently producing rapid results, have demonstrated in several conflict episodes over the past two decades to be effective levers of dispute preemption and resolution. Improvements in coordination among external parties, greater financial commitment to incentive approaches by these parties, and adroit implementation of carrot and stick programs, will likely further enhance the effectiveness of economic statecraft as an instrument of conflict resolution.

Notes

1. Thucydides, *History of the Peloponnesian War*, trans. Rex Warner, intro M.I. Finley (London: Penguin Books 1972).

2. On Adam Smith and Thomas Jefferson see David Baldwin, *Economic Statecraft* (Princeton, NJ: Princeton University Press, 1985), 81-93; on the Abbe de Saint-Pierre, see Jean Jacques Rousseau, "Critique of the Peace Project of the Abbe' de St. Pierre," in Grace Roosevelt, *Reading Rousseau in the Nuclear Age* (Philadelphia: Temple University Press, 1990).

3. Johann Galtung, "On the Effects of International Economic Sanctions: With Examples from the Case of Rhodesia," *World Politics* 19, no. 3 (April 1967): 378-416; Donald Losman, *International Economic Sanctions: The Cases of Cuba, Israel, and Rhodesia* (Albuquerque: University of New Mexico Press, 1979); and Anna Schreiber, "Economic Coercion as an Instrument of Foreign Policy: US Economic Measures Against Cuba and the Dominican Republic," *World Politics* 25, no. 3 (April 1973): 387-413.

4. Henry Bienen and Robert Gilpin, "Economic Sanctions as a Response to Terrorism," *Journal of Strategic Studies* 3 (1980):89-98.

5. Baldwin, *Economic Statecraft*, 38.

6. Baldwin, *Economic Statecraft*, 38.

7. Preclusive buying involves excessive purchases of a product in order to prevent its acquisition by third parties.

8. Direct purchase involves payment for specific items. Baldwin notes the Louisiana Purchase, in which territory was transferred in exchange for cash. Baldwin, *Economic Statecraft,* 42.

9. "Economic Sanctions Reconsidered: History and Current Policy," by Gary Clyde Hufbauer, Jeffery J. Schott, and Kimberly Ann Elliot, remains the most prominent study on the effectiveness of economic sanctions. Gary Clyde Hufbauer, Jeffery J. Schott, and Kimberly Ann Elliot, *Economic Sanctions Reconsidered: History and Current Policy*, 2nd ed. (Washington, D.C.: Institute of International Economics, 1990). An updated edition was released in 2007.

10. Kimberly A. Elliott, "Economic Sanctions," in *Intervention in the 1990s: US Foreign Policy in the Third World*, ed. P.J. Schraeder, (Boulder: Lynne Rienner, 1992),102.

11. Elizabeth Rogers, "Economic Sanctions and Internal Conflict," in *The International Dimensions of Internal Conflict*, ed. Michael Brown, (Cambridge, MA: The MIT Press, 1996), 434.

12. Elizabeth Rogers, "Using Economic Sanctions to Control Regional Conflicts," *Security Studies* 5, no. 4 (Summer 1996):72.

13. Michael Brown, "Internal Conflict and International Action," in *The International Dimensions of Internal Conflict*, ed. Michael Brown (Cambridge, MA: The MIT Press, 1996), 608-13, 623-24.

14. John Cookson, "How Much Does the Libya Intervention Cost the U.S.?," August 23, 2011, http://globalpublicsquare.blogs.cnn.com/2011/08/23/question-how-much-does-the-intervention-in-libya-cost-the-u-s/ (accessed March 12, 2012).

15. Rogers, "Economic Sanctions and Internal Conflict," 426, 427.
16. Rogers, "Economic Sanctions and Internal Conflict," 412.
17. Rogers, "Economic Sanctions and Internal Conflict," 412, 413.
18. Abel Escriba Folch, "Economic Sanctions and the Duration of Civil Conflicts," *Journal of Peace Research* 47, no. 2 (March 2010):129-141.
19. Risa Brooks, "Sanctions and Regime Type: What Works and When?" *Security Studies* 11, no. 4 (Summer 2002): 1-50.
20. Chantal du Jonge Oadraat, "Making Economic Sanctions Work," *Survival: The IISS Quarterly* 42, no. 3 (Autumn 2000): 105-127.
21. Daniel Drezner, "Conflict Expectations and the Paradox of Economic Coercion," *International Studies Quarterly* 42, no. 4 (December 1998): 709–731.
22. David Cortright, "Sanctions and Stability Pacts: The Economic Tools of Peacemaking," in *Peacemaking in International Conflict*, ed. William Zartman (Washington, DC: United States Institutes of Peace, 1997), 394, 395.
23. Donald Rothchild, "Third-Party Incentives and the Phases of Conflict Prevention," in *From Promise to Practice: Strengthening UN Capacities for the Prevention of Violent Conflict*, eds. Chandra Lekha Sriram and Karin Wermester (Boulder, CO: Lynne Rienner, 2003), 55, 56.
24. Some theorists, including Risa Brooks, maintain that omnibus sanctions are less effective against authoritarian regimes.
25. Donald Rothchild, "Third-Party Incentives and the Phases of Conflict Prevention," 41.
26. Rogers, "Economic Sanctions and Internal Conflict," 424-25; Victor Comras, "Economic Sanctions and US Foreign Policy," Statements to the Open Forum, February 25, 2002, http://www.state.gov/s/p/of/proc/tr/9128pf.htm (accessed August 12, 2009).
27. Morton H. Halperin and Kristen Lomasney, "Guaranteeing Democracy," *Journal of Democracy* 9, no. 2 (April 1998): 134-47.
28. Joseph Kahn, "Salvaging the Reputation of Sanctions," *The New York Times*, October 15, 2000, 4(3).
29. Freedom House, *Freedom in the World – 2000-2001* (Washington, DC: Freedom House, 2001): 590; Joseph Kahn, "Salvaging the Reputation of Sanctions."
30. On sanctions' impact on Yugoslavia, see Stephen D. Collins, "Democracy Sanctions: An Assessment of Economic Sanctions as an Instrument of Democracy Promotion," *Taiwan Journal of Democracy* 5, no. 2 (December 2009): 81-83.
31. Halperin and Lomasney, "Guaranteeing Democracy,"134-47; Gordon Crawford, *Foreign Aid and Political Reform* (New York: Palgrave McMillan, 2001), 194; Joan M. Nelson and Stephanie J. Eglinton, "The International Donor Community: Conditioned Aid and the Promotion and Defense of Democracy," in *Beyond Sovereignty: Collectively Defending Democracy in the Americas*, ed. Tom Farer (Baltimore, MD: Johns Hopkins University Press, 1996),177-78.
32. Stephen D. Collins, "Regional Trade Agreements and Democracy Promotion: Measuring the Influence of Democracy Requirements in Regional Trade Agreements," *Politics & Policy* 38, No. 4 (August 2010): 751-752.
33. Collins, "Regional Trade Agreements and Democracy Promotion," 745.
34. Cortright, "Sanctions and Stability Pacts," 410.
35. Collins, "Regional Trade Agreements and Democracy Promotion," 748-51.
36. Collins, "Democracy Sanctions," 80-81.
37. Collins, "Democracy Sanctions," 80-81.
38. Collins, "Democracy Sanctions," 81.
39. Rothchild, "Third-Party Incentives and the Phases of Conflict Prevention," 55.

40. Adam Nossiter, "After Massacre Guinea Sees Hope of Lifted Chains," *The New York Times,* Feb 3, 2010, 1(A).

41. Stephen D. Collins, "The Efficacy of Economic Sanctions: Economic Sanctions and American Foreign Policy in the Unipolar Era," *New England Journal of Political Science* 3, no. 2 (November 2009): 247.

42. Gary Clyde Hufbauer, "Sanctions Happy US," *Washington Post*, July 12, 1998.

43. CBC News, "Canadian Sanctions Working in Burma, Sui Kyi Says," February 29, 2012, http://www.cbc.ca/news/politics/story/2012/02/29/pol-cp-aung-san-suu-kyi.html (accessed July 29, 2012).

44. Cortright, "Sanctions and Stability Pacts," 398.

45. On the use of incentive measures as a foreign policy tool to support political reform abroad, see Stephen D. Collins, "Can America Finance Freedom?: Assessing U.S. Democracy Promotion Via Economic Statecraft," *Foreign Policy Analysis* 5, no. 2 (October 2009): 367-389.

46. Brown, *The International Dimensions of Internal Conflict*, 610.

47. Rothchild, "Third-Party Incentives and the Phases of Conflict Prevention," 39.

48. Rothchild, "Third-Party Incentives and the Phases of Conflict Prevention," 39.

49. Francis Fukuyama, "The Future of History: Can Liberal Democracy Survive the Decline of the Middle Class, " *Foreign Affairs* 90, no. 1 (January-February 2012): 56.

50. Fukuyama, "The Future of History," 56.

51. Eli Berman, Joseph H. Felter, and Jacob N. Shapiro, "Constructive COIN: How Development Can Fight Radicals," *Foreign Affairs*, June 1, 2010. http://www.foreignaffairs.com/articles/66432/eli-berman-joseph-h-felter-and-jacob-n-shapiro/constructive-coin# (accessed April 8, 2012).

52. Carol Lancaster, "Redesigning Foreign Aid, " *Foreign Affairs* 79, no. 5, (September/October 2000): 76.

53. Rothchild, "Third-Party Incentives and the Phases of Conflict Prevention," 50-51.

54. Krishna Kumar skillfully examines the converse; that is, how elections can sometimes increase intrastate violence. See Krishna Kumar, "International Assistance for Post Conflict Elections," in *Democracy Assistance: International Co-operation for Democratization*, ed. Peter Burnell (London: Frank Cass, 2000), 192.

55. Kumar, "International Assistance for Post Conflict Elections," 192.

56. Collins, "Can America Finance Freedom?," 380; Kumar, "International Assistance for Post Conflict Elections," 193.

57. Collins, "Can America Finance Freedom?," 380.

58. Thomas Carothers, *Aiding Democracy Abroad: The Learning Curve* (Washington, D.C.: Carnegie Endowment for International Peace, 1999),129.

59. Collins, "Can America Finance Freedom?," 380-83; On external support for the Arab Spring revolutions, including in Egypt, see Ron Nixon, "US Groups Helped Nurture Arab Uprisings," *The New York Times*, April 14, 2011, 1(A).

60. Collins, "Can America Finance Freedom?," 383.

61. See Michael Brown, "Internal Conflict and International Action," 623-34.

62. Cortright, "Sanctions and Stability Pacts," 410; Collins, "Regional Trade Agreements and Democracy Promotion," 745.

63. Frank Schimmelfennig, Stefan Engert, and Heiko Knobel, "Costs, Commitments, and Compliance: The Impact of EU Democratic Conditionality on Latvia, Slovakia, and Turkey," *Journal of Common Market Studies* 41, no. 3 (2003): 514.

64. Cortright, "Sanctions and Stability Pacts," 410.

65. Collins, "Regional Trade Agreements and Democracy Promotion," 746-47.

66. Rothchild, "Third-Party Incentives and the Phases of Conflict Prevention," 41-42.

67. Rothchild, "Third-Party Incentives and the Phases of Conflict Prevention," 61.

68. Cortright, "Sanctions and Stability Pacts," 400.

Chapter 10

Externally Mandated Economic Liberalization and the Onset of Civil Conflict

Matthew Hoddie
Caroline Hartzell

This chapter considers the relationship between economic liberalization and civil conflict. The argument we advance is that the process by which economic liberalization takes place plays an important role in determining the degree to which liberalization is linked to domestic instability. We suggest that the greatest potential for a turn towards violence is associated with the deep, extensive, and formulaic model of economic liberalization favored by the international financial institutions (IFIs). Often referred to as a form of "bitter medicine" to be consumed by inefficient economies, the orthodox package of prescriptions advocated by these institutions has the potential to foment conflict, we argue, because it generates losers at a faster rate than it produces winners while also compromising the state's ability either to compensate or check those who lose as a result of the reform process.

To develop the claim that economic liberalization via the far-reaching package of institutional reforms called for by the IFIs increases the risk of violence, we focus on the International Monetary Fund's (IMF) Structural Adjustment Programs (SAPs). Based on existing quantitative and case study evidence, we find that states that follow the IMF's economic liberalization prescriptions are at heightened risk of experiencing an outbreak of civil conflict.

We divide the chapter into three sections. The first section describes the basis for the conventional expectation that liberal economies will enjoy political stability. In the second section we present evidence for the claim that process matters when considering the effects of liberalization programs. Identifying a contrast between the comprehensive liberalization programs called for by the

IMF and more modest and incremental liberalization programs that have been nationally designed, we consider the reasons why externally-mandated programs, sometimes called "shock therapy" because of the speed with which they are applied, heighten the risks of internal violence. In the third and final section of the chapter we note the policy implications of these findings, particularly as they relate to states emerging from civil conflict.

Liberal Economics and Peace

An established literature notes an association between open economic systems and economic growth. States that allow for relatively unfettered interactions with the global economy through trade and foreign direct investment also tend to be the states that enjoy the greatest levels of wealth accumulation.[1] It is the wealth created by liberal economies that is thought to make states defined by these economic systems relatively peaceful.

The association between wealth and domestic peace exists for reasons both obvious and more obscure. One obvious reason for this relationship is that the citizens within wealthy states are less likely to engage in violence given their relative contentment with the established political and economic order. An economy effective at creating jobs for citizens makes it challenging for opposition leaders to convince individuals to forgo readily-available economic opportunities in favor of the more risky strategy of rebellion.[2]

It is also uncontroversial to observe that wealthy states typically enjoy the tax base necessary to support both an extensive government bureaucracy and security apparatus. The size and power of government in wealthy states thus serves as a substantial deterrent to rebellion. If an opposition movement does emerge, it is likely to be readily identified and easily controlled.[3]

A less straightforward explanation for the association between wealth and peace within a state's borders relates to the issue of dependence on primary commodity exports. Research suggests that countries with undiversified economies, focused on a limited number of primary commodities such as oil, diamonds, or precious metals, are particularly vulnerable to experiencing rebellion. This is the case as rebels may fund their armed opposition to the government by taking control of these resources, using the money they generate to fund the rebellion.[4] This was true in Sierra Leone during the 1990s as the revenue generated by diamond mines was appropriated by rebels and used to support their movement. Given that wealthy states tend to enjoy diversified economies, there are fewer lootable resources that rebels might monopolize to fund their drive for power.

Two quantitative studies demonstrate the existence of an association between liberal economies, the wealth that these open economies generate, and peace. In each of these analyses, the focus centers on globalization; globalization tends to be correlated with more liberal economic systems as open economies are also those that have greater levels of interaction with the international economy. Håvard Hegre, Ranveig Gissinger, and Nils Peter Gleditsch present an analysis of states' experiences with globalization between 1960 and the mid-1990s. They operationalize the level of openness of a state's economy using two indicators: trade as a percentage of Gross Domestic Product (GDP) and foreign direct investment as a percentage of GDP.[5] Employing duration models, the authors find that neither of these measures of globalization is associated with an increased risk of a country experiencing civil war across time. Instead, their analyses suggest that economic openness enhances political stability and that this association between globalization and stability is most apparent in the context of democratic systems.[6]

Katherine Barbieri and Rafael Reuvney report a similar finding in their study of states during the period between 1970 and 1999. Beyond using measures of trade and foreign direct investment that mirror those of Hegre *et al.*, Barbieri and Reuvney specify two additional indicators that they consider important aspects of globalization: the net inflow of portfolio investment into a state as a percentage of GDP and internet usage per 1000 people. Based on a series of tests employing time series data, they conclude that none of their globalization indicators is associated with an increased risk of civil war onset. Their central finding is instead that states defined by higher rates of trade and portfolio investment have a reduced risk of experiencing war within their borders.[7]

The Importance of Process

While the empirical studies we describe above present convincing evidence of a relationship between open economic systems and peace, an issue that neither of these articles addresses is the implications for stability associated with the processes by which a country liberalizes its economy. These quantitative tests may serve to indicate that *liberal* economies enjoy stability, but this does not demonstrate that *liberalizing* economies do so as well. The argument we develop here is that the process by which liberalization takes place has important implications for whether or not a state proves capable of maintaining stability.

This claim concerning the importance of process has parallels to the dialogue that has evolved concerning the theory of the democratic peace. The central claim of this theory is that established democracies enjoy a "separate peace" and do not fight one another in war. The theory anticipates that a world comprised of democracies would also be one defined by universally peaceful relations among countries.[8] While the observation that democracies do not fight one another in war may be "the closest thing we have to an empirical law in international relations," critics argue that its claims only apply to established democratic governments.[9] States undergoing a process of democratization may actually have a heightened risk of experiencing wars within their own borders and conflict with other states.[10] Scholars who note that democratizing states are at heightened risk of violence emphasize that the different processes by which democratization takes place can have implications for whether or not a transition proves both peaceful and successful.

The argument concerning the significance of process that we develop in this chapter is that the method by which an economy liberalizes has important implications for the degree to which these efforts prove destabilizing or not. Liberalization programs that encourage a rapid, deep, and extensive process of economic transformation enhance the risk of a turn to conflict; by contrast, more gradual and modest liberalization programs have a greater potential to maintain social stability while serving to promote economic growth. To further develop this claim, the discussion below draws a contrast between these two processes of liberalization.

Externally Mandated Liberalization: "Bitter Medicine" and "Shock Therapy"

International financial institutions (IFIs) have often taken the lead in promoting an economic liberalization process that is both aggressive and far ranging in scope. This process, which has been labeled "the Washington Consensus," reflects a standard economic reform package for countries in economic crisis promoted by the Washington D.C.-based institutions of the IMF, the World Bank, and the U.S. Treasury Department.[11] Countries embark on this path to liberalize their economies when they agree to adopt an IMF SAP.

Economic liberalization via structural adjustment programs became increasingly common following the onset of the debt crisis in 1982. While 172 IMF loan programs were approved for the period between 1970 and 1979, the 1980s witnessed 271 such programs approved with an additional 282 loan programs agreed to during the next decade. These statistics suggest that the vast majority of developing countries have received IMF financial support at least once since 1970.[12]

While SAPs are supposed to be tailored to the circumstances of each borrowing country, there is a set of common objectives associated with these programs. *Reduction of aggregate demand* is called for in those instances in which governments face a budget deficit. Cutbacks in imported goods, decreases in government expenditures, devaluation of an overvalued currency, and a reduction in the money supply may all be implemented with the goal of reducing domestic consumption and accumulating foreign exchange that can be used to purchase the goods and services needed to promote economic growth. An *expansion of production*, particularly of foreign exchange-earning exports, is achieved via trade liberalization and the use of controls on wage increases in order to encourage the exploitation of low-cost labor. *Changes in government institutions and economic policies* involve the sale of state-owned enterprises, the elimination of subsidies, and the imposition of higher taxes.[13]

How does this process of liberalization increase the potential for instability within a state? Here we suggest that there are two means by which SAPs contribute to the breakdown of stability. First, the transformation required by these programs changes the rules of economic interaction within a society and reorders expectations about which individuals and groups will be the "winners" and "losers" in economic competition. This shift is most apparent in the negative impact on society's most vulnerable citizens who face financial hardships in the form of a dramatic loss of government support and services. Second, SAPs diminish state capacity as indicated by cuts to both the bureaucracy and military. This undermines the ability of government to respond to existing armed challenges and those that might develop with the emergence of new economic hardships. A detailed discussion of these two items follows.

Economic Hardships

In terms of economic hardships, one of the most immediate harms felt by the citizens of a country adopting SAPs is a rapid rise in prices for essential goods. This is a result of the SAP requirement that governments quickly end the practice of using subsidies and price controls to maintain artificially low prices for items such as food and energy. While the new prices may more accurately reflect the actual costs of production, these prices put needed goods beyond the reach of many citizens.

The discontent generated by a rapid rise in prices has been most starkly illustrated in the form of demonstrations and riots in affected countries. Writing in 1994, John Walton and David Seddon describe the phenomenon of mass protests in response to rising prices in the following terms:

> In most countries, these new policies have met with stiff opposition, including political demonstrations, strikes, and riots. In fact, a wave of austerity protests has occurred in 39 of the approximately 80 debtor countries. Between 1975 and late 1992, some 146 incidents of protest occurred, reaching a peak from 1983 to 1985 and continuing to the present without attenuation.[14]

While government buildings proved to be a favored site for protests, demonstrators also targeted markets and gasoline stations to highlight their discontent with the rising prices for goods sold at these locations.[15]

In a similar vein, the World Development Movement (WDM) has produced a series of "States of Unrest" reports in which they document more recent instances in which protests have been motivated by the imposition of austerity programs by the IMF and World Bank.[16] In an April 2003 report, the WDM identifies twenty five countries in which wide-ranging protests took place in the wake of the imposition of SAPs. The report notes that protests in approximately half of these countries were motivated by the rising prices of goods.[17]

Beyond increasing prices for essential goods, countries participating in an SAP typically experience a dramatic reduction in the government services provided to the public. This is most notably represented by cuts to government spending for the provisions of health care and education. Irfan Nooruddin and Joel Simmons find that democratic states that are signatories to an IMF SAP cut spending for these two items to an extent that they have levels of expenditure that become comparable to non-democratic countries. They suggest that health and education spending are favored targets for early and deep cuts in the wake of an SAP as these reductions in expenditures disproportionately affect the poor who typically lack an organized political voice to protect their interests.[18]

Unsurprisingly, the consequence of such a reduction in government health care spending is higher incidences of disease and mortality rates among a country's citizens. One piece of research that focused a great deal of attention on this issue is a 2008 study that considers the health effects of IMF SAPs in the post-Communist states of the former Soviet Union and Eastern Europe. Examining the period between 1991 and 2003, the authors compare states in this region that were subject to an IMF SAP to those countries that were not. Their central finding is that states that were party to an IMF agreement had noticeably higher levels of tuberculosis; rates of tuberculosis infection grew by 13.3 percent and levels of mortality attributable to tuberculosis increased by 16.6 percent.[19]

The recent experience of Greece also serves to underscore the harmful effects of a rapid decline in government spending that can result from structural adjustment. Confronted by a debt crisis that emerged in 2008, the government of Greece agreed to a series of austerity measures required by the IMF and European Union in return for their financial assistance. Included in the austerity measures were reductions in government health care spending. The *New York Times* reports that over a two-year period the government was forced to cut medical care spending by 13 percent and commit to greater reductions in the future. The newspaper describes the effects of these cutbacks in the following terms:

> At public hospitals, doctors report shortages of all kinds of supplies, from toilet paper to catheters to syringes. Computerized equipment has gone unrepaired and is no longer in use. Nurses are handling four times the patients they should, and wait times for operations—even cancer surgeries—have grown longer. Access to drugs has also been affected, as some drug manufacturers, owed tens of millions of dollars, are no longer willing to supply Greek hospitals. At the same time pharmacists, afraid that the government might not reimburse them, are asking for cash payments, even from those with insurance.[20]

A similar story is apparent in terms of the loss of educational opportunities that follow in the wake of IMF-initiated SAPs. Reductions in government spending for teacher's salaries facilitate a tacit and incremental privatization of education. David Keen describes this phenomenon in Sierra Leone, noting that in the aftermath of a late-1980s SAP, teachers sought to supplement their income by charging students for examination tuition and private lessons.[21] In some cases, teachers engaged in strikes to protest their poor wages. The harm done to the society was apparent in the growing gap in educational attainment between the small number of students who could afford to continue their education and the majority who lacked these resources and were left behind as a result.[22]

Reductions in Government Capacity

Coupled with the economic hardships that are generated by SAPs, these programs also have the effect of diminishing the ability of government to maintain order within their societies. This is the case as the advocates of liberal reforms place a priority on reducing the influence of the state over the economy with the expectation that the state's withdrawal will create opportunities for the efficient provision of goods and services by profit-driven entrepreneurs. Yet these strategies unintentionally serve to weaken the government entities considered vital to maintaining stability, including the police and military.

One means by which the SAPs serve to limit the capacity of the state is by mandating the privatization of public corporations. Taking these companies out of the hands of government is understood to be an opportunity to address problems such as state-based corruption and mismanagement. While efficiencies may be introduced, it also limits the ability of government to claim the revenue that was once generated by state-dominated companies. This dynamic is again illustrated by the case of Sierra Leone. William Reno notes that privatization encouraged by the IFIs during the 1970s and 1980s reduced government involvement in such industries as diamond exports, agricultural marketing, and banking.[23] With privatization, government revenue dropped dramatically; revenue in 1985-1986 was only 18 percent of levels collected during 1977 and 1978.[24]

As government revenues decline in the aftermath of an SAP, states find it increasingly difficult to employ and pay their workers.[25] This includes those responsible for maintaining security and order. Keen reports, for example, that it was poor pay for soldiers during the 1990s in Sierra Leone that allowed for the success of a rebel uprising.[26] He further suggests that this is part of a larger pattern in which the requirement that states cut back on their capacity has the potential to undermine counterinsurgency efforts that are forced to rely on "underpaid and under motivated state officials (whether police or soldiers)."[27]

Externally Mandated Liberalization and Civil War

SAPs harm the economic interests of a large number of citizens, with the most pronounced harm done to the poor. These conditions are likely to generate discontent among the population and emerge at the same time as the government confronts new financial limitations with the potential to undermine its ability to maintain security and order. In our view, this toxic combination of factors creates an environment ripe for the outbreak of violence.

The challenge in demonstrating that this particular process of liberalization increases the risks of violence is that countries that adopt SAPs are states already confronting economic difficulties as indicated by the debt crisis that motivated the initial decision to seek the assistance of the IMF. It thus proves difficult to disentangle which factor increases the potential for conflict: the original financial crisis or the SAP intended to address the economic downturn.

Caroline Hartzell, Matthew Hoddie, and Molly Bauer attempt to address this issue in their quantitative analysis of the relationship between the adoption of IMF SAPs and the onset of civil war for the years between 1970 and 1999. The study uses a bivariate probit model which has the advantage of allowing for the simultaneous estimation of two outcomes: 1) a state's agreement to participate in an IMF SAP and 2) the onset of civil war. By accounting for the economic conditions that determine the signing of the IMF SAP in the first stage of the equation, the bivariate probit model thus allows for a consideration of the independent effect of the IMF SAP on civil war in the second stage.[28]

The core finding of this analysis is that IMF SAPs increase the odds that a country will experience the onset of civil war.[29] It should be emphasized that the definition of civil war they adopt in their analysis is indicative of a widespread breakdown of order and intense violence. While studies of civil conflict have increasingly employed the relatively narrow criterion of twenty five battle deaths to identify instances of instability in the state, the definition employed by Hartzell *et al.* centers on conflicts that have resulted in at least 1,000 total battle deaths with at least 100 killed on each side of the dispute.[30]

The findings that we describe above are based on a consideration of all countries around the globe for which data were available. Yet there are reasons to anticipate that this association between SAPs and the emergence of violence is most likely to prove apparent in those states that are in the early, fragile period of transition towards peace following a previous bout of domestic conflict. In other words, the states that may be at the greatest risk of civil war are those that may experience a relapse back into conflict rather than those countries that have enjoyed stability for an extended period of time.

This claim that the SAPs of the IMF and World Bank may undermine efforts to foster stability in post-civil war states was first highlighted in the work of Alvaro de Soto and Graciana del Castillo. Their analysis considers the efforts of the United Nations and IFIs to assist with the implementation of the peace accords to end the civil war in El Salvador. They note that fulfilling the expectations of the Salvadoran peace accords and building the capacity of the post-war state was a process that demanded high levels of government spending. They describe the expenses associated with the peace process for a single year in the following terms: "For 1993 alone, El Salvador needed about $250 million to reintegrate ex-combatants into society (through the purchase of land, agricultural credit, housing, credit for small enterprises, pensions for the disabled, etc.) and to promote democratic institutions (National Civil Police, National Public Security Academy, human-rights activities, and activities related to the coming elections)."[31] Yet at the same time that the state was in need of resource to fulfill these obligations, it was subject to IMF and World Bank conditions intended to cut back on the size and reach of the state. The result was a heightened risk of a failing peace process given the contradictions that existed between the UN's priority of establishing peace through the development of state capacity and the IFIs' emphasis on facilitating economic liberalization.[32]

The dangers associated with foreign-initiated economic liberalization in states emerging from civil war are also considered in the work of Roland Paris. Based on case studies of all fourteen major peacekeeping operations initiated between 1989 and 1998, he identifies three reasons why SAPs have the potential to unintentionally sabotage a nascent peace. First, in keeping with our earlier consideration of the economic hardships linked to SAPs, he suggests that many of the cuts in government spending required by these reforms disproportionately harm the interests of a country's poor and serve to widen the income gap between rich and poor. Second, he notes that cutbacks make it challenging for the state to provide an immediate peace dividend to citizens. Instead, the emergence of peace is associated with a precipitous decline in economic well-being or "peace penalty" accompanied by vague assurances of future economic growth. Third, he suggests that post-war states lack the government capacity to oversee market-oriented reforms, and this heightens the risk that the benefits of liberalization will be hijacked by elite and/or criminal elements with little benefit to the population as a whole. These three factors generate sufficient economic hardship and societal upheaval to endanger an emerging, post-civil war peace.[33]

Taken together, these studies suggest that the process of liberalization favored by the IMF heightens the prospects of political instability. This is true in all states, but there are particular dangers associated with the "shock therapy" process of economic liberalization within states that are emerging from civil war.

Incremental Liberalization: Crossing the River by Stepping from Stone to Stone

If the process of economic liberalization favored by the IFIs serves to foster conflict, why might an alternative set of efforts towards the same goal not also produce the same effects? Our view is that a process that eschews a rapid and formulaic approach to liberalization in favor of a more limited and nuanced approach should serve to minimize, but not fully eliminate, the harm done to society and state associated with this transformation of the economic system. If this more limited approach to liberalization is coupled with efforts to mitigate the harmful aspects associated with the process of liberalization, a turn towards widespread violence should become less likely.

In order to provide a brief illustration of how an incremental, indigenously led economic liberalization program might serve to stem the possibility of political violence we consider the case of the People's Republic of China (PRC), which has increasingly opened its economy since the late 1970s. As we seek to demonstrate in our discussion below, this process of liberalization is still ongoing and incomplete. The value of this slow and modest approach to liberalization, sometimes described as "crossing the river by stepping from stone to stone," is that it allowed for liberalization without mass violence.[34]

One means by which this incremental approach to liberalization is apparent concerns the Chinese government's approach to ending price controls. As noted previously, the strategy favored by the IFIs is a rapid end to government interventions into the marketplace that serve to distort prices that would otherwise be determined solely by the interaction between supply and demand. By contrast, the approach of the PRC's government to removing price controls began in the 1980s and took years to accomplish. Incremental price liberalization initially took the form of a dual price system. A fixed amount of goods produced by enterprises was sold at government-mandated prices, but anything produced beyond the quota could be sold at the market rate. The government then slowly decreased the percentage of goods under price controls relative to market-determined prices, with the expectation that a gradual transition would serve to minimize inflation. By 2004, approximately 90 percent of all goods in the PRC were sold at market-determined prices.[35]

Yingyi Qian describes this transformation of the pricing system as a strategy of reform that had the value of not creating economic losers. He notes that the introduction of market prices "provides the opportunity for economic agents who participate in it to be better off, whereas the maintenance of the plan track provides implicit transfers to compensate potential losers from the market liberalization by protecting the status quo rents under the preexisting plan."[36] By contrast, the abandonment of the dual price system would have had immediate consequences for the "economic losers" in that scenario: those unable to cope with the immediate and unanticipated rise in prices.

The PRC's strategy for reducing the scope and influence of state-owned enterprises (SOEs) over the economy has also followed a gradual course that sharply contrasts with the emphasis on rapid privatization associated with the IFI-led process. To the present day, SOEs remain a key feature of the Chinese economy, but through a series of reforms their influence has become progressively attenuated. The most important of these changes was legitimizing private businesses in China that allowed for competitors to the SOEs to emerge without requiring the immediate closing of government-owned firms. According to Lawrence Lau, Yingyi Qian, and Gérard Roland, the percentage of workers in China that were permanent state employees dropped from 60 percent in 1978 to 26 percent ten years later.[37] During the mid-1990s, further strategies were adopted to reduce the influence of government-owned business, including efforts to privatize smaller SOEs while maintaining state control of larger operations (referred to as "grasping the large and retaining the small") and the laying off of redundant SOE workers.[38]

Finally, an emphasis on gradual economic liberalization is apparent in the PRC's approach towards allowing foreign direct investment (FDI) into the country. FDI was first allowed in the PRC in 1980, with initial foreign investment only being authorized in four special economic zones located on China's southeast coast: Zhuhai, Shenzhen, Shantou, and Xiamen. These zones were largely isolated from the rest of the economy and were considered laboratories for evaluating the effects of FDI.[39] Since this initial experiment in the special economic zones, FDI has progressively expanded over the years. Yet economists point out that FDI over the decade of the 1980s remained relatively modest and that at its peak during the 1990s only accounted for 10 percent of all investment within China.[40]

These reforms associated with pricing, SOEs, and FDI are all representative of a much broader, incremental approach to liberalization favored by the Chinese government. Andrew Walder summarizes this process in the following terms:

> For many, China's transitional economy is an intriguing anomaly; a transition heralded as difficult and painful has sparked an economic boom. As a gradual rather than abrupt transition to the market, with public industry protected rather than subject to privatization, China's reform path has confounded the widespread and deeply held belief that gradual reform and public ownership simply cannot work, not even as a transitional strategy.[41]

If this statement by Walder points out the economic success of these reforms, it is also notable that China has to a degree sidestepped the widespread violence that is often associated with rapid and aggressive economic liberalization. This should not be taken to mean, however, that liberalization has proven to be a seamless process within the PRC. Critics point out that, with the opening of the economy, China has become a society in which inequality is becoming increasing apparent. Minxin Pei, for example, notes that income inequality among citizens has increased by approximately 50 percent since the start of the reform era and that "less than 1 percent of Chinese households control more than 60 percent of the country's wealth."[42] This inequality has fueled the perception that China now has a crony capitalist system in which those connected to the Communist Party disproportionately claim the wealth generated through the new economic system.[43]

With inequality, China has experienced growing tensions within the society as reflected in reports of "mass incidents" or protest.[44] Data from China's Ministry of Public Security (MPS) indicate a steady rise in the number of "mass incidents" over the years. Based on MPS data, the China Academy of Social Science estimates a total of over ninety thousand "mass incidents" in 2006.[45] The most recent of these events to garner international attention were riots during September 2011 in the city of Shanwei within the Guangdong province. The *New York Times* reports that residents signaled their displeasure with the seizure of farmland by the local government by encircling public buildings, overturning vehicles, and attacking police officers.[46]

It would be a mistake, however, to draw a parallel between the "mass incidents" reported for China and the widespread and intense violence that approximates a civil war. The "mass incidents" reported by the MPS describe a range of activities that may fall short of violence. Will Freeman notes that "mass incidents" data reflect activities such as "mass public speeches, physical conflicts, airing of grievances or other forms of group behavior that may disrupt social stability."[47] While significant, these actions fall far short of the level of conflict considered in the Hartzell *et al.* study of the relationship between foreign-initiated liberalization and the onset of civil war.

The fact that China has experienced social strains with its incremental adoption of economic liberalization is a further demonstration of the sense of dislocation and distress fostered by efforts to promote economic openness. However, these strains might well have proven more pronounced if the state's leaders had pursued a much more rapid and wide-ranging approach to liberalization.

Conclusions

As noted at the outset of this chapter, countries with liberal economies tend to enjoy both greater prosperity and peace. Yet the process of liberalization itself has the potential to prove profoundly destabilizing. This chapter has sought to demonstrate that the degree to which liberalization is accompanied by instability is largely dependent on the model employed for promoting an open economy. The "shock therapy" form of liberalization favored by the IFIs generates hardships for citizens and diminishes government capacity to a point that violence becomes more likely. By contrast, an approach to liberalization that is more modest, incremental, and that identifies context-appropriate changes rather than the "one size fits all" liberalization model the IFIs have been accused of employing, has a greater potential to minimize the possibility of a turn towards widespread conflict.[48]

Based on these findings, we present our conclusions in the form of four policy prescriptions. First, a country's elites should have a stronger voice in any liberalization process. State leaders, in contrast to the IFIs, are more likely to be aware of which particular reforms might impose unacceptable levels of hardship on citizens and enhance the risk of violence.[49] IFI leaders should take seriously the objections of state leaders about the pace and scope of "shock therapy"-style reforms. To a certain extent, this may already be occurring through a slow but increasing recognition among the IFIs themselves that there is not a "one size fits all" set of policies that puts countries on a path towards prosperity.[50]

Second, and related to the above, poor countries or countries in economic crisis can identify growth-promoting policies and institutions, "but doing so often requires experimentation, willingness to depart from orthodoxy, and attention to local conditions."[51] Although some of the liberalizing policies governments arrive at through the process Dani Rodrik describes above may differ from the "best practices" advocated by the IMF and other reform-minded actors, government leaders are much more likely to implement policies that, although imperfect, are politically feasible. The question of political feasibility is not one that has ranked high on the IFIs' lists of concerns. Clearly, though, if national actors are able to design reforms that have a "high ratio of economic benefits to political costs," they will be much more likely to remain committed to the course of reform.[52]

Third, incremental liberalization, in comparison to "shock therapy," is most likely to minimize the risk of political violence and thus increase the odds that these economic reforms attain their ultimate goal of creating a more prosperous society and stable political system.[53] In this sense, states undergoing liberalization might be better served by borrowing something akin to the Chinese model for opening up its economy rather than following in the footsteps of Russia and other Eastern European states that adopted shock therapy models of economic reform. While all liberalization processes will inevitably create hardships, these harms may be more attenuated if adopted in an incremental fashion that preserves the state's ability to compensate losers from the reform process.

Fourth and finally, the states for which the "shock therapy" model of economic liberalization is most inappropriate are likely to be those countries emerging from civil war via a negotiated settlement. These are countries in which governments are in desperate need of resources to develop new political institutions and the capacity to meet the needs and expectations of citizens. Governments that help to broker or emerge from negotiated settlements of civil wars also have a need to prove their legitimacy to their suspicious and war-weary populations. Liberalization policies that promote austerity and limit the ability of government to provide a "peace dividend" to the population may prove threatening to the legitimacy of such governments and enhance the risk that the country will experience a return to conflict.

Notes

1. Indra de Soysa and John R. O'Neal, "Boon or Bane? Reassessing the Productivity of Foreign Direct Investment," *American Sociological Review* 64, no. 5 (1999): 766-82.

2. Paul Collier and Anke Hoeffler, "Greed and Grievance in Civil War," Washington, DC: World Bank, 2001, http://econ.worldbank.org/programs/conflict/library/doc?id=12205. (accessed April 27, 2012).

3. James D. Fearon and David D. Laitin, "Ethnicity, Insurgency, and Civil War," *American Political Science Review* 97, no. 1 (2003): 75-90.

4. Collier and Hoeffler, "Greed and Grievance in Civil War."

5. Both of these measures are transformed using their natural logarithm to decrease the influence of extreme values.

6. Håvard Hegre, Ranveig Gissinger, and Nils Petter Gleditsch, "Globalization and Internal Conflict," in *Globalization and Armed Conflict*, eds. Gerald Schneider, Katherine Barbieri, and Nils Petter Gleditsch (Lanham, MD: Rowman and Littlefield, 2003), 251-75.

7. According to Barbieri and Reuvney, neither foreign direct investment nor internet usage proved to have a statistically significant influence on civil war onset or presence. Katherine Barbieri and Rafael Reuvney, "Economic Globalization and War," *Journal of Politics* 67, no. 4 (2005): 1228-47.

8. See Michael Doyle, "Liberalism and World Politics," *American Political Science Review* 80, no. 4 (1986): 1151-69; Zeev Maoz and Bruce Russett, "Normative and Structural Causes of the Democratic Peace," *American Political Science Review* 87, no. 3 (1993): 624-638; and John O'Neal and Bruce Russett, "The Kantian Peace: The Pacific Benefits of Democracy, Interdependence, and International Organizations, 1885-1992," *World Politics* 52, no. 1 (1999): 1-37.

9. This quote is found in Jack S. Levy, "Domestic Politics and War," in *The Origin and Prevention of Major Wars*, eds. Robert I. Rotberg and Theodore K. Rabb (New York: Cambridge University Press, 1989), 79-100, 88.

10. See Edward L. Mansfield and Jack Snyder, "Democratization and the Danger of War," *International Security* 20, no. 1 (1995): 5-38; Jack Snyder, *From Voting to Violence: Democratization and Nationalist Conflict* (New York: W.W. Norton and Company, 2000); and Edward Mansfield and Jack Snyder, *Electing to Fight: Why Emerging Democracies Go to War* (Cambridge, MA: MIT Press, 2005).

11. The term "Washington Consensus" originates with the work of John Williamson, "What Washington Means by Policy Reform," in *Latin American Readjustment: How Much Has Happened?*, ed. John Williamson (Washington, DC: Institute for International Economics, 199), 7-20.

12. Barro and Lee provide the data on IMF loan program approval. Their study indicates that Botswana, Iraq, Kuwait, and Malaysia were among the few developing states not to have received IMF assistance since 1970. Robert J. Barro and Jong-Wha Lee, "IMF Programs: Who is Chosen and What are the Effects?" *Journal of Monetary Economics* 52, no. 7 (2005): 1245-69, 1249.

13. See Eliana Cardoso and Ann Helwege, *Latin America's Economy: Diversity, Trends, and Conflicts* (Cambridge, MA: The MIT Press, 2003); John W. Peabody, "Economic Reform and Health Sector Policy: Lessons from Structural Adjustment Programs," *Social Science and Medicine* 43, no. 5 (1996): 823-35; and Anna Breman and Carolyn Shelton, "Structural Adjustment Programs and Health," in *Globalization and Health*, eds. Ichiro Kawachi and Sarah Wamala (Oxford: Oxford University Press, 2007), 219-33.

14. John Walton and David Seddon, *Free Markets and Food Riots: The Politics of Global Adjustment* (Cambridge, MA: Blackwell, 1994), 42. Concerning the relationship between SAPs and protests, see also Juha Y. Auvinen, "IMF Intervention and Political

Protest in the Third World: A Conventional Wisdom Redefined," *Third World Quarterly* 17, no. 3 (1996): 377-400.

15. Walton and Seddon, *Free Markets and Food Riots*, 43.

16. "States of Unrest" reports were issued in 2000, 2002, and 2003.

17. Mark Ellis-Jones, *States of Unrest III: Resistance to IMF and World Bank Policies in Poor Countries* (London: World Development Movement, 2003).

18. Irfan Nooruddin and Joel W. Simmons, "The Politics of Hard Choices: IMF Programs and Government Spending," *International Organization* 60, no. 4 (2006): 1001-33, 1010-11.

19. David Stuckler, Lawrence P. King, and Sanjay Basu, "International Monetary Fund Programs and Tuberculosis Outcomes in Post-Communist Countries," *PLoS Medicine* 5, no. 7 (2008): 1079-90. These findings have been the subject of controversy. See, for example, Murray and King's (2008) criticism of the study. Megan Murray and Gary King, "The Effects of International Monetary Fund Loans on Health Outcomes," *PLoS Medicine* 5, no. 7 (2008): 1011-13.

20. Suzanne Daley, "Fiscal Crisis Takes Toll On Health Of Greeks," *New York Times*, December 27, 2011, A4 (NY edition).

21. David Keen, "Liberalization and Conflict," *International Political Science Review* 26, no. 1 (2005): 73-89.

22. While our discussion focuses on hardships experienced by an economy's "losers" as a possible source of instability, Bussman, Schneider, and Wiesehomeier suggest that the new economic "winners" following liberalization may also become the source of upheaval. In their words, the "...winners will see an increase in their personal wealth. This will enhance their willingness to call for political reform that acknowledges these changes. The groups that profit from foreign economic liberalization may consequently challenge the incumbent." In a democracy this challenge may take place in the context of an election; in a non-democratic regime, Bussman et al. suggest a challenge will likely take the form of violence. Magrit Bussman, Gerald Schneider, and Nina Wiesehomeier, "Foreign Economic Liberalization and Peace: The Case of Sub-Saharan Africa," *European Journal of International Relations* 11, no. 4 (2005): 551-79.

23. William Reno, *Corruption and State Politics in Sierra Leone* (New York: Cambridge University Press, 1995): 141-42.

24. Reno, *Corruption and State Politics in Sierra Leone*, 76. A summary of Reno's findings concerning Sierra Leone is also presented in Keen, "Liberalization and Conflict," 76.

25. See Auvinen, "IMF Intervention and Political Protest in the Third World," 377, and Reno, *Corruption and State Politics in Sierra Leone*, 8-9.

26. Keen, "Liberalization and Conflict," 81.

27. Keen, "Liberalization and Conflict," 85. Nooruddin and Simmons report the finding that democracies actually increase the share of spending on the military when the state is under an IMF SAP. It is important, however, to keep this finding in context. While the percentage of the budget dedicated to the military may increase, this takes place in a context in which government spending is typically in substantial decline. "The Politics of Hard Choices," 1023.

28. Caroline A. Hartzell, Matthew Hoddie, and Molly Bauer, "Economic Liberalization via IMF Structural Adjustment: Sowing the Seeds of Civil War?" *International Organization* 64, no. 2 (2010): 339-56.

29. Other studies have reached a different finding concerning the relationship between SAPs and civil violence. Studies by Bienen and Gersovitz, Sidell, and Snider each conclude that SAPs do not enhance the risks of a turn towards conflict within a state. It

should be noted, however, that none of these studies addresses the issue of distinguishing between the effects of the initial economic crisis from the effect of signing an SAP. See Henry S. Bienen and Mark Gersovitz, "Economic Stabilization, Conditionality, and Political Stability," *International Organization* 39, no. 4 (1985): 729-54; Scott R. Sidell, *The IMF and Third-World Political Instability: Is There a Connection* (New York: St. Martin's Press, 1988); and Lewis W. Snider, 1990. "The Political Performance of Governments, External Debt Service, and Domestic Political Violence," *International Political Science Review* 11, no. 4 (1990): 403-22.

30. These criteria for defining a civil war are drawn from the work of James D. Fearon and David D. Laitin, "Ethnicity, Insurgency, and Civil War." Research employing a relatively low threshold for identifying conflict is based on the use of the UCDP/PRIO Armed Conflict Data set. This data set identifies all domestic and international conflicts with at least twenty five battle deaths. See Nils Petter Gleditsch, Peter Wallensteen, Mikael Eriksson, Margareta Sollenberg, and Håvard Strand, "Armed Conflict 1946–2001: A New Dataset," *Journal of Peace Research* 39, no. 5 (2002): 615–37.

31. Alvaro de Soto and Graciana del Castillo, "Obstacles to Peacebuilding," *Foreign Policy* 94 (1994): 69-83, 72.

32. De Soto and del Castillo suggest this is analogous to two doctors (the UN and IMF/World Bank) performing unrelated and contradictory surgeries on the same patient. "Obstacles to Peacebuilding," 74.

33. Roland Paris, *At War's End: Building Peace after Civil Conflict* (New York: Cambridge University Press, 2004), 199-202.

34. This quote is drawn from Thomas G. Rawski, "Implications of China's Reform Experience," *The China Quarterly* 144 (1995): 1150-73, 1151.

35. Kenneth Lieberthal, *Governing China: From Revolution to Reform* (New York: W.W. Norton and Company, 2004), 262.

36. Yingyi Qian, "How Reform Worked in China," in *In Search of Prosperity: Analytic Narratives on Economic Growth*, ed. Dani Rodrik (Princeton, NJ: Princeton University Press, 2003), 307.

37. Lawrence Lau, Yingyi Qian, and Gérard Roland, "Reform without Losers: An Interpretation of China's Dual-Track Approach to Transition," *Journal of Political Economy* 108, no. 1 (2000): 120-43.

38. Qian, "How Reform Worked in China," 327.

39. Mary E. Gallagher, "Reform and Openness: Why China's Economic Reforms Have Delayed Democracy," *World Politics* 54, no. 3 (2002): 338-72, 348.

40. Qian, "How Reform Worked in China."

41. Andrew Walder, "China's Transitional Democracy: Interpreting Its Significance," *The China Quarterly* 144 (1995): 963-79, 963.

42. Minxin Pei, "The Dark Side of China's Rise," *Foreign Policy* 153, no. 1 (2006): 32-40.

43. Pei, "The Dark Side of China's Rise," 37.

44. Tanner draws a connection between China's economic reforms and rising unrest. See Murray Scot Tanner, "China Rethinks Unrest," *The Washington Quarterly* 27, no. 3 2004): 137-56.

45. Will Freeman, "The Accuracy of China's 'Mass Incidents,'" *Financial Times*, March 2, 2010. Available at: http://www.ft.com/intl/cms/s/0/9ee6fa64-25b5-11df-9bd3-00144feab49a.html#axzz1tFVEUJ2A (accessed April 27, 2012).

46. Andrew Jacobs, "Farmers in China's South Riot Over Seizure of Land." *New York Times*, September 24, 2011, A5 (NY edition).

47. Will Freeman, "The Accuracy of China's 'Mass Incidents.'"

48. See Joseph E. Stiglitz for an example of the "one size fits all" critique of the global financial institutions. *Globalization and Its Discontents* (New York: W.W. Norton and Company, 2002).

49. The possibility always exists that a handful of leaders in different states will prove unconcerned about the damaging effects of rapid economic liberalization and thus promote a set of programs that reflect those favored by the IFIs. However, it seems reasonable to expect that the vast majority of political elites recognize the threat to their continued governance that is posed by the onset of sudden economic dislocation and favor strategies that minimize this risk.

50. Rodrick notes that the IFIs themselves acknowledged that the policies associated with the Washington Consensus did not have the desired results and describes the current period as one of confusion concerning what alternative policies should be promoted in the future. Dani Rodrick, "Goodbye Washington Consensus, Hello Washington Confusion? A Review of the World Bank's Economic Growth in the 1990s: Learning from a Decade of Reform," *Journal of Economic Literature* 44 (2006): 973-87.

51. Dani Rodrik, "Introduction: What Do We Learn from Country Narratives?" in *In Search of Prosperity: Analytic Narratives on Economic Growth,* ed. Dani Rodrik (Princeton, NJ: Princeton University Press, 2004), 12.

52. Rodrik, "Introduction: What Do We Learn from Country Narratives?" 13.

53. Paris, *At War's End: Building Peace after Civil Conflict*, 204.

Chapter 11

Conditional Conditionality: The European Union, International Justice, and the Democratic Transition in Serbia

Victor Peskin and Mieczysław P. Boduszyński

In March 2012, Serbia finally became a candidate for European Union (EU) membership, nearly twelve difficult years since the fall of Slobodan Milošević, a period during which Serbia lagged behind its Balkan neighbors in the quest for Euro-Atlantic integration. Serbia's progress toward EU accession was delayed mainly because of its failure to meet its legal obligations to cooperate with the International Criminal Tribunal for the Former Yugoslavia (ICTY) in The Hague. However, the 2011 arrests of Ratko Mladić and Goran Hadžić, the two remaining fugitives indicted by the ICTY, cleared Serbia's path to EU candidacy.

For some observers, this outcome signals a triumph for the EU as a committed supporter of the ICTY as well as the norms of international law and human rights. The EU has indeed won high praise for employing a policy of conditionality to support the ICTY's mission by making Serbia's progress toward EU membership contingent on its cooperation with the tribunal.[1] Bereft of police powers, the ICTY must turn to powerful international actors to act as "surrogate enforcers"[2] to press targeted states to hand over their nationals for trial. Among all of today's international tribunals, the ICTY has enjoyed a privileged position owing to the EU's support. Specifically, the EU has used the promise of membership as leverage to bolster the tribunal in its quest to elicit cooperation from the Yugoslav successor states.[3]

Yet, EU conditionality has not always been the consistent policy it appears from a distance.[4] Nor has it been without its complications for European leaders confronted with the persistent dilemma of whether, when, and how to adjust the terms of the policy to accommodate changing political circumstances in the

Western Balkans. Serb nationalists have long reviled the ICTY for focusing its prosecutorial scrutiny primarily on Serbian atrocities in Croatia, Bosnia, and Kosovo. At key junctures, backlash against the tribunal has strengthened their political fortunes, imperiling Serbian moderates as well as their political and economic reforms. That, in turn, has threatened to derail the EU's objective of bringing Serbia into the European fold and ensuring the stability of the region. Thus, even as European leaders hail the tribunal as "an essential element of reconciliation,"[5] there is deep concern among some EU policy-makers that an uncompromising conditionality policy could undermine peace and democratization in the region. These concerns have been heightened during moments of great uncertainty in Serbia.

The EU is beset by an enduring quandary arising from its quest for justice in The Hague and for stability in the Balkans. This has led Brussels to play a complex balancing act with regard to its conditionality policy in the former Yugoslavia. This chapter focuses its attention on Brussels' use of conditionality vis-à-vis Serbia, a country of particular importance and difficulty for both the tribunal and the EU.[6] Our aim is to explain how and why the EU has strengthened or diluted its ICTY conditionality policy at critical moments in Serbia's post-Milošević transition. An examination of the EU's changing approach to conditionality is crucial to understanding the fortunes of the ICTY and its ability to fulfill its mandate.

The EU as a Community of Values

The rationale for EU expansion to the Western Balkans has been framed in terms of ensuring stability and democratic consolidation in the region. The notion of the EU as more than just an economic union, indeed as a force for human rights and democracy, played a role in the earliest rounds of enlargement to include Spain, Portugal, and Greece in the 1970s and 1980s.[7] In more recent years, the EU has come explicitly to describe itself as "a community of law and a community of values."[8] The Union has put increasing emphasis on the advancement of human rights within and beyond its borders. When it comes to the question of enlarging the Union eastward, this commitment finds expression in the EU's 1993 Copenhagen criteria, a list of political, economic, and human rights requirements that countries in Eastern and Central Europe must meet in order to gain membership.

In addition to meeting the Copenhagen criteria, the states of the former Yugoslavia face obligations that stem from their complicity in the human catastrophe of the recent Balkan wars. To demonstrate their human rights bona fides, these states must confront their responsibility for wartime atrocities by providing full cooperation to the ICTY, particularly in the arrest and transfer of suspects for trial in The Hague. The *raison d'être* of the tribunal is to determine individual responsibility for atrocities, and not cast blame on states or societies. But, for the EU's conditionality policy, the central question is whether states will fulfill their legal responsibility to cooperate with the tribunal. For a state to obstruct justice is a tangible rebuke of The Hague and Brussels (and the UN Security Council, which makes full cooperation a binding legal obligation). A state's decision to hand over suspects does not, as we have seen in Serbia and Croatia, necessarily mean that it has accepted the norms of international justice.[9] Indeed, the EU's conditionality policy and the material incentives offered in exchange for the handover of suspects may actually foster compliance at the expense of a true reckoning with state and societal responsibility.[10] Still, for the EU, cooperation is the litmus test of a state's moral readiness to join Europe.

In an ideal world, the EU's desire for trials in The Hague and a stable, democratic Balkans would seem to go hand in hand. In fact, EU officials frequently amplify the tribunal's contention that justice fosters peace and stability.[11] Beyond a normative commitment to justice for its own sake, these sentiments also suggest a pragmatic interest in it; namely, that the process of adjudicating war crimes suspects in a legitimate forum will help war-torn societies come to terms with their past and live together peacefully. Trials are also seen to have other benefits, such as delegitimizing and removing indicted suspects whose nationalist politics pose a continuing threat to the new democratic order.[12]

The EU's inconsistent implementation of conditionality belies a more complex view of the relationship between justice and stability. This, in turn, speaks to the negative standing of the ICTY in the Balkans, where there are often sharp tensions between the imperatives of international justice and ensuring domestic stability. Anti-tribunal sentiment did not disappear with the 2000 demise of the Milošević and Tuđman regimes in Serbia and Croatia, respectively. The new democratic governing coalitions in both countries initially indicated a willingness to aid the tribunal. Yet, the power of nationalist groups and their ownership of matters of national memory have remained salient. Nationalists have bitterly protested what they view as the state's willingness to collaborate with the tribunal, which is seen as facilitating Western attempts to undermine sovereignty and dishonor the nation's wartime conduct. Thus, even as the tribunal focuses its scrutiny on the misdeeds of select individuals, nationalists have argued that the tribunal is damning all of their countrymen.[13] For staunch nationalists, holding on to such a view is both a matter of deep conviction and a political opportunity to take back the reins of power from moderate politicians.

Nationalist attacks on the ICTY have placed great stress on fragile governing coalitions and sparked wider political turmoil. When faced with a tribunal request for the handover of suspects, governments must choose between domestic opponents and international proponents of state cooperation. At the very least, the controversy surrounding these decisions constitutes a major political distraction. The more troubling scenario is that political crises spawned by tribunal indictments of high-level suspects threaten to derail the reform agenda, bringing anti-European nationalists back to power. This, in turn, may bring all cooperation with the ICTY, not to mention democratization, to a halt.

In respect to the tribunal, states in the former Yugoslavia and the EU grapple with parallel dilemmas. The policy dilemmas that arise in the Balkan capitals over whether to cooperate with the tribunal also present a quandary for the EU when it comes to deciding the extent to which to pressure states to cooperate, given the extensive reform agenda of the international community. On the one hand, the EU has stood firmly behind its conditionality policy, even blocking Serbia's advancement toward Brussels when cooperation has been deemed insufficient. On the other hand, at critical periods of turmoil and uncertainty in Serbia, the EU has softened the terms of its conditionality policy to keep the country on track toward membership, while continuing to present EU conditionality on behalf of the tribunal as unwavering. Political pressure—from Serbia and even within the Union itself—has compromised the terms of the conditionality policy. Yet the pressure to dilute conditionality has, at other times, been successfully countered by the tribunal's chief prosecutor, international human rights organizations, and pro-tribunal EU states. Above all, as we aim to show, EU conditionality has employed flexibility to bend to the political imperative of the moment. In practice, therefore, EU conditionality is inherently conditional.

The EU and the Democratic Transition in Serbia

Well before the fall of Slobodan Milošević, the conflict between the EU's dual imperatives of prodding Serbia to cooperate with the ICTY and fostering stability in the region were evident. During the 1990s, the EU and the U.S. issued unsuccessful calls for Milošević to cooperate with the ICTY. However, until the end of the Kosovo war in June 1999, the West's most pressing concern was garnering Milošević's cooperation to reach a negotiated settlement to the devastating Bosnian war and the deteriorating situation in Kosovo. Only when Milošević refused to forgo his campaign of mass violence against ethnic Albanians in Kosovo did the North Atlantic Treaty Organization (NATO) go to war against Serbia in the spring of 1999.

The tribunal's May 1999 indictment of Milošević for war crimes and crimes against humanity served to solidify the new view of him in the West as an international outlaw.[14] In the wake of the NATO war against Serbia, Milošević came to be seen as the impediment to a stable Balkans. In this new political climate, regime change in Belgrade, as well as Milošević's trial in The Hague, became a growing imperative in Brussels and Washington. In turn, Western leaders increasingly saw the tribunal as a way to marginalize nationalists in the region. More important, the focus shifted from ending war to securing a successful transition to a stable democracy. As such, this goal, and not the tribunal, became the overarching priority.

In the aftermath of the Kosovo war, the West intensified its efforts to foster a domestic consensus for political transformation in Serbia by signaling the benefits of embracing democracy. In the run-up to Serbia's national elections in

September 2000, the EU offered Serbs immediate rewards, such as loans, if they voted Milošević out of power. Vojislav Koštunica's electoral victory as president of the rump Federal Republic of Yugoslavia in late September—and Milošević's belated acquiescence in the face of massive protests in early October—was hailed as a triumph of democracy. But many vestiges of the Milošević regime remained intact, particularly in the military and state security apparatus. From the start, therefore, Serbia faced stark dangers to its fledgling democracy. Therein lay the EU's abiding interest in preventing the reemergence of nationalism that could reawaken conflict, especially in Bosnia and Kosovo.

In this political context, the tribunal represented a double-edged sword for the EU. While the ICTY could rid Serbia of the vestiges of Milošević's regime, too much pressure on Serbia to cooperate with the ICTY could spark an anti-Western backlash that might embolden right-wing nationalists and ensure their return to power. The Serb nationalist parties could vilify the ICTY as an enemy of Serbian national dignity for substantial political gain. Thus, in the aftermath of Milošević's fall, the EU's concern about ensuring a soft landing for Serbia's fragile democracy led it to reward Serbia for its recent democratic turn. A few days after Koštunica took power, British Foreign Secretary Robin Cook said the EU would grant the new government a "swift, generous, and welcoming" response.[15] A "generous" welcome entailed providing Serbia with aid, ushering it back into the UN and other international institutions, and signaling that handovers of accused war criminals were not urgent. Some in the EU, such as Cook, indicated that it was premature to decide whether cooperation with the tribunal should be a condition of aid. Others, like German Foreign Minister Joschka Fischer, announced that Serbian cooperation was "not a top priority."[16] Correctly gauging the mood in Brussels and seeking political cover in the EU's warm embrace of the new government, Koštunica did not hide his animosity to the ICTY, and declared that the Yugoslav Constitution did not permit the handover of suspects to an international tribunal.[17]

In this permissive atmosphere, the tribunal's chief prosecutor, Carla Del Ponte, acknowledged in the fall of 2000 that it was not the right time to press strongly for arrests, while also noting that the ICTY could not wait forever. Indeed, the UN Security Council's consideration of a so-called Completion Strategy to close the tribunal by decade's end highlighted the urgency of receiving cooperation from Belgrade. By the start of 2001, Del Ponte's patience had come to an end. In a visit to Belgrade in January, she signaled her intention to lobby vigorously for the handover of the prime suspect, Milošević.[18] In the following months, she campaigned for his arrest and transfer, forcefully ruling out compromise proposals, advanced by Serbian authorities as well as EU leaders, to prosecute Milošević in Serbia on unrelated domestic charges. Under pressure from Del Ponte, some EU officials favored a future policy of rendering aid conditional on Milošević's handover. Yet, other officials strongly criticized aid conditionality as a misguided policy that would undermine the imperatives of stability and democracy.[19]

Del Ponte's bid for Milošević found a more receptive audience in Washington than in Brussels. It was Washington rather than Brussels that used conditionality for the first time to prod Serbia to take action. The U.S. Congress required the Bush administration each year to certify adequate cooperation in order to release aid to Serbia. This led to Milošević's arrest in early 2001. The U.S. later threatened not to participate in a donors' conference for Serbia, effectively withholding $100 million.[20] The EU then also indicated it might withhold a significant amount of aid. These moves led Prime Minister Zoran Đinđić to engineer the transfer of Milošević to The Hague on 28 June 2001.[21]

State Cooperation and the Role of Prime Minister Đinđić[22]

Western concerns about instability in Serbia reemerged after the Koštunica-Đinđić coalition collapsed following Milošević's handover. By the spring of 2002, it was evident that Serbia's political reforms had stalled in a climate of corruption, criminalization, and political infighting.[23] The grip exerted by the war criminal/organized crime nexus, and the volatility of the war crimes issue were violently underscored by the March 2003 assassination of Đinđić by suspects who feared their handover to The Hague.[24] Western leaders were also seriously concerned about the security of the region, particularly given Serbia's meddling in Bosnia and the unresolved status of the rump Yugoslavia composed of Serbia, Montenegro, and Kosovo (under UN administration since the end of the NATO war).[25] The central concern was Kosovo's unresolved status and the postwar acrimony between Belgrade and Pristina. Kosovo, as one Western diplomat observed, was a "mythic albatross"[26] around the necks of nationalist and moderate Serbian leaders alike.

Notwithstanding its obstructionist policies, Serbia remained intent on reaping the benefits of closer ties to Europe and sought Brussels' agreement to begin negotiating a Stabilization and Association Agreement (SAA) in order to catch up with its Balkan neighbors, which had made strides on the long road toward EU membership. This provided the EU with the leverage it needed to press for domestic reforms and work toward a comprehensive resolution of Yugoslavia's borders. Yet, until the end of 2002, a conciliatory EU had been reluctant to deal strongly with Belgrade and establish firm conditions in regard to domestic political reform or cooperation with the ICTY.[27]

With flagging Serbian reforms and Koštunica's open defiance of the ICTY, the EU began to apply a more stringent form of conditionality, making cooperation with the tribunal a precondition of signing an SAA. In so doing, it created a tangible reward for Serbia, as the SAA would be a milestone on the path to EU membership and a contractual agreement yielding direct economic benefits. This new EU stance, along with concerted pressure from Washington, raised expectations for increased Serbian cooperation. These inducements helped compel Đinđić to promise cooperation, and played a role in the series of events that led to his assassination. Đinđić's successor, Zoran Živković, instituted a crackdown on the mafia and sent a number of war crimes suspects to The Hague. As domestic elections approached in the fall of 2003, however, Živković backed away from cooperation. In the elections in a reconstituted federal arrangement,[28] Koštunica won and became prime minister in early 2004, albeit in a tenuous coalition with the Socialist Party, which, along with the resurgent anti-western Radical Party, had captured nearly sixty percent of the vote.

Koštunica as Prime Minister

Koštunica's return to power did not bode well for the stalled reform process or the tribunal's need for additional war crimes suspects. During 2004, Belgrade's cooperation deteriorated.[29] Moreover, the international community grew increasingly concerned about Kosovo, where interethnic riots in March 2004 led to the deaths of nineteen people and the destruction of scores of Serb Orthodox churches.[30] Even as the wars in Iraq and Afghanistan and the atrocities in Darfur replaced the Balkans on the front pages of newspapers, EU officials remained concerned about the region's uncertain future. It became apparent that the EU had to play a leading role in the Balkans, particularly as Washington's attention shifted elsewhere.

For the EU, the key to increasing its leverage was to make the requirements for compliance—in regard to the ICTY and the reform process—more immediate and the rewards more tangible. Toward that end, the EU decided in late 2004 to offer separate SAA negotiations to Serbia and Montenegro, even though the two entities were at the time in a political union.[31] Offering this twin-track approach rendered the SAA more attainable because it did not have to await the resolution of the future status of Serbia and Montenegro. With SAA negotiations in sight, the reality of EU membership no longer seemed an elusive goal to Serbian leaders. Yet, to reap the reward in the short term, Serbia now had to demonstrate sufficient cooperation with the ICTY.

The prospect of entering into SAA negotiations provided incentive enough for Koštunica. Although he refused to arrest fugitives, Koštunica worked to arrange the "voluntary" surrender of a dozen ethnic Serb suspects in the first four months of 2005.[32] In this period, the number of Serb suspects transferred to The Hague surpassed the number in the previous three years combined. Despite evidence that the Serbian government had directly obstructed the course of international justice by shielding Ratko Mladić and providing him with a pension, the EU did not make his handover a condition for starting SAA negotiations.[33] In April 2005, Brussels approved a feasibility study, an important precursor to SAA negotiations. In October 2005, the EU Council of Ministers authorized the start of the SAA negotiations. While Serbia had demonstrated its capacity to provide significant cooperation to the tribunal in early 2005, the prospect for continued compliance was arguably diminished now that the EU had decided to reward Belgrade by entering into the negotiations.

The Difficult Road to the EU

When the 10th anniversary of the Srebrenica massacre approached in 2005, EU Enlargement Commissioner Olli Rehn called the failure to hand over Karadžić and Mladić "unacceptable."[34] The EU appeared in no mood to punish Belgrade for turning off the cooperation tap, however.[35] The EU's softening approach and the drought in handovers after the feasibility report's approval spurred the tribunal and human rights organizations to heighten their criticism of Belgrade's non-cooperation. This may have been a factor in the EU's decision to warn Serbia of the negative consequences of not resuming cooperation. On the eve of the actual start of the SAA negotiations in October 2005, the EU Council called on Serbia to hand over Karadžić and Mladić and signaled that it would closely monitor Serbia's compliance before concluding the negotiations.[36]

From 2005 to early 2006, the EU's conditionality policy toward Serbia vacillated between lenience, reflecting Brussels' desire to keep Serbia on the EU road, and a stronger form of conditionality, which reflected the frustration of Brussels and the ICTY with the failure to apprehend Karadžić and Mladić. Del Ponte heightened her criticism of Serbia's non-cooperation, specifically in regard to Mladić. Her criticism resonated in no small part because the EU had informally deputized the chief prosecutor as the authority best suited to assess state cooperation.[37] Del Ponte's criticisms constituted growing pressure on the EU to suspend the SAA talks.[38] Still, when Del Ponte called Serbia's cooperation unsatisfactory in late February 2006, the EU Council balked at delivering Serbia an ultimatum. Nevertheless, it signaled that it would "remain in close contact with the Chief Prosecutor."[39] Under pressure, Koštunica pledged to arrest Mladić in the coming months, which was particularly significant as he had previously denied that Mladić was in Serbia and was thus beyond the reach of Serbian authorities.[40] In its clearest sign of support for the tribunal, the EU established an end-of-March deadline by which the SAA talks would be suspended if Mladić was not arrested. This cast Serbia's choice in stark relief. Amid the fallout in Serbia over Slobodan Milošević's death in March, shortly before the end of his long trial in The Hague, the EU extended the cooperation deadline by a month. When the new deadline passed without Mladić in custody, however, the European Commission suspended the SAA negotiations in early May 2006.

The EU was by no means decided on how long to suspend the EU negotiations with Serbia. Ambivalence grew stronger in the following months, as EU leaders feared a rightward turn in Serbian politics and as the specter of instability in Kosovo loomed. Now, more than ever, EU leaders perceived a conflict between pursuing their dual imperatives of international justice and regional stability. The Union had anticipated the need for a quick resumption in the SAA negotiations in order to get Serbia quickly back on the road to Brussels. This is why the European Commission, rather than the EU Council, suspended the talks. This would allow for a quicker resumption of talks, as only the go-ahead of the enlargement commissioner, rather than the unanimous decision of all twenty-seven EU member states, would be required. Technically, Rehn could resume the talks at any point, but doing so in the absence of compliance could undermine the credibility of the EU's conditionality policy and even encourage Serbia's defiance. Moreover, the European Commission's suspension of the talks had been explicitly tied to Serbia's failure to arrest and transfer Mladić. The Commission had established a firm and unambiguous conditionality policy, or so it seemed.

Diluting Conditionality

Well aware of European ambivalence over the suspension of the SAA negotiations, Koštunica appeared to exploit the EU's fears of losing Serbia to nationalism and instability. For tribunal advocates, dealing strongly with Serbia was seen as a principled policy to realize the determination of individualized guilt in the courtroom trials of defendants. But Koštunica argued that "it is wrong to place an entire country into isolation and suspend the Stabilization and Association talks only because it is impossible to resolve the technical issue of the capture of the several remaining indictees."[41] He also suggested that reengaging Serbia in the SAA talks would do more to encourage cooperation. Privately, some EU officials complained that Serbian leaders often spent more time lobbying the EU to relax conditionality than cooperating with the tribunal.[42] Still, Koštunica appeared to understand that the EU's decision to suspend the talks was in fact open to contestation and negotiation.

The EU, for its part, did not relish entirely blocking Serbia's long path to membership, especially in light of destabilizing events in 2006. In that year, leaders in Belgrade were confronted with two major blows: the May victory of an independence referendum in Montenegro and the increasing likelihood that the UN would soon recommend some form of independence for Kosovo. In this context, EU officials interviewed in December 2006 expressed concern that the suspension of the SAA talks would further weaken Koštunica and increase the chances of the Radical Party prevailing in the January 2007 parliamentary elections.[43]

In light of the coming elections, the EU worked to find a way out of the Mladić impasse. The dilemma it faced was how to restart the SAA negotiations without being seen, in the eyes of tribunal supporters and Serbia, to be abandoning its firm approach to conditionality. To be seen in this light would threaten the EU's reputation as a defender of human rights as well as embolden Serbian politicians to continue to thwart the tribunal. Yet, Rehn had reduced the EU's room for maneuver in May 2006 when he announced that progress on the SAA was not possible in the absence of Mladić's arrest and handover.

In the second half of 2006 and the first half of 2007, EU officials appeared to recast their definition of cooperation, privileging efforts over results when it came to the arrest of Mladić.[44] This shift can be seen in the consequential EU Council conclusions of February 2007 stipulating that SAA talks could be restarted as long as Serbia demonstrated "a clear commitment and takes concrete and effective action for full cooperation with the ICTY."[45] Specifically, the EU indicated to Belgrade that talks could resume if Koštunica presented a credible "action plan"[46] for arresting Mladić. Koštunica tried to provide evidence that the government was actively searching for Mladić by circulating a plan for his capture, staging a raid purportedly aimed at arresting him and several people who helped protect him. Still, some European diplomats remained skeptical that this would quickly lead to Mladić's capture. "I will believe it when I see it," said Dutch Foreign Minister Bernard Bot, whose government has been the strongest European ICTY supporter.[47] In speeches to the Security Council in June and December 2006, Del Ponte faulted Belgrade for not seriously pursuing Mladić. In December, Del Ponte dismissed Koštunica's arrest plan as "just another smokescreen."[48] Nevertheless, in June 2007, the EU Commission announced the resumption of negotiations on the SAA.[49]

Conditional Conditionality

At the start of 2007, another international court handed down a decision that would seem to bolster Del Ponte's campaign for Karadžić and Mladić. In February, the International Court of Justice (ICJ) issued its long-awaited decision in Bosnia's genocide lawsuit against Serbia, ruling that Serbia was not guilty for the genocide in Srebrenica and did not owe reparations to Bosnia. The Court also ruled, however, that Serbia was in violation of the Genocide Convention of 1948 for not handing over Karadžić and Mladić.

Rather than interpret the ICJ ruling as a moral imperative to renew pressure on Serbia, some EU officials appeared to see it as an opportunity to leave the Bosnian war behind. Rehn said that the ICJ decision had reaffirmed Serbia's obligation to cooperate. However, mention of Serbia's obligation to hand over the two suspects was conspicuously absent from his remarks. Rehn also downplayed the urgency of Serbia's obligation by saying that full cooperation would only be needed to conclude the SAA talks.[50] Over the next several months, the chief prosecutor's leverage diminished as the EU and the West grew increasingly concerned about the prospect of instability in Kosovo.

The first-place showing of the Serbian Radical Party in the January 2007 elections and the uncertain composition of the new government heightened Europe's concerns. It would take almost four months of negotiations until a new coalition was formed, led again by Koštunica. However, in early May, the Serbian parliament's election of Radical Party leader Tomislav Nikolić as its speaker raised fears in the West that the pro-Moscow ultranationalists might join with Koštunica. Just before the deadline to form a new government expired in mid-May, Koštunica and Boris Tadić, Serbia's pro-Western president, agreed to a power-sharing deal that excluded the Radical Party.

To bolster the new pro-Western government and ease Serbia's adamant opposition to the growing likelihood of Kosovo's independence, European diplomats indicated that the SAA talks would soon resume. In a bid for political cover, the EU looked to Del Ponte to render a positive assessment of Serbia's cooperation. With the EU prepared to compromise its conditionality criteria, Serbia had new incentive to demonstrate some goodwill by facilitating the handover of low-level suspects. Del Ponte, in turn, provided a positive assessment of Serbia's cooperation, a conciliatory approach apparently aimed at encouraging yet more cooperation. At the end of May 2007, the Serbian government facilitated the arrest and handover of Zdravko Tolimir, a top aide to Mladić, indicted for genocide and crimes against humanity at Srebrenica. Not long afterward, Serbia arranged the arrest of another suspect, Vlastimir Đorđević.[51] Rehn then announced that Brussels would restart the talks later in June, but did not set an actual date. The handover of these two suspects fell far short of full cooperation. Still, in the EU's estimation, Serbia had done what it needed to do: "shown clear commitment. . . for full cooperation."[52]

By agreeing to restart the talks with Mladić still at large, the EU Commission reneged on its own condition, demonstrating to Serbia the flexibility of its conditionality policy. The Commission's decision to resume the SAA talks came as a relief to the growing number of European states eager to place Serbia back on the road to Brussels. Still, as EU officials often noted, the road ahead for Serbia was long.

EU officials maintained that the SAA talks would not be concluded without Serbia first bringing Karadžić and Mladić into custody.[53] Knowing full well that the EU could later back away from its promise, Del Ponte pressed Brussels to hold to this commitment. In early 2008, as elections in Serbia once again brought the prospect of a nationalist victory, EU officials underscored that an SAA agreement was in reach. Rehn signaled that the EU was working to prepare the agreement to be signed as soon as Serbia provided "full cooperation with the ICTY leading to the arrest of the remaining indictees."[54] Thus, Serbia would be rewarded with a signed SAA agreement even if it did not hand over suspects, as long as the EU deemed this cooperation was sufficient *to lead* to future arrests. Once again, the EU strategically altered the meaning of "full cooperation" to dilute what the tribunal's Security Council-established statute presented as an unwavering legal obligation.

EU officials had a clear interest in influencing the course of the presidential elections in January 2008. In the first round, Nikolić came out ahead of Tadić. In a bid to bolster Tadić and his promise to bring Serbia closer to Europe, momentum grew in Brussels to grant the major concession of concluding the SAA agreement. Such a move required unanimity among the EU's twenty-seven countries. In a sign of the growing anxiety over losing Serbia, even formerly staunch tribunal backers favored an early signing of the SAA agreement. Only the Netherlands held firm in opposition.

As pressure mounted on the Netherlands to acquiesce to the SAA agreement and the Serbian government collapsed in the wake of Kosovo's declaration of independence in mid-February, the prospect of an EU compromise emerged. Days before parliamentary elections in May 2008 and with the moderates behind in the polls, the EU Council signed the SAA agreement with Serbia. It stipulated, however, that the agreement would not be implemented without evidence of full cooperation with the ICTY. This move is a paradigmatic example of EU balancing.

In signing the SAA, the EU bolstered the moderates' chance of electoral success by granting the intermediate award of closer ties with Europe. To legitimize this decision and maintain its image as a principled supporter of human rights, the EU claimed that Serbia had demonstrated sufficient commitment to cooperating with the tribunal. Some EU officials privately conceded that this was dubious given that Belgrade had not facilitated any handovers in close to a year. "It is stretching [it] a bit to say cooperation [was] satisfactory when it is not," said an EU official familiar with the negotiations with Serbia. The official maintained that the Union had not abandoned the tribunal insofar as its action was just "the symbolic gesture of the signature"[55] and the actual implementation of the SAA would be delayed. That argument was hardly convincing for tribunal officials and their supporters in international human rights organizations.[56]

The EU's partial granting of the SAA strengthened Serbian moderates locked in a tight electoral race. In the May 2008 elections, Tadić's moderate Democratic Party scored a major victory. It would take several months of negotiations with other parties, however, to determine whether the moderates would form a coalition government, especially given the Radical Party's strong showing. In June, the Democratic Party formed a government with the backing of the now more moderate Socialist Party. So concerned were some EU officials about a nationalist resurgence that they remained skeptical about their ability to influence the election. One EU official recalled, "I said [to myself], 'Will the public buy it?' And apparently they did." The efficacy of the EU's concession, the official said, shows how many Serbs "look for symbols to see they're not excluded from Europe."[57]

Given the dangerous confluence of events in early 2008 (Kosovo's declaration of independence and the prospect of the ultranationalists gaining power in Belgrade in both the presidential and the parliamentary elections) a range of EU officials[58] and even a number of Dutch officials[59] clearly supported the decision to sign an SAA with Serbia. They also insisted that what was good for Serbian democracy would also, in time, be good for the ICTY. Bolstering the electoral prospects of the moderates would strengthen those forces most likely to cooperate with the tribunal. In this argument, we see an effort to demonstrate that advancing democracy and stability can also serve the interests of international justice. Still, in the short term, EU officials and human rights activists alike agreed that the concession of signing the SAA would diminish the EU's leverage to prod Serbia to hand over more suspects. "We're obviously not in a strong position" in relation to Mladić and Karadžić, one EU official said, adding, "It's obvious it is the wrong climate to get [them] to The Hague."[60]

The Serbian political climate soon changed, however. Not long after Tadić's Democratic Party formed a new government, it took action in support of the tribunal. First came the June arrest of Stojan Župljanin.[61] As the new government took office after weeks of post-election negotiation, Serbian leaders expressed their resolve to expedite the process of EU accession, as the momentum for an EU decision on whether to implement the pre-membership agreement increased. These developments seemed to be key factors leading to Karadžić's arrest in July 2008. For many in Brussels, Tadić's electoral victory, followed by the Karadžić arrest, vindicated the EU's decision to sign the SAA before the elections.

It would be tempting to call the arrest of such a major figure as Karadžić a turning point in Serbia's troubled relationship with the tribunal and the EU. The significance of the arrest notwithstanding, there were limits to Tadić's political courage. In the months that followed, the Serbian government did not arrest Mladić or Goran Hadžić, the other remaining fugitive sought by the ICTY. The malleability of the EU's conditionality policy may well have given Belgrade incentive to withhold further cooperation in order to gauge whether the EU's resolve would diminish. Further incentive for delay was provided by the EU's diluted requirement that Serbia had to provide full cooperation leading to the arrest of indictees. The inclusion of the phrase "leading to" signaled that it would be sufficient for Serbia to demonstrate its efforts to arrest Mladić without actually doing so. In 2008, the government again staged raids for Mladić.[62] Even as Serbian officials tried to signal a commitment to arrest Mladić, they sought to further downplay their responsibility for bringing him into custody by repeating their dubious claims of several years earlier that he was not hiding in Serbia.[63]

Serbian officials understood that the arrest of Karadžić alone would not lead the EU to implement the SAA, especially given opposition from the Netherlands. Still, they continued to devote more energy to lobbying the EU than to arresting Mladić.[64] Reviving the often-used argument of Serb victimization at the hands of the West, Serbian officials argued that Serbia was being unfairly denied the right of EU integration, and even was being punished despite its apprehension of Karadžić.[65]

The EU and Serbia after Koštunica

In 2008 and 2009, the EU grappled with whether to move Serbia one step closer to Brussels. Most of the twenty-seven EU states favored implementing the SAA, a move that would in effect weaken its conditionality policy vis-à-vis the ICTY. The Netherlands continued to insist that the SAA not be implemented until the two remaining fugitives were in ICTY custody. Meanwhile, in Belgrade, significant power shifts were underway as EU membership became a more realistic prospect and the public mood turned against extreme nationalism. A faction led by Nikolić, the Radical leader, split from the party over its refusal to vote in favor of ratifying the SAA. Taking many members with him, Nikolić founded a new party, the Progressives, who do not fundamentally question the pro-European direction of Serbia. In terms of strengthening the pro-Western segments of the Serbian political scene, this "political earthquake"[66] can be seen as vindicating the EU's concessions during the critical 2008 election.

The EU offered a number of concessions to Belgrade in 2009, albeit ones that did not entail full implementation of the SAA. In June 2009, it announced it would lift visa requirements for citizens of Serbia, Montenegro, and Macedonia. In December 2009, with the agreement of the Netherlands under substantial pressure from other EU member states, the EU unblocked the implementation of a trade pact with Serbia, a key part of the SAA. The EU's concessions were facilitated in part by a generally positive assessment delivered by ICTY Chief Prosecutor Serge Brammertz in a December 2009 speech to the Security Council.[67] His speech credited Serbia's efforts to pursue Mladić without criticizing its continued failure to apprehend him. In his early Security Council speeches, Brammertz avoided strong criticism of Serbia's cooperation record. To some observers, these were acts of prosecutorial conciliation that gave the EU political maneuvering room to grant Serbia concessions.[68]

Moreover, the yearly EU Commission progress report on Serbia released in November 2009 painted a generally optimistic picture of Serbia's democratic and EU prospects.[69] On 22 December 2009, Serbia formally submitted its application for EU membership, an unprecedented move for a state that had yet to conclude an SAA. It was likely made with an eye to domestic constituencies, to whom the government badly needed to show progress on the EU front. Initially, Brussels reacted coolly.

In 2010, Brussels granted further rewards to Belgrade. Together, they signaled the EU's strongest embrace of Serbia in the post-Milošević period up until that point. First, in June 2010, EU foreign ministers gave member states, with the support of the outgoing Dutch government, the green light to proceed with full ratification of the SAA. Second, in October 2010, European foreign ministers voted to request a formal study of Serbia's membership bid by the European Commission. In September 2010, an accommodating Serbian government had agreed to support a compromise UN resolution that dropped its earlier demands to reopen talks on the status of Kosovo and promised cooperation with Kosovar authorities. The new European Commissioner for Enlargement, Stefan Füle, said that Serbia's cooperation on the UN resolution was a "critical element" in the EU decision to send Serbia's membership bid to the European Commission.[70] To satisfy the Netherlands and tribunal supporters, the decision included an explicit requirement that Serbia continue to pursue Mladić. Yet, in the EU Council's deliberations, the need to assuage Serbia was evident. Swedish Foreign Minister Carl Bildt, for instance, argued that if the wording of the decision on assessing Serbia's membership application was too negative, it would send the message that Brussels' commitment to EU enlargement had waned.[71]

Tadić and other Serbian leaders were acutely aware, however, that the major reward of EU candidate status could not be realized as long as the two remaining ICTY fugitives, Mladić and Hadžić, were not apprehended. In April 2011 in Paris, Tadić pledged that he would arrest both men soon. After nearly sixteen years as a fugitive, in May 2011, Serbian authorities arrested Mladić in a small village in northern Serbia. Hadžić's arrest followed in July 2011. Both men were handed over to the tribunal soon after their capture, to great fanfare in The Hague and Brussels.

From Belgrade's perspective, the handover of Mladić and Hadžić should have cleared the way for immediate EU candidacy. However, in late 2011, Kosovo emerged as a major obstacle to Serbia's membership bid, in light of clashes in the Serb-majority north and increasing calls by some EU members for normalized relations with Pristina as a condition for further progress toward EU accession. After Belgrade conceded to allowing Kosovo's participation in regional meetings, and returned to an ongoing dialogue, Brussels gave the green light to Serbia's candidacy at an EU summit in March 2012. The EU declared that Belgrade had reached a "fully satisfactory" level of cooperation with the ICTY while emphasizing that progress on the Kosovo issue and strengthening the rule of law in Serbia will be closely watched by Brussels as key criteria for full membership.[72]

The new coalition government that took power in Belgrade in summer 2012, despite its former nationalist credentials, has pledged to continue the reform-minded agenda approach of its predecessor, including dialogue with Kosovo. However, the hard reality is that full EU membership is still years away, not only because of the need to implement further economic and political reforms, but because of the current recession and atmosphere in Brussels, there is little appetite for further expansion.

Conclusions

As a European-based international tribunal with a mandate to prosecute perpetrators of atrocities that occurred on Europe's doorsteps in states that now seek membership in Euro-Atlantic structures, the ICTY has called upon key actors, such as the EU and the U.S., to act as surrogate enforcers on its behalf. By contrast, the International Criminal Court faces far greater difficulties in motivating a similar level of international pressure on defiant states, particularly Sudan. In the place of actual military intervention, the EU has come to see its political intervention on behalf of the tribunal's judicial intervention as a way to become an effective force in shaping a peaceful and prosperous Europe.

Over time, the EU has played an increasingly important role in prodding Serbia and other Balkan states to aid the ICTY.[73] Indeed, the gravitational pull of the EU's policy of conditioning progress toward membership on increased cooperation has proven critical in Serbia's significant, albeit reluctant and delayed cooperation, with the tribunal. Yet, EU conditionality vis-à-vis the ICTY is more complex and lenient than many accounts allow.[74] Rather than being a resolute policy composed of clear conditions and firm deadlines, the EU's conditionality policy has been crafted to allow for continual renegotiation in light of changing political circumstances. This has rendered conditionality inherently conditional. The contingent nature of the policy has allowed the EU to balance its support of international justice with its interest in promoting democratization and stability in the region. The effort at such balancing is, of course, inherently political.[75] In the EU's quest for balance, the norms of international justice do not necessarily trump other interests.

The EU's fluctuating approach to conditionality is a product of deep conflict and uncertainty within the Union over whether the pursuit of international justice may undermine the pursuit of democratization and regional stability. For the EU, the ICTY has become a paradox insofar as it is viewed as both an essential instrument and a formidable obstacle to Serbia's democratic development and quest to join Europe. Even as EU officials hail cooperation as a litmus test for the rule of law in Serbia and for reconciliation in the region, they view it as an obstacle to reform and a trigger of instability, given the extent to which anti-tribunal sentiment has emboldened nationalists and threatened the standing of moderate, pro-European politicians in Serbia. Recently, concern over the destabilizing potential of international tribunals has been on display in the context of Libya, as well as Lebanon.[76]

The question that remains to be answered is how we should evaluate the EU's balancing efforts. No doubt Serbia is a more stable and democratic nation than it was just several years ago. Its institutions are stronger, the majority of its people and politicians support a European future,[77] and its economic growth was robust until the current recession. Even the nationalist parties that ignited fears in Brussels just a few years ago have adopted a liberal and pro-EU platform. This includes the coalition of parties that took power in the summer of 2012, composed of the reformed Socialist Party of former President Milošević and the Progressive Party of Tomislav Nikolić, who once inspired dread in Western capitals but ultimately retreated from ultranationalism.

Thus, one could argue that the EU's conditional conditionality has enjoyed unbridled success in terms of accomplishing the dual goals of supporting the tribunal and keeping Serbia on the democratic and European paths. However, there is another side to the coin. Serbia's compliance with the ICTY has not brought widespread acceptance of the tribunal in the country.[78] In fact, linking material benefits to compliance may undercut a true reckoning despite recent signs of Serbia's emerging confrontation with its past.[79]

The fact that Mladić and Hadžić are now finally in detention in Scheveningen Prison near The Hague is clearly a triumph for the ICTY, and by extension, for EU conditionality. Yet, justice delayed may yet be justice denied, owing to Mladić's age and poor health. Moreover, ninety of the 196 charges against

Mladić have been dropped in the interest "of a fair and expeditious trial."[80] An earlier trial would have enhanced its truth-telling function, an important component of transitional justice. This may affect how historians judge the tribunal and the EU itself. How will they interpret the EU's self-styled role as a defender of human rights, both within and beyond its borders?

Regardless of the scope of charges against Mladić and the outcome of the trial, the EU has played an indispensable role in advancing international justice in The Hague. Yet, this does not negate the fact that Mladić and Karadžić eluded justice for so many years. Carla Del Ponte said that the failure to capture Karadžić and Mladić was a "permanent stain" on the tribunal.[81] To be sure, political imperatives at times trump legal ones. Compromises in the conditionality policy that take the form of intermediate rewards and decreased pressure may in fact bolster cooperation with the tribunal in the long run by providing liberal, pro-European elites with the political capital they need to pursue a reformist and pro-tribunal agenda.

There is a thin line, however, between compromises that bolster and those that undermine the tribunal and EU values. The EU's concessions in 2009 and 2010 in its conditionality policy toward Serbia may have undercut both institutions for two reasons. First, while the likelihood of instability in Serbia and a takeover by hardline nationalists was high in the past, it no longer appeared to be a serious threat in 2010.[82] Second, and most important, the ICJ's ruling that found Serbia was in violation of the Genocide Convention for its failure to arrest and transfer Mladić underscored the moral imperative to deal firmly with Belgrade.

For human rights purists, the policy of conditional conditionality undermined the tribunal and the integrity of the EU's support for it. Interestingly, however, tribunal officials are not above supporting such compromises. Even Del Ponte realized that at times adopting a conciliatory approach to Serbia (and Croatia) offered the best prospects of eliciting cooperation. In this vein, Del Ponte in June 2007 actually called on the European Commission to resume SAA negotiations with Serbia in the hopes that this intermediate award would bring a new spirit of reciprocity from Belgrade. Similarly, Chief Prosecutor Brammertz initially appeared to proceed cautiously in securing cooperation from Serbia for Mladić's arrest. Rather than strongly criticize Serbia for not arresting Mladić, Brammertz, early in his tenure, was measured in his assessments of Serbia's failure to deliver the fugitive. However, over the course of 2010 and the first half of 2011, Brammertz grew increasingly critical of Belgrade, culminating in his influential spring 2011 report to the Security Council, which unequivocally faulted the Serbian government's failure on the Mladić issue. Thus, the route to compliance does not necessarily rely on an adversarial approach alone. Striking a balance between adversarial and conciliatory approaches and between rewards and punishments has been at the heart of the EU's attempts to achieve both justice and stability, and thereby to draw Serbia and the Balkans away from the legacy of war and nationalism and into a united Europe.

Notes

1. The former ICTY chief prosecutor has been one source of this praise. Address to the Security Council by Carla Del Ponte (16 December 2006). http://www.icty.org (accessed 13 December 2010).

2. See, Victor Peskin, *International Justice in Rwanda and the Balkans: Virtual Trials and the Struggle for State Cooperation* (New York: Cambridge University Press, 2008), 12.

3. Successive EU annual progress reports have highlighted ICTY cooperation among the criteria for advancement toward membership.

4. Carla Del Ponte, with Chuck Sudetic, *Madame Prosecutor: Confrontation with Humanity's Worst Criminals and the Culture of Impunity* (New York: Other Press, 2009).

5. European Union at the UN, "Speech by Commissioner Olli Rehn: Commission Declaration on the Balkans 10 Years after Srebrenica" (6 July 2005), http://www.eu-un.europa.eu/articles/en/article_4866_en.htm (accessed 13 December 2010).

6. Serbia is the most important country for the ICTY because its armed forces and proxies are linked to a majority of the wartime atrocities in Croatia, Bosnia, and Kosovo. Despite its increased cooperation, the question of Serbian compliance remains a major problem for the tribunal.

7. See, Erik O. Eriksen, *The Unfinished Democratization of Europe* (New York: Oxford University Press, 2009).

8. European Union at the UN, Speech by Commissioner Olli Rehn on "The Next Steps towards Europe" lecture at Belgrade University (18 April 2005), http://www.europa-eu-un.org/articles/en/article_4582_en.htm (accessed 13 December 2010).

9. Peskin, *International Justice in Rwanda and the Balkans*, 12.

10. See, Jelena Subotić, "The Paradox of International Justice Compliance," *International Journal of Transitional Justice* 3, no. 3 (2009): 362-83.

11. Victor Peskin interviews with EU officials, Brussels, Belgium, December 2006 and May 2008. From 2006 to 2009, Peskin conducted thirty qualitative, open-ended interviews with EU officials working on enlargement and the Balkans in Brussels. During the same period, he also conducted open-ended interviews with ICTY officials in The Hague (ten), international human rights activists in The Hague and Brussels (seven), and Dutch Foreign Ministry officials in The Hague (five). Snowball sampling was used to identify key players in these organizations. The interviews were read for patterns and themes that illustrate the dilemma we explore in this chapter.

12. Diane F. Orentlicher, *Shrinking the Space for Denial: The Impact of the ICTY in Serbia* (New York: Open Society Institute, 2008).

13. Victor Peskin and Mieczysław P. Boduszyński, "International Justice and Domestic Politics: Post-Tudjman Croatia and the International Criminal Tribunal for the Former Yugoslavia," *Europe-Asia Studies* 55 no. 7 (2003): 1117-42.

14. Milošević's ICTY indictment was subsequently amended to include genocide charges.

15. "EU Prepares to Lift Yugoslav Sanctions," *BBC News*, 9 October 2000.

16. "EU Prepares to Lift Yugoslav Sanctions."

17. Europa Publications, *The Europa World Year Book 2004* (London: Europa Publications, 2004), 3698.

18. Peskin, *International Justice in Rwanda and the Balkans.*

19. *Tanjug*, 24 January 2001, http://www.tanjug.rs (accessed 13 December 2010).

20. International Crisis Group, *Milosevic in The Hague: What It Means for Yugoslavia and the Region* (July 2001).

21. See "U.S. Calls Milosevic Extradition 'Great News,'" *CNN*, 28 June 2001.

22. Until a 2003 EU-brokered agreement that loosened the federation between Serbia and Montenegro, the rump Yugoslavia continued to operate under a complex constitutional arrangement it inherited from both the communist Yugoslav federation and the Milošević era. In this arrangement, real power was shared in Belgrade by the federal president (at the time, Koštunica) and the Serbian prime minister (Đinđić).

23. International Crisis Group, *Serbia after Đinđić* (March 2003).

24. John B. Allcock, "The International Criminal Tribunal for the Former Yugoslavia," in *Confronting the Yugoslav Controversies: A Scholars' Initiative*, ed. Charles Ingrao and Thomas A. Emmert (West Lafayette, IN: Purdue University Press, 2009).

25. See International Crisis Group, *Belgrade's Lagging Reform: Cause for International Concern* (March 2002).

26. Peskin interview, western diplomat, Pristina, Kosovo, May 2007.

27. International Crisis Group, *Serbia after Đinđić*.

28. In this new arrangement, the position of federal president was eliminated and the post of Serbian prime minister became the most powerful one.

29. Peskin, *International Justice in Rwanda and the Balkans*.

30. See "A Survey of the EU's Eastern Borders: Taming the Balkans," *Economist*, 25 June 2005.

31. "EUHR Solana Met with the Prime Minister of Serbia" (16 December 2004), http://europa-eu-un.com/articles/en/article_4164_en.htm (accessed 13 December 2010).

32. Peskin, *International Justice in Rwanda and the Balkans*.

33. See Igor Jovanovic, "Serbia and Montenegro: Slow SAA." *Transitions Online*, 16 April 2006.

34. European Union at the UN, "Speech by Commissioner Olli Rehn: Commission Declaration on the Balkans."

35. European Union at the UN, "Speech by Commissioner Olli Rehn on Progress in the Western Balkans' (13 April 2005), http://www.eu-un.europa.eu/articles/fr/article_4561_fr.htm (accessed 13 December 2010).

36. European Union at the UN, "EU Council Conclusions on Western Balkans" (3 October 2005), http://www.eu-un.europa.eu/articles/es/article_5083_es.htm (accessed 13 December 2010).

37. Peskin interviews, EU officials, Brussels, Belgium, May 2008.

38. Ahto Lobjakas, "Serbia: EU Sets Deadline for Belgrade to Arrest War Crimes Suspects," *Radio Free Europe/Radio Liberty*, 27 February 2006.

39. European Union at the UN, "EU External Relations Council Conclusions on the Western Balkans" (27 February 2006), http://www.eu-un.europa.eu/articles/fr/article_5739_fr.htm (accessed 13 December 2010).

40. Peskin interviews, EU officials, Brussels, Belgium, December 2006.

41. *Tanjug*, 9 June 2006, http://www.tanjug.rs (accessed 13 December 2010).

42. Peskin interviews, EU officials, Brussels, Belgium, May 2008.

43. Peskin interviews, EU officials, Brussels, Belgium, May 2008. Concern with instability in Serbia appears to have been the motivation behind NATO's decision in November 2006 to invite Serbia to join the Partnership for Peace, a coveted stepping stone for membership in the military alliance.

44. See the EU Commission's 2006 progress reports. Also see Brussels European Council, *EU Presidency Conclusions* (8 November 2006). http:// ec.europa.eu/enlargement/ (accessed 13 December 2010).

45. European Union at the UN, "EU Western Balkans Relations," speech by EU Commissioner Rehn' (12 February 2007), http://www.eu-un.europa.eu/articles/fr/article_6770_fr.htm (accessed 13 December 2010).

46. European Union at the UN, "EU Council Conclusions on the Western Balkans" (15 September 2006), http://www.europa-eu-un.org/articles/en/article_6252_en.htm (accessed 13 December 2010).

47. "Serbian Proposed 'Mladic Plan' in Plea to EU," *Financial Times*, 17 July 2006.

48. Address to the Security Council by Carla Del Ponte (15 December 2006). http://www.icty.org (accessed 13 December 2010).

49. While Mladić drew increased Western scrutiny in the spring of 2006, interest in Karadžić seemed to fade, to Del Ponte's chagrin.

50. European Union at the UN, "Introductory Remarks on Western Balkans by EU Commissioner Rehn" (21 March 2007), http://www.europa-eu-un.org/articles/en/article_6881_en.htm (accessed 13 December 2010).

51. Đorđević was a Serbian military commander indicted for crimes against Kosovar civilians in 1999.

52. European Union at the UN, "EU Council Conclusions on Western Balkans" (18 June 2007), http://eu-un.europa.eu/articles/en/article_7115_en.htm (accessed 13 December 2010).

53. European Union at the UN, "EU Presidency Statement—United Nations General Assembly: Reports of the ICTY and ICTR" (15 October 2007), http://www.eu-un.europa.eu/articles/en/article_7419_en.htm (accessed 13 December 2010).

54. European Union at the UN, "'Serbia's European Road'—Speech by EU Commissioner Rehn" (24 October 2007), http://www.eu-un.europa.eu/articles/en/article_7432_en.htm (accessed 13 December 2010).

55. Peskin interview, EU official, Brussels, Belgium, May 2008.

56. Peskin interviews, representatives of international human rights organizations, Brussels, Belgium, May 2008.

57. Peskin interview, EU official, Brussels, Belgium, May 2008.

58. Peskin interviews, EU officials, Brussels, Belgium, May 2008 and June and December 2009.

59. Peskin interviews, Dutch foreign ministry officials, The Hague, Netherlands, December 2008.

60. Peskin interview, EU official, Brussels, Belgium, May 2008.

61. Župljanin, a Bosnian Serb, was indicted by the ICTY in 1999 for crimes against humanity during the Bosnian war.

62. Juliana Mojsilović, "We Don't Know Where War Criminals Are, Dacic," *Balkan Insight*, 4 November 2008, http://www.birn.eu.com (accessed 13 December 2010).

63. "Jeremić: EU Should Stop with the Conditioning," *Radio Beograd*, 6 November 2008, http://glassrbije.org/ (accessed 13 December 2010).

64. Dragoljub Žarković, "Mala Nočna Straža" (A Little Night Guard Duty), *Politika Online* (19 September 2008), http://www.politika.co.yu (accessed 13 December 2010).

65. "Ljajić unsatisfied with EU decision," *B92*, (10 December 2008), http://www.b92.net (accessed 13 December 2010).

66. Tim Judah, "At Last, Good News from the Balkans," *New York Review of Books*, 11 March 2010, 47.

67. See address to the UN Security Council by Serge Brammertz, 3 December 2009. http://www.icty.org (accessed 13 December 2010).

68. It is important to note that in his June 2010 report to the Security Council, Brammertz took a more critical view of Serbia's cooperation, calling for more concerted

action to arrest Mladić. See, International Criminal Tribunal for the former Yugoslavia, "Prosecutor Brammertz's Address before the Security Council" (18 June 2010), http://www.icty.org/sid/10423 (accessed 13 December 2010).

69. The most recent progress report, released in November 2010, was also positive, but firm in calling for further reforms, including cooperation with the ICTY. European Commission, *Enlargement Strategy and Progress Reports 2010: Serbia* (2010).

70. Stephen Castle, "Serbia's E.U. Aspirations Face Long Road Ahead," *New York Times*, 28 October 2010.

71. Stephen Castle, "Serbia's E.U. Aspirations Face Long Road Ahead."

72. See http://ec.europa.eu/enlargement/pdf/key_documents/2011/package/sr_ conclusions_2011_en.pdf (accessed 13 December 2010).

73. Peskin interviews, EU officials, Brussels, Belgium, May 2008 and December 2009.

74. For example, see Patrice C. McMahon and David P. Forsythe, "The ICTY's Impact on Serbia: Judicial Romanticism Meets Network Politics," *Human Rights Quarterly* 30, no. 2 (2008): 412-35.

75. Peskin interview, EU official, Brussels, Belgium, May 2008.

76. See International Crisis Group, "Trial by Fire: The Politics of the Special Tribunal for Lebanon," (2 December 2010). http://www.crisisgroup.org (accessed 13 December 2010).

77. See Gallup Balkan Monitor, http://www.balkan-monitor.eu (accessed 13 December 2010).

78. In a 2009 poll, when asked what role the ICTY plays in the future of the region, only 10 percent of Serbs responded that the ICTY "helps reconciliation and strengthens peace," a figure that has decreased over time. See, Gallup Balkan Monitor, http://www.balkan-monitor.eu; Eric Stover and Harvey M. Weinstein, eds., *My Neighbor, My Enemy: Justice and Community in the Aftermath of Mass Atrocity* (Cambridge: Cambridge University Press, 2004).

79. Denisa Kostovicova, ed., *The European Union and Transitional Justice: From Retributive to Restorative Justice in the Western Balkans* (Belgrade: Humanitarian Law Center, 2009). At the end of March 2010, the Serbian parliament narrowly approved a resolution that condemned the Srebrenica massacre.

80. "Mladic gets some charges dropped," United Press International, 3 December 2011. The charges relating to Srebrenica are still in place.

81. Address to the Security Council by Carla Del Ponte (18 June 2007). http://www.icty.org (accessed 13 December 2010).

82. The July 2010 ICJ ruling that Kosovo's 2008 declaration of independence did not violate international law provoked strong condemnation from the Serbian political elite but did not spur large demonstrations or violence.

Chapter 12

The EU and Roma Rights

Neil Cruickshank

A "security" measure introduced by France in August 2010 culminated in the deportation of hundreds of Roma (Gypsies) to Romania and Bulgaria, their respective countries of origin. According to French officials, Roma had been living illegally in France for a number of months preceding the removals, and were engaged in criminal behaviour and other anti-social activities. As the BBC reported on 19 October 2010, "the [French] president's office said the camps were 'sources of illegal trafficking, of profoundly shocking living standards, of exploitation of children for begging, of prostitution and crime.'" What France did (and in fact had done several times before), other than perpetuating an all too familiar stereotype, was violate several European Union (EU) directives, notably 2004/38/EC, which states "the free movement of persons constitutes one of the fundamental freedoms of the internal market, which comprises an area without internal frontiers, in which freedom is ensured in accordance with the provisions of the Treaty" (§ 2). Nongovernmental organizations (NGOs) such as the European Roma Rights Centre (ERRC) were quick to condemn France's callousness, but the overriding concern was with the overall lack of legal protections being extended to Romani travellers. Here was a clear-cut case of discrimination, the ERRC argued.

In a letter sent to President Sarkozy, the executive director of the ERRC wrote: "the ERRC. . . is deeply concerned about the measures announced by your office on 28 July 2010 which collectively implicate French Travellers and migrant Roma in crimes and call for their eviction and expulsion."[1] With all the publicity surrounding these deportations, and the involvement of the ERRC, the Commission could not ignore what was happening. A series of statements released that September and October made the Commission's position abundantly clear. Justice Commissioner Viviane Reding was quoted in *The New York Times*, saying "My patience is wearing thin. Enough is enough. . . no member state can expect special treatment when fundamental values and European laws are at stake."[2]

Though publicly critical of France and their use of enticements (of up to €300 per Rom) to facilitate removal, the Commission decided against formal infringement procedures. The European Parliament was less forgiving, however. On September 9th it passed a strongly worded resolution affirming the EU's commitment to mobility, equality, and minority rights, while at the same time condemning Paris for its failure to respect EU law and the Charter. It also took umbrage with the collection of fingerprints that preceded deportation and the Commission's "late and limited reaction" to the whole episode.[3] Along with European parliamentarians, various NGOs decried the actions as racist and illegal, calling out French lawmakers and President Nicolas Sarkozy in particular, for indiscriminately expelling Roma from France.

Most troubling to Europhiles is the fact that these evictions, which occurred in July and August, directly contravene European law. It is important to recognise as well, the law in question, free-movement/mobility, is perhaps (at least symbolically) the most important of all European laws. Moreover, deportations of this kind really cast doubt on the European culture of "rights" that has supposedly (and purportedly) developed lock-step with economic integration. In part, this chapter argues that a gulf still remains between what the EU says, in terms of minority protections and human rights, and what it can actually do, in terms of compelling member-states to adhere to EU law.[4] However, this chapter also argues that in many ways the EU *is* managing ethnic conflict, specifically conflict between Roma and non-Roma, through its various institutions, rules, and decision-making mediums. There is a tendency to overlook non-coercive intervention or at least downplay it. But as this chapter suggests, since the early 1990s the EU has managed to both exert influence over member-states in the area of Roma rights, and construct a discourse that shapes the trajectory of this on-going continental-wide ethnic conflict.

But why did not the Commission intervene more forcefully if the above is true, and France flouted European law? The Commission's reticence to initiate formal infringement proceedings against France likely owes to a perceived political need on its part to balance member-state sovereignty (and members' "national" security) with EU derived rights, including "free movement rights" (i.e. mobility rights) and "equality rights." Such is the nature of the EU that non-retributive mechanisms are routinely employed to force compliance, though this is not always the case. In 2007, for instance, its commissioner for the environment threatened Poland with severe sanctions if it continued with an infrastructural project it said would violate European law.[5] One can infer from this episode that the Commission is perfectly capable of threatening member-states should they ignore explicit instructions or violate EU law.

Justice Commissioner Viviane Reding was clear in her condemnation and in the steps France needed to take to rectify the situation.[6] In the end France did what the Commission asked. European laws were eventually transposed; the directive on freedom of movement is now codified in French law. However, the deportations highlight a systemic problem in inter-institutional relations, and pinpoint a deficiency that could limit what the EU can do in terms of managing ethnic conflict. As witnessed with France, member-states can play the "security card" when their actions are called into question. Even after the Commission had publicly chastised France, condemned their methods, and asked them to change what they were doing, French officials were *still* adamant that the forced removal of Roma was "legal and necessary to ensure public order."[7]

The EU can only do so much. But what it has done, in terms of establishing an atmosphere of tolerance and a policy framework that supports Roma integration, political rights, and social inclusion, is an important step in managing conflict between Roma and non-Roma, and between Roma and member-states. The norm-creating aspects of Europeanization[8] have thus far worked to (a) reposition the Roma "problem" from that of an exclusively national concern to one that is fundamentally "European," and (b) reconceive Roma as a "European" national minority requiring assistance from the EU (and other European organizations). The French deportations capture this new reality and offer a glimpse into how third party intervention will likely occur from this point forward. The "intervention" initiated by the Commission was neither coercive nor strictly hyperbolic, but a mix of enticements, public shaming, and soft power. And, despite public obstinacy, in the end, France bowed to the pressure being exerted by the Commission, Parliament, and NGOs, and changed its "Roma policy" so that it was no longer discriminatory.

As the above example suggests, human rights and mitigation of ethnic conflict are important parts of the European project. The Preamble of the *Charter of Fundamental Rights of the European Union*,[9] for example, reads: "Conscious of its spiritual and moral heritage, the Union is founded on the indivisible, universal values of human dignity, freedom, equality, and solidarity; it is based on the principles of democracy and the rule of law." Cognizant of the ethnic, linguistic, religious, and cultural differences found in Europe, the Framers (i.e. authors of the Charter) seem intent on establishing a European human rights regime, of sorts, that will draw all Europeans together under one political-cultural umbrella, potentially giving rise to a European demos. That may be overstating it a bit, but it is important to recognise similar language can be found in other foundational documents, such as the *Declaration of the Rights of Man and Citizen*, and the *American Declaration of Independence*. There is every indication that EU directives, whether strictly binding or not, have changed the way political actors think, act, and engage in contentious politics. This extends to ethnic conflict as well. By framing debate and presenting previously unanticipated options to state and non-state actors, it can be said that European law (along with governing structures) has had a strong empirical *and normative* influence on ethnic conflict resolution and the strategies employed to abate xenophobia and racism in the EU and accession countries.

The question is: can human rights "ideas" and "pronouncements" of the sort contained in the *Charter of Fundamental Rights of the European Union* and EU directives, and the development of a governance framework and human rights regime, combine to end (or mitigate) ethnic conflict between Roma and non-Roma in EU countries?

The EU and the Roma

This chapter, like others in this volume, concerns third party management of ethnic conflict. In this case the "third party" is the EU, which will be discussed below as a discrete political actor, even though directives, programmes, and recommendations concerning Roma emanate (and have emanated) from several institutions and organs, both at the supranational and intergovernmental levels. The EU Commission, European Parliament, European Council, European Network on Social Inclusion and Roma under the Structural Funds (a.k.a. EU Roma), and the European Union Agency for Fundamental Human Rights have all become involved with the Roma "problem." The Commission, through two Directorates General, (i) Employment, Social Affair and Inclusion, and (ii) Justice, has been able to coordinate European Roma Summits and the Platform for Roma Inclusion, and other *ad hoc* programmes in the sphere of Romani culture, employment, and integration. Two other European intergovernmental organizations will be discussed, the Organization for Security and Cooperation in Europe (OSCE) and Council of Europe (CoE), though only briefly and only to suggest that *all* European organizations have dedicated time and resources to managing this particular ethnic conflict. Along with the EU, the OSCE and CoE have been instrumental in developing policy guidelines/"action plans" for European governments. In many cases, the OSCE has taken a lead role both in investigating violent incidents involving Roma and issuing recommendations on how to solve the on-going socio-economic problems faced by Roma.[10]

This chapter will: first, briefly speak to the historical and socio-political context of ethnic conflict between Roma and non-Roma in Central Europe, paying particular attention to how this acute and protracted ethnic conflict developed and has been perpetuated; second, examine the pre-accession period to demonstrate how the European Commission, by way of "carrot" *and* "stick," managed to bring new democracies, e.g. the Czech Republic and Slovakia, into alignment with EU law and its culture of rights and; third, isolate examples post-accession to show that, like turning a ship at sea, mitigating ethnic conflict altogether will take some time, especially when the conflict has gone on undiminished for centuries. Institutional convergence has led to the development of a concrete human rights framework in Europe, which among other things, encourages European institutions and NGOs to investigate the policies and practices of local and national governments. This is perhaps the only way to change the culture of impunity that surrounds anti-*ziganism* in many parts of Europe.

The Context

Now that Roma are EU citizens and the states where they reside (e.g. the Czech Republic, Bulgaria, Hungary, Poland, Slovakia, and Romania) enmeshed in a regular regime *par excellence*, it seems more appropriate than ever to consider how various EU instruments, including the Charter, anti-racism/equality Directives, and the Council Framework Decision on combating racism and xenophobia (2008/913/JHA), have worked to alter repertoires of contention at the European and nation-state levels.[11] Without doubt, EU institutions and directives have fundamentally altered political opportunity structures available to Roma advocacy organizations and/or human-rights NGOs, and have facilitated the development and delivery of inclusion/integration programmes in several post-communist member-states. An equally important advance, and one that should not be overlooked when investigating the emergent Roma rights discourse in Europe, is the introduction of the Charter of Fundamental Rights into European primary law. Taken together they have contributed greatly to the ideational and normative fabric of the EU. A fabric, in the end, that encourages associational affiliation, collective action, and non-traditional forms of conflict management involving states, NGOs, and a constellation of other political actors at the local, national, and European levels.

Ethnic conflict usually involves (a) a claim-maker, normally a discernible ethnic group (or minority group), and (b) a state, or similarly sovereign political unit. Rodolfo Stavenhagen, for instance, argues "ethnic conflicts usually pit a specific ethnic group against an ethnocratic state—that is, a nation-state controlled essentially by a majority or dominant ethnic group, which is able to exercise cultural hegemony over the rest of the nation."[12] Other "types" of ethnic conflict do occur, Stavenhagen suggests, many of which involve neither states nor governments, nor even intergovernmental organizations for that matter. For instance, conflict can develop horizontally between two or more ethnic groups in the same state without the "state" figuring into the conflict, as either an initiator or recipient of contentious collective action. Such conflict, as Stavenhagen points out, would "not directly implicate the state as one of the antagonists."[13] In the case of European Roma, conflict exists between Roma and the state on one level, and Roma and majority populations on the other.

Neo-Nazi/skinhead hate crimes and physical attacks are an obvious manifestation of this cleavage. Though perpetrated by a small minority, such violence contributes to the overall climate of fear. In the Czech Republic between 1990 and 1998, for instance, fifteen hundred separate attacks were reported, resulting in nearly thirty deaths.[14] Because of this widespread, encompassing antiziganism, Roma have become marginalised at both societal and political levels, possessing few citizenship rights and almost no social advantage. Joseph Rudolph argues "where they [Roma] reside, the Romany continue to live in the worst conditions of any community, and their poverty continues to grow."[15]

What is challenging about this case, and why pinpointing dependent variables (or identifying causal pathways) can feel like guesswork sometimes, is because, in the EU, ethnic conflict between Roma and non-Roma involves a multitude of actors and agencies, protagonists and antagonists, from far-right political parties like Jobbik[16] to encompassing, long-established intergovernmental organizations like the OSCE. These European actors, and many others, exist in a highly stratified polity with many loci of power. When you combine this multi-level arrangement with Europe's only pan-European nation, the Roma, you end up with a very complex and complicated conflict spanning twenty-seven member states, involving at least four intergovernmental organizations (the United Nations, EU, OSCE, and CoE), and countless NGOs, advocacy organizations, and philanthropic associations. Moreover, the ethnic conflicts of today, in Slovakia, Hungary, the Czech Republic, and France for that matter, are rooted in cleavages that predate the EU by nearly seven hundred years.

Who are the Roma?

Roma, a heterogeneous group numbering between 12-15 million, have lived in all parts of Europe from around the 14th century (or earlier). Since their introduction to Europe from northern India, Roma have experienced all manner of cruel and inhumane treatment. More recently (i.e. the twentieth century), Roma have been targeted for "liquidation" and "assimilation." During the Holocaust, for example, Roma were forcibly relocated and murdered by occupying Nazi forces (and pro-Nazi governments). During the Nazi occupation, Czechoslovakia's Romani population was nearly liquidated, with only about 5 percent of the pre-war population surviving the "devouring" (or *porajmos*).[17] During the communist period, attempts were made to fully assimilate Roma, in many instances forcing the abandonment of traditional Roma vocations and nomadism, not to mention the Romani language. Many countries tried to control Romani population growth though the sterilization of Romani women.

In 1972, for example, Czechoslovak authorities initiated a "formal" programme of non-voluntary sterilization. The dissident group Charter 77 called attention to this practice in the late 1970s, making many Czechs aware of a policy they knew nothing about. One of their reports, Charter 77 Document No. 23/1978, references the practice of forced sterilization. It reads:

> Particularly serious is the sterilization issue, which is admissible in cases with proper medical justification, sometimes perhaps necessary, although always dubious in moral terms. The consent of Romani women to sterilization is obtained through persuasion, the impartiality of which is not guaranteed. . . . Thus sterilization becomes one of the policies of the majority population against the minority population directed at preventing childbirths in the minority ethnic group.

Charter 77 was not able to stop the practice. After the collapse of communism in 1989, many NGOs actively sought to put an end to the practice of coercive or forced sterilization once and for all. Czech NGOs, IQ Roma Servis, ERRC, *Ligalidskýchpráv* (League of Human Rights), and *Vzájemnésoužití* (Living Together) initiated a claim on behalf of ten Romani women and subsequently helped the Czech Public Defender of Rights collect information from the complainants. A total of eighty-seven cases were presented to the Minister of Health before a final report on this matter was released in 2005.

The Czech Ministry of Health still maintains that all sterilizations that were carried out by doctors were both medically necessary and non-discriminatory, and neither a racial nor nationalistic policy. However, the Regional Court in Ostrava ordered the City Hospital in Ostrava to pay one of the complainants, Iveta Červeňáková, Kč 500,000 (approximately £16,600) in damages. According to her lawyer, this is the first time a Czech court awarded damages to a Romani woman for being coercively sterilized. NGOs played a vital role in bringing about this particular settlement and also bringing this once "accepted" practice to the attention of the European and international community. Many people were shocked to learn such barbarism continued long after the collapse of communism.

Roma have managed to survive *in spite* of a never-ending series of social, political, and economic obstacles, and policies intended to bring about their demise. Barany captures this dynamic:

> Marginality–the condition of being subordinated to or excluded by others–is the central theme in the Romani experience. Indeed, Romani marginality is far more comprehensive than that of the Jews, Kurds, or other traditionally excluded or disadvantaged groups. Since their arrival in Europe about seven centuries ago, the Gypsies have been politically, socially, culturally, and economically marginalised by the dominant populations of the region. . . . although political systems and their policies toward Roma have changed, these variations have had little apparent effect on Gypsy marginality.[18]

Roma have also borne the brunt of transitional angst and anger. With the introduction of liberal democracy and the free market, socio-economic conditions actually worsened for Central and Eastern European Roma. Unemployment went up while their political capital went down. Whereas under communism Roma were guaranteed employment, an apartment, and subsistence income, post communism they have been left to languish in what amount to Roma ghettos, very often miles away from urban centers, infrastructure, and public transit. As Istvan Pogány reports, "hundreds of thousands of Roma, particularly in Slovakia, Romania, Bulgaria and in parts of the former Yugoslavia, live in settlements with limited access to clean drinking water, sanitation or basic medical care."[19] Awareness of these problems does not seem to correlate with purposeful action on the part of lawmakers to ameliorate them. Awareness is at an all-time high, but poor living conditions remain a feature of the Roma condition.[20] In this way democratization has not been entirely enabling for Roma. However, since the collapse of communism, the wars in the former Yugoslavia, and EU expansion, particularly eastward in 2004 and 2007, minority rights have gained a level of acceptance previously unfathomable. The liberal philosopher Will Kymlicka argues that "since 1989 we have witnessed a remarkable trend toward the internationalization of minority rights issues in the European context."[21] The irony is, despite impressive institutional change and a focus on minority rights and multiculturalism, all economic and political indicators would suggest things are progressively getting worse for Roma.

As Rick Fawn argues, "if one group of people seems today to be consistently verbally derided, subjected to physical abuse, social marginalization and even legal disenfranchisement in the post-communist space, it is them [Roma]."[22] As a recognizable minority group (but not always), Roma in all parts of Europe continue to experience abuse. But as a heterogeneous and dispersed (and at the same time insular) group, Roma still lack the sort of national identity, and by extension political clout, needed to dismantle impediments to substantive societal change. And, unlike the Scots or Welsh, Roma are without a delimited territory to call "their own." The conditions may therefore be ripe for the development of a pan-European Romani nation.[23] Part of the reason for this mobilization lag is on-going uncertainty around the size and shape of Europe's Roma community. Demographic problems are not easily overcome, as many

> "ethnic Roma" (to use an imprecise term) seem unwilling and/or unable to self-identify as Roma. In a recent interview with the *International Business Times*, NidhiTrehan suggested, "because of centuries of persecution, many Roma are loathe to reveal their identity, as it could be tantamount to social suicide; this holds true for many Roma who can 'pass' or assimilate (either because of lighter skin colour or better education). Over generations, some Romani families have completely assimilated."[24]

Census data have been used to control Roma, monitor their movement as justification for assimilatory policy, and as a way for the deporting authority to justify forcible relocation or renationalization. It has often been argued, and recent events in France and Italy seem to confirm this, that Roma are from "somewhere else" and as a result do not (and should not) normally qualify for residency and/or citizenship. This was certainly the case in late 1992 when Czechoslovakia was set to split along federal lines, as many Roma living in the Czech half were effectively prohibited from obtaining citizenship in the "new" sovereign Czech Republic. Roma living in the Czech lands were forced to relocate there from Slovakia decades earlier. So it seemed odd (and seemingly discriminatory) that Czech officials in 1992 were all of a sudden demanding proof of residency from Roma.

The Pre-Accession Period

Since the early 1990s the pre-accession period has become for the European Union a way to prepare non-member states for membership, and in more fundamental ways than just harmonising tariffs, currency, and weights and measures. It gives older member states in Western Europe an opportunity to share their socio-political and economic habits with accession states. Accession is therefore more than just juridical harmonization and economic symmetry. It is an opportunity for existing members to bring future members around to their position; a way to instil new members (and new democracies, as it were) with a particular set of norms and values. This period offers Commissioners a chance to evaluate structures and processes of accession states, critique existing law and institutions, and pressure national lawmakers into conformity. It was during this process in the late 1990s and early 2000s that the issue of Romani integration and rights gained momentum and a place on the political agenda.

In 1993 the European Council (EC) responded to the collapse of Soviet communism and resulting geo-political changes in Central and Eastern Europe by issuing a concrete, albeit porous, statement concerning Eastward expansion. The EC declared "membership requires that the candidate country has achieved stability of institutions guaranteeing democracy, the rule of law, human rights and respect for and protection of minorities."[25]

An Immediate Test of Resolve: Usti nad Labem's "Separation Wall"

The maltreatment of Central European Roma was on the accession agenda almost immediately, and the Commission had singled out the Czech Republic and Slovakia as persistent violators of Roma human rights. In 1999 the EU pledged to support "both financially and politically, social programmes aimed at improving the situation of the Roma minority in the Czech Republic." A year earlier the EU was confronted with a rather clear-cut case of racism in a potential candidate country. In the Czech towns Usti nad Labem and Plzen, the town council approved the building of "separation walls," which would have in effect ghettoised the Roma populations of those towns. Usti nad Labem's Mayor, Ladislav Hruska, was quoted as saying:

> The wall is about one group that obeys the laws of the Czech Republic and behaves according to good morals, and about a group that breaks these rules—doesn't pay rent, doesn't use proper hygiene and doesn't do anything right. . . . This is not a racial problem. It is a problem of dealing with decent and indecent people.[26]

This controversial project drew criticism from national Roma associations, international human rights groups, and the EU, with the latter suggesting that the

Czech Republic's membership bid would be harmed if the physical segregation of Roma were permitted to continue. As the BBC reported on 26 February 1999, "the gypsies of Usti nad Labem believe what can help them now is the Czech Republic's eagerness for membership of the European Union. . . . As the accession talks continue, the diplomatic pressure is growing on Prague to improve its record on human rights."[27] With the central government's prompting (and financial assistance), the wall separating the Roma from the non-Roma was eventually torn down. Five years later the Czech Republic joined the EU.

At the time, Usti nad Labem's "Roma wall" was a cause of consternation amongst the Czech Republic's friends and allies. Then, only a decade into democratization, the Czech Republic was still very much in the process of discovering a place in the new, post-Soviet (post-Cold War) world order. They joined the North Atlantic Treaty Organization (NATO) only a couple of months before the "Roma wall" controversy erupted. The United States Agency for International Development (USAID) had closed their mission in Prague two years earlier, after delivering approximately US $ 169 million in transitional aid to Czech authorities between 1990 and 1997.[28] Drawing criticism from the United States, a vocal proponent of their candidature for NATO and WTO membership, was not a terribly good thing.[29] The Czech government of Miloš Zeman was feeling pressure from European and international NGOs, the UN, the EU and OSCE, and the Americans. They really had no choice but to intervene.

Here then was a clear case of a candidate country (with the Czech Republic having begun accession negotiations 31 March 1998) flouting the Copenhagen Criteria. Perhaps the lure of Union membership was enough to compel Czech authorities to intervene and order the wall's demolition. While this incident is an acute example of bigotry, it is consistent with how Roma are generally viewed, treated, and dealt with throughout the Czech Republic and much of Central Europe. The solution, according to the Commission, involves cooperation between all levels of government.

> The European institutions and Member States have a joint responsibility to improve the social inclusion of Roma by using all the instruments and policies for which they have the respective competence. . . . The European Union has a strong legal framework to combat Roma discrimination, based among others, on article 13 of the Treaty of the European Community and the Directive 2000/43/EC on racial equality. Member States have the duty to translate the Directive into their own national legislations.[30]

The myriad institutions, actors, organizations, and associations monitoring the implementation of European law make it virtually impossible for governments to ignore the "legal framework" and get away with it.

European Integration and Citizenship

From the outset the European project oscillated between intergovernmentalism, premised on inter-state negotiation, sovereign equality, and consensus decision making, and supranationalism, which led to the construction of European institutions, Community directives, and ideational or normative networks (i.e. Europeanization). A recent report on EU citizenship, discussing some of the problems associated with Europeanization and extension of rights to all member-states, provides a good summary of how EU citizenship is construed.

> The concept of citizenship of the European Union, introduced by the Treaty of Maastricht in 1992, added a new political dimension to the hitherto primarily economic nature of European integration. Every person holding the nationality of an EU Member State is now also automatically a citizen of the European Union. EU citizenship does not replace national citizenship. Instead, it confers upon all EU citizens an *additional* set of rights, guaranteed by the EU Treaties, which lie at the heart of their everyday lives.[31]

The polycentric nature of post-Maastricht Europe, replete with new and different loci/spheres of political power, judicial (and judicial-like) institutions and ideational frameworks, has significantly altered the nature and scope of contentious politics.[32] When the Czech Republic, for instance, acceded to the *acquis communautaire* in 2004, it was joining a polity with established transnational pathways. It would no longer be politics as usual. First, issue salience emerged as the most important determinant of political action. Interest groups and NGOs seem unconstrained by political and/or geographic barriers and are more willing to support local campaigners. They see benefit in collaborative enterprise. Second, advocacy groups now have multiple access points from which to enter and/or influence the policy process, and importantly are not beholden to "normal" lobbying techniques; money is also less important. Traditional forms of collective action, lobbying, and protest have given way to non-traditional forms, which are characteristically episodic, transnational, and multidimensional. As Laura Cram suggests "the decision to embark on any form of collective action is, of course, made within the context of a set of opportunities facilitating collective action and of a set of constraints inhibiting the prospect of collaboration."[33] And third, an impressive corpus of European and international law has had an equalizing effect, as many member-states are entirely unsure about the nature and function of human rights law.

Governance and Europeanization

In some respects the EU is a polity *sui generis*. The NGOs, advocacy organizations, and professional associations that inhabit European civil society have been instrumental in determining its structure and function. Roma are utilising EU institutions, European-level judicial bodies (i.e. European Court of Human Rights), and other European and non-European organizations, namely the United Nations and the OSCE,[34] to advance grievances and ultimately change discriminatory policy and practice. Central to post-accession Romani activism and repertoires of contention, then, is the notion of European governance, which offers groups institutional opportunities, a new ideational framework and/or participant-friendly political culture, and ultimately a more extensive network of human rights NGOs and related policy communities.[35]

As a result of the EU Commission's 2001 *White Paper on Governance*, the European space (or polity), and chiefly the European Commission, Parliament, and ancillary agencies, became much more accommodating to civil society associations, NGOs, lobbyists, and in particular minority groups. The *White Paper* sought to ameliorate many of the problems, both real and perceived, that were contributing to the Union's democratic deficit. In this instance "deficit" refers to the apparent gulf between decision makers in Brussels and the European citizenry, and a corollary of this, the absence of input legitimacy in the development of Union law. To make the Union more relevant, accountable, and connected to Europeans, governance was proposed and subsequently incorporated into the European Constitutional Treaty and the Treaty of Lisbon, with the latter having taken effect December 2009.

Governance is a much more inclusive decision-making model than government as it includes both traditional political institutions and actors, e.g. legislatures and political parties, and third sector organizations, social movements, and supranational bodies in policy making. It reflects the reality of Europe's multilevel programme with its emphasis on consensus, non-zero-sum bargaining, and shared goals. As G.P.E. Walzenbach argues, "European governance has become the most appropriate overarching term to capture the complex, dynamic and fast-changing features of the interdependent institutional ensembles operating at subnational, national, and supra-national levels."[36] Here, governance has proven a cost-effective solution to the Union's looming (or existing) legitimation crisis, a way of encouraging the development of a participant political culture, improving the Union's image, and ultimately injecting "democracy" into the decision-making process.

European political integration has been hastened by a whole host of considerations and developments that have for the most been dealt with *ad hoc*. Beate Kohler-Koch identifies a very real conundrum:

> The transfer of decision-making power to Brussels may take it out of reach for local grassroots activists. But European governance may also open opportunities for societal groups that so far had been excluded. . . . That is to say, new opportunity structures may distribute the chances for political actors to raise their voice in the decision-making process unevenly.[37]

Institutions therefore have an enabling and/or constraining effect on the actors who utilise them. Changes in procedure, either official or unofficial, can dramatically change the political opportunities available to a given constituency, interest sector, or lobby. Equally important are rule changes and/or new regulation, which impact intergovernmental relations and accepted practice. Europeanization, in a word, encapsulates the European project. With multiple venues, Europe is redefining the nature, scope, and character of contentious collective action and, by extension, how rights are articulated and understood. Among other things this means marginalized "Europeans" are able to utilise European institutions, lobby European officials (and parliamentarians), and pressure national lawmakers vis-à-vis European policy communities and minority rights networks. Citizenship at the European level could be construed as encouragement (a carrot), inviting individuals and groups (NGOs. etc.) to recalibrate strategies and tactics for a highly disaggregated, fluid, and "open" policy arena. EU citizenship confers rights; EU institutions offer Roma (and Roma organizations) political opportunities. The combination of the two, a new rights discourse coupled with receptive institutions, has encouraged third party intervention—orchestrated by EU and European institutions and European NGOs, in episodes of ethnic conflict. Moreover, inaction or non-intervention is now viewed disparagingly by the same stakeholders. The French example, again, speaks to this new reality.

Post Accession

A wall very similar to the one erected in Usti nad Labem was recently constructed in the Slovak town, Ostrovany. The conditions in these so-called Romani settlements are very poor indeed. For instance, "there are more than 600 Roma settlements in Slovakia where people live without electricity, sewage or running water, most located far from the relatively affluent capital Bratislava."[38] As reported in the *Sunday Times*, "the most solidly built structure in the Roma ghetto in Ostrovany is the wall dividing it from the rest of the village, built with €13,000 (£11,300) of public funds to separate those living in conditions of medieval squalor from their better-off non-Roma neighbours."[39] The concrete wall is a stark reminder of the schism that exists between the majority Slovak and minority Roma populations, though Roma comprise nearly 10 percent of the total population. Like Usti nad Labem, the wall in Ostrovany is causing EU officials to think twice about existing Roma policy and the sincerity of member states when it comes to its numerous Roma initiatives. However, unlike Usti nad Labem, the EU has been relatively quiet about the wall in Ostrovany. The ERRC reports "The lack of legal or political condemnation of the wall in Ostrovany sent a signal to other municipalities. The wall in Ostrovany has been tolerated for more than a year and in the meantime similar walls have been built in other localities in Slovakia."[40]

A similarly disquieting example of chauvinism (or callousness) comes via a pig farm in Lety, south Bohemia Czech Republic, which today operates on the site of a WWII era "gypsy" concentration camp. In 1998 the Czech government agreed with Romani advocates that a permanent museum should be built on the Lety site to commemorate the Romani holocaust (or *porajmos*[41]) and specifically those who died at Lety. However, recently government "shelved" the idea of relocating the pig farm and constructing a commemorative museum on the site. As reported, "PM Petr Nečas has announced his government will not be moving the pig farm from the site of the former concentration camp at Lety."[42]

In a statement issued by the European Parliament on anti-discrimination, it called for sweeping policy reform in several sectors, with housing, healthcare, and education atop the "most pressing" list. The EP press release concluded, "MEPs urge the Commission to shape a Community Action Plan on Roma Inclusion, to give one Commissioner [sole] responsibility for coordinating a policy and to promote Roma staff within its structure."[43] According to the EP, "ghettoization" of the Roma is a very real concern, as many Roma exist at the periphery of society. The EP suggested the nearly 10 million Roma, the majority of which gained EU citizenship after the 2004 and 2007 enlargements, deserve special protection. Parliamentarians believe "the situation of European Roma communities is distinct from other national minorities, they say, arguing that this justifies specific measures at European level."[44] The press release did not specifically mention the Czech Republic, but it did say something concrete about coercive sterilization. "In addition, extreme human rights abuses. . . including racial segregation in health facilities and coercive sterilisation of Romani women must be ended."[45]

The Other European Organizations

While the EU has taken up the issue of Roma political disenfranchisement and social marginalization, it is by no means the only European-based organization working with Roma and European governments to solve the so-called Roma "problem." The Council of Europe, and its court, the European Court of Human Rights (ECHR), along with the OSCE, have done a great deal to help create Europe's new human rights regime. For example, in *D. H. and Others vs. the Czech Republic*, the ECHR found the Czech Republic to be in violation of the European Convention of Human Rights. By permitting the *de facto* segregation of Romani school children, Czech officials were condoning what the Court saw as discriminatory policies. Remarkable for several reasons, this decision goes a long way in shirring up the European "human rights regime."

The OSCE and Commission on Security and Cooperation in Europe (CSCE) have been involved in a number of ways. The U.S. Department of State, for example, publicly chastised the Czech government for its poor treatment of Roma. At a hearing on 15 August 2006, the CSCE discussed the matter of eugenics and coercive sterilization in Slovakia and the Czech Republic. The commission report, *Accountability and Impunity: Investigations into Sterilization without Informed Consent in the Czech Republic and Slovakia,* was informed by the testimony of two NGO representatives, Gwendolyn Albert from the League of Human Rights and Claude Cahn of the ERRC. It subsequently issued reservations and recommendations to the Czech and Slovak governments. The report was particularly critical of the way the Czech government investigated allegations of coercive sterilization, as the Czech Ministry of Health was in effect investigating itself. The CSCE called this a "conflict of interest."[46]

The OSCE has published numerous reports on Roma maltreatment, in political custody and more generally, and remains an active third party to the conflict. The Office for Democracy and Human Rights has taken a keen interest in how member states treat Roma and the proposals they have put forward to hasten Roma integration. Their website offers a comprehensive list of activities, from working "with interior ministries and law-enforcement institutions to build trust and understanding between police and Roma and to encourage young Roma to join police forces" to reviewing the "implementation of the OSCE's Action Plan on Improving the Situation of Roma and Sinti Within the OSCE Area."[47]

Conclusions

In trying to establish an encompassing human rights regime, ameliorate ethnic conflict in accession countries, and bring twenty-seven distinct systems into conformity, the European Commission and ancillary offices (e.g. European Network on Social Inclusion and Roma under the Structural Funds—EU Roma;[48] European Union Agency for Fundamental Human Rights[49]) have been forced to confront and deal with widespread, often disquieting forms of racism directed at Roma. The Commission is in an awkward position, as frequently its desire for accelerated political integration is at odds with its stated commitment to human rights and equality, especially in relation to citizen and mobility rights. Also, its desire to develop a European demos, discover input legitimacy, and solve the so-called democratic deficit, appears to be at odds with its deference to state sovereignty in matters relating to Roma. What is clear is that the EU's inability or unwillingness to sanction states like France, Slovakia, and Italy (to name a few) over Romani maltreatment and discrimination is leading many NGOs to wonder just how serious the Commission really is when it comes to curtailing ethnic conflict in post-communist Europe. For example, it seems few member states have taken the *Council Framework Decision* (2008/913/JHA) *of 28 November 2008 on Combating Certain Forms and Expressions of Racism and Xenophobia by Means of Criminal Law* very seriously. As Amnesty International reported in 2010, Hungary has yet to develop a comprehensive database or policies that would permit Hungarian and European officials to track and evaluate hate crimes (especially crimes directed at Roma), which is an expressed feature of several agreements to which it is a party.[50]

What the EU has done thus far, in terms of establishing policy and "best practice" guidelines in the sphere or Roma rights, could either be hailed as an extraordinary accomplishment or a decidedly underwhelming start, depending upon the criteria one uses. An underwhelming start because the EU has only just begun to seriously push states to use structural funds for the development and administration of inclusion and integration programmes, which would help offset some of the costs incurred by NGOs, philanthropic bodies, and European Union funding agencies. This is disquieting, as many of the problems identified by the Commission and NGOs (i.e. ERRC) date back to the pre-accession period (or before).On the other hand, what the Commission has been able to accomplish in less than a decade is extraordinary, considering the complex and complicated nature of the problem (i.e. coordination among levels of government), and the fact that at least three levels of government come into play in most policy areas. It does appear, however, that not only is policy convergence beginning to occur but also the EU's value as a norm entrepreneur is starting to pay off in dividends.

Anti-Roma sentiment, common in many post-communist states, is best characterised as racism and hostility toward European gypsies (i.e. Roma), and a general dislike of Romani custom and tradition. The EU is essentially battling hundreds of years of often hardened, institutionalised, and entrenched forms of Roma-phobia. So to think it can end social marginalization and disenfranchisement of Roma in a couple decades is, unfortunately, unrealistic. Over the past few years, however, more and more people have come to learn of the hardships experienced by Roma, in Central Europe as well as in other accession countries, and how their story reads more like a tragedy than anything else.

When the EU agreed to admit post-communist states in 2004 and 2007, it was fully aware of the Roma "problem" and the many ethno-linguistic (and religious) cleavages criss-crossing Central and Eastern Europe.[51] Anticipating problems, it hastily introduced the Copenhagen Criteria in 1993. Around the same time, Community leaders began to assist with democratization and harmonization by initiating the PHARE (or Phare[52]) programme and several other pre-accession instruments. The concern of ethnic conflict was borne out during the accession process, when xenophobia, intolerance, and racism seemed to dominate newspaper headlines in Europe and North America. A page one *Toronto Star* headline of 15 April 1995, which reads "Violent Racism Spreading Like Wildfire Across Europe," speaks to the severity of it all. And the Usti nab Labem separation wall, documented cases of coercive sterilization, policies of segregated schooling, and the growing frequency of neo-Nazi demonstrations and attacks seem to support such an interpretation. This being said, integration and institutional isomorphism has been responsible for establishing a rights discourse that clearly and unequivocally condemns racism and any other practice that lead to the marginalization of Roma.

In the end, one is left wondering how "governance" and "economic integration" can alter longstanding ethnic and socio-economic cleavages that, in some European states, have recently deepened. Exacerbated by recession and rising unemployment, anti-Roma rhetoric has been used to fuel populism and right-wing political campaigns (e.g., Jobbik in Hungary). But this is only one side of the story. The other side, a more hopeful side, has seen an increasing awareness of Roma issues, especially in the sphere of human rights, and the contribution made by Roma in all sectors in all European countries. The Decade of Roma Inclusion, 2005-2015, the annual Roma summits organised by the Commission and its NGO partners, the development of the Fundamental Rights Agency in 2007, and investigations into the causes and consequences of Roma-phobia point to a stakeholder-driven process that is trying to fundamentally change the nature of Roma/non-Roma relations. This will definitely take time. But facilitated through a supranational institution like the European Commission, and aided by countless NGOs in Europe and elsewhere, chances are good that discrimination and ethnic violence directed at Roma will decrease over time, with the caveat that the EU continues to emphasise human rights and citizenship.

Notes

1. The full letter can be found at the European Roma Rights Centre website, http://www.errc.org/cms/ upload/file/france-sarkozy-evictions-expulsions-july-2010.pdf (accessed 18 October 2012).

2. See Katrin Bennhold and Stephen Castle, "E.U. Calls France's Roma Expulsions a 'Disgrace,'" *The New York Times*, 14 September, 2010. On-line http://www.nytimes.com/2010/09/15/world/europe/15roma.html (accessed 18 October 2012).

3. For a summary of the resolution, see http://www.europarl.europa.eu/sides/ get-Doc.do?language=en&type=IM-PRESS&reference=20100909IPR81794 (accessed 19 October 2012).

4. See Michael Johns, "'Do as I Say, Not as I Do: The European Union, Eastern Europe and Minority Rights," *East European Politics and Societies* 17, no. 4 (November 2003): 682-699.

5. EU commissioner for the environment, Stavros Dimas, threatened to deny Poland structural monies if it proceeded with a bridge project over the Rospuda valley in north-east Poland. The Commission deemed the valley an ecologically sensitive area and did everything it could to quash the project. According to Dimas, Poland was, among other things, in violation of the Birds Directive (2009/147/EC) and Habitats Directive (92/43/EEC). Contentious politics lasted from 2007 to 2009, and was resolved only when Prime Minister Donald Tusk ordered the road re-routed away from the valley.

6. See BBC "EU warns France of action over Roma" (29 September 2010), http://www.bbc.co.uk/news/world-europe-11437361 (accessed 19 October 2012).

7. "EC suspends actions over France Roma expulsions," *The Telegraph,* October 19, 2010. On-line version: http://www.telegraph.co.uk/news/worldnews/europe/france/ 8073216/EC-suspends-action-over-France-Roma-expulsions.html (accessed 19 October 2012).

8. Claudio Radaelli provides a useful definition of Europeanization: "Europeanization consists of processes of (a) construction, (b) diffusion, (c) institutionalization of formal and informal rules, procedures, policy paradigms, styles, "ways of doing things" and

shared beliefs and norms." See Claudio Radaelli, "The Europeanization of Public Policy," in *The Politics of Europeanization*, eds. K.Featherstone and C. Radaelli (Oxford: Oxford University Press, 2003), 30. This is a particularly illuminating conception of Europeanization because it regards institutional change and changes to the normative order as reinforcing phenomena. Kohler-Koch discusses a similar phenomenon but relates it to governance. For her, "governance has an ideational dimension as well as an organizational one." See Beate Kohler-Koch, "The Evolution and Transformation of European Governance," in *The Transformation of Governance in the European Union*, eds. Beate Kohler-Koch and Rainer Eising (UK: Routledge, 1999).

9. Hereafter, "the Charter."

10. See OSCE, "Addressing Violence, Promoting Integration: Field Assessment of Violent Incidents Against Roma in Hungary, June-July 2009," (Warsaw, 15 June 2010).

11. Charles Tilly and Sidney Tarrow define "contentious repertoires" as "arrays of contentious performances that are currently known and available within some set of political actors" in *Contentious Politics* (Boulder Co.: Paradigm Publishers 2007), 202.

12. Rodolfo Stavenhagen, *Ethnic Conflicts and the Nation-State* (New York: St. Martin's Press, 1996), 9.

13. Stavenhagen, *Ethnic Conflicts and the Nation-State,* 9.

14. Rick Fawn, "Czech Attitudes Toward the Roma: Expecting More of Havel's Country," *Europe-Asia Studies* 53, no. 8 (2001): 1198.

15. See Joseph Rudolph, *Politics and Ethnicity: A Comparative Study* (New York: Palgrave Macmillan), 154.

16. Jobbik, a right-wing political party in Hungary, gained prominence by way of anti-Semitic and anti-Roma rhetoric.

17. See http://www.ceskapozice.cz/en/news/society/holocaust-%E2%80%98 devouring%E2%80%99-czech-roma (accessed 19 October 2012).

18. Zoltan Barany, *The East European Gypsies: Regime Change, Marginality, and Ethnopolitics* (Cambridge, MA: Cambridge University Press, 2002), 2.

19. See Istvan Pogány, *The Roma Café: Human Rights and the Plight of the Romani People* (London: Pluto Press, 2004), 1.

20. For a more detailed analysis of European Roma, see Will Guy, ed, *Between Past and Future: the Roma of Central and Eastern Europe* (Hertfordshire: University of Hertfordshire Press, 2001); Ian Hancock, *We are the Romani People* (Hertfordshire: University of Hertfordshire Press, 2005); Den Ringold, Mitchell A. Orenstein, and Erika Wilkens, *Roma in an Expanding Europe: Breaking the Poverty Cycle* (Washington: The World Bank Press, 2005); Isabel Fonseca, *Bury Me Standing: The Gypsies and their Journey* (New York, NY: Random House, 1996).

21. Will Kymlicka, "National Minorities in Post-Communist Europe: The Role of International Norms and European Integration," in *Ethnic Politics After Communism*, eds. Zoltan Barany and Robert Moser (Ithaca: Cornell University Press, 2005), 191.

22. Fawn, "Czech Attitudes Toward the Roma," 1193.

23. For an overview of Romani political mobilization and socio-economic conditions, see Guy, *Between Past and Future: The Roma of Central and Eastern Europe*; Peter Vermeersch, *The Romani Movement: Minority Politics and Ethnic Mobilization in Contemporary Central Europe* (Berghahn Books, 2007); and Barany, *The East European Gypsies*.

24. Palash R. Ghosh, "Interview: The Status of Roma, Part I," *International Business Times*, 8 September 2010.

25. "Presidency Conclusion: Copenhagen European Council, 21-22 June 1993." European Council. http://www.europarl.europa.eu/enlargement/ec/pdf/cop_en.pdf (accessed August 21, 2012).

26. Jane Perlez, "Usti nad Labem Journal; A Wall Not Yet Built Casts the Shadow of Facism," *The New York Times*, July 2, 1998, On-line: http://www.nytimes.com/1998/07/02/world/usti-nad-labem-journal-a-wall-not-yet-built-casts-the-shadow-of-racism.html.

27. Janet Barrie, "World: Europe Hiding Gypsies Behind a Wall." *BBC*, February 26, 1999. http://news.bbc.co.uk/2/hi/europe/286704.stm (accessed August 21, 2012).

28. See USAID, http://www.usaid.gov/locations/europe_eurasia/countries/cz/index.html (accessed 19 October 2012).

29. Rep. Christopher H. Smith, Chairman of the Commission for Security and Cooperation in Europe, along with his co-chair, Senator Ben Nighthorse Campbell, released a damning statement in October 1999. One section reads: "The wall in Usti nad Labem is a symbol of intolerance and racism against Roma that cannot be allowed to stand in today's Europe." In another section Smith said, "The human rights situation in the Czech Republic has taken an alarming turn for the worse."

30. See European Commission: Employment, Social Affairs and Inclusion web page. http://ec.europa.eu/social/main.jsp?catId=518&langId=en (accessed September 25, 2010).

31. http://ec.europa.eu/justice/policies/citizenship/docs/com_2010_603_en.pdf (accessed September 25, 2010).

32. The notion of ideational framework refers to a cluster of ideas, norms, and even practices that impact politics and political action. An ideational framework constitutes a separate, albeit interconnected sphere that shapes behavior and influences institutionalized politics. The "idea" of governance is just as important as the institutions of governance; the "idea" of advocacy is just as important as the institutions that enable it.

33. Laura Cram, "The EU Institutions and Collective Action: Constructing a European Interest," in *Collective Action in the European Union: Interest and the New Politics of Associability,* eds. Justin Greenwood and Mark Aspinwall (New York: Routledge, 1998), 64.

34. OSCE's Office for Democratic Institutions and Human Rights has published several reports and "action plans" summarizing the plight of Roma and proposing short and long-term policy to help mitigate some of the institutionally generated prejudices that negatively affect Roma and Sinti. A report entitled *Implementation of the Action Plan on Improving the Situation of Roma and Sinti Within the OSCE Area* emphasizes human security, police brutality, and educational opportunities.

35. Referencing J.N. Rosenau, Rhodes contends "government refers to 'activities that are backed by formal authority,' whereas governance refers to 'activities backed by shared goals.' Governance is 'a more encompassing phenomenon' because it embraces not only governmental organizations but also 'informal, non-governmental mechanisms.'" Quoted in R.A.W. Rhodes, "The New Governance: Governing without Government," *Political Studies* 44 (1996): 652-667, 657-658. This is an important distinction to make, because the EU is both open to lobbying and non-traditional forms of decision-making.

36. G.P.E. Walzenbach, "Introduction: The Ambiguity of Multi-level Governance," in G.P.E. Walzenbach , ed., *European Governance: Policy Making between Politicization and Control* (Franham, UK: Ashgate, 2006), 1.

37. Kohler-Koch, "European Governance and System of Integration," European Governance Papers (EUOGOV), No. C-05-01, 6. http://www.connex-network.org/euro

gov/pdf/egp-connex-C-05-01.pdf (accessed 19 October 2012).

38. Tatiana Bednarikova, Anti-Roma Wall through Slovak Village Provokes Outcry" *The Telegraph,* November 25, 2009. http://www.telegraph.co.uk/expat/expatnews/6650958/Anit-Roma-wall-through-Slovak-village-provokes-outcry.html (accessed March 3, 2010).

39. Adam LeBor "Slovakian Council in Ostrovany Funds Wall to Isolate Roma Community," *The Sunday Times* , February 18, 2010.

40. ERRC, "Standards Do Not Apply" (December 2010): 19. Available at http://www.romadecade.org/files/downloads/standards-do-not-apply-01-december-2010.pdf (accessed 19 October 2012).

41. This term, which translates into English as "devouring," is often used to describe the Romani holocaust.

42. Romea.cz, "Czech Government to Leave Smelly Pig Farm on the Lety Holocaust Site," http://www.romea.cz/english/index.php?id=detail&detail=2007_1949 (accessed 19 October 2012).

43. European Parliament (EP) Press Release, "MEPs highlight 'ghettoization' of Roma and call for EU anti-discrimination measure" (January 28, 2008).

44. EP, MEPs highlight 'ghettoization' of Roma."

45. EP, MEPs highlight 'ghettoization' of Roma."

46. CSCE, "Accountability and Impunity: Investigations Into Sterilization Without Informed Consent in the Czech Republic and Slovakia" (Washington: OSCE, 2006).

47. http://www.osce.org/odihr/roma (accessed June 21, 2010).

48. From the EU Roma website, http://www.euromanet.eu/.: "EURoma, a European Network made up of representatives of twelve Member States, is determined to promote the use of Structural Funds (SF) to enhance the effectiveness of policies targeting the Roma and to promote their social inclusion." Current Member States include: Bulgaria, the Czech Republic, Finland, Greece, Italy, Hungary, Poland, Portugal, Romania, Spain, Slovakia, and Sweden.

49. See their website for recently released reports on the status of Roma in the EU: http://www.fra.europa.eu/fraWebsite/roma/roma_en.htm (accessed June 21, 2010).

50. See Amnesty International, "Violent Attacks Against Roma in Hungary: Time to Investigate Racial Motivation" (Amnesty International Publications, 2010): 16-18. At http://www.amnesty.org/en/library/ asset/EUR27/001/2010/en/7ee79730-e23f-4f20-834a-deb8deb23464/eur270012010en.pdf (accessed 19 October 2012).

51. The Commission estimates that 70 percent of the EU's Roma citizens live in the new member states added in 2004 and 2007. See "European Commission, Improving the tools for the social inclusion and non-discrimination of Roma in the EU" (Brussels: Directorate-General for Employment, Social Affairs and Equal Opportunities, June 2010).

52. As the European Commission notes: "The Phare programme is one of the three pre-accession instruments financed by the European Union to assist the applicant countries of Central and Eastern Europe in their preparations for joining the European Union. Originally created in 1989 to assist Poland and Hungary, the Phare programme currently covers 10 countries—the eight new Member States: the Czech Republic, Estonia, Hungary, Latvia, Lithuania, Poland, Slovakia and Slovenia—as well as Bulgaria and Romania, assisting them in a period of massive economic restructuring and political change. Until 2000 the countries of the Western Balkans (Albania, Bosnia-Herzegovina, and the former Yugoslav Republic of Macedonia) were also beneficiaries of Phare. However, as of 2001 the CARDS programme (Community Assistance for Reconstruction, Development and Stability in the Balkans) has provided financial assistance to these countries." See http://

ec.europa.eu/enlargement/how-does-it-work/financial-assistance/phare/index_en.htm (accessed 27 June 2010).

Part 4

Military Operations and Communal Conflict

Chapter 13

Military Intervention as a Tool of Conflict Resolution and Institution Building

William J. Lahneman

Throughout history, groups have used military force to gain power in the form of territory, plunder, and cheap (slave) labor. Those who did not engage in such activities nevertheless had to maintain military forces to defend against the depredations of others. Today, military force has a multitude of uses beyond aggression and defense against attack. After outlining the nature and different uses of military force in today's world, this chapter focuses on its employment for "peace operations," including third party humanitarian military interventions. The aim of these activities is no longer the accretion of wealth and power but rather the protection and enhancement of human rights even when one's own security is not directly threatened.

Anyone who proposes to play a role on the world stage—in diplomacy, economics, law, or nongovernmental organizations—without taking the time to understand the many nuances that affect the sober, responsible uses of modern military force is doing themselves, their constituents, and the world a severe disservice. Death and destruction usually accompany the actual use of military force and, even when coercion is threatened rather than used, the nature of war means that escalation into violence is always a possibility whenever military forces are employed. Despite this fact, actors continue to rely on coercion in many instances. One important reason for its persistence as a tool of world politics is that military force sometimes achieves the goals of those wielding it. Additionally, actors who feel passionately about their causes are reluctant to surrender before exhausting all options, including the resort to violence. The multifaceted nature of the military tool makes it possible for even weak parties to prevail given the right conditions, strategies, and tactics.

Employing the military tool, however, can and often does make matters worse. Accordingly, taking the time to study the many ways that governments and other actors employ military force is essential if policymakers are to improve its responsible use.

The Nature of Military Force and Its Role in International Relations

Decision makers should remember three cardinal rules when contemplating the use of military forces. First, military force is a tool of international relations; it is a means to an end. Therefore, its use should be clearly tied to concrete political goals. Second, the employment of military force should be a last resort. Its use inevitably causes death and destruction, harms civil society, and makes resumption of nonviolent behavior in affected societies difficult. Third, the fact that military force is a last resort does not automatically mean that its use will succeed when other methods of conflict resolution have failed. Not every case has a military solution.

In the absence of clear political objectives to guide its employment, a successful military campaign is all but precluded. Carl von Clausewitz said it best: "We see, therefore, that war . . . the continuation of political intercourse, carried on with other means. What remains peculiar to war is simply the peculiar nature of its means."[1] Clausewitz used the term "war" because of the kinds of military action he experienced in the Napoleonic era, but his thoughts on the nature of war remain applicable to the employment of military forces today.

Clausewitz' observations about military operations as a means for achieving political leaders' desired ends remain instructive. He speaks of the enemy's "center of gravity," i.e., that thing that, if captured or neutralized by military operations, causes the enemy to concede. In the eighteenth, nineteenth, and much of the twentieth centuries, strategists considered a country's capital city to be its center of gravity. This view was never completely accurate, and it is almost always inaccurate today. However, the lesson is clear—determining the enemy's center of gravity and thus the objective of military operations needs to be a critical first step when policy makers are considering the efficacy of military operations.

Violence is the peculiar "other means" of which von Clausewitz speaks, and the purpose of violence is coercion: "War is thus an act of force to compel our enemy to do our will."[2] Clausewitz characterizes war as a "duel on a larger scale."[3] His point is not that war is exciting or chivalrous—although many often associate these qualities with war—but rather that war is an extreme measure. Two persons fight a duel to satisfy some matter of honor that is sufficiently serious to warrant risking their lives!

Its violent nature imparts a dynamic to war that is absent in other tools of international relations. This dynamic rests on the fact that violence prompts a strong emotional response from both participants and observers alike. Two of the chief emotions involved are hatred and fear. After soldiers have seen their comrades blown up or civilians have seen their family members tortured and brutally killed, they come to hate their opponent and want revenge. Military operations take on a new intensity following these events. While policymakers might choose to escalate military confrontation for purely logical reasons, the emotional component of war adds another source of escalation beyond what policymakers might have intended. Clausewitz observes that this dynamic tends to drive combat toward more and more extreme measures. Fear is another strong emotion that accompanies military operations. Fear arises when combat places combatants—and increasingly civilians as well—in grave danger. Fear degrades thought processes and reduces performance.

Clausewitz considers "risk" to be the third important factor to keep in mind when contemplating and executing military operations. He explains that war involves risks because things inevitably occur that are impossible to foresee. These risks stem not only from the enemy's actions to surprise and confuse its opponent, but also from two factors inherent in military action, "friction" and the "fog of war." They can derail even the most brilliantly planned military operation.

Friction refers to the fact that military operations, even small ones, involve a series of complex events, most of which are interdependent. When something goes wrong, it often causes delays and other problems throughout the operation. Of course, things do go wrong. Communications break down, logistical problems develop, and simple operations take longer than originally estimated. In fact, everything becomes more difficult to perform as the fear factor grows under combat conditions. "Friction, as we choose to call it, is the force that makes the apparently easy so difficult."[4]

The fog of war refers to the fact that military commanders never have complete information about what is happening in their area of operations. This increases the difficulty of making good decisions. It also means that subordinates might not execute decisions as commanders intend. Clearly better intelligence about the area of operations and better communications among units are two of the principal ways to reduce the fog of war. The vast amount of effort that military establishments expend in these two areas testifies to their importance, as well as to the continuing difficulty in getting these areas right despite advancements in information sharing, communications, and battlefield management technologies. "War is the realm of uncertainty; three quarters of the factors on which action in war is based are wrapped in a fog of greater or lesser uncertainty."[5]

Given these factors, Clausewitz summarizes war as a "paradoxical trinity."

> As a total phenomenon, its dominant tendencies always make war a paradoxical trinity – composed of primordial violence, hatred, and enmity, which are to be regarded as a blind, natural force; of the play of chance and probability within which the creative spirit is free to roam; and of its element of subordination, as an instrument of policy, which makes it subject to reason alone.[6]

Clausewitz' theory underscores that employing military forces—whether in combat operations or in some other capacity—involves handling a cocktail made up of extremely unstable and potentially toxic ingredients. The military instrument should be used with care, even when military forces are employed in a role that is not envisioned to include combat operations.[7] Once military operations have begun, the situation will undergo rapid, repeated change, including surprises. Thus, constant adjustment to plans and policies is necessary if the military option is to be a successful policy tool. Three popular sayings in today's U.S. military serve as good reminders of the continued applicability of Clausewitz' dictums:

- "The first report is always wrong."
- "The first casualty of war is the war plan."
- "Hope for the best but plan for the worst."[8]

Legitimate Employment of Military Coercion

The clearest and most generally accepted standard concerning the legitimate use of military force is summarized in the "just war criteria." Policymakers, legal scholars, and others routinely use just war criteria to determine if a particular employment of military forces is justifiable and thus legitimate under international law.

Just war criteria are divided into two main components. The first is *jus ad bellum* (the just cause of war), which addresses legitimate reasons for initiating the use of force. *Jus ad bellum* consists of the following guidelines:

1. Armed force must be used as a last resort.
2. The use of armed force must be initiated by legitimate authority.
3. The purpose of initiating the use of armed force must be in self-defense or to promote justice.
4. The ultimate goal of using armed force must be to restore peace.

Note that these criteria prohibit the use of military force for aggressive purposes. Wars of aggression are illegitimate and illegal under international law.

The second component of just war criteria, *jus in bello* (the just conduct of war), addresses the manner in which armed forces should conduct combat operations. It contains two principal dictums:

1. Proportionality – The amount or intensity of military coercion must be proportionate to the provocation that caused the need for a military response.
2. Discrimination – Military forces must target the opponent's military forces rather than its civilian population.[9]

Just war criteria originated with Christian philosophers during the late Roman Empire and the Middle Ages and, since then, scholars and practitioners of international law have further developed and refined them. They thus reflect western philosophical thought, which sometimes leads critics with different philosophical heritages to dispute their universality. However, just war criteria permeate the United Nations Charter and many important multilateral treaties. Furthermore, scholars, other experts of international law, and governing elites throughout the world behave as though the criteria are universally applicable. For example, even when leaders decide to pursue a blatantly aggressive and thus illegitimate and illegal military action, they take care to develop narratives that describe their actions as meeting just war criteria.

Following the end of the Cold War, the international community experienced an eruption of internal conflicts as various governments, ethnic groups, and other subnational actors sought to settle old scores and fill power vacuums created by the collapse of Soviet power. The most serious cases of these conflicts went far beyond traditional civil war in their scope by incorporating genocide, ethnic cleansing, and other forms of systematic human rights violations.[10] In response, the international community has come to accept third party humanitarian military intervention as a legitimate means for dealing with such atrocities.

> Under Chapter VII of the UN Charter, the UN Security Council can impose coercive measures and disregard the general principle of non-intervention in the domestic affairs of states if it determines that a particular problem poses a "threat to international peace and security." In the 1990s, the Security Council showed great creativity in defining such threats. It increasingly deemed internal conflicts and gross violations of human rights to be legitimate reasons for international action. By the end of the 1990s, the idea that states should not be allowed to hide behind the shield of sovereignty when gross violations of human rights take place on their territory had firmly taken root.[11]

This line of reasoning has become formally expressed and legitimized in the UN's "Responsibility to Protect," or R2P, standard,[12] which is discussed in detail in Section 2. As a result, the number of third party humanitarian military interventions has grown, and they have become an enduring feature of international relations.

Traditional Uses of Military Power

While this chapter focuses on the use of military power in third party humanitarian interventions, it is useful to place this employment of military power in context by surveying the range of ways that military forces can be used. Each case of military intervention typically ends up employing military forces in several different ways, many of which are not foreseen at the beginning of the mission. Any use of military power should be part of larger, integrated strategies that incorporate diplomacy, economic measures, and other instruments of statecraft.

Uses Not Involving Combat

The least coercive way that military power can be used is as *diplomatic backdrop*. Policy makers use military forces to symbolize and emphasize national power. The famous Soviet-era May Day parades in Moscow's Red Square are perhaps the best example of this type of use. Foreign port visits by a country's naval forces—often called "show the flag" visits—are another good example. Note that in both of these instances there is no implication that these forces will be employed in any particular way. Rather, these highly visible displays send signals to other countries that the state making them is powerful, and other countries should act accordingly when dealing with it.

In addition to creating a general sense of a country's power and prestige, military forces can also provide diplomatic backdrop in ways that are more specific. Military exercises are one example. For instance, when a country is being obstinate about reaching an agreement with the United States on an important issue, US policymakers might decide to hold a large-scale naval exercise off that country's coast. The targeted country cannot help but conclude that an indirect threat has been made. Holding negotiations on military bases is another example of using diplomatic backdrop in a focused manner. For example, the 1995 Dayton Peace Agreement that stabilized conditions in Bosnia and Serbia is so named because the Clinton administration held negotiations at Dayton Air Force Base. The base conducted air operations throughout the negotiations, which meant that negotiators were constantly reminded of US military power by the imposing roar of military aircraft screaming overhead.

Directly threatening to use military force is the next step up the escalatory ladder. While coercive force is not yet used, policy makers threaten to use military force against an adversary in a particular fashion. Usually the state issuing the threat must move its forces into a position to conduct attacks in order to make its threat credible. For example, to make its 1991 threats to liberate Kuwait and its 2002 threats to overthrow Saddam Hussein credible, the United States and its allies spent months and considerable expense moving large numbers of forces into Mideast states. One problem with making threats in this way is that it becomes difficult for the country issuing the threat to back down if the target state does not yield because national prestige will be tarnished and countries will perceive future threats as hollow. Also, various external conditions can affect decisions. For instance, military planners might stress that the likelihood of a successful operation will be jeopardized if intervention occurs during the summer or after the rainy season has started. These kinds of considerations tend to impose a perceived deadline that can adversely affect negotiations.

The next kind of employment, *indirect intervention*, marks the transition from using the presence or threatened use of military force as a bargaining chip to actually using it, although in various ways that do not involve combat. Providing military assistance in the form of equipment and training to another country's armed forces is a widely used approach. Such assistance can be open or secret, although keeping ongoing operations secret has proven difficult. Providing military assistance not only helps to support governments that are allies but also makes these governments dependent to some degree on the donor government. This condition gives the donor state a degree of influence over recipient state policies and actions. The recipients of military assistance pledge to use it for defensive purposes only, but this is not enforceable once the assistance has been delivered except by threatening to halt future shipments.

Uses Involving Combat

Limited Demonstrations

Limited demonstrations represent the first overt use of force against an opponent to achieve policy goals. A demonstration is usually conducted in response to some attack or other hostile action, although it can occur without provocation. The Clinton administration's cruise missile attacks on terrorist targets in Afghanistan and Sudan following terrorist attacks on the US embassies in Kenya and Tanzania are examples of the former, while North Korea's 2011 artillery bombardment of a South Korean island and its earlier sinking of a South Korean naval vessel are examples of the latter. In any case, the demonstration is "limited" because the country performing the attacks makes it clear that it does not plan to conduct any further military operations unless the opponent chooses to escalate.

Covert Action and Special Operations

Covert actions or "grey operations" involve a number of both non-violent and violent techniques that fall between diplomatic measures and overt military actions. They include paramilitary operations that employ force on a small scale and strive to keep the involvement of the authorizing state secret. Traditionally, a country's intelligence service conducts covert action using its own personnel or proxy agents (foreign nationals in the intelligence service's employment), but they can also be conducted by military forces. Use of military units is more common in wartime, when "special warfare" forces, such as U.S. Navy Sea, Air, Land units (SEALs) conduct very small-scale, highly specialized operations that depend primarily on surprise and stealth rather than firepower to achieve their objectives. The May 2, 2011 U.S. military operation that resulted in the killing of Osama bin Laden at his compound in Abbottabad, Pakistan is a recent case in point.

Conventional Warfare

The next two categories of military force employment, conventional and unconventional warfare, involve the use of military coercion in a sustained combat role. Conventional warfare encompasses all forms of warfare that utilize conventional weapons, i.e., that do not involve the use of weapons of mass destruction (WMDs). As such, it encompasses a very wide range of combat activities that often defy rigid classification. Usually conventional warfare involves regular military forces on the part of at least one party to a conflict, although exceptions occur.

One way to classify conventional warfare is in terms of the *intensity* of combat operations. *High intensity conflict* refers to combat between two military forces that are heavily armed with conventional weapons (tanks, artillery, combat aircraft—so-called "heavy" weapons). While individual engagements can range in size, small engagements, when they occur, are usually part of a larger battle or campaign involving large numbers of troops. Armored divisions, heavy infantry divisions, air force bomber wings, and large naval warships are typical examples of forces configured for high intensity warfare. In addition to these types of units, modern high intensity warfare depends upon extensive command control, communications, computers, intelligence, surveillance, and reconnaissance (C4ISR) assets, which modern militaries use in conjunction with precision, often self-guided (or "brilliant") weapons to achieve and maintain battlefield dominance. The marriage of brilliant weapons and advanced C4ISR capabilities has produced such sweeping advances in the effectiveness of high intensity combat that many experts have dubbed this development a Revolution in Military Affairs (RMA).[13] One significant result of the RMA is that militaries that have not adopted the techniques of the RMA cannot prevail in high intensity conflict with the handful of western militaries that have embraced it.

Low intensity conflict, in contrast, refers to operations at the lower end of the spectrum of conventional warfare. It involves combat between small, lightly armed (rifles, machine guns, grenades) military units. These units can consist of regular military forces, such as light infantry divisions, air mobile forces, and special operations forces, as well as irregular forces, such as militia and insurgency groups, on one or both sides.

Classifying conventional warfare according to the intensity of combat is useful because it describes the range of armaments and organizational units that might be available to the parties to an armed conflict. However, this information alone is not sufficient for appreciating the effectiveness of each type of unit (heavy vs. light) and the kinds of tactics warring parties actually employ. These factors depend in large measure on how opposing forces compare to each other in a given situation. The concepts of *symmetric and asymmetric warfare* are useful concepts for sorting out such issues. *Symmetric warfare* refers to combat between two heavily armed or two lightly armed forces. In symmetric warfare, both forces are equipped in roughly the same way and use similar tactics (both engage in either high or low-intensity conflict). In contrast, in *asymmetric warfare*, each side is differently equipped, with one side being much more heavily armed than the other. This imbalance means that the weaker party cannot hope to win against its stronger opponent using symmetric tactics, i.e., meeting the enemy's stronger forces in large battles. Instead, the weaker side must look for innovative ways to perform successful attacks of some kind. The weaker party does this by identifying the weak points in the stronger party's defenses and designing ways to exploit them that do not involve direct confrontation with the forces of its stronger opponent, thus largely neutralizing the stronger enemy's advantage in fire power. If performed by insurgents in the countryside this form of warfare is called *guerilla warfare*; if conducted in cities it is called *urban warfare*. Usually insurgents waging asymmetric warfare target government forces and the forces of any allied intervening or occupying power. *Terrorists*—who operate at the lowest end of the spectrum of violent conflict—engage exclusively in acts of asymmetric warfare. They avoid contact with opposing military forces whenever possible, choosing to attack unarmed civilians instead. The widespread use of improvised explosive devices (IEDs) in Iraq and Afghanistan is a prime example of an asymmetric warfare tactic used by both terrorists and insurgents.

The idea of exploiting an opponent's weaknesses is as old as war itself because it can succeed. Consider the case of a modern military force that is conducting third party humanitarian intervention. Normally its primary goal is to assist in stabilizing a war-torn society by fostering a security environment capable of supporting nation-building efforts. A faction opposed to such a program does not need to defeat the intervening forces to derail this plan; it only needs to produce enough instability to make nation building efforts falter. To the degree that spoilers can prevent the establishment of an effective security environment through asymmetric warfare tactics, they win and the intervening forces lose; the longer that security remains elusive, the more likely that intervening forces will depart as public support for the prolonged intervention wanes. Note that the technological superiority and high intensity combat capabilities of the intervening force, if so equipped, do not come into play in such a situation because there are no large enemy formations to attack.

Unconventional Warfare[14]

Unconventional warfare refers to combat operations in which some form of weapon of mass destruction (WMD) is used. Each type of WMD employs a different chemical, nuclear, or biological principle to inflict mass casualties of varying magnitude. WMDs are also referred to as CBRNE weapons (chemical, biological, radiological, nuclear, and explosive) because of the five categories that comprise them:[15]

- Chemical weapons (CW) produce death or incapacitation by interrupting autonomous nervous system operation (nerve agents); creating painful blisters on skin and respiratory tract tissues (blister agents); interfering with the blood's ability to transport oxygen to the body's cells (blood agents); or producing nausea, disorientation, or unconsciousness (incapacitating agents).
- Biological weapons (BW) are biopathogens that have been deliberately engineered to create high morbidity in targeted populations and weaponized to improve their delivery and persistence once delivered.

- Nuclear weapons are weapons that use an uncontrolled nuclear chain reaction from plutonium or enriched uranium to produce an extremely large blast and overpressure effect, making them extremely destructive to lives and property. Nuclear devices can employ nuclear fission (splitting atoms of plutonium-239 or enriched uranium-235), such as the bombs detonated over Hiroshima and Nagasaki, or they can utilize a nuclear fusion reaction (combining or "fusing" tritium atoms, a radioactive isotope of hydrogen). These latter weapons are known as "hydrogen" or "thermo-nuclear" bombs; they use a fission weapon as their detonating device, and are many times more powerful than fission weapons.
- Radiological weapons, or so-called "dirty bombs," use fissionable materials (plutonium enriched uranium, or other radioactive isotopes) but do not employ a nuclear reaction. Instead, they use a conventional high explosive charge to disperse radioactive material, thus rendering an area radioactively contaminated. This category of WMD is thought to be something that a group possessing nuclear material might employ if they were not able to fabricate a working nuclear weapon. Some have labeled these weapons "weapons of mass *disruption*" because, although the conventional explosive produces only limited casualties, the blast disperses radioactive contamination over an area. The contamination would make the affected area off limits until it was surveyed for radioactivity and then was successfully decontaminated. Exploding a dirty bomb could spread panic through a population and impede economic and other activity in a large area until authorities determined the extent and intensity of the contamination. Even then, citizens might not be in a hurry to reoccupy the affected area.[16]
- Explosive weapons refer to weapons that use conventional explosive reactions to achieve mass destruction effects. This category of WMD was added to the WMD list following the 9/11 attacks, when the destructive effects that airliners filled with jet fuel could produce when used as weapons became apparent.

Except for radiological weapons, which have never been employed, the other four categories of WMD have been used but, in general, various technical, ethical, organizational, and operational considerations have prevented their widespread employment. Today, while one cannot rule out use of WMDs by one state against another (e.g., India vs. Pakistan or Israel vs. Iran), the probability of such unconventional warfare continues to be low; a state that employed such weapons would incur severe international censure and virtually guarantee retaliation in kind from the attacked party and its allies. Rather, most experts feel that a terrorist attack using one or two WMDs against a population center is the most likely scenario. This is the reason that preventing nuclear proliferation is at the top of most developed states' security strategies. As the U.S. *National Security*

Strategy states, "The American people face no greater or more urgent danger than a terrorist attack with a nuclear weapon."[17]

Expanding the Roles and Missions of Military Forces: Military Operations Other Than War (MOOTW)

While the traditional uses for military force are certainly extensive, the last thirty years have seen military roles and missions expand considerably. The increase in the number of third party humanitarian military interventions following the end of the Cold War has contributed substantially to this expansion. In the mid-1990s, the U.S. Department of Defense categorized these activities as "Military Operations Other Than War" or MOOTW. Like the term "post-Cold War world," the MOOTW designation indicates more about what the new employments are *not*—i.e., war—rather than what they are. MOOTW encompass a wide range of activities, including

> arms control; combatting terrorism; [U.S.] Department of Defense support to counterdrug operations; enforcement of sanctions/maritime intercept operations; enforcing exclusion zones; ensuring freedom of navigation and overflight; *humanitarian assistance*; *military support to civil authorities*; *nation assistance/support to counterinsurgency*; noncombatant evacuation operations; *peace operations*; protection of shipping; recovery operations; show of force operations; strikes and raids; and support to insurgency. [emphasis added][18]

Many of the new missions listed above are things that militaries had traditionally performed but were now performing more frequently and in new contexts. Distinguishing the implications of MOOTW roles and missions from traditional employments has challenged national military establishments. For example, the U.S. Joint Chiefs of Staff have described the differences as follows:

> Although MOOTW and war may often seem similar in action, MOOTW focus on deterring war and promoting peace while war encompasses large-scale, sustained combat operations to achieve national objectives or to protect national interests. MOOTW are more sensitive to political considerations and often the military may not be the primary player. More restrictive rules of engagement and a hierarchy of national objectives are followed.[19]

When these numerous MOOTW employments are added to the list of traditional military roles and missions, the sheer number and diversity of activities that policy makers expect military forces to be ready to perform is striking. It is important to note that not all military units are equally capable of performing every mission. National military establishments handle this potential "mission overload" situation in different ways. Some militaries specialize in certain kinds of missions. Others try to develop specialized units within their forces that focus on particular types of missions. Despite attempts at specialization, the fact remains that members of today's military forces—particularly western ones—are expected to perform a wider range of missions than their predecessors of only a decade or two ago, and maintaining force proficiency in all mission areas is challenging.

Third Party Humanitarian Military Interventions

Third party humanitarian military interventions occur when military forces from one or more states deploy into a region experiencing violent communal conflict for the purpose of helping to resolve the conflict and reestablish law and order. These operations fall under the broad heading of "peace operations." While the concept of peace operations is still being refined (meaning, among other things, that scholars and practitioners sometimes argue over terminology), it is useful to think about the concept as possessing four main categories—monitoring, peacekeeping, peace enforcement, and peace making.[20] In practice, the boundary where one category ends and another begins is often indistinct. On some occasions (e.g., Bosnia), a single intervention has resorted to all or most of these categories at various times.

In the first two categories of peace operations, *monitoring* and *peacekeeping operations*, the parties to a communal conflict have signed a peace or ceasefire agreement. Intervening forces do not anticipate employing military force except for purposes of self-defense. As a result, they are lightly armed and deliberately assume a non-threatening posture. For instance, UN-sponsored missions drive vehicles that are painted white and are clearly marked to identify them as peacekeepers.

Monitoring missions are at the low end of the peace operations spectrum. These missions monitor conditions at strategic locations following a conflict. For example, the monitoring mission on the Golan Heights at the contested border between Israel and Syria uses this vantage point to observe Israeli and Syrian military operations in the region. The awareness that these impartial monitors are likely to detect and report any aggressive moves by either side is intended to deter such action. There is nothing that mandates the use of military units for such missions. Their use stems from the fact that, historically, the United Nations has favored military forces because of their ability to respond rapidly to new tasking, their mobility, and their logistics capability. These qualities make military forces ideal candidates for establishing self-sufficient bases of operations on short notice.

Peacekeeping operations are one step up the peace operations ladder from monitoring missions. The goal of peacekeeping is the same as monitoring, i.e., to deter resumption of hostilities by impartially reporting peace agreement violations. Peacekeeping forces are larger than monitoring units because, in addition to reporting violations, they serve as a "barrier" along a ceasefire line or between previously warring units or areas. This barrier is a psychological rather than a substantive one because peacekeepers are only lightly armed. Potential violators of a peace agreement know that it is likely that violating the agreement will probably involve confronting peacekeepers in some way because they are interposed between the formerly warring forces. If confronted, peacekeepers' rules of engagement usually require them to step aside and allow belligerent troops to pass or, if directly threatened with violence, to surrender or, as a last resort, to defend themselves. The point is that the need to deal with peacekeepers in some way before violating a peace or ceasefire agreement deters a resumption of hostilities between formerly warring factions. The logic behind this assumption has failed on occasion. For instance, in both Bosnia and Sierra Leone, one of the warring factions has taken peacekeepers hostage and used them as bargaining chips in their internal conflict. Attempts to solve this problem, which stems, among other things, from the lightly armed nature of peacekeeping forces and their non-military role in strengthening peace agreements, have led in two directions. In the military dimension, peace enforcement operations represent a more coercive approach for enforcing agreements.

In *peace enforcement operations*, as with monitoring and peacekeeping operations, intervening forces enter a country following the signing of a ceasefire or peace agreement. However, unlike peacekeepers, peace enforcement forces are heavily armed and capable of defeating any indigenous forces that violate the agreement. Peace enforcement includes traditional peacekeeping functions but makes the decision to violate a peace agreement far more costly and less likely to succeed because intervening forces will use whatever degree of coercion is required to defeat the violators. In addition to enforcing an agreement, forces configured for peace enforcement operations can help to implement the provisions of peace accords that require the presence or participation of heavily armed military forces. These roles can include participation in disarmament programs, the apprehension of accused war criminals, and policing or other security-related duties until local government institutions can assume these responsibilities. Note that, as with monitoring and peacekeeping missions, peace enforcement missions do not assume that combat will be necessary. The point is to provide a stronger and thus more effective deterrent to a resumption of hostilities.

Peace making operations are the most intrusive form of peace operation. In this category, no peace agreement exists and internal conflict is ongoing. Intervening forces conduct combat operations directed at bringing hostilities to an end by demonstrating that not only will warring parties fail to achieve their goals, but they also will suffer destruction of their military forces until they agree to stop fighting. The best example of peace making in action is the NATO-led air campaign against Serbian targets with the purpose of getting the Serbian regime to cease its attacks against Kosovars.

As this survey demonstrates, peace operations use many forms of military force employment from both the traditional and MOOTW categories for purposes of conflict resolution and protection of human rights. To be effective, policymakers must understand the range of uses for the military tool and appreciate the dynamics at work.

The Dynamics of Third Party Humanitarian Military Interventions

Conducting effective third party humanitarian interventions has proven difficult. This is because such interventions usually become much more complex than originally envisioned. And, as Clausewitz notes, one should expect the situation to undergo constant change after intervention occurs. Such developments can reduce the effectiveness of an intervention and produce criticism, much of it well deserved. When assessing such critiques, it is important to remember that, in general, interventions save lives; given reasonably coherent and correct political objectives, interventions, even those beset with problems, usually achieve better results than allowing internal conflicts to play out.

The remaining chapters in this section provide specific examples of the successes, failures, and difficulties encountered in third party humanitarian intervention. This chapter offers four generalizations about intervention based on a survey of humanitarian interventions in the 1990s for consideration while assessing these specific cases.[21]

Too Little Too Late

The majority of interventions in the 1990s were "too little" in the sense that intervention was performed by military forces that were insufficiently configured in numbers, equipment, and command-and-control capabilities to prevail in combat operations. These characteristics also rendered them inadequate, at least in the opening phases of military intervention, to reestablish law and order in the wake of internal conflict so that reconstruction could begin in earnest. They were "too late" in the sense that military intervention occurred only after violent internal conflict had been underway for some time and had caused widespread destruction and human rights abuses.[22]

The Legitimacy Factor

It is in the long-term interests of all countries to strengthen international regimes that regulate the use of force and foster the rule of law, including those aspects that pertain to human rights. Additionally, an intervention perceived as legitimate will garner the support of more countries, thus providing more partners to share the cost of intervention and hopefully increase the chance that the intervention will succeed in its policy goals. The Responsibility to Protect doctrine[23] is the most visible manifestation of the international legitimacy given to humanitarian interventions. As detailed in several other chapters, it requires states to intervene in the domestic affairs of a state that is either unwilling or unable to halt human rights abuses within its territory.

The existence of a UN Security Council resolution authorizing intervention is the most desirable way to achieve legitimacy for an intervention because, among other things, it means that none of the permanent members of the Security Council (USA, UK, France, Russia, and China) objects to the action. However, given the complexity and unique circumstances that accompany each potential case of intervention—as well as the national interests of each state considering intervention—achieving this consensus for a particular intervention can be difficult.

In the absence of consensus among the permanent Security Council members (or in the absence of a majority of the fifteen Security Council members), the next preferable option is to use a regional IGO such as the African Union (AU) or an alliance such as the North Atlantic Treaty Organization (NATO) to direct the intervention. A third option is to employ a so-called "coalition of the willing," i.e., a group of states that agree with the intervention's goals and volunteer to participate in and otherwise support it. In cases when these options have been used, the organizers have tried to gain UN support after the fact to bolster the intervention's legitimacy.[24]

Defining Success

Discussions about whether to conduct a military intervention and how to initiate it typically capture center stage. However, it is just as important to address how to terminate one, since this is what determines how to conduct the intervention and allows policymakers to gauge success. Developing such an "exit strategy"[25] should occur before military intervention takes place. Ideally, policymakers decide on a set of goals that the intervention must achieve to produce the desired results, including when to withdraw intervening forces. Then they establish a method for measuring progress toward these goals and determine a point at which progress toward the goals would be sufficient to declare the intervention a success. Specific actions for achieving success form the exit strategy. To be effective, any exit strategy must also include the nonmilitary dimensions of intervention. For example, if military forces have been providing law and order following internal conflict, what civil organization will take over this function from them when forces withdraw? An exit strategy that withdraws intervening troops too soon might lead to the decay of law and order and even to a resumption of internal conflict.

No two interventions will have identical exit strategies because each case possesses different situational dynamics. Should territory remain integrated or separated? Should intervening forces avoid changing the local balance of power? Do intervening countries want to influence the behavior of one or both sides in the internal conflict? Should the intervening force try to remain impartial or should it back one of the warring factions? Should the population or one or both factions be disarmed? The answers to these and a host of other questions will vary according to the situation.

Once an exit strategy has been determined, the intervening powers must track progress toward success based on trends in security, economic conditions, the status of government institutions, and developments in civil society. It is important to remember the baseline from which to make assessments. It is all too common to use an absolute standard, to ask whether things are worse now than they were prior to intervention. The implication is that, if conditions have worsened since the intervention began, then the intervention is moving further from success and runs the risk of failing. However, the correct question should be a relative one: "Are things worse now than they would have been in the absence of intervention?" Of course, this question is difficult to answer. First, there usually is a paucity of reliable information about local political, economic, and social conditions. Second, analysts must estimate what conditions would have been in the absence of intervention, which opens the door to honest disagreements and debate about progress toward success. Third, any deterioration in conditions following intervention creates skepticism among segments of the public in both the intervening and host countries, which adversely affects their enthusiasm for ongoing efforts.

Even under ideal planning conditions, it is unlikely that any exit strategy determined in advance will remain completely intact once intervention has begun. Day-to-day events will change the situation in unforeseen ways and will require alterations to the original exit strategy. Despite this fact, comprehensive and realistic planning prior to intervention offers the best chance for ultimate success at the lowest cost in lives, material, and national prestige.

Military Intervention and Nation Building[26]

In countries that are experiencing or have recently experienced internal conflict, civil society will be in ruins, physical infrastructure will be damaged, and government institutions will be compromised to some degree. While the immediate goal of third party humanitarian military intervention in these cases will be to end communal conflict and reestablish a stable, secure environment, a successful exit strategy for terminating military intervention must include the ways that military forces interface with the political, economic, and civil aspects of nation-building efforts. This is because it is the nonmilitary aspects of nation building that lead to a sustainable peace. To the extent that intervening forces are withdrawn before significant progress has been made in these dimensions of nation building, the resumption of internal conflict becomes more likely.

Accordingly, intervening forces should hand over authority to appropriate civilian leaders and organizations as soon as the situation is stable and remain as the "junior partner" to help reestablish law and order. The military's role as junior partner is an extremely important one. If intervening forces are unable to reestablish law and order, it is virtually certain that the process of nation building will fail. However, even when military forces are able to achieve security, the hand-off of control for other functions is rarely a smooth exercise because identifying *properly trained and equipped* appropriate civilian authorities can be difficult. As a result, in practice, military forces often have retained responsibility for several of the non-military aspects of nation building (this phenomenon is partly responsible for the addition of many MOOTW functions to the list of military roles and missions).[27]

Nation building efforts are further complicated by the fact that not only must interveners create a peaceful, stable, functioning state, but they also must create a peaceful, stable, functioning, *democratic* state. After all, what is the point in intervening to protect human rights if the new government is authoritarian and does not respect the rule of law? While there is general agreement in the west that democracy is a desired outcome for all peoples, debate continues about how best to create a functioning democracy from the ashes of authoritarian and even totalitarian political traditions. When one considers that humanitarian military intervention occurs in those states that are most ravaged by war and human rights abuses, it should come as no surprise that democratization is a lengthy process.

Choosing Where to Intervene

Recalling von Clausewitz' dictum that military action is "the continuation of political intercourse, carried on with other means," this chapter closes with observations about the political motives that drive third party humanitarian military interventions. After all, at any given time there are far more cases that merit intervention to halt human rights abuses than actually occur. Why do states perform humanitarian interventions in some cases and not in others? As several other chapters have noted, it appears that, while systematic human rights abuses are a *necessary* condition for intervention to occur, they often are not a *sufficient* reason. Other factors are sometimes involved.

First, only certain kinds of states are eligible for humanitarian intervention. Neither policy makers nor western publics have supported humanitarian interventions in large countries because doing so would require large commitments of troops and resources. Rather, interventions occur in small states in cases where policy makers believe that the need for actually using coercion is slight or, when the need to use some form of coercion appears likely, intervening forces will be able to meet their objectives with a relatively small force size. These views are arguably a logical result of two interrelated attitudes. First, many western policy elites do not believe that intervention on strictly humanitarian grounds involves vital national interests. Second, elites believe that public support for humanitarian objectives is strong in the abstract but would evaporate if intervening forces were to suffer significant casualties. Taken together, these factors lead policymakers to conclude that publics will not support high casualties in interventions for strictly humanitarian reasons. This does not mean that western powers do not intervene for strictly humanitarian purposes, but it inclines policy makers to contemplate intervention only in cases of human rights violations in weak states where the actual hazard to intervening forces seems low.

Second, most cases of intervention involve other considerations besides the human rights dimension alone. Western powers have been more likely to respond to cases of human rights violations when more traditional interests have also been threatened.[28] On the one hand this is understandable. Public support—including willingness to accept casualties—is more dependable when vital interests are threatened. Also, intervening in cases where both human rights abuses are occurring and vital or major interests are threatened makes sense given the resource constraints discussed below. However, on the other hand, this tendency appears to constitute a double standard that opens western powers to charges of inconsistency, neoimperialist practices, racism, and religious persecution. While western audiences tend to downplay or discount such claims, many others believe them, which can lower an intervention's legitimacy.

Third, the decision to intervene in a particular case depends on the availability of appropriate forces. The meaning of "appropriate" forces goes beyond force levels alone. There is also the matter of matching forces to the mission, which has become more challenging as experience with humanitarian interventions has accumulated. While most states can supply troops able to perform monitoring or peacekeeping duties, both peace enforcement and peace making operations require the kinds of heavily armed forces that only the militaries of western states can provide. In this regard, the employment of large numbers of American and other countries' ground forces in Afghanistan and Iraq for the last ten years has made policymakers from these countries more reluctant to commit troops to potential candidates for humanitarian intervention.

Fourth, while the R2P doctrine has been widely accepted, there remain a few states that continue to emphasize a more traditional, absolutist view of sovereignty that emphasizes that events occurring within a state are internal matters and not subject to direction by other states. For example, China has been a prime adherent to this view. Its position as a permanent member of the UN Security Council allows China to use its veto to prevent any UN-sponsored intervention that it feels is inappropriate. Since a UN mandate for a humanitarian intervention is considered the highest form (and many believe the only form) of legitimacy for such operations, the ability of a lone permanent Security Council member to veto action is significant.

Conclusions

The uses of military force are extremely varied, with a large number of employments applicable to peace operations. In fact, many functions that do not involve the use of coercion are relatively recent additions that are directly associated with third party humanitarian military interventions. Regardless of their intended role in such interventions, policy makers should never lose sight of the fact that the core function of military forces is the employment of coercion through organized violence. This fact makes military force unique among the tools of statecraft.

Anyone responsible for decisions involving the employment of military forces should keep three main facts in mind. First, military force is a means to an end, where the end should be a coherent political goal and the means, once again, is violence, either actual or implied. Second, the employment of military force should be a last resort. Its use inevitably causes death and destruction, harms civil society, and makes resumption of nonviolent behavior in affected societies difficult. Third, the fact that military force is a last resort does not automatically mean that its use will succeed when other methods have failed. Not every case has a military solution.

To appreciate fully the implications of these three maxims, it is important to study the military option in some detail. This chapter has briefly outlined von Clausewitz' principal thoughts on the nature of war, including the tendency for violence to escalate, the role played by the emotions of fear and hatred, and the concepts of friction and the fog of war. It also has described the many roles and missions that military forces can perform and attempted to provide insights into the difficulties this wide range of activities poses for military force planning, readiness, and effectiveness.

Third party humanitarian intervention is an umbrella term that encompasses monitoring, peacekeeping, peace enforcement, and peacemaking missions. While there are commonalities among these activities, each makes unique demands on military forces. However, regardless of which category policy makers choose to employ, four general tendencies stand out. First, there is a tendency for interventions to be underfunded relative to their missions (the "too little too late effect"). Second, a failure to achieve legitimacy for an intervention will reduce the chances of success. Third, failure to design a coherent, appropriate exit strategy based on a clear, achievable definition of success, will prolong an intervention, increase its costs, and decrease its overall effectiveness. Fourth, it is important to design a plan for handing off responsibility for non-military activities from military to civilian actors at the earliest opportunity.

This chapter has described many pitfalls that can impede third party military interventions, and the complexity and relative novelty of this form of activity means that setbacks will be commonplace. However, when one asks the appropriate question—"Are conditions better now (after intervention) than they would have been without intervention"—the answer is almost always "yes." Most would agree that, despite their mistakes, setbacks, ambiguities, and inconsistencies in their application, military humanitarian interventions have reduced the toll in deaths, suffering, and economic destruction that would have occurred if the international community had not adopted this tool as a standard practice in international relations.

Notes

1. Michael Howard and Peter Paret, eds. *Carl von Clausewitz: On War* (Princeton, NJ: Princeton University Press, 1976), 87.
2. Howard and Paret, *Carl von Clausewitz*, 75.
3. Howard and Paret, *Carl von Clausewitz*, 75.
4. Howard and Paret, *Carl von Clausewitz*, 121.
5. Howard and Paret, *Carl von Clausewitz*, 100.
6. Howard and Paret, *Carl von Clausewitz*, 89.
7. M.S. Wallace's chapter on the Nonviolent Peace Force in Sri Lanka includes a discussion of the negative dynamics that can occur when military forces are employed in supposedly non-combat roles during peacekeeping and monitoring missions.
8. Based on the author's twenty year career as a Surface Warfare Officer in the U.S. Navy.
9. Most introductory international relations texts contain a discussion of just war criteria. See, for example, John T. Rourke, *International Politics on the World Stage*, 11th ed. (New York: McGraw-Hill, 2006), 285-287.
10. An earlier version of this material is contained in William J. Lahneman, ed. *Military Intervention: Cases in Context for the Twenty-First Century* (Lanham, MD: Rowman and Littlefield Publishers, 2004): 173-177.
11. Chantal de Jonge Oudraat, *Intervention in Internal Conflicts: Legal and Political Conundrums*, a working paper of the Global Policy Program of the Carnegie Endowment for International Peace, Nr. 15, August 2000, 4.
12. *World Summit Outcome Document*, High Level Plenary Meeting of the United Nations General Assembly, September 2005, paragraphs 138 and 139.
13. For a description of the development and significance of this latest RMA, see William J. Lahneman, *Keeping U.S. Intelligence Effective: The Need for a Revolution in Intelligence Affairs* (Lanham, MD: Scarecrow Press, 2011), 60-68.
14. Some experts also use "unconventional warfare" as a synonym for asymmetric warfare.
15. For details about each type of WMD, see James L. Forest and Russell D. Howard, ed. *Weapons of Mass Destruction and Terrorism*, 2nd ed. (New York: McGraw Hill, 2013), 85-254.
16. See Michael A. Levi and Henry C. Kelly, "Weapons of Mass Disruption," *Scientific American* (November 2002): 77-81.
17. *National Security Strategy*, Washington, DC: The White House, May 2010, 23.
18. *Joint Doctrine for Military Operations Other Than War*, Joint Publication 3-07. Washington, D.C.: J-7 Operational Plans and Interoperability Directorate, Joint Chiefs of Staff, U.S. Department of Defense, June 16, 1995: ix.
19. *Joint Doctrine for Military Operations Other Than War*, vii.

20. Sometimes the term "peacemaking" is used to denote pre-intervention diplomatic attempts at halting violence.

21. These conclusions resulted from a project on internal conflict commissioned by the National Intelligence Council in 2001. The project case studies and conclusions were later published in Lahneman, *Military Intervention.*

22. Lahneman, *Military Intervention*, 167-72.

23. "'The Responsibility to Protect,' the idea that sovereign states have a responsibility to protect their own citizens from avoidable catastrophe—from mass murder and rape, from starvation—but that when they are unable or unwilling to do so, that responsibility must be borne by the broader community of states." See *The Responsibility to Protect: Report of the International Commission on Intervention and State Sovereignty* (Ottawa, Canada: The International Development Research Center, 2001), viii.

24. Lahneman, *Military Intervention*, 173-77.

25. I. William Zartman observed that perhaps the very use of the term "exit strategy" sends a misleading signal to policymakers. Rather, intervening powers should look upon military intervention as part of an *engagement strategy* rather than an exit strategy, particularly in cases where no government exists or opposing groups have no political program to implement if the government falls. In such cases, only constructive engagement to reestablish basic institutions will lead to a sustainable peace. There is no *military solution* to the problem, only a *military dimension*. See Lahneman, *Military Intervention*, 133-50.

26. "Nation building" is used in this chapter as an umbrella term to refer to post-conflict reconstruction activities. Section 5 describes the various aspects of nation building, state building, institution building, and stabilization and reconstruction operations in detail.

27. Lahneman, *Military Intervention*, 183-86.

28. See William J. Lahneman, "Explaining Post-Cold War Humanitarian Military Intervention: Theory and Practice" (paper presented at the *28th Political Studies Students' Conference—Twenty Years of Western Military Intervention: Protecting Whose Rights?*, Winnipeg, Canada: University of Manitoba, February 1, 2012), 7-8.

Chapter 14

Somalia: Intervention in Internal Conflict[1]

David D. Laitin

Massive international efforts beginning in 1992 to ameliorate the devastating effects of the Somali civil war and to reconstitute a functioning government in that country brought some notable achievements, but they were overshadowed by grievous failures. This chapter in section I provides background information on the Somali conflict that precipitated the international intervention. In section II, it delineates the special problems for military intervention in the current era in civil wars like Somalia's. In sections III-V, it develops three points, listed here, that have implications for future international interventions in civil wars:

- Early decisive diplomatic attention to the Somali crisis, backed by fiscal and military threats, probably could have nipped the civil war in its bud, averting the catastrophe that followed.
- The goals of the humanitarian relief mission, while impressively fulfilled, undermined the chances for a political settlement, and therefore set the stage for an ignominious exit by the international gendarmerie.
- The strategic situation in the United Nations Security Council, between the leading permanent members (the P-5) and the Secretary General (SG) creates a bias towards ambitious goals combined with paltry resources. The UN's Somali operations reflected that unfortunate bias.

In section VI, an evaluation of the international effort in Somalia is offered.

Background Information

In the late 1980s, President Maxamad Siyaad Barre's inner coalition of three clans (Marreexaan, Ogaadeen, and Dhulbahante, called "MOD") were in full scale war against the Isxaaqs of the former British colony in the northwest (organized into the Somali National Movement, the SNM), the Majeerteens in the northeast (organized as the Somali Salvation Democratic Front, the SSDF), and the Hawiyas to Mogadishu's immediate west and south (organized as the United Somali Congress, the USC). The USC army drove Siyaad out of the country in 1991 and a Hawiya businessman, Cali Mahdi, was installed as president, with the encouragement of the Italian ambassador. The Isxaaq and the Majeerteen armies refused to accept Hawiya rule (proximity to the capital and old colonial ties to the Italians were not sufficient justification for non-Hawiyas) and continued to fight. The issue was especially complex for the SNM. The Isxaaqs fought Siyaad Barre with the greatest loss in personnel (and their major metropolis, Hargeisa, leveled) and were angry that their army did not get to Mogadishu (where Isxaaqs had major land holdings) before the armies of the USC. They were thus reluctant to return to their homeland in the north but eventually did, creating a rump state. Meanwhile, a military leader of the USC army from a different sub-clan than Mahdi, Maxamad Faarax Aideed, challenged Mahdi's right to the presidency. By late 1991, not only was there an inter-clan war for control over Somalia but an intra-clan war for control over Mogadishu. Throughout the south, and in Mogadishu especially, warlords (*waraanle*) claimed control over bands of well-armed youths who, with their armed Land Rovers (called "technicals"), roamed the cities and roadways plundering, extorting, and killing. By late 1992, due to the civil war, the entire infrastructure of the country was ruined, mass killing, starvation, and disease afflicted much of the population, there was no central government that could negotiate on behalf of the state, and international relief workers were nearly as vulnerable to attack as was the Somali population.

The United Nations (UN), more than a year after Siyaad fell from power, brokered a cease-fire in February 1992 between Mahdi and Aideed. Six weeks later, the Security Council established the United Nations Operation in Somalia (UNOSOM I) to monitor the cease-fire and to provide emergency humanitarian assistance. The Secretary General appointed Mohamed Sahnoun, a well-respected Egyptian diplomat, as his special representative (SRSG) and he was provided with a staff of fifty unarmed monitors. In Resolution 751 (April 1992), the UN promised to send a 500-man security force as well, but it was not until September when lightly armed Pakistani troops arrived. The cease-fire did not last. Continued fighting in this impoverished country created massive numbers of starving and diseased victims. The unspeakable horrors of the war, broadcast through international media, gained international attention. Reports on this situation led U.S. President George H. W. Bush to commit U.S. forces to airlift relief supplies to the civil war's victims. In this U.S.-support operation of UNOSOM I, called "Provide Relief," more than 28,000 metric tons of relief supplies were delivered to Somalia.

By November, President Bush agreed to up the ante and to offer U.S. troops to lead a UN military action to avert an even greater human tragedy. On December 3, the Security Council, combining language of Chapters VI (on peacekeeping) and VII (on peace enforcement) of the UN Charter, passed Resolution 794 creating the United Task Force (UNITAF) with a mandate to create a permanent UN peacekeeping operation to provide humanitarian assistance and to restore order to southern Somalia once the UNITAF ameliorated the human tragedy. From December 1992 through May 1993, UNITAF had about 38,000 troops from twenty-one nations, including 28,000 Americans, whose parallel operation during the UNITAF period was called "Restore Hope." President Bush insisted that "Restore Hope" be seen merely as a humanitarian mission to save civilian lives and promised that the mission would be over in a few months' time.

The UN was reluctant to manage the transition in which UNITAF would be replaced. But in March 1993, with Security Council Resolution 814, crafted by President Clinton's foreign policy team, UNOSOM II was mandated to replace UNITAF. This was an ambitious resolution calling for the rebuilding of state institutions. Moreover, it was the first ever Chapter VII resolution that was explicit about enforcement, including the disarming of Somali clans. Aideed took advantage of weak administration of the mission in June 1993 when some of his supporters ambushed and killed twenty-four Pakistani soldiers. In response, the UN authorized (through Security Council Resolution 837) U.S. Rangers to apprehend those responsible. This led to a disaster for UNOSOM II. In an operation conducted on October 3, eighteen Americans were killed and seventy-five wounded in their manhunt for Aideed. President Clinton forthwith announced the phased withdrawal of American troops that would be completed by March 1994, thus ending the role of the international gendarmerie in the Somali civil war.

A New Kind of Mission

The collapse of weak states in the post Cold War world and the concomitant humanitarian tragedies bring new challenges for diplomatic and military operations. For one, many actors involve themselves in these operations, each with its own program, leading to considerable coordination issues. Second, the goals of any operation are ambiguous from the beginning and tend to change in the course of its implementation. Third, rarely do these wars affect the interests of the intervening powers in a direct way. Humanitarian horrors rather than national threat drive the intervention. Therefore, goals are often more ambitious than resolve.

The most evident operational problem for this new type of intervention (clearest in UNOSOM II) comes from the divided command structure, with each part of the command having somewhat different goals. UNOSOM II was under nominal UN control. However, the U.S. had its own parallel command structure. U.S. Major General Montgomery was both Commander of U.S. Forces Somalia (USFORSOM) and a deputy to the UN Force Commander in Somalia, Lieutenant General Cevik Bir. Furthermore, the U.S. command was itself divided, with a complex command structure that, for example, separated the land forces inside Somalia from the Navy and Marine Corps forces that remained under United States Central Command (CENTCOM). When the Task Force Ranger was deployed to capture Aideed, it had its own chain of command that did not go through either the U.S. or the UN channels in Somalia.

Then there was a problem of command over a diverse multinational army. Several countries besides the U.S. provided troops to these UN operations. In UNOSOM I, a brigade of uniformed but unarmed Pakistani troops was stationed at the airport, unable to carry out its mission. With U.S. troops leading UNITAF, support contingents from France, Canada, Belgium, Italy, Australia, Pakistan, Botswana, Nigeria, Zimbabwe, Saudi Arabia, Kuwait, the United Arab Emirates (UAE), and six other countries were sent to Somalia. UNOSOM II included troops from Italy, France, Belgium, and Pakistan. In UNOSOM II, different national armies interpreted the Rules of Engagement differently, as to whether technicals should be engaged without provocation or whether they should first be asked to surrender weapons voluntarily. However, the bigger problem was the tendency of national contingents to seek guidance from their governments before carrying out orders. This reached levels of near treachery when the commander of the Italian contingent opened negotiations with Aideed when the SC had instructed UNOSOM II to hunt him down. There was no way the Italians could be policed or punished. Nearly all of the problems in plan implementation can be traced at least in part to this ambiguous command structure.

The coordination issues that stymied military command were equally problematical in relations between the military command and the humanitarian operations. Foreign non-governmental organization (NGO) personnel were ubiquitous. Throughout the period, thirty NGOs were active in providing humanitarian relief. These included Catholic Relief Services (CRS), International Medical Corps (IMC), Abu Dhabi Welfare Organization (AWO), Diakonic Care Germany (DGC), CARE International (CARE), Adventist Relief and Development Agency (ADRA), Africa Muslims Agency (AMA), Coordination Committee of Organizations for Voluntary Service (CCOVS), International Action Against Famine (AICF), Children's Emergency Services (SOS), Mercy International (MERCY), Doctors Without Borders (MSF), Muwafaq Charity (MCF), Pharmacists Without Borders (PSF), Revival Islamic Heritage (RIHS), Swedish Church Relief (SCR), Nordic Red Cross (NORCROSS), International Committee of the Red Cross (ICRC), Federation of the Red Cross Society (FRCS), Oxford Famine Relief (OXFAM), Church World Services (CWS), Agency for Cooperation and Research Development (ACORD), American Friends Service Committee (AFSC), Islamic African Relief Agency (IARA), International Islamic Relief (IIRO), International Development and Relief Agency (IDRA), Munzamai Islamic Society (DAWA), Muslim Aid UK (MAUK), Save the Children (SCF), and African Charity Society for Maternity and Childhood (ACSSOM). In October 1992, Philip Johnston, president of CARE, helped to create a security coordination mechanism for all NGOs, and this became the US-led Civilian-Military Operations Center (CMOC). Besides the NGOs, several UN Humanitarian Agencies were also active during the civil war, including the United Nations High Commissioner for Refugees (UNHCR), UNICEF, United Nations Educational, Scientific, and Cultural Organization (UNESCO), United Nations Development Program (UNDP), United Nations Conference on Trade and Development (UNCTAD), and United Nations Economic and Social Council (ECOSOC).

The goals of the NGOs have rarely been examined in a systematic way. Based on the stinging exposé of these goals written by Michael Maren, we can say that oftentimes their publicly stated humanitarian goals are overshadowed by their organizational desires to raise private money and to procure international contracts for their activities.[2] For several of these organizations Somalia was a perfect site for advertising to potential donors the need for greater financial support. Their personnel were there despite an inability to provide the aid that would have justified their presence. In reality, personnel from these humanitarian contingents were constantly in danger from their own (Somali) personnel as well as from militias. There was no clear way that the military command could provide security services to the NGOs. Giving IDs to registered NGO personnel only created a market for such IDs and these IDs were considered a license to bear arms. The CMOC was established in December 1992 to ameliorate some of these problems, but the larger problem was that military commands had to expand goals or be faced with the blood of humanitarian relief workers on their hands. The multiplicity of humanitarian agents without a clear structure of command is a constant in military/humanitarian interventions, and participating organizations need to adjust to this new reality. The CMOC is evidence that the U.S. armed forces are cognizant of the problems and able to adjust to this new reality.

Missed Opportunities for Early Decisive Action

In retrospect it seems clearer than it did at the moment that decisive diplomatic action backed by fiscal and military promises and threats could have cauterized the Somali civil war. There were several propitious points for significant diplomatic intervention, but they were squandered.[3]

In 1988, when only small insurgencies were evident, the international community had an opportunity to stem the civil war in its bud. In that year, Somalia made a formal agreement with its arch-enemy Ethiopia forming the Inter-Governmental Agency on Drought and Development (IGADD). Ethiopia was then housing insurgents from Somalia's north (the Isxaaq-led SNM). In light of this "conflict management agreement" between Mengistu and Siyaad, Ethiopia forced the repatriation of the SNM into Somalia. The SNM was thereby pressured into military action for survival. Meanwhile, Siyaad brutally bombed Hargeisa, the commercial capital of the Isxaaqs. At this point the U.S. could have condemned the massacre in Hargeisa and withheld financial support for Somalia, including arms shipments, to compel a cease-fire and an internal dialogue for reconciliation. In part because the U.S. remained interested in Berbera for CENTCOM, it ignored the signs of disaster.

In 1990 an Abgal-led "Manifesto Group" wrote an open letter to Siyaad calling for national reconciliation and democratization. The writers were arrested, but when their trial began riots broke out, and they were released. Italy quietly tried to negotiate on behalf of the Manifesto Group. The U.S., had it understood the severity of the crisis, might have pushed the opposition groups to accept mediation and not wait for military victory. Instead, the U.S. maintained its support for the Siyaad regime.

In January 1991 Siyaad and his entourage escaped from the Presidential compound, and the forces of the USC took control over what was left of the administrative apparatus. In the chaos of governmental collapse the U.S. airlifted its personnel to Kenya. Italy maintained a shadow mission, and its ambassador urged Ali Mahdi to declare himself President (Italy was a longtime ally of the Abgal clan, going back to the days of the Colony and the Trusteeship). If the Cold War were still being fought, Mahdi would have then declared himself an ally of either the West or East and received consequential military backing from either the U.S. or the Soviets. The other superpower (having learned the lesson in Congo-K in 1960 that African states are not worth fighting over) would have acquiesced. All parties in Somalia would then have had to reconcile themselves to procuring positions in an Abgal-led government. No democracy would have resulted, but there would have been order. That Mahdi received no more external support than his opponents meant that there was no preferred leader who could decisively defeat opposition. This opened the possibility for a war of attrition in which all parties, to prove their resolve, refuse to negotiate a solution, as showing interest in a cease-fire would be an unwanted sign of the lack of resolve. The Cold War tactic of backing the first leader to occupy the presidential palace and then mollifying opposition was not taken, and this created the conditions for a war of attrition.

In June 1992 (and reconvened in July with wider participation) there was a reconciliation conference in Djibouti with Saudi financial support. Despite widespread Somali public opinion that the time was ripe for a negotiated settlement, the Djibouti conferences failed. The UN did not participate. The organizers (a group of mediators from *inter alia* Italy, Egypt, and Djibouti) were all interested parties one way or another. The conference reaffirmed the 1960 constitution and the unity of Somalia (thus alienating the SNM) and sought to build a fair transitional government around Mahdi (and thus the Habar Gidirs refused to join in). There was no sufficiently skilled negotiator to capitalize on the de facto cease-fire and to overcome the presumption of Mahdi's presidency so that

Aideed could attend. There was also no backing of any sort of military force to enforce any agreement. This was an opportune moment squandered due to lack of leadership.

The Secretary General's special representative, Sahnoun, was entrusted with the administration of Security Council Resolution 751, creating UNOSOM I. While working in Somalia, he learned that his superiors had allowed a Russian plane with UN markings to deliver shipments to Mahdi, thus undermining the UN's impartiality. Later, the UN announced a deployment of 3,000 troops to Somalia while he was in delicate negotiations concerning the first 500. Exasperated with the UN's inability to articulate and sustain any policy, Sahnoun quit in October 1992.

Sahnoun has argued that more decisive international involvement in mediating the political crisis after the fall of Siyaad would have enabled the installation of a regime capable of legitimate domination, thereby forestalling a civil war. There is clear merit to Sahnoun's argument. If decisive support were given to one of the faction leaders or to a coalition group shortly after the collapse of the Siyaad government, it is likely that other factions would have bargained for positions in the Cabinet rather than fought a war of attrition.[4]

In retrospect, the Somali faction leaders were weak and desperate for a compelled solution. They would have yielded early on to a deal brokered by the U.S. or the UN, if it had substantial fiscal and military backing. But once the war of attrition got underway, none of the parties could accept a negotiated settlement without appearing to have lost resolve, thus making them more vulnerable to attack by rival clans.

Humanitarian Relief and a Political Solution

From an operations point of view, UNITAF was a success. In this operation, 986 airlift missions moved over 33,000 passengers and more than 32,000 short tons of cargo to Somalia. Eleven ships moved 365,000 tons of cargo as well as 1,192 containers of sustainment supplies. To be sure, there were logistical problems. The Mogadishu airport had limited capacities and there was no central airlift control coordinating U.S. government and NGO charters. Additional problems were incurred with the supply of hazardous cargoes on chartered planes and the issue of diplomatic clearance. Furthermore, documentation of sustainable supplies was subject to different accounting systems and failure to have consistent documentation wasted airlift assets. Equally complex problems occurred with the sea-lift, and a lack of clear priorities when only one ship could be unloaded at a time led to confusions. Overall, what Allard calls extensive "work-arounds" enabled the UNITAF command to pursue its mission with impressive skill.[5]

However, humanitarian success required compromises that undermined political reconciliation. The biggest problem for the relationship of military to nonmilitary aspects of the intervention is that the military goal of providing rapid distribution of food and medical supplies required accommodation with warlords. The civilian goal of establishing legitimate government in Somalia required challenging those warlords. This dilemma, often posed as one of an "exit strategy," was never successfully resolved in UNITAF (which emphasized the need to cooperate with the warlords and therefore empowered them) and in UNOSOM II (which sought to diminish the power of those warlords).

There was never a clear exit strategy for the UN operation. Amid the early discussions within the U.S. State Department, John Bolton wrote a memo called "Somalia: Easier to Get into than to Get Out Of." He was correct, and for two reasons. First, the goal of providing immediate relief tended to undermine the later goal of building legitimate authority. Oakley faced a difficult decision in his attempt to "restore hope." The warlords had the capacity to terrorize anyone who ventured into the countryside. Although the anarchy in the bush made the success of humanitarian efforts precarious even with warlord acquiescence, they were the principal threats to the security of the refugee centers that the humanitarian agencies sought to reach. Eliminating the warlords would be a major military and political undertaking, and if that were the first step in a U.S. plan, nearly the entire population of the south would have been put in jeopardy. Such a strategy would have been counter to the presidential admonition that all U.S. troops be gone from Somalia within three months. Although Oakley made several efforts to trim the warlords' sails, for example in the appointment of governors in the localities and in the appointment of women in all local councils, he necessarily became hostage to the order that the warlords could provide, as this order was the key to the success of the humanitarian effort. The long term consequence of such a strategy was to make legitimate governance of Somalia (or even illegitimate governance by a hegemonic warlord) virtually impossible. Thus the best strategy for restoring hope undermined a reasonable strategy of exit under peaceful conditions.

Second, the need for a peaceful effort led to mission creep (even by the Oakley team), and expanded goals made exit ever more distant. By the end of January 1993 Oakley's mission had already expanded beyond relief. Oakley had engaged in building local councils and engaging in some level of mediation. Brigadier General Anthony Zinni (UNITAF Deputy for Operations) said, "We did creep outside our mission a lot. . . . I think we went as far as we could go given what we were." General Johnston said, "To the extent that the hand-off was becoming more difficult to execute, the prospect of mission creep became greater. . . . I resisted it strongly, but I also knew that the standup of a police force. . . were stabilizing actions by themselves." Bush resisted for a while, but after the first U.S. casualty, a marine shot in an alleyway, Oakley wrote a stinging message saying that a Somali police force would be crucial for U.S. troop security. Bush relented. The UN was against this, as it was too minimal, but they went along. By late February, interim police forces were operating not only in Mogadishu but in dozens of towns, and courts began to take shape. Oakley later tried to extend the cantonment program to the outlying areas, but the Department of Defense (DOD) objected and only wanted cantonment near U.S. troops.

Oakley lost this battle. The greatest controversy was on the issue of disarmament, and UNITAF refused a proactive disarmament program. One relief official said, "The fact that weapons were cantoned and then not destroyed probably sent quite a message of comfort to the warlords that, well, yeah, we're just temporarily on hold while these guys are here."[6]

UNITAF believed that its mission had succeeded by January 1993 as the deaths in the camps had stopped. With hostility toward Americans beginning to be felt, many in UNITAF believed this was the opportune time to go. But Boutros-Ghali refused to allow his people to engage in many of the police and civic programs until UNITAF left the scene, so there was no transition for these efforts. Neither the U.S. nor the UN was thinking about a viable exit strategy at this time.

The U.S. mission under the UNOSOM II rubric (which, if it succeeded, would have enabled exit) was led by Admiral Jonathan Howe. Given pressure from the Secretary General, from the international lobby of humanitarian agencies, and from the realization that the Oakley strategy provided no easy exit, Howe became further implicated in "mission creep"—the move from humanitarian intervention to nation building. But with entrenched war-lords surviving on predation, UNOSOM II did not have civilian leaders with sufficient authority to negotiate a political solution. Those with authority—earned by force and recognized by UNITAF—had little interest in legitimate governance.

The Fundamental Strategic Dilemma in International Peace Keeping Operations

The fundamental strategic dilemma for international peacekeeping operations is that the leading members of the P-5 have an interest in mandating operations that they do not want to fulfill. This leads to systematic underfunding of ambitious mandates. To see how this operates, it is first crucial to analyze the goals of the major actors.

In regard to Somalia, the U.S. goals must be broken down into two periods. From the viewpoint of President Bush, the original U.S. intervention into UNOSOM I and UNITAF was principally for humanitarian purposes, to address the massive starvation and illness that resulted from the Somali civil war. The U.S. Ambassador to Kenya, Smith Hempstone, Jr., had sent a cable to Bush called "A Day in Hell" on a visit to a Kenya refugee camp. Bush was moved and told Acting Secretary of State Lawrence Eagleburger to be "forward leaning" on Somalia, with an eye to airlifting supplies. At the U.S. Department of State, there developed a consensus (as opposed to the DOD, which was largely against such a mission) that the U.S. could help save several hundred thousand people's lives, and no one else could, so the U.S. should do it. Eagleburger later said, "There was no one in the Bush administration who thought of this as anything other than fundamentally a humanitarian mission. . . . we were prepared to concede that once we fed people and left, it could turn into a mess again. But we consciously were unprepared to try to solve the political mess." Although there was some initial ambiguity about the goals of the mission, eventually Bush wrote to Secretary General Boutros-Ghali, "I want to emphasize that the mission of the coalition is limited and specific: to create security conditions which will permit the feeding of the starving Somali people and allow the transfer of these security functions to the UN peacekeeping force."[7] The expectation of the Bush administration was that after UNITAF finished its mission, UNOSOM II would deal with the issue of disarmament of the factions and a transition to civilian administration.

From the point of view of the U.S. armed services, led by General Powell as Chairman of the Joint Chiefs of Staff, there was a grudging acceptance of the mission. Powell was reluctant to have the U.S. intervene in Bosnia, a much more dangerous operation, and he may have felt that the operation in Somalia would take political pressure off of quick entry into the Bosnian war. He therefore was much more positive to the UNITAF operation than was the DOD. It might be said, then, that a secondary goal of the U.S. in its entry into Somalia, replacing UNOSOM I with UNITAF, was to deflect public pressure for a military intervention into Bosnia.

In the second period, the Clinton administration was handed the extraordinarily delicate task of exit. This required a rethinking of goals. It decided that the best way to exit would be through a reconstitution of a legitimate government in Somalia under conditions of peace. This was the goal as set in UNOSOM II, a document largely drafted by members of the Clinton administration. Some commentators associated with the Bush administration (e.g. John Bolton) exaggerated the differences in philosophy of the Clinton administration, calling it "assertive multilateralism." While there is some truth to this charge, the change was also due to an inexorable logic of mission creep and to the extraordinary difficulty of developing an exit strategy. When the Aideed forces took advantage of poor surveillance by UN forces, killing twenty-four ill-equipped Pakistani soldiers, the goal of the Clinton administration changed, in support of revenge. When revenge turned into disaster for American Rangers, the goal changed again to immediate exit without any concern for the implications of that exit for Somalia.

The UN had its own perspective. Despite the Charter that mandated that the UN act to end the scourge of war, the UN initially was against any operational involvement in Somalia. The Organization of African Unity (OAU) advised against such an operation because there was no sovereign government requesting help, and thus it could not be justified within the context of the UN Charter. Article 2(7) of the UN Charter, OAU representatives further argued, prohibits intervention in the internal affairs of member states. Secretary General Pérez de Cuéllar showed little interest in a proactive policy.

De Cuéllar's successor as Secretary General, Boutros Boutros-Ghali, had a keener interest in Somali affairs. Furthermore, the new Secretary General was adamant that the international community react to crises in Africa with the same concern as in Europe and shamed the Security Council into active consideration of the crisis in Somalia. In February 1992, the two faction leaders went to UN Headquarters and agreed to a cease-fire. In April, through UN Resolution 751, the Security Council established UNOSOM I to monitor the cease-fire. Sahnoun was deputized as the SRSG, but the Secretary General several times undermined the authority of his Special Representative, who eventually resigned. (The resignation illustrated some internal differences in goals within the UN. The Secretary General, who had as Foreign Minister in Egypt worked closely with Siyaad Barre, was despised by faction leader Aideed, and the feeling became mutual; meanwhile Sahnoun was negotiating closely with Aideed, and this created friction between the SG and the SRSG.)

With the chaos in Somalia when the cease-fire broke down, the Bush plan (as demanded by Powell) called for a massive military operation. Boutros-Ghali had reservations, but given the catastrophe, he had no choice but to accept the U.S. plan. On December 3 the Security Council unanimously passed Resolution 794, under Chapter VII, allowing for "all necessary means" to get relief food to the refugee camps. This set the basis for the U.S.-led UNITAF. Once in the field, the SG sought to enlarge UN goals, seeking to change the UNITAF mandate to include the disarmament of all factions.

Some consideration should be given to the goals of the P-5, the permanent representatives in the UN Security Council. UNOSOM I was created by Security Council Resolution 751 on 24 April 1992. It was a compromise. It established a peacekeeping operation, but it was modest. It called for fifty unarmed UN observers to overlook the cease-fire, a longer term commitment to five hundred armed peacekeepers to protect relief supplies, and a ninety day plan to be created to coordinate humanitarian aid. Ambitious resolutions but low funding have been endemic for UN peacekeeping operations (PKOs). In part this was caused by the failures in the Somali intervention, but even UNOSOM I was ambitious in words and quite modest in support.

We can infer P-5 goals from their consistent actions. At least in the 1990s, and with the horrible failure of the Somali operation in their minds, the rich states have been mindful of five goals in mandating UN peacekeeping policies. First, they (and this is especially true of the European states) do not want refugees. Civil wars produce refugees in large numbers who can become threats to the efficient provision of social services and the national self-images of the developed states. Second, the leading powers in the West will not countenance "private" rule in foreign countries by mercenary armies such as "Executive Outcomes." Therefore, it is desirable that countries suffering from civil wars be "on track" to some form of self-rule. Third, leaders of liberal societies increasingly empathize with civilian victims of civil wars, massacres, and genocides, and cannot callously sit and watch these horrors (e.g. on CNN) without taking ameliorative action. Finally, in light of the psychological effects of media coverage of civil wars, leaders of rich states at least want to be "seen" by their populations as "doing something" about the human tragedy in whatever country is facing massive civilian starvation and death. These goals need to be pursued under a remarkable constraint, especially when military operations are called for. Leaders of rich states do not want body bags of their own citizens as a consequence of their playing the role of international gendarme. If peace is to be bought through combat, the troops whose lives would be on the line should not be from the rich states. The death of U.S. Rangers in Somalia was sufficient cause for President Clinton to end U.S. military engagement. The result of these goals along with the no-deaths constraint is to push for missions under the auspices of the Department of Peacekeeping Operations (DPKO) but to underfund them, as showing interest and stemming refugee flows is more important than sustaining peace. Furthermore, if combat troops are needed, it is best to recruit battalions from the Group of 77 (third world) armies rather than from the countries that are mandating the mission. While the Somali PKOs were in part the cause of the goals now pursued by the P-5, even in 1992, there was a clear reluctance by the permanent representatives to the SC to fund and to man fully what they mandated.

In light of the unconscionable mismatch between mandates and resources, the UN showed itself unable to assume leadership of an international military engagement. It could not take the lead when member states entrusted it with leadership. This was not merely a failure at the top. The UN's staffing was at that time an international embarrassment. During the negotiations between the U.S. and the UN over the establishment of UNITAF, for example, the Secretary General did not develop a serious plan (as Resolution 794 called for) for transferring power to UNOSOM II after UNITAF's withdrawal. When a U.S. interagency team went to New York to connect with the UNOSOM team, they were shocked that the Secretary General had virtually no staff working on the problem. The best the UN team could do was to drag its feet, in the expectation that if it did nothing, the Americans would continue keeping guard. There was no command center in the UN committed to getting the operation done correctly. Under UNOSOM II, no UN planners were sent on site before the arrival of the Commander (Admiral Jonathan Howe) and his Deputy Commander. With the UN Command operating with twelve thousand fewer troops than authorized, and many of the troops under strong restrictions as to what kinds of activities they could legally engage in, there was no way Admiral Howe could develop a coherent tactical plan. Furthermore, Howe was authorized to have a staff of eight hundred, but it took months to reach one hundred, and he described the applicant pool as a bunch of "people that nobody else wants." Stories of UN incompetence in the field are legion. Major-General Lewis Mackenzie, a Canadian and former head of UN forces in Sarajevo, made this comment about UN managerial capacity: "a UN commander in the field should not get into trouble after 5 p.m. in New York, or Saturday and Sunday. There is no one to answer the phone."[8]

A far more powerful intervention force was needed for UNOSOM II success. UNOSOM II was asked to carry out with about 18,000 troops a much more complex mission than UNITAF, which had about twice that number of troops. Furthermore the UNITAF troops were better trained and equipped and under a more coherent command structure. The basic point here is that a disarmament mission is far different from arms control.

> Removing or limiting the major weapons of an inferior or defeated military force can be thought of as a form of arms control, *but to commit military forces to the mission of forcibly disarming a populace is to commit those forces to a combat situation that may thereafter involve them as an active belligerent. . . . If the disarmament of the population becomes an objective, then there should be no mistaking the fact that the troops given this mission have been committed to combat.*[9]

It should be asked if the failures in Somalia are inherent in UN operations, or are they just examples of poor management that can be fixed? Under the leadership of Secretary General Kofi Annan, the UNDPKO has been strengthened, and the Brahimi Report issued in August 2000 went a long way to identifying the problems that were evident in Somalia but repeated in Sierra Leone. Suggestions for improvement were both feasible and useful. While the UN seems to be on the road to improvement, I have serious doubts as to whether it should have command and control power in chapter VII type operations.[10]

Despite the Brahimi Report's acute analysis, bold recommendations, considerable Security Council (and less so, the General Assembly) support, and renewed optimism at the DPKO, several problems lie ahead. First, there is a P-5/Secretary General commitment problem that remains unsolved. In humanitarian crises, the Secretary General will face enormous pressures to seek some form of provisional settlement (as in the Mahdi/Aideed cease-fire of February 1992). If he achieves one, no matter how papered over it is, the Security Council cannot say no or else their members look callous. So instead they say yes but underfund a mission with little concern for its success. Once the Security Council agrees, even with underfunding, the Secretary General can hardly turn his back. After all, he had only a thin strand of a peace agreement originally. In the words of Stephen Stedman, "The Secretary General reasons that once we get a PKO on the ground, 'I can shame [the great powers] to give me the resources to save the day.'"[11] This is mission creep. At best, the Secretary General will hope for "mission creep" to get more resources.

The logic of "mission creep" weakens Brahimi recommendations. Suppose there is a rebel group that signs a peace accord but sees itself being squeezed by the UNPKO forces (as was the case with Aideed). The rebels can then renounce the agreement and become "spoilers." By the terms of the original mission, one that requires agreement on both sides, the UN should leave once there is a spoiler. But when the rebels have caused real damage to the UN troops, the option of just pulling out looks like an ignominious defeat for the UN that would undermine its reputation and credibility in other PKOs. So there is a strong temptation to expand, even without the necessary resolve, to ensure success. This logic explains the call for the U.S. Rangers after Aideed's men ambushed UN troops.

This critical analysis of the logic of mission creep needs to be modified a bit. As one DPKO staff person analyzed the strategic situation of Mr. Annan

> The Secretary General does *not* have an incentive to misrepresent the costs, as doing so plays directly back into his office. So the idea that he would be motivated by an ideology of "give peace a chance" is not correct. He has discouraged any mission to Congo-B, and has been cautious with MONUC, and pulled out of Angola when the mission was going nowhere. He catches the flak when things go really wrong.[12]

This response is not wholly convincing. The logic of mission creep is more immediate and short-term and thus more decisive than the long term worries about the integrity of the Secretariat.

The UNDPKO's answer to the spoiler issue is a doctrine of deterrence that reads like the Powell Doctrine in the U.S. The UN force should be strong enough so that no group has an incentive to be a spoiler. Furthermore, no original party to the agreement should have the resources to compel the UN mission to leave. Thus, even though an agreement between warring parties still serves as a near necessary condition for a new UNDPKO, if one of the parties pulls out from the agreement the new doctrine of deterrence requires the PKO to hold its course. With sufficient force and presence, the doctrine goes, spoilers disappear into the proverbial woodwork.

The international gendarmerie is demonstrating this more aggressive approach to peacekeeping in Kosovo and even Sierra Leone. In Kosovo, with the UN, North Atlantic Treaty Organization (NATO), and Organization for Security and Cooperation in Europe (OSCE) involved in operations there, it has become clear that the international presence will not disappear even if the Provincial Government demands that all international organizations leave the country. Under these conditions radicals cannot successfully play spoiler, and they have increasingly agreed to accept the electoral game. After its May 2000 debacle, the United Nations Mission in Sierra Leone (UNAMSIL) faced a similar situation in Sierra Leone. The UN effectively ignored the Revolutionary United Front (RUF) when it played the role of spoiler and would not leave even if RUF demanded it.

However successful UN deterrent effects, these strategies take resources and long term commitments that the P-5 states are reluctant to provide. Since failures of the UN due to mission creep will not be consequential for the P-5, they will already have been seen to have "done something." Furthermore, the UN will take the heat from a gaggle of critics that will sustain its image as an inefficient organization. Under these conditions, the UN does not provide a credible deterrent.

In light of this analysis, the best role for the UN is to vote for interventions, whether of Chapter VI or VII (or some hybrid), and then to subcontract the operation out to a state or regional organization capable of carrying it out. This is how UNITAF was organized as opposed to the two UNOSOMs. An equitable share-the-burdens taxation scheme for member states would of course be necessary, and this might be facilitated by the Secretariat, but the UN should not be directly involved in the command and control over combat operations.

Conclusions

The initial humanitarian goals of UNITAF achieved some success but at enormous cost. A ballpark figure is hard to come by. Steven Hansch et al. provide reasonable statistical evidence that UNITAF input saved between 10,000 and 25,000 lives, with total lives saved by international efforts during the course of the civil war amounting to 110,000. Supporters of American efforts have given wildly inflated figures. Chester Crocker gives a figure (without any empirical support) of 250,000. Michael Mandelbaum gives the figure of 500,000, again without any empirical justification. Meanwhile, detractors of the policy err in the other direction. Alex De Waal asserts without statistical evidence that the rains of 1991 were the principal cause of the miracle that saved thousands. The overall cost of the operation for the U.S. from 1992 to 1994 was $2.3 billion, as estimated by John Sommer.[13] We should not be embarrassed or defensive about the costs paid. UN- and U.S.-led efforts showed a profound respect for human life.

However, in part the result of a mismatch between goals and resources, the goals of bringing peace to Somalia and nation-building were failures. Somalia remains without a state. Two regions (Somaliland in the North and Punt in the Northeast) have seceded from Somalia and have attained a degree of peace and prosperity without any UN attention. In the South, where most of the international action took place, the two factions remain entrenched in different parts of Mogadishu. There is a modicum of peace but as yet no government. While the goals of UNITAF were partly, albeit expensively, met, the goals of UNOSOM II were not attained.

The analysis herein of the international intervention into the Somali civil war yielded three insights that can be applied in future episodes of state breakdown. First, decisive diplomatic action in constituting state authority can help avert a costly and gruesome civil war. In the Somali case, the international community put insufficient diplomatic pressure, and none backed with fiscal and military threats, to reconstitute state authority in the late Siyaad and the early post-Siyaad periods. Second, humanitarian missions should not be planned in absence of a strategy of reconstituting political authority once the humanitarian crisis is solved. In the Somali case, reliance on warlords to implement the humanitarian program certainly eased the crisis in an efficient way, but the cost was the ceding of authority in Somalia to military units whose leadership had little interest in legitimate government. Third, the P-5 powers have an interest in creating mandates for the UN that P-5 countries have little interest in implementing. This means that missions are underfunded and weakly staffed. In the

Somali case, the mandate for UNOSOM II was far more ambitious than the resources provided to fulfill it. This was not a mistake, but is built into the structure of the relationship between the P-5 and the SG. Addressing this issue is crucial for the success of future peace-keeping missions.

Notes

1. This chapter is based on research that went into my chapter "Somalia—Civil War and International Intervention," published in Barbara Walter and Jack Snyder, *Civil War, Insecurity, and Intervention* (New York: Columbia University Press, 1999). This version was previously published in *Military Intervention: Cases in Context for the Twenty-first Century*, ed. William J. Lahneman (Lanham, MD: Rowman and Littlefield, 2004), 29-46.

2. Michael Maren, *The Road to Hell: The Ravaging Effects of Foreign Aid and International Charity* (New York: Free Press, 1997).

3. I. William Zartman, in a chapter in press, develops some of these themes more fully. Terrence Lyons and Ahmed I. Samatar, *Somalia: State Collapse, Multilateral Intervention and Strategies for Political Reconstruction* (Washington D.C.: Brookings, 1995) also emphasize missed diplomatic opportunities that could have forestalled the civil war.

4. Mohamed Sahnoun, *Somalia: The Missed Opportunities* (Washington, D.C.: United States Institute of Peace Press, 1994).

5. Kenneth Allard, *Somalia Operations: Lessons Learned* (Washington, D.C.: National Defense University Press, 1995), 51.

6. Quotes from Susan Rosegrant, "A 'Seamless' Transition: United States and United Nations Operations in Somalia—1992 – 1993," Case Program (Part A), John F. Kennedy School of Government, Harvard University, CO9-96-1324.0 (1996): 26-28.

7. Quotes from Rosegrant, "Seamless Transition," 13-15.

8. Ramesh Thakur, "From Peacekeeping to Peace Enforcement: the U.N. Operation in Somalia," *Journal of Modern African Studies* 32, no. 3 (1994): 393. This changed a bit in 1993 with a 24-hour Situation Room phone in New York.

9. Allard, *Somalia Operations: Lessons Learned*, 64, 90.

10. "Report of the Panel on United Nations Peace Operations," A/55/305, S/2000/809, chaired by Lakhdar Brahimi.

11. In remarks delivered at the annual meeting of the Association for the Study of Nationalities, New York, 5 April 2001.

12. Confidential interview with a member of the staff of the Secretary General, April 3, 2001.

13. See: Steven Hansch et al. *Excess Mortality and the Impact of Health Interventions in the Somalia Humanitarian Emergency* (Washington, D.C.: Refugee Policy Group and Centers for Disease Control and Prevention, 12 August 1994); Chester Crocker "Lessons of Somalia," *Foreign Affairs* 75, no. 3 (1995); Michael Mandelbaum, "Foreign Policy as Social Work," in *Foreign Affairs* 75, no. 1 (1996): 30; Alex de Waal, *Times Literary Supplement* (December 1995), 29; and John G. Sommer, *Hope Restored? Humanitarian Aid in Somalia 1990-1994* (Washington, D.C.: Refugee Policy Group, Center for Policy Analysis and Research on Refugee Issues, 1994).

Chapter 15

Intervention in Internal Conflict: Lessons from Bosnia and Kosovo

Steven L. Burg

The interventions in Bosnia and Kosovo illuminate the complex issues affecting the decision making and behaviors of third party states, multilateral organizations, and local warring actors in cases of intervention in internal conflict. Indeed, even the distinction between "internal" and "external" might be considered problematic in these cases. For the purposes of this analysis, they are defined as internal conflicts over the status and internal political organization of the territory. These conflicts erupted as part of the larger set of conflicts surrounding the disintegration of the former Yugoslav federal state, of which Bosnia and Herzegovina was a federal "republic," and Kosovo an "autonomous province" of the Serbian republic. However, the larger conflict is treated here only as context and not subjected to detailed analysis.

The direct and indirect involvement of the neighboring states of Serbia and Croatia in the internal Bosnian conflict, as well as the penetration of Kosovo by the externally-organized and funded Kosovo Liberation Army (KLA), could be defined as "external" interventions, but are instead treated here as dimensions of internal conflict. The involvement of these actors, and their very real interests in the outcome of the conflict, were critical factors in the decisions of U.S. and other third party policymakers concerning intervention.

In both cases, intervention culminated in military occupation and *state-building* intended to implement a settlement imposed on the warring parties. Even after more than fifteen years, however, the institutional character of the Bosnian state remains in doubt. After more than ten years, intervention in Kosovo has not yet produced a stable democratic state in Kosovo, or resolved the status of Serbs within that state, or the relationship between Kosovo, Serbia, and the Kosovo Serbs. These issues, however, are outside the scope of this paper, which focuses on the decisions and actions of external policymakers, U.S. policymakers in particular, to intervene in these conflicts, and the immediate outcomes of their interventions. It examines the gradual escalation of direct involvement from peacemaking, to peacekeeping, deterrence, coercive diplomacy, and coercion, and argues that national self-interest, rather than commitment to more abstract principles, played the determinative role in shaping policies.

Interventions in these conflicts fall into several distinct categories. *Peacemaking* included diplomatic/political efforts intended to find a solution to each of these conflicts, either before or after the outbreak of violence. *Peacekeeping*, included efforts in Bosnia at first to facilitate the delivery of humanitarian relief, then to secure and maintain the limited agreements reached by the parties during the course of the conflict and, finally, to carry out UN decisions taken without the support of the warring parties. In Kosovo, an international observer mission carried out some peacekeeping functions. Intervention in Bosnia also included *humanitarian relief* operations carried out with the support of peacekeeping forces and intended to redress the suffering of the civilian population, while in Kosovo "humanitarian relief" constituted more of a post-hoc justification rather than motivation for intervention. In both cases, intervention also took the form of economic and other *sanctions* imposed under the authority of the UN Security Council. In both Bosnia and Kosovo, external actors engaged in the threat or use of force to prevent specific actions by the warring parties. The failure of these efforts hastened the resort to a strategy of *coercive diplomacy*. In this chapter, I argue that coercive diplomacy succeeded in Bosnia, but failed in Kosovo, giving way to simple *coercion*, because policymakers ignored the lessons of Bosnia.

Peacemaking, or "Baseball without a Bat"

The initial involvement of the European powers in the Yugoslav conflict(s) was motivated by a clearly articulated desire to prevent armed conflict. European negotiators pursued a straightforward security interest in preventing armed conflict in a neighboring state; the political interest of some states in advancing the role of common European (EC and, later, EU) foreign policy making institutions in international security affairs; the concern of several states to prevent an influx of significant numbers of refugees, with potentially destabilizing consequences; and the pressure of domestic ethnic and ideological constituencies calling for action. Relatively early in the conflict, the European states rejected military intervention in favor of a diplomatic effort to negotiate a peaceful settlement among the Yugoslavs. Thus, the initial intervention by outside actors took the form of diplomatic and political peacemaking activities, without the backing of a credible threat of force.[1]

The Europeans expressed their support for existing internal and external borders while the U.S. discouraged secession. Although the U.S. left the door open to border changes by "peaceful consensual means," it offered no support for such changes.[2] The European and American positions reflected a mechanistic application of existing Helsinki principles. But these were designed for a period of relative stability, made possible by détente between the superpowers.[3] Their application to intra-state or inter-group relations under conditions of enormous uncertainty and instability was ineffective. It was already clear to many academic and other experts, after a January 1991 meeting of the Serbian and Slovenian leaders, that a negotiated agreement among the regional leaders of Yugoslavia over internal borders would be essential to maintaining peace in that country, that such an agreement was likely to involve changes, perhaps substantial changes, to the status quo, and that such an agreement would be difficult to achieve by consensual means without external pressure in the form of (negative) incentives for the Yugoslavs (in the initial stages of dissolution, primarily the Serbs) to avoid the use of force.[4] Little of this thinking appears to have been incorporated into official responses to the emerging crisis.

Convocation of the EC's Conference on Yugoslavia in September 1991 came against the background of escalating conflict in Croatia and the European decision not to intervene militarily. The fighting in Croatia was not seen by Western policymakers as threatening their national security interests. In the absence of any prospect of external military intervention, the Serbian and Yugoslav Army (JNA) leaderships were free to pursue a strategy of seizing Serb-populated regions of Croatia, and Western pressure in the form of negative sanctions, including the United Nations Security Council's adoption of Resolution 713 (25 September 1991) imposing an arms embargo against all of (former) Yugoslavia, was insufficient to reverse Serbian military actions. Cooperation by the Serbs extended only as far as accepting an UN-sponsored cease-fire in November 1991 and establishment of UN-protected areas in those regions of Croatia seized by the Yugoslav army, thus "freezing" Serbian gains and ending Serbian interest in further negotiations. Serbia ignored other provisions of the UN-sponsored Vance plan for Croatia. Similarly, once Croatia achieved international recognition in January 1992, it also had no further interest in negotiations, as these might have compromised its now internationally-recognized claim to sovereignty over the protected areas.

This pattern of intransigence on the part of local actors once they had extracted political or formal diplomatic or legal recognition of their claims repeated itself in Kosovo. In both Bosnia and Kosovo, external actors failed to use the leverage of such recognition to push local actors toward a settlement short of war, thereby increasing political pressures at home for intervention.

In Bosnia, international recognition of the state came in the absence of a negotiated agreement among the conflicting parties. As in Croatia, recognition offered the single most powerful positive inducement to cooperation, and granting it (denying it, with respect to the Bosnian Serbs) without first seeking to extract cooperation had the effect of ending any incentives for the parties to negotiate. The timing of recognition was a matter of intense diplomatic maneuvering by the U.S. and its European allies, the Bosnian government, and Serbia, as well as intense political maneuvering among the Bosnian Muslims, Croats, and Serbs in the period between December 1991 and March 1992.[5]

In the absence of *either* a constitutional agreement on status among the conflicting Bosnian parties (and their neighbors) *or* an international commitment to defend the newly-recognized government of Bosnia or, better yet, *both*, recognition in early April contributed to a rapid escalation of the conflict. Eleventh-hour negotiations to achieve such an agreement, conducted for the EC by Jose Cutiliero, ended in failure. The lack of U.S. interest in, or support for the process signaled to the Bosnian Muslim leadership that they had only to withhold their agreement in order to win eventual U.S. support. In effect, the U.S. had provided the Muslim-dominated Bosnian government, wittingly or not, with a positive inducement to intransigence.

It is by no means certain, of course, that these negotiations would have succeeded even if recognition had been linked to an agreement. The negotiations began after the Muslim political leadership in control of the government declared Bosnian independence, Serbian and Bosnian Serb preparations for war were already well-advanced, and countervailing military action by the U.S. or the European powers to avert Serbian (and Croatian) aggression against the newly-recognized state had already been ruled out. Successful negotiations, even if supported by delayed recognition, would almost certainly have had to have begun much earlier, before the onset of dissolution.[6]

The approach taken in these early Western peacemaking efforts was based on the fundamentally flawed principle that the existing internal borders of the constituent units of the Yugoslav federation should become internationally-recognized borders. This ignored the lack of correspondence between borders and identities in much of the Yugoslav federation and the dynamic of political conflict that this produced. Even this flawed approach was not implemented consistently, however. The demand for recognition by the Kosovar Albanians, for example, who comprised 90 percent of the population of an autonomous province that had dual status as a constituent unit of the federation and an integral part of the Serbian republic, and thus could arguably have received the same treatment as the republics, was rejected.

Although it could be said that the disintegration of Yugoslavia began in Kosovo in 1981, the West excluded Kosovo from its efforts to negotiate an end to the crisis in the former Yugoslavia. The United States issued what has become known as the "Christmas warning" in December 1992, declaring that the United States would act against Serbia if violence broke out in Kosovo and could be attributed to the Serbs, but did little else. With the end of fighting in Bosnia, the need for proactive efforts to avert a crisis in Kosovo was clear. The reports of several NGO initiatives made apparent the hard political bargaining, and support of the major powers, that would be required to achieve any agreement over Kosovo.[7] But major international actors, especially the United States, showed little interest.

American indifference can be attributed, first of all, to the fact that Milosevic's support remained essential for implementation of the Dayton agreement, and especially for imposing political changes in the Bosnian Serb republic (Republika Srpska). During the most promising period of Kosovar-Serbian contact and communication, policymakers in the United States appear to have been preoccupied with developments in Bosnia. Dependence on Milosevic also blinded Western policymakers to opportunities for change in Serbia, manifest in mounting democratic opposition to Milosevic on the streets and at the polls that created additional incentives for Milosevic to achieve a negotiated settlement in Kosovo. Although the Contact Group, which provided the diplomatic mechanism for ending the war in Bosnia, called for dialogue over Kosovo in September 1997, there was no concerted U.S. diplomatic effort to address the conflict until rising violence in the province compelled the United States to dispatch Special Representative Robert Gelbard to Belgrade and Prishtina in early 1998.

As Paul Shoup and I have argued, the initial effort at peacemaking in Bosnia might have succeeded had the European strategy been formulated differently; in essence, holding the nationalist ambitions of dominant nations in each Yugoslav republic for international recognition hostage to prior agreement on borders and internal political order, including the effective protection of minority rights. By doing so the Europeans, with support from the U.S., could have defined a peaceful path by which each of the Yugoslav nations might have pursued its nationalist goals, a path that not only would have required each to negotiate, but would have enabled them to do so rather than resort to force. Nonetheless, for this strategy of peacemaking to succeed, the intervening powers would have needed to mount an effective threat to use countervailing force against any party that violated the peace. Neither the Europeans nor the Americans were prepared to make such a threat in the early stages of the Yugoslav conflicts. Indeed, the military option was explicitly dismissed on both sides of the Atlantic.[8]

Senior U.S. policymakers saw no strategic U.S. national interests at risk.[9] As a result, the United States not only resisted the use of force, but remained at the margins of diplomatic efforts to end the conflict in Bosnia for almost two years. The International Conference on the Former Yugoslavia (ICFY) was established in August 1992 under the co-sponsorship of the United Nations and the European Community and co-chaired by former U.S. Secretary of State Cyrus Vance (for the UN) and former British Foreign Minister Lord David Owen (for the EC).[10] Each of the warring parties sought to use the negotiations as means to pursue their own goals, rather than to find a genuine solution. The absence of any capacity to compel the parties to compromise led negotiators to offer last-minute concessions to the Serbs in April 1993 that moved the proposal toward a strategy of partition. However, not even a partition plan could work as long as parties on the ground remained wedded to force and major outside powers remained uninterested in compelling them to agree. The absence of any Western threat of force—either to implement an agreed settlement or to impose a solution in the absence of agreement—led one member of the Vance-Owen team to liken the negotiations to playing "baseball without a bat."[11] The lack of engagement on the part of the U.S. and a concomitant absence of a credible threat of force continued to plague later negotiators even as they moved toward an explicit plan for partition in 1993 and 1994.

Humanitarian Relief and Peacekeeping

Western intervention in Bosnia first took the form of UN-authorized peacekeeping and humanitarian relief efforts. Humanitarian intervention began in February 1992 with establishment of the United Nations Protection Force (UNPROFOR) for those areas of Croatia from which Yugoslav (Serbian) forces were to withdraw under the Vance plan. The mandate of UNPROFOR in Croatia was gradually expanded both territorially and functionally. Similarly, the deployment of UN troops to Bosnia began with the June 1992 action to re-open Sarajevo airport for humanitarian supply efforts and expanded both territorially and functionally over time.

The deployment of a humanitarian relief mission to Bosnia in the midst of continuing fighting reflected both the understanding of Western policymakers that the conflict was not going to end quickly and their reluctance to intervene in it militarily. Nonetheless, UNPROFOR gradually took on the characteristics of a limited military intervention. In an effort to secure delivery of humanitarian relief to Bosnian civilians, Security Council Resolution 757 (30 May 1992) imposed sanctions on Yugoslavia under Chapter VII authority, and called for the opening of Sarajevo airport. Although not intended as such, the agreement to open the airport offered an important positive inducement to the Serbs: control of the airport by a neutral force that would prevent it from falling into the hands of Bosnian government, or Muslim, forces. There is some evidence to suggest that Milosevic pressured the Bosnian Serb leadership to accept the agreement in an effort to avert implementation of the sanctions called for in Resolution 757.[12] Indeed, the compelling effect of sanctions on Serbian (Milosevic's) behavior would grow stronger over time. It would come to play an important, if not critical, role in the success of coercive diplomacy in 1995.

Continued Bosnian Serb resistance to the delivery of humanitarian relief to Bosnian Muslim populations under siege resulted in further expansion of Western intervention through UNPROFOR. Steps toward a widening intervention in the conflict were contradicted however, by highly restrictive rules of engagement that reflected the original Chapter VI authorization of the UNPROFOR mission, which made it dependent on the cooperation of local forces.[13] As events in Srebrenica in July 1995 would make painfully obvious,[14] these deployments did little to protect threatened populations but did expose UNPROFOR troops to heightened risks and thus inevitably drew them more directly into the military conflict. As the mandate of UNPROFOR expanded, the distinction between "humanitarian" and "peacekeeping" activities, and even military intervention, became blurred. As most of the UNPROFOR troops were drawn from European NATO-member states, the distinction between UN involvement and Western intervention also became blurred.

Threats, and Use, of Force

Bosnia

Over the course of the war in Bosnia, the U.S. participated in five attempts to use the threat of force to persuade or compel the Bosnian Serbs either to cease or to refrain from certain actions. Although these were limited in scope and intent, together they had the effect of expanding the Western commitment of resources to the conflict. First, in response to increased Serb shelling of Sarajevo and ground action that suggested an imminent frontal assault on the city in the summer of 1993, and rising domestic pressure to "do something,"[15] NATO issued a vague threat of future action, leading the Bosnian Serbs to end their immediate threat. Second, in February 1994, the threat of NATO air attack in response to a shelling of the Markala marketplace in Sarajevo led the Serbs to withdraw their heavy weapons from around the city and to establishment of a heavy weapons exclusion zone around Sarajevo.

These actions can be considered successful but limited acts of intervention. In each case, a threat of air attack was employed to compel the Bosnian Serbs to pull back from Sarajevo and reduce, at least temporarily, their attacks on the city. Issuance of an ultimatum was accompanied by crisis negotiations, but in each case, special circumstances secured Serb compliance. Shoup and I have pointed out that the Bosnian Serb agreement was secured in no small part by the fact that in 1993 the Serbs were not required to withdraw so far as to prevent them from renewing artillery fire on the city; were able to secure UN occupation of strategic territory, thereby denying it to the Muslims; and appeared to have pushed resolution of the conflict in the direction of a UN-patrolled partition based on the *status quo*.[16] Similarly, in 1994 negotiators agreed to prevent the Muslims (Bosnian government) from gaining control over territory relinquished by the Serbs by deploying Russian peacekeepers to the territory. In each case the demand advanced by the NATO allies was one to which the Serbs could agree, and the agreements kept alive negotiations for a comprehensive cease-fire that would freeze existing Serb territorial gains.

Neither of these episodes advanced the conflict toward resolution, however. The threat of force reflected the desire on the part of Western policymakers to contain the conflict, and to respond to media pressure to "do something," rather than a commitment on their part to end it. There is no evidence that policymakers had changed their view that the conflict did not threaten strategic interests and therefore did not warrant a significant commitment of resources to its resolution. In some respects, these attempts to use force made matters in Bosnia worse. The apparent increase in U.S. and NATO involvement and the threat of force against the Serbs contributed in each case to a hardening of Bosnian Muslim positions in the negotiations over a political settlement taking place at the same time in Geneva under the auspices of the ICFY. This contradictory outcome suggests one of the difficulties of intervening against only one party to a conflict involving multiple actors.

Because the interests of the Bosnian actors were most often in opposition, threats applied against one in order to encourage that party to negotiate or comply would make one or more of the others less willing to negotiate or comply. The fact that these threats were not actually carried out, and the Serbs were able both to keep their immediate concessions modest and to reverse them later, weakened the credibility of subsequent U.S. and NATO threats in the eyes of both the Serbs and the Muslims. In effect, both these "successful" cases of limited intervention actually "upped the ante" for the later, more comprehensive intervention intended to bring the conflict to an end.

The third example of deterrence in Bosnia, in April 1994, consisted of three limited air attacks, which were carried out against Serb forces threatening to overrun the Muslim-held enclave of Gorazde in eastern Bosnia. The air attacks were followed by another NATO ultimatum to the Serbs to withdraw and at least some consideration of the use of more extensive force against them. However, in response to the air strikes, the Serbs took two hundred UN and civilian personnel hostage. Concern for their fate contributed to the reluctance of Yasushi Akashi, the special representative of the UN Secretary General who exercised "dual key" control over the use of force (because the West was operating in Bosnia under a UN mandate), to authorize additional air strikes. The concern among contributing states that UNPROFOR troops should not be put at risk by the use of air power had led the Europeans to reject an earlier U.S. proposal to "lift and strike," i.e., to lift the arms embargo against the Bosnian government and use air power against the Serbs. An exclusion zone was established around Gorazde in 1994, but the confrontation was allowed to wind down without a definitive conclusion.

The fourth example of deterrence through use of force, in November 1994, consisted of NATO air attacks against a Serb airbase and three Serb surface-to-air missile (SAM) sites in the Bihac area in response to Serb attacks that threatened to overrun the Muslim-held enclave in Western Bosnia. UNPROFOR forces were caught in the fighting, suffering several casualties. The involvement of Serb ground and air forces operating from the Serb-held territories of Croatia just across the nearby border threatened to draw the Croatian regular army into the battle, with the potential to re-ignite fighting in Croatia. NATO planes struck the Serb airbase in Croatia and then, two days later, three Serb SAM sites in the Bihac area. Once again, the Serbs seized UN personnel as hostages to deter further NATO attacks. NATO leaders convened to consider proposals to demilitarize and secure the Bihac safe area, as well as proposals to carry out wide-ranging air strikes against the Bosnian Serbs. But, they could not agree on a course of action due to continuing differences between the U.S. and at least some of its NATO allies with troops on the ground in UNPROFOR. The Serbs allowed UN aid convoys into the pocket, and Bosnian Muslim troops began slipping out, bringing this crisis too, to an inconclusive end.

The fifth and final attempt at deterrence consisted of the use of airpower against Bosnian Serbs in May 1995, in response to an escalation of fighting on the ground and increased Serb shelling of Sarajevo. The UNPROFOR commander warned both the Muslims and the Serbs to halt the use of heavy weapons and issued an ultimatum to the Serbs to withdraw from the exclusion zone around Sarajevo. When they failed to comply, NATO carried out air strikes against Serb ammunition bunkers in Pale, east of Sarajevo. These attacks failed to compel the Serbs. Rather, they responded by shelling Tuzla and seizing UN personnel as hostages, using them as human shields against further attack—a response that could have been anticipated in light of Serb actions at Bihac and Gorazde. This time, they compelled NATO to cease its use of force, and forced UNPROFOR to renounce the future use of force by reaffirming its adherence to strict peacekeeping principles. Thus, while the earlier instances of the use of force did have at least a short-term deterrent effect on the Serbs, the May 1995 events had no such effect. On the contrary, they contributed to both the collapse of the UN mission in Bosnia and the emergence of a comprehensive, U.S.-led strategy of coercive diplomacy.

More extensive, direct intervention, considered at various times during 1993 and 1994, or proposals for intervention around Sarajevo and Gorazde, were rejected either by European actors concerned they might subject their troops in UNPROFOR to increased risk; by U.S. policymakers concerned that direct intervention represented a "slippery slope" of involvement in a potential quagmire; or by UN officials concerned not to put UNPROFOR at greater risk. The threat to NATO cohesion evident in these differences, media criticism that NATO lacked resolve, the growing threat to UNPROFOR and, especially, repeated failures of the use of limited force, led policymakers to conclude that strategic interests had been put at risk, and to adoption of a strategy of coercive diplomacy in 1995.

Kosovo

In Kosovo, the West was unprepared for the appearance of the Kosovo Liberation Army (KLA), within a few months of Dayton, and the outbreak of violence. The KLA transformed the Albanian nationalist movement in Kosovo from a peaceful resistance to an armed insurgency. This closed the door to ending the struggle in Kosovo by securing minority rights in Serbia. By this time, however, the West had committed itself in Bosnia to opposing secessionism and partition as solutions to ethnic conflicts within states, and to opposing the consolidation of ethnic irredenta with their national states.

The rise of the KLA gave Ibrahim Rugova, and others in the leadership of the more moderate Democratic League of Kosovo (LDK), a powerful new incentive to negotiate. Milosevic also had new incentives to negotiate, as he now had to achieve progress on Kosovo in order to win the lifting of the sanctions that still remained in place in the wake of Dayton. But, for Rugova and the LDK to have negotiated with Milosevic would have accelerated their loss of popular support in Kosovo. As one Albanian commentator for the Helsinki Committee suggested, "the belligerent option is gaining more followers, at the expense of the peaceful one."[17] For Milosevic, Rugova no longer represented a credible negotiating partner. It was the KLA insurgency that now constituted the threat to Serbian control over Kosovo.

Escalation of the Yugoslav effort to root out the KLA, and its consequences for the civilian population in Kosovo, captured the attention of Western policy-makers, particularly following clashes in the Drenica region of Kosovo in February-March 1998 that resulted in at least eighty-five civilian deaths. U.S. Special Representative Gelbard, in his Prishtina press conference on 22 February, rightly attributed "the great majority" of the violence to the Serbian police. But he also condemned the violence perpetrated by the KLA. "I consider these to be terrorist actions," he declared, and called upon "the responsible, democratic Kosovar Albanian leaders to condemn this terrorism and to show which side they are on."[18] The Contact Group called in March for an end to violence against civilians and the withdrawal of special police units from the province while also condemning terrorism; for the granting of greater autonomy and self-administration for the province while continuing to support the territorial integrity of the Federal Republic of Yugoslavia; and for dialogue. The Contact Group also adopted relatively mild sanctions, including an arms embargo, visa restrictions, and the cutting-off of financial assistance to the Yugoslav government. These were strengthened in April by the freezing of Yugoslav funds held abroad. The Contact Group actions gained international authority through their incorporation in UN Security Council resolution 1160, adopted 31 March 1998, which condemned both the excessive use of force by the government and all acts of terrorism by the KLA.

By this time, however, Milosevic would settle for nothing less than re-affirmation of Kosovo as an integral part of Serbia, while Kosovar Albanians would settle for nothing less than independence. At the same time, the United States and the other members of the Contact Group concluded that the KLA would have to be represented in any negotiations. The dilemma inherent in this approach was reflected in the unfortunate symbolism of a widely-published photograph of Holbrooke meeting with a local KLA commander still holding his Kalashnikov.[19] The photograph sent a clear message that the KLA was unprepared to compromise on methods and goals that were completely incompatible with the diplomatic/political approach adopted by U.S. policymakers, and which made it a natural competitor rather than partner to the LDK, and enemy of the Serbs. Nonetheless, Gelbard reported to Congress in July "we have opened a dialogue with the UCK [KLA]. The UCK is a reality on the ground, and however much we condemn the use of violence by either side, they will have to be a party to any cessation of hostilities."[20]

Thus, unlike Bosnia, where the United States and its allies enjoyed direct or, in the case of the Bosnian Serbs, indirect leverage over all the warring parties, in

Kosovo the United States and its allies exercised no leverage over the KLA, and rapidly declining leverage over the LDK and Milosevic. A KLA offensive in spring and early summer 1998 gained control of some 40 percent of the province. A Serbian counteroffensive in late summer and early fall employed disproportionate levels of force, directed not only against the KLA itself, but against the civilian populations of villages and towns in areas of KLA activity, displacing over 230,000 Albanians from their homes.[21]

The flow of refugees into neighboring and West European countries, the increasing number of internally displaced persons and the rapid deterioration of humanitarian conditions in Kosovo, and the "excessive and indiscriminate use of force by Serbian security forces and the Yugoslav Army" led the UN Security Council to adopt Resolution 1199 (September 23, 1998), calling for "the withdrawal of security forces used for civilian repression," the establishment of "effective and continuous international monitoring in Kosovo," the safe return of refugees and displaced persons, "free and unimpeded access for humanitarian organizations and supplies to Kosovo," and full cooperation with the International War Crimes Tribunal. The resolution called upon the Yugoslav government and Kosovo Albanian leadership to "take immediate steps to improve the humanitarian situation" and "enter immediately into a meaningful dialogue without preconditions and with international involvement, and. . . a clear timetable, leading to an end of the crisis and to a negotiated political solution to the issue of Kosovo."

The NATO allies backed up the demand for an immediate end to the fighting by adopting an "activation *warning*" for an air campaign against Yugoslavia. But Resolution 1199 did not authorize the use of force, and the activation warning constituted, in the words of NATO Secretary General Javier Solana, only "an important political signal of NATO's readiness to use force if it becomes necessary to do so,"[22] rather than a threat to use force.

A massacre of twenty-one civilians in Gornji Obrinje in late September 1998,[23] only days after the NATO activation warning, prompted a simultaneous escalation of threat and diplomacy. This was the context in which Richard Holbrooke returned to Belgrade in October 1998 in an effort to end the conflict by negotiating once again with Milosevic. The Contact Group demanded that Milosevic comply with Resolution 1199, backed up by a NATO "activation *order*" on 12 October, authorizing the military to carry out the attacks, but delaying its implementation for ninety-six hours in order to allow Milosevic to demonstrate compliance.[24] Unlike NATO threats in Bosnia, this action came in the absence of an explicit Security Council authorization to use force, and can be seen as an effort to sidestep Russian opposition to use of force and its willingness to veto any Security Council action.

The October 1998 negotiations in Belgrade produced what appeared to be an agreement to comply with Resolution 1199, and the verification demands of the Contact Group. The key concessions extracted from the Serbs[25] consisted of an increase in the number of international observers on the ground in Kosovo; the return to barracks and/or withdrawal of Yugoslav military and special police units; unimpeded access for humanitarian relief organizations; cooperation with international war crimes investigators; and agreement to pursue a political, rather than military solution to the conflict. The October agreements established an OSCE verification mission consisting of two thousand Western observers on the ground in Kosovo, a NATO air verification mission, an OSCE training program for the mostly ethnically Albanian local police expected to take over from Yugoslav special police, and called for OSCE-supervised elections within nine months.[26] The Yugoslavs also accepted Contact Group provisions for a political settlement to be concluded by 2 November.[27] However, the Serbian leadership still refused to accept anything more than cosmetic changes in the basic political status of the province and its subordination to Serbia.[28]

The initial October agreement thus had all the makings of a successful exercise in coercive diplomacy: demands that can be accepted, backed up by a credible threat of force that remained in effect until acceptance of the demands and the reversal of objectionable actions, followed by restraint from the use of force. On the surface, it looked very much like the February 1994 NATO ultimatum in Bosnia, and State Department officials tried to characterize it as such.[29] British Foreign Secretary Robin Cook argued that Milosevic would not "have gone into these arrangements, and gone so far, if he had not been convinced that NATO meant business."[30] Implementation of the NATO activation order was further delayed, but the order was not rescinded.

The October agreement built upon an agreement reached between Milosevic and Russian President Boris Yeltsin in Moscow in June that had established a fifty-member Kosovo Diplomatic Observer Mission (KDOM). The additional October demands were limited, and did not challenge fundamental Serbian interests. Similarly, the threat to Milosevic was limited: In the midst of the October talks, U.S. National Security Advisor Sandy Berger publicly downplayed the prospect of deploying U.S. troops, and Senate Majority Leader Trent Lott warned of public opposition to such deployment, making it clear that the threat of a NATO ground invasion, if it existed, was a distant one.[31]

But compliance with the October agreement was acceptable to Milosevic and the Serbs only as long as it did not result in gains for the KLA. The Serb counteroffensive in Kosovo in summer and fall had reduced the KLA military and political threat significantly. This was a view shared by some U.S. officials, who reportedly now viewed the KLA as "of little relevance to the negotiations."[32] The field reports of international observers on the ground in Kosovo make it clear that the Serbs, in fact, did carry out the reductions and withdrawals called for by the agreement. Secretary of State Albright declared on 27 October that the Serbs were "in very substantial compliance with Security Council Resolution 1199, and. . . this compliance is sufficient to justify not launching any strikes at this time."[33]

These developments suggest that, if the KLA could have been contained, Milosevic might have been persuaded to reach a compromise with the Rugova leadership in Kosovo. Unlike the agreements negotiated in Bosnia in September 1995 that provided the basis for the later Dayton agreement, however, the agreements negotiated in Belgrade in October did not define a settlement acceptable to both the Serbs and the Kosovar Albanians, and especially not to the KLA. The KLA, in fact, exploited the Serb pullback. According to reports of the verification mission, the KLA expanded its visible presence in areas from which the Serbs withdrew, and increased its provocations, becoming more overt and assertive in its efforts to exploit the advantage offered by Serb withdrawals.[34] Western governments openly criticized the KLA for violating the ceasefire established by the October agreement even though the KLA was not formally a party to the agreement.[35] But they did not have the capacity, perceived no compelling interest, and almost certainly did not have the inclination, to oppose the KLA on the ground. Western leaders continued to recognize this as a fundamental problem even as they moved toward coercion in January 1999,[36] but took no action to address it.

The resurgence of the KLA in the wake of the October agreement posed a direct threat to Milosevic's leadership in Belgrade. In response, the Serbs adopted a plan to "cleanse" the province by force. A *Washington Post* analysis published in April 1999 suggested that the plan, identified as "Operation Horseshoe," was put in place in November 1998, after the post-October resurgence of the KLA, with internal Yugoslav troop movements and other operations associated with the plan beginning in December.[37] International observers on the ground in Kosovo did note in December that violence was increasing in the province, and the Yugoslav army was undertaking offensive operations and meeting KLA resistance.[38]

It was thus clear by the end of 1998 that negotiations were futile. U.S. officials reported at the time that "key players in the Kosovo conflict are all still confident that they know best, that others are at a larger disadvantage and that the international community in the end will force their opponents to yield more ground." As a result, "neither side is ready for a deal right now." According to another official, "neither side understands that the other side has a point of view. They each say that you [the United States] have to just tell the other side what to do." The Kosovar Albanian negotiators, for example, finally rejected U.S. efforts to draft a compromise solution that would have given Kosovo extensive autonomy, but not independence.[39]

Toward Coercive Diplomacy in Bosnia

The Bosnian example reinforces the view that limited interventions motivated by humanitarian concerns or policymakers' perceived need to "do something" in the face of mounting public and/or media pressure, rather than by clearly-defined national interests, result in poorly conceived and inadequately implemented actions. These efforts were of limited military value and were not accompanied by a serious effort to extract larger political concessions from the Serbs. Their net effect, if any, appears to have been to deepen divisions within

NATO over the use of force and erode the effectiveness of any future threat to do so. Paradoxically, however, the prospect of irreparable damage to the internal cohesion and external credibility of the NATO alliance created a powerful U.S. national interest in bringing the war to an end.

The divisions within the alliance that followed the limited use of force against the Serbs at Bihac in November 1994 led U.S. policymakers to adopt a more comprehensive approach. Shoup and I have examined in detail the process by which the U.S. finally became seriously engaged in a strategy of coercive diplomacy in Bosnia in late 1994, when policymakers finally came to perceive the fighting as threatening U.S. national interests.[40] U.S. policymakers concluded that the use of force alone was futile, that the Serbs had to be given incentives to accept a settlement and that, if force were to be used, it had to be used to support a political settlement. U.S. diplomats entered into direct negotiations with both Milosevic and the Bosnian Serbs and prepared to back up their negotiating positions with a more credible threat of force. The establishment of a credible threat required intensive diplomatic efforts with NATO allies and Russia, primarily in the context of the Contact Group, so as to establish a set of shared perceptions, commitments, and goals. It also required the continuation of efforts to change the military balance on the ground in Bosnia.

In order to exercise control over negotiations, the U.S. had to shift negotiations over a political settlement away from the EU-UN controlled ICFY and to the Contact Group. Rather than mediating exchanges among the warring parties in search of a mutually acceptable solution, the Contact Group powers negotiated among themselves in search of a solution they all could accept and then impose on the warring parties. The United States can thus be said to have laid the basis for a strategy of coercive diplomacy in Bosnia in late 1994. But it was not until July 1995 that policymakers appear self-consciously to have committed themselves to such a strategy.

The decision by U.S. policymakers to intervene more directly in Bosnia was driven for the most part by concern that U.S. troops would be drawn into a potentially costly operation to evacuate UN forces, including those of the NATO allies. According to Holbrooke, following the fall of Srebrenica and Zepa in July 1995 and the realization that the UN operation was heading for failure, "the President saw the degree to which involvement was now inevitable, and how much better it would be to have involvement built on success rather than failure."[41] The resort to coercive diplomacy in 1995 was thus driven by a clear sense of national interest in avoiding a potential military catastrophe that might threaten the survival of the NATO alliance. Policymakers in the Clinton administration, including the President, also turned to coercive diplomacy out of a narrower sense of political self-interest; that is, their interest in resolving the Bosnian issue in time to prevent the presumed Republican candidate for president from using it against the administration in the 1996 election.[42]

Unlike the earlier uses of force in Bosnia, outlined above, the U.S. intervention that unfolded in late 1994 and 1995 was directed toward a specific, comprehensive goal: achieving an agreement that would put an end to the fighting. This was a goal shared by the U.S. and its allies, who were also concerned about the consequences of a collapse of the UN mission. This convergence of allied goals around a clear shared interest in avoiding catastrophe made the management of alliance politics over Bosnia more tractable in the period July–October 1995 than it had been at any point in the previous three years.

The success of coercive diplomacy in Bosnia in 1995 was built on changes in the military situation on the ground in the direction of a stalemate or standoff between the parties. In the literature on conflict resolution, the emergence of such a stalemate is seen as "ripening" and is characterized as "hurting" when each party is assumed to be neither willing or capable of enduring it, nor able to overcome it.[43] In Bosnia, the "ripening" process was manufactured or engineered by the United States. U.S. support for the development of the regular Croatian army and its war-fighting capacity began more than a year earlier, before coercive diplomacy was adopted as a strategy. Moreover, the stalemate in Bosnia was clearly not "hurting;" it was a stalemate enforced by the U.S., which was determined not to allow the strategic balance between Croatia and Serbia essential to regional stability to be tipped in favor of Croatia. It should be noted that the tragedies in Srebrenica and Zepa played a major role in establishing the conditions for this stalemate, which involved genocidal killing of Muslims by Serbs, but which were greeted by some U.S. officials as events that eliminated heretofore thorny map problems.[44]

For a strategy of coercive diplomacy to succeed, the demands imposed on the object of coercion must in the end be ones that can be accepted. In the case of Bosnia, this required the U.S. to alter its demands from those based on one-sided support for the Bosnian Muslims (and Bosnian Croats, to the extent that these two parties could be kept in agreement) to those based on recognition of the need to address the real and often conflicting interests of all sides, including the outside actors, Serbia (Milosevic), and Croatia (Tudjman). A December 1994 NATO declaration calling for "equitable and balanced arrangements" signaled the onset of this transformation.[45] It was completed by the *de facto* recognition of "Republika Srpska" and partition of Bosnia, incorporated in a 1 September agreement negotiated by Holbrooke with Milosevic and the Bosnian Serbs. This provided the general framework for the later Dayton settlement.

The key to securing Milosevic's cooperation from this point on, including his dramatic role at Dayton,[46] appears to have been the combination of a credible threat that the Bosnian Serbs would be defeated on the battlefield, thereby tipping the larger balance of power in the region against Serbia, and the positive inducements of recognition for the Bosnian Serb republic and a promise to lift sanctions against Serbia (formally the Federal Republic of Yugoslavia, or FRY). The threat was made credible by the successes of the Croatian army and by the application of limited but significant U.S. and NATO air power. As noted earlier, Milosevic's interest in lifting sanctions had been clear since 1993. Milosevic's cooperation at Dayton appears to have been secured in an apparent deal with Holbrooke in exchange for sanctions-lifting.

The final factor in the successful application of coercive diplomacy to end the war in Bosnia was, of course, the use of airpower. These words are often followed by the phrase "against the Serbs," but air power was used not only to pressure the Serbs into specific action on the ground—primarily a withdrawal from around Sarajevo—but also to pressure the Muslims into accepting the emerging partition of Bosnia. It was the end of bombing that opened the door to a cease-fire agreement and negotiations, not its onset. The agreement on "basic constitutional principles" for Bosnia, signed by the foreign ministers of Croatia, Serbia, and Bosnia on 8 September in Geneva, was reached while the bombing was still in progress, but the bombing did not, in fact, "bring the Serbs to the negotiating table." Milosevic was already moving in early August toward establishing control over the Bosnian Serbs so as to bring them to the negotiating table and had completed his moves before the bombing began. It appears that it was the Bosnian Muslims who were brought to the negotiating table by the bombing or, more accurately, by the threat that it would be ended if they did not agree to the U.S. settlement. The initial decision to "suspend" the bombing on 14 September came in exchange for Bosnian Serb agreement to withdraw their heavy weapons from the exclusion zone around Sarajevo and end the siege of that city.

At the same time, the United States did not allow the combined Croatian-Muslim offensive in western Bosnia that followed the ouster of the Krajina Serbs to inflict too great a defeat on the Bosnian Serbs. Doing so might have drawn Serbia into the conflict directly and threatened the strategic balance in the region. A military analyst points out that the air campaign in Bosnia "equated to just about a busy day's sorties count for coalition air forces during the Gulf War" and characterizes it as "a strategically limited, tactically intense, high-technology, coalition air campaign, conducted under tight restraints of time and permissible collateral damage. . . aimed at coercing political and military compliance from a regional opponent who had no airpower."[47] The United States and its NATO allies thus were careful not to use so much force as to lead either side to believe that all was won or lost, thereby creating real incentives on all sides to accept the U.S. settlement.

To a certain extent, the "balancing act" carried out by U.S. diplomats during the bombing was necessitated by the pressures exerted by the British, French, and Russians. However, "balancing" reflected to a far greater extent the difficulties of applying the techniques of coercive diplomacy to the behaviors of multiple parties with conflicting interests. By facilitating the emergence of a Croatian ground army and using air power against the Bosnian Serb army, the U.S. encouraged the political and territorial ambitions of the Croats and the Muslims. The United States, therefore, did not prevent the Bosnian Serbs from using artillery withdrawn from Sarajevo and Serbian air power to stop the Croatian and Muslim advance in western Bosnia. Whereas Holbrooke had blamed the Serbs for the difficulties of negotiations in August and September, for example, by October he was blaming the Muslims for blocking the conclusion of a cease-fire agreement and threatening to abandon them to their fate. The Bosnian Muslims agreed to a cease-fire only after they had extracted a commitment from the United States to provide them with military assistance after the settlement. Thus, the United States was compelled to supply positive incentives to cooperation as well as applying threats of force to all the parties directly involved in the conflict in order to turn negotiations into a non-zero sum game for all participants.

From Coercive Diplomacy to Coercion in Kosovo

The U.S. response to the escalating conflict in Kosovo was formulated in the context of a mounting domestic political crisis over the impeachment of President Clinton. A political advisor to the President, commenting on this period in a later press report, said "I hardly remember Kosovo in political discussions. It was all impeachment, impeachment, impeachment. There was nothing else."[48] The House of Representatives voted to impeach in mid-December, and the Senate trial of the President took place in early 1999. One consequence of this crisis appears to have been a significant increase in the influence of the Secretary of State over U.S. responses to developments in Kosovo. A more cautious actor who played a key role up to then, head of the policy planning staff Greg Craig, was, for example, transferred to the President's impeachment defense team in Congress. During Bosnia, then-Ambassador Albright had been an outspoken advocate of the use of force. Secretary Albright supported air strikes in Kosovo as early as May 1998. But air strikes were rejected by the national security advisor, Samuel Berger, because there were no plans in place for specific follow-up actions[49]—a key deficiency of early attempts to use force in Bosnia.

Secretary Albright and others appear to have been motivated very largely by a desire to punish Milosevic for his actions in Kosovo, and in no small part by a desire to atone for what some felt to have been their failure to act early enough in Bosnia. In March 1998 Secretary Albright had pressed the Contact Group foreign ministers to act by arguing that "history is watching us, and we have an opportunity to make up for the mistakes that had been made four or five years ago."[50] When the motivation for the use of force is punishment, there are likely to be few constraints on its use, and few incentives to be flexible in diplomacy or to accommodate the interests of one's opponent—key factors contributing to the success of coercive diplomacy in Bosnia. While there can be no doubt that a humanitarian crisis was developing in Kosovo at the time, Western policymakers do not appear to have been motivated by humanitarian concerns. It appears that Western diplomatic and political rhetoric shifted to "humanitarian disaster" as justification for the threat and, later, use of force because Russian and Chinese opposition precluded legitimation by the Security Council.

One participant in a December 1998 discussion of the events then unfolding in Kosovo argued "as long as there were no atrocities committed in Kosovo that might conjure up memories of ethnic cleansing in Bosnia, the West would not intervene."[51] But the Serbs appear to have crossed this perceptual threshold by perpetrating a massacre of forty-five civilians in the Kosovo village of Racak in January 1999, conjuring up images and memories of Bosnia and diverting attention away from the actions of the KLA. The massacre at Racak galvanized Secretary Albright to action. According to "confidants" of the Secretary, quoted in an April 1999 media analysis of the decision to use force, Albright "realized that the galvanizing force of the atrocity would not last long. 'Whatever threat of force you don't get in the next two weeks you're never getting,' one advisor told her, 'at least until the next Racak'."[52] U.S. policymakers adopted a strategy consisting of four elements: a demand that the conflicting parties attend a meeting; presentation at the meeting of demands—including deployment of a NATO implementation force in Kosovo—decided upon in advance by the Contact Group, including Russia; non-negotiability of these demands; and, a credible threat of military force to back up the demands.[53] These elements correspond almost precisely to Alexander George's definition of a full-fledged ultimatum: "1) a demand on the opponent; 2) a time limit or sense of urgency for compliance with the demand; and 3) a threat of punishment for noncompliance that is both credible to the opponent and sufficiently potent to impress upon him that compliance is preferable."[54]

Whether an ultimatum will succeed depends heavily on the relative stakes for each actor. The interests articulated by American policymakers were, for the most part, abstract, or distant.[55] Unlike the situation in Bosnia in 1995, there were as yet no allied troops on the ground and at risk in Kosovo, threatening alliance cohesion and the survival of NATO. For Milosevic, in contrast, it was clear that the territorial integrity of his country was at risk. But, for him, the overriding interest at stake in the conflict appears to have been his own personal power. In the case of Kosovo, therefore, the interests at stake appear, at least at the outset, to have been relatively greater for Milosevic than for U.S. policymakers. The demands placed upon Milosevic proved unacceptable, and the threat behind the ultimatum lacked, from Milosevic's perspective, sufficient credibility or potency (or both) to require compliance.

On 29 January the Contact Group, after reiterating past demands on both the Serbs and Albanians, "summoned" representatives of both sides to negotiations at Rambouillet. The demands, and call for talks, were backed up by an explicit NATO threat to "take whatever measures are necessary. . . to avert a humanitarian catastrophe, by compelling compliance with the demands of the international community and the achievement of a political settlement." The NATO Secretary General was empowered to "authorize air strikes against targets on FRY territory." But, cognizant of the fact that the conflict in Kosovo had become (at least) three-sided, the NATO Secretary General was to "take full account of the position and actions of the Kosovar leadership and all Kosovar armed elements in and around Kosovo in reaching his decision on military action. NATO will take all appropriate measures in case of a failure by the Kosovar Albanian side to comply with the demands of the international community."[56]

Unlike Bosnia, given Russian and Chinese opposition to intervention, there could be no UN Security Council resolution authorizing NATO's use of force in

Kosovo. Nonetheless, UN Secretary General Kofi Annan delivered a clear, and unprecedented, endorsement of the NATO threat, emphasizing the "combination of force and diplomacy" as "the key to peace in the Balkans," and "the need to use force, when all other means have failed." He declared "We may be reaching that limit, once again, in the former Yugoslavia."[57] Thus, the strategy adopted by the United States and its allies in January 1999 had all the characteristics of an ultimatum, directed against Milosevic and the Serbs, but was contingent on cooperation by the Kosovar Albanians, including the KLA.

The Contact Group then promulgated a list of "non-negotiable principles/basic elements for a settlement".[58] Unlike the Dayton conference that ended the Bosnian war, not only had neither side agreed to the basic principles or concepts of an agreement, both sides had already in late 1998 rejected the approach adopted by negotiators. The Albanian delegation, which included representatives of the KLA, was unhappy with the efforts of negotiators to accommodate the Serbs, and was persuaded to accept the proposed agreement only under intense pressure from the United States. Secretary Albright traveled to Rambouillet to pressure the Kosovar Albanian delegation to agree.[59] NATO air strikes against the Serbs were made contingent on Kosovar Albanian acquiescence to the Rambouillet Accord in much the same way that air strikes against the Serbs in Bosnia had been made contingent on Bosnian Muslim acquiescence to the agreements that later were incorporated in the Dayton Accords. This represented both a positive and a negative inducement to cooperation. The Kosovar Albanians were also offered a more clearly positive inducement to cooperate in the form of a *de facto* roadmap to independence. For the Serbs, however, there appear to have been few, if any, positive inducements to cooperate.

The proposed settlement put on the table by the United States at Rambouillet may be viewed as either a valid peace plan, a flawed peace plan that nonetheless represented a genuine effort to reach a settlement, or a "turn down" proposal. From the latter perspective, the events at Rambouillet are seen not as an effort actually to negotiate a settlement as had been the case at Dayton, but as an effort to gain support for, and legitimate use of force that had already been decided, by presenting an ultimatum known in advance to be unacceptable to the Serbs so as to frame the Kosovo conflict as one in which the Serbs "rejected peace." The statement of the primary U.S. negotiator, Ambassador Chris Hill, that there was "zero point zero" chance of the Serbs accepting the proposed settlement[60] lends some support to this interpretation. Moreover, Secretary Albright suggested in a later interview with the *New York Times* that the purpose of the Rambouillet process was "getting [the Europeans] to agree to the use of force."[61] However, the last phase of the Rambouillet process involved what appears to be a genuine effort by U.S. negotiators to meet Serb objections, which nonetheless failed.

Secretary Albright's apparent eagerness to turn to force was matched by Milosevic's willingness to accept bombing by NATO rather than sign the agreement. The threat of NATO air strikes had been an important element in the successful effort in October 1998 to get Milosevic and the Serbs to withdraw forces. But, as the chairman of NATO's military committee at that time, General Klaus Naumann, explained to a U.S. Senate committee in November 1999, by Rambouillet "our threat was not as credible as it used to be in October. We had threatened too often and hadn't done anything."[62] Publicly-articulated Russian and Chinese diplomatic opposition to Security Council authorization of the use of force, which in Bosnia had been an essential step in the establishment of credibility, was likely just as important for Milosevic's estimate of the credibility of the NATO threat. Moreover, the relatively limited air campaign conducted in Bosnia in 1995, and the similarly limited action taken by the United States and Britain against Iraq in December 1997, may also have undermined the effectiveness of the NATO threat in Kosovo. Daalder and O'Hanlon argue that these campaigns suggested NATO bombing "would likely last only a few days."[63] Some senior US policymakers, in fact, suggested publicly that "Milosevic would probably back down after a few visible targets were hit."[64] Secretary Albright stated publicly at the outset of the bombing "I don't see this as a long-term operation. . . . I think this is something. . . achievable within a relatively short period of time."[65]

The apparent violation of Serbian sovereignty inherent in the provisions of the security annex to the Rambouillet agreement, rejected by the Serbs, may have been less significant for the Serb position than their opposition to foreign troops—as opposed to an international "presence"—in Kosovo. Moreover, developments following the October 1998 agreements had made it clear that the United States and its allies could not control or even influence the KLA, as it had the warring parties in Bosnia. The KLA, in contrast, was not under the control, and was subject to only limited influence by any outside actor. Its medium and long-term interests were not served by peace, and certainly not by any arrangements that preserved a Serbian presence in and sovereignty over Kosovo, although it was prepared to, and did accept short-term cease-fires in order to gain further advantage. Although represented at Rambouillet, the KLA was not a party to the negotiations over the draft proposal leading up to the meeting and remained a competitor or even adversary to the Americans' main negotiating partner in Kosovo, the LDK. There was little reason to believe that the KLA would comply with the disarmament provisions of the Rambouillet proposal. Acceptance of Rambouillet therefore raised the specter, from Milosevic's perspective, of the occupation of Kosovo by foreign troops, and the takeover of power in Kosovo by the KLA. Alternately, initiating war, in the case of Kosovo, entailed Serbia's enduring an air attack by NATO expected not to do much damage, while conducting operations to eliminate the KLA and expel a large proportion of the ethnically Albanian population from Kosovo by force, confident that no ground attack by NATO would occur during this process.

As in Bosnia, concern to protect civilians from the use of force by the Serbs did play a role in Western policy making. President Clinton, in his speech announcing the start of air strikes, stated that one of the three goals of the operation was "to deter President Milosevic from continuing and escalating his attacks on helpless civilians by imposing a price for those attacks."[66] But, as Kelly

Greenhill has demonstrated, the scale, tempo, and geographic sources of forced expulsions from Kosovo escalated after NATO initiated its air campaign.[67] Expulsions increased the humanitarian costs of the crisis; undermined the already weak Serbian claim to "victimhood;" provided a concrete threat to the stability of neighboring states; threatened to create a refugee crisis in the West; and posed a challenge to the prestige of the United States and senior U.S. policymakers. These created concrete interests and motivations to keep policymakers committed to the bombing, to intensifying it, and to remaining steadfast in their demands. As in the case of Bosnia, intervention itself created incentives to use more force to ensure success, contributing to a shift in strategy from coercive diplomacy to straightforward coercion. Within ten days of the start of the bombing, U.S. and European policymakers were considering adding the removal of Milosevic from power to the list of NATO objectives, making it "a condition for stopping the war."[68]

The central lesson of the endgame in Bosnia for U.S. policymakers should have been that the creation and deployment of a credible ground force—in the case of Bosnia, the army of Croatia and its operations to expel the Serbs from the Krajina region and take control of much of western Bosnia—was critical to the success of coercive diplomacy. Nonetheless, the military and civilian leaderships of the Pentagon were reported "firmly opposed" to sending U.S. ground forces into Kosovo.[69] A later analysis of the U.S. decision to engage in bombing argues that it was "for fear of a divisive congressional and allied debate"[70] that President Clinton accompanied announcement of the air campaign with the declaration that "I do not intend to put our troops in Kosovo to fight a war." It is almost certainly the case that the absence of any threat of a ground assault lowered Milosevic's estimate of the potency of the NATO threat.

Although a media analysis on 2 June 1999 reported that a decision to use ground troops was only a few days or week away, preparations for the invasion, including positioning of troops, could not have been completed before September 1999.[71] The threat of a NATO ground invasion was, at the time of the capitulation, therefore still a distant threat, and the Yugoslav capacity to make such an invasion costly was still substantial.[72] Thus, the more immediate threat to Milosevic was posed by the intensifying air campaign and its domestic social and political consequences. Escalation of the air campaign affected not only the Yugoslav military, but large segments of the urban civilian population.[73] The indictment of Milosevic for war crimes in late May seemed to reduce the constraints on Western action even further.

In response to Russia's continued opposition to a purely NATO deployment as part of a settlement, NATO foreign ministers on 12 April demanded that Milosevic "agree to the stationing in Kosovo of an international military presence" rather than a NATO force. On 14 April the German government advanced a proposal, endorsed the same day by EU leaders, for a Security Council resolution outlining the steps to peace. This opened the door to Russian participation in a search for a negotiated end to the bombing, which seems to have been a more immediate factor in Milosevic's decision to capitulate than the anticipation of a NATO ground invasion. The appointment on 14 April of Viktor Chernomyrdin as the Russian diplomatic point man initiated a period of intense, direct East-West diplomacy over ending the war.[74] After meeting with Milosevic in Belgrade, Chernomyrdin announced on 22 April that Milosevic would accept an "international presence" in Kosovo under UN auspices.[75] By 6 May, Russia was supporting deployment of an "effective international civil and security presence. . . capable of guaranteeing. . . the common objectives." This formulation, contained in the 6 May G-8 statement, represented diplomatic code for NATO forces.[76] More important, Chernomyrdin is reported to have advised Milosevic on 2 June that the threat of an eventual NATO ground invasion was, in fact, real, and that Russia would not help Milosevic resist such an invasion.[77] This is likely to have made the distant threat of an invasion politically more immediate for Milosevic, and accepting the NATO-EU-Russian demands more attractive.[78]

The NATO-EU-Russian principles for resolution of the crisis accepted by Milosevic and later incorporated as annex 2 to Security Council Resolution 1244 (10 June 1999) included "establishment of an interim administration. . . under which the people of Kosovo can enjoy substantial autonomy within the Federal Republic of Yugoslavia to be decided by the Security Council of the United Nations." This re-introduced the UN Security Council into the process of authorizing and legitimating arrangements for the administration of post-conflict Kosovo and, more important, adoption of a long-term solution. This created diplomatic leverage for Russia and/or China over independence for Kosovo, and the accommodation of Serbian/Yugoslav interests. Echoing Milosevic's willingness, even eagerness to accept United Nations authority over intervention in the Bosnian conflict, capitulation came the following day in the form of a Yugoslav parliamentary endorsement of the NATO-EU-Russian demands.[79] It is beyond the scope of this chapter to explain the Russian change in position. The reasons for the Russian change are, however, less important for understanding the dynamics and effect of intervention than the fact of the change, and its consequences for the Serbian calculation of costs.

Conclusions

Intervention in Bosnia represented the continuation of Western efforts to contain the destabilizing consequences of the dissolution of former Yugoslavia, rather than an effort to facilitate meaningful settlement of the issues driving Bosnia toward violence. Such an effort appeared to be closed off by recognition of the former internal borders of the Yugoslav federation as if they were inter-state borders, and of the Bosnian state they defined, prior to negotiation among the conflicting parties of an agreement on either new borders or, more likely, agreement on a new political order within the existing borders that recognized the legitimate claims of conflicting groups. *A priori* treatment of the internal border that separated Kosovo from the rest of the Serbian republic as if it were an inter-state border similarly closed off any approach to negotiating an agreement between Serbia and the secessionist Albanian nationalist movement to exchange redefined borders for independence, or an agreement between Kosovo Serbs and Albanians recognizing their respective claims within the framework of an independent Kosovo.

The interests that in the end compelled armed intervention as part of a strategy of coercive diplomacy were not the product of the conflicts in Bosnia and Kosovo themselves. Some in the U.S. argued at the time, and continue to argue today, that the Serbs were committing genocide against the Muslims in Bosnia and the Albanians in Kosovo, and that the U.S. was not only obligated to intervene, but had a (moral) interest in doing so. The debate over the place of moral values in the definition of American national interest remained unresolved, however. It was instead limited intervention, increasing commitment of national resources and prestige over time, domestic American politics and, in the Bosnian case, the increasing vulnerability of allied troops on the ground that created the impetus for further intervention by raising the political cost of inaction.

Ultimately, escalating risks to troops from NATO-member states on the ground in Bosnia led to Chapter VII authorization to use force by UNPROFOR, and created the impetus for direct U.S. and NATO military intervention to end the fighting. The threat to NATO cohesion posed by the prospect that these troops might be overwhelmed in the absence of support from the U.S., and the cost of waiting to assist them until they were already under attack, created a compelling U.S. national interest in bringing the fighting in Bosnia to a rapid conclusion. While policymakers' initial assessments that no strategic national interest was at stake limited engagement in the conflict, over time that engagement tended nonetheless to expand incrementally in response to events on the ground and, in part, media coverage that created pressure on policymakers to "do something" in response to egregious developments. The gradual expansion of resources committed to the conflict, in turn, created a real national interest in ending it. Thus, the decision to intervene directly in the conflict with military force in support of a strategy of coercive diplomacy reflected a change in national decision-makers' calculations of the interests put at risk by the conflict.

Coercive diplomacy in Bosnia and Kosovo can be considered successful because it achieved the primary goals of Western policymakers. It put an end to the fighting and Serbian violence against civilian populations; averted a threat to the NATO alliance; stemmed the flow of refugees to neighboring states and the West; and, punished Milosevic. But these cases suggest the difficulty of intervening in conflicts involving multiple warring parties: Threats or coercion applied against one party in order to encourage it to negotiate or comply makes the other(s) less willing to do so, or may even be exploited to the other's advantage, thereby potentially worsening the situation rather than moving it toward a solution. In Bosnia, the United States enjoyed direct or, in the case of the Bosnian Serbs, indirect leverage over all the parties. In Kosovo, in contrast, the United States and its allies exercised no leverage over the KLA, and rapidly declining leverage over the LDK and Milosevic. The absence of leverage over the KLA undermined the October 1998 Belgrade agreement, which initially had all the makings of a successful exercise in coercive diplomacy. That agreement looked very much like the coercive diplomacy exercised by NATO in summer 1993 and February 1994 in Bosnia that led to pullbacks of the Bosnian Serbs around Sarajevo. But the key to securing Bosnian Serb compliance with the NATO ultimatums was preventing the Serbs' adversary—the Bosnian Muslims—from taking advantage of their withdrawals. Compliance with the October 1998 Belgrade agreement was acceptable to Milosevic and the Serbs only as long as it did not result in gains for the KLA.

The interventions in Bosnia and Kosovo were characterized by repeated failures to deter, compel, or coerce local actors, until the United States and its allies finally achieved a clear unity of purpose. This did not occur until both U.S. and European policymakers shared the perception of a real threat to their respective national and shared interests. That threat, of course, derived from the fact of intervention itself. The resort to coercive diplomacy by the United States in Bosnia in 1995 avoided a potential military catastrophe that might have threatened the survival of the NATO alliance. This national interest was reinforced by the strong political interest of President Clinton in resolving the Bosnian issue well before the 1996 presidential election campaign. The Europeans were concerned about the consequences of a collapse of the UN mission for their troops on the ground, as well as the implications of unrestrained warfare on their southern flank. This shared interest in avoiding catastrophe facilitated alliance consensus over Bosnia after July 1995. Similarly, in the case of Kosovo, it was clear by the April 1999 NATO summit that policymakers perceived a potential threat to the coherence, if not the survival of the alliance. As in the case of Bosnia, preservation of the NATO alliance was a powerful motivation for the use of force to ensure success.

In the Bosnian case, military intervention to impose a settlement was accompanied by positive inducements to the conflict parties to cooperate. These included U.S. promises to lift sanctions on Serbia (Yugoslavia), concessions to the Bosnian Serbs in the form of *de facto* partition of Bosnia and establishment of the Bosnian Serb Republic, and a commitment to the Bosnian Muslims to provide military assistance after the settlement. The Bosnian case thus provides clear evidence of the importance of positive inducements to a successful strategy of coercive diplomacy.

In the case of Kosovo, U.S. intervention came in support of Albanian demands, although in the end, the allies did not, in the short term, fulfill the Albanian demand for independence. For Milosevic and the Serbs, there were few positive inducements to cooperate until Russian diplomacy secured a settlement that placed military occupation of Kosovo under UN instead of NATO authority and, at least in the short term, denied independence to Kosovo and affirmed the formal sovereignty of Serbia (Yugoslavia) over the territory.

Some U.S. policymakers appear to have been motivated in Kosovo largely by a desire to punish Milosevic, for his actions in Kosovo and his earlier actions in Bosnia, and to make amends, at least in their own minds, for their own inaction in Bosnia. With this motivation, there were few incentives to be flexible in diplomacy or to accommodate Serbian interests. Escalation of the air campaign against Milosevic was consistent with the full-fledged ultimatum strategy on which the United States and the European allies embarked at Rambouillet. In the absence of negotiation, however, escalation can end only with the military defeat of the adversary. This was an outcome that threatened to become very costly for the NATO alliance, and especially for a sitting president facing a re-election campaign. In order to avoid a ground war, the need to defeat and occupy Serbia, and untold casualties, the United States and its allies moved from a full-fledged ultimatum to a strategy involving at least limited, mediated negotiations facilitated by Russian participation, which was crucial to the success of this effort. Nonetheless, unlike the negotiated settlement in Bosnia that addressed and balanced the real interests of all three warring parties, intervention in Kosovo was brought to an end only by the capitulation of Milosevic and the Serbs.

Notes

1. Steven L. Burg and Paul S. Shoup, *The War in Bosnia-Herzegovina: Ethnic Conflict and International Intervention* (Armonk, N.Y.: M. E. Sharpe, 1999), 80–81, 84–88.

2. *U.S. Department of State Dispatch* 2, no. 22 (3 June 1991): 395–396.

3. For discussion of the uncertainties surrounding these principles at the moment of Yugoslavia's dissolution, see Steven L. Burg, *War or Peace? Nationalism, Democracy, and American Foreign Policy in Post-Communist Europe* (New York: New York University Press, 1996), 45–55.

4. Steven L. Burg, "Nationalism and Democratization in Yugoslavia," *The Washington Quarterly* 14, no. 4 (Autumn 1991): 5–19.

5. Burg and Shoup, *The War in Bosnia-Herzegovina*, 92–102.

6. For a detailed account of these negotiations, see Burg and Shoup, *The War in Bosnia-Herzegovina*, 108–117.

7. See, for example, International Commission on the Balkans, *Unfinished Peace: Report of the International Commission on the Balkans* (Washington, DC: The Brookings Institution Press, for the Aspen Institute and the Carnegie Endowment for International Peace, 1996) and Barnett R. Rubin, ed., *Toward Comprehensive Peace in Southeast Europe* , Report of the South Balkans Working Group of the Council on Foreign Relations Center for Preventive Action (New York: Twentieth Century Fund Press, 1996).

8. Kofi Annan, "Agreement of 5 June 1992 on the reopening of Sarajevo airport for humanitarian purposes," *Report of the Secretary General Pursuant to Security Council Resolution 757*, S/24075, (6 June 1992).

9. Burg and Shoup, *The War in Bosnia-Herzegovina*, 120–127, 200–203.

10. These negotiations are examined in detail in Burg and Shoup, *The War in Bosnia-Herzegovina*, 189-262.

11. Herbert S. Okun, as cited in *New York Times*, 11 July 1993, IV: 7.

12. Burg and Shoup, *The War in Bosnia-Herzegovina*, 207–208.

13. See Security Council Resolution 819 (16 April 1993), establishing Srebrenica as a "safe area," and Resolution 824 (7 May 1993), extending this status to five additional areas. Andrew Winner points out this source of the contradiction between UNPROFOR

mission/mandate and rules of engagement in his doctoral dissertation, "You and What Army? Coalitions and Coercive Diplomacy," (Ph.D. diss., University of Maryland, College Park, 2002).

14. See Norbert Both and Jan Willem Honig, *Srebrenica: Record of a War Crime* (New York: Penguin Books, 1997).

15. For a careful examination of the impact of media coverage of these events on Western policymakers, see Nik Gowing, *Real-Time Television Coverage of Armed Conflicts and Diplomatic Crises: Does It Pressure or Distort Foreign Policy Decisions?* Working Paper 94-1, The Joan Shorenstein Barone Center on the Press, Politics and Public Policy (Cambridge, MA: John F. Kennedy School of Government, Harvard University, 1994), which is based on extensive interviews with Western policymakers. These events are also examined in greater detail in Burg and Shoup, *The War in Bosnia-Herzegovina*, 140–159, 329, 340–341. These events, as well as those addressed in the following section on coercive diplomacy, are examined from the perspective of coalition theory and the politics of coercive diplomacy in Winner, *You and What Army?*

16. Peter Viggo Jakobsen makes the same point in *Western Use of Coercive Diplomacy After the Cold War: A Challenge for Theory and Practice* (New York: St. Martin's Press, 1998), 92.

17. Behlul Begaj, "'Drenica's Homogenization of Albanians," *Helsinki Charter* (March 1998) as reprinted in Helsinki Committee for Human Rights in Serbia, *Helsinki Charter* Special English Edition on Kosovo (Belgrade: January 1999), 4-5.

18. Special Representative Robert Gelbard, *Press Conference*, Prishtina, Serbia and Montenegro (22 February 1998) and *Press Conference*, Belgrade, Serbia and Montenegro (23 February 1998), as published at www.state.gov.

19. *Washington Post*, 25 June 1998

20. Robert S. Gelbard, *Statement before the House International Relations Committee*, Washington, DC, 23 July 1998 as published at www.state.gov.

21. UN Security Council document S/1998/834 (4 September 1998), 2.

22. *Statement to the Press*, Villamoura, 24 September 1998 as published at www.nato.int.

23. For contemporary news reports, see *New York Times*, 30 September 1998, A1 and *Washington Post*, September 30, 1998, A1 as published at www.washingtonpost.com. For a more detailed, later analysis, see Human Rights Watch, *A Week of Terror in Drenica* (New York: Human Rights Watch, 1999).

24. *Statement to the Press of the Secretary General*, NATO HQ, 13 October 1998 at www.nato.int

25. For an overview of the October agreements, see Tim Youngs, *Kosovo: The Diplomatic and Military Options* Research Paper 98/93 (London: House of Commons Library, 27 October 1998), 15-19.

26. US Department of State, *Ambassador Richard Holbrooke, Special Envoy, and Ambassador William Walker, Director of the OSCE Kosovo Verification Mission, On the record briefing released by the Office of the Spokesman*, Washington, DC, 28 October 1999 as published at www.state.gov

27. UN Security Council document S/1998/953 (*Letter dated 14 October 1998 from the Charge d'Affairs. . . of Yugoslavia. . . to the President of the Security Council*) (14 October 1998)

28. UN Security Council document S/1998/953.

29. James P. Rubin, "Excerpt from the Daily Press Briefing," Washington, DC, 13 October 1998. As released by the Office of the Spokesman, US Department of State.

30. "Milosevic Backs Down on Kosovo," Press Conference by the Foreign Secretary. . . ," 13 October 1998, at www.fco.gov.uk.

31. *Washington Post*, 12 October 1998, A14 as published at www.washingtonpost.com.

32. *Washington Post*, 3 September 1998, A48 as published at www.washingtonpost.com.

33. Secretary of State Madeleine K. Albright, "Remarks on Kosovo," 27 October 1998, Washington, DC. As released by the Office of the Spokesperson, U.S. Department of State.

34. For reports of KLA activity, see KDOM reports of 31 October, and 2,3,4 November 1998, as posted on the State Department website special section on Kosovo (www.state.gov/regions/eur); UN Security Council document S/1998/1068 (November 12, 1998), paragraphs 13-17; *Washington Post*, 18 November 1998, A1 as published at www.washingtonpost.com, and *New York Times*, 8 December 1998, A3.

35. Foreign & Commonwealth Office, *Edited Transcript of a Press Conference by the Foreign Secretary, Mr. Robin Cook, Ljubljana, Slovenia, Monday 23 November 1998*, at www.fco.uk/news. Daalder and O'Hanlon suggest that NATO military and U.S. diplomatic officials assured Milosevic during the October meetings that NATO would control the KLA. See Ivo Daalder and Michael E. O'Hanlon, *Winning Ugly: NATO's War to Save Kosovo* (Washington, DC: Brookings, 2000), 58. However, an American participant in the October meetings has reported to the author that no such assurance was given, because "I would not have made such an assertion as we knew too little about the KLA to begin with. We only began to get some sense of the structure, leadership, and size of the KLA after the so-called cease-fire went into effect. None of us, including [Gen.] Clark, were in a position to make such claims and all of us, including Clark, knew that." This American diplomat pointed out to the author that the negotiating team that met with Milosevic in October "all knew the October agreement was a huge risk as KVM had no enforcement mechanism and the KLA was not party to it. I spent the next five months trying to persuade the KLA to honor something it did not sign or was consulted on. We all knew the agreement was shot full of holes. There was no alternative to open war, however. So we signed, took a deep breath, and did our best." (Personal communication from Shaun Byrnes (25 August 2001).)

36. *Washington Post*, 19 April 1999 as published at www.washingtonpost.com.

37. *Washington Post*, 11 April 1999, A1 as published at www.washingtonpost.com. For a less detailed analysis that nonetheless argues the campaign was well-organized in advance, see *New York Times*, 29 May 1999, A1.

38. See KDOM reports of 12, 14, 16, 18, 19, 20, 21, 22, 27 December 1998, as posted on the State Department website special section on Kosovo at www.state.gov/regions/eur.

39. *Washington Post*, 30 December 1998, A16 as published at www.washingtonpost.com.

40. Burg and Shoup, *The War in Bosnia-Herzegovina*, 307–360.

41. Burg and Shoup, *The War in Bosnia-Herzegovina*, 325.

42. Bob Woodward, *The Choice* (New York: Simon and Schuster, 1996), 253–270.

43. See I. William Zartman, *Ripe for Resolution: Conflict and Intervention in Africa*, 2nd ed. (New York: Oxford, 1989); "The Unfinished Agenda: Negotiating Internal Conflicts," in *Stopping the Killing: How Civil Wars End*, ed. Roy Licklider (New York: New York University Press, 1993), 20–34.

44. Burg and Shoup, *The War in Bosnia-Herzegovina*, 326.

45. Cited in Burg and Shoup, *The War in Bosnia-Herzegovina*, 321.

46. Burg and Shoup, *The War in Bosnia-Herzegovina*, 363–364.

47. Col. Robert C. Owen, USAF, "The Balkans Air Campaign Study," part II, *Airpower Journal* XI, no. 3 (Fall 1997): 8, 20. Part I of the analysis is to be found in *Airpower Journal* XI, no. 2 (Summer 1997): 5–24.

48. *New York Times*, 18 April 1999, 1.

49. *New York Times*, 18 April 1999, 1.

50. *Washington Post*, 18 April 1999 as published at www.washingtonpost.com.

51. Steven L. Burg, "The Failure of Early Warning in Kosovo," in *The Application of Prevention* Report of the Center for Preventive Action's Fifth Annual Conference (New York: Council on Foreign Relations, 11 December 1998), 8.

52. *Washington Post*, 18 April 1999, A1 as published at www.washingtonpost.com and *New York Times*, 18 April 1999, 13.

53. *Washington Post*, 18 April 1999 as published at www.washingtonpost.com.

54. Alexander L. George, *Forceful Persuasion: Coercive Diplomacy as an Alternative to War* (Washington: United States Institute for Peace Press, 1991), 7.

55. See, e.g., *The Guardian* (London), 6 April 1999 at www.newsunlimited.co.uk.

56. *Statement by the North Atlantic Council on Kosovo* (Brussels, 30 January 1999).

57. *Secretary-General Calls for Unconditional Respect for Human Rights of Kosovo Citizens, in Statement to North Atlantic Treaty Organization*, United Nations Press Release SG/SM/6878 (28 January 1999). Note that the sub-title of the press release ("Kofi Annan Stresses Peaceful Negotiation Only Way to Resolve Kosovo Conflict") contradicts the substance of Annan's remarks, and may represent an attempt by UN staff to distance the organization from the NATO threat.

58. These are reproduced in Marc Weller, "The Rambouillet Conference on Kosovo," *International Affairs* 75, 2 (1999): 225-6.

59. James Rubin, Department of State Spokesman, *Press Briefing on the Kosovo Peace Talks*, Rambouillet, France, 21 February 1999. As released by the Office of the Spokesman, Paris, France. U.S. Department of State at http://secretary.state.gov/www/statements/1999.

60. *Washington Post*, 27 March 1999, A15 as published at www.washingtonpost.com.

61. *New York Times*, 18 April 1999, 13.

62. United States Senate, Armed Services Committee, *Hearing on Operation Allied Force and Relief Operations in Kosovo*, 3 November 1999 as published by Federal Document Clearing House, Inc. on CIS Congressional Universe (Lexis-Nexis).

63. Daalder and O'Hanlon, *Winning Ugly*, 95.

64. *Washington Post*, 7 April 1999, A1 as published at www.washingtonpost.com.

65. *Washington Post*, 8 April 1999, A26 as published at www.washingtonpost.com.

66. *Full text of President Clinton's statement*, as published at www.cnn.com (March 24, 1999). For the European statement of goals, which fails to mention the NATO air strikes, see *The Guardian*, 24 March 1999 as published at www.newsunlimited.co.uk.

67. Kelly M. Greenhill, "People Pressure: The Coercive Use of Refugees in the Kosovo Conflict" (unpublished paper). See also the map and timeline of expulsions in *New York Times*, 29 May 1999, A4 and A5.

68. *Washington Post*, 5 April 1999, A12 as published at www.washingtonpost.com.

69. *Washington Post*, 23 January 1999, A1. See also the testimony to Congress by the Secretary of Defense, reported at 4 February 1999, A21; both as published at www.washingtonpost.com.

70. *Washington Post*, 18 April 1999, A1 as published at www.washingtonpost.com.

71. *New York Times*, 2 June 1999, A12.

72. *New York Times*, 28 June 1999, A8; *Washington Post*, 19 September 1999, A1 as published at www.washingtonpost.com, and John Barry and Evan Thomas, "The Kosovo Cover-Up," *Newsweek*, 15 May 2000, 22.

73. See, e.g., the report in *Washington Post*, 4 May 1999, A1 as published at www.washingtonpost.com.

74. *New York Times*, 8 June 1999, A13A and A13B (Northeast edition).

75. *Washington Post*, 23 April 1999, A1 as published at www.washingtonpost.com.

76. *The Guardian*, 7 May 1999, as published at www.newsunlimited.co.uk.

77. *New York Times*, 7 November 1999, 4.

78. Some sources suggest that a British businessman with close ties to the Russian government may also have played a role in convincing Milosevic to accept the demands. See, e.g., *New York Times*, 13 June 1999, A15.

79. Associated Press, "Text of the Kosovo Peace Plan," 3 June 1999, as published at www.washingtonpost.com.

Chapter 16

The Bosnian Intervention: Stabilization without Guidelines

Brigid Myers Pavilonis[1]

> [Bosnians, Serbs, and Croats] have asked for America's help as they implement the [Dayton] peace agreement. America has a responsibility to answer that request, to help to turn this moment of hope into an enduring reality. To do that, troops from our country and around the world would go into Bosnia to give them the confidence and support they need to implement their peace plan. I refuse to send American troops to fight a war in Bosnia, but I believe we must help to secure the Bosnian peace. . . . Securing peace in Bosnia will also help to build a free and stable Europe. Bosnia lies at the very heart of Europe, next door to many of its fragile new democracies and some of our closest allies.[2]
>
> —President Clinton on the eve of the November 1995 troop deployment to Bosnia

On August 28, 1995, a mortar round exploded in a market place in Sarajevo. The blast killed thirty-seven civilians, most of whom were Bosnian Muslims. The Clinton Administration interpreted this as a hostile Serbian action[3] that explicitly challenged America's emergent Bosnia policy. In response, America began its direct support to NATO's Operation Deliberate Force. Two days later, thirteen Tomahawk cruise missiles destroyed several major Serbian command posts and placed increased pressure on Serbian air defenses. The total air campaign lasted three weeks and involved eight countries.[4] Significantly, the heretofore uninvolved United States supplied two-thirds of the flights. These events in the summer of 1995 marked the first meaningful American military response—almost three years after Serb forces entered neighboring Bosnia.

Three main factors influenced both the U.S. decision to intervene and its operational effectiveness once involved. First, the United States simply did not perceive the Bosnian crisis as having any real and immediate effect on U.S. national security. Two years prior to the U.S. intervention, in March of 1993, Secretary of State Warren Christopher appeared on *Face the Nation* and described the situation as "really a tragic problem" and "a problem from hell."[5] Despite the Clinton Administration's stated concern, at the outset, they perceived the situation in the Balkans as a horrific civil war, but interpreted the crisis as having a limited effect on U.S. national security. In 1993, when the Europeans enthusiastically stepped forward to take responsibility for the devolving situation in Bosnia, the U.S. was satisfied to step aside and let Europe take the lead.

Second, as Americans in the early 1990's reveled in the victory over communism and success in Iraq, major military efforts were deemed as having vital importance, while "nation-building" efforts were relegated to secondary importance. Piecing together a Bosnian society racked by internecine warfare was labeled a "nation-building" exercise—and one that was not only less important but also held little promise for success. Therefore, in the early years of the unfolding Bosnian crisis, the U.S. undertook limited planning for the operation that it would eventually accept in 1996. Thus, when the combat portion of Operation Deliberate Force ended, U.S. forces had little guidance on how to conduct the stabilization effort that followed.

Third, the Bosnian stabilization effort lacked a solid and thoughtful design to address the common problems occurring in a post-combat society. One of the major problems with the stabilization operation was that it failed to consider the complexities of Bosnian history, society, and internal ethnic relationships. Instead, Americans generally reverted to the ethnic cleansing of the World War II period as the marker of Bosnian society, which led many Americans and some U.S. policy makers[6] to conclude that peace in Bosnia would not come easily, and might never come at all. Indeed, these perceptions of Bosnians not only delayed U.S. intervention, but also led to the entrenched American pessimism regarding the long-term stabilization of Bosnia. This pessimism, coupled with the disinclination for nation-building exercises, complicated America's ability to succeed long after committing intervention forces in November of 1995.

In short, the United States operation struggled to assist in the stabilization of Bosnia due to a failure to interpret Bosnian instability as a challenge to U.S. national security, unpreparedness of U.S. forces, and the absence of an effective stabilization plan specifically designed for the intricacies of Bosnia. As the war unfolded, the West, and in particular, the United States, failed to understand the relationship among the warring groups and underestimated the impact of regional destabilization. Yet by 1995, as the shocking news of the Srebrenica massacre spread, the U.S. was compelled to action[7]—with a limited plan and insufficient knowledge of relationships among Bosnian ethnic groups.

A Raging War, Reticent Europe, and a Reluctant Partner

> The United States should take the lead in seeking United Nations Security Council authorization for air strikes against those who are attacking the relief effort. The United States should be prepared to lend appropriate military support to that operation. . . . We should make clear that the economic blockade against Serbia will be tightened, not only on weapons but also on oil and other supplies that sustain the renegade regime of Slobodan Milosevic.
>
> —Governor Bill Clinton, on the presidential campaign trail, July 26, 1991[8]

> [The declaration] represents the Road to Hell, in which the Muslim nation may disappear altogether.
>
> —Co-founder of the Serbian Democratic Party Radovan Karadzic's response to the October 1991 Declaration of Bosnian Sovereignty as supported by Bosniacs and Bosnian Croats[9]

There were three main factors that influenced the United States efforts to stabilize Bosnia-Herzegovina (hereafter Bosnia) during the 1990s. First, westerners did not perceive the Bosnia conflict as influencing regional or international security. Indeed, although the conflict was fierce and terrifying, at least initially, the crisis was understood as having little impact outside the borders of Bosnia. Second, because westerners understood the conflict in Bosnia to be a civil war, the intervention was deemed a peacekeeping operation, albeit with little guidance for these soldiers on how to do the job and little desire on their part to be there. Finally, because neither Europe nor the U.S. developed a well-orchestrated plan for stabilization, the violence extended and impeded long-term operational effectiveness.

Inaction, Delays, and Questions: Impacts on Regional and National Security

Luxembourg Foreign Minister Jacques Poos uttered this now famous phrase, "The hour of Europe has dawned," as he disembarked his plane on the way to negotiate the Slovene secession from the former Yugoslavia in early 1991. While the statement may have sounded a bit lofty at the time, it was not entirely unbelievable. The Soviet Union had dissolved. The need for an American defense umbrella no longer seemed necessary to preserve European security. Indeed, many questioned the need for NATO—or any version of an Atlantic partnership. The Europeans deemed the crisis in the Balkans "a European problem" and declared their leadership role in stabilization of the region. The United States, perceiving no direct threat to its own national security, was comfortable with Europe taking charge. The problem was that neither the Europeans nor the

United States viewed the Bosnian conflict as having the potential to create larger security challenges. That mindset resulted in the European adoption of an ineffective neutral approach to diplomatically solve the conflict and nearly virtual disengagement by the United States.

In the early days of the crisis and prior to U.S. involvement, the Europeans perceived the conflict in Bosnia too narrowly. As the breakaway republics declared their independence, the Europeans underestimated the massive destabilization caused by the Bosnian crisis and gravely miscalculated the international security threat that a fractured southeast Europe presented. As a result, Europe severely underestimated the need for a forceful intervention. When Europe declared its impartiality, the Bosnians, suffering at the hands of Serbs, interpreted this declaration as European favoritism for their sworn enemy.[10] This position set the wrong tone for the conflict and degraded Europe's ability to assist in the stabilization of Bosnia.

As the Balkans unraveled and the Europeans scrambled to identify the appropriate action, the United States debated whether and how it should become involved. Foremost in U.S. policy-makers' minds was the relationship between Bosnian instability and U.S. national security. Many in the Clinton administration, including U.S. Ambassador Warren Zimmerman, argued that Balkan instability would not influence U.S. security.

Policy makers offered two key defenses for non-intervention in Bosnia. First, compared with the important U.S. commitments elsewhere in the world, the crisis in Bosnia seemed to have limited significance. America had just fought a fabulously successful military campaign in the Persian Gulf. In its aftermath, the U.S. concerned itself with the disposition of the post-war Iraqi government and Iraq's adherence to UN no-fly zones and weapons inspections. Stability in the Middle East was the focus; the crisis in Bosnia was comparatively much less important.

In addition, the United States had suffered public embarrassment in its stinging retreat from Somalia in the early 1990's. As the U.S. military and the newly elected Clinton Administration struggled to identify what went wrong in Somalia, taking on another "humanitarian emergency" seemed unwise for America. Furthermore, popular wisdom of the day, growing out of the World War II experience, suggested that fighting was endemic in the region. Although the situation was "tragic, dangerous, full of violence, and confusing," it was perceived that little could be done by outsiders to resolve the conflict.[11]

Although these arguments held great sway among U.S. decision makers at the time, as the conflict persisted, discussions of U.S. intervention grew in frequency and seriousness. David Owen, EU Co-chairman for the Conference on the Former Yugoslavia, argued that the Balkan wars surrounded

> a fuse line which runs from Sarajevo to Sandzak Muslims to the Albanians in Kosovo, to the Albanians in Macedonia to Albania itself and then Greece and Turkey. This powder keg could have ignited in 1991 and then again in 1992 af-

ter the appalling rapidity with which the Serb ethnic cleansing campaign developed.[12]

In other words a war in Bosnia, could have served as a catalyst for the entire region to devolve into war. In 1994, Secretary of State Warren Christopher termed this idea as the "wider war thesis," in which he argued that a massive collapse of southern Europe threatened economic viability and political stability for the whole of Europe.[13] By 1995, policy makers concluded that instability in Europe threatened U.S. security.[14] The challenge was what to do about it.

Sending the Troops: Problems with Readiness and Guidance

The second major challenge in stabilizing Bosnia was that the United States lacked a clear understanding of the role their troops should play. The United States' difficulty with mission execution was, in part, caused by the UNPROFOR mandate regarding Bosnia.[15] While the overarching mission goal was to quell the violence, impartiality toward both sides remained a key directive. In other words, its requirement for impartiality limited UNPROFOR soldiers' ability to stop Serbian aggression because the Europeans perceived the Bosniaks, Serbs, and Croats as having legitimate claims of grievance against the others and rejected support for one group over another. Their unwillingness to act, however, became increasingly dubious as the Serbian attacks on the Bosniacs grew in intensity, frequency, and brutality. By 1995, the Bosnian conflict was clearly not a civil war; it was an attempt by the Serbs to eradicate the Bosniacs and Croats from the entire region.

On May 8, 1995, a vicious attack on the central Sarajevo market place propelled Lieutenant General Rupert Smith, the NATO military commander, to request air support for civilian protection against Bosnian Serb attacks. In his steadfast devotion to impartiality, the Special Representative of the Secretary General for UNPROFOR, Yasushi Akashi, denied his request. General Smith, recognizing the impending seriousness of the situation, presented the Bosnian Serbs with an ultimatum; he ordered them to cease the use of heavy weapons. Ignoring the ultimatum, Bosnian Serbs littered Sarajevo with attacks two days later.[16] Then, in July, Bosnian Serbs launched a military operation to cleanse Srebenica of its Croat and Muslim inhabitants. When the U.S. learned of what later became known as the "Srebenica Massacre," it felt compelled to act.

Shortly thereafter, the U.S. lent direct military support to NATO's Operation Deliberate Force to "provide a continued military presence in order to deter renewed hostilities, stabilize and consolidate the peace, contribute to a secure environment and maintain broad support for civilian implementation plans."[17] U.S. military forces were well-trained and prepared to perform these traditional tasks associated with combat, and as a result were superbly effective in maintaining a deterrent military presence, ensuring compliance with the no-fly zones, engaging in force protection, and preventing major hostilities.

The challenge for U.S. forces was that they were also assigned the task of creating “a secure environment for civilian organizations to carry out their responsibilities.”[18] In the mid-1990’s, U.S. forces had little recent experience in understanding that mandate and had little doctrinal guidance to direct them how to do so.

This lack of understanding on how to do the assigned task among U.S. soldiers can be attributed to the fact that peacekeeping, although not entirely new, was not a typical task assigned to the military during the Cold War. As such, soldiers had little understanding of its practice. Moreover, little guidance existed for soldiers. Policy makers struggled to catch up, and one of the first attempts at establishing guidance was the promulgation of Presidential Decision Directive 25, U.S. Policy on Multilateral Peacekeeping Operations.

The goal of PDD-25 was to provide direction on the conduct of peacekeeping missions. It addressed situations in which the U.S. would support UN peacekeeping missions, reiterated U.S. command and control over its troops, and recognized the unique demands presented by peacekeeping operations—most critically the relationship between military and civilian components of the operation.[19] PDD-25 stated that the U.S. government is adopting a new way to manage peacekeeping operations through a “shared responsibility" approach, giving the Department of Defense “lead management and funding responsibility” while assigning the State Department “responsibility for the conduct of diplomacy.”

While this construct for peacekeeping operations demonstrated a visionary first step, the problems in Bosnia persisted due to a lack of practical guidance on the ground. PDD 25 incompletely addressed the issues of interagency cooperation and misunderstood the complexities in designing, what was then termed a peace-keeping[20] operation. In a peacekeeping operation, it is difficult to assign responsibility to U.S. agencies for each task, as most tasks are riddled with elements drawing from both the civilian and military realms. For instance, the return of displaced people in Bosnia was a responsibility for both civilian aid workers and the military forces, as refugees needed both resettlement help and protection in returning to homes they had left months or years ago.[21] There was no clear guidance for soldiers in the field, USAID, or State Department personnel on how to work through commonalities and differences in their approaches.

As a result, U.S. soldiers in Bosnia never completely understood their performance of duties. More precisely, while they easily accepted and effectively performed their traditional combat roles of force protection, prevention of major hostilities, and enforcement of no-fly zones, U.S. forces in Bosnia never fully understood how to act in support of the peacekeeping mission because so little guidance existed which outlined their role. This confusion compromised the effectiveness of U.S. soldiers in stabilizing Bosnia. Another major reason for the difficulty was associated with the plan itself, which we will now explore.

Stabilizing Bosnia: Challenges and Opportunities

> The decision to keep U.S. troops in Bosnia beyond June 1998 is critical to ensuring the success of the Dayton Accords. It also lies squarely in the national self-interest of the United States. The stability of southeastern Europe depends on the ability of the Bosnians, working with the international community, to create a self-sustaining, peaceful, democratic system in the country.
>
> —Senator Joe Biden, July 1998[22]

While the United States was immediately effective in achieving cessation of violence, it overestimated the capacity and power of a negotiated settlement in resolving the region's long-term problems. The problem was that the resulting operational plan was inextricably linked to the negotiated solution at Dayton—which ultimately served as both a help and a hindrance in its effective execution.

In late 1995, the Clinton Administration committed well over ten thousand U.S. forces to the stabilization of Bosnia. The depth and breadth of the atrocities committed by Bosnian Serbs were horrifically offensive—and the "do-something" effect burgeoned throughout the American public. Furthermore, the wider war thesis, the notion that a destabilized central Europe could affect U.S. national security, became an increasingly convincing argument among policy makers. By staving off collapse and corruption in Bosnia, the U.S. could support its European allies and save itself. Instability in Bosnia had introduced the notion that failed and failing states are dangerous. A Bosnia run by the "warlord" Slobodan Milosevic could have become a ripe breeding ground for a growing terrorist threat.

After committing U.S. assistance to the stabilization effort, the Clinton administration had to decide how to act. Interestingly, the U.S. never established a formal stabilization plan. Rather, the work of stabilizing Bosnia was detailed in the Dayton Peace Accords which ended the fighting, discussed the causes of war, and outlined the way forward. While the agreement was a tremendous triumph in its foremost goal of ending the violence, in many ways the Accords neglected the long-term stabilization of Bosnia in that it dealt incompletely with the underlying causal factors that had jumpstarted the war. Indeed, the Dayton Peace Accords, which were signed on December 14, 1995, were a compromise settlement among Serbian President Slobodan Milosevic, Croatian President Franjo Tudjman, and Bosnian President Alija Izetbegovic. It formally re-established the unified state of Bosnia-Herzegovina but de facto created a 51:49 percent division between the Bosnian/Croat federation and Republic of Srpska. Bosnian Serbs retained their hold on captured territories taken during the war and Bosnian Muslims were bestowed the land around Sarajevo, capitol of Bosnia-Herzegovina.[23] Thus, although Dayton served as a seemingly reasonable administrative solution, stopped the violence, and undoubtedly saved countless future lives, it was a settlement plan, not a stabilization plan. It ended the hostilities but it did not achieve the critical outcomes that effective stabilization plans should.

As a stabilization plan, the Dayton Peace Accords had several major weaknesses. It struggled to address the difficulties associated with long-term security, management of the internal civil administration, and reconstruction of the state. It also failed to address such factors vital to long-term success, such as the effective use of intelligence and an historical understanding of obstacles to a unified effort for Bosnia's reconstruction.

Dayton's stabilization of Bosnia largely involved a military solution that portioned the groups into ethnic enclaves. When the war ended the militias of the three ethnic groups remained in place and peoples of each ethnicity returned to living with one another. The "soft partition" agreement allowed for the existence of divided ethnic communities. The republic of Sprpska and the Bosnian/Croat federation appointed their own presidents and created independent legislatures. As Craig Nation argues "the creation of ethnically pure enclaves had been a major war aim of all belligerents, and progress toward reversing the consequences of years of ethnic cleansing was negligible."[24] The stabilization plan did not address the original impetus for war: the identity of the Bosnian state. It was not a political solution in that it accomplished little in resolving problems among those who were fighting.

In addition, the Bosniak (Bosnian Muslims) and Croat forces retained much of their equipment and soldiers after the fighting had ended. In fact, although Serb forces and weaponry had been greatly diminished during the large-scale fighting in late 1995, all groups retained some capability.[25] Moreover, because the stabilization did not achieve a political solution but relied on a military-enforced ethnic division, the region remains at risk today for renewed violence.

Finally, the stabilization effort was difficult because it failed to satisfactorily address the reconstruction and development of post-war Bosnia. After three years of fighting, Bosnia's GDP had been reduced to a third of pre-war levels. Industrial plants had closed and a majority of workers had lost their jobs. The countryside was devastated, making agricultural recovery just as difficult as the return to industrial productivity. "Two-thirds of homes, one-half of schools and one-third of hospitals were damaged or destroyed."[26] The Dayton Peace Accords physically separated those who were fighting and used the military to enforce the cessation of hostilities; however, it should have also included a unified effort to bring together the expertise of both military and civilians to solve the endemic problems of a troubled inter-ethnic society.

Conclusions

An examination of the intervention in Bosnia-Herzegovina serves as an important case study in understanding the circumstances under which the United States should take action, how its troops should be deployed, and how to develop an effective stabilization plan. Many of the problems in the stabilization of

Bosnia were directly related to the indecision of the West in its initial response, the ambiguity of the soldier's role, and the effectiveness of the stabilization plan.

The United States, when initially faced with the conflict in the Balkans, was unsure how to respond. Indeed, in the 1990s, Americans observed a public debate emerge among the Clinton administration, members of Congress, and other key policy makers regarding the purpose and value of U.S. troop presence in Bosnia.[27] The debate became even more heated once the initial IFOR mission ended and the UN formally reconstituted the mission into a stabilization operation that was to accomplish the reconstruction of the civilian society. Those who disagreed with a sustained U.S. presence in Bosnia pointedly questioned the mission's purpose and doubted the effect that an unstable Bosnia could have on U.S. national security.

At the outset, the Clinton administration argued that the need for U.S. troops in Bosnia was fueled by humanitarian aims and consistent with national security goals. In an address to the American people, President Clinton argued that:

> In fulfilling this mission, we will have the chance to help stop the killing of innocent civilians, especially children, and at the same time, to bring stability to central Europe, a region of the world that is vital to our national interests. It is the right thing to do.[28]

President Clinton's point was that stoppage of the violence in Bosnia would assist in avoiding a larger European War.[29] While the movement of refugees and challenges to economic stability were typically offered as items of major concern, I argue that the real risk was the deterioration of Bosnia into a severely weakened state. The challenges of the post-9/11 world have offered a consistent and painful reminder of the danger of failed and failing states, where warlords rise, terrorist groups operate, and underground economies develop. In the 21st century, these threats to U.S. national security are some of this era's most complex and challenging.

The second lesson to be learned from the Bosnian conflict is that a determination of soldiers' tasking and the limits of their responsibility must be clear prior to entry. In Bosnia, the role for UNPROFOR and U.S. soldiers were never clearly defined. The UNPROFOR soldiers were constrained in their ability to act due to the UN's overriding commitment to impartiality—despite the situation on the ground. For the U.S. soldiers, the role was incompletely defined and changed as the mission progressed. This lack of clarity was due to the complexity of the operation in support of the NATO Deliberate Force mission, the UN peacekeeping operation Joint Endeavor, and the disagreements about the relationship between and duties of civilian and military entities.

The issue of impartiality is a difficult one in dealing with cases of interethnic violence in that interveners typically should not presuppose outcomes or force a mandated solution on other peoples. The problem, in the case of Bosnia, was that the conflict had taken a troubling turn in that one warring group had grown increasingly powerful and did nothing to self-police its wartime actions. Karadzic and Milosevic had become warlords who resorted to brutal tactics to win the war. When the Europeans misperceived the transformation of the fighting, they failed to understand not only their enemy but also the kind of war they were fighting. In effect, they rendered their troops useless, through their imposition of absolute impartiality, as the UNPROFOR soldiers were not permitted to fight effectively.

The U.S. soldiers experienced a different sort of problem in that they were assigned responsibility for tasks that they neither fully understood nor were trained to do. When the UN created the Implementation Force (IFOR), they were assigned responsibility for security in post-combat Bosnia. IFOR, initially composed of 54,000 NATO soldiers[30] focused on the military elements of the stabilization plan outlined in Dayton: enforcement of the cease-fire, demobilization of the remaining militia forces, and security protection for Bosnian civilians. By 1996, the UN had also assigned to IFOR forces the traditionally "civilian tasks" of stabilization: the conduct of elections, return of displaced persons, and support for the International Criminal Tribunal. The mission was renamed SFOR, or Stabilization Force. At the same time, the UN created the Office of the High Representative (OHR) for Bosnia Herzegovina, whose formal responsibility was the resolution of any difficulties arising in connection with civilian implementation.[31]

The main problem was that neither group fully understood or appreciated the work of the other. Military forces grew resentful of their civilian counterparts because the civilian effort lagged behind the forward leaning military pieces of the operation. The OHR office was largely ineffectual due to understaffing and underfunding. As such, many traditionally "civilian" tasks fell to the military, as these forces were present in greatest number and had the broadest capacity for action. In addition, no formal guidance existed for the coordination between SFOR and OHR. While some ad hoc relationships developed between SFOR commanders and OHR personnel, the stabilization of Bosnia moved forward with limited influence by civilians.[32]

US soldiers therefore gradually assumed responsibility for many of the traditionally civilian tasks, and they did so with little guidance from national directives like PDD-25 or from joint documents detailing SFOR responsibilities. As a result, the U.S. soldiers' role in Bosnia lacked clarity. This constituted one of the significant oversights of the stabilization plan and leads me to my final observation.

The de facto stabilization plan for Bosnia was the Dayton Peace Accords, which were a negotiated settlement to stop the violence with the usual shortcomings of a diplomatic compromise. It was definitively not a long-term plan for stabilization of Bosnia. Dayton stopped the fighting but failed to reconstitute Bosnia's multi-ethnic society, and in so doing neglected an essential political element of any stabilization plan. Although the region has maintained a basic level of civic order and has eschewed the resort to war, Bosnia's political structures remain unstable, with weak civic organizations and politicians prone to the pursuit of pure self-interest.[33] As a result, Bosnia's economy has recovered slowly and with unsteady progress. The major reason for these persistent political and economic problems is that a peace accord cannot be substituted for an operational stabilization plan with a sound joint political-military approach.

Despite these problems, Dayton was fabulously successful in a single, significant way—it stopped Milosevic and Bosnia's de-evolution into disorder. In the 1990's Milosevic adopted many "war-lord" characteristics in terms of the tactics he used and the power he wielded over non-Serbian minorities in Kosovo as well as Bosnia. Had he been allowed to proceed unchecked, the disorder and instability had catastrophic potential. The bottom line is that the U.S. took proper action in its troop deployment to Bosnia in 1995, because it stopped the emergence of budding warlords, tit-for-tat violence by paramilitaries on all sides, and suspended Bosnia's collapse.

The U.S. also learned a valuable lesson in Bosnia in that it demonstrated the existence of an emerging national security challenge—one in which armed groups and warlords cause weakened states that, in turn, threaten U.S. stability. In this way, the conflict in Bosnia situated the U.S. on the precipice of a reconceptualization of vital national security interests. Indeed, Bosnia forced the U.S. to think differently about how we understand warring groups and the danger they can cause. It also began, even if very slowly, some reflection in military and diplomatic circles about how forces should be trained to function successfully in these ambiguous environments that remain a feature of the post 9/11 world.

Notes

1. The views expressed in this paper are those of the author alone and do not necessarily reflect the positions of the U.S. Coast Guard or the United States Government.

2. President William Clinton, Weekly Radio Address, Washington, D.C., November 27, 1995, http://www.cnn.com/US/9511/bosnia_speech/speech.html, (accessed July 23, 2011).

3. Robert F. Baumann, George W. Gawrych, and Walter E. Kretchik, *Armed Peacekeepers in Bosnia* (Fort Leavenworth, Kansas: Combat Studies Institute Press, 2004), 29.

4. Thierry Domin, "History of Bosnia and Herzegovina: From the Origins to 1992," *SFOR Informer* #117, http://www.nato.int/SFOR/indexinf/117/p03a/chapter1.ht, (accessed August 19, 2011).

5. Warren Christopher, *Face the Nation,* Interview with Bob Schieffer, October 22, 1995, http://dosfan.lib.uic.edu/ERC/briefing/dossec/1995/9510/951022dossec, (accessed July 23, 2011).

6. Robert Kaplan, *Balkan Ghosts: A Journey through History* (New York: St. Martin's Press, 1993), 23.

7. Baumann, Gawrych, and Kretchik, *Armed Peacekeepers in Bosnia*, 36.

8. Quoted in David Owen, *Balkan Odyssey* (New York: Harcourt Brace and Company, 1995), 13.

9. Quoted in Laura Silber and Allan Little, *Yugoslavia: Death of Nation* (London: TV Books, 1996), 215.

10. Timothy L. Thomas, "United Nations Crisis Management in Bosnia: Problems and Recommendations," Foreign Military Studies Office, Fort Leavenworth, 1995, http://fmso.leavenworth.army.mil/documents/unbos.htm, (accessed July 7, 2011).

11. This argument is closely associated with the strongly-held notion by Europeans that the situation in the Balkans was best characterized as "civil unrest" and a candidate for humanitarian assistance. Peace operations were neither applicable nor workable in the region. Craig Nation, *War in the Balkans, 1991-2002* (Carlisle: U.S. Army War College, 2003), 171.

12. Owen, *Balkan Odyssey,* 11.

13. Warren Christopher, "Statement at the Opening of the Balkan Peace Talks," in *The Stream of History: Shaping U.S. Foreign Policy for a New Era,* (Stanford; Stanford University Press, 1998), 360.

14. Ted Galen Carpenter, "The Domino Theory Reborn: Clinton's Bosnia Intervention and the 'Wider War' Thesis," *CATO Foreign Policy Briefing*, No. 42, August, 1996, http://www.cato.org/pubs/fpbriefs/fpb-042.html (accessed July 10, 2011).

15. "The United Nations Protection Force Mission Description," *Department of Public Information, United Nations.* 31 August 1996, http://www.un.org/Depts/dpko/dpko/co_mission/unprof_p.htm (accessed July 10, 2011).

16. Karen Von Hippel, *Democracy by Force: U.S. Military Intervention in a Post-Cold War World* (Boston: Cambridge University Press, 2000), 137.

17. Stephen Bowman, "Bosnia: U.S. Military Operations," Congressional Research Service, July 8, 2003, http://www.au.af.mil/au/awc/awcgate/crs/ib93056.pdf (accessed July 8, 2011).

18. Bowman, "Bosnia: U.S. Military Operations."

19. "U.S. Policy on Multilateral Peacekeeping Operations," Presidential Decision Directive 25, Washington, D.C. May 6, 1994, http://www.fas.org/irp/offdocs/pdd25.htm (accessed July 8, 2011).

20. Joint Publication 3-07.3, Peacekeeping Operations, October 2007, http://www.fas.org/irp/doddir/dod/jp3-07-3.pdf, (accessed September 1, 2011).

21. Frederick Fleitz, *Peacekeeping Fiascoes of the 1990s: Causes, Solutions, and U.S. Interests*, (New York: Praeger Publishing, 2002), 112.

22. Joseph R. Biden, "Bosnia: Why the United States Should Finish the Job," *SAIS Review* 18, no.2 (Summer 1998).

23. "Dayton Peace Accords," Wright Patterson Air Force Base, November 21, 1995, http://www.state.gov/www/regions/eur/bosnia/bosagree.html (accessed July 10, 2011).

24. Nation, *War in the Balkans, 1991-2002,* 202.

25. James Dobbins, *America's Role in Nation-building from Germany to Iraq* (Santa Monica: RAND Corporation, 2003), 90.

26. Dobbins, *America's Role in Nation-building,* 92.

27. A very public discussion emerged among congressional leaders regarding the decision to send troops. While some questioned their safety, efficacy, and interest, others pointed out that the U.S. had already committed through Operation Deliberate Force and support for the Commander-in-chief was their responsibility. Stanley Meisler, "GOP Leaders Support Sending Troops to Bosnia," *Los Angeles Times,* December 1, 1995.

28. President William Jefferson Clinton, "Address to the American People," November 27, 1995, http://www.cnn.com/US/9511/bosnia_speech/speech.html (accessed July 12, 2011).

29. Warren Christopher, "Send Troops to Bosnia," *USA Today*, October 18, 1995.

30. Thirteen thousand of IFOR forces were American soldiers. Steven Bowman, "Bosnia: U.S. Military Operations." Congressional Research Service, July 8, 2003, http://smallwarsjournal.com/documents/crl2.pdf (accessed July 8, 2011).

31. "The Mandate of the OHR," UN Office of the High Representative to Bosnia Herzegovina, http://www.ohr.int/ohr-info/gen-info/default.asp?content_id=38612 (accessed July 8, 2011).

32. George A. Joulwan and Christopher C. Shoemaker, *Civilian-Military Cooperation in the Prevention of Deadly Conflict: Implementing Agreements in Bosnia and Beyond* (New York: Carnegie Commission, 1998).

33. Robert Benjamin, "Regional Politics: Political Transition and Institution Building," *Transforming the Balkans: Security, Political Stability and Economic Development,* National Democratic Institute, May 10, 2010, http://www.ndi.org/files/Transforming_the_Balkans_051010.pdf (accessed July 13, 2010).

Chapter 17

Rebuilding a Democratic Iraqi Police Force: The Effects of the Militia on the Rebuilding Process

DiJon Jones[1]

On March 20, 2003 an international coalition, led by the United States, invaded Iraq because of Saddam Hussein's defiance in the supposed continuance of a Weapons of Mass Destruction (WMD) Program, and to free the Iraqi citizens from a brutal dictator. Many reasons were given for the invasion, but the operation was symbolically named "Operation Iraqi Freedom." Although no WMD programs have been found, the ensuing war crippled the government system and the one agency responsible for providing domestic order, the Iraqi Police Services (IPS). Since the toppling of the Saddam regime, the international community has provided millions of dollars in cash and resources for advising and assisting the Iraqi Ministry of Interior (MoI) with rebuilding the IPS. Unfortunately, the international community did not fully appreciate the problems posed by the influence of violent militias in their process of rebuilding the IPS. The U.S. must rethink its policing transference strategy in response to such challenges in Iraq and elsewhere.

In post-conflict Iraq, a vacuum in policing, judiciary, and government legitimacy emerged almost immediately after initial hostilities ended. After the toppling of Saddam's regime, the international community failed to seize the opportunity to instill law and order as the lull in violence turned to lawlessness and societal and sectarian divisions grew. This eroded the public's trust in the international military force and the Government of Iraq (GoI). International Military Forces subsequently assumed police functions in order to create a secure environment as civil unrest and the sectarian divide consumed Iraq.

It is axiomatic that governmental legitimacy and citizen prosperity are intimately tied to security and stability, as is increased citizen participation in government and access to commerce. Max Weber cited "the protection of personal security and public order (police)" as one of the most important functions of the State, and that has not changed since his time. Yet in Iraq the institutions of law enforcement and criminal justice, and the ability to enforce security, were for all intents and purposes destroyed in March of 2003. Since then, the international community and the IPS have faced numerous challenges in rebuilding a capable police force that can provide modern and democratic services to the citizens of Iraq. Current and future adversaries of the Republic of Iraq, however, have been increasingly proficient in undermining Iraqi Security Forces (ISF) operations and national politics. Iran, in particular, is active in promoting civil unrest, corruption, supporting extremist militias, and encouraging elements from the previous regime in a range of destabilization activities.

This chapter focuses on the ability of the international community, specifically the U.S. and the IPS to rebuild a police force faced with these and other challenges.

Post-Invasion Iraq: Lawlessness and Disorder

The Iraqi Police Service: An Historical Perspective

The Iraqi Police Services (IPS) under Saddam Hussein were well known to be corrupt and brutal implementers of oppression. The Iraqi security apparatus was a complex muddle of security organizations that permeated all layers of the government, including the police. Saddam purposefully staffed certain positions with relatives or members of the Sunni Arab Triangle.[2] These forces provided a vehicle for Saddam to keep tabs on members of the GoI and citizens around the country, and were created to keep him in power.[3] The majority of individuals spent more time spying on other members of the government than providing services to the Iraqi people as Saddam piled on layers of distrust in order to keep Iraqis in line.

Under the previous regime, three levels of police, or "Shurta," existed: the Enlisted and Non-Commissioned Officer (NCO) Corps; Assistant Officers; and Officers. Most Enlisted and Non-Commissioned Officers had little education and were given little police training. The Enlisted and NCO Corps were the first responders to calls for service and dealt with the citizens on a daily basis. Assistant Officers usually had completed secondary school or the Police High School courses and normally were responsible for administrative functions across the IPS. Officers were typically from well-to-do families, attended the Baghdad Police Professional College, and served in traditional leadership roles of management and command staff in the provinces. This system typically led to corruption because of the Enlisted and NCO Shurta's inability to have a voice.[4]

Corruption was not new to the police under Saddam; it had long played a role within the Iraqi Security apparatus and the government. It was widely accepted as normal practice, prima facie. Corruption occurred at all levels within the IPS and ranged across the spectrum of criminal activity. Provincial Chiefs of Police would take cuts from salaries from the junior employees or make them purchase their weapons and ammunition. In order for the Enlisted Shurta to be admitted to training, they would have to pay special middlemen a fee. Citizens were cheated, beaten, wrongly arrested, and killed to protect the regime and the corruption of those in power. After developing many relationships with staff officials, it was discovered that Officers made what was equivalent to $20-$30 USD per month, Assistant Officers made $7-$10 USD per month, and Enlisted/NCO's made much less. The Shurta could not afford to support their families on salaries like this and, as a result, many resulted to taking bribes.[5]

The environment of corruption was a "top down" function within the GoI. Under Saddam, a complicated, clandestine procurement network was created during the Iran-Iraq War to purchase controlled weapons and technologies for his war effort, which included chemical, biological, and nuclear weapons. Saddam supported smuggling operations and he was able to circumvent many of the United Nations (UN) sanctions that were placed on Iraq.

Operational Conditions Prior to 2003

In short, prior to 2003 the operational conditions in Iraq were brutal, corrupt, and fueled by a need to maintain power. The IPS was not a democratic force but woven into the vast web of Saddam's security apparatus. It was highly unlikely for junior IPS officials to make decisions of any kind without the direction of the most senior official. It was widely known that Saddam would use chemical weapons to quell opposition, as he had on the Kurdish people seeking autonomy for a homeland that they hoped would eventually unite Kurds in Iraq, Iran, and Turkey. After the invasion, most of the crime data were lost or burned. Therefore, assessing the capabilities of the police using empirical data is impossible. James Morrill, who served as a Civilian Police Advisor in Iraq from 2008-2010, indicated that much of the "information obtained came from the Council of Elders, or the police generals with more than thirty to forty years of policing experience in Iraq."[6]

Criminal investigations and those who were responsible for carrying them out were not trained in modern investigative techniques. The police felt that confessions were the only way to prosecute criminals and rarely relied on the use of physical evidence in conducting criminal investigations. Morrill indicates that advisors were told on numerous occasions by the lead IPS criminal investigator/Ministry of Interior (MoI) legal advisor that solving crimes started with the arrest and then the case was built from that point, which generally meant having the arrested subject confess to the crime.[7] The use of brutal interrogation techniques usually led to a confession and at times death. The official line throughout the IPS, because of a manual written by a senior IPS official, was that all crimes were committed by "Gypsies" and not Iraqi citizens. This thinking resulted in a police force that was not capable of providing the needed services to its constituents. The IPS was wrought with corruption, lacked modern police proficiency, and was plagued with human rights violations. Interestingly enough, it was able to keep extremist violence, civilian unrest, and sectarian violence at bay as an arm of the dictatorship, but the Shurta did not serve the communities in which they policed.

Since extremist violence, civil unrest, and sectarian violence were quickly and harshly answered by Saddam's regime, police were not afraid of operating in their local environments. They were not the targets of assassinations (except those carried out under orders by the regime) and despite their primary charge they were able to provide some level of service to the citizens of Iraq, although the service would possibly not have been acceptable using democratic law enforcement standards. Regardless, the streets of Iraq were relatively safe from criminal, terrorist, and sectarian activities. The citizens were more afraid of GoI officials' harsh and brutal activities.

Within its limited capabilities, the IPS provided services based on the culture, law, religious practice, and the environment in which they worked. Captain Rousseau (U.S. Army) indicated that the "primary mission of the IPS was to protect the government from the people, and anyone, or country, that wanted to harm the government" and to "maintain order with security as opposed to law enforcement." Thus, the IPS were effective at their jobs in a closed border society, living under a dictatorship.[8]

With the rampant corrupt practices of officials and the inability for citizens to participate in the governmental process, the conditions in Iraq were ripe to explode. The only thing missing was the source of ignition. The U.S. and its coalition of the willing provided the ignition to this long and festering sectarian and violent extremism. Although many understand and agree that Saddam probably needed to go, there is no doubt that he provided stability during his regime.

The Coalition Provisional Authority (CPA) disbanded the Iraqi Army and other Security agencies within the GoI, but spared the IPS. "Unfortunately, the IPS had been at the bottom of Saddam's bureaucratic hierarchy of security agencies and suffered from years of mismanagement, deprivation of resources, and lack of professional standards" and what advisors later found was an agency that did not understand or use basic policing techniques.[9]

The Militias

The Mahdi Army and the Sadrist Movement

The Sadrist movement is an Iraqi Islamist National Movement (mainly Shi'ites) dedicated to returning Iraq to the use of a system of religious political ideologies in which Islam provides the guiding principles for government. Its history predates the U.S.-led invasion. Saddam Hussein and the Ba'athist Party did not tolerate any rival parties or sources of power, particularly the Kurdish (Kurds) and Shi'ites (Shi'a). Ayatollah Mohammed Baqir al-Sadr developed his own version of the Sadrist Movement. Given the ruthlessness of Saddam Hussein and the Ba'ath party, he remained in the shadows and was not very vocal. In 1980, Baqir was killed after Saddam identified him as a threat to his regime and power. In the absence of Baqir, Ayatollah Mohammed Sadiq al-Sadr took the helm. He believed in a more vocal presence in the Shi'a communities and began to strengthen his alliances in the Sadr City neighborhood in Baghdad. Because Saddam understood that Sadiq had a following, after an uprising in 1991, he tolerated Sadiq in order to prevent more violence. Sadiq was hardly a Saddam loyalist and his style did not fit with the supreme Islamic power in Iran; he was not liked much by either group. Eventually, he was assassinated along with two of his sons in 1999.[10]

Immediately following those assassinations, a rebellion took place in which Sayyid Muqtada al-Sadr emerged as the leader of the Sadrist Movement. Because of his family's long history in the movement and his new leadership role, he was able to exploit the power vacuum caused by the U.S.-led invasion in 2003, and Sadr soon emerged as a leading figure capable of masterminding a violent uprising. His Militia, better known as the Mahdi Army or Jaysh al-Mahdi (JAM), is extremely violent,[11] and he is responsible for very violent battles fought with U.S. and British soldiers in 2004 that could have possibly thrust the country into the violence that swept the country in 2006.

By 2007, JAM became the most "dangerous accelerant of potentially self-sustaining sectarian violence in Iraq."[12] The good news for the Coalition of the Willing was that the political infighting within the Shi'ite coalition party caused tribal uprisings that suppressed al Qaeda in Iraq (AQI). The bad news was that the Mahdi Army attacked rival militias and coalition forces, as well as ISF. Prime Minister Nouri al-Maliki (also Shi'a) went on the offensive in the southern province of Basra to take control of the oil facilities, ports, and smuggling operations after the British left Basra unsecured. According to some officials in the Iraqi Police Services, it is believed that Sadr was gaining political influence in the provinces and Maliki needed to respond in order to limit Sadr's political successes, though only temporarily. Sadr City became the major battle ground soon after the Basra operations as JAM members launched rockets and mortars into the Green Zone. After several weeks, U.S. and Iraqi Security Forces entered

Sadr City to neutralize the threat. Al-Sadr eventually came to a ceasefire agreement with Maliki, which allowed ISF full access to patrol Sadr City.[13]

Meanwhile, Sadr created a formidable fighting machine capable of fighting the U.S. and ISF in small-scale, neighborhood battles. JAM attacked police officers at check points, killed new recruits waiting to apply for police positions, and fought ISF in limited engagements after the so called ceasefire. Although Sadr was handed some losses, he has not lost his ability to mobilize, and he "owes his authority to the reverence with which his family of Shi'a clerics is regarded by millions of poor Iraqis." He also had assistance from the Iranian Quds Force, which played a role in equipping and training the Mahdi.[14]

Nor were the Mahdi and other militias the only serious challenge to restoring order. With the fall of the Saddam regime, criminal groups also took advantage of the power vacuum, and subsequently crime and lawlessness have aggravated many problem areas. Criminals have aided terrorists with services like "money laundering, forging documents, obtaining illegal weapons," and have stolen vehicles which were later used as Improvised Explosive Devices (IEDs).[15] Kidnappings are another problem facing the ISF. And Saddam, in his efforts to create problems for the U.S. and its invading allies, released approximately seventy-five thousand to one hundred thousand criminals from prison to complicate any effort by the United States to install a new regime in Iraq.[16]

Political and Governmental Influence in Iraq

Grand Ayatollah Sayyid Ali al-Husayni al-Sistani is another prominent figure within the regional religious and political affairs movement. Before Sadr, Sistani issued a fatwa shortly after the U.S. invasion, advising Shi'a to become more involved in politics. Sistani is linked to the petitioning of international forces for a constitutional convention which is most likely linked to the Shi'a dominated government. During an operation where Iraqi and U.S. Forces cornered Muqtada al-Sadr and his Mahdi Army at the Imam Ali Mosque in Najaf, Sistani brokered a truce to allow Sadr to leave the area. Sistani has a huge following and his followers are very active in the political arena. At some point in 2004 Sadr began to distance himself from Sistani and actively challenged him for more influence over the Shi'a in Iraq.

The Badr Brigade is a key Shi'a rival to Sadr's JAM. Much of the Shi'a infighting has occurred between the Sadr followers and the Badr Brigades, and it has affected much of the political landscape in parliament and several Ministries. The Badr Brigades are part of the Da'wa Party, which was and is currently led by Prime Minister Nouri al-Maliki. The Badr Forces were "trained and equipped in Iran by the Iranian Revolutionary Guard."[17] Many of the Badr forces, because of their support for the Da'wa party, have obtained positions within the ISF, including the Ministry of Interior (MoI) where the IPS functions. Some of these positions are within the Patrol Police, the Baghdad Police College, and other police agencies. The concessions that Maliki made with Sadr during visits to the Ministry of Interior have been widely apparent, and probably allowed him to stay in office, as well as provided Sadrists with additional seats and political appointments to certain positions within the Government and Iraqi Security Forces.

On June 13, 2008, Muqtada al-Sadr announced that he planned to create a political wing for JAM that would consist of many of his followers, and a special group responsible for expelling all foreign occupiers or for fighting the government. With his announcement and many Sadr supporters (albeit quietly) already in government, he was able to infiltrate many aspects of government even while running his political activities during his self-imposed exile in Iran. Thus, during the rocket and mortar attacks on the Green Zone, JAM would continuously attack the Baghdad Police College and the Ministry of Interior complex. Eventually, Sadr agreed to end the attacks if the Ministry of Interior would allow JAM members to hold positions within it.[18] This effectively ended the rocket and mortar attacks on the Baghdad Police College, the Ministry of Interior Complex, and several key U.S. facilities located in this area.

JAM has been very effective at gaining support from Shi'a citizens by providing "some much-needed services, such as generators."[19] In a country where electricity is scarce, where citizens may only receive four hours of electricity a day from the government, a generator supplied by JAM had an important impact. JAM also used thug-like tactics to extort money from local businesses. They controlled many neighborhoods through exploitation, threats, and even violence. The police did not patrol these neighborhoods out of fear that they would be killed.

In a conversation with Key Leader Engagement (KLE), a Brigadier General from the IPS advised that individuals from extremist groups throughout Iraq had infiltrated the ranks of the local police, the IPS, and throughout the government.[20] Since the ceasefire between JAM in Sadr City and the Government, there has been a feeling that Sadrists are gaining too much control of certain aspects of the MoI. A 2011 article published in the Al-Iraqi News observed that, "Prime Minister Nouri Al-Maliki is at present restructuring his Interior Ministry for the purpose of making them more loyal to him. . . . the Prime Minister has felt that the ministry was going out of his control and he intends to tighten his grip" by appointing members of the Da'wa group (or Badr Brigades).[21]

Staying Alive in Iraq

Assassinations remain a daily occurrence in Iraq and are used to influence the direction of government activities. Between January and November 2011, U.S. advisors worked with IPS officials who were the targets of assassination attempts, but some of these attempts remain successful. This form of violence directed at MoI police officials has created an environment in which senior police officials refuse to take action. Meanwhile, the assassinations are being carried out by any number of groups and are being waged by both ends of the religious and political spectrum as part of a renewed positioning for power as the American pullout continues to proceed as planned.[22] Many believe that the groups responsible for these incidents are sponsored by Iran, former Saddam Hussein party members, or AQI. Ali al-Dabbagh, Iraq's chief government spokesman,

> acknowledged that the sheer number of killings of high-placed government officials has become a serious problem. . . . Major General Hussein Kamal, the domestic intelligence chief, said the government has information suggesting that remnants of the country's Ba'athist regime might have returned to Iraq in recent months from Syria.[23]

These assassination attempts take many forms. Some are conducted at or near Iraqi Army (IA) checkpoints using assault rifles while others occur as a result of Magnetically Attached Improvised Explosives Devices (MAIEDs) attached to the undercarriage of the target vehicles. Other attempts involve quick strikes with silenced pistols. While advising one senior Iraqi official from IPS during the summer of 2010, I was informed that one of my Iraqi counterparts was the target of a MAIED attack. After speaking with the official, I found that he was traveling with his two children (both under the age of ten) and stopped at a store. He left his children in the car (but could see them from the window) and went into the store to make a quick purchase. Less than four minutes later when he returned to his car, he was informed by his eldest child that someone had stuck something underneath the vehicle. He immediately checked underneath and found a MAIED attached, got his children out of the car and ran to safety just seconds before the vehicle blew up. Fortunately, this IPS official had just learned about these devices during training conducted by his American counterparts a few days prior.

In order to protect themselves, IPS officials change vehicles daily and alter their routes to and from work. Some have even been forced to abandoned their homes and live within their offices because they are afraid to go home. Instead of a proactive policing posture, many of the police officials hide in stations waiting to be called to respond to a crime or take a report. Recruiting events have been the target of some of the worst insurgent attacks and are aimed at derailing security forces as well as destabilizing the fragile government. One such attack took place at a police recruitment center in Tikrit on January 18, 2011, when a "suicide bomber wearing an explosive-packed vest attacked. . . and killed at least sixty five people and wounded 160 others."[24] Not surprisingly, data from recruitment efforts in 2010 indicate that many individuals are just not showing up to become Shurta. These issues further cripple security-building efforts. With these events taking place, IPS officials focus their efforts on personal security rather than working on police reforms, recruitment, training, and fielding of highly qualified people that would help to sustain a democratic police force.

Al-Sadr and Recent Iraqi Politics

Moqtada al-Sadr spent three years of self-imposed exile in Iran. During that time, Iraq held elections to elect a new Prime Minister and Parliament, and Iraqi citizens courageously made their way to polling stations to vote while being rocketed and mortared in many cities. In a close election between al-Maliki and Ayad Allawi, neither provided a coalition that could pull together a new government. With the stalled government process, Maliki traveled to Qom in Iran in order to meet with Sadr. Historically, these two men have been bitter enemies and have waged violent battles against each other. During the elections, Sadr supporters won forty seats. The coalition Maliki formed with Sadr enabled Maliki to gain an additional forty seats, which moved him closer to forming a government. In late 2010, after many months of impasse, Prime Minister Nouri al-Maliki retained his position, a government was formed, and he established a coalition to include Sadr, which took many additional months and promises. This coalition drew sharp criticism and one Member of Parliament stated "the enemy of Maliki is not his friend. . . . The Sadrist went with Maliki under pressure from our neighbor," referring to Iran's influence.[25]

In January 2011, we were informed by our Iraqi counterparts that al-Sadr had returned to Najaf from Iran with the notion that he had brokered a deal with Maliki and that many of his followers would be returned to prominent positions. Many believed that Sadr wanted to have one of his followers take control of the MoI. Then came the "Arab Spring" of 2011, with many countries within the Arab World experiencing problems with civil unrest. Even Iraqi citizens took to the streets for a "day of rage," demanding not the regime change sought elsewhere, but for basic services to be provided by their government and for the corruption to end. Maliki pledged that his cabinet would respond to the people and provide the services needed within one hundred days. Still, many of the protesters turned to violence and "seized provincial offices and burned others, forcing officials around the country to resign, or in some cases, flee."[26] Even though overall violence somewhat slowed during this period of uncertainty, the frequency of suicide attacks, vehicle borne IEDs (VBIEDs), and assassinations increased in late April and early May of 2011.

In an attempt to retrieve some of his control, Nouri al-Maliki "nominated members of the Wasaat Alliance, Minister of Culture Saddoun Al Dulaimi, to the post of Minister of Defense, Twafiq Al Yasiri to the Ministry of Interior, and Riyadh Gharib for the National Security" in early May, 2011.[27] With the nomination of Twafiq Al Yasiri for the MoI, Maliki made yet another attempt to regain control. Even after the announcement of these names, however, militias continued their wave of violence in an attempt to derail the government process. On May 9, 2011, for example, an assassination attempt was made on a Police Chief and a police recruit was wounded as a result of a sticky bomb in Sadr City. That violence continues, frequently on a greater scale.

The Department of State Bureau of Diplomatic Security issued a report on April 21, 2011, declaring Iraq to be a critical threat area for terrorism and political violence.[28] It goes on to report that

> Terrorists and insurgent groups continue to conduct large-scale, lethal attacks that often target personnel and facilities associated with both American organizations and the Government of Iraq. Insurgents also continue to carry out effective small-scale attacks throughout Iraq that cause fewer casualties but hinder free movement and influence public opinion regarding safety and security.[29]

With the ongoing basic humanitarian issues in Iraq, these groups and their violence continue to influence citizens, discredit the government, and undermine its legitimacy along with the rule of law. Meanwhile, efforts to recruit, train, field, and sustain a democratic police force continue to suffer, even as the militias and their members have won prominent political positions.

Building a Police Force: The Advise and Assist Mission

After their successful military operation that toppled the Saddam regime, international forces failed to take advantage of the opportunity to provide order. Instead, after a brief lull in violence the country lapsed into lawlessness. The U.S. military made a public appeal to the police to return to duty, proposing joint patrols composed of U.S. soldiers and Iraqi Police.[30] What was not known to U.S. military commanders at the time was that the IPS officials who returned to duty were unorganized, lacked leadership, and neither understood nor utilized logistical support in law enforcement efforts.

In late 2003, a Department of Defense (DoD) request was made to assess the capabilities and shortcomings of the Iraqi Police Assistance Program. It was found that the effort was not properly funded, and was itself disorganized and incapable of producing a professional IPS. Also included in the assessment was a recommendation that the U.S. military take over the training program for the police along with the one for the Iraqi Army. In 2004, "President George W. Bush signed National Security Presidential Decision Directive 36, which formally transferred responsibility for the IPS train-and-equip program from the State Department to the Department of Defense."[31] In response, the U.S. military created the Civilian Police Advisory Training Team, or CPATT, that would be under the control of the Multi-National Force-Iraq, which later became the Multi-National Security Transition Command-Iraq or MNSTC-I. All of this occurred during the CPA's return of sovereignty to the Iraqis.There was a huge gap in the understanding of this mission, however, as there was no coordination and agreement between the DoD, Department of State (DoS), Department of Justice

(DoJ), U.S. commanders on the ground, the Iraqis, or the contract advisors who were responsible for the program. In fact, there were fundamental disagreements on the main task, the mission of the Iraqi Police, its relationship to U.S. military forces, and its role in countering the insurgency.

The fundamental issue between the civilian and military components from the U.S. was that the civilian officials (DoS, DoJ, and contract advisors) saw the need to create a community policing apparatus that operated under the Provincial Chiefs of Police, whereas the military felt that the situation on the ground required the creation of a militarized police force capable of battling the insurgency. On the ground, no U.S. official took into account what the Iraqis felt should be done to combat the growing violence. Eventually the Iraqis acted on their own.The crux of the matter was the differing philosophy and the understanding of law enforcement activities versus military activities. The DoS, DoJ, and civilian law enforcement contractors believed that the military just wanted to put more Iraqi forces on the ground to relieve the stress from the U.S. forces.

The DoJ civilian police advisors thought that it would help the situation if they changed the name of the force from the Saddam-era National Police to what we see today, the Iraqi Police Services (IPS).[32] The goal was to change the atmosphere from one of a dictatorship to a more participatory form of government that acted on behalf of the Iraqi people. The community policing concept, as designed for Iraq, was to use Western operating standards and techniques. The security environment in Iraq, however, was most definitely not the environment for a western style community policing strategy.

A training Academy was created in Amman, Jordan, and many police officers were sent there from Iraq to obtain police training.[33] There they were trained for community policing and given a few basic police techniques; many Iraqi Police looked forward to the training because it was held in a safe environment. Unfortunately, they were not prepared for the operational roles which they were handed upon their return to Iraq,[34] where the U.S. military used them to fight the insurgents and sectarian militias. They were not trained in this capacity, and the U.S. military was not convinced that the community-policing effort was the right direction. Not surprisingly, with only their side arms, no training, and weak leadership, the police officers were not effective against the insurgents and the militias.

Meanwhile, the U.S. military created heavily armed police units that could bring a higher level of force to fight the insurgents. These units, made up of approximately 750 men, mainly former Sunni Special Forces, were based in the U.S. civilian tactical unit SWAT, for Special Weapons and Tactics. The problem was that these units were not trained with any policing theory, only in tactical operations to provide fire power above and beyond that of a regular Iraqi street officer. At the time, the U.S. did not realize that the MoI had begun its own recruitment of police commando-type units totally independent of U.S. forces. The U.S. failed to put a sufficient number of advisors in the MoI and thus did not pick up on this issue; coordination between the two operations was non-existent.

Nor did the IPS perform well when engaged with al-Sadr's Mahdi Army. As a consequence, the MoI began to develop their own units, motivated in part by the fact that the U.S. and International Community had not assisted the MoI as much as other Ministries. These units were able to fill the void where the U.S.-trained police were lacking. Falah al-Naqib, the Minister of Interior in 2005, had great success in providing security during the elections that created the Transitional Government, and as he was leaving office expressed his concern that the incoming Shi'a government would use these commando units to further its cause, instead of for the people.

Naqib was perhaps right. Soon after the Shi'a led government took over they appointed Bayan Jabr Solagh as the Minister of Interior. He was a senior member of the Shiite Supreme Council of the Islamic Revolution of Iraq or SCIRI. This led to many Badr Brigade members obtaining positions within the MoI and special police units such as the Iraqi Emergency Response Team (ERU), SWAT, and others. At the same time, Muqtada al-Sadr's militia forces infiltrated the police at all levels. "Members of the Sadrist Mahdi Army used police uniforms and their official status to pass through checkpoints and as cover for sectarian violence."[35] These units eventually conducted assassinations, kidnappings, and began to kill many Sunnis, some of whom were police officials. Secret prisons were used to detain and torture prisoners, mostly Sunnis.

In 2006, it became evident that something needed to be done and thus the "Year of the Police" effort was launched to reinvent the Iraqi Police. Training, equipment, vehicles, and lots of money were diverted to the Ministry of Interior. The names of many units were changed, but the people were the same. Human rights training was conducted and the MoI was warned that the U.S. could not provide assistance to those units that committed torture and violations against human rights. Nonetheless, the U.S. and Iraqi inspection teams continued to find secret facilities, even within the MoI complex, and "On July 30, 2007, the Los Angeles Times reported that Iraq's interior ministry had become an 'eleven-story powder keg of factions' where hostile militias and criminal organizations controlled various floors and settled their differences by assassinations in the parking lot"[36] The handful of U.S. advisors assigned to the MoI spent most of their time on the eleventh floor as they did not have any influence over the different factions that took control of their own floors.

The police were once again taken offline and retrained. Basic police skills were taught, and the "graduates" were paired with U.S. troops to conduct joint operations. The Italian Carabinieri assisted with leadership and riot control training, and were successful significantly in getting the Iraqi Police to understand and distinguish themselves from the Army. The roles were different and they needed to take a different approach to be successful. Meanwhile, change again took place in Baghdad with the success of the U.S. troop surge, the rise of the Sons of Iraq, and al-Sadr's decision to put himself in self-exile to Iran, all of which contributed to a decrease in violence. Still, while the names of units were again changed, more money continued to be spent on building police stations instead of building the capacity of the force.

Conclusions

Whether one agrees with the invasion of Iraq or not, it is important to understand the aftermath of the toppling of the Saddam regime and the issues confronted by the Advise and Assist officials. The United States military apparatus has not historically taken on police advisory missions and does not operate in the same ways as do civilian law enforcement officials. This is not to stay that the DoD is not capable of providing advisors and mentors to assist police, but it should be understood that the primary mission of the U.S. military does not parallel that of law enforcement. An example of this is that soldiers take orders from their chain of authority whereas police respond to the needs of the citizen.

The effectiveness of militias has dramatically impacted the rebuilding of the Iraqi Police Services and is at the heart of the issues facing the GoI. Although there are numerous factors that affect the development of a democratic police force, violent sectarian militias such as those led by Sayyid Muqtadā al-Sadr's Shi'a paramilitary force have proven to be the biggest impediment to overall Iraqi police reform efforts, domestic order, and citizen participation. Until the GoI and the International Community, specifically the United States, find a successful method to instill domestic order, the GoI will continue to be unstable and possibly collapse. The U.S.'s strong military presence avoided a complete collapse of the GoI in the past; however, as the military drawdown is complete, the rebuilding of the IPS will need to adhere to a strategic and defined policy aimed at providing all citizens of Iraq the ability to participate in government and commerce.

Domestic order is key to the government's legitimacy in as much as it provides the ability for participation to all of its citizens, not one religion or another, not based on gender, and not based on the social-economic status of the individual. Because of the extreme ideologies of some and the corrupt practices of others, domestic order in Iraq has not been realized. Deal making and bribes rule the political landscape where the rule of law falls short.

For their part, the militias have destabilized the effectiveness of the GoI in establishing a bond with the people. If the government cannot provide the necessities and security to the communities, then individuals and communities find other ways to have the necessities and security provided to them. Thus, the influence wielded by the militias is far more powerful than that of the GoI. Services like electricity, vehicle fuel, food, clean water, and schools have not been provided to the citizens of Iraq by the GoI, and that has opened the door to the militias gaining the support of the local communities.

The U.S. has poured millions of dollars into the law enforcement infrastructure for the purchase of equipment that was not needed or probably wanted, and training without taking into account religion, tribal influences, and the socio-economic issues of the Iraqi people. The money that was spent on equipment, the building of police stations, and the salaries of police officers did not meet the needs of the community. Similarly, the time that the police spent in training programs was not adequate, and the curriculum changed depending on what military unit or international group was in charge. That inconsistency and quality of training is unacceptable in building an effective police service, but can be explained by the prevailing belief that the quantity of police was more important than the quality. Inadequate vetting of police officials also caused serious problems that allowed militias and different groups to create their own sections within the MoI and police. This caused advisors to spend more time trying to bring IPS officials together than on practical, administrative, and operational tasks.

What lessons, then, can be learned from the United States' experience in police-building in Iraq?

First, in a peace-building process, creating an effective, professional police force is not an independent variable. For it to succeed in Iraq, the central government in Baghdad must provide the basic necessities of sustaining life to its citizens. Electricity, water, food, security, and employment are aspects of the framework that leads to legitimacy, participation, and prosperity. Militias have experienced great success within the communities that they otherwise terrorize by providing generators, water, and food. If the government cannot provide these basic necessities, they will not be able to maintain public order. As for the international advisors, they must change their approach so as not to be seen as colonial administrators, but rather as mentors providing guidance while allowing the decisions to be made by the local officials.

Second, for a professional police service to emerge, police operations need to be transparent, follow procedures, and be visibly respectful of the rule of law. At present this remains an elusive goal. The GoI, which has been infiltrated by members of extremist groups and militias, and the IPS are notorious for arresting everyone within the general area of an incident and failing to take into account that most of these people are not involved in the incident, but are probably their best witnesses. This not only creates hatred and disrespect for police and government, but aids militias in elevating their status and recruiting political supporters and would be terrorists. To counter these trends, as the first representatives of government and those that make citizen contacts daily, the police must be open to outside observation and accepting of reports from the community of official abuses. In practice, this means that the Ministry of Interior also needs to take an active role, starting at the top, in reforming the culture within its ranks. The militia debilitates the IPS' effectiveness and ability to perform its duty. Moreover, "many of the IPS share the same beliefs that are represented by the militias and this naturally limits the effectiveness of the law and order process."[37]

Third, community policing as it has developed in Western democracies will not work in today's Iraq. There needs to be a considerable amount of social change before it could be effective as we know it, but there are segments of community policing that would benefit the IPS in their efforts to fight crime and terrorism. Intelligence-led policing requires only changing the police mentality and not the public's culture to improve effectiveness. Problem-oriented policing would enable the IPS to look at the core of the problem to solve the insurgency and/or crime. Arresting a few terrorists has not solved the problem because it is deeply rooted in more than just Americans having boots on the ground in this Arab country. Bringing religious clerics, tribal elders, and Mullahs to the table and providing them with an avenue to join the process is an important step in creating participation.

Finally, a personal observation: for long term undertakings of this nature, the selected international advisors themselves need more training and vetting to understand the culture and environment in which they will operate. In particular, as international advisors work to improve security on the ground, one must understand that many who wish for the return of Sharia may not be militant or extremist, and the advisors need to consider how they might make use of Sharia as they advise their counterparts. Furthermore, the selection of advisors should be based on results and not connections; not many people have the ability to motivate or deal with an immersion in diverse cultural locales. Advisors need to remember that they are not there to determine the host country's police future, but to provide assistance.

Notes

1. This chapter in part draws on the author's firsthand experience while serving as a Civilian Police Advisor assigned to U.S. Forces-Iraq (USF-I), Iraq Train and Advise Mission (ITAM), Iraqi Police Transition Team (IPTT), and the Ministry of Interior (MoI).

2. The Sunni triangle encompassed Tikrit, Dur, Sharqat, Huwayja, Bayji, Samarra, and Ramadi. Based on interview with IPS Colonel Rasheed Mohammed, (October 2010).

3. I. Al-Marashi, "Iraq's Security and Intelligence Network: A Guide and Analysis," *Middle East Review on International Affairs* 6, no. 3 (September 2002). http://meria.idc.ac.il/journal/2002/issue3/jv6n3al.html (accessed September 29, 2011).

4. Based on numerous personal interviews with Iraqi police officials during 2010 and 2011. Names and specific dates of interviews withheld to protect those still in Iraq.

5. IPS Col. Rasheed Mohammed, Personal Interview, October 2010.

6. James Morrill, field advisor and trainer. Personal Interview, October 16, 2011.

7. Morrill, Personal Interview, October 16, 2011.

8. USA CPT d. Rousseau, Personal Interview, 2011.

9. Robert M. Perito, "The Iraq Federal Police: U.S. Police Building under Fire." United States Institute of Peace Special Report. http://www.usip/org/files/resources/SR291_The_Iraq_Federal_Police.pdf (accessed October 20, 2011).

10. IPS Brigadier General Zehad, Personal Interviews, November/December 2010.

11. Anthony H. Cordesman, and Jose Ramos, *Sadr and the Mahdi Army: Evolution, Capabilities, and a New Direction* (Washington, DC: Center for Strategic & International Studies, 2008).

12. Kenneth Katzman, "Iraq: Post Saddam Governance and Security." CRS Report RL31339, 9 May 2008. http://www.fas.org/sgp/crs/mideast/RL31339.pdf (accessed October 18, 2012).

13. Patrick Cockburn, "Sadr's militia may live to fight again," *The Independent*, 14 July 2008. http://www.independent.co.uk/news/world/middle-east/sadrs-militia-may-live-to-fight-again-8668866.html (accessed October 1, 2011).

14. Cockburn, "Sadr's militia may live to fight again."

15. W. Andrew Terrill, "Regional Spillover Effects of the Iraq War." The Strategic Studies Institute, December 2008. http://www.strategicstudiesinstitute.army.mil/pdffiles/PUB901.pdf (accessed October 18, 2012)

16. Terrill, "Regional Spillover Effects of the Iraq War."

17. Cordesman and Ramos, *Sadr and the Mahdi Army.*

18. IPS Brigadier General Sadiq, Personal Interview, December 2010.

19. Cordesman and Ramos, *Sadr and the Mahdi Army.*

20. IPS Brigadier General Zehad, Personal Interview, March 2011.

21. Badr Brigades, *Al-Hurriyya News*, 2011.

22. Aaron C. Davis, "In Iraq, assassinations are a nightly event," *The Washington Post*, 3 May 2011. http://www.wasingtonpost.com/world/middle-east/in-iraq-assassinations-are-a-nightly-event/2011/04/26/AFEWfVgF_story.html (accessed October 1, 2011).

23. Davis, "In Iraq, assassinations are a nightly event."

24. Mohammed Tawfeeq, "At Least 65 die in attack at recruitment center in northern Iraq," *CNN World*, 18 January 2011. http://articles.cnn.com/2011-01-18/world/iraq.violence_1_recruitment-center-tikrit-residents-sunni-muslim-city?_s=PM:WORLD (accessed September 29, 2011).

25. John Leland, "Iraq Prime Minister Visits Egypt and Iran," *New York Times*, 20 October 2010. www.nytimes.com/2010/10/21/world/middleeast/12iraq.html (accessed October 5, 2011).

26. Stephanie McCrummen, "Iraqi PM Maliki pledges reform after 'Day of Rage,'" *The Washington Post*, 27 February 2011. http://www.washingtonpost.com/wpdyn/content/article/2011/02/27/AR2011022700985.html (accessed September 28, 2011).

27. "MP calls on parliament to vote on Maliki's candidates for security ministries," *National Iraqi News Agency*, 5 May 2011. http://www.ninanews.com/english/News_Details.asp?ar95_VQ=FGIELG (October 6, 2011).

28. United States Department of State, Bureau of Diplomatic Security-OSAC, "Iraq 2011 Crime and Safety Report: Baghdad," https://www.osac.gov/Pages/ContentReportDetails.aspx?cid=10884 (accessed October 1, 2011).

29. United States Department of State, "Iraq 2011 Crime and Safety Report."

30. Perito, "The Iraq Federal Police."

31. Perito, "The Iraq Federal Police."

32. Perito, "The Iraq Federal Police."

33. Perito, "The Iraq Federal Police."

34. Perito, "The Iraq Federal Police."

35. Perito, "The Iraq Federal Police."

36. Perito, "The Iraq Federal Police."

37. Griffin, Peter, field adviser and trainer, Personal Interview, 4 October 2011.

Chapter 18

Security Without Weapons: Nonviolent Peaceforce in Sri Lanka

M.S. Wallace

Once we reached the roads east of Habarana, the Sri Lankan countryside started to feel different: military and police checkpoints became much more common, and we began to spot small bulwarks emerging from the earth, mounds of clay and timber patched together to provide just enough room for a solitary soldier to peer out with his rifle poised. This was the part of the country that had recently been "liberated" (in 2007) by the Sri Lankan government (GoSL) in its war against the LTTE (Liberation Tigers of Tamil Eelam), the armed Tamil movement that had been fighting for a separate state in the North and East of Sri Lanka for the previous twenty-five years. At the time of this visit to the East in October 2008, the frontlines of the war had moved north to the Vanni,[1] but violence in the East continued, and the armed presence of the Sri Lankan Army (SLA) and other groups[2] was ubiquitous.

Also ubiquitous was the "no-gun" symbol found on most non-governmental organization (NGO) vehicles and office doors, including those of Nonviolent Peaceforce (NP), the international NGO I spent the fall of 2008 researching.[3] This sign marks spaces that are to be kept free of the intrusion of weapons in a society that is heavily militarized. As I was travelling to the East for the first time on that October day—in an NP van marked with this symbol—an NP staff member pointed out two SLA soldiers riding on the back of a motorbike with a civilian, explaining that it is common for soldiers to demand rides from civilians, since they often do not have their own transportation, and their guns mean that those asked are unlikely to refuse. This observation prompted her to recount an experience that a friend of hers had had recently in relation to his work with a local educational organization for children of all ethnicities. The friend had been driving a group of children in the organization's bus, when they were stopped by some soldiers who asked for a ride despite the "no-gun" symbol displayed.

When the friend told them "no," the soldiers were taken aback, basically saying, "What do you mean, no? We're getting on the bus." And the friend said, "Well, here are the keys," and turning to the children: "Children, we're getting off the bus now. These soldiers will be taking it." The soldiers were so surprised and embarrassed that they backed down and left.[4] Somehow, the friend, though unarmed, was able to make these soldiers change their course of action, thereby carving out and maintaining a demilitarized zone in the midst of militarizing forces.

This anecdote provides a useful opening for exploring a little-known paradigm of protection work and security provision that is taking root in Sri Lanka and elsewhere, through either the courageous unarmed defiance and resistance of local civilian actors or the international proactive presence of unarmed groups such as Nonviolent Peaceforce and Peace Brigades International (which also worked in Sri Lanka in the late 1980s/1990s).[5] Whereas the predominant assumption is that peacekeepers should be soldiers and that protection requires armaments, those engaged in civilian peacekeeping (also known as nonviolent intervention) protect civilians in the face of violence without themselves carrying weapons.[6] In contexts like Sri Lanka in the fall of 2008, where politics and day-to-day realities are dictated by the logic of violence, NP employs a different logic in its efforts to create space for demilitarized politics, providing nonpartisan unarmed protection for civilians so they feel secure enough to work for peace and justice on the local and national levels—or simply to go along with their normal lives.

NP and others doing similar work embody a response to recent critiques of military peacekeeping and military humanitarian intervention. These critiques can be divided into two broad types. First, there is the concern that deploying soldiers as peacekeepers is a fundamentally flawed proposition, as the militarized masculinity required to form soldiers is antithetical to most of the tasks required of peacekeepers and may result—as it has in Cambodia and Somalia—in peacekeeping missions fraught with "sexual abuse and racist violence."[7] More broadly, militarized peacekeeping/intervention, like the armed groups it seeks to stop, depends on threat power to function and hence reinforces a zero-sum conception of security.

Second, there is the post-colonial critique of military humanitarian intervention and, more recently, of the emerging "responsibility to protect" norm insofar as it justifies such intervention. Here, military humanitarian intervention is viewed as a violation of sovereignty and a nice-looking cover for the West's continued control of post-colonial countries. Mamdani thus notes how calls for humanitarian intervention echo colonial discourses that identified victims to be saved and perpetrators to be civilized, thereby casting these contemporary *missions civilisatrices* as re-enactments of colonial violations of sovereignty.[8] Anne Orford deepens this critique by drawing attention to the way legal texts frame humanitarian crises as being caused solely by local actors motivated by "premodern tribalism, ethnic tensions, and religious factionalism" and as being solved by international actors portrayed as the "bearers of peace, democracy, and human rights" who must come in to fix things—as if the "international community" had nothing at all to do with the causes of the crisis in the first place.[9] Furthermore, by focusing on the *international* response to atrocities and getting caught up in debates about "responsibility to protect," foreign commentators lose sight of the agency of local actors in the midst of atrocities.[10] Not only does this focus risk casting local civilians as powerless and in need of outside rescue, but there is the perhaps graver risk of dehumanizing the "perpetrators" by assuming that "all they understand is force" and denying them any status as reflexive, thinking, moral agents capable of changing their course of action.

These concerns point to the need for a radical reconceptualization of protection efforts: a form of action, first, that does not rely on the very logic of violence and militarism that both peacekeeping and humanitarian intervention are meant to counter, and, second, that supports local capacities for protection and political action rather than disregarding and/or supplanting these capacities, and that allows for the complexity and reflexivity of *all* actors, civilian and armed alike. Nonviolent Peaceforce is particularly well suited to fulfilling these criteria. It self-consciously and explicitly rejects the use of weapons to protect civilians or even its own staff, and its staff is composed of civilian actors who bring various human relations skills—rather than military skills—to their work. Its unarmed and nonpartisan status means that NP is able to carry out its protection work without implicating itself directly in the substantive issues at stake in a conflict, an approach that supports rather than directs or supplants local political agency. Furthermore, because its security provision does not depend on weapons—and therefore does not require one person's security to be ensured at the expense of someone else's—NP is able to engage with all actors as complex human beings, not as one-dimensional caricatures of perpetrators and victims.

But even if NP's unarmed status and particular activities make it more able to avoid the serious shortcomings—dangers, even—of military forms of peacekeeping and intervention, NP is still an international NGO intervening from the outside and therefore subject to a variant of the sovereignty critique above. Why this assumption on the part of the "international community" that outside actors are needed at all, and why my own emphasis on the role of an international NGO rather than on local movements or actors? My graduate student colleagues at the University of Colombo confronted me with this question during my first week in Sri Lanka, sharing, as they did, the widespread impression that NGOs were only in it for the money and that international NGOs, in particular, dampened the voluntarism of local actors (a view repeated frequently in the media and government, often in more extreme form). As a tentative response, one way in which NP distinguished itself from other NGOs "working on the conflict" in Sri Lanka is that it limited its focus to security provision rather than also providing material aid or engaging in more substantive Track I conflict resolution activities. Its lack of substantive "content" in this sense set it apart from the larger liberal peacebuilding project that seeks to impose a "desired end state" on conflict zones.[11] And security provision is something for which *international* unarmed actors are particularly well suited; the protective effect of their international status is something distinctive they can offer as compared to what local actors can provide. Nonetheless, their question lingered with me throughout my research, leaving me critical of the INGO community that I still felt was worthy of study.

There are a few ways, then, in which this chapter and the case it explores push up against the framework of this volume, the first being my uneasiness with an emphasis on the role of *international* actors in the management of communal conflict (even as I recognize the usefulness of such an emphasis). Second, the term communal (or ethnic) conflict itself in the context of such intervention highlights the schisms between ethnic communities and also casts a conflict as predominantly internal. The conflict in Sri Lanka, however, resists both of these descriptions.[12] Although in important respects about competing Tamil and Sinhala nationalisms,[13] the conflict has also been characterized by intense *intra*-communal violence as illustrated by the LTTE's violence over the years against other Tamil groups/individuals critical of it, the Marxist Sinhala nationalist JVP insurrections of the 1970s and 1980s against the Sinhala-dominated government, and government-linked intimidation, abduction, and assassination of Sinhalese journalists and human rights defenders critical of the government.[14] Additionally, the conflict was not strictly internal but internationalized in significant ways through Sri Lanka's economic liberalization and globalization after 1977, the role played by India, international development policy impacts on ethnic polarization, diaspora funding, and the discursive context of the global "war on terror."[15] Finally, the inclusion of this chapter in the military operations section of this volume immediately flags it as a misfit. Although Nonviolent Peaceforce most certainly does not engage in military operations, it also does not fit under either more traditional conflict resolution efforts or more substantive nation-building projects. Instead, NP's interventions—like military action in this respect only, perhaps—are meant to provide security rather than to address the more substantive issues underlying the conflict itself; indeed, NP focuses on the former so that local actors can have the space to engage with the latter. And, importantly, NP's security provision is both less intrusive and less costly than military operations that also aim to protect civilians.

The obvious questions to address with such a radical departure from traditional military modes of protection and security provision are a) what sorts of civilian protection and violence prevention has NP been capable of in Sri Lanka, and b) what mechanisms operate in its work? Perhaps more fundamentally, in light of the opening anecdote, what happens when the logic of nonviolence comes up against the logic of violence? Why does this encounter not simply result in the submission and vulnerability of those without weapons? The coercive and transformative mechanisms I discuss map roughly onto the mechanisms identified by Liam Mahony, who has done extensive work on unarmed international protective accompaniment and presence: deterrence (of abusers), encouragement (of civil society actors), and influence (on more "progressive" voices within the "abusive or negligent institutions" in question).[16] What my analysis adds to his and others' studies of unarmed protection efforts is special attention to the effect that the absence or presence of weapons has on these protective mechanisms and an explicit challenge to the presumed link between weapons and protection. A civilian peacekeeping force's unarmed status is crucial to the operation of these mechanisms: such a presence can be subtly coercive without being perceived as overtly threatening (as an armed peacekeeping force might be), which would risk retaliatory violence and hence decreased protection; such a presence can *also* support transformative processes because of the comparative ease with which unarmed international actors can engage and build trust with local actors on all sides of the conflict. In light of these findings, NP's unarmed status emerges as a strength, enabling NP to win the trust of local actors and build relationships, to remain nonpartisan, to protect its staff and the civilians with whom it works, and, ultimately, to help challenge the dominant logic of violence and militarism.

Nonviolent Peaceforce at Work

In late 2008, the Sri Lankan Army was executing a military campaign in the North to defeat the LTTE. NP was working in five field sites: three in the Eastern Province (Batticaloa, Valaichchenai, and Trincomalee), one in the northernmost town of Jaffna, and one (a smaller "response team") in Colombo—none of which were along the frontlines of the war. This marks an important limitation to NP's work: NP did not view its role in Sri Lanka as interpositioning between the warring parties per se, and certainly not with its limited human and financial resources.[17] Rather, NP defused violence and protected civilians at the community level beyond the "battlefield"—but where threats to human security were just as devastating and no less real for those affected.[18] In 2008, so-called "white van abductions" were frequent, especially for Tamils. Former child soldiers or adult combatants who had been (often forcibly) enlisted by either the LTTE or the TMVP but escaped feared being re-recruited, disappeared, or killed. Unknown armed actors—who may or may not have had some connection to the government—operated largely with impunity, and civilians often felt insecure going about their daily activities. Additionally, inter-ethnic suspicions (across Tamil/Muslim lines, but also between the Sinhalese-dominated government forces and the Tamil-speaking majority population they controlled) escalated tensions when there were acts of violence in the community. In this context, NP's civilian protection and community violence prevention work filled a notable gap in human security provision.[19]

With headquarters in Brussels and regional offices around the world, NP is clearly an international NGO and its field teams in Sri Lanka were truly international in composition. An NP staff member accompanying someone at risk or creating links between two communities during a crisis was just as likely to be from the Global South as from the Global North. This international composition was not incidental. NP's activities worked precisely *because* of the status of most of its staff as outsiders to the Sri Lankan conflict. As *national* staff members at one of the field sites told me, "International presence is very essential, because...they [locals] trust internationals. [Those] who are affected by war, violence, they will trust internationals, not local[s]."[20] Another national staff member added, on the other hand, that *armed* actors are wary of internationals—in particular, the ramifications that might follow from international observation of their activities—which is what prompts threatened individuals to request international presence.[21] In other words, civilians trust internationals more than they do locals and armed actors fear internationals more than they do locals. This is the golden combination that made NP's work viable—both in building the trust and confidence of civil society actors and in deterring armed actors from carrying out extra-legal abductions and killings.

At the same time, national staff members played a key role in NP's field work, thereby complicating NP's status as a purely external, international intervention. In fact, NP intentionally employed national staff members evenly from all of the ethnic communities represented in the local area, and these national staff members, in their capacity as field officers, contributed fully to the *substantive work* of the field teams.[22] Indeed, national staff members filled a role that could not be filled by international staff, particularly insofar as national staff members understood the nuances on the ground in a way outsiders would be unable to do, were closer to information sources because of their close and long-term relationships in the community, provided a sense of continuity for the communities where NP worked, and, most obviously, operated fluently in Tamil or Sinhala, depending on the situation.[23] In late 2008, field teams, drawing on the strengths of their national and international members, carried out the following kinds of protection and violence prevention work.

Protecting Individuals at Risk of Abduction, Forced Recruitment, or Targeted Killing

NP's accompaniment work aimed at preventing abductions, forced recruitment, and targeted killings of child soldiers (who had escaped armed groups), human rights defenders, adult former combatants, or other threatened civilians; accompaniment enabled them to travel to a safer place, confront armed groups about the whereabouts of loved ones, or simply access government services safely. NP's greatest accompaniment successes, according to one international Field Team Member (FTM), happened when it coordinated effectively with other agencies, most often the International Committee of the Red Cross (ICRC) and UNICEF, allowing each to play the role it played best. This FTM pointed to a recent case where, after two months of repeatedly badgering one particular armed group about the presence of under-age cadres, ICRC was able to get them released. But that is where ICRC's mandate ended, so it coordinated with NP to take over from there, at which point NP identified what, for these boys, would constitute a "safer place" and accompanied them there so as to prevent re-recruitment.[24]

In addition to providing direct protection, NP's accompaniment had further *indirect* effects on protection, as when it created the space for individuals to take action themselves to protect loved ones. In one case, a diminutive but courageous grandmother decided she would like NP to accompany her to the nearby TMVP camp to tell them not to take her grandson back. And though she was scared and though her tiny stature contrasted with that of the "six foot four, bullet-proof" young TMVP officer she confronted, she went ahead and spoke for herself on behalf of her grandson.[25] NP's presence gave the grandmother the protection she needed to confront the TMVP about her grandson, empowering her to challenge an armed group that otherwise might feel entitled to take whatever youth it needs from the community. Enabling one grandmother to feel safe enough to confront an armed group can also have "ripple effects" on the broader community, emboldening others to do the same.[26]

Protecting Communities Under Threat

NP's protective presence work was also sometimes performed on behalf of whole communities at risk. NP field teams occasionally stayed with communities overnight or for several days; other times, they simply visited a community, an Internationally Displaced Person (IDP) camp, or an organization on a regular basis to show whoever was watching that they were monitoring the situation.[27] One international FTM understood NP's effectiveness in such cases to be reflected in "the fact that people call [us] back," keeping NP in the loop when "strange things" happen in the village and asking NP to "give international presence."[28] Even if it is impossible to know for sure whether targeted killings, indiscriminate shelling, or other forms of violence would have been carried out had NP not shown up on a regular basis, what we can know with certainty is that if people kept requesting NP's presence then they *felt* safer with NP there. And this *sense* of security may be what matters most if people are going to feel like they have the space to demand their rights or work towards a peaceful and just political solution.

Preventing Inter-communal Violence

Additionally, by facilitating communication and "rumor control," NP helped prevent the escalation of inter-communal violence.[29] NP's ability to do so was evident in the case of Valachchenai during and after the provincial elections of May 2008 (elaborated further below). As inter-communal violence escalated in Batticaloa and surrounding areas, Valachchenai—historically a prime site for inter-communal violence—remained calm. In fact, Valachchenai is where NP had invested much time and energy into supporting and nurturing a multi-ethnic network of community groups called the Community Information Network (CIN; later renamed the Organizations' Council for Peace and Coexistence, OCPC)—a structure that provided a space for community members to interact and communicate across communal lines during the post-election crisis.[30]

Preventing Security Force Violence

Finally, more recently, NP facilitated first steps towards a sustainable security structure to help prevent violence between the (predominantly Sinhalese) Sri Lankan security forces and community members (with suspected LTTE ties). Capitalizing on the successes of the multi-ethnic organizational structure of the CIN/OCPC and the on-going meetings it enabled, "some members of the OCPC" developed "tight links with the SLA and police officers" in the area.[31] According to the international FTM who highlighted this development, direct contact could reduce threats from the security forces because it reduced suspicion. "[S]pecific officers in the SLA understand that somehow the people who approach them through us are filtered. . . so through direct contact between these 'good' leaders and these 'good' officers, at least some of the threats that come. . . by the security forces may be a little bit reduced."[32] As an intermediary, NP supported the emergence of trust between the community leaders and the security forces, making them less suspicious of each other and therefore less threatening to each other.

Mechanisms

If these are some of the ways in which NP protected civilians and prevented violence, what were the mechanisms that enabled it to do so? Two mechanisms emerged in my research: deterrence and relationship-building.

Deterrence

One question I asked NP staff was what sort of internal process they thought was occurring when would-be perpetrators did not carry out—because of NP's presence—abductions or targeted killings that they might otherwise have: were they deterred, or was there some deeper transformation at work? The overwhelming response was that they were deterred: "Someone's watching, and they're not exactly sure on what kind of. . . what we're doing there. . . and how far we go to report and who we're going to tell. . . . And how often do we come back and how strong we are. It's more the fear of being monitored."[33] One international FTM illustrated the effectiveness of NP's deterrence with regards to armed groups—in this case, the so-called "white van unit."[34] NP was involved in a high-profile case of a person who had been accused of killing an SLA officer but had been proclaimed innocent by a Sri Lankan judge. Nonetheless, this person was still at risk of being killed extra-judicially, and NP was providing an international protective presence for this person at a "safe place" that local actors[35] had provided for him in Colombo while he was seeking asylum from a nearby embassy. When security forces started to show up daily, NP decided to "tighten the security measures,"[36] arranging to be contacted by the staff at the "safe place" whenever the security forces showed up and to arrive immediately thereafter. The security forces, having been told that NP was about to arrive—and what its mandate was—were always gone by the time NP did.[37] This international staff member also highlighted the role that communication—especially with high-level police/security officials—played in effective deterrence in this case, echoing NP's common practice of being transparent about its work and purpose with all stakeholders in a spirit of nonpartisanship.[38] NP's message of its complete support for Sri Lanka's *above-the-board* legal structures and processes drew attention to—and therefore helped deter—any extra-legal measures that the "white van unit" might have taken under NP's watch.[39] Furthermore, NP's cultivation of relationships with government officials and armed actors at *all* levels was meant to make it harder for higher-level decision-makers in such situations to deny a link with on-the-ground perpetrators.[40]

The deterrent effect described here is intensified if the onlookers are internationals, as illustrated in the experience of one NP staff member who was accompanying mothers to an LTTE camp where they were trying to get their recruited sons back. The LTTE told the mothers that if it were not for the presence of the "foreigners" they had brought with them, they would have "str[u]ng them from the highest tree" for having had the gall to come to the camp and request their sons—a statement that, of course, completely validated the mothers' choice to bring foreigners with them.[41] Would-be perpetrators in this and other cases might think—rightly or wrongly—that NP would publicize an act of wrongdoing and thereby bring about negative repercussions.[42] Whether NP would actually report such a violation is beside the point and, for the record, NP does not normally engage in "naming and shaming" campaigns, in order to maintain the nonpartisan status so crucial to its work. What matters is that perpetrators might anticipate such repercussions—and the fact that these potential repercussions may remain unspecified and ambiguous to perpetrators has its advantages. That they *could* include the withdrawal of needed resources by foreign state or non-state actors, as Mahony asserts, provides a compelling reason to refrain from human rights violations when internationals are watching.[43] The bottom line for NP, though, is that *something* worked: in five years of protection work in Sri Lanka (as of late 2008), NP staff members had never had someone they were accompanying—someone with reason to fear abduction or worse—taken from their vehicle.[44]

Relationship-building as Effective Intervention and Preventive Diplomacy

Beyond deterrence, the second mechanism operating in NP's work was relationship-building, which both facilitated the acceptance of NP's presence in the community by armed and civilian actors alike, and created direct links between potential antagonists that could defuse violence during a crisis.

Relationship-building with armed actors (for instance, a particular officer at a nearby checkpoint) was crucial to successful protection. According to NP staff, developing a good relationship with these individuals through respectful and congenial interactions (evidence of which I observed on my trips to the East) made it more likely that nothing would go wrong when NP staff were accompanying someone through these checkpoints. Furthermore, NP staff would often identify common ground with armed actors as a rhetorical strategy for enhanced protection: in a tense situation with a government soldier or police officer during an accompaniment, an NP staff member could draw on the *shared* purpose of protecting the security of Sri Lankan people and/or of abiding by the laws of Sri Lanka, a reminder of his/her stated commitments that would rule out extra-legal abduction. Similarly, in interactions with the LTTE or TMVP about a child abduction case, NP staff could capitalize on the fact that all armed groups wanted to maintain a reputation for not recruiting children.[45] Thus NP staff members could expose a potential disjuncture between identity and practice on the part of state actors or other armed groups as a tool for civilian protection by strategically reminding actors of their *stated identities*—and the discursive incoherence that would follow if they were to carry out some action that violated these identities.

Relationship-building with and between community leaders was also crucial to NP's efforts at inter-communal violence prevention. In May 2008, for example, just after the provincial elections in the newly "liberated" Eastern Province, the situation was tense after President Rajapaksa appointed a TMVP official as chief minister when the Muslim community had been led to believe that he would appoint someone from the Sri Lanka Muslim Congress (SLMC). Two TMVP-affiliated Tamils were killed in a Muslim area near Batticaloa, followed by the killing of three Muslim civilians later that day in a Tamil area, sparking a spate of violence in Batticaloa.[46] During this period, local NP field team members were busy trying to organize meetings and sustain contact among mutually suspicious community groups and leaders with whom the teams had developed relationships over the years. Whereas a key meeting fell through in Batticaloa, in Valaichchenai NP's efforts at organizing a meeting were successful and may have helped stem the violence. One international FTM characterized NP's immediate violence-prevention impact as the product of NP's long-term engagement with the community through the formation in Valachchenai of the aforementioned multi-ethnic network of community groups (CIN, later OCPC). According to him, "a guy got kidnapped. . . —which could've started the violence—but a few phone calls [were] made between the different members of this network and he was released."[47] Another was more direct in elaborating upon what happened in these meetings that made the defusing of potential violence possible:

> NP8: In Vala[chchenai]...the teams were able to create meetings that included the police, the Special Task Force, the Sri Lankan Army, and the TMVP, Muslim groups, religious leaders, community leaders. . . all in the same room, all talking. They exchanged phone numbers with each other. "Oh yeah, yeah, yeah, here's my mobile number, you call if you have problems." "Somebody disappears, you know, you call me and let me know."[48]

Even the Divisional Secretary attributed the lack of violence in Valachchenai to NP's work.[49]

In this case, two types of relationships are evident—those between NP and various members of the community and those that NP facilitated between the different community groups themselves. The former enabled a positive and trusting response when NP called upon these groups to meet during a crisis (in a context where a meeting was no small accomplishment). It developed gradually and stemmed from the fact that NP field teams not only worked in the community but lived there, too, giving them special status over time as "insiders" who could be trusted more than *real* insiders/locals precisely because they were internationals (due to the mutual suspicion that developed within/between local communities during the war).[50] The latter is that which directly defused potential violence, as evidenced in the sharing of mobile phone numbers among community leaders to create a direct communication channel so that any spark that might be used to justify an inter-communal attack could be extinguished before starting a conflagration.

The example of the CIN/OCPC in Valachchenai bears out Ashutosh Varshney's thesis that inter-ethnic networks, especially "associational forms of engagement," encourage peace in multi-ethnic societies. But a further point he makes affirms NP's crucial role—that these "organizations [are] difficult to form in cities where everyday interaction [does] not cross religious lines, or where Hindus and Muslims live. . . in highly segregated neighborhoods. Sustained prior interaction or cordiality facilitate[s] the emergence of appropriate, crisis-managing organizations."[51] If creating these organizations capable of stemming inter-ethnic violence requires a context of trust and coexistence—precisely the qualities missing in societies where there is a history of inter-ethnic violence—then it is clear why a trusted catalyst would be necessary. As an outside actor with insider status, NP could gain (and build) the trust that was otherwise so sparse in relations both between and within ethnic communities in Sri Lanka,[52] crossing inter-communal boundaries and creating spaces where others were encouraged—and made to feel safe enough—to do the same, thereby enabling these violence prevention mechanisms to emerge.

Armed Versus Unarmed Intervention and Peacekeeping

Despite the impact NP was able to have on human security at the community level, it did not intervene directly in the war between the GoSL and the LTTE. Does this necessarily mean that nonviolent intervention is ultimately inadequate when compared to military humanitarian intervention? To think through this question, one must start with a fair appraisal of military intervention's abilities. Immediately stopping the fighting on the battlefield is rarely expected even of humanitarian intervention forces. Instead, military humanitarian intervention involves taking sides, as in the case of armed "peace enforcement" missions, to disarm, overwhelm, or oust the putative aggressor (e.g., Kosovo in 1999 or Libya in 2011). Intervention forces in such missions become a party to the conflict, escalate the violence, and implicate themselves in the substantive political objectives of the side on behalf of whom they are fighting.[53] In the case of traditional "peacekeeping" operations, neutral military forces are involved in less "robust" ceasefire monitoring and enjoy the consent of the parties, between whom there is no longer active violence. Neither "peace enforcement" nor "peacekeeping" operations are expected or able simply to cease on-going hostilities.

In addition, as in the case of the Indian Peace-Keeping Forces (IPKF) who arrived in Sri Lanka in 1987 to oversee the implementation of the Indo-Lankan Accord, the latter may dissolve into the former as a ceasefire disintegrates. Within months, the IPKF was fighting the LTTE who were supported by the Tamil population as resentment simmered in response to being occupied by a foreign army. After the martyrdom by cyanide tablets of seventeen LTTE cadres who were held jointly by the IPKF and the SLA, and the subsequent Tamil violence against Sri Lankan soldiers, police, and (Sinhalese) civilians, the IPKF, according to its commander, "was told that it was required to train its guns on the LTTE to whom the IPKF then became an enemy."[54] That Tamil civilians started to view the Indian Army as no better than the Sri Lankan Army[55] suggests that the fact of being armed can create seeming aggressors even out of forces who are originally meant to serve humanitarian purposes, inciting resistance from the community they were meant to serve.

Curious about what difference the presence or absence of weapons actually makes to the ability of peacekeepers to protect civilians or prevent violence (other obvious differences in size, resources, and institutional status notwithstanding), I asked NP field team members to reflect on how having weapons would change what an international (UN) armed peacekeeping force mandated with protecting civilians would be able to do as compared to NP. First, there was strong consensus among NP interviewees that an armed peacekeeping force's access to the community—both civilians and armed actors—would be limited by virtue of its arms. One international FTM put it this way:

> NP16: Not carrying a gun—I find it a lot easier to gain people's trust and to create relationships with people. Because they're not afraid of me, why should they? People feel, of course, it's easier, and it's safer, and it's more natural to approach me, or for me to approach someone when I'm not like dragging around some *thing* that could kill or seriously injure people. Because I think the perception of someone with a gun is also, this person is carrying this gun, or this weapon, *to* kill or *to* injure, not only for protection. But it's the possibility of the violence there that makes it impossible for people to approach and trust. . . . I know it's easier for me to be invited into someone's house for. . . whatever, than if I would be carrying a gun. Definitely. And it's easier for me to go into a village and have a meeting with so many people and talk about, "Can we get together? What's your security issues?" than if I would be carrying a gun. . . . If you carry a gun, you're suspicious to everyone. Including military forces.[56]

In other words, it was precisely the fact of being unarmed that enabled NP to do the work that it did. Not only did being unarmed make NP field team members less threatening to community members and therefore easier to trust and to communicate with—essential components of NP's relationship-building work key to its effectiveness—but it also enabled NP to be perceived as truly nonpartisan.[57]

Additionally, the post-colonial context of Sri Lanka and the sheer proliferation of armed groups on the island since its independence would influence the ability of armed peacekeepers to operate effectively, as the arrival of a foreign military force would be read against Sri Lanka's colonial and militarized history.[58] Thus, despite their benign intentions, members of an armed international peacekeeping force would have great difficulty gaining the trust of community members in large part because of the negative feelings associated with armed groups and colonial forces historically. Furthermore, being armed would perpetuate the logic of violence that has been maintained by a proliferation of armed groups over the years. So something absolutely crucial that NP could do that an armed peacekeeping force could not was to model a different logic of power in the face of a highly militarized society,[59] to demonstrate "solidarity with what it's like to live, to try to not be violent in a violent conflict" and to provide a "different kind of space" marked off by the "no-gun" signs.[60] This ability to model a different way of living in and responding to violent conflict points to the longer-term implications of the presence of one sort of peacekeeping force over another: one that contributes to a culture of peace through its actions and one that simply perpetuates a culture of violence through its reliance on the deterrent force of arms.

Nevertheless, some NP staff members did mention advantages an armed peacekeeping force could have, including the fact that a UN peacekeeping force (in particular) would have more space in which to operate by virtue of its legitimacy, given a UN Security Council resolution authorizing its existence.[61] There was, however, some disagreement on this point, due to the common view of the UN as a western-dominated institution and because of the UN's inflexible regulations on the ground.[62] Another international FTM saw the strength of armed

UN peacekeepers as being a combination of this institutional identity and the deterrence power of arms as a back-up.[63]

Other FTMs framed the potential advantage of armed peacekeeping forces in terms of short-term versus long-term effects. To this international staff member, violence "only works—to the extent it works—it only works in the very short term. And most of us, I think, are, you know, in it for the long haul—and that ultimately nonviolence is more powerful, more permanent, more stable."[64] Another international FTM came to a similar conclusion, thinking through this distinction with the example of what it would be like if she entered a TMVP camp armed, demanding to get a particular boy released. Even if she would seem to have more initial leverage to get the boy out, she asked, "what good's going to [come] of it? I get shot? The boy gets shot? Other boys get shot?. . . . It's way more sustainable if I don't force people to do something. . . if I negotiate someone out."[65] In this case, the advantage gained from having weapons is extremely short-term. As she noted, there is likely to be almost immediate retribution and/or re-abduction of the boy shortly thereafter.[66]

In this sense, the short-term and immediate deterrent capability so commonly and unquestioningly associated with arms collapses into their greatest liability. As indicated above, many felt that being armed would put them, as well as the people they are trying to protect, at *greater* risk than when unarmed. Most NP staff spoke emphatically when making this point, insisting, "Hell yeah!. . . . I mean, if I carry a gun around. . . having so many security forces and military around, I mean, I'm sorry: *it does not make me feel safer.* Quite on the—au contraire. . . . If I carry a gun—no, if I'm known to carry a gun and I make a strange movement, I'm going to be shot."[67] Another in a different interview added, "If we were out there carrying guns, we would be being shot at. . . I have no doubt at all that the TMVP or the LTTE or the army or the police, some Muslim gang, or who the hell knows who, would definitely be shooting at us."[68] In other words, the main advantage most people think of when they think of armed actors—that the threatening appearance and capability of their arms mean that they can better protect themselves and others than unarmed actors can—may, in fact, be a liability insofar as individuals are just as likely to resist/retaliate in the face of threatened or actual harm as they are to be deterred by it.

To summarize, then, not only would being armed mean hindered access to the community and the perpetuation of a logic/culture of violence in a society already inundated with it, but being armed, though in certain cases an immediate deterrent or source of control, might also actually make the peacekeeping force and those it tries to protect less safe by inciting violent resistance against it.

Conclusions

As K.M. Fierke reminds us, "intervention" is a much broader phenomenon than the physical, military form we most often associate with the term. A whole host of actions can "modif[y] the existing state of affairs."[69] Instead of being stuck in the old idea that the only way to stop violence is to counter it with more violence—because military action is the only form of intervention we can *recognize* as such—we can use Fierke's lens to look at NP's work and recognize *as intervention* the myriad forms of action (from organizing meetings to accompanying grandmothers) that are capable of stemming violence. My research on Nonviolent Peaceforce in Sri Lanka has found that it is possible to protect civilians and prevent violence without weapons. Where nonviolent intervention comes up against limitations, however, a fair comparison between unarmed and armed intervention compels us to look anew at what military intervention can actually do and to question whether its ability to stop violence is any more evident than NP's. As history—both in Sri Lanka and elsewhere—suggests, military interventions are fraught with inadequacies as well, inadvertently inciting violence or actively escalating violence before being able to stop it. Nonviolent intervention is able to deter some violence without this same danger; and it is also able to carry out relationship-building functions that provide a more sustainable foundation for violence prevention, something military intervention is handicapped from doing by virtue of its arms.

That said, it is worth reflecting in these concluding paragraphs on the types of contexts in which nonviolent intervention is most likely to function effectively. First, because it operates through a potential perpetrator's fear of being monitored or fear of publicity, an international presence is more likely to deter violence with which actors do not want to be associated, most notably violence against civilians. Second, a group like NP can only deter violence where it has access. This may be an obvious point, but it bears repeating as it draws attention to the fact that international NGOs are dependent on host governments in crucial ways, and therefore nonpartisanship is not only a principled but also a pragmatic position for such groups to take. Third, the international presence of groups like NP is more likely to deter violence by actors—both state and non-state—who are somehow dependent on global support (moral or material) for their survival. Geopolitical concerns enter in here in two ways: first, by drawing attention to the way in which nonviolent intervention can work if certain states or non-state actors are more or less dependent on others in the international system and therefore sensitive to international presence, and, second, by pointing to the impact that shifts in international economic relationships can have on the kinds of pressure that can be exerted.[70]

Although nonviolent intervention may not be a panacea, it does address some of the concerns regarding military humanitarian intervention and peacekeeping noted at the beginning of this chapter. First, it is clear that NP's refusal to depend on the threat power of weapons enables NP to model a completely different way of being in the world, one that does not accept security as a zero-sum enterprise where some people's security is expendable for the sake of others' security. Second, with regards to post-colonial critiques of military humanitarian intervention, NP's unarmed INGO status means that it sidesteps the debate to some extent, insofar as an INGO presence is less invasive than a foreign military one. The absence of weapons, as well as the focus on security rather than on more substantive issues, means that nonviolent intervention groups do not force particular political outcomes, and hence their actions resist old colonial tropes of Westerners swooping in to civilize the savages. Rather, NP's limited scope of action—limited to civilian protection and violence prevention—opens up space for local actors to act. Therefore, rather than framing the conflict as one where all the problems are local and all the solutions are international, NP offers the aspect of its international identity that is most helpful and then steps back so local solutions can emerge. Finally, engaging with all actors nonviolently and as complex beings, rather than, say, monolithically evil perpetrators, opens up room for these actors to be more reflexive about their own participation in violence—even if the mechanism of deterrence means that the protective function of NP's presence does not *depend* on this sort of reflexivity and deeper transformation to work.

I asked earlier, what happens when the logic of violence and the logic of nonviolence come up against each other? And how is this different from what happens when the logic of violence is pitted against the logic of violence? Returning again to the story at the beginning of this chapter, what would have happened if the driver of the bus had been armed while transporting Tamil and Muslim kids to school through SLA-controlled areas? It is likely that if his goal were still to keep the SLA soldiers off the bus, the battle of wills may have ended in someone actually using a gun, as this would be the form of power being depended on by both sides: either the driver would have felt that the children were threatened and this would be his only option for protecting them, or the SLA soldiers would have understood his armed resistance as an affront to their control over the area and their credibility maintained only if proved through the use of force. A child might have been killed by a stray bullet; the relationship between the different communities might have deteriorated. As it was, the unarmed bus-driver was able to stand up to the armed soldiers, insisting on the maintenance of a certain type of space and protecting the children and himself at the same time. Of course, no kind of action, violent or nonviolent, comes with guaranteed results, but as this man and NP have demonstrated in their own ways, we need not be limited to thinking that violence is the only resource we have to counter violence.

Notes

1. The name for the forested area across northern Sri Lanka.

2. Notable among these was the TMVP, a Tamil armed group that split from the LTTE in 2004, helped the government win control of the East, and became a political party despite its retention of arms.

3. I carried out ethnographic research predominantly in Colombo, at the main offices of NPSL (Nonviolent Peaceforce Sri Lanka), keeping regular field notes, interviewing field team members passing through on their way to/from field sites, and reading through

internal documents. The other part of my time in Colombo was spent as a visiting scholar at the University of Colombo where I had access to a video archive of thirty-two interviews with Sri Lankan women about their experiences in the war. I took two trips to NP's field sites in the East, first to Trincomalee and then to Batticaloa and Valachchenai, where I interviewed NPSL's international field team members and national field officers. I conducted interviews with a total of eighteen NPSL staff members altogether, and I also attended various multi-day staff strategizing meetings.

4. Field notes, October 5, 2008.

5. See Patrick Coy, "Cooperative Accompaniment and Peace Brigades International in Sri Lanka," in *Transnational Social Movements and Global Politics,* eds. Jackie Smith, et al (Syracuse: Syracuse University Press, 1997), 81-100; and Liam Mahony and Luis Enrique Eguren, *Unarmed Bodyguards* (West Haven, CT: Kumarian Press, 1997).

6. See Mahony and Eguren, *Unarmed Bodyguards,* Liam Mahony, *Proactive Presence* (Geneva: Centre for Humanitarian Dialogue, 2006); Yeshua Moser-Puangsuwan and Thomas Weber, eds., *Nonviolent Intervention Across Borders* (Honolulu: Spark M. Matsunaga Institute for Peace, 2000); Lisa Schirch, *Civilian Peacekeeping* (Uppsala: Life & Peace Institute, 2006); Tim Wallis and Claudia Samayoa, "Civilian Peacekeepers: Creating a Safe Environment for Peacebuilding," in *People Building Peace II,* eds. Paul van Tongeren et al (Boulder, CO: Lynne Rienner, 2005), 263-268; and Thomas Weber, *Gandhi's Peace Army* (Syracuse: Syracuse University Press, 1996).

7. Sandra Whitworth, *Men, Militarism and UN Peacekeeping* (Boulder: Lynne Rienner, 2004), 186.

8. Mahmood Mamdani, "The Politics of Naming: Genocide, Civil War, Insurgency," *London Review of Books,* March 8, 2007: 6-7, & 12.

9. Anne Orford, *Reading Humanitarian Intervention* (Cambridge: Cambridge University Press, 2003), 82-83.

10. Frederic Mégret, "Beyond the 'Salvation' Paradigm: Responsibility To Protect (Others) vs. the Power of Protecting Oneself," *Security Dialogue* 11, no. 6 (2009).

11. Jonathan Goodhand and Oliver Walton, "The Limits of Liberal Peacebuilding? International Engagement in the Sri Lankan Peace Process," *Journal of Intervention and Statebuilding* 3, no. 3 (2009): 306.

12. Goodhand and Walton, "The Limits of Liberal Peacebuilding*,"* 304-305.

13. See Qadri Ismail, *Abiding by Sri Lanka: On Peace, Place, and Postcoloniality* (Minneapolis: University of Minnesota Press, 2005); and Jayadeva Uyangoda, "Review Essay: Reinterpreting Tamil and Sinhalese Nationalism," *South Asian Bulletin* 7 (1987): 39-46.

14. Human Rights Watch, "Recurring Nightmare: State Responsibility for 'Disappearances' and Abductions in Sri Lanka," *Human Rights Watch Report,* March 5, 2008, and "Sri Lanka: End Harassment, Attacks on Journalists: Post-Election Crackdown Feared," *Human Rights Watch Press Release*, January 29, 2010.

15. See Sunil Bastian, "Politics of Social Exclusion, State Reform and Security in Sri Lanka," *IDS Bulletin* 40, no. 2 (2009); Goodhand and Walton, "The Limits of Liberal Peacebuilding;*"* and Molly Wallace, "Confronting Wrongs, Creating Wrongs: Official Discourses and the Legitimation of Violence," paper presented at the annual meeting of the International Studies Association, New Orleans, February 17, 2010.

16. Liam Mahony, *Proactive Presence,* 16-27.

17. Field notes, September 30, 2008; Interview, November 25, 2008. Note, however, that the frontlines of the war *were* in the Eastern Province in 2004 where the fighting intensified in 2006-2007. NP staff members were, therefore, very much working and

living on the frontlines, even if they still did not see themselves as an interpositioning force. Email communication with NP staff member, February 10, 2009.

18. Keith Krause and Jennifer Milliken, "Introduction: The Challenge of Non-State Armed Groups," *Contemporary Security Policy*, 30 no. 2 (2009): 205.

19. Interviews, November 6, 2008, November 23, 2008, December 6, 2008, December 7, 2008, and December 15, 2008.

20. Interview, October 7, 2008.

21. Interview, October 7, 2008.

22. Email communication with NP staff member, January 29, 2010.

23. Interview, December 6, 2008; Interview, December 15, 2008.

24. Interview, December 6, 2008.

25. Interview, December 6, 2008.

26. Email communication with NP staff member, January 29, 2010.

27. Interview, October 7, 2008.

28. Interview, October 6, 2008.

29. Interview, October 6, 2008.

30. Interview, December 4, 2008.

31. Interview, December 7, 2008.

32. Interview, December 7, 2008.

33. Interview, December 6, 2008.

34. The "white van unit" is thought by many to be connected to the Sri Lankan security forces and to be responsible for disappearances and extrajudicial killings. See Human Rights Watch, "Recurring Nightmare: State Responsibility for 'Disappearances' and Abductions in Sri Lanka," *Human Rights Watch Report*, March 5, 2008.

35. NP partnered in such cases with Sri Lankan actors/organizations who were themselves working to keep threatened people safer. Email communication with NP staff member, March 26, 2010.

36. Interview, December 7, 2008.

37. Interview, December 7, 2008.

38. Interview, December 7, 2008.

39. Interview, December 7, 2008.

40. Meeting notes, November 7, 2008.

41. Interview, November 23, 2008.

42. Interview, October 7, 2008.

43. Liam Mahony, *Proactive Presence,* 18.

44. Meeting notes, November 6, 2008.

45. Meeting notes, November 6, 2008.

46. Nonviolent Peaceforce, *Monthly Team Progress Report*, Batticaloa, May 2008.

47. Interview, November 4, 2008.

48. Interview, December 4, 2008.

49. Interview, November 4, 2008.

50. Email communication with NP staff member, February 10, 2009.

51. Ashutosh Varshney, "Ethnic Conflict and Civil Society: India and Beyond," *World Politics* 53, no. 3 (2001): 375.

52. Interview, December 6, 2008.

53. As Kaufmann argues, "No outside force, no matter how great its advantage in combat power, can pacify ethnic hostilities inflamed by war." Instead, humanitarian intervention forces must choose a side and fight to military victory, even if this means killing civilians on the "enemy" side. "Intervention in Ethnic and Ideological Civil Wars," in

The Use of Force: Military Power and International Politics, eds. Robert J. Art and Kenneth N. Waltz (Lanham, MD: Rowman and Littlefield, 2009), 406-426, 421-422.

54. Harkirat Singh, *Intervention in Sri Lanka* (Colombo: Vijitha Yapa Publications, 2006), 75.

55. See interviews 13, 15, 18, 23, and 29 of the *Bearing Witness* video archive: Neloufer de Mel and Robert Crusz, *Bearing Witness: Women's Experience of Armed Conflict in Sri Lanka* (Kelaniya: Tulana Media Unit, 2005).

56. Interview, December 6, 2008.

57. Interview, October 14, 2008; Interview, November 25, 2008.

58. Interview, December 4, 2008.

59. Interview, October 6, 2008.

60. Interview, November 23, 2008.

61. Interview, October 6, 2008.

62. Email communication with NP staff member, January 29, 2010; Interview, October 14, 2008.

63. Interview, October 4, 2008.

64. Interview, November 23, 2008.

65. Interview, December 6, 2008.

66. Interview, December 6, 2008.

67. Interview, December 6, 2008.

68. Interview, December 4, 2008.

69. K.M. Fierke, *Diplomatic Interventions* (Basingstoke: Palgrave MacMillan, 2005), xiii-iv.

70. Jonathan Goodhand and Oliver Walton, "The Limits of Liberal Peacebuilding?," 312.

Part 5

Mediation, Political Tutelage, and Nation-building as Tools of Conflict Prevention and Management

Chapter 19

Third Party Nation-Building Today: Fifth Time Charmed?

Joseph R. Rudolph, Jr.

As several essays in this volume note, by the 1990s "peacekeeping" had become an umbrella term for a variety of quite different undertakings. Often used indiscriminately, it sometimes contributed to the under-preparation of third party efforts to manage conflict because of the war-free environment it suggested. The subsequent refinement in the terminology of third party military activity has restored it to its original, literal meaning of neutrally keeping an *existing* if tenuous peace, as opposed to peace-making, peace-enforcement, or side-taking.

A similar fate befell the term "nation building" during the 1990s, when it acquired a great deal more currency in use than precision of meaning in referring to what is now more commonly referred to as "peace-building," itself an umbrella under which are encamped a considerable assortment of tasks, including; 1) community building, with its focus on altering attitudes; 2) capacity building, more often than not associated with security and economic affairs; and 3) institution building emphasizing non-corrupt governing devices with a chance of acquiring legitimacy. The latter has also entailed a commitment to democratic institutions, although as Thomas Carothers has observed, "democratization" has itself been endowed with two separate definitions. There is "political democratization," which has centered on holding elections as means of creating governments, and the long term "process" of democratization, which involves creating broad support for human rights, equality before the law, and those other facets of political life associated with democratic government in the developed Western democracies, discussed below in this chapter as "Constitutional Government."[1]

What "nation building" has not very often been perceived to be is what it literally means. Although in common parlance and journalist reports the terms country, state, and nation tend to be used interchangeably,[2] within the exacting terminology of certain areas in the social sciences, those words distinguish between an area's geographical territory (the country), its governmental entity (the state, which theoretically if not always in fact controls that territory and the people living in it), and the members of society (the nation or nations). In this construct, as Rupert Emerson phrased it in his classic volume, *From Empire to Nation*, to which in title this book pays homage, the nation is "the largest community which, when the chips are down, effectively commands men's loyalty, overriding the claims both of the lesser communities within it and those which cut across it or potentially enfold it within a still greater society."[3] Artificially building *that* sense of national identity is a feat many have tried with few results, including the Soviet Union in its seventy year effort to replace Armenians, Georgians, *et al* with a common identity built around the New Soviet Man. A map of the former U.S.S.R. aptly reflects the success of that venture.

Meanwhile, in its current incarnation, third party nation-building has become a global growth industry stretching from the Balkans to Baghdad and East Timor to Kabul, quite literally for corporations like Halliburton as well as the policy planners who have committed themselves to creating an environment in which former blood enemies, immediately emerging from civil wars, can come to terms with the past, deal productively with the imperatives of the present, and prepare for a democratic future. In this design, democratization is in turn linked with the long term security of a region based on the belief that democratic forms of government are not only the best means of protecting minority rights, but also for maintaining regional security because of the reduced likelihood that democratic regimes will choose war with one another (the democratic peace theory), or non-democratic states unless their own security is imperiled.

In the shorter term, the development of democratic institutions has itself been linked by American policy makers to a military occupation/presence, in contrast to the soft power assistance tendered to the democratization projects in the peaceful, post-communist countries of Central and Eastern Europe during the 1990s.[4] As William Lahneman has noted in referencing a 2001 study by the Army War College, the U.S. was late to embrace the broader approach to nation-building accepted by most of its allies, and focused instead on the military dimensions of peacemaking and peacekeeping during the 1990s, while downplaying the humanitarian and nation-building aspects of intervention.[5] Hence, the majority of reforms, whether in Bosnia, Kosovo, Iraq, or Afghanistan, were based at least initially on the muscle of a gun and with third party troops overseeing and sometimes enforcing those reforms as well as the peace. The reach of the military in nation-building efforts, however, is limited if extraordinarily important.

Wars can be ended by third party military assistance or even direct peacemaking intervention in force, and a relatively safe environment can be provided in the immediate aftermath of the conflict by peacekeeping forces. Beyond imposing a peace and enforcing it, the military can also be useful in other areas. Its presence may enable outside overseers of democratization to cut through initial opposition to change and to avoid a lengthy wave of score-settling by the "victors" over their former enemies where secession succeeds in reversing the majority-minority numbers in the state. Peacekeepers can provide a safe environment for returning refugees, though experience in both Bosnia and Kosovo has indicated that the latter may develop a psychological dependency on the former's continued presence. But in the long term, as Lahneman has elsewhere summarized, "there is no *military solution* to the problem; only a *military dimension*" to the reconstruction and society transformation processes.[6] The protection of human rights and establishment of stable democracies depends on the emergence of local leaders and institutions committed to those objectives and imbued with a sense of legitimacy by the local populations. And the road to that destination can be a long one mined with politically explosive choices if not with actual explosive devices, that can test any third party's willingness to maintain a military security blanket throughout that undertaking.

Nor is there a nation-building design of universal or proven utility for making that journey. But it is not a trek lacking in history.

Two Thousand Years of "Nation Building"?

Nation-Building in the Roman and Holy Roman Empires

Had they been inclined to look, the "nation-builders" in the administrations of Presidents George H.W. Bush, William Jefferson Clinton, and George W. Bush might have learned from the efforts of others stretching over the centuries to erect, of late in a democratic form, durable, system-wide institutions of governance in areas composed of communities whose peoples' diverse histories and ways of life gave them little reason to like one another and even fewer reasons for trusting one another. The issue would have been where to begin, and Lahneman has argued that a good place might be Rome, two millennia ago.[7]

Apart from introducing the first paved roadways to facilitate communication, trade, and the use of its military to maintain order in the realm, plus spreading the tenets of Roman law where it ruled, the Romans were interested in producing "stable regimes to help them achieve their policy goals," and to transform "disparate peoples with vastly different cultural and social attributes into loyal and enthusiastic supports of the empire."[8] Towards those ends, the Roman Empire offered positive (rewards) and negative (death for open defiance) incentives to locals to Romanize. As in the case of contemporary nation building efforts, Lahneman notes that the Roman Empire relied first on overwhelming military superiority and then on soft power to accomplish their goals, demonstrated a "firm commitment to pursuing nation-building efforts for as long as necessary to achieve its goals," understood the need to induce local elites to cooperate in those efforts, and sought to "accommodate as many of an occupied people's traditional values and customs as possible without impeding progress toward vital nation-building objectives."[9] In short, there are lessons to be learned from its experience.

By contrast, the Holy Roman Empire lacked military muscle (its Imperial Army was composed of the armies of its member units, reflecting its 1422 origin in the late Middle Ages) or any centralized governmental system. But its survival over centuries in which Germany and other parts of Central Europe were effectively controlled by numerous localized rulers indicates the utility of devolution as a short and middle term strategy for holding together territorialized peoples of diverse identities. By bestowing on the rulers of these areas a "motley and variable collection of powers" involving legislative, executive, judicial, international, and feudal authority, the Empire demonstrated the integrative potential of local autonomy in system-maintenance efforts.[10]

Nineteenth Century European Empires

Although the term was still yet to be coined, the first Western states to undertake "nation-building" activities as they came to be defined in the 1990s were perhaps the European colonial powers, whose empire-making had resulted by the eve of World War I in 84 percent of the globe's land being under European control.[11] During the high point of their empires, they needed to fashion tools of administration and often inclusive, if only advisory, representative bodies in order to placate their subjects. Britain, in particular, had to devote considerable energy to these tasks given its frequent use of local authorities in the service of the Crown in its indirect rule approach to managing much of its empire. And, especially in the multinational acreage of empire, the challenges of governance did not end there. Communal conflict, under the best of circumstances one of the most difficult of political problems to manage, often had to be addressed. Consequently, institutions capable of accommodating rival communal claims frequently had to be devised, with federal-like forms emerging as devices for institutionally accommodating territorialized ethno-linguistic communities in India, Malaysia, and later Nigeria generations before the architects of the Dayton Accords employed federalism as a means of fusing together the Serb Republic and the Croat and Bosniak (Bosnian Muslims) Federation in Bosnia-Herzegovina.

Peacekeeping, too, was a common duty of empire; for example, Britain's action in responding to the Arab-Jewish riots in Jerusalem and elsewhere in Palestine throughout the 1920s,[12] and to the various Muslim riots in India in protest of, among other things, the British effort to build a neutral, multi-communal police force there, albeit heavily staffed with Hindu recruits.[13]

Then came the end of empire, and except where the colonial authority was driven out (France in Indo-China and Algeria for example) or pressured to liquidate its empire before it had a chance to plan a transition (Belgium, in the Congo), the departing colonial authorities became actively engaged in designing democratic institutions for post-colonial governance as their last act of empire.

In doing so, they often embraced the same type of compromise arrangements designed to hold together multinational states that have been a part of the institution-building schemes of those concerned with devising constitutions for independent Bosnia, Kosovo, and post-occupation Iraq; most frequently, federalism-like autonomy formulae that leave each territorialized community with control over sensitive topics, proportionality schemes in creating system-wide police forces, and torturous ethnic balancing acts that give each of the major communities a highly visible office at the center.

Finally, in introducing democracy as part of the decolonization process, the departing European powers also often learned a fact of multinational political life with which the "nation-builders" of the 1990s and the early years of the twenty-first century have had to contend: that in multinational states the introduction of democracy below frequently begets political parties organized to serve the interests of the individual ethno-political communities, and rarely concludes with the election of moderate politicians at the top who are interested in, or capable of the long term collaboration across communal lines that is desired by the nation-builders. On the other hand, there is ample evidence that the nation-builders in the British Empire were aware of the limits of institutional design as a means of eradicating inter-communal distrust and equally well aware that the creation of stable states would also require a democratic spirit. As the Commission on Nigeria's independence constitution phrased it in rejecting the demands of Nigeria's smaller tribes for states of their own as a means of protecting themselves from the majority tribes in the three regions that were to compose independent Nigeria's federal system,

> The whole structure of the proceedings leading to independence is based on the belief that Nigeria means to follow the road to liberal democracy and parliamentary government; to base parts of the structure on the opposite assumption is to invite governments to do their worst.[14]

Post-World War II Nation-Building in Europe and Asia

Chronologically, the next round of nation-building occurred following the Second World War. In a 2002 article in *The Washington Post*, former National Security adviser and Dayton Peace Accords negotiator Richard Holbrooke cited United States "success at nation building most notably during the Cold War in countries from Greece and Japan to Korea" in defending the commitment of American resources to nation-building efforts in Afghanistan and their continued commitment to Bosnia-Herzegovina.[15] As contentions go, his argument was not quibble free. Japan developed an essentially one-party system for two generations, Greece lapsed into authoritarian rule by the Generals during the 1960's, and General Park's South Korea was hardly a model of pluralistic democracy. Overall, however, he had a point. The United States was instrumental to the successful reconstruction of these countries, and in laying the foundations for a functioning democracy in occupied Germany and Japan. On the other hand, as precedents for the 1990's nation-building undertakings, there are at least two major problems with the cases that Holbrooke cites.

First, none of these post-war nation-building products was a multinational state. Rather, nation-building could proceed on the basis of an existing, single national identity in each country, however much that national community might have been divided by ideological differences or even, in the case of Greece, a recent civil war between contending sides. Reconstructing a multinational state after a bloody ethnic civil war is another matter, especially where crimes against humanity were committed by all parties.

Secondly, even among these states there is only one—pre-unification West Germany—in which it can be credibly argued that the political culture was thoroughly remade to the point where the operating norms of society came to fit the democratic constitution that third parties drafted for it. But West Germany's political culture was uniquely malleable in 1945 in ways that have no parallel in the targets of nation-builders since 1990. Geographically, a sizeable portion of the country was lost to communist occupation (East Germany), profoundly shifting the country's demographics because the east had been both its agricultural heartland and heavily Catholic in religion. West Germany had to survive economically on industrial power. Equally important, old Germany had Berlin, but West Germany did not because West Berlin was inside East Germany. European capitals are usually also their countries' cultural, economic, communications, and social centers, and Berlin was all of that to Germany. Hence, as an influence on the development of political culture, geography hardly operated as it traditionally had in Germany and does in other countries.

Nor was history an influence upon which West Germans wanted to draw. Germany's prior history had been short, traumatic, and culpable. Most preferred to treat the Third Reich (1933-1945) as a twelve year gap in German history, and start anew in 1945. And, in terms of the economy, it was truly Zero Year. Germany's money was worthless and one of the first acts of the Federal Republic's government was to wipe out all savings accounts.

Finally, the allies were able to recruit national leaders likely to lead the Germans in a democratic direction. Men like Konrad Adenauer, who were free of taint from the old regime, well respected and loved, and willing to urge the Germans to participate in their new democracy. With the exception of Kosovo's first president, Ibrahim Rugova, who died in office in 2006, such leaders have been in short supply in the current world of nation building.

Nation-Building in the Post-Colonial Multinational World

It was during the early years of independence of the multinational states in Asia, which began with the partition of the Indian sub-continent in 1947, and Sub-Saharan Africa, beginning with Ghana in 1956, that the term "nation-building" first appeared, as defined in Emerson's sense of instilling a common, paramount sense of national identity in the diverse peoples populating them. Like the colonial powers before them, the governments of these new states engaged in a broad search for workable forms of government, democratic and non-democratic. They, too, embraced federal power sharing schemes as means of allaying communal fears of domination by the other ethnic fellow, along with ethnic balancing formulae (for example, the National Pact between the Maronite Christian, Sunni, and Shi'a communities in Lebanon) and other accommodation devices. But in the newly independent states of Asia and Africa, where colonially-drawn borders had often left behind a bewildering assortment of different ethnic, religious, tribal, and/or linguistic groups in the newly born states, the focus was frequently on trying to build a broader sense of identity that would link the various communities together. The working assumption was that, for those multinational entities that had become sovereign states internationally without having become cohesive nations within, "purposeful planning" would enable them to draw their diverse groups together into a common community.[16] In the optimistic words of one Indian scholar at the time, "the evolution of human society. . . has now reached a stage where it is possible to give conscious and purposeful direction to the trend of evolution."[17]

More often than not their efforts, and their democratic independence constitutions, were abandoned, or succumbed to a wave of communally-motivated coups, the breakdown of inter-communal trust, and/or separatist movements. Thus, of the four large federations that Britain fashioned in departing its empire between 1947 and 1963—India, Nigeria, Pakistan, and Malaysia—within a quarter century of independence Singapore had been expelled from Malaysia (whose Malay majority was concerned about the large numbers of Chinese in *their* country), Nigeria had lapsed into long term military rule following the failed secessionist effort of its Eastern Region (whose majority still thought of themselves as Ibos, not Nigerians), and East Pakistan (whose Muslim citizens thought of themselves as Bengalis, not Pakistanis) had successfully seceded from the Pakistan created when the Indian sub-continent was itself partitioned along the lines of its religious divide into (predominantly Hindu) India and a Muslim West Pakistan composed of numerous ethnically distinct communities and East Pakistan. Only India remained a functioning democracy, and a quarter century after that country's independence Prime Minister Indira Gandhi was invoking the emergency provisions of its Constitution to place more than 90 percent of its federal units under central rule.

Problems and Pitfalls of Contemporary Nation-Building

Measured against this backdrop, contemporary operations represent at least the fifth round of nation-building endeavors, and the challenges have expanded with the expanding definition of the term. At present, even a short list of the problems confronting third parties and the host states engaged in a nation-building process would include the following, each of which is fraught with potential pitfalls.

The Everything-at-Once Conundrum

Aside from repairs to or construction of infrastructure following a civil war, new and recovering states often need to commit to political, economic, social, and cultural rehabilitation, to use Krishna Kumar's terminology.[18] Currencies may have to be created, financial grids established, choices made in terms of the structure of the state (e.g., unitary or federal? parliamentary or presidential?). Add a commitment to democratization and the "to do" list expands. Not only must constitutions be written but political parties organized, elections scheduled, and voters registered in some fashion, even if warfare has erased most proofs of birth. If ethnic cleansing has been practiced, refugees must be returned, but to where? Their houses may have been bulldozed to prevent their return, or occupied by others. Moreover, much of this should not be rushed, but it nonetheless has to be done in a hurry. This includes the writing of the constitution. As the Chief Justice of the newly independent Slovak Republic's Constitutional Court noted, "the Constitution is the legal basis of national, civil, social, economic, cultural, and spiritual life," as well as "the source or focus of the legal system, the quality of which depends to a significant degree on the quality of the constitution."[19] Yet in many postwar settings, the constitution has itself been written by third parties as a part of the peace conference settling the conflict, and lacks support in the post-war zones.

Developing a Stabilization Strategy

Adhering to the due process of the law standard while maintaining order was not of great concern to previous peacekeepers and nation-builders. But, to repeat the observations of other contributors to this volume, the creation of a safe environment is *the* essential first step in moving societies emerging from war to an environment in which nation-building and democratization efforts have a chance to succeed. Furthermore, democratic states and international organizations are expected to practice what they preach. Yet, doing so can be especially difficult in the aftermath of an ethnic civil war or the ouster of a tyrant. Score-settling by those victimized may be much more important to communities than adhering to democratic niceties. Extremists may exploit the freedom of speech, press, and assembly to urge non-compliance with imposed reforms, or to mobilize crowds for violent action. Balancing freedom and order is an entirely different problem in such circumstances than it is in established democracies.

There is also an issue here involving the means of maintaining order. Experience has taught, sometimes with tragic results, that the heavily armored military forces that can be important in ending a war are often both untrained and ill-equipped with the instruments for crowd control necessary to protect local minorities from angry majorities. Thus, when Kosovo Albanians violently reacted to the false rumors in March of 2004 that Serbs in the north were responsible for the deaths of three Muslim youth, the failure of NATO's forces to protect Kosovo's Serbs and Romani was all too apparent. As Human Rights Watch noted in its report on this round of ethnic cleansing five years after NATO intervention paved the way for Kosovo autonomy, the nearly system-wide violence involved more than thirty riots, 50,000 protesters across Kosovo, destroyed 550 homes and nearly thirty Orthodox churches and monasteries, cost nineteen lives, and displaced more than four thousand. Yet,

> The security organizations in Kosovo—KFIR, UNMIK, international police, and the KPS—failed catastrophically in their mandate to protect minority communities during the March 2004 violence. In numerous cases, minorities under attack were left entirely unprotected and at the mercy of the rioters. In Svinjare, French KFOR failed to come to the assistance of the besieged Serbs, even though their main base was only a few hundred meters away. . . and the ethnic Albanian crowd had walked right past their base on their way to burning down the village. French KFOR troops similarly failed to respond to the rioting in Vucitrn, which is located between two major French bases. In Prizren, German KFOR troops failed to deploy to protect the Serb population and the many historic Serbian Orthodox churches, despite calls for assistance from their UNMIK international police counterparts, who later accused German KFOR commanders of cowardice. In Kosovo Polje, UNMIK and KFOR were no where to be seen as Albanian crowds methodically burned Serbian homes. The village of Belo Polje, rebuilt on the outskirts of Pec to house returning Serbs, was burned to the ground even though it was almost adjacent to the main Italian KFOR base. . . . Even in the capital Pristina, Serbs were forced to barricade themselves into their apartments, while Albanian rioters shot at them and looted and burned the apartments below and around them, for up to six hours before KFOR and UNMIK came to their assistance.[20]

Developing a Democratization Plan

Designing Democracy may or may not be an oxymoron, as Donald Horowitz has discussed;[21] however, its birth via a top down model does seem a bit contradictory. But even beyond that, the commitment to democratization is not to create just any form of democratic government. To those viewing nation-building as a long term process as opposed to "political nation-building" with its narrower focus on holding elections, nation-building means laying the foundation for the highly developed form of democracy once described by Carl Friedrich as Constitutional Government: "the process by which government action is effectively restrained."[22] As such, it embraces the rule of law, protection of minority rights, regular procedures for checking the power of government, and respect for the fundamental rules of the game, which include protection of minority rights. All of these tenets are exceedingly difficult to implement in the aftermath of a civil war, when there is much to be done in a hurry and therefore an ill time to commit to a restrained governmental system. Indeed, it is a daunting commitment that had many critics essentially saying "Good Luck" in the 1990s,[23] and that led George W. Bush to shy away from "nation-building" both in running for the presidency and during the pre-9/11 days of his administration. But once the commitment to rebuild and remold a society is taken, the questions pile up quickly.

There is the issue of how far and quickly to push democratization efforts, which arises early and deliberations do not get much easier with the passage of time. Should elections be held immediately, when the leaders of ethnonationalist parties are far more likely to be elected in the aftermath of an ethnic civil war than coalition parties composed of moderates from different communities? If not, how long, then, can you delay holding elections and claim to be democratizing? How soon should you return refugees to the ethnically cleansed areas from which they were driven, and should you do so even if there will be no jobs for them there? How quickly should you try to change society; for instance, by requiring parties in Muslim states to offer the voters as many women candidates as men? Perhaps above all, how soon should you try to implement unpopular reforms involving the integration of the formerly warring national communities? And how much say should local leaders have in these reforms, and how soon? Overcoming opposition among communities who have emerged from committing acts of violence and perhaps war crimes against one another is a challenge whose resolution can stretch across generations. Eighteen years after the Dayton Accords ended the war in Bosnia-Herzegovina, for example, the Croat-Muslim Federation is only now contemplating a school plan that will result in multiethnic classrooms, replacing the fully segregated schools and the recently repudiated "two schools under one roof" system of separate entrances, playgrounds, and classes for Muslims and Croats in the same building.[24]

Building and Maintaining Stake Holders

For nation-building to work and the troops to leave a secure environment behind, almost as essential as creating that initial, outsider-enforced security is the task of building and maintaining local stake holders in a multinational state whose communities may wish to remain apart and where power sharing arrangements may enable dissenters to stall or prevent the development of vigorous state institutions, as has occurred in Bosnia. It is a challenge with both inside and outside facets.

The outsider issue revolves around the third party maintaining its troops in the country long enough for a sufficient number of local stakeholders to emerge in support of the system so that the presence of the troops is no longer needed. Third parties may be under strong pressure at home to re-deploy the forces elsewhere because of the deadly nature of the environment (occupied Iraq, Afghanistan), or because other issues, including a debt crisis, have reordered the third party's priorities.[25] Paradoxically, the very success of pacification operations may make the troops appear superfluous to outsiders when in fact the peaceful environment still depends on their presence.

The internal dimension of building stake holders is more complex. As Marie-Joelle Zahar has pointed out, there are stakeholders and then there are the stake holders. More precisely, there are those who develop a genuine commitment to the new system, and there are those who are mostly committed to it because of the status and influence that it gives them, and some of the latter can become quite adroit at manipulating the presence and the power of the third parties to entrench their own power. In Zahar's words, "[t]he association of local elites to liberal peace building processes provides these elites with access to the resources of the international communities. This strengthens the hands of these elites against opponents on the national scene, transposing the asymmetry from the local-international nexus to local politics."[26] The "local capital" gained by local leaders who cooperate with the internationals can thus be exploited for personal advantage, and at a minimum, some of the authority that was acquired by the third parties who intervened and are pursuing democratization projects can be "recuperated."[27]

The Transference of Security Affairs to Local Authorities

Finally, in our short list of priority issues, the restoration of law and order services involving the creation of countrywide, impartial police and judicial bodies is essential. Indeed, rebuilding a country's domestic security system is one of the first tasks in reconstructing any state after the collapse of a repressive regime or the ending of hostilities following a civil war. International peacemaking and peace-keeping units like SFOR in Bosnia-Herzegovina and KFOR in Kosovo can provide security, but not legitimacy for a regime.[28] That can only occur when it has an effective domestic police force that makes its citizens feel secure, but building one is another thoroughly daunting task. Where an authoritarian regime has collapsed or been overthrown, those associated with the old order are nearly always stigmatized by their identity with it and replaced. Similarly, in the aftermath of a civil war, not only may tension remain high and the disaffected seek payback, but the previously existing legal conflict resolution system has often been among the first casualties of the war. In either case, securing the streets with trustworthy personnel is a necessary step if the new regime is to have legitimacy. A government that cannot protect its citizens from violence has little reason to expect their support.

The good news for a postwar society is that finding men and women to recruit into a police force is rarely a problem because unemployment invariably runs high in such settings and job applicants are aplenty. The problem is usually providing *them* with security when they are applying, and insuring that the police services are not infiltrated to the point where the recruits become threats to the peacekeeping forces, as has occurred in Afghanistan.[29] Recruitment centers and police stations are prime targets for rejectionists on all sides seeking to undo ceasefires or shape the new order, and long lines of hopeful job seekers are easy prey for suicide bombers.[30] Ironically, standing in line can be as deadly for a would-be police infiltrator as for a good faith job applicant.

Nor are these the only matters to be addressed. Despite the availability of literally hundreds of relevant articles and "how to" books such as Donald Bayley's *Democratizing the Police Abroad: What to Do and How to Do It*,[31] there is no more a universal "Police-Building" model that fits all circumstances than there is a cookie cutter "Nation-Building" design. Even where the government is supportive of the efforts and resources exist, strategies must be tailored to the needs and conditions of individual countries, and the process frequently proceeds on a slow, trial-and-error basis.[32]

But what do you do when the party resisting the creation of an effective security system is one of the previously contentious parties who has come out of the war in control of a government? Here, control over the security apparatus is likely to be one of the very last items that government is willing to cede to a central authority committed to building a multinational police force.[33]

Finally, there is the issue of justice, and what to do when the "winners" are unwilling to prosecute their own war criminals and disproportionately prosecute the losing minorities once tribunals are established to try to clear away the paralyzing memories of the past through legal proceedings.

Our contributors to this section offer no solutions to such dilemmas, but the set that follows takes you into the Balkans and elsewhere in pursuit of answers.

Notes

1. Thomas Carothers, "Democracy Assistance: Political vs. Developmental?" *Journal of Democracy* 20, no. 1 (January 2009): 5-19.

2. See, for example, Matthew Lee, "Clinton arrives in South Pacific to begin six-nation Asian Tour," *The Washington Post*, September 1, 2012, A9.

3. Rupert Emerson, *From Empire to Nation: the Rise of Self-Assertion of African and Asian Peoples* (Cambridge, MA: Harvard University Press, 1960), 95-96.

4. On outside assistance to democratization efforts in post-communist Eastern Europe, see Geoffrey Pridham, Eric Herring, and George Sandord, eds. *Building Democracy? The International Dimension of Democratisation in Eastern Europe* (New York: St. Martin's Press, 1994).

5. William Lahneman, "Military Intervention: Lessons for the Twenty-First Century." In *Military Intervention: Cases in Context for the Twenty-First Century*, ed. William J. Lahneman (Lanham, MD: Rowman & Littlefield, 2004), 185-200, 194.

6. Lahneman, "Military Intervention: Lessons for the Twenty-First Century," 184, referencing remarks made by I. William Zartman, National Intelligence Council project *Workshop on the Future of Internal Conflict*, College Park, MD, August 11, 2000.

7. See William Lahneman, "The Nation Building Strategy of the Roman Empire: Lessons for Today" (paper presented at the Annual Convention of the International Studies Association, New Orleans, Louisiana, February 17, 2010).

8. Lahneman, "The Nation Building Strategy of the Roman Empire," 1.

9. Lahneman, "The Nation Building Strategy of the Roman Empire," 13-14.

10. See "The Medieval Era: Nation Building—Holy Roman Empire," http://themedievalera.wikispaces.com/Nation%20Building%20%20Holy%20Roman%20Empire (accessed September 13, 2012). Citation at page 3.

11. Daniel R. Headrick, *The Tools of Empire: Technology and European Imperialism in the Nineteenth Century* (New York: Oxford University Press, 1981), 3. The great growth in empire occurred during the second half of the nineteenth century. The figure for 1800 was only 35 percent of the world's land surface, but by 1878 that had nearly doubled to 67 percent.

12. On these communal conflicts, see especially Bernard Wasserstein, *The British in Palestine: The Mandatory Government and the Arab-Jewish Conflict 1917-1929* (London: Royal Historical Society, 1978), and *Report on the Palestine Disturbances of August, 1929* (London: His Majesty's Stationery Office, 1930).

13. "From 1923 through 1928 there were 112 riots which the Government of India classified as serious *communal* disorders." Approximately 450 people died in these incidents, and more than five thousand were seriously injured, and "They occurred nearly any place where Hindus and Muslims lived in proximity." G. R. Thursby, *Hindu-Muslem Relations in British India* (London: E. J. Brill, 1975), 80.

14. *Nigeria – Report of the Commission Appointed to Enquire into the Fears of Minorities and the Means of Allaying Them* (London: H.M.S.O., 1958), Section 10.

15. Richard Holbrooke, "Rebuilding Nations," *The Washington Post*, April 1, 2002.

16. Lucien Pye, *Aspects of Political Development* (Boston, MA: Little, Brown Company, 1966), 5. On the same theme, see also the extensive collection of essays by influential academic thinkers assembled in Karl Deutsch and William J. Foltz, eds, *Nation Building* (New York: Atherton Press, 1963).

17. Jayaprakash Narayan, *Three Basic Problems of Free India* (Bombay: Asian Publishing House, 1946), 15.

18. Krishna Kumar, ed., *Rebuilding Societies After Civil Wars: Critical Roles for International Assistance* (Boulder, CO: Lynne Rienner Press, 1997).

19. Milan Cic, "About the Constitution and Constitutionalism," in *Constitutionalism & Politics*, ed. Irena Grudzinska Gross, (Bratislava: Slovak Committee of the European Cultural Foundation, 1994), 53-59, 53. On the range of institutional options available, see Vojislav Stanvocic, "Problems and Options in Institutionalizing Ethnic Relations" *International Political Science Review* 13, no. 4 (1992): 359-79.

20. Human Rights Watch, *Failure to Protect: Anti-Minority Violence in Kosovo, March 2004*, 26 July 2004, D1606, http://www.unhcr.org/refworld/docid/421eec8b4.html (accessed September 4, 2012), 2.

21. Daniel L. Horowitz, "Constitutional Design: An Oxymoron?" in *Designing Democratic Institutions*, eds. Ian Shapiro and Stephen Macedo (New York: NYU Press, 2000), 253-84.

22. Carl J. Friedrich, *Constitutional Government and Democracy: Theory and Practice in Europe and America* (Boston: Ginn and Company, 1946), 129.

23. See, for example, Michael Lind, "In Defense of Liberal Nationalism," *Foreign Affairs* 73, no. 3 (1994): 8-99.

24. Elvira M. Jukic, "Bosnia Vows to End Ethnically Divided Schools," *IEWS*, 31 August 2012, available from Balkan Insight, http://www.balkaninsight.com/en/article/bosnia-plans-uniting-divided-schools (accessed September 6, 2012). The plan is to phase in the new design over a two year period in schools willing to accept the proposal.

25. See Matthew Parish, "Depressed West Averts Gaze from Bosnia's Demise," Balkan Independent Reporting Network (BIRN), available through Balkan Insight Premium Weekly, August 15, 2012.

26. Marie-Joelle Zahar, "Norm Transmission in Peace- and State-building: Lessons from Democracy Promotion in Sudan and Lebanon," *Global Governance: A Review of Multilateralism and International Organizations* 18, no. 1 (January-March 2012): 73-88.

27. Zahar, "Norm Transmission in Peace- and State-building."

28. See Alice Hills, "The Inherent Limits of Military Forces in Policing Peace Operations," *International Peacekeeping* 8, no. 23 (2001): 70-98.

29. On the "green on blue" violence involving Afghan police and NATO troops, see Heidi Vogt and Kay Johnson, "NATO troops targeted again: U.S. ambassador calls 5th attack by Afghan police 'troubling,'" *The Washington Post*, August 14, 2012.

30. See, for example, Salman Masood, "Deadly Bombings Strike Pakistani Police," *The New York Times* February 1, 2011; Josh Kron, "Recruits for Police in Sudan are Abused," *The New York Times*, February 25, 2011; Joshua Partlow and Sayed Salahuddin, "Afghan Police targeted in attack," *The Washington Post*, May 23, 2011; and Ed O'Keefe and Aziz Alwan, "Iraqi police, soldiers targeted in wave of attacks," *The Washington Post*, July 5, 2011.

31. United States Department of Justice, Office of Justice Programs, Issues in International Crime Series, Washington, DC, June 2001 (NCJ 188742).

32. See, for example, International Crisis Group Asian Report No. 138, "Reforming Afghanistan's Police" (30 August 2007); International Crisis Group Asian Briefing No. 85, "Policing in Afghanistan: Still Searching for a Strategy" (18 December 2008); and International Crisis Group Asian Report No. 180, "Handing Back Responsibility to Timor-Leste's Police" (3 December 2009). All reports are available at the ICG website, www.crisisgroup.org. (accessed 19 October 2012)

33. For information on the lingering policing problem in Bosnia-Herzegovina nearly a decade after the author's departure, see the International Crisis Group European Report No. 164, "Bosnia's Stalled Police Reform: No Progress, No EU" (6 September 2005), www.crisisgroup.org. (accessed 19 October 2012)

Chapter 20

"Nation-Building" and Democratization in Afghanistan: The Need to Rethink the "Democratic Reconstruction Model"

Mohammad Ashraf

The Soviet Union's invasion of Afghanistan on 27 December 1979, which resulted in the installation of a Marxist-Leninist government—The Democratic Republic of Afghanistan—was the turning point in the contemporary history of Afghanistan. Initially, the Soviet Union's invasion was successful in overthrowing President Mohammed Daud Khan's regime (1973-1978) and installing an Afghan regime that pushed for socialist changes, backed by the Soviet army, with little or no regard for prevalent socioeconomic, cultural, and religious conditions in Afghan society or support from the masses. The military occupation and the top-down enforcement at gun-point of socialist changes under the banner of development and modernization, which were at odds with the core values and institutions of traditional conservative Muslim Afghan society, fueled insurgency and plunged the country into a brutal civil war. After ten years of occupation, war, and violence that achieved little in terms of development but caused death, destruction, and displacement of the majority of the Afghan population, the development and modernization programs were aborted and the Soviet Union withdrew from Afghanistan in February 1989. An accurate estimate of human loss is not available but reports indicate that the Soviet war inflicted over two million deaths[1] and created over five million refugees among the estimated fifteen million population of Afghanistan.[2]

Following the Soviet Union's withdrawal, the Marxist regime of Dr. Mohammad Najibullah, which was left behind by the Soviet Union, was overthrown in 1992 by the *Mujahedeen*, the Afghan resistance. The *Mujahedeen* were mainly supported and armed by the United States and were comprised of various tribal, religious, and ethnic groups. However, after Najibullah's regime collapsed, the *Mujahedeen*, who could not agree on a coalition government, turned their guns on each other and a brutal war and struggle for power ensued, creating a power vacuum that eventually brought the Taliban to power in 1996. The Taliban, who wanted to create an Islamic state in Afghanistan, were mostly educated in Madrassas (religious schools) in Afghanistan and refugee camps in Pakistan. In spite of their strict interpretation of Islam and views about women, they were welcomed by the Afghan people because they effectively ended anarchy, eliminated corruption, and restored security by crushing brutal and abusive warlords.

In the wake of Al Qaeda's terrorist attacks against America on September 11, 2001, the United States, with the backing of the United Nations and the international community, invaded Afghanistan. The mission of the United States was to kill or capture Osama bin Laden, the head of Al Qaeda, to deny the Al Qaeda terrorist organization a safe haven, and to build a liberal democracy in Afghanistan. Initially, the mission was successful in overthrowing the Taliban regime (for refusing to hand over Osama bin Laden), destroying terrorist camps and chasing foreign terrorists out of the country, concluding the Bonn Agreement (2001), creating a new constitution (2004), conducting presidential (2004, 2009) and parliamentary (2005, 2010) elections, and undertaking emergency humanitarian and reconstruction projects.

After ten years of military occupation, nation-building, and pouring billions of dollars into the country, however, the results and reality on the ground indicate that Afghanistan is headed toward a bleak future. Security has been deteriorating, the Taliban-fueled insurgency has been on the rise, the ineffective and corrupt Afghan state has virtually lost its legitimacy in the eyes of its citizens and the international community, and violence is increasingly claiming significant numbers of military and civilian lives. According to the 2010 Corruption Perception Index, Afghanistan is "highly" corrupt, with a ranking of 176th among the 178 countries included in the study.[3] In addition, seventy-six percent of the Afghans who were recently polled said that corruption is a major problem in the country.[4]

On December 1, 2009, American President Barack Obama announced the deployment of thirty thousand additional troops to Afghanistan to stabilize the government and reverse the Taliban's momentum. In an address to the nation, from the United States Military Academy at West Point, President Obama said "Afghanistan is not lost, but for several years it has moved backwards. There's no imminent threat of the government being overthrown, but the Taliban has gained momentum. Al Qaeda has not reemerged in Afghanistan in the same numbers as before 9/11, but they retain their safe havens along the border."[5]

The killing of Osama bin Laden by U.S. Special Forces in Abbottabad, Pakistan on May 2, 2011 was a significant symbolic blow to the Al Qaeda organization. However, bin Laden's death will have little effects on the insurgency in Afghanistan or the day-to-day operations of the Al Qaeda organization, which has become decentralized since 2001. For the past ten years bin Laden was in hiding and remained as a spiritual iconic figurehead of the Al Qaeda organization rather than its operational chief. His death was not the "game changer" claimed by US Secretary of Defense Robert Gates.

The main purpose of this paper is to expand understanding of the root causes of the increasing instability, insurgency, and lack of security that are threatening peace and nation-building in Afghanistan. It is anticipated that students of nation-building and conflict management will learn from the mistakes and missteps of nation-building in Afghanistan, which teaches us that local ownership lies at the heart of a successful and sustainable nation-building process and that local actors are central to the design, management, and implementation of the political process.

Democratic Reconstruction Model

Since World War II, the United States has been involved in nation-building; that is, restructuring political, economic, and social institutions in post-conflict societies according to Western standards and "best" practices. In the context of nation-building, the US framework is known as the democratic reconstruction model.[6] The core vision of the model is shaped by promoting the rule of law, human rights, economic liberalization, and democratization as understood and practiced in the West.[7] According to this model, nation-building is about transforming the political, economic, and social institutions of post-conflict societies into functioning liberal democracies. In this context, nation-building is best understood by Western experts, and war-affected societies are expected to accept and adopt top-down prescriptive changes as dictated by these foreign experts. The democratic reconstruction model is based on the premise that disconnected failed, failing, or weak states are a major threat to the globalized world and its values. The architects of the model have theorized that the mission of the United States in the twenty-first century is to integrate disconnected states into the global system by restructuring their institutions through military, economic, and political means.

Unfortunately, empirical evidence from South Vietnam to Cambodia to Afghanistan indicates that any approach to nation-building, no matter how well defined, that does not emphasize local ownership and participation has rarely produced a successful and sustainable peace, much less a democracy. This is due to the fact that sustainable peace cannot be achieved by a top-down prescriptive approach designed and driven by foreign experts and military occupation. Such an approach to nation-building erodes state legitimacy, alienates the locals, misguides the process and mission, and creates serious tension between the internal and external actors. Afghanistan is a textbook example of why a top-down approach to conflict management and nation-building by third parties has had such an uneven record over the past two decades.

The Bonn Agreement and the Political Settlement

The Bonn Agreement was signed on December 5, 2001 in Bonn, Germany by the delegates of four anti-Taliban groups from Afghanistan, and under the auspices of the United Nations (UN). The Bonn Agreement established that the international community would empower the people of Afghanistan to determine their future according to their history and social, religious, and cultural values. It constituted a partnership between the people of Afghanistan and the international community, with the UN as a bridge between the two. It was, however, understood by the international community that Afghanistan's development and reconstruction would be as a liberal democracy and that the democratic reconstruction model would serve as a road map for this process.

The Bonn Agreement was not a peace agreement between warring factions because the defeated Taliban government was not invited. The four groups invited to the Bonn Agreement by the United Nations—the Northern Alliance, Rome group, Peshawar group, and Cyprus group—consisted of various ethnic leaders, Jihadi leaders, and powerful warlords with questionable pasts, including several with blood on their hands. At the time, only the Northern Alliance group had troops inside Afghanistan and was helping the United States in overthrowing the Taliban government. The rest of the groups were living outside the country and were only brought together by their opposition to the Taliban. Nevertheless, the four anti-Taliban groups were invited and portrayed by the international community and the United Nations as a united and cohesive delegation that best represented the Afghan people and their interests, given the circumstances under which the Bonn Agreement was organized and signed. However, these delegates did not consult the Afghan people and had serious rivalries and mistrust among themselves, which had resulted in the failure of the prior Rawalpindi Accord (1989), Peshawar Accord (1992), and Macca Accord (1993).

Although the international community agreed to provide an enabling environment for the Afghan people to rebuild their war-torn country according to their own history, and political and economic institutions, the political settlement that was agreed upon and signed in Bonn was not consistent with establishing an effective and stable government in Afghanistan. The Northern Alliance, a loose coalition of the Tajik, Uzbek, and Hazara minority ethnic groups, was over-represented in the Bonn Agreement and in the subsequent political process, where members of these groups filled seventeen of the thirty top government positions, including the key ministries of Defense, Foreign Affairs, Interior, Intelligence, Planning, and Commerce. This was resented by the other ethnic groups, especially the Pashtuns. Giving a leading role to the Northern Alliance in the Bonn Agreement and in the makeup of the subsequent Afghan government was interpreted by the Afghan people in general, and the Pashtuns in particular, to be an ethnicization of the military victory against the Taliban. In other words, the Afghans saw the US- and international community-supported reinstatement of the Northern Alliance, which was overthrown by the Taliban in 1996, in a dominant role in the Afghan government as a reward for its cooperation and support in overthrowing the Taliban regime, not as a result of the Northern Alliance's record or character. Afghans also viewed this move as a way to further punish the Pashtuns for their association with and support of the Taliban. Reflecting on the past record and character of the Northern Alliance, Robert Fisk wrote:

> I ask myself, why the Northern Alliance is our friend? Not because it is a loyal ally but because it hates the Taliban?. . . But it remains a fact that from 1992 to 1996, the Northern Alliance was a symbol of massacre, systematic rape and pillage. Which is why we, and I include the US State Department, welcomed the Taliban when they arrived in Kabul. The Northern Alliance left the city in 1996 with 50,000 dead behind it. Now its members are our foot soldiers. Better than Mr. bin Laden, to be sure. But what—in God's name—are they going to do in our name?[8]

In contrast, the Pashtuns, who constitute over fifty percent of the Afghan population, were underrepresented in the Bonn Agreement and in the subsequent state formation and political process. The Taliban and Pashtuns in general felt that the United States and the international community were marginalizing the Pashtuns due to their support for and affiliation with the Taliban. Indeed, the Taliban were Pashtuns and they derived their support exclusively from the Pashtuns. Now, for the first time, the Pashtun political dynasty has been overthrown by non-Pashtun minority groups. The Bonn Agreement and subsequent governments have been dominated by non-Pashtuns, especially the Northern Alliance, which the Pashtuns take as a body blow from their so-called "international friends." As a result, a large percentage of the Afghan society, especially Pashtuns, has been unhappy and essentially marginalized from the start of the peace and nation-building process.

The Bonn Agreement was the classic top-down approach to nation-building. The simplistic assumption was that power-sharing by the four anti-Taliban groups would set the framework and environment to deliver peace, development, and democracy to the rest of the society. However, the legitimacy and character of the four anti-Taliban groups were an issue from the start. Lakhdar Brahimi, the United Nations special representative for Afghanistan, who led the Bonn 2001 conference, stated at the conclusion of the Bonn Agreement "upon the founding of a legitimate and representative government in Afghanistan at the Bonn meeting, nobody would question whether the Bonn Agreement represented the actual Afghan people or even remember the participants in the meeting."[9] Indeed, it was a crucial mistake: a simplistic assumption and an inaccurate understanding and interpretation of the ethno-political dynamics of the Afghan society and conflict—which has had trickledown effects on the outcome and nature of nation-building in Afghanistan. In short, the Bonn Agreement marginalized the Taliban, created tension among various ethnic groups, and caused the alienated Pashtuns to question the legitimacy of nation-building and democracy in Afghanistan. In turn, the marginalization of the Taliban, and ethnic tension and polarization have been major factors giving rise to insurgency and contributing to the failure of the disarmament, demobilization, and re-integration of warlords and ex-combatants. Moreover, important steps toward peace-building and conflict resolution have failed because the Taliban boycotted the government and powerful warlords did not properly disarm, claiming they needed their weapons to protect themselves against possible Taliban attacks.

Disarmament, Demobilization, and Reintegration of Ex-combatants (DDR)

Political stability, the success of nation-building efforts, and economic development are intimately linked to bringing peace and security to post-conflict societies. Security is the most critical factor in post-conflict societies because it not only affects nation-building, but also affects the renewal of war and the credibility and legitimacy of the state. Fukuyama and Smith argue that security is the key precondition for successful nation-building.[10] Without security there is no stability and without stability there is no nation-building or development. The Russian invasion and occupation of Afghanistan (1979-1989) led to civil war and gave rise to different armed groups, warlords, and militias that initially formed a resistance front and fought the Soviet Union. However, after the withdrawal of the Soviet Union in 1989, the warlords kept their weapons and often fought each other for control of resources and territory. Therefore, disarming the warlords was a crucial step in building peace, implementing the democratic reconstruction model, and thus a prerequisite for nation-building and liberal democracy in Afghanistan.

It is widely accepted that the process of Disarmament, Demobilization, and Reintegration (here after DDR) has economic, political, and social aspects. In the case of Afghanistan, three decades of war have transformed the combatants into war-hardened militants with little to no memory or understanding of peace, justice, and law and order. The lack of education, skills, and opportunity to earn a stable income makes the DDR process very difficult in Afghanistan, requiring a carefully drafted long-term approach. Empirical evidence from Nicaragua (1909-1933) and Cambodia (1991-1995) indicates that failure to successfully reintegrate ex-combatants and ex-military personnel into society leads to a renewal of war and conflict.[11] In both cases, lack of a proper approach, employment, income, and government support were key elements that made ex-combatants and ex-military officers revert to war and revolt against their governments.

The DDR program, with funding from Japan, started in 2003 in Afghanistan with the aim of disarming and reintegrating warlords, combatants, and militia groups into society by providing them proper training and jobs. The $141 million US program had two main goals: 1) to disrupt the clientele relationship between the powerful warlords and various militia and armed groups that had been undermining law and order; and 2) to expand government control and legitimacy beyond the capital, Kabul City. Both approaches have proved to be essential for sustainable nation-building in Afghanistan.

Nevertheless, in the 2001 Bonn Agreement, the Northern Alliance and warlords from other anti-Taliban groups argued that they would not agree to the disarming of their militias, claiming that they were *Mujahedeen* who fought against the invading Red Army (i.e., the Soviet Union) to restore the honor and freedom of the Afghan people. Disarming the *Mujahedeen* would be disrespectful to these national heroes. To protect themselves against possible future prosecution for war crimes, the Northern Alliance and *Mujahedeen* leaders also demanded that the Bonn Agreement acknowledge and accept the *Mujahedeen* as national heroes or they would withdraw from the peace talks. The United States and the international community agreed, because they needed the Northern Alliance in their fight against the Taliban and for creating a new government in Afghanistan. As a result, the disarming issue was not properly addressed in the Bonn Agreement and it was left for further and future discussion. In addition, in response to the demands of the Northern Alliance and *Mujahedeen* leaders, the parties to the Bonn Agreement expressed

> their appreciation to the Afghan mujahidin who, over the years, have defended the independence, territorial integrity and national unity of the country and have played a major role in the struggle against terrorism and oppression, and whose sacrifice has now made them both heroes of jihad and champions of peace, stability and reconstruction of their beloved homeland, Afghanistan.[12]

As a result, in most cases, powerful warlords with connections to the Northern Alliance or other power brokers in the government either refused to disarm, claiming that they needed their arms to defend themselves against the Taliban, or partially disarmed in return for high level positions with the government, national army, or police forces. Furthermore, since various warlords were helping the United States to locate and arrest Al Qaeda and Taliban operatives in Afghanistan, the DDR program was implemented with the assistance and collaboration of warlords.[13] Therefore, warlords not only influenced the implementation of the DDR program from the start, but they also masterfully channeled their loyal militia and combatants into government, military, and police ranks. These tactics, which contributed to the rise of warlordism, corruption, and insecurity, have had major trickledown effects on the nation-building process and the legitimacy of the central government.

In summary, the DDR was intended to disarm militias, ex-military officers, and other combatants to reduce the strength and influence of warlords, improve security, and enhance the legitimacy of the central government in rural Afghanistan. However, the DDR process not only failed to properly disarm powerful warlords and power brokers but it also ushered them into the central government by cutting deals and offering them high ranking civil and military positions. Failing to disarm warlords was bad enough. Expecting them to set aside their personal greed, rivalries, ethnic and political differences, and to promote peace, unity, and respect for civil liberty—all goals in keeping with democratic principles and the expectations and wishes of the Afghan people—was even worse, given the lack of incentives for them to do so.

The inclusion of the warlords and militia leaders in the government, national army, and police forces further consolidated their social and political positions. Since these warlords were not properly disarmed, rural Afghanistan today is virtually controlled either by warlords or by the Taliban. They are involved in drug trafficking, human rights abuses, kidnapping, and extortion, all of which undermine security, the legitimacy of the government, and the nation-building process in the country. The United States and the government of Afghanistan cannot use force against these warlords, fearing that it may drive them into the arms of the Taliban. Therefore, warlords undermine security, challenge the legitimacy of the state, and benefit from the reconstruction projects. The lack of security and the abusive behaviors of the warlords are the critical factors that continue to drive Afghans to join and support the Taliban insurgency.

In response to an increasing Taliban insurgency and the lack of security, the US and the government of Afghanistan have initiated a number of local defense and security programs such as the Afghan Public Protection Force (2010), Afghan Public Protection Program (2009), Afghanistan National Auxiliary Police (2006), Community Defense Initiative (2009), Local Defense Initiative (2010), Village Security Program (2010), and others. These programs are based on the Arbakai concept, which has a long history and tradition in Afghanistan. Arbakais are militia; more precisely, young men from a village, who have traditionally protected their village and provided security on a voluntary basis under the guidance of their community leaders. However, the current community defense and security initiatives are different in a number of ways from the traditional Arbakai concept. First, members of the community defense groups and community elders are well paid and supported by US Special Forces units. Second, local community defense programs have attracted mostly ex-fighters and military officers, militias, and warlords. The goal is that these programs and militias will provide security in rural Afghanistan by denying the Taliban a base to operate. While the community defense initiative, as a concept and in practice, is in its initial stages, some within and outside the Afghan government argue that, since the program is attracting existing militias, warlords, and power brokers, it will be difficult for the government of Afghanistan to control and command them and maintain their loyalty. According to Ahmad Nader Nadery, a Commissioner at the Afghanistan Independent Human Rights Commission, arming rural communities will serve as a source of insecurity and will create warlords who will be difficult for the weak central government to integrate into its security system.[14]

Donor-Led Nation-Building

Afghanistan is faced with the enormous tasks of providing security, employment, food security, and the reconstruction of physical and institutional infrastructures. Indeed, these are all urgent and crucial tasks. However, Afghanistan, like most post-conflict states, lacks capacity and functioning institutions to manage aid funds and carry out the complex and challenging tasks of nation-building. As a result, the architects of the democratic reconstruction model at the Tokyo Conference in 2002 decided that donors would fund and lead the nation-building process, creating a donor-led approach to nation-building in Afghanistan. It was also decided that nongovernmental and international humanitarian organizations (here after NGOs), which have the capacity and considerable knowledge and experience in promoting development and democracy in many post-conflict states, would implement these nation-building projects. As a result, in the aftermath of the Tokyo Conference, about 3,000 NGOs were funded to carry out various reconstruction and emergency aid projects in the country, in consultation and coordination with donors. But if the NGOs are the primary service providers and the main source of disbursing the aid funds, with little meaningful voice or ownership for the Afghan state, how can the central government still be locally perceived as legitimate? Most Afghans resent the fact that their own government is a silent passenger in the back seat while "foreigners" with little to no knowledge of their country and needs are doing the driving. The donor-led approach to nation-building has sidelined the state and eroded its capacity, visibility, and legitimacy in the eyes of its citizens because the state, no matter how weak or fragile, is still accountable to its citizens, but the NGOs are not.

The following three points question the viability of the donor-led approach to nation-building currently being implemented in Afghanistan.

NGOs in Afghanistan reduce the capacity of the government

The decision that NGOs would implement nation-building projects, in consultation with donors, essentially sidelined the weak and embryonic state of Afghanistan right from the start of the nation-building process. As noted, due to a lack of security and capacity in the central government, most of rural Afghanistan remains under the control of warlords. As a result, the NGOs have to cooperate with the warlords in order to implement nation-building projects. Otherwise, NGOs cannot operate beyond the capital.[15] Warlords have continued to benefit from reconstruction projects and programs to further consolidate their political and social positions. This has led to a situation in which the planning and implementation of reconstruction projects has been done in consultation with the donors at the "top" and the warlords at the "bottom," with the Afghan state mostly out of the loop. In addition, NGOs are not only doing the government's job but, in working outside the government system, they have also created parallel government-like structures, thus undermining the visibility, development, and legitimacy of the central government.[16] By working outside the government system, the NGOs have contributed very little to capacity-building within the state. In fact, by creating government-like structures, the NGOs have reduced the capacity of government institutions, given that the NGOs normally offer much higher salaries and better benefits than the government can give for the same job. The NGOs, therefore, compete with government to attract and hire the most qualified, skilled, and talented employees, which has had a "brain drain" effect on the government.

NGOs lack historical and cultural knowledge

Post-war reconstruction and nation-building are complex processes, demanding careful navigation through political, economic, and social institutions. This requires unique and unusual compromises and interventions. Historical, cultural, ethnic, linguistic, religious, and social endowments are important factors that must be understood and taken into account during the nation-building process. The development of policies and the implementation of projects must be based on realities on the ground, with the consultation and partnership of local communities. Cultural, linguistic, and religious factors dictate and drive the domestic political process by shaping the perceptions, attitudes, and values of the individual and society.[17] Like formal institutions, informal institutions play a crucial role in the implementation and outcome of the domestic political process.[18] The challenge is to package the domestic political process in such a way that it is more consistent with, and less confrontational to informal institutions, cultural and religious practices, and values. Therefore, proper understanding of historical, cultural, and religious factors is extremely important for designing and implementing successful and sustainable nation-building projects. In most cases, NGOs do not have the much needed background knowledge to do so in close consultation and cooperation with the national government and local communities. This lack of background information, in the case of Afghanistan, has led to resource mismanagement, project duplication, waste of aid funds, and implementation of projects and policies that are not sustainable. In Afghanistan, NGOs usually hire their personnel to develop a policy or implement a project after their proposals are funded by donors. Proposals are time sensitive; within a fixed time frame projects have to be implemented, activities have to be carried out, results have to be reported to donors, and the budget has to be spent. In such cases, the NGOs quickly recruit, mostly from Western countries, the needed personnel to implement a specific project or draft a specific policy. These experts, or the so-called advisors, have the necessary technical skills, but seriously lack the political, cultural, economic, and social understanding and knowledge of the country for which they are supposed to develop a policy or implement a project.

To be cost effective, the NGOs recruit their personnel for a fixed period of time with a well-defined and outlined term of reference. As a result, these experts, under time pressure, complete their tasks as soon as possible, with little or no consultation with the national government or local communities, and move quickly to their next assignment, wherever it might be. Obviously, these experts cannot speak the local languages, so they rely on local interpreters, who typically speak very little broken English, to communicate with local people or collect data, resulting in misunderstanding and misleading conclusions. At the end of the project, the NGOs submit the final report not to the government of Afghanistan, but to the donor that has funded the project. As a result, the government is out of the loop and in most cases has neither the idea where or why a particular project was implemented, nor the necessary funds to sustain it.

At the Afghanistan Development Forum 2007, which was a major conference between donors and the government of Afghanistan to discuss development outcomes and future needs, Praful Patel, South Asia Regional Vice-President of the World Bank, acknowledged that inconsistencies between the NGOs and the government of Afghanistan exist. In his words

> we get cases when a school is built but no teachers are available simply because the ministry did not know about it and did not staff it. Or infrastructure is provided that will deteriorate rapidly because the ministry is unaware of it and does not include maintenance costs in the budget. So we gain in speed but we also shoot ourselves in the foot. Donors ask me—"why doesn't the Bank do more on aid coordination; no one knows where the money is being spent?"[19]

NGOs lack accountability, cooperation, and coordination

The major reason for the donor-led approach to nation-building in Afghanistan was that it allowed the donors to dictate how their aid money should be used, what projects should be funded and where. Unfortunately, this has translated, in most cases, into a situation where the policy of a donor country, working in a particular sector, became the policy of the Afghan state in that sector and the priority of the donor country became the priority of the Afghan state; again, a top down process with the Afghan state on the receiving end. In addition, according to the government of Afghanistan and donors, two thirds of the aid money has been directly provided to various NGOs, bypassing the Afghan government.[20] The Donor Assistance Database for Afghanistan does not track expenditures by the NGOs. It only records donors' disbursements—the transfer of funds by the donors into the NGOs' accounts. Therefore, the government of Afghanistan cannot ask for accountability because it does not know exactly how the aid funds are "spent" by the NGOs. Rubin argues that:

> This method of giving aid fails to build the legitimacy and capacity of the recipient government. The government cannot make decisions about what ser-

> vices are to be provided, track expenditures, or gain experience in providing public goods. Multilateral operations risk creating elected governments fragmented among clienteles of different aid agencies, with no political authority having the power to pursue a coherent strategy for building sovereignty. Elected governments without budgetary authority or control over security provision hardly merit the term "democracies."[21]

In most cases, the multilateral operations in Afghanistan have resulted in fragmented projects with various levels of scope, impact, and sustainability being implemented in the country. After a project is completed and final reports are submitted to the donor, the NGO closes the book and moves on to a different country or different sector or different project. As a result, the government agencies that inherit NGO roles cannot find the departed NGO officials to answer questions or provide the needed information. Therefore, the government has little knowledge of the project, or the funds or personnel to sustain it, which has a devastating effect on the legitimacy and capacity of the state.

The lack of coordination and cooperation has also given rise to a waste of resources, fraud, and mismanagement. The 2010 polls show a significant decline in confidence in international NGOs (fifty-four percent) compared to sixty-five percent in 2009. This is due to the perception among Afghans that the donors and the international NGOs make decisions that are in their best interest rather than the interest of the Afghan people and country.[22] On April 4, 2005, Afghan President Hamid Karzai, frustrated with the unaccountability and squandering of resources by the NGOs, voiced his concern in a meeting with foreign ambassadors and representatives of the United Nations, donors, and NGOs saying that "we have a responsibility towards the Afghan people, as well as the taxpayers in the donor countries, to stop NGOs that are corrupt, wasteful and unaccountable."[23] According to Arnold Fields, former head of the Special Inspector General for Afghanistan Reconstruction, "what starts out as a dollar whose interest is to provide a major support and reconstruction effort and by the time that dollar reaches a bona fide reconstruction effort, it is twenty or thirty cents."[24]

Rethinking the Democratic Reconstruction Model

For more than ten years the United States and the international community have supported nation-building in Afghanistan. In spite of tremendous support and effort, the nation-building process has failed to take root in the country. While this failure is well recognized by the US and its allies, the source of the problem is not. The international community blames the Karzai government, which indeed has many shortcomings and weaknesses, for this failure. However, the root of the nation-building problems in Afghanistan is the top-down approach of the democratic reconstruction model. A significant aspect of democratization is the "right to self-determination;" here, the Afghan people's right to reconcile their differences, rebuild their country, and introduce changes consistent with their own political, economic, cultural, and religious institutions. From the start, though, the democratic reconstruction model has envisioned and worked toward a specific outcome in Afghanistan: a statehood based on Western-style political, economic, and social institutions. As a result, the democratic reconstruction model has directly or indirectly promoted and supported the inclusion or election of those individuals, ethnic groups, and political parties that are ostensibly sympathetic to the imposition of Western values and ideals in Afghanistan. This is why the Bonn Agreement failed to lay the groundwork for establishing a legitimate and broad-based government that reflects the will of the majority of Afghans. The spillover effect of this failure is that the DDR process has actually strengthened and ushered the warlords into the government and security forces, thus undermining peace, security, government authority and legitimacy, and losing the trust of the Afghan people in both the nation-building process and the international community.

The donor-led approach to nation-building and the design, management, and implementation of development projects by the NGOs, with little to no say or control by the central government, have further convinced the Afghan people that the Karzai government is a puppet regime with no authority, legitimacy, or control of nation-building affairs, much like the government of Dr. Mohammad Najibullah, which was installed and controlled by the Soviet Union. This is a major reason why the Karzai government has lost its legitimacy and support among the Afghan people, and why the Taliban have repeatedly stated that they will not talk with a government that cannot make its own decisions.

The democratic reconstruction model has fueled ethnic conflict and provoked Islamic and nationalist insurgencies as a consequence of designing, managing, and implementing democratic transitions from above, while sidelining the Afghan state, religion, culture, and voice. For example, the Constitution of Afghanistan clearly states that "in Afghanistan, no law can be contrary to the beliefs and provisions of the sacred religion of Islam" (Chapter 1, Article 3), a commitment that explains much as to why the promotion of secular democracy and Western-style gender equality is difficult to implement and impossible to sustain. It is reasonable to assume that the Afghan people want peace, security, economic development, and prosperity according to their vision and history and consistent with their political, economic, cultural, and religious institutions. But to assume that a predominantly conservative Muslim society wants a secular state and Western-style gender equality and freedom is, in this view, more an expression of ignorance, power, and arrogance than a valid judgment.

In addition, the democratic reconstruction model has failed to harness the established complex ethnic, cultural, and religious networks and informal institutions that have long been the backbone of Afghan society for resolving conflicts, and introducing social and political changes. Historically, these networks and informal institutions have been an important vehicle connecting central governments with civil society so that the will and voice of the people are reflected in the design and implementation of government policies. Indeed, the essence of a legitimate government is to reflect the will of the people in the design and implementation of public policies. The need to reconcile the democratic reconstruction model with the existing traditional network of civil society was recognized and recommended in the 2007 Afghanistan Human Development Report.[25] It was reported that more than eighty percent of the Afghan people use and prefer the local traditional mechanisms of *Jirga* (meeting of representatives), *Maraka* (meeting of elders), and *Shura* (council) for dispute resolution and justice to a formal court system. According to a public opinion poll recently conducted in Afghanistan by the Asia Foundation, the majority of the respondents (seventy-three percent) indicated that local *Jirga* and *Shura* are fair and trusted, follow their local customs and norms (seventy percent), effectively deliver justice (sixty-nine percent), and promptly resolve cases (sixty-six percent). Furthermore, more than half (fifty-two percent) of the respondents indicated that they do not trust state courts and the judicial system.[26] The Bonn Agreement acknowledged the central role that the traditional system of justice and conflict resolution has played, over centuries, in Afghan society by mandating the convening of an emergency *Loya Jirga* (grand assembly) within six months of the establishment of the Afghan Interim Authority to decide on the Transitional Government of Afghanistan "to lead Afghanistan until such time as a fully representative government can be elected through free and fair elections."[27]

The Bonn Agreement also called for the creation of a Judicial Commission to rebuild the Afghan judicial system, with the assistance of the United Nations, according to Islamic principles, international standards, rule of law, and the "Afghan legal traditions," which is defined by the United Nations Assistant Mission for Afghanistan as "the customs, values, and senses of justice acceptable to and revered by the people of Afghanistan."[28] Truly, justice, conflict resolution, or any other practice or system that is "imposed" by the state, ruler, or foreign models, on a society or nation will remain, at the end, as a concept on paper in the drawer of a desk or on a shelf collecting dust.

Lastly, the democratic reconstruction model has incorrectly assumed that traditional values and practices in Afghanistan are contrary to international standards and norms, so they should be replaced with Western "best" practices and "blue prints" for democracy and development to take root in the country. For example, after September 11, 2001, the burqa-shrouded woman of Afghanistan was the subject of heated debate. The international community and the democratic reconstruction model equated "burqa" with oppression, and the aim was to "liberate" Afghan women from their attire and their culture. The West failed to realize that burqa or any other form of women's cover has been a manifestation of Afghan religion and culture and a product of Afghan history. In fact, empirical evidence since 2001 indicates that lack of security, employment, and education, and fear of being kidnapped or raped by warlords are the major problems facing Afghan women, not the burqa. The pictures of burqa-shrouded women casting their votes in the 2010 presidential and parliamentary elections, broadcast in the Western media, made the point that the burqa, like bikinis or blue jeans, is a manifestation of a different culture. Such mistakes, misinterpretations, and invalid assumptions have alienated the Afghan people and created serious obstacles to and suspicion about the mission of foreign-driven nation-building in Afghanistan. The Taliban has capitalized on the mistakes and missteps of the democratic reconstruction model to generate broad support and sympathy based on the notion that the main purpose of the foreign occupation and nation-building is to impose Western ideals and practices that deprive the Afghan people of their religion and culture. The rise and spread of the Taliban insurgency since 2001 is the consequence. According to the International Council on Security and Development, in November 2007, the Taliban had a permanent presence in fifty-four percent of the country, but by December 2008, the Taliban increased their presence to seventy-two percent of the country, and they continue to expand their influence.[29] The deployment of thirty thousand additional troops by the United States to Afghanistan in 2010 to "stabilize the government and reverse the Taliban momentum" punctuates the point.

To summarize, the resilient Taliban insurgency, the declining legitimacy and popularity of the central government among the Afghan people, and the lack of long-term commitment by the donors and the international community necessitate a rethinking of the democratic reconstruction model. These realities require that the current top-down theoretical approach to nation-building based on a foreign vision of statehood and best practices, problematic both in terms of implementation and sustainability, must give way to bottom-up practices that put the Afghan state and people in the driver's seat. A bottom-up rather than top-down approach to nation-building is consistent with the essence of democracy, supported by the Afghan people, and can be both successful and sustainable. It is essential for the international community to realize that Afghanistan stands at a critical juncture, and that the decision to stay the current course most likely will lead Afghanistan toward failure. Afghanistan at present seriously lacks the preconditions that are needed to support a sustainable democratic transition consistent with Western vision and practices. Contrary to Western societies, Afghanistan is a tribal society where religious, family, and cultural values are deeply rooted in society and define social relationships, values, and perceptions, which in turn define and determine the kinds of institutions that can be developed and sustained in the country. The question is no longer whether, but to what extent the democratic reconstruction model adjusts to local circumstances and accepts a vision of statehood that is by the Afghans and for the Afghans. The answer will determine the fate of democracy and nation-building in Afghanistan.

Conclusions

The core objectives of sustainable nation-building are to restore the state's capacity and legitimacy, to reconstruct old or create new institutions consistent with local circumstances, and to repair the state-society relationship. From Japan to Germany to Afghanistan, the democratic reconstruction model has viewed post-conflict nation-building as an opportunity to make political, economic, and social changes to post-conflict societies according to a Western vision and blueprints.

The United States and the international community alike need to rethink that model to avoid repeating the recent disaster of Soviet-led nation-building in Afghanistan (1979-1989). While the Western media portrays the Soviet-led nation-building in Afghanistan as an "occupation" and the US-led nation-building (2001 to present) as "peace-building," both approaches involve a static top-down pathway to nation-building that imposes foreign models and practices while claiming to know what is best for Afghanistan. In both cases these have been key problems that have fueled Islamic and nationalist insurgencies in the country. Soviet-led nation-building failed because the model was a statehood based on a communist vision and theoretical framework which had to be forced at gunpoint because there was virtually no demand or precondition for communism in Afghanistan.

Since 2001, the international community has repeatedly claimed that tribalism, warlordism, ethnic division and rivalry, and lack of a functioning state and institutions are the major problems facing post-conflict nation-building in Afghanistan. However, empirical evidence since 2001 indicates that foreign-driven top-down prescriptive approaches, inconsistency between the vision of the democratic reconstruction model and local realities, and multilateral operations are the key impediments to nation-building in Afghanistan. They have further ethnicized the Afghan nation, ushered warlords into the Afghan state, ignored the role and voice of the Afghan people, and given rise to ethnic and religious insurgencies.

The international community and the democratic reconstruction model should make every effort to learn from past mistakes and avoid the Soviet experience by empowering the Afghan state and society to take ownership of the nation-building process. To undo the mistakes and missteps of the Bonn Agreement, the international community should stop supporting the warlords and bring the perpetrators of past war crimes to justice. This will not just curb the power of warlords, the culture of human rights abuse, and corruption. It will also contribute to security, conflict resolution, state legitimacy, nation-building, and democracy. The Asia Foundation's 2010 public opinion survey shows that less than half of the Afghans (forty-seven percent) believe that things are moving in the right direction in the country. Insecurity, corruption, and bad governance are cited as the main reasons for the pessimism.[30]

Only a strong and legitimate government in Afghanistan can effectively combat warlordism, protect individual rights, and provide the needed security and services to all citizens. For this to happen, the main focus of nation-building must be establishing a legitimate government, which has the full support, trust, and cooperation of the international community, donors, and NGOs. Donors and NGOs should work through the government not for the government, contribute to government agendas and priorities, and strengthen its capacity to take control and ownership of the development process. By teaming up with the government, the NGOs would effectively overcome the "outsider problems" and improve their effectiveness in terms of costs, delivering services, and building capacity in the government. Such an approach will foster an enabling environment for the government and local institutions to grow and take charge of the nation-building process. This will in turn allow the international community, donors, and NGOs to eventually vacate the country, which is the essence of successful and sustainable nation-building. In short, the NGO-led approach to nation-building is not the right answer to the problems of central government because NGOs cannot achieve sustainable nation-building and democracy without a strong and legitimate state.

Furthermore, integrating human rights principles and modern justice and conflict resolution systems into the traditional conflict resolution and justice system will not only ensure that the justice and conflict resolution system in the country is consistent with the Afghan religious and cultural practices that are understood, trusted, and practiced by the majority of Afghans, but it will also ensure that the traditional conflict resolution and justice system is in line with the principles of human rights and international standards. Such a conflict resolution and justice system will fully utilize the existing traditional networks and informal institutions and, therefore, be owned by the Afghan people and closely tied to their daily life practices and social and religious customs.

In sum, a bottom up approach to democracy and nation-building that is led by the Afghan state, owned by the Afghan people, and supported by the international community would be consistent with the essence of democracy and nation-building and the wishes of the Afghan peoples. Such an approach to democracy and nation-building would be successful and sustainable because it would be building a statehood based on the dynamics of the Afghan society, which is by the Afghans and for the Afghans rather than a statehood that is based on foreign vision, models, and "best" practices.

Notes

1. Lee Michael Katz, "Afghanistan's president is ousted," *USA Today* (April 17, 1992).

2. See M. Hassan Kakar, *Afghanistan: The Soviet Invasion and the Afghan Response, 1979-1982* (Berkeley: University of California Press, 1995).

3. Transparency International, "Global Perception Index 2010," 2010 http://www.transparency.org/policy_research/surveys_indices/cpi/2010/results (accessed April 5, 2011).

4. The Asia Foundation "Afghanistan in 2010: A Survey of the Afghan People," http://asiafoundation.org/country/afghanistan/2010-poll.php (accessed April 5, 2011).

5. Office of the Press Secretary, "Remarks by the President in Address to the Nation on the Way Forward in Afghanistan and Pakistan" *The White House*, December 1, 2009, http://www.whitehouse.gov/the-press-office/remarks-president-address-nation-way-forward-afghanistan-and-pakistan (accessed December 2, 2010).

6. See Charles T. Call and Susan E. Cook, "On Democratization and Peacebuilding," *Global Governance* 9, no. 2 (April-June 2003):233-46; Marina Ottaway, "Promoting Democracy After Conflict: The Difficult Choices," *International Studies Perspectives* 4 (2003): 314-22; and Minxin Pei and Sara Kasper, "Lessons from the Past: The American Record on Nation Building," *Carnegie Endowment for International Peace,* Policy Brief 24 (2003): 1-8.

7. See Oliver Richmond, "Emancipatory Forms of Human Security and Liberal Peacebuilding," *International Journal* 62, no. 3 (2007):459-472.

8. Robert Fisk, "What will the Northern Alliance do in our name now? I dread to think," *The Independent* (United Kingdom), http://www.independent.co.uk/opinion/commentators/fisk/robert-fisk--what-will-the-northern-alliance-do-in-our-name-now-i-dread-to-think-616866.html (accessed December 13 2010).

9. Bulent Aras and Sule Toktas, "Afghanistan's Security: Political Process, State-Building and Narcotics," *Middle East Policy Council* 15, no. 2 (Summer 2007).

10. See Francis Fukuyama, *State-Building, Governance, and World Order in the 21st Century*. (New York: Cornell University Press, 2004), and B. C. Smith, *Understanding Third World Politics: Theories of Political Change and Development* (Bloomington: Indiana University Press, 2003).

11. See Charles T. Call and Susan E. Cook, "On Democratization and Peacebuilding," and Minxin Pei and Sara Kasper, "Lessons from the Past: The American Record on Nation Building."

12. United Nations, "Agreement on Provisional Agreements in Afghanistan Pending the Re-establishment of Permanent Government Institutions, 2001," http://www.un.org/News/dh/latest/afghan/afghan-agree.htm (accessed January 10, 2011).

13. Shamsul Hadi Shams, "Assessing the Role of DDR in Afghanistan: Internal Security Revision and External Environment*," Toward Bringing Stability in Afghanistan: A Review of the Peacebuilding Strategy,* 2010, http://home.hiroshima-u.ac.jp/heiwa/Pub/E24/yujiuesugied.pdf (accessed February 25, 2011).

14. Spence Ackerman, "Afghanistan Human Rights Official Criticizes McChrystal 'Tribes' Initiative," *Washington Independent*, December 1, 2009, http://washingtonindependent.com/69131/afghan-human-rights-official-criticizes-mcchrystal-tribes-initiative (accessed December 15, 2010).

15. Spence Ackerman, "Afghanistan Human Rights Official Criticizes McChrystal 'Tribes' Initiative."

16. See Andreas Wimmer and Conrod Schetter, "Putting State-Formation First: Some Recommendations for Reconstruction and Peace-Making in Afghanistan," *Journal of International Development* 15 (2003):525-39.

17. B. C. Smith, *Understanding Third World Politics.*

18. See Gretchen Helmke and Steven Levitsky, "Informal Institutions and Comparative Politics: A Research Agenda," *Perspectives on Politics* 2, no. 4 (December 2004):725-40, and Christopher J. Coyle, "Reconstructing Weak and Failed States," *The Journal of Social, Political and Economic Studies* 31, no.2 (2006):143-62.

19. World Bank, "Afghanistan Development Forum 2007" *World Bank* (2007), http://www.worldbank.org.af/WBSITE/EXTERNAL/COUNTRIES/SOUTHASIAEXT/AFGHANISTANEXTN/0,,contentMDK:21314955~pagePK:141137~piPK:141127~theSitePK:305985,00.html (accessed January 17, 2011).

20. United Nations Office of the High Commissioner for Human Rights, "Human Rights Dimension of Poverty in Afghanistan," March 31, 2010,

http://www.humansecuritygateway.com/documents/OHCHR_HumanRightsDimensionOfPovertyInAfghanistan.pdf (accessed February 25, 2011).

21. Barnett Rubin "Peace Building and State-Building in Afghanistan: Constructing Sovereignty for Whose Security?" *Third World Quarterly* 27, no. 1 (2006):177-85, 182.

22. The Asia Foundation, "Afghanistan in 2010: A Survey of the Afghan People."

23. Ramtanu Maitra, "The Party's over for Afghan NGOs,"*Asia Times Online*, April 21, 2005, http://www.atimes.com/atimes/Central_Asia/GD21Ag01.html (accessed February 27, 2011).

24. Cited in Kimberly Halkett , "US Combats Afghan Aid Corruption," *Al Jazeera News,* 2009, http://english.aljazeera.net/news/americas/2009/12/2009123042621747107.html (accessed February 27, 2011).

25. Ali Wardak *et al*, "Afghanistan Human Development Report 2007," *Center for Policy and Human Development,* 2007, http://hdr.undp.org/en/reports/ nationalreports/asiathepacific/afghanistan/nhdr2007.pdf (accessed February 26, 2011).

26. The Asia Foundation "Afghanistan in 2010: A Survey of the Afghan People."

27. United Nations, "Agreement on Provisional Agreements in Afghanistan Pending the Re-establishment of Permanent Government Institutions, 2001": 4.

28. International Council on Human Rights Policy, "When Legal Worlds Overlap Human Rights, State and Non-State Law," (2009): 12, http://www.ichrp.org/ (accessed March 30, 2011).

29. The International Council on Security and Development, "Struggle for Kabul: The Taliban Advance," *Afghanistan Reports*, December 2008, http://www.icosgroup.net/report/report-afgh/page/2/ (accessed December 20, 2011).

30. The Asia Foundation "Afghanistan in 2010: A Survey of the Afghan People."

Chapter 21

International Intervention and Ethnic Tolerance in Bosnia-Herzegovina: Evidence from Public Opinion

Sam Whitt

To what extent can civil war intervention enhance prospects for long-term cooperation and shared statehood among former rivals? This essay considers the case of Bosnia-Herzegovina and how U.S./NATO-led intervention has likely impacted Bosnian public opinion since the war. I argue that international intervention has helped facilitate the revitalization of important foundations for social cooperation, but failure to make progress on institutional reforms has restricted the ability for cooperation to evolve beyond ethnic boundaries. While an analysis of public opinion is helpful to shed light on this point, it does not offer a clear process or solution for getting beyond the status quo. While Bosnians are no longer divided by hate, they have meaningful and possibly irreconcilable differences regarding any roadmap for the future, and Bosnia still relies on international commitments to maintain state unity and social cohesion.

This essay is divided into three main parts. First, I examine pre-war attitudes using what data are available from the late Yugoslav period. I then move to the immediate aftermath of the Bosnian war and consider the damage done to basic foundations for cooperation in Bosnian society. Finally, I look at how attitudes have changed over the course of Bosnia's post-war reconstruction from the war's end to the present. Based on evidence from public opinion data, I assess whether international intervention in the Bosnian conflict has resulted in positive social transformations and support for multi-ethnic state unity. I conclude by considering what broader lessons could be drawn from the Bosnian case and offering suggestions, based on public opinion, for breaking the current political stalemates that have hindered Bosnia's movement from an international protectorate to a viable multi-ethnic state.

Ethnic Relations before the Yugoslav Collapse

One problem of studying the effects of international intervention on civil war violence is often a lack of pre-war baselines. Without pre-war data, it is difficult to evaluate the changes conflict might have affected, if any, in a society's basic norms and values. Thanks to pioneering work by a number of Yugoslav scholars, this is not the case in Bosnia. Yugoslav authorities established a network of social science institutes within the constituent republics and conducted routine polling from the late 1950s onward.[1] One of the most extensive pre-war studies of public opinion in Bosnia was conducted by the Yugoslav Consortium for Social Research in 1989 with a nationwide sample of over 13,400 respondents, of which 2,123 were sampled in Bosnia. The survey was one of the last major attempts to measure public opinion across Yugoslavia on sensitive social and economic issues before the war.[2] I look to this survey to identify important baselines of social cooperation before the onset of the war.

Given the type of questions that are commonly asked in Bosnia and throughout much of the former Yugoslavia today, it is striking how few questions in this survey deal with issues of ethnic relations and national identity. Instead, the 1989 survey focuses, like much of the scholarship of the time, on Yugoslavia's economy, standards of living, and unique challenges of sustaining market socialism in a period of transition.[3] However, the survey authors had the foresight to include a battery of sensitive questions on ethnic identity and tolerance, without which we might draw very misleading conclusions about the meaning and salience of ethnic identity, not just in Bosnia but throughout the former Yugoslavia.

When conflict broke out over the collapse of Yugoslavia in 1991, some were quick to blame the violence on underlying ethnic hatred.[4] The logic of their argument was rooted in the region's contentious social and political history. According to their historical reading, people in former Yugoslavia nursed deep-seated ethnic grievances going back to the Second World War—if not centuries earlier. Under the authoritarian grip of the Yugoslav regime, ethnic tensions were kept at bay by suppressing the voice of ethnic nationalists, which grew louder after Tito's death in 1981. The collapse of communism in Yugoslavia's Warsaw pact neighbors gave nationalists the momentum to demand multi-party elections, which they won, and subsequently enacted a series of referenda, where majorities in Slovenia, Croatia, Macedonia, and then Bosnia voted in favor of independence from Yugoslavia. These actions were strongly opposed by Serbia as well as by ethnic Serb minority populations living in Croatia and Bosnia. The wars that subsequently broke out in Croatia and then Bosnia were essentially territorial struggles between rival ethnic groups, fueled by centuries of religious and cultural rivalry, mutual fear, hatred, and distrust—or so the story goes.

The main point I would like to make is that while there is ample evidence (in the form of voting behavior) that public opinion in Bosnia was ethnically divided over the issue of breaking up Yugoslavia, it is less evident that these divisions were driven by widespread or underlying hatred for one another.[5] Here I provide an overview of major findings from a 1989 nationwide survey in Yugoslavia and then discuss what I think the study can and cannot tell us about the "ethnic hatred" assumption.

Some of the most important insights on pre-war public opinion in the former Yugoslavia were documented by Randy Hodson et al. as the conflict in Bosnia was still unfolding.[6] At a time when the world was shocked and horrified by the brutality of ethnic cleansing in Bosnia, they offered compelling evidence of a strong foundation for ethnic tolerance in Bosnia before the war. They based their analysis on the Yugoslav Consortium's 1989 nationwide survey data. The 1989 survey contained a number of broad indicators of ethnic inclusivity, which Hodson et al. used to create a broad index of national tolerance.[7] Across Yugoslavia, they found positive associations between tolerance and the ethnic diversity of one's region, age (older), gender (female), urban dwellers, and a weak positive effect of education. Religiosity, unemployment, and "reading the news" were negative correlates of tolerance. In comparison to all other Yugoslav republics, Bosnians were the most tolerant people in the study. Inside Bosnia, the results did not vary significantly by ethnicity. For example, Bosnian Serbs were not seen as less intolerant than Bosniaks or Bosnian Croats. Bosniaks/Muslims were not more tolerant than Bosnian Serbs or Croats.

Table 1 shows the frequency distributions for components of the Hodson et al. index of tolerance by ethnicity. The total sample size for Bosnia was 2,123, of which 43 percent identified as "Muslims," 16 percent as "Croats," 26 percent as "Serbs," and 14 percent as "Yugoslavs" in addition to other minority groups. The table presents question responses as percentages using these identity categorizations. The table shows that while some Bosniaks, Croats, and Serbs were concerned about nationalities trusting one another, a majority supported mixed marriages, said they felt safe outside their ethnic communities, and upheld ideals of multi-ethnic statehood. Many also did not think nationality should be an important criterion for choosing a spouse, especially those who identify as "Yugoslav." While people who identify as Yugoslavs were more trusting across ethnicity and more supporting of mixed marriages, comparisons across the three ethnic groups do not suggest that one had a greater propensity for intolerance than the others. Bosnian Serbs, Croats, and Bosniak/Muslims answered questions about tolerance very similarly. Overall, if someone were analyzing these data in 1989, they would not have drawn alarming conclusions that Bosnian society was deeply divided, ethnically polarized, and on the brink of war.[8]

Some may disagree and question the reliability of any pre-war survey data on Bosnian tolerance. Some might be convinced that respondents in 1989 were simply posturing—giving socially desirable answers to questions rather than revealing their true preferences. Others may wonder what explains the war if the Bosnian public was as open and tolerant as these data suggest. With regard to the last point, we do not have the ability to track changes in public opinion over time to say whether Bosnian society's tolerant values rapidly disintegrated from

Table 1. Survey Evidence of Prewar Ethnic Tolerance in Bosnia (1989)

	Muslim/ Bosniak	Bosnian Croat	Bosnian Serb	Yugoslav
Every nation should have its own state				
Agree	6	14	5	4
Disagree	87	80	88	91
People can only feel completely safe when they are the majority nationality in their country				
Agree	11	17	13	5
Disagree	82	76	81	91
Among Nations it is possible to create good cooperation, but not full trust				
Agree	40	45	41	39
Disagree	49	42	48	57
Nationally mixed marriages are more unstable than others				
Agree	25	29	23	9
Disagree	69	61	70	87
How important is nationality to you personally when choosing a spouse?				
Important	51	59	43	13
Not important	48	41	57	87

Consortium for Social Research Institutes of Yugoslavia survey, 1989

the time of the 1989 study until the start of the conflict.[9] We also do not have reliable measures of public opinion during the war, and if any government or international organization has conducted polling during that period, they have not made the results publically available. Hence, public opinion data cannot provide a compelling explanation for why the war began, and so that question is unfortunately beyond the purview of this discussion. On the first point, however, I would argue that public opinion studies conducted in the former Yugoslavia are a valid indicator of the public mood at that time and should not be readily dismissed or discounted.

In authoritarian regimes, public opinion may be sensitive to self-censoring biases due to fears that revealing one's true beliefs could be costly or dangerous if they contradict the reigning dogmas of the regime. There are also questions about the feasibility and reliability of sampling methods if interviewers are restricted from traveling freely to sampling locations throughout the country. This problem may have been more apparent for the countries of the former Soviet

Union and Eastern Bloc, even after liberalization in the late 1980s.[10] Concerns about self-censorship in Yugoslavia, however, are less apparent by this period. In prior decades, nationalists and liberal dissidents had faced exile or imprisonment for voicing their views. While the official mantra of Yugoslavia was still "brotherhood and unity," the regime no longer had the willingness or capability to prevent nationalist dissidents from speaking their mind, which they were increasingly doing with impunity.

If we can discount the fear of authority that would lead the Bosnian public to self-censor their views, then the 1989 survey becomes a more convincing indicator of Bosnian society's pre-war tolerance.[11] The methodology of the survey is otherwise sound, relies on random sampling, and provides a snapshot of Bosnian public views at the time. Taking these data as a credible pre-war baseline, I now turn to the question of whether the war fundamentally destroyed foundations for social cooperation in Bosnia and whether those pre-war norms of tolerance could recover from violence on the destructive and brutal scale of Bosnia.

Ethnic Relations and the Effects of the War

Two elections and two referendums serve as important preludes to the Bosnian war. On November 18, 1990, Bosnians voted in the first multi-party general elections, where ethnic nationalist parties triumphed over multi-ethnic, cross-national groupings. Municipal elections of that same year also resulted in big wins for nationalist parties with majority control in areas of ethnic concentration.[12] With nationalists in charge, the central government broke down in less than a year, with ethnic Serbs proclaiming their own separate Bosnian Serb Assembly in Banja Luka in October 1991. On November 9 and 10, 1991, ethnic Serbs staged a referendum wherein 96 percent voted in favor of remaining part of Yugoslavia. Three months later, between February 29 and 2 March 2, 1992, 90 percent of Bosnian Croats and Bosniaks voted in favor of Bosnia's independence.

While coercion during the elections and referendums was a factor, the results are still a behavioral indicator of where the majority might have stood on the issue of nationalist party support and Bosnian independence.[13] After all, majorities did not vote for cross-national coalitions in multi-party elections. Serbs did not defy the April 1992 boycott and vote nor did Bosniaks and Bosnian Croats rally *en masse* with the Bosnian Serbs to remain in Yugoslavia. However, it is less clear whether the political division over Bosnia's future status also reflected growing intolerance, fear, or hatred across ethnicity within the broader society. While there are many narrative accounts that could shed light on this question, the focus here is on public opinion, where immediate pre-war data are sadly lacking or have yet to be discovered, shared, or publicized. In 1992, we still do not know the extent to which the political divisions are reflective of a growing intolerance in the population.

What we do know is that between April 1992 and December 1995, nearly one hundred thousand people were killed in Bosnia and more than one million displaced by ethnic cleansing. Much of Bosnia's infrastructure had been destroyed, especially in towns and villages along the front lines. The war ended in 1995 with a negotiated settlement that became known as the Dayton Agreement. International intervention was critical to bringing all sides to the negotiating table and international monitors would play a leading role in Bosnia's post-war restructuring. As part of the agreement, NATO deployed a Stabilization Force (SFOR) of more than sixty thousand soldiers to enforce the Dayton Agreement and keep the peace. Dayton also created a new complex set of domestic institutions, including a three-member Bosnian presidency with representation for each ethnic group, a separate ethno-territorial entity (RepublikaSrpska) for ethnic Serbs, and a canton-based power-sharing system for Bosniaks and Croats (the Federation). An international High Representative was established with broad authority to direct post-war reconstruction, including the power to veto legislation, call and validate elections, and appoint/remove Bosnian representatives. Hence, from the onset, international actors were imbedded in Bosnia's post-war institutional development and reconstruction effort.

While much ink has been spilled detailing the course of the Bosnian war, no studies of which I am aware make use of inter-war public opinion data. If public opinion surveys were conducted during the war, none are publically available. To my knowledge, the earliest post-war survey data in Bosnia were collected by the United States Information Agency's Office of Research, now part of the State Department. The Office of Research ran its first survey in Bosnia in December 1995 as the Dayton Accords were finalized, providing a rare early glimpse at a post-conflict society and illustrating in stark terms the challenges ahead for building a viable, multi-ethnic, post-war Bosnian state.[14]

We do not know how long the process took, but by the war's end, Bosnia was a divided, polarized society. The effects of ethnic cleansing are grimly apparent in the post-war data. Before the war, a majority of Bosniaks and Serbs and half of Croats reported living in multi-ethnic communities, but by April 1996, those numbers had plunged due to ethnic cleansing and post-war population resettlements. Table 2 indicates self-reported localized ethnic diversity before and after the war. In 1989, 72 percent of Bosnian Serbs claimed to live in neighborhoods with other ethnic groups. That dropped to 3 percent after the war. Nearly half of Bosnian Croats claimed to live in ethnically mixed neighborhoods before the war, but only 13 percent thereafter. Furthermore, many Bosnian Croats and Serbs believed their communities were now better off as a result. An overwhelming majority (91 percent) of Bosnian Serbs and Croats believed that it was better for their local communities if everyone were of the same ethnicity. Few thought they could live in harmony again with others.

Even though Bosnian Muslims disagreed in principle about the ideal of ethnic integration, in reality, they too now lived increasingly segregated from

Table 2. Tracing the Impact of Ethnic Cleansing on Communities

	Bosniaks	Bosnian Croats	Bosnian Serbs
Four years ago (before the war started) did you live in a neighborhood with many people of another nationality, some people, a few or none of a different nationality?			
Many/Some	81	47	72
Few/None	19	53	28
Do you live in a neighborhood with many people of nationalities other than your own, some people, a few, or none of a different nationality?			
Many/Some	42	13	3
Few/None	57	87	96
Some people say it is better for our village/town/city to be composed of only one nationality group. Others say that different nationality groups can live together in harmony in our village/town/city. Which view is closer to your own?			
One nationality better	12	91	91
Many nationalities better	79	7	5

Office of Research survey, April 1996

Bosnian Croats and Serbs, and none of Bosnia's ethnic groups viewed each other favorably after the war. Based on Office of Research polling, a large majority of Bosnian Serbs had unfavorable views of Bosniaks (89 percent) and Bosnian Croats (87 percent). Most Bosniaks (76 percent) and Bosnian Croats (79 percent) felt the same about the Bosnian Serbs (see Appendix Figures 1-6). Many Bosnian Croats and Serbs also now projected the bitterness of the war onto their assessment of pre-war relations. In August 1996, majorities of Bosnian Croats and Serbs claimed that they never trusted one another—despite pre-war evidence of the contrary (see Table 3). Furthermore, few Bosnian Croats and Serbs thought that they would be able to live together peacefully again, citing that too much damage has now been done from the war.

While majorities of Serbs and Croats had rejected ethnically exclusive rhetoric in 1989, many in 1996 felt strongly that people could be safe only when they were in the ethnic majority of their country, and that every nation should have its own state (see Table 4). Even though Bosniaks still supported the ideal of a multi-ethnic state, they no longer believed they could feel safe unless they were the majority nationality. The multi-ethnic framework agreed to under the Dayton agreement left much to be desired by all three groups.

The Dayton agreement brought peace, but it failed to resolve fundamental questions about Bosnian state unity.[15] When the war ended, virtually all Bosniaks (99 percent) and a majority of Croats (65 percent) supported keeping Bosnia a unified state, while as many Serbs (96 percent) were opposed.[16] Hence, from perspective of the 1992 referenda, the Bosniaks and Serb positions had not changed over the course of the war. Bosnian Croat support, however, had eroded so that by August 1996 only one-third still favored Bosnian unity.

Table 3. Bosnians Disavow Earlier Trust

	Bosniaks	**Bosnian Croats**	**Bosnian Serbs**
Even before the war, I never trusted Bosnian Muslims			
Agree	-	73	71
Disagree	-	25	27
Even before the war, I never trusted Bosnian Serbs			
Agree	63	19	-
Disagree	36	70	-
Even before the war, I never trusted Bosnian Croats			
Agree	14	-	64
Disagree	85	-	34
Bosnian Muslims, Croats, and Serbs have hated each other for centuries			
Agree	16	66	80
Disagree	83	34	17
Given our history, Bosnian Serbs, Croats, and Muslims will never be able to live peacefully together			
Agree	15	77	91
Disagree	83	21	7
Do you believe Croats, Muslims, and Serbs can live together again in the country or has the war done too much damage for them to live peacefully together anymore?			
Can live together peacefully	65	10	6
Too much damage has been done	34	88	89

Office of Opinion Research survey, August 1996

Despite opposition to Bosnian unity in principle, a majority of Serbs (67 percent), Croats (74 percent), and Bosniaks (85 percent) supported the Dayton Agreement in practice. Though many felt the Dayton accords were "forced on us by the West,"[17] as many also said that accepting Dayton was a better option than continuing the war.[18] Still, nearly half of Serbs (48 percent) and Croats (49 percent), and a large minority of Bosniaks (36 percent) were not confident that Dayton would result in a lasting peace.[19] An overwhelming majority of Serbs

(91 percent) and a majority of Croats (62 percent) and Bosniaks (68 percent) thought that fighting would again break out in the next few years.[20]

Table 4. Assessing the Damage Done by Conflict on Ethnic Tolerance

	Bosniaks/Muslims		**Bosnian Croats**		**Bosnian Serbs**	
	1989	1996	1989	1996	1989	1996
People can feel safe only when they are the majority nationality in their country						
Agree	11	55	17	93	13	96
Disagree	82	39	76	7	81	3
Every nation should have its own state						
Agree	6	17	14	88	5	98
Disagree	88	80	80	11	88	1
Nationally mixed marriages are unstable/generally not a good thing						
Agree	25	54	29	81	23	65
Disagree	69	31	61	17	70	32

Consortium for Social Research Institutes of Yugoslavia survey, 1989; Office of Research survey, August 1996

While the Serbs were eager to end the war, they were also wary of governing with former adversaries. Although virtually all Serbs (98 percent) favored the creation of the Serb Republic under Dayton, as many (98 percent) agreed that the Serb Republic should ideally be part of Serbia.[21] In January 1997, 91 percent said it would be better to be independent than to remain part of Bosnia and 95 percent agreed that their future lies more with Serbia than with Bosnia-Herzegovina.[22] Virtually all Bosnians Serbs also held strong negative views of the United States, the EU, and NATO for their role in the conflict and post-war mission in Bosnia (see Appendix Figures 7-12).

Within the Federation, Bosnian Croats and Bosniaks were growing weary of one another as well. Many Bosnian Croats (56 percent) viewed Bosniaks unfavorably at the war's end which only grew worse over the following year (up to 88 percent unfavorable) as the difficulties of shared-governance became more apparent to both. Though most Bosniaks (77 percent) had favorable views of Bosnian Croats when the war ended, half (51 percent) soured within a year as cooperation in the Federation broke down. In December 1995 a majority of Croats (58 percent) had supported the Muslim-Croat Federation, but by January 1997, a majority (57 percent) opposed it. Instead, most Croats (74 percent) wanted the Herzegovina section of the Federation to become part of Croatia, 84 percent would choose independence over remaining in Bosnia if given the chance, and 90 percent felt their future lies more with Croatia than Bosnia. Though the war had ended, Bosnia's future as a multi-ethnic state remained in peril.

Ethnic Relations after International Intervention

Post-war Bosnia exists as a product of international intervention where institutions are endogenous to a broader international framework of support. Without a strong international civilian and military presence on the ground in Bosnia to enforce the Dayton agreement, 1996 might have ended differently, possibly with the collapse of the Dayton framework and recurrence of ethnic violence. Though Bosnian Serbs vilified and Bosnian Croats were wary of NATO, the EU, and the United States, they did not trust each other to abide by the terms of the peace agreement and therefore turned to international monitors as a pragmatic alternative to more violence. The international presence was also agreeable to Serbia and Croatia, and it is likely that both countries would have heightened tensions within Bosnia if not for a deterring international presence. Still, when the war ended, Bosnia was internally divided and not capable of functioning without international guidance and pressure. Today, this essential feature of Bosnian politics is still true, reflected most recently in the inability to form a national government for over a year and a half. However, some important aspects of Bosnian society have shown improvement since the war, and public opinion has become a vital metric for gauging the success of international intervention.

The scarcity of pre-war data on Bosnia is matched by an abundance of post-war opinion monitoring.[23] Among many organizations conducting opinion polling in Bosnia today, the Office of Research at the State Department has some of the best tracking data on social attitudes across ethnicities. Between 1995 and 2005, survey respondents were asked whether they had favorable or unfavorable views of other ethnic groups living in Bosnia. The trends on this question are illuminating of the remarkable changes in social attitudes that have taken place since the war ended (See Appendix Figures 1-6).

Bosniaks emerged from the war allied with their former adversaries, the Bosnian Croats.[24] Though tensions arose over power sharing governance in 1996, it only had a short-term negative impact on otherwise positive attitudes toward their co-equals in the Federation. The same cannot be said of the Bosnian Croats—a majority of whom held unfavorable views of both Bosniaks and Bosnian Serbs until 2001. The period between 2001 and 2002 was an important tipping point for Bosnian Croat opinion, possibly brought about or reflected in the short-lived multi-ethnic coalition, *Alliance for Change*, which broke through war-time divisions. Though the coalition would ultimately collapse, it may have signaled to ordinary Bosnian Croats that shared governance can be possible.

This also marks the point where Bosniak majorities begin to express favorable views of Bosnian Serbs.

For Bosnian Serbs, the path toward social reconciliation has taken much longer. In 1997, for a brief moment, the trajectory of Bosnian Serb opinion looked as though they were warming to Bosnian Croats and Bosniaks, but conflicts over governance likely caused Bosnian Serbs to reverse course. Trend data from 1997-2005 show little positive movement in Bosnian Serb attitudes toward the other ethnic groups. However, by 2011, when this trend question was again re-examined, Bosnian Serbs had undergone a major transformation in social attitudes in the past five years, but it is not clear exactly when or how quickly the change has occurred.

At the end of 2011, polls show for the first time that a majority of all three major ethnic groups view each other favorably (see Figure 1). At least half of Bosnians also say they would now feel safe within each other's ethnic communities (Appendix Table 1).[25] At the very least, Bosnians believe they can avoid another war, live peacefully as neighbors, respect one another's religion, work together in business, and possibly even be close friends (see Table 5). Though Bosnians may never truly forgive the crimes of the past, they appear able and willing to co-exist peacefully.[26]

Figure 1. Despite Political Divisions, Bosnians View Each Other Favorably

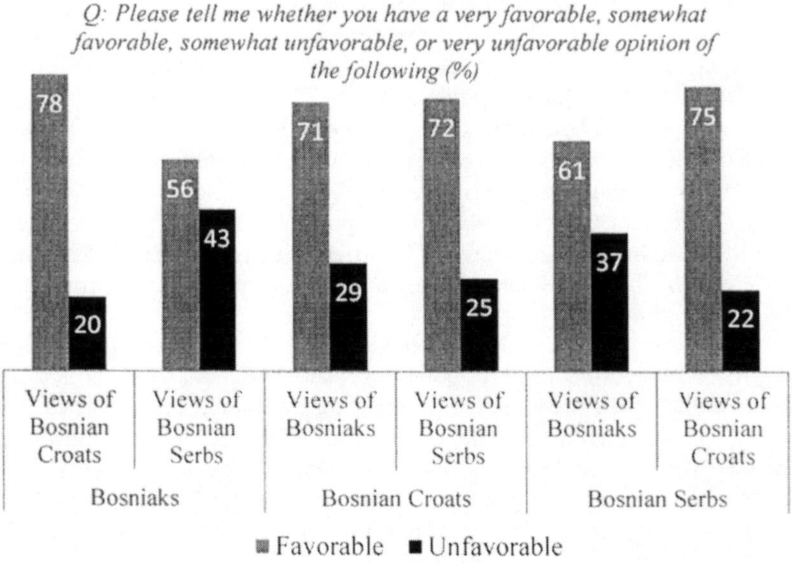

Source: Office of Research surveys, Nov.2011

Table 5. Bosnians Can Reconcile Socially, not Politically

Q: Given the way things are now, to what extent do you think Bosnian Serbs, Croats, and Bosniaks will be able to do the following? (percent)

	Bosnian Serbs		Bosniaks		Bosnian Croats	
	Yes	No	Yes	No	Yes	No
Avoid another war	80	18	75	21	86	11
Respect each other's religion	69	30	78	21	79	19
Live peacefully as neighbors	69	30	74	25	73	24
Work together in business	83	15	88	10	88	11
Be close friends	55	42	63	35	45	52
Forgive the crimes of the past	22	76	21	77	23	73
Support the Same Political Leaders	32	66	32	67	20	78

Source: Office of Research Survey, Nov. 2011

Though social tolerance is only one part of the broader story of Bosnian public opinion, it is nonetheless an important milestone in Bosnia's post-war history. This may be little consolation to policymakers who are focused on resolving Bosnia's perennial political stalemates. While Bosnians may be reconciling on a personal level, some still see major ethnic divisions in their society. More than half of Bosniaks (55 percent) and Bosnian Serbs (61 percent) think relations between the two groups are still bad, and four-in-ten Bosnians and Bosnian Croats feel the same about their groups' relations.[27] While Bosnians believe they might be able to put aside differences for the sake of business, a majority do not think they can support the same political leadership, which is divided along ethnic lines.

When asked what they think is the greatest threat to stability in Bosnia-Herzegovina today, the most popular response was "our own politicians."[28] Looking through the list of leading political figures and political parties in Bosnia today, not one has the confidence and trust of a majority of all three ethnic groups (see Table 6 and Appendix Table 2). Instead, each group tends to support and trust their own, and there is little chance that one will emerge from the current crop of contenders as a political unifier. However, many Bosnians are also dissatisfied with their own group's leadership. When asked in open-ended questions "who is the most trusted politician in Bosnia today?," "no one" is an ever-popular response (see Table 6).

Table 6. No Common Consensus on Political Leadership, or Trust

Q: Please tell me whether you have a very favorable, somewhat favorable, somewhat unfavorable, or very unfavorable opinion of... (percent with favorable opinion)

	Bosnian Serbs	Bosniaks	Bosnian Croats
Bakir Izetbegovic	3	47	13
Zlatko Lagumdzija	5	56	19
Zeljko Komsic	9	80	29
Dragan Covic	23	10	57
Nebojsa Radmanovic	60	7	14
Milorad Dodik	63	3	21

Q: Which political figure in Bosnia do you trust the most? (percent)

	Bosnian Serbs	Bosniaks	Bosnian Croats
Zeljko Komsic	1	40	5
Milorad Dodik	25	0	1
Dragan Covic	1	0	28
No one	43	31	33

Source: Office of Research Survey, Nov. 2011

One of the over-arching concerns today is the inability to make progress on resolving Bosnia's final status, where each group holds mutually unacceptable views (see Figure 2). A large majority of Bosniaks want reforms that will further deepen integration and unity. Bosnian Serbs are divided between keeping things as they are under the Dayton Accords or quitting Bosnia either for independence or unification with Serbia. While most Bosnian Serbs (88 percent) support the Dayton framework in principle, a large minority (45 percent) oppose the provision of the Dayton Agreement that Bosnia must remain a unified state, and eight-in-ten are opposed to any transfer of power away from RepublikaSrpska.[29] If provoked, most Bosnian Serbs (78 percent) feel they have the right to declare independence from Bosnia if they choose to, and six-in-ten would vote in favor of independence if given the chance.[30]

Bosnian Croats are also deeply dissatisfied with institutions created under the Dayton Agreement. Only a quarter (24 percent) desire greater integration in a unified Bosnian state. Instead, about half (53 percent) want to divide Bosnia

Figure 2. Bosnians Can't Agree on Roadmap for the Future

Q: Of the following political arrangements, which would you say is your ideal choice for the future? (%)

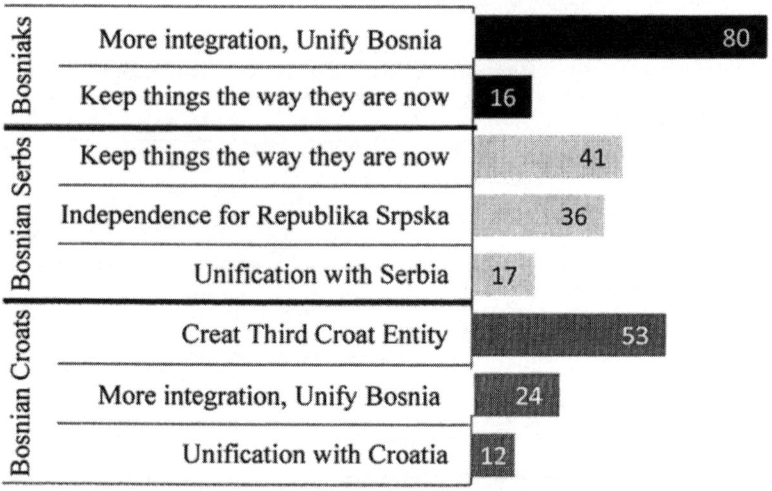

Source: Office of Opinion Research survey, Nov. 2011

even further by creating a separate regional entity for Bosnian Croats. Only a small minority now say unification with Croatia (12 percent) is their ideal choice. Bosnian Croats are also regionally divided. Croats in Central Bosnia are stronger supporters of Bosnian unity and integration and less supportive of establishing a third entity than those in Herzegovina.[31] Support for unification with Croatia is strongest in Herzegovina, where a majority (66 percent) believes they have—in principle—the right to declare independence from Bosnia in the future if needed. While talk about constitutional changes and reforms are ongoing, Bosnians are doubtful that any major changes in the status quo will take place in the next decade (see Table 7). More Serbs think RepublikaSrpska will not declare independence than will. More Bosnian Croats in Herzegovina predict that they will get a third entity but those in Central Bosnia disagree. Finally, though six-in-ten Bosniaks predict greater unity in the future, seven-in-ten Bosnian Croats and Serbs disagree and would vote against greater integration in a hypothetical referendum.[32]

Finally, though eight-in-ten Bosnians want to believe they are capable of avoiding another war, some are still fearful for the future. A sizable minority of Bosnian Croats (35 percent), a large minority of Serbs (42 percent), and more than half of Bosniaks (56 percent) worry about possible conflict in the next few years.[33] Nearly half (46 percent) of Bosnian Croats and Serbs also think it is unlikely that Bosnia will be a unified state ten years from now, compared to only a minority of Bosniaks (26 percent). Hence, even though Bosnians have made tremendous strides reconciling socially in the fifteen years since the war, fundamental questions about Bosnia's future as a multi-ethnic unified state are still being raised.

Table 7. Predictions for the Future—More of the Same

Q: Given the way things are now, to what extent do you think the following events are likely to happen in Bosnia—would you say definitely yes, probably yes, probably no, or definitely no (percent)

RepublikaSprksa will vote for independence			
	Bosnian Serbs	**Bosniaks**	**Bosnian Croats**
Yes	42	17	35
No	51	79	61
The Federation will split into separate Bosniak and Bosnian Croat entities			
	Bosnian Serbs	**Bosniaks**	**Bosnian Croats**
Yes	38	7	43
No	55	90	53
Bosnian Croats will declare independence from Bosnia			
	Bosnian Serbs	**Bosniaks**	**Bosnian Croats**
Yes	30	8	28
No	60	90	67
The Federation and RepublikaSrpska will become more fully integrated into Bosnia			
	Bosnian Serbs	**Bosniaks**	**Bosnian Croats**
Yes	24	59	26
No	70	37	69

Source: Office of Research Survey, Nov. 2011

Dissatisfied with the Status Quo

While Bosnians disagree on whether or not to pursue constitutional reforms, they agree that the current system is not working. Though ethnically divided on many fronts, Bosnian citizens are united in their frustration over the dismal state of the economy and perception of widespread corruption.[34] Most Bosnians (77 percent) point to the economy over ethnic tensions (2 percent) or political reform (5 percent) as the critical issue facing the country today. In general, nine-in-ten Bosnians think their country is headed in the wrong direction and believe authorities are doing a poor job promoting economic development, creating jobs, and fighting corruption (see Figure 3).

Figure 3. Bosnians Speaking with One Voice on Economy, Corruption

Q: Please tell me whether you think that the authorities in the Federation/RS have been doing a good job or a poor job on the following? (% who say poor job)

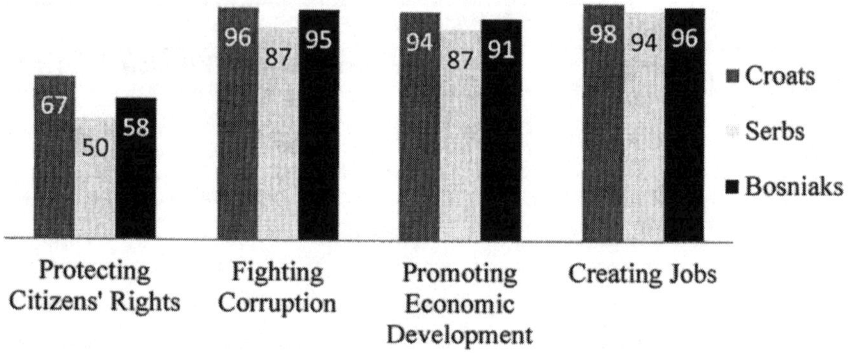

Source: Office of Research survey, Nov. 2011

With one of the highest unemployment rates in Europe (officially 43 percent in 2010), half (53 percent) say that lack of jobs is the most important issue facing Bosnia today. Virtually all (95 percent) think the current Bosnian economy is performing poorly and that authorities are failing to create jobs. Nearly half (47 percent) feel their current household financial situation is bad, where three-in-ten say they only have enough money for food. Bosnians see little hope that the economy will improve. Four-in-ten think that the economy will remain the same at least over the next year, and even more (46 percent) fear it will become worse. In a desperate economy, a large majority (86 percent) is also worried about growing corruption, and nearly half (49 percent) think corruption levels have gotten worse in recent years.

Path for European Integration

Many Bosnians increasingly look to European integration as the solution to domestic political stalemates, economic malaise, crime, and corruption. The emergence of a shared desire for EU inclusion could be the best hope for pressuring consensus on institutional reforms. Bosnian Serbs, in particular, appear to be making peace with the European Union, setting aside old animosities in favor of increasing economic and security partnerships. For the first time since the war in Bosnia ended, a majority of Bosnian Serbs (60 percent) view the EU favorably, (Appendix Figure 7). There is also now strong support among Bosnian Serbs for future EU membership (73 percent), up from about half (52 percent) just a year ago. Even though most lack confidence in specific aspects of the EU's police mission (74 percent) and military force (79 percent) in Bosnia, more than half (55 percent) say the EU's *overall* impact on Bosnia is positive.[35]

Bosnian Croats and Bosniaks are also strong advocates of EU integration.[36] An overwhelming majority of Bosniaks (98 percent) and Bosnian Croats (94 percent) want EU membership for Bosnia. Bosniaks have shown strong support for EU integration since the war, and nine-in-ten Bosniaks view the EU favorably today (Appendix Figure 8). Though many Bosnian Croats lacked confidence in the EU in the past, attitudes have shifted within the last decade as Croatia made progress on EU accession. Now eight-in-ten view the EU favorably (Appendix Figure 9).

The European Union is the *only* important economic and security partnership that Bosnian Serbs, Croats, and Bosniaks can all agree upon (Appendix Table 3). However, it is unclear whether the European Union, facing its own internal crises, sees Bosnia's candidacy as a serious priority. While Bosniaks and Bosnian Croats also support NATO membership and security ties to the United States, Bosnian Serbs still look primarily to Serbia and Russia and oppose NATO (Appendix Figure 10). Though the United States has made strong commitments to preserving a multi-ethnic Bosnian state, it has credibility problems with the Bosnian Serbs (Appendix Figure 13). Hence, while Bosnians may be increasingly speaking with one voice on the economy and EU integration, the same cannot be said of the broader international community and Bosnia's neighbors. More than fifteen years since the post-war reconstruction began, Bosnia's future in Europe remains uncertain.

Conclusions

International intervention brought an end to the war, but Bosnia became an international protectorate rather than transitioning into a fully self-governing multi-ethnic state. Though Bosnia appears to be making important progress on rebuilding foundations for social cooperation following the war, political divisions remain, stymieing prospects for constitutional reform.[37] In the meantime, Bosnians are fed up with the state of their economy, and look to the EU for a better future, but EU integration may be delayed indefinitely by failure to make progress on domestic institutional reforms. Serbia and Russia may also find cause to strengthen ties over NATO expansion and Kosovo, undermining prospects for a comprehensive strategy for integrating all the former Yugoslav successor states into a common economic and security framework.

The lessons I draw from examining public opinion in the Bosnian case are that international intervention has helped Bosnians to overcome polarizing ethnic divisions in their society as a result of the war. By monitoring and enforcing the terms of the Dayton Agreement, international intervention provided stability necessary for revitalizing foundations for social cooperation. However, more effort needs to be applied to post-war institutional development. If integrating former rivals into a common state is a realistic and desirable goal, the question is how to create institutions that will give rival parties enough incentives not only to stop fighting but also start them on a path toward greater trust, cooperation, and shared governance? This is challenging because institutions are often forged in an environment where mutual trust and credibility are lacking. If post-war institutions are a product of the divisions people held at the time, then they are unlikely to maximize opportunities for cooperation. Rather than alleviating problems, institutions could further entrench social divisions where they exist and possibly lead groups back into conflict. Moreover, post-war institutions may not be easily amenable to change further down the road, as is now the case in Bosnia. Even if foundations for social cooperation emerge or revitalize, as in Bosnia, would institutions nurture them or simply leave them to stagnation? If the latter is true, it is unclear how long such an arrangement could or should last.

Finally, public opinion suggests that Bosnia's dependence on international actors for security and stability could continue indefinitely under the current political arrangements. While Bosnians appear to be putting aside war-time divisions, they are still living under rigid postwar institutional arrangements that inhibit social cooperation from crossing over into the political realm. The problem and consequences of ethnic division and stalemate is something the Bosnian public understands all too well. They agree that the current system is not working and share a common vision for a European future, but acknowledge that they lack the political environment to make things happen. Fifteen years after the end of the war, Bosnians still seek international leadership to bridge ethnic political divides and move Bosnia toward greater European economic and security integration.

Notes

1. For details on Yugoslav polling, see S. Woodward, "How Not to End a Civil War," in *Civil Wars, Insecurity, and Intervention,* eds. B. Walter and J. Snyder (New York, Columbia University Press, 1999). For details on Yugoslav polling, see Gabor Toka, *An Inventory of Political Attitude & Behavior Surveys in East Central Europe & the Former Soviet Union (1989-1997)* (Bergisch Gladbach, Germany: Erwin Ferger, 2000).

2. A smaller follow-up study was conducted by the Yugoslav Consortium in 1990 with a sample size of 4,232 of which only 675 were sampled in Bosnia. See Government of Yugoslavia, "Public Opinion Survey on the Federal Executive Council's Social and

Economic Reform," *Yugoslav Survey* 31, no. 3 (1990): 3-26. Here I will focus on the results from the more extensive 1989 survey.

3. See Woodward, "How Not to End a Civil War," for a discussion regarding Yugoslav-era survey research topics

4. See R. Kaplan, *Balkan Ghosts: A Journey Through History* (New York: St. Martin's Press, 1993) as an early example and, more recently, J. Mueller, "The Banality of 'Ethnic War,'" *International Security* 25, no. 1 (2008): 42-70.

5. In the municipal and general elections of 1990, ethnic-nationalist parties won pluralities over multi-ethnic or cross-national parties. Voters were subsequently polarized along ethnic lines in the 1991 and 1992 referenda on remaining in Yugoslavia or voting for Bosnian independence. It is a fascinating question as to why Bosnians fractured along ethnic lines on party identification and voting, but it is sadly not a question that can be adequately answered by available public opinion data and is beyond the scope or ability of this chapter to answer.

6. See opinion studies by: R. Hodson, D. Sekulic and G. Massey, "National Intolerance in the Former Yugoslavia," *American Journal of Sociology* 99, no. 6 (1994): 1534-58; S. Burg and M. Berbaum, "Community, Integration, and Stability in Multinational Yugoslavia," *The American Political Science Review* 83, no. 2 (1989): 535-54; Sekulic, Massey, and Hodson, "Who were the Yugoslavs? Failed Sources of a Common Identity in the Former Yugoslavia," *American Sociological Review* 59, no. 1 (1994): 83-97; Massey, Hodson, and Sekulic, "Ethnic Enclaves and Intolerance: The Case of Yugoslavia," *Social Forces* 78, no. 2 (1999): 669-91; and R. Kunovich and R. Hodson, "Ethnic Diversity, Segregation, and Inequality: A Structural Model of Ethnic Prejudice in Bosnia and Croatia," *Sociological Quarterly* 43, no. 2 (2002): 185-212.

7. The index consisted of responses to the following agree/disagree questions. "Nationally mixed marriages are more unstable than others," "Every nation must have its own state," "Among nationalities it is possible to create good cooperation, but not full trust," and the question "How important is nationality to you personally in choosing a spouse."

8. A follow-up 1990 Yugoslav consortium survey highlights growing concern about the governing crisis, but Bosnians did not think the crisis at the national level had affected "communal relations" at home. While only a small minority of Bosnians thought relations were either good or satisfactory at the national level in 1990, most (80%) thought relations were either good or satisfactory inside Bosnia. See Government of Yugoslavia, "Public Opinion Survey on the Federal Executive Council's Social and Economic Reform," (1990), 25.

9. For further insights into the question of whether norms broke down leading up to the war, see S. Woodward, *Balkan Tragedy: Chaos and Dissolution After the Cold War* (Washington, DC: Brookings Institution, 1995); S. Burg, *The War in Bosnia-Herzegovina: Ethnic Conflict and International Intervention* (New York, M. E. Sharpe, 1999); J. Mueller, "The Banality of 'Ethnic War;'" and V. Gagnon, *The Myth of Ethnic War: Serbia and Croatia in the 1990s* (Ithaca: Cornell University Press, 2004).

10. For overviews of survey research elsewhere in Eastern Europe and the former Soviet Union, see William A. Welsh, ed., *Survey Research and Public Attitudes in Eastern Europe and the Soviet Union.*(New York: Pergamon Press, 1981): 80-135; G. Toka, *An Inventory of Political Attitude and Behavior Surveys in East Central Europe and the Former Soviet Union 1989-1997* (Bergisch Gladbach, Germany: E. Ferger Verlag, 2000); and John G. Geer, ed., *Encyclopedia of Public Opinion.*(Santa Barbara, CA: ABC-Clio Press, 2004).

11. Voters were not deterred by social desirability concerns from supporting nationalist parties in the 1990 municipal and general elections. While voters do not face the same social-desirability pressures in a voting both as in a face-to-face interview, many interviews in the 1989 survey were conducted with same-ethnicity enumerators. Hence, if everyone were secretly harboring hostile views of one-another, the social-desirability bias should work *against* tolerance rather than toward tolerance. Survey respondents could have given unfavorable responses toward other ethnic groups as a way of signaling ethnic solidarity—but they did not.

12. More Bosnians also identified themselves by ethnicity and fewer as "Yugoslav" in the 1991 population census (6 percent) than in the 1989 survey (14 percent). With the next census scheduled for April 2013, it will be interesting to see how people identify on the question of ethnicity, or whether there will be irregularities in the conduct of the census.

13. The turnout rate for the March 1992 referendum was estimated at 63% of adult Bosniaks and Croats. Serbs enforced a boycott of the March referenda in their communities. I have not found information about the November 1991 turnout rate for Serbs. I suspect it was above half of the adult population. See Burg, *The War in Bosnia-Herzegovina*, for a discussion of the referendums.

14. The Office of Opinion Research conducted opinion polls annually or semi-annually in Bosnia from 1995 through 2005. These surveys were based on stratified random samples of one thousand Bosnian Serbs, one thousand Bosnian Croats, and one thousand Bosniaks. Respondents were randomly sampled within the Serb Republic and Bosnian Federation in municipalities proportionate to the population size based on post-war population estimates, since 1991 census data were no longer representative. Brcko district was only periodically surveyed as a separate sample and is not represented by these data. In the few remaining ethnically mixed neighborhoods and communities, respondents were interviewed only by enumerators of their ethnicity. A new census is currently needed to establish clear population parameters from which to draw samples. The next census was scheduled for April 2013, but because of political disagreements had to be postponed to a later date.

15. For criticism of the Dayton agreement, see S. Woodward, "How Not to End a Civil War;" R. Belloni, "Civil Society and Peacebuilding in Bosnia and Herzegovina," *Journal of Peace Research* 38, no. 2 (2001): 163-80; D. Chandler, *Bosnia: Faking Democracy after Dayton* (London: Pluto Press, 2002); S. Bose, *Bosnia after Dayton* (London: Hurst, 2002); F. Friedman, *Bosnia and Herzegovina: A Polity on the Brink* (New York: Routledge, 2004); and P. McMahon, 'Rebuilding Bosnia: A Model to Emulate or to Avoid? *Political Science Quarterly* 119, no. 4 (2004): 569-94

16. Respondents were asked in this December, 1995 survey, "What is your opinion of the provision of the Dayton Accords that Bosnia-Herzegovina will remain a unified state?"

17. When asked if you Agree or Disagree that "The Dayton Accords were forced on us by the West." virtually all Serbs (96 percent), Croats (91 percent), and an overwhelming majority of Bosniaks (87 percent) agreed with this statement in a December 1995 USIA poll.

18. Respondents were asked to choose between the following: "Some people say that whether the Dayton peace accords are just or not, the accords are better than the continued war. Others say that we should continue fighting for a just conclusion of the war, regardless of the accords." In December 1995, 76 percent of Serbs, 78 percent of Croats, and 85 percent of Bosniaks believed that the accords were better than a continued war.

19. The question was "How much confidence do you have that that these accords will result in a lasting peace?" December, 1995 survey.

20. The question was "How concerned are you that fighting might start again in a few years?" December, 1995 survey.

21. The queries here were the following: "Do you favor or oppose the existence of the Serb Republic?"(December 1995), and do you Agree or Disagree that "The Bosnian Serb Republic really should be part of Serbia." (August 1996).

22. The Agree or Disagree question was "It would be better for us to be independent than to remain part of Bosnia." "Our future lies more with Serbia than with Bosnia Herzegovina." (January 1997)

23. Many organizations have conducted public opinion surveys in Bosnia since the war, especially since 2000 when USAID/United Nations Development Programme began a regular tracking poll. Other groups have followed suit.

24. Under the March 1994 Washington Agreement, Bosnian Croats and Bosniaks established the framework for the joint Federation of Bosnia-Herzegovina that would later be incorporated into the Dayton Agreement.

25. However, three-in-ten Bosnian Serbs admit they never travel to areas outside the RepublikaSrpska. Half of Bosniaks and Bosnian Croats never travel outside the Bosniak-Croat Federation.

26. For other studies showing promising signs of trust and cooperation, see P. Pickering, "Generating Social Capital for Bridging Ethnic Divisions in the Balkans: Case Studies of Two Bosniak Cities," *Ethnic and Racial Studies* 29, no. 1 (2006): 79-103; P. Håkansson and F. Sjöholm, "Who Do You Trust? Ethnicity and Trust in Bosnia-Herzegovina," *Europe-Asia Studies* 59, no. 6 (2007): 961-976; S. Whitt and R. Wilson, "The Dictator Game, Fairness, and Ethnicity in Postwar Bosnia," *American Journal of Political Science* 51, no. 3 (2007): 655-668; K. Bakke, X. Cao, J. O'Loughlin, and M. Ward, "Social Distance in Bosnia-Herzegovina and the North Caucasus Region of Russia: Inter and Intra-Ethnic Attitudes and Identities," *Nations and Nationalism* 15, no. 2 (2009): 227-253; and Sam Whitt, "Institutions and Ethnic Trust: Evidence from Bosnia," *Europe-Asia Studies* 62, no. 2 (2010): 271-292.

27. The question was "How would you describe relations today between the following ethnic groups in Bosnia—would you say they are very good, somewhat good, somewhat poor or very poor?"

28. Respondents were given the open ended question "What do you think is the greatest threat to the existence and continuity of Bosnia today?"

29. "Do you favor or oppose the Dayton peace accords? Are you strongly in favor, somewhat in favor, somewhat opposed, or strongly opposed to Dayton?;" "What is your opinion of the provision that Bosnia Herzegovina will remain a single state—do you strongly support, somewhat support, somewhat oppose, or strongly oppose this provision?;" "There is often talk in Bosnia about increasing the authority of the central government in Sarajevo and decreasing the authority of the Federation and RS. Is this something you would strongly support, somewhat support, somewhat oppose, or strongly oppose?"

30. "Do you think Bosnian Serbs should have the right to hold a referendum on whether to become independent from Bosnia?;" "If there were a referendum today to decide the following questions, would you vote in favor or would you vote against independence for the RS from Bosnia?"

31. Six-in-ten Croats in Herzegovina desire a third entity as their ideal arrangement for the future compared to only a minority (36 percent) of Croats in Central Bosnia. A plurality of Croats in Central Bosnia (44 percent) see deeper integration as their ideal.

Only a small minority of Croats in Herzegovina (17 percent) prefer deeper integration. As many (17 percent) in Herzegovina would prefer unification with Croatia as an ideal goal. Hardly any (1 percent) Croats in Central Bosnia want to unify with Croatia.

32. "If there were a referendum today to decide the following questions, would you vote in favor or would you vote against transferring power away from the Federation and giving the central government more control?"

33. "How concerned are you that the fighting might start again in the next few years—very concerned, somewhat concerned, not very concerned, or not concerned at all?;" "In your opinion how likely is it that Bosnia and Herzegovina will be a unified state ten years from now—very likely, somewhat likely, not very likely or not at all likely?"

34. For broader discussion on the problem of corruption, see B. Divjak and M. Pugh, "The Political Economy of Corruption in Bosnia and Herzegovina," *International Peacekeeping* 15, no. 3 (2008): 373-386.

35. While Bosnian Serbs have warmed to the EU, they continue to see the United States and NATO as adversaries. Seven-in-ten Bosnian Serbs have unfavorable views of the United States and eight-in-ten feel the same about NATO.

36. In contrast to the Bosnian Serbs, they also have warm feelings toward NATO and the United States as security partners. An overwhelming majority of Bosniaks (95 percent) and a large majority of Bosnian Croats (84 percent) also want NATO membership for Bosnia, which most Serbs (72 percent) oppose. Nine-in-ten Bosniaks and eight-in-ten Bosnian Croats view NATO favorably, while eight-in-ten Bosniaks and Bosnian Croats view the United States in a positive light.

37. For further discussion on problems of constitutional reform, see P. McMahon and J. Western, "The Death of Dayton: How to Stop Bosnia from Falling Apart," *Foreign Affairs* 88 no. 5 (2009): 69-83, and T. Gromes, "Federalism as a Means of Peacebuilding: the Case of Postwar Bosnia and Herzegovina," *Nationalism and Ethnic Politics* 16, nos. 3/4 (2010): 354-374.

Appendix

Table 1. Many Bosnians Feel Safe Outside their Ethnic Communities

Q: In general, how safe do you (or would you) feel in the following places: Do you feel very safe, somewhat safe, not very safe, not at all safe? (percent)

In Bosnian Serb Communities		
	Bosniaks	**Croats**
Safe	59	57
Not Safe	37	42
In Bosnian Croat Communities		
	Bosniaks	**Serbs**
Safe	56	65
Not Safe	39	33
In Bosniak Communities		
	Serbs	**Croats**
Safe	48	62
Not Safe	47	36

Source: Office of Research Survey, Nov. 2011

Table 2. No Political Party in Bosnia Has Multi-Ethnic Support

Q: If the parliamentary elections were held tomorrow, which party would you vote for? (percent)

	Nationwide Support		
	Bosnian Serbs	Bosniaks	Bosnian Croats
Party of Democratic Action (SDA)	0	18	0
Social Democratic Party of Bosnia (SPD-BiH)	1	29	4
Alliance for a Better Future (SBB-BiH)	0	5	0
Party for Bosnia-Herzegovina (SBiH)	0	4	0
Croatian Democratic Union (HDZ)	0	0	45
Croatian Democratic Union-1990 (HDZ-1990)	0	0	16
Croatian Party of Rights (HSP)	0	0	7
Serbian Democratic Party (SDS)	15	0	0
Alliance of Independent Social Democrats (SNSD)	30	0	0
Party of Democratic Progress (PDP)	5	0	0
Other	5	3	2
Will not vote	23	23	15
Refuse to answer	13	7	5
Undecided	5	7	2
Don't know	3	4	4
Total	100	100	100

Source: Office of Research survey, Nov. 2011

Table 3. Bosnians Agree EU is an Important Security and Economic Partner

Q: Which country do you think is currently Bosnia's most important security partner? (percent volunteered)

Most Important Security Partner	Bosnian Croats	Bosnian Serbs	Bosniaks
EU	42	27	41
United States	22	3	44
Serbia	0	29	1
Croatia	29	0	4
Russia	0	27	0
Turkey	0	0	2

Q: Which country do you think is currently Bosnia's most important economic partner? (percent volunteered)

Most Important Economic Partner	Bosnian Croats	Bosnian Serbs	Bosniaks
EU	35	23	51
United States	14	2	24
Serbia	1	40	2
Croatia	44	4	9
Russia	1	22	1
Turkey	0	0	4

Source: Office of Research survey, Nov. 2011

Figure 1. Bosnian Croat Views of Bosnian Serbs (1995-2011)

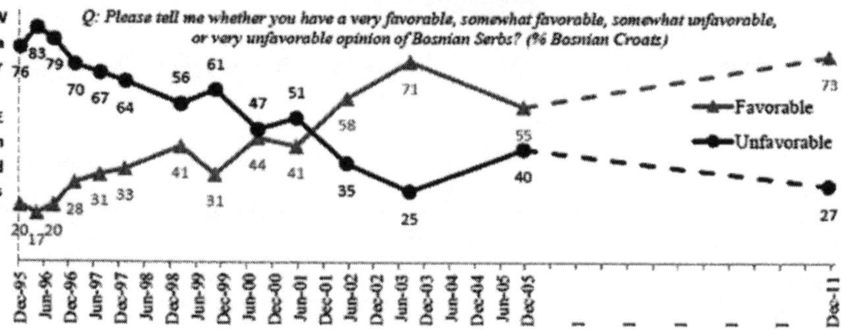

Source: Office of Research surveys, 1995-2011

Figure 2. Bosnian Croat Views of Bosniaks (1995-2011)

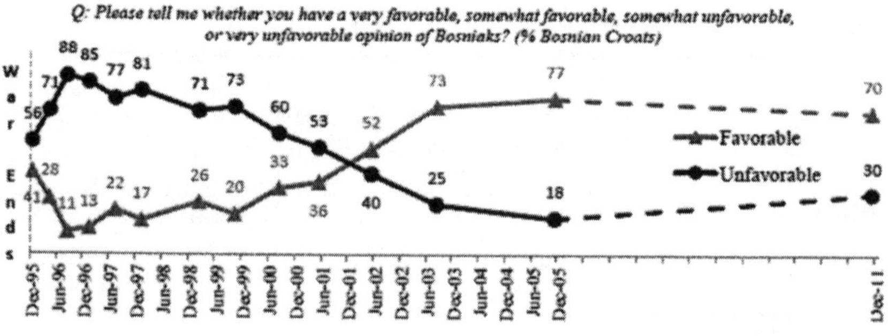

Source: Office of Research surveys, 1995-2011

Figure 3. Bosniak Views of Bosnian Croats (1995-2011)

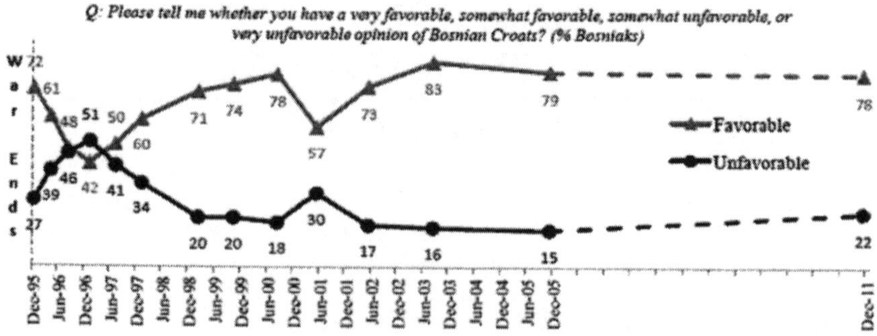

Source: Office of Opinion Research surveys, 1995-2011

Figure 4. Bosniak Views of Bosnian Serbs (1995-2011)

Q: Please tell me whether you have a very favorable, somewhat favorable, somewhat unfavorable, or very unfavorable opinion of Bosnian Serbs? (% Bosniaks)

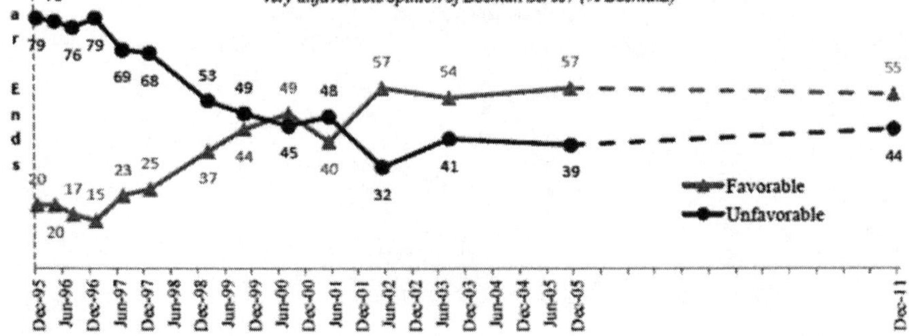

Source: Office of Research surveys, 1995-2011

Figure 5. Bosnian Serbs Views of Bosniaks (1995-2011)

Q: Please tell me whether you have a very favorable, somewhat favorable, somewhat unfavorable, or very unfavorable opinion of Bosniaks? (% Bosnian Serbs)

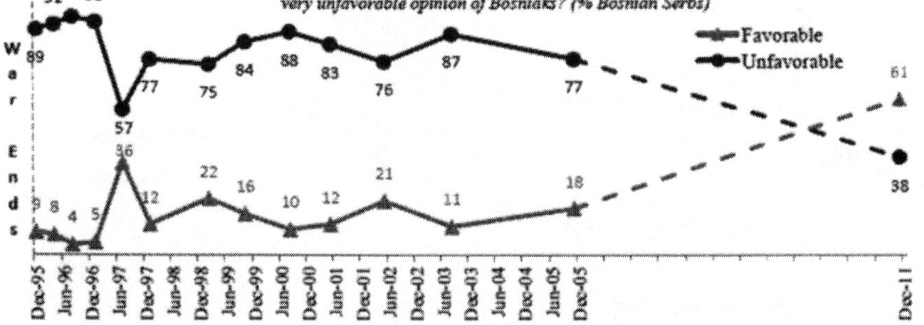

Source: Office of Research surveys, 1995-2011

Figure 6. Bosnian Serb Views of Bosnian Croats (1995-2011)

Q: Please tell me whether you have a very favorable, somewhat favorable, somewhat unfavorable, or very unfavorable opinion of Bosnian Croats? (% Bosnian Serbs)

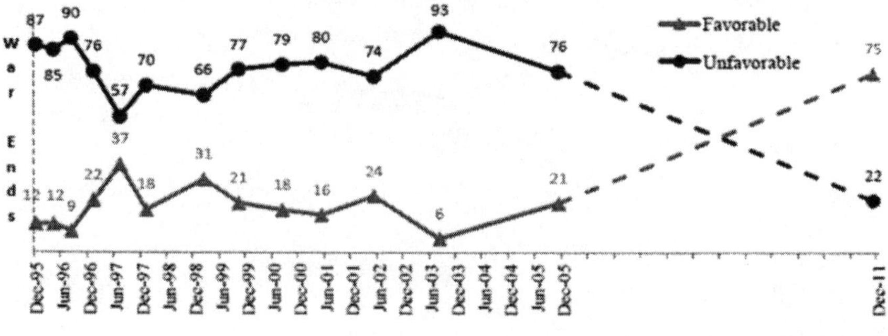

Source: Office of Research surveys, 1995-2011

Figure 7. Bosnian Serbs Now Favor EU

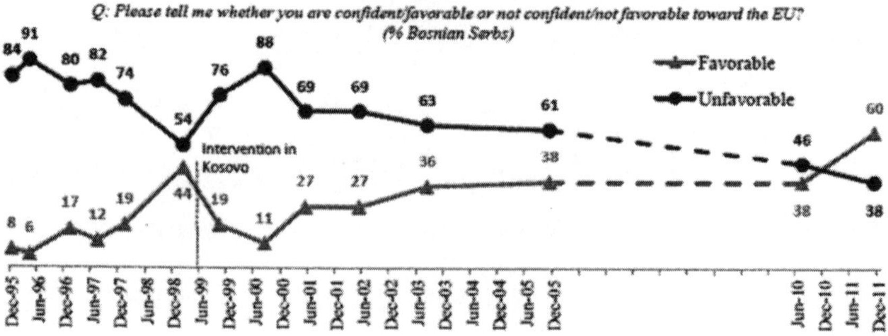

Source: Office of Research surveys, 1995-2011

Figure 8. Bosniaks Highly Favorable Toward the EU (1995-2011)

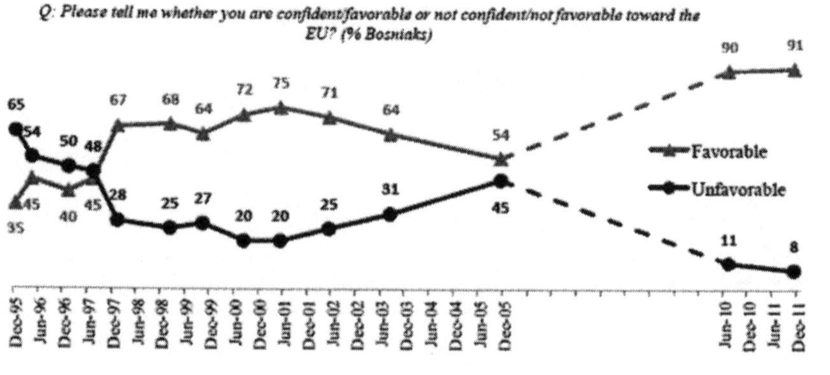

Source: Office of Research surveys, 1995-2011

Figure 9. Bosnian Croats Now View EU Favorably (1995-2011)

Source: Office of Research surveys, 1995-2011

Figure 10. Bosnian Serbs Still Opposed to NATO (1995-2011)

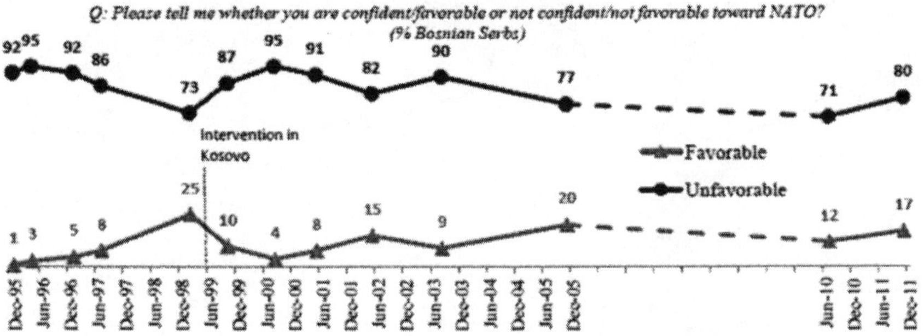

Source: Office of Research surveys, 1995-2011

Figure 11. Bosniaks Support for NATO (1995-2011)

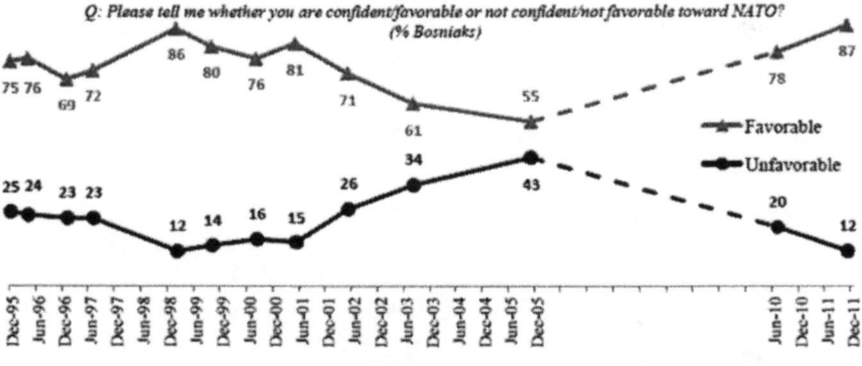

Source: Office of Research surveys, 1995-2011

Figure 12. Bosnian Croats Now Support NATO (1995-2011)

Source: Office of Research surveys, 1995-2011

Figure 13. Bosnian Serb Views of the United States (1995-2011)

Q: Please tell me whether you are confident/favorable or not confident/not favorable toward the United States? (% Bosnian Serbs)

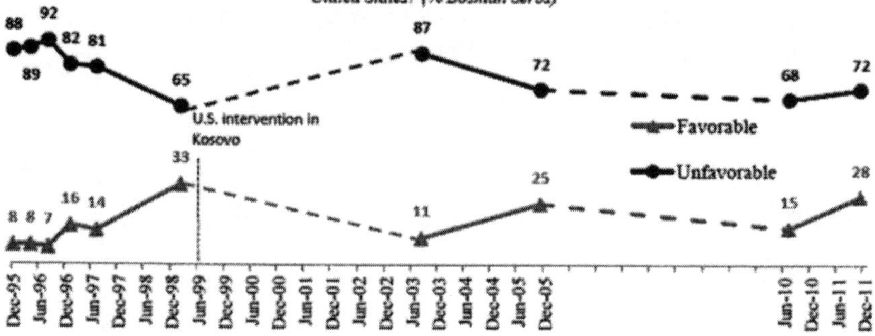

Source: Office of Research surveys, 1995-2011

Chapter 22

Whither Sovereignty? The Limits of Building States through International Administrations

Mateja Peter[1]

Peacebuilding and state-building have repeatedly been identified as one of the main challenges faced by the international community. Be it the inability to secure environments for the purposes of peace implementation or how to manage transitions and power-sharing after open conflict has ended, the topic has preoccupied both academics and practitioners. On any given day, it would be impossible to open a newspaper without reading about governance problems in countries emerging from civil wars.

This chapter examines the most extreme type of peace operation—international administrations. Through these, the international community assumes some or most of the governance roles in states emerging from violent conflict. These kinds of state-building exercises present a substantial innovation in the post-Cold War order, challenging normative ideals that a sovereign territory should always govern itself. The brutality of civil wars in the 1990s and growing humanitarian concerns foregrounded the argument that the international community should intervene when the state is incapable of governing itself through a transition period. The increasing legitimization of international intervention has undermined sovereignty as a normative ideal.

We begin with an overview of how the thinking and practice of peace operations have changed, leading to the emergence of international administrations. It continues to explore what international administrations are in greater depth before focusing on the example of Bosnia and Herzegovina, which illustrates how international administrations operate in practice and how they develop their functions and assume governance roles. This chapter teases out some of the problematic assumptions about external governance, highlighting the limits of external interventions. It concludes with thoughts on how to understand international administrations in the twenty first century.

From Keeping Peace to Building States

In the late 1970s James Crawford observed that terminology in post-conflict studies tends to be confused.[2] Although international conflict settlement and peace operations have comprised one of the more burgeoning research areas in political science, the basic terminology in the field remains contested and constantly reworked. This is largely due to the fact that the missions undertaken following the Second World War and inception of the United Nations (UN) have differed tremendously. They therefore defy straightforward categories. At the same time, these issues over terminology relate to how scholars and practitioners formulate their inquiries around particular agendas that are driven by tacit preconceptions about peacebuilding activities and the spaces in which these activities take place.

Literature in the field of keeping peace expanded gradually and came in several stages, largely reflecting developments in practice. Virginia Paige Fortna and Lisa Morje Howard (2008) write of the three waves.[3] The first and the smallest wave covers a long period of sporadic works during the Cold War, the second coincides with the newfound interest in peacekeeping around the end of the Cold War, and the third, the most systematic inquiry of the three, starts roughly at the turn of the millennium. This expansion of peacekeeping scholarship reflects the expansion and changes in peacekeeping missions since the fall of the Berlin Wall. Many studies now distinguish between "traditional" or "first generation" peacekeeping from the Cold War era and "multidimensional" or "second generation" missions of the post-Cold War era.[4] Traditional modes of peacekeeping rest on the principles of consent, neutrality, and non-intervention in internal affairs, and have largely been deployed to monitor peace agreements between two states. Conversely, multidimensional operations involve the implementation of complex peace agreements and encompass security mandates and a multitude of civilian tasks, such as organizing elections, overseeing refugee return, police training, setting up institutions, as well as various economic and developmental goals.[5] They include elements of peace enforcement and the consent of belligerents is often absent.

These missions are a response to what Mary Kaldor refers to as "new wars," that is, civil wars that defy the boundaries of sovereign territories, involve entire populations, are conducted through guerrilla and terrorist activities, and are self-financing through illicit trade.[6] While the newness of new wars has rightfully been contested,[7] there is no doubt that a new wars ideology has emerged and that this ideology has had a strong influence on the approaches taken by the international community, and particularly the institutions of the global North, to conflicts in the global South. Alternatively, some scholars have argued that the increase in the number and complexity of peace operations cannot be primarily attributed to changes in conflict areas themselves, but that the primary change came from within the intervening states themselves.[8] Nevertheless, what is generally not disputed is that these so-called "complex emergencies"—often arising around and out of new wars—have resulted in more complex intervention.[9]

Not surprisingly, these new and more complex missions brought along new vocabulary. Conflation of peacekeeping and peace enforcement, and the expansion of the areas peacekeepers were involved in, meant that the international community was now engaged less in keeping and monitoring peace and more in building peace, states, and/or nations. What used to be referred to as peacekeeping is now often equated with peacebuilding, state-building, nation building, or their substantive agendas: democratization and liberalization. These terms can take on several different meanings according to the context and the objectives for which they are used.

An early definition of the term peacebuilding can be found in the *UN Agenda for Peace*, where post-conflict peacebuilding refers to "action to identify and support structures which will tend to strengthen and solidify peace in order to avoid a relapse into conflict."[10] This kind of a broad and unsubstantive definition allowed for a plethora of different interpretations on the levels and areas of interventions in post-war societies.[11] Nevertheless, some clarifications of the original definition occurred. The 1995 *Supplement to An Agenda for Peace* emphasized the link between peacebuilding and state-building, arguing that "international intervention must extend beyond military and humanitarian tasks and must include the promotion of national reconciliation and the re-establishment of effective government."[12]

One of the most important macro-level shifts in peacebuilding strategy occurred in the late 1990s and early 2000s, when major peacebuilding agencies started stressing the construction or strengthening of legitimate governmental institutions in countries emerging from civil conflict. Peacebuilding has thus come to mean "extended international involvement that goes beyond traditional peacekeeping and peacebuilding mandates, and is directed at constructing or reconstructing institutions of governance capable of providing citizens with physical and economical safety,"[13] that is, state-building. State-building—creation of new governance institutions and/or the strengthening of existing ones with an aim to provide citizens with physical and economic security—has been recognized by both practitioners and scholars as one of the main concerns faced by the international community today.[14]

Mandates of peacekeeping/peacebuilding operations launched in the late 1980s and early 1990s encompassed quick elections and rapid bursts of economic privatization. They were heavily influenced by the triumph of democracy and capitalism with the end of the Cold War, which resulted in the expectation that "at the end of history," everyone would welcome these "universally accepted" ideas.[15] But the assumption that quick solutions could take root in post-conflict societies that lack functioning and legitimate institutions proved to be flawed.[16] In the hopes that a larger and longer-term international presence would lead to more sustainable outcomes in countries emerging from wars, the mandates of international missions expanded.

In the most extreme cases of contemporary peacebuilding, the international community has temporarily taken over the functions of sovereign governments through the mechanism of international administrations. These administrations comprise the most comprehensive peacebuilding missions and can have direct legislative, executive, and judicial powers over the governed territory. Building on the labels of "first" and "second" generation operations, it has been suggested that, given the complexity of contemporary international administrations, we could even talk about a further generation of peacekeeping.[17] Conversely, Ralph Wilde has argued that labeling international administrations as a "third generation" peacekeeping is problematic as it presents them as a natural evolution through successive steps of increasing complexity and consequentially disguises the political nature of the external governance of a territory by an international actor.[18] This criticism points to an important distinction. Besides the regulative tasks of "traditional" peace operations, the scope of authority afforded to international administrations demonstrates the international community's wish to directly influence and shape local actors in accordance with broader sets of social and political principles.

There is no universal agreement within the international community on the specific purposes of peace operations. Despite this heterogeneity, however, some general trends in the practices of peace operations have emerged. Contemporary multidimensional peacebuilding operations—and international administrations in particular—are based on an assumption that certain modes of governance can be transposed from the global North to the global South. Exogenous state-building is perceived as being able to supplement (and in the most extreme cases substitute) endogenous solutions.

These missions have also been fundamentally shaped by the democratic peace thesis. This thesis, articulated in the 1980s by Michael W. Doyle and based on numerous quantitative studies, holds that democracies rarely go to war with each other.[19] Promotion of democracy therefore becomes an integral element of peacebuilding and peace maintaining. Democracy is often presented as a panacea for peace. Piki Ish-Shalom argues that *theoretical constructions* of the democratic peace thesis are transformed into *public conventions* and then into *political convictions* that are exhibited in the real-world politics of interventions.[20] This finding can also be observed in policy works and scholarly literature where peacebuilding is often used interchangeably with democratization.

Economic liberalization is another policy that is considered to promote peace, based on the idea that economic growth reduces hatreds of previously fighting factions and trade becomes too beneficial to disrupt through armed conflict.[21] A free-market orientation is considered the best recipe for the development of societies whose economies have been devastated in the conflict. Liberalization therefore becomes the third component of the "Wilsonian Triad"—meaning peace, democracy and, free markets.[22] The underlying logic of interventions is that democratization through elections and human rights protection, and free market reform through privatization and developmental policies, will ultimately create peace and stability in post-conflict societies. While strong neo-liberal policies have come under severe criticism, and the sequencing, speed of reform, and degrees of outside intervention are constantly contested, the content of the peacebuilding agenda of international institutions remains fairly consistent. The main change is in the increasing complexity of these missions and the tasks they undertake.

International Administrations

International administration is a particular form of peacebuilding and state-building exercise, and is the best example of the so-called "heavy footprint" peace operations. Through international administration some or all of the traditionally sovereign powers are temporarily transferred from the hosting state to an actor representing the international community. Although not entirely without precedent,[23] their emergence and subsequent proliferation in the 1990s was a substantial innovation in post-conflict management and poses a challenge to the post Second World War order, which is premised on the idea of a community of sovereign states.[24]

Precisely because international administrations challenge contemporary understandings of sovereignty, while at the same time resembling historical forms of overseas domination, they have often been referred to as military occupations or neo-colonial enterprises.[25] Nevertheless, these brandings, because they are so transparent and immediately reveal the critical nature of their authors, are probably less problematic from the perspective of academic research than terms more closely associated with legal management of foreign territories—especially trusteeships and protectorates.

International administrations are often falsely branded as trusteeships.[26] Although sharing many characteristics with contemporary international administrations, trusteeship has a very clear meaning, as defined in Chapter XII of the United Nations Charter. Article 77 of the Charter confines the territories, which may be placed under a trusteeship agreement to three precise categories: mandate territories, territories seized from enemy states in the Second World War, and those voluntarily placed under the trusteeship system by states responsible for their administration. It leaves no space for contemporary administration of territories emerging from a violent conflict. Moreover, while international administration is under control and answerable to some kind of an international body, this body is not necessarily the United Nations. An example of this is the international administration of Bosnia and Herzegovina, where the Office of the High Representative (OHR) is accountable to a multilateral body called the Peace Implementation Council (PIC). The composition of these contemporary supervisory bodies differs from the UN Trusteeship Council in ways that impact the management of the territory. Confusing the two concepts is therefore not only erroneous but also misleading.

International administrations should also not be confused with protectorates or protected states. A protectorate is a political entity that consents through a treaty to enter in a relationship with another, stronger, state, from which it derives protection against other states in exchange for some obligations. While most of these criteria also apply to international administrations—treaty based, protection against other parties, and some kind of reciprocal obligation—a substantial difference is the multilateral character of contemporary administrations. Protectorates were traditionally governed by a single state. However, the development of legal and political norms in the second half of the twentieth century brought along an understanding that, for an administration to be legitimate, it needs to be accountable to a multilateral body.[27]

Although there is no conclusive definition on what contemporary international administrations are, and in practice they have taken various forms assuming different degrees of authority, some common characteristics can be discerned.

International administrations are always part of larger international efforts to address post-conflict reconstruction. They are established in those territories where local governance structures are either missing or are deemed unable to govern the territory. These operations often take over civilian functions, replacing or complementing administrative tasks of national governments, normally leaving the broader security concerns to a separate military mission. At the same time, they operate alongside other multilateral and single-state civilian organizations and agencies, making them only one of the international actors on the ground.

International administrations are also always multilateral and answerable to an international body. With UN Security Council authorization they have a legal right to operate even in territories where the hosting state would object to their establishment; an example of this would be the UN Interim Administration Mission in Kosovo (UNMIK). Arguments in favor of these mechanisms emphasize their multilateral character and accountability structures, which differentiate them from occupations and protectorates. Under what conditions these operations possess legitimacy and whether it is ever possible for an external actor unaccountable to the local population to be legitimate are questions of substantial debate among both lawyers as well as political philosophers. Topics range from practical issues of accountability to discussions on influences international administrations have on the social contract between people and the state.

Another common characteristic of international administration is their transient nature. All international administrations are temporary arrangements and even those of seemingly infinite duration envisage an end state. In some cases, their termination is clearly defined, as in the case of UN Transitional Administration in East Timor (UNTAES), where it was agreed that the transitional administration would cease with the proclamation of independence of Timor-Leste from Indonesia. Some, specifically those in Bosnia and Herzegovina and Kosovo, seem more open-ended; their completion is contingent on successful implementation of a broader agenda. But even in these seemingly endless missions, the end goal is to relinquish complete authority to the local population.

Contemporary international administrations entail the most comprehensive governance of all peace operations. Even in those cases where their mandates and responsibilities are limited—such as in the case of the UN Transitional Authority in Cambodia (UNTAC)—these operations involve aspects of governance beyond traditional peacekeeping. The scope of authority afforded to international administrations specifically mandates intervention into the domestic order and the creation of local actors and political systems according to a particular normative agenda—one that rests on the (liberal) peacebuilding consensus.[28]

International administrations serve as arbiters and openly confer or withdraw legitimacy from local actors and processes. Richard Caplan refers to this as governance of a comprehensive nature.[29] Through varying degrees of executive, legislative, and/or judicial power, international administrations provide solutions that the "international community" deems most desirable for war-torn countries. All peace operations are able to employ a range of instruments of intervention into the territory to which they are designated—such as, monitoring and verification, good offices and mediation, and sometimes conditionality. However, international administration is unique in that it can also rely on direct enforcement mechanisms. These are part of its mandate.

The International Administration of Bosnia and Herzegovina

In November 1995, an American city of little significance to international audiences received unprecedented media coverage. Dayton, Ohio—or more precisely a United States Air Force base lying on its outskirts—was the site of US-led three week negotiations that produced the document ending the war in Bosnia and Herzegovina (Bosnia, BiH).[30] By the time the Dayton Peace Agreement[31] was initialed and signed, the wars in the former Yugoslavia had been raging for more than four years. Sarajevo, the capital of Bosnia and Herzegovina, had after 1,479 days of shelling become the longest besieged capital city in the history of modern warfare. The bloodiest war that Europe had seen since the end of the Second World War was happening right on the doorsteps of a Western world that was celebrating its victory over communism and anticipating a new order in which everyone accepted the Wilsonian ideals of peace, democracy, and free markets.

Throughout the wars in the former Yugoslavia, the international community was heavily involved in negotiating and proposing peace agreements. A series of peace plans—some initially adopted—were eventually rejected by one party or another.[32] Disagreements inside the international community over what kind of settlement was desirable further impeded the success of these initiatives. So when the Dayton Accords were being negotiated, the breakdown of negotiations or the failure to translate the document into reality would not have come as a big surprise. Lacking a decisive victory ending in unconditional surrender, the drafters needed to carefully balance the interests of all sides. The agreed accords, with their eleven annexes, detailed a multi-level political structure at state, entity, and cantonal levels. They effectively divided a country of roughly four million into small pockets of influence, each controlled by one of the three main ethnic groups—Bosniaks,[33] Croats, and Serbs. Linking these was a weak state-level structure with a heavily circumscribed list of responsibilities, with most of the powers remaining at entity and cantonal level.[34]

It was partly this intricate institutional structure and partly the guilt of not preventing the conflict by intervening earlier that led to an extraordinary influx of international humanitarian and state-building resources. The fragile peace explicitly called for an unprecedented involvement of international actors, giving rise to the understanding that Bosnia operates as a compromise between four parties—the three previously warring ethnic groups and the internationals. The military part of the international presence was organized under a unified chain of command. The United Nations Protection Force (UNPROFOR) deployed to the territory during the wars was replaced by the Implementation Force (IFOR), a North Atlantic Treaty Organization (NATO) led coalition comprised of both alliance members and non-members. Conversely, the civilian implementation was envisaged as a dispersed endeavor, with the Dayton Accords referring to four key civilian institutions: the Organization for Security and Co-operation in Europe (OSCE), the UN Mission in Bosnia and Herzegovina (UNMIBH), the United Nations High Commissioner for Refugees (UNHCR), and (the Office of) the High Representative (OHR).[35] Of the four, the latter is in a privileged position, tasked with a dual role of "facilitat[ing] the Parties' own efforts" and "mobiliz[ing] and, as appropriate, coordinat[ing] the activities of the organizations and agencies involved in the civilian aspects of the peace settlement."[36] Additionally, the High Representative (HiRep) was designated as "the final authority in theatre regarding interpretation of this [Dayton] Agreement on the civilian implementation of the peace settlement,"[37] a provision that in essence gave the institution of the HiRep the ability to interpret its own powers. The High Representative therefore acts not only as a coordinator of international civilian engagement but also as the international administrator of the country.

The range of powers available to the High Representative is not clearly spelled out in the Dayton document and has shifted over time. The rest of this chapter looks at how enforcement mechanisms were developed and why; how these enforcement measures were used; and how they resulted in local and international discontent. Rather than attempting to provide a complete picture of this transition, I use illustrative examples to map out the rise and decline of the international administration in Bosnia.

All Bark and No Bite

During the first year of the operation, the civilian implementation was undergoing numerous problems. While the military part met every early deadline and provided for a fairly secure environment, the civilian implementation was steadily falling behind. Local actors cooperated with the IFOR mission, for example by withdrawing their forces or transferring territories, but when it came to civilian progress on the Dayton Agreement, such as refugee return, voter registration, and constructive participation in joint committees, problems arose.

At the insistence of the US administration, the High Representative was created as a lean institution with weak powers *vis-à-vis* other international actors. Although the US saw a need for a coordinator of multiple agencies involved in the civilian implementation, it feared a strong actor outside of its control. The expectation was that the High Representative would assist both locals and internationals and serve as a central coordinating point for international endeavors but that the institution would soon be abolished. During the first months of peace implementation, the High Representative—a position at that time occupied by Carl Bildt—and his staff primarily acted as mediators/negotiators. They provided good offices and expert advice to local parties, while at the same time keeping the international community up to date on the developments in Bosnia and Herzegovina.

The initial priority for the civilian implementation was to hold elections allowing Bosnia to transition from an internationally supervised territory to a self-governing state. The Dayton Peace Accords provided that elections were to take place no more than nine months after the agreement entered into force.[38] The organization and oversight of the elections were entrusted to the OSCE. The timing of the Bosnian elections had much to do with the US presidential elections in November 1996. President Bill Clinton, who was running for re-election, was aware of the low support for the mission in both Congress and among the American public and therefore campaigned on the promise to close down the military part of the operation by the end of 1996. In order to provide for some stability in the country after the international troop withdrawal, Bosnia had to hold elections and set-up common institutions as envisaged by the peace agreement.

There is now virtually universal agreement that holding elections so soon after the war did more harm than good. Not only were there serious problems with their fairness, but they also reified and legitimized the three nationalist parties in power, making it difficult to seek compromise and continue the state-building process.[39] But at the time, despite some loud calls for postponement,[40] the views of all the key players were the opposite. Not only was there a wide agreement in the capitals[41] and between the OSCE and IFOR in support of elections, the scheduling of the first elections for September 1996 was also supported by the highest civilian implementer—the High Representative.[42] For Carl

Bildt, the decisive phase of peace implementation—setting up the country's common institutions—could only start after the elections.

Empowering the High Representative

After the elections civilian implementation was to take priority, with local parties expected to assume increasing responsibility. Although it was clear that there was still a need for troops amidst the highly unstable and potentially insecure political environment, IFOR duly completed its mission of implementing the military annexes of the Dayton Agreement. In December 1996 it was replaced by the Stabilization Force (SFOR) of 32,000 troops—approximately half the size of IFOR. On the civilian side, problems started becoming more obvious. In short, the elections marked the transition from interim arrangements to permanent institutional structures, but also brought much of the same, both in terms of people and the speed of reform, challenging the expectations held by the international community at Dayton.

To facilitate the initial functioning of the state's common institutions, the OHR prepared a Quick Start Package comprising the minimal legislative basis for the government and the country to operate. The package included laws covering foreign economic relations, citizenship and passport regulations, the setting up of the Central Bank of Bosnia and Herzegovina, the duration of the parliamentary mandate, immunity and Presidency succession, air traffic regulations, and a draft budget for 1997.[43] However, since the institutions were barely operational, the laws in the Quick Start Package failed to be adopted. Throughout 1997 the international community and the High Representative in particular urged and cajoled local parties as well as negotiated and mediated among them to try to get the country running and parties to abide by their commitments.

In May 1997 the High Representative's international supervisors, the PIC Steering Board countries, announced a new set of provisions that allowed the HiRep to ensure better co-operation of local parties. The HiRep was charged to pursue deadlines adopted by the Steering Board and to take measures in cases of non-compliance. These included introducing visa restrictions for travel abroad for obstructive politicians,[44] recommending the denial of economic assistance to municipalities that continued to tolerate persons indicted by the International Criminal Tribunal for the former Yugoslavia in public office,[45] as well as suspending media networks whose output contravened the spirit or letter of the Dayton Peace Agreement.[46] Although the international intervention was getting more intense and individuals and municipalities started feeling the consequences of non-cooperation with the internationally sponsored peace plan, the final decisions on whether to comply with conditions laid out by the High Representative remained with local politicians. This conditionality approach failed to produce significant momentum and implementation woes continued. The international community was getting more impatient with the intransigence of the local parties, in the end resorting to enforcement measures.

At a conference in Bonn in December 1997 the Peace Implementation Council "welcome[d] the High Representative's intention to use his final authority in theatre regarding interpretation of the Agreement.... in order to facilitate the resolution of difficulties by making binding decisions, as he judge[d] necessary."[47] The Bonn conclusions enabled the HiRep to pass binding interim legislation, which would remain in force until Bosnian institutions reached agreement. The final document specifically named a number of laws and set clear deadlines for the parties to agree on them. It also asked the High Representative to take appropriate measures in cases of non-compliance.[48] The so-called *Bonn powers* also gave the HiRep an authority to dismiss public officials who were obstructing the peace process.[49]

Although not clearly defined in the Dayton Accords and initially resisted by the United States, the peace agreement that ended the war in Bosnia was flexible enough to accommodate such extensions. Enforcement powers were strongly opposed to by Bosnian Serbs, who were the main obstructionists at the time, but received wide international support and thus became a reality. At a meeting in June 1998, the PIC Steering Board confirmed that the interim binding decisions were "in accordance with his [High Representative] authority under Annex 10 of the Peace Agreement."[50] While the Office of the High Representative might not have been envisaged as an international administration at the signing of the Dayton Accords, it became a reality at a review conference two years later.

Increasing Confidence of the High Representative

The Bonn powers caused a substantial buzz in both Bosnian and international circles. Nowhere before had the international community assumed such vast legislative, executive, and judicial powers over a sovereign country. Because they were a novelty in international state-building practice, neither local implementers nor their supporting capitals had a clearly developed plan for their use.

During the first year and a half, the High Representative—then Spanish diplomat Carlos Westendorp—used his enforcement powers primarily to build the external contours of the new country. The international community had set this agenda during the first two years after the Dayton Accords, yet the local parties never implemented it. The Bonn powers were therefore seen as a corrective mechanism to make up for time lost during the early days of peacebuilding. However, they had little to do with addressing the sources of obstructionism in the country.

The PIC Bonn conclusions explicitly identified a number of key laws for the HiRep to impose if not agreed upon by the parties. These laws were already part of the Sintra Communiqué from May 1997. For example, in Bonn, the PIC stipulated that a law on citizenship had to be adopted by local institutions by 15

December 1997.[51] When that did not happen, the High Representative imposed it a day later.[52] The PIC also instructed parties to reach an agreement on uniform license plates by 31 January 1998.[53] The HiRep intervened on 20 May the same year to remedy the delay.[54] The oversight body asked the HiRep to decide on a new flag and state symbols if the parties could not agree on them by themselves by 31 December 1997.[55] In February 1998 the HiRep passed a law on the flag.[56] In March he confirmed the design of bank notes.[57] Two months later he imposed the coat of arms[58] and in June 1999, a national anthem.[59] The external signifiers of a sovereign country were starting to take shape, although largely at the behest of international administration. Nevertheless, the international community had less of a plan on how to systematically address obstructionism.

The Bonn powers allowed the High Representative to dismiss public officials that were delaying peace implementation. In the first year and a half Westendorp dismissed eleven officials for a variety of reasons—individual parties often being guilty of several—indicating the multitude and the interconnectedness of problems experienced by Bosnia and Herzegovina and its international peace implementers. The main reasons for these removals were the obstruction of refugee return, corruption, and threats to the international community. But these decisions were not linked to the wider strategic policies of the international community. Although some of the offending individuals were removed, there was little change, as they would either be replaced by other obstructionist politicians or refuse to leave their positions. In one of the more high-profile instances, the President of the Republika Srpska, Nikola Poplasen, took half a year after the HiRep issued a decision on his removal to move his "presidential office" to his party headquarters.[60]

It was only two years after their inception, after the arrival of Westendorp's successor Wolfgang Petritsch, that the Bonn powers started being used more consistently and strategically. The enforcement powers left the biggest impact in the field of refugee and internally displaced persons return, especially the return of property in areas where returnees would constitute an ethnic minority. Assessments differ on the success of minority return in Bosnia,[61] but Petritsch's approach to using the Bonn powers in this area provided a coherent international policy that produced some results for the first time.

Although his predecessor had already imposed a series of decisions repealing legislation that enabled quick transfers of "abandoned" property to preferred groups[62] and the Human Rights Chamber issued a number of verdicts asking for the restitution of property, no proper enforcement was put in place. In order to remedy this situation and expedite the return process, the OHR took it upon itself to coordinate the actors that would develop the Property Law Implementation Plan (PLIP). Participating agencies besides the OHR were the UNHCR, the OSCE, the Commission for Real Property Claims, and the UNMIBH. The PIC Steering Board officially endorsed the plan at the end of November 1999.[63]

In sum, the PLIP strengthened field monitoring and reporting and provided the High Representative sufficient information on officials obstructing minority return. Besides repealing the controversial legislation, the HiRep also dismissed thirty nine officials based on the reports he received from the field. This provided enough of a deterrent for parties to cooperate and by the time PLIP concluded at the end of 2003 more than 92 percent of claims had been resolved. Although on the surface four years seem like a long time to address property restitution, it is relatively short compared to the speed with which both entities would solve cases without direct international intervention. Prior to the PLIP process, it was estimated that at the rate the cases were being resolved, the process could have taken another twenty two years in the Federation of Bosnia and Herzegovina and forty in Republika Srpska.[64]

Transcending the Limits of Enforcement Powers

By the time Paddy Ashdown became the High Representative in 2002, both the international community and locals had grown accustomed to the use of enforcement powers and the new HiRep did not shy away from using them either. Although individual decisions were still resisted and there were increasing references to local ownership, interventions by the High Representative became part of how the international community ensured Bosnia progressed in its reform process. At the same time, almost seven years after the war had ended and with new conflict spotlights emerging, the international community was losing its interest in the Balkans and wanted to close down the operation.

The institutional setup negotiated at Dayton provided for a highly decentralized state where a broad consensus was needed for reforms to take place. Over the years the High Representative attempted to serve as an actor concerned with the common interest of the country as a whole, enforcing decisions on which the parties themselves could not agree. However, these powers could not be used to bring about structural institutional changes. The role of the HiRep is to uphold the Dayton Accords and so its legal powers stop at the limits of Dayton. As the Constitution of Bosnia and Herzegovina forms an integral part of the Dayton Agreement[65] any changes to it or the wider Agreement would have to be adopted in the Parliamentary Assembly of Bosnia and Herzegovina and not by the HiRep. It was because of this that the international community started linking enforcement measures with conditions for accession to international organizations. This strategy was most successfully employed in defense reform.

A common security policy and state level defense had been on the agenda of the international community since at least 1998.[66] However, not much had been done to provide for comprehensive defense reform. As the Constitution of Bosnia and Herzegovina did not explicitly provide for a defense competency at the state level, the entities assumed the lead role in defense, including the formation of separate armed forces. In 2002 a major scandal broke out exposing that Republika Srpska defense structures had sanctioned the illegal trading of weapons to Iraq. The High Representative responded by outlining a number of steps to be taken by the local authorities in response.[67] Although some progress was made, the international community remained concerned. Reacting to this, the High Representative issued a number of decisions concerning defense issues, including amendments to the constitutions of both entities and to their defense laws.[68] In May 2003 he also established the Defense Reform Commission that was to plan the entire reform and propose the changes that he could not enact through his Bonn powers.[69] As an outside incentive, defense reform became a condition to join NATO's Partnership for Peace program. With this in mind, parties negotiated and, by the end of 2003, a Defense Law passed through both the state and entities parliaments.[70]

Coming Full Circle

On the wings of its successes with defense reform, the High Representative wished to continue its reform agenda, attempting to combine enforcement powers and conditionality in other areas. For example, there were attempts to replicate defense reform strategies for negotiating police reform—making this a precondition for the signing of the Stabilization and Association Agreement with the European Union. However, in contrast to defense reform, these plans were less successful. There are several interrelated reasons for why this happened[71] but one major factor seems to have been an increasing dissatisfaction with the international administration's efforts to prescribe and enforce desired outcomes. This feeling has only strengthened since.

Resistance to the use of enforcement powers comes not only from the side of the local actors, who have started to resent what they see as the patronizing behavior of the international community, but also from some key international actors. The European Commission, in particular, and a number of EU member states are beginning to vocally oppose the use of Bonn powers by the High Representative. They see them as an unnecessarily invasive measure, inappropriate in the context of a country that has been peaceful for more than a decade. At the same time, the abolition of international administration or at least the enforcement measures has come to be seen as a condition for Bosnia to progress in its negotiations with the EU. Brussels has always negotiated with potential members that were fully sovereign and is reluctant to change this policy for Bosnia. On the other hand, some actors, in particular the US and the OHR itself, are more concerned with the consequences of leaving the country solely in the hands of local actors. They believe that the EU pull is not strong enough to push for reform and overcome the obstructionism in the country. They therefore argue for the continued presence of these special powers, seeing them as the only guarantee to prevent parties from violating the peace agreement.

This division has left the international administration in Bosnia in limbo. On one side the enforcement powers remain in existence, on the other the ultimatums issued by the OHR carry less weight. Implementation of any comprehensive reform through targeted interventions of the High Representative is no longer realistic. That time has passed. The main role now occupied by the institution is as a watchdog of the Dayton Agreement, returning to its earlier position of intervening only in cases of outright breaches. Some would want to see even this role abolished soon.

Conclusions

Although a slightly unusual case among international administrations, the Office of the High Representative and the experiences of its use of enforcement powers in Bosnia provide us with a number of insights on how to think about international administrations at the beginning of the twenty-first century. The most important of these concern the complex relationships between the international community and the local population in post-war contexts.

There is a broad disagreement in the International Relations literature over whether international administrations represent an imperial enterprise or are a welcome form of providing governance for states emerging from conflict. This is a discussion unlikely to be settled, as the conclusions often stem from the normative positions of the authors weighing in. But what can be seen in practice is that the idea of sovereignty and independence from external interference is so firmly entrenched that any international administration necessarily has an expiration date. Unlike some other international administrations with built-in timelines for their closure, the High Representative in Bosnia has a more open-ended mandate. Nevertheless, the gradual loss of powers by the HiRep shows that territories can only be externally managed for so long. Even if international administration retains formal powers, its actual powers will be increasingly contested at the local level and will eventually wither away. Any delegation of sovereign powers is temporary.

At the same time, international administrations require broad international support if they want to achieve their objectives. By definition an international administration is given an almost insurmountable task of governing a territory that lacks the ability to govern itself. Established in a highly volatile post-war situation, these govern in a state whose local populations often lack even a basic consensus about governance issues. Since there is no local consensus on the reforms needed, the legitimacy of decisions that the international administration wants to pass therefore stems from external consensus on the types and degrees of intervention. This is especially relevant for the use of enforcement powers. Recent experiences in Bosnia show that as soon as the broad external support diminished, the role of the High Representative changed. Although they can become sources of innovation, international administrations rely on external consensus.

Additionally, the experience from Bosnia also shows that while some reform can be externally directed, international administration cannot substitute for a domestic political process. International administration can act as a corrective mechanism but cannot push through structural transformations. If imposed, these kinds of reforms would not be sustainable in the long run. Structural transformations and revisions of power distribution among different groups need to be rooted in the domestic processes. One way international administration has been trying to encourage these processes is through combining enforcement powers with conditionality. The experience with using external incentives in Bosnia shows a mixed record. While they can assist in building domestic momentum for change, such as in the case of the defense reform, they can also generate local resistance if they are interpreted as a patronizing measure. Even in the cases where external actors are afforded extraordinary powers over the given territory, the limits of external intervention can soon be seen.

Notes

1. The author would like to thank Jonathan Agensky and Brendan Simms for their invaluable comments.

2. James Crawford, *The Creation of States in International Law* (Oxford: Clarendon Press, 1979), 185.

3. Virginia Paige Fortna and Lisa Morje Howard, "Pitfalls and Prospects in Peacekeeping Literature," *Annual Review of Political Science* 11, no. 1 (2008): 283-301.

4. See, for example: John Mackinlay and Jarat Chopra, *A Draft Concept of Multinational Operations* (Providence, RI: Thomas J. Watson Institute for International Studies, Brown University,1993); Michael W. Doyle and Nicholas Sambanis, "International Peacekeeping: A Theoretical and Quantitative Analysis," *American Political Science Review* 94, no. 4 (2000): 779-801; and Trevor Findlay, *The Use of Force in UN Peace Operations* (Oxford: SIPRI and Oxford University Press, 2002).

5. These operations have been greatly influenced by former UN Secretary General Boutros Boutros-Ghali's *An Agenda for Peace: Preventive Diplomacy, Peacemaking and Peace-keeping* (New York: United Nations, 1992) and rethought after the Brahimi *Report of the Panel on United Nations Peace Operations* (New York: United Nations, 2000).

6. Mary Kaldor, *New and Old Wars: Organized Violence in a Global Era* (Cambridge, MA: Polity Press, 1999).

7. See Alex J. Bellamy, "The 'Next State' in Peace Operations Theory?," *International Peacekeeping* 11, no. 1 (2004); Mark Duffield, *Global Governance and the New Wars: The Merging of Development and Security* (London: Zed Books, 2001); and Martin Shaw, "The Contemporary Mode of Warfare? Mary Kaldor's Theory of New Wars," *Review of International Political Economy* 7, no. 1 (2000): 171-80.

8. See Bellamy, "The 'Next State' in Peace Operations Theory?," 28.

9. See Mark Duffield, "Complex Emergencies and the Crisis of Developmentalism," *IDS Bulletin* 25, no. 4 (1994): 37-45; David Keen, *Complex Emergencies* (Cambridge, MA: Polity Press, 2008); and S. Neil MacFarlane, "Humanitarian Action and Conflict," *International Journal* 54, no. 4 (1999): 537-61.

10. Boutros-Ghali, *An Agenda for Peace*, paragraph 21.

11. In their analysis of twenty four governmental and intergovernmental agencies operating in the spheres of peacebuilding, Michael Barnett, Hunjoon Kim, Magdalene O'Donnell, and Laura Sitea (2007) conclude that there are almost as many mandates as

there are agencies. See Barnett *et al.* "Peacebuilding: What is in a Name?," *International Governance: A Review of Multilateralism and International Organizations* 13, no. 1 (2007): 35-58.

12. United Nations, "Supplement to an Agenda for Peace: Position Paper of the Secretary General on the Occasion of the Fiftieth Anniversary of the United Nations," A/50/60-S/1995/1, 3 January 1995, http://www.un.org/Docs/SG/agsupp.html (accessed 5 July 2012).

13. Simon Chesterman, *You, the People: the United Nations, Transitional Administration, and State-building* (Oxford: Oxford University Press, 2005), 5.

14. For more detailed discussion on this see Chesterman, *You, the People*; David Chandler, *Empire in Denial: the Politics of State-building* (London: Pluto, 2006); and Roland Paris and Timothy D. Sisk, eds., *The Dilemmas of Statebuilding: Confronting the Contradictions of Postwar Peace Operations* (New York: Routledge, 2009).

15. See Francis Fukuyama, *The End of History and the Last Man* (New York: Free Press, 1992).

16. See Roland Paris, *At War's End: Building Peace after Civil Conflict* (Cambridge: Cambridge University Press, 2004).

17. See Christine Gray, *International Law and the Use of Force: Foundations of Public International Law* (Oxford: Oxford University Press, 2000), 159.

18. Ralph Wilde, "Taxonomies of International Peacekeeping: An Alternative Narrative," *ILSA Journal of International and Comparative Law* 9, (2002): 391-8.

19. Michael W. Doyle, "Liberalism and World Politics," *American Political Science Review* 80, no. 4 (1986): 779-801.

20. Piki Ish-Shalom, "Theory as a Hermeneutical Mechanism: The Democratic-Peace Thesis and the Politics of Democratization," *European Journal of International Relations* 12, no. 4 (2006): 565-98.

21. See Keen, "War and Peace," 11.

22. For more on the "Wilsonian Triad," see Michael Mandelbaum, *The Ideas that Conquered the World: Peace, Democracy, and Free Markets in the Twenty-first Century* (New York: Public Affairs, 2002).

23. For historical accounts of international administrations see Edward Mortimer, "International Administration of War-Torn Societies," *Global Governance* 10, no. 1 (2004): 7-15; Carsten Stahn, *The Law and Practice of International Territorial Administration: Versailles to Iraq and Beyond* (Cambridge: Cambridge University Press, 2008); and Ralph Wilde, *The Administration of Territory by International Organizations* (Oxford: Oxford University Press, 2005).

24. The principle of sovereign equality is the first principle on which the United Nations Charter is based, as indicated in the UN Charter, Article 2 (1), signed on 26 June 1945, in force since 24 October 1945, available at http://www.un.org/aboutun/charter (accessed July 7, 2012).

25. See for instance, Alejandro Bendana, "From Peacebuilding to State Building: One Step Forward and Two Steps Back," *Development* 48, no. 3 (2005): 5-15; Omar G. Encarnacion, "The Follies of Democratic Imperialism," *World Policy Journal* 22, no. 1 (2005): 47-60; and Gerald Knaus and Felix Martin, "Travails of the European Raj," *Journal of Democracy* 14, no. 3 (2003): 60-74.

26. See William Bain, *Between Anarchy and Society: Trusteeship and the Obligations of Power* (Oxford: Oxford University Press, 2003); Tonny Brems Knudsen and Carsten Bagge Laustsen, eds., *Kosovo between War and Peace: Nationalism, Peacebuilding, and International Trusteeship* (London: Routledge, 2006); and Peter

Lyon, "The Rise and Fall and Possible Revival of International Trusteeship," *Journal of Commonwealth & Comparative Politics* 31, no. 1 (1993): 96-110.

27. For more on the terminology and differences between various forms of management of foreign territories see Richard D. Caplan, *International Governance of War-torn Territories: Rule and Reconstruction* (Oxford: Oxford University Press, 2005) and Ralph Wilde, *The Administration of Territory by International Organizations.*

28. See Oliver P. Richmond, "UN Peace Operations and the Dilemmas of the Peacebuilding Consensus," *International Peacekeeping* 11, no. 1 (2004): 83-101.

29. Richard Caplan, *International Governance of War-torn Territories*, 21.

30. For comprehensive accounts of the negotiations at Dayton see Carl Bildt, *Peace Journey: The Struggle for Peace in Bosnia* (London: Weidenfeld and Nicolson, 1999); Ivor H. Daalder, *Getting to Dayton: the Making of America's Bosnia Policy* (Washington DC: Brookings Institute Press, 2000); and Richard Holbrooke, *To End a War: Sarajevo to Dayton, An Inside Story* (New York: Random House, 1999).

31. The General Framework Agreement for Peace in Bosnia and Herzegovina, variously known as the Dayton Peace Agreement, the Dayton Agreement, and the Dayton Accords, was initialed in Dayton, Ohio on 21 November 1995, and signed in Paris on 14 December 1995.

32. For more on the history of international attempts to negotiate peace in the former Yugoslavia and Bosnia and Herzegovina see James Gow, *Triumph of the Lack of Will: International Diplomacy and the Yugoslav War* (Oxford: Oxford University Press, 1997).

33. Bosniak is a term for the predominantly Muslim population of Bosnia and Herzegovina. In the English language literature this ethnic group is also referred to as (Bosnian) Muslim or Bosnian. Here I use the term Bosniak for two interrelated reasons: firstly, it is the term that the group itself uses to distinguish itself from other groups, and secondly, while there is a substantial overlap between Bosniaks and Bosnian Muslims, the two groups are not identical. Many Bosniaks, while having Islamic ancestry, consider themselves non-believers. Bosnians is used to denote all citizens of Bosnia, that is, the three main ethnic groups and other minorities. See Mitja Velikonja, *Religious Separation and Political Intolerance in Bosnia-Herzegovina* (College Station: Texas A&M Press, 2003): 161.

34. Dayton Peace Agreement, Annex 4, Art. III.

35. Another key civilian implementation agency, the International Criminal Tribunal for the former Yugoslavia (ICTY), is not mentioned in the main text of the Dayton Agreement. This was a deal struck so as not to explicitly embarrass Bosnian Serb leadership, in particular Radovan Karadzic, who had at the time already been indicted by the tribunal. Author's interviews, Washington, February 2009.

36. Dayton Peace Agreement, Annex 10, Art. I. 2.

37. Dayton Peace Agreement, Annex 10, Art. V.

38. Dayton Peace Agreement, Annex 3, Art II.4.

39. See James A. Goldston, "Role of the OSCE in Bosnia: Lessons from the First Year," *The Helsinki Monitor* 8, no. 3 (1997): 6-36.

40. The International Crisis Group (ICG), a leading think-tank on Balkan developments, issued a damning report claiming that even the minimum conditions for the elections to be effective were nowhere in sight, and the same message was widely reported in the world media. See International Crisis Group, "Why the Bosnian Elections Must be Postponed," *Europe Report* No. 14 (1996) at www.crisisgrojup.org (accessed 5 July 2012).

41. PIC Main Meeting, Conclusions, Florence, 13 June 1996, Art. 8.

42. See Office of the High Representative, *Bulletin No. 8*, 23 June 1996.

43. *Third Report of the High Representative for Implementation of the Bosnian Peace Agreement to the Secretary-General of the United Nations*, 1 October 1996.

44. PIC Steering Board Ministerial Meeting, Communiqué, Sintra, 30 May 1997, Art. 35.

45. PIC Steering Board Ministerial Meeting, Communiqué, Art. 36.

46. PIC Steering Board Ministerial Meeting, Communiqué, Art. 70.

47. PIC Main Meeting, Conclusions: Bosnia and Herzegovina 1998: Self-sustaining Structures, Bonn, 10 December 1997, Part XI. High Representative, Art. 2.

48. PIC Main Meeting, Conclusions: Part II. Constitutional and Legal Matters, Art 1. a, b, e.

49. PIC Main Meeting, Conclusions: Part XI. High Representative, Art. 2.c.

50. PIC Steering Board Ministerial Meeting: Declaration, Luxembourg, 9 June 1998, Art. 5.

51. Bonn Conclusions, II. Constitutional and Legal Matters, Art. 1.a.

52. The High Representative, Decision imposing the Law on Citizenship of BiH, 16 December 1997.

53. Bonn Conclusions, II. Constitutional and Legal Matters, Art. 1.b.

54. The High Representative, Decision on the deadlines for the implementation of the new uniform license plate system, 20 May 1998.

55. Bonn conclusions, II. Constitutional and Legal Matters, Art. 1.e.

56. The High Representative, Decision imposing the Law on the Flag of BiH, 3 February 1998.

57. The High Representative, Decision imposing the design of bank notes, 27 March 1998.

58. The High Representative, Decision on the shape and design of the coat-of-arms of BiH, 18 May 1998.

59. The High Representative, Decision imposing the Law on the National Anthem of BiH, 15 June 1999.

60. The High Representative, Decision removing Mr. Nikola Poplasen from the Office of President of Republika Srpska, 5 March 1999.

61. For various assessments and more detailed accounts of minority return see Carl Dahlman and Gearoid O. Tuathail, "The Legacy of Ethnic Cleansing: the International Community and the Returns Process in post-Dayton Bosnia-Herzegovina," *Political Geography* 24, no. 5 (2005): 569-99; Marita Eastmond, "Transnational Returns and Reconstruction in Post-war Bosnia and Herzegovina," *International Migration* 44, no. 3 (2006): 141-66; Ayaki Ito, "Politicization of Minority Return in Bosnia and Herzegovina: The First Five Years Examined," *International Journal of Refugee Law* 12, nos. 1-2 (2001): 98-122; and Charles Philpott, "Though the Dog is Dead, the Pig Must be Killed: Finishing with Property Restitution to Bosnia-Herzegovina's IDPs and Refugees," *Journal of Refugee Studies* 18, no. 1 (2005): 1-24.

62. Notable examples include The High Representative, Decision imposing the Law on Amendments to the Law on Housing Relations in the Federation, restoring to displaced persons and refugees occupancy rights cancelled under Article 47 of the old law and extending from six to twelve months the deadline for requesting, of 17 September 1998; and The High Representative, Decision cancelling all permanent occupancy rights issued in the RS during and after the war in BIH and converting them into temporary occupancy rights, of 14 April 1999.

63. PIC Steering Board Meeting, Communiqué, Brussels, 30 November 1999.

64. PLIP, Non Negotiable Principles In The Context Of The Property Law Implementation, 1 March 2000.

65. Dayton Peace Agreement, Annex 4.

66. PIC Main Meeting, Declaration, Madrid , 16 December 1998.

67. Office of the High Representative Press Release: "High Representative Outlines Required Action Following 'Orao' Scandal," 28 October, 2002.

68. Office of the High Representative Press Release: "High Representative Acts to Ensure that Military in BiH are under Effective Civilian Control," 2 April 2003.

69. The High Representative, Decision Establishing the Defence Reform Commission, 9 May 2003.

70. Bosnia and Herzegovina Law on Defense, *Official Gazette of Bosnia and Herzegovina*, 43 (29 December 2003).

71. For more on the police reform in Bosnia and Herzegovina see Gemma Colantes Celador, "Police Reform: Peacebuilding through Democratic Policing?," *International Peacekeeping* 12, no. 3 (2005): 364-76; Thomas Muehlmann, "Police Restructuring in Bosnia-Herzegovina: Problems of Internationally-led Security Sector Reform," *Journal of Intervention and Statebuilding* 2, no. 1 (2008): 1-22.

Chapter 23

Bosnia-Herzegovina and the Development of Democratic Policing[1]

Donald R. Zoufal[2]

The current difficulties in restoring order in Iraq and Afghanistan are just the most recent reflection of the need to examine the process of restoring civil order in post-conflict situations. While the breakdown of order in Iraq and Afghanistan is the result of externally generated regime change, their problems are similar to those of internally generated breakdowns in law and order. Countries like Kosovo, Liberia, and Haiti all provide relatively recent examples of the ominous implications of the breakdown of public safety in modern societies.

In the search for a solution to the problem of restoring public order and re-establishing public safety services, an examination of the internationally sanctioned process for re-establishing public order in Bosnia and Herzegovina (BiH) may be helpful. The BiH experienced the almost complete breakdown of conventional law and order functions, and as hostilities raged the police became part of paramilitary units, many of whom were engaged in atrocities against civilians. This chapter examines the international community's initial efforts to restore public order there.

The Settlement of the War

In negotiating the terms of the 1995 General Framework Agreement for Peace (GFAP), which ended the hostilities and provided a blueprint for peace in BiH, issues of public safety were a central focus. The parties to the GFAP recognized that, without a secure environment, attempts to encourage repatriation of refugees, elections, and freedom of movement were ephemeral. To restore the country to normalcy, the restoration of public confidence in the safety and security of their environment was critical.

Under the GFAP, this restoration process was to be accomplished by two separate components operating simultaneously. The first, operating as the initial focus under the GFAP, was an international military Implementation Force (IFOR) directed to separate the combatant military forces in BiH, supervise their disarmament, and supervise the transfers of certain areas, which had been hotly contested during the hostilities. These tasks were scheduled to be completed by mid-April 1996.

The second component involved the introduction of an international police force to monitor and assist in democratizing the policing function in BiH. Under Annex 11 of the GFAP, an International Police Task Force (IPTF), operating under the auspices of the United Nations, was empowered to monitor policing operations and assist in the restructuring and training of police forces. The logic of the GFAP was that the monitoring and restructuring of the police by an international police presence would provide both a short and long-term solution to the issue of public safety. The restructuring of the police was to be conducted in both of the subnational entities, the *Republika Srpska* (RS) and the Federation of Bosnia-Herzegovina (the Federation hereafter), as well as at the national level of the Republic of Bosnia Herzegovina (BiH).

IPTF's initial monitoring efforts were to be conducted in conjunction with IFOR. As greater stability in the security environment was achieved, attention shifted. Under the GFAP, a wide range of civil efforts was to be coordinated to bring the country back to normalcy. To coordinate that effort, the GFAP created the Office of the High Representative (OHR).

As the military environment stabilized, growing emphasis was placed on the IPTF's duty to assist the parties in providing a safe environment through the development of indigenous law enforcement mechanisms capable of addressing issues of public safety. As these indigenous structures developed, IFOR's presence could be reduced.

Addressing the Challenge

The challenge which confronted IPTF planners in restructuring security in BiH was a formidable one. Information such as the size of police forces, the location of stations, armaments, etc., which in a peacetime democracy are matters that are readily available for both public scrutiny and analysis by police planners, was considered a state secret in both pre-war and post-war BiH. The ability to gather data was further constrained by the absence of a planning staff at the IPTF Headquarters dedicated to that task until after mid-March 1996. Even after that date, the ability to gather data was extremely limited and largely restricted to voluntary compliance on the part of the former warring parties despite the fact that the GFAP required that they provide detailed information to the IPTF Commissioner. An initial survey conducted by UN personnel provided general numbers as to the deployment of police; however, breakdowns by regional and local levels were not available until the late spring of 1996.

Those initial numbers were undoubtedly under-reported; however, even they were indicative of the overriding problem facing IPTF planners in creating a democratically oriented policing force. The number of police had swelled to three times the pre-war complement of police; to 44,750 police throughout BiH. Within the Federation, 29,750 Bosnian Muslim (Bosniak) police were identified in areas of Bosniak control, with an additional 3,000 Bosnian Croat police in Bosnian Croat areas. Twelve thousand police were identified in the RS.

Despite their number, police throughout the country were ill-equipped for peacetime policing. Simple items such as pistols and uniforms were unavailable. The firearm generally carried by police officers throughout the country was the AK-47 assault rifle and police inventories in even small communities included items such as hand grenades, machine guns, and, in some cases, armored vehicles. In short, arsenals were stocked more for warfare than policing.

Uniforms were also at a premium. Many police, especially in outlying areas, wore fatigue-style military uniforms, and those who were associated with one faction or another wore the uniform of that faction. Consequently, the issue of selecting a common uniform for the Federation was an emotionally charged one and, like many issues of unification, the symbolic issue of uniforms was disputed even though a common uniform was specifically mandated in the Federation's constitution.

More substantively, there were shortages in almost every category of equipment used in modern policing. Vehicles and communications equipment were in chronic short supply. Equipment used in crime detection even as basic as fingerprint and crime scene processing kits was almost nonexistent. Also nonexistent were comprehensive criminal records and other related criminal justice information, since records and information centers had been targeted during hostilities.

In addition, the bloated policing apparatus in both the Federation and the RS was staffed with young and poorly trained officers. Central training had been located in Sarajevo. Early in the war, its headquarters was attacked and closed. Meanwhile, almost from the war's onset, the police, especially those in Bosniak areas, became the only organized resistance forces, and young untrained recruits augmented their numbers. After hostilities, there was considerable UN concern that these young, untrained police officers might turn to crime or seek revenge for lost family members.

Finally, there was the issue of police compensation. During the war, the police had received little in the way of wages. Compensation occurred in allotments of food or personal comfort items like cigarettes. As the country returned to normalcy following the war, the compensation of police officers became a critical issue. Absent a system for compensating police, graft and other corruption-related misconduct was certain to occur.

The Development of the Plan

Prior to March 1996, the focus of much of the effort of IFOR, the IPTF, and various other international organizations was on the smooth transition of the Sarajevo suburbs from Serb control to control by the Federation. With that task completed on March 19th scarce IPTF assets could be turned to address the more long-term strategies for accomplishing IPTF tasks, especially the restructuring of police forces throughout BiH.

The initial discussion on developing a plan for that restructuring began with a meeting in Zagreb on March 23rd between the Deputy Commissioner of the IPTF and the IPTF Acting Chief of Plans. Eight principal tasks were identified: 1) Establishing links with key leaders; 2) Assessing current structures and operations; 3) Developing an overall structure for the new police force; 4) Determining resource needs for policing; 5) Developing a restructuring strategy for new police; 6) Developing a supportive training strategy; 7) Developing an implementation plan; and 8) Designing a supportive civil information plan.

From its inception, the IPTF had suffered from the absence of a separate planning section. Recruitment of IPTF monitors did not include recruitment based on skill set identification or plans expertise. Moreover, the IPTF mission's organizational design was focused on day-to-day monitoring operations, with little thought to strategic or long-range planning. If the IPTF were to create mechanisms whereby it could work with the former warring parties, a planning cell had to be established to develop the base plan. This would involve research regarding the existing police structures, analysis of those structures, structural redesign commensurate with the requirements of democratic policing, and ultimately the implementation of the plans.

In early April 1996, the IPTF Commissioner approved the establishment of that planning cell with a multinational representation (U.S., Argentinean, Irish, Swiss, Dutch, and Turkish) that drew from very divergent policing traditions, including common law and code systems, systems with national and local police, and systems where the military and civil police are integrated. Additionally, IFOR seconded a reserve officer with civil police and legal experience to serve as the acting chief of plans. The planning process also required the input and participation of the former warring parties through the creation of commissions on restructuring.

Creation of the Commissions on Restructuring

Consonant with the first of the principal tasks outlined in the March Zagreb meeting was the development of organizational structures designed to elicit support and participation of key decision-makers. Two such organizations (designated commissions on restructuring) were formed (one each for the Federation and RS) and charged with two principal objectives: to increase information flow from the parties concerning their current policing structures; and to engage and invest key police policymakers in the restructuring process. The RS's commission met only once and received nominal support from government officials. The Federation commission met on several occasions and through its efforts moved the Federation forward in the restructuring process.

The process began on April 10, 1996, when the Commissioner forwarded correspondence to the RS Minister of the Interior and the Federation Minister and Deputy Minister of the Interior inviting their participation in the commissions. The commissions included members from these Ministries, as well as the IPTF Chief of Staff, an IFOR representative, and a representative from the OHR, thereby acknowledging the importance of involving the parties in the restructuring process; however, the commissions themselves were advisory in nature. They were to provide input to the Commissioner in formulating his guidance, thus allowing the parties to have access to the decision-making process but without the ability to obstruct it.

The commission concept was successful in increasing information flow, providing a communication channel that afforded the IPTF plans staff with better access to information concerning the local police. Prior to their establishment, repeated requests to both the Federation and the RS for detailed information concerning their policing operations had largely been ignored. Afterwards, flow improved from all parties and the information provided proved to be extremely useful in assessing the existing policing structures.

The second objective, engaging key decision-makers in a meaningful discussion as to restructuring the existing police organizations, was much more successful in the Federation. In formulating the Federation Commission, careful attention was paid to creating an ethnic balance in participation. Both the Minister (Bosniak) and Deputy Minister (Croatian) were made members, as were two additional policing professionals from each ethnic group. In contrast, the RS Commission had only Serb representatives, held only one commission meeting, and although it adopted the principles of policing and the code of ethics outlined in the Commissioner's guidance, it consistently maintained that IPTF had no mandate to advise them concerning internal police affairs. The Federation Commission, however, met several times and agreed on a restructuring program that it proceeded to implement.

The Organizational Meetings

Organizational meetings for both commissions were held in April 1996. At them, the Commissions' basic objectives were outlined by the IPTF. Plans staff prepared presentations on the existing policing structures and sought comment from those present as to their validity. Ministry officials were presented with documents requesting information on policing strength at each *opstina*, which is similar to counties in the United States and forms the basic governmental unit in the RS and Federation. In addition to survey instruments, ministry officials were presented with an instruction sheet which IPTF monitors were planning to present to the chiefs of police in each *opstina* to acquire information about police strength, structure, training, and equipment.

Both Federation and RS Commission representatives indicated a willingness to cooperate with IPTF efforts to collect information on policing operations. However, there was some concern expressed by all regarding the IPTF's proposed practice of directly approaching the local chiefs of police. Ultimately, Federation officials acceded to that request but the RS indicated that *it* would gather the information from the local chiefs. Elsewhere, ministry representatives agreed that they would make key members of their policing structures available to IPTF planners to facilitate information-gathering. Tours of Federation and RS facilities, including their police training facilities were arranged, as were interviews with public safety officials with information relevant to the IPTF survey.

The IPTF employed a two-track approach in gathering information. First, it was gathered directly by IPTF monitors at the local level through survey instruments, and then checked against the information provided by the ministries and key officials. While this was not a perfect means of verification, the two-tracked approach helped validate IPTF data even though compliance with the IPTF requests for data was spotty. The RS refused to allow monitors to contact local police chiefs, and although the Federation imposed no such prohibition, as a practical matter its local officials would not provide information except through their superiors at the Ministry of Interior. Information gathering was also hampered by the absence of a trained group of IPTF personnel to conduct the assessments. Reliance on already overtaxed IPTF field resources often yielded poor results.

Assessment Data

The data collection and assessment process revealed policing systems much more in the nature of military militias than modern democratic police forces, with maintaining state secrecy and security as their primary functions. The central ministries unquestionably exercised hierarchical control over local policing organizations. In the Federation there was a "dual key" system of control. The Bosniak Minister of the Interior controlled police in the areas of the country that had been controlled by the forces of the BiH (Bosniak Forces). Areas that had been under the control of the HVO (Croat Forces) reported to the Croatian Deputy Minister. The Bosniaks seemed to have the most trouble controlling their subordinate chiefs. It is hard to know whether this was a function of inferior communications systems or greater local autonomy. The Croatian police, while tightly controlled, unquestionably had reporting links that ran not only to Sarajevo but to Zagreb. Centralized control was much stronger in the RS. There, as throughout the Federation, police were organized in a paramilitary fashion based largely on the pre-war organizational structure.

The RS government reported a policing strength of 12,786, organized into eight regional departments. These regional departments each covered three or four municipalities or *opstinas*. Each municipality had its own local police. In addition to the regional departments for local policing operations, there was a centralized unit of special police, whose functions included riot control and anti-terrorism.

The Agreement on Restructuring the Federation Police

At the first formal meeting of the Federation's Commission, held on April 25, 1996, the "Agreement on Restructuring the Police in The Federation of Bosnia and Herzegovina" was adopted. In it, the Commission committed to restructuring the Federation's police forces at the direction of the IPTF Commissioner and in accordance with generally accepted standards of policing, which guarantee internationally accepted human rights.

Adopted at the Federation's highest level of political leadership, the Agreement authorized the Commission to provide input to the IPTF Commissioner in his formulation of the restructuring plan. Key members of the political leadership and Commission members also committed themselves to a series of "concrete steps" to advance the restructuring process. These steps, under the IPTF Commissioner's leadership, included the accomplishment of most of the principal tasks identified by IPTF planners as necessary to a successful restructuring, such as: a reduction in the numbers of police; reorientation of policing structures to reflect democratic values; demobilizing, disarming, and re-employing police; and the development and implementation of training standards and curricula.

The Agreement also included a timeline for accomplishing the identified tasks that was extremely compressed and overly optimistic, especially in the area of implementation. Still, it did provide a series of guidelines and goals for planning and implementation purposes. More broadly, with the Agreement in place, the IPTF cemented the support of the key leadership in the Federation in the restructuring process.

Establishing the Principles of Policing in a Democratic State

Early in the planning process it was recognized that a change had to occur in the basic philosophic underpinnings of the delivery of police service insofar as the central and overriding focus of the existing police structure was the protection of the state. In order to make meaningful progress, it was decided that there needed to be a codification of the essential elements of democratic policing. Once these principles were agreed upon and codified, they would serve as the guide for recommendations in reorganizing the Federation police and in reorienting the police to serve Federation citizens consistent with the requirements of a democratic state.

At the Bonn-Petersburg meeting the Federation Commission adopted a set of "Internationally Accepted Principles for Policing in a Democratic State" (the "Principles") as prepared by the IPTF plans staff based on applicable human rights standards and the staff members' common experiences in policing. Stressed, and carefully explained, were the operation of the police "in accord with the principles of democracy" and as prescribed "by a professional code of conduct," that the police "must have as their highest priority the protection of life," that they are "accountable to the community they serve," and that they must, without discrimination, "conduct their activities with respect for human dignity and basic human rights."

For its part the RS refused to engage in any discussion of the principles but unilaterally adopted and published them throughout its Ministry of Internal Affairs. While this publication was a minor success, the RS's failure to engage in a consideration of how to implement the guidelines made that success a hollow one; RS's abject failure to implement those principles is a testament to the weakness of engaging in a restructuring process with an entity that is completely uncommitted or invested in it. This lack of commitment by the RS resulted in a refocusing of efforts and limited planning resources shifted to the Federation, where the adoption of the Principles was viewed as only a first step in a more comprehensive process of restructuring.

With these guiding principles in place, emphasis then turned toward the more difficult task of structuring an organization to implement those principles. While the RS viewed the Principles as an end, they were, in fact, only designed to be a beginning.

Establishing the Standards of Democratic Policing

The Principles provided a touchstone to guide the development of a policing structure, but did not provide concrete measures that planners could use in developing them. The skeleton of the Principles had to be fleshed out with more tangible measures. The development of the "Standards of Policing in a

Democratic State" document provided those concrete measures.

The process for developing those measures was similar to that employed in developing the Principles. Additionally, the IPTF retained the services of Professor David Bailey, a renowned scholar and expert in the field of policing. Together with the IPTF Acting Chief of Plans, Professor Bailey created an outline of functions and measures necessary for a police organization to achieve the Principles' goals. The IPTF plans staff then reviewed this outline before it was submitted for approval.

As with the review procedure for the Principles, the review process for the Standards was of critical importance. It allowed policing professionals with widely divergent backgrounds to discuss and agree on a core set of measures necessary to determine whether a policing structure met the goals of the agreed-upon principles. This unity of effort was an extremely difficult part of the process.

The complete text of the Standards is attached as an Appendix. The Standards were not designed to encompass every function relating to a given Principle. Rather, the Standards were designed to address the essential functions necessary to achieve each of the Principles. For example, for the principle that the police be oriented and operate in accord with the principles of democracy, there are only four standards stressing that the police must enforce the law in accordance with its terms. The police must know what the law is and be trained in it. They must be governed by identifiable written procedures. Compliance with the law and procedures must be monitored and misconduct be punished. Citizens must be able to recognize their police and have some redress for a violation of their rights. Nonetheless, the Standards provided a basis for evaluating existing structures and developing new ones.

The Code of Professional Conduct

Having developed the Standards, the IPTF plans staff turned its attention to developing a Code of Conduct to address the individual officer component of the restructuring process. The overarching concern was to make the Code a simple document that each individual officer could understand and accept, could be reduced to pocket size, and carried by each police officer as he or she performed his or her duties. In this endeavor the code of the Garda Siochana (Irish Police) became the IPTF's model.

The final product, the "Code of Ethics for Professional Police Officers" adopted by the Commission at its May 7th meeting, was developed by merging the requirements of the seven "Principles for Policing in a Democratic State" with such common requirements of police professionalism as selfless service, rejection of corruption, personal integrity, and pursuit of continuing professional training.

Reducing Policing Levels

Once the more philosophic underpinnings of restructuring were addressed, attention focused on such practical concerns as the size of the policing apparatus, which was also an issue of substantial concern to the Federation. The need to maintain a substantial police presence for "state security" was uppermost in the minds of the Commission's Federation representatives, and although this concern was understandable given the recent past in Bosnia, it was not conducive to the democratization of policing.

The size of the existing Federation police force was clearly a function of the internal conflict in Bosnia, and the level of policing (1:75 citizens) was at wide variance with the European average of 1:250 to 400 people. It was the consensus of the IPTF command staff that a transition to democratic policing would not occur without substantial reduction in the police ranks.

Beginning with the Federation Commission's May 7, 1996 meeting, negotiations were conducted between the acting chief of plans and representatives from the Interior Ministry during which proposals and counter-proposals for reductions and personnel ceilings were exchanged. A smaller working group was soon established to address the issue of defining and realigning the policing structure.

The Croatian members of the Commission were generally more favorably disposed to reductions in the number of police than the Bosniaks. This was doubtless a result of their confidence in the security forces of the neighboring Croatian government to address their security concerns. However, all members of the Commission agreed that limits had to be placed on both the cantonal (state) police assigned to each *opstina* as well as on the police assigned to the Federation's Ministry of the Interior, thus ensuring a balance acceptable to local constituencies. This was particularly important in light of the fact that the police forces in several areas of the Federation had engaged in combat operations against each other.

In order to secure the support and cooperation of the police at the local level, the Minister of the Interior and the Deputy Minister called a meeting of all the police chiefs from *opstinas* across BiH. The meeting was held in Sarajevo on May 13, 1996, and constituted the first time since the outbreak of hostilities that all the chiefs, some of whom had fought against one another, had met together. For some, it was the first time since the outbreak of the war that they had returned to Sarajevo. Hence, this gathering in and of itself was a significant move toward restoring normalcy to the country's policing structure.

At the meeting the chiefs were apprised of the Agreement, the work of the Commission to date, and the proposals for reducing police forces. Proposals for redefining and realigning police functions in the Federation were also discussed. The meeting allowed the Federation Interior Ministry officials to gauge the relevant feelings of local police officials as Ministry officials reviewed their proposals on a canton-by-canton, *opstina*-by-*opstina* basis with the chiefs.

In an attempt to resolve the issues involving reductions and the appropriate functions for the restructured police, a Federation Commission met May 16th in Zagreb, it being felt that moving the meeting place outside Sarajevo to a place where the members could work and socialize away from their daily work environments would be helpful. There, the reduction of police forces, the appropriate functions for police, training, and vetting and implementation issues were discussed. While some progress was made on the issues of training and vetting, the reduction issue went unresolved. The meeting did, however, provide a key to its ultimate resolution by linking functions performed by police to the numbers issue. Civilianizing and eliminating certain functions traditionally performed by police greatly facilitated the process of negotiating reductions.

The working group continued to meet subsequently. By May 20th an agreement was finally reached as to appropriate policing levels and functions. The numbers were as follows: ten thousand police allocated to cantonal and *opstina* policing functions; and one thousand for functions assigned to the Federation police. An additional five hundred police were allocated for border functions. Because the issue of border control was in dispute between the Federation and cantonal authorities, the decision on control of these forces was deferred.

Defining and Realigning Policing Functions and Structures

Perhaps as critical as the reduction in numbers of Federation police were the elimination, realignment, and restructuring of policing functions within the Federation. Simple acceptance of the Principles and reduction in the numbers of police would not be sufficient to democratize the policing. Only through change in the organizational structures and functions of the existing policing establishment could that goal be achieved.

The focus of the existing organizational structures was on population control and anti-terrorist operations. Large numbers of personnel and many resources were allocated to heavily armed "anti-terrorist" policing units and to population control, particularly through the use of "traffic police" maintaining checkpoints to monitor the movement of the populace. In fact, 70 percent of personnel resources at the cantonal level were reserved for "traffic police." The existing structure also contained extensive police "reserves" that had been activated during the war.

The discussion of these matters was undertaken by the same small working group that was addressing the issue of reduction of forces. The IPTF plans staff prepared a set of draft proposals for new organization, with materials clearly delineating the function of the police at the Federal, cantonal, and *opstina* levels.

The preparation of the proposed organization charts also necessitated review of the GFAP and Federation Constitution to determine the appropriate competencies of each level of government. Here, the IPTF consulted the UN mission's legal advisors, and the IPTF Chief of Staff arranged for a constitutional law expert to be brought from Germany to provide input. The general consensus was that the new Federation Constitution relegated most of the domestic policing function to cantonal control, and the IPTF proposal reflected that consensus.

Ministry representatives of the working group also prepared organization charts. These largely reflected the existing structures. Along with those prepared by the IPTF staff, they were discussed by the working group, and presentations were prepared for the May 16th Federation Commission meeting in Zagreb. On the technical issues, both sets of proposals were similar; hence, the discussion focused on the operational practices of the anti-terrorist units, the traffic police, and the registration of persons and the issuance of identity paperwork. The latter two functions had an impact not only on democratic principles in policing but also freedom of movement within the Federation, which was central to both the GFAP and the Federation's constitution. It was agreed that the function of these anti-terrorist units and the traffic police be reduced or eliminated altogether, and that heavily armed anti-terrorist police should be extremely limited in number and controlled by the Federation Interior Ministry. At the cantonal level a smaller number of police (thirty to fifty) were authorized for enforcement activities such as riot control, hostage negotiation, and search and rescue.

As to the extensive records-keeping function then being performed by police, which revolved around the issuance of identity papers and was enforced by the traffic police and plainclothes special police, the group agreed that record-keeping functions were not police functions and did not require persons with executory law-enforcement powers to carry them out. While it was agreed that the Federation Interior Ministry should temporarily continue to perform this function, the work was to be done by non-sworn personnel.

Meanwhile, some functions that were viewed as essential to democratic policing by the IPTF plans staff were either non-existent or underdeveloped; for example, investigation of citizen complaints, internal investigations, and internal auditing. These were added to the Federation policing structure, as was an accreditation board responsible for establishing standards and vetting police. Training functions, particularly in the area of curriculum development, were enhanced.

Perhaps as significant as the addition and deletion of functions were the reorientation of resources and the articulation of responsibilities agreed to at the Zagreb meeting. Consonant with the Federation Constitution, authority was decentralized at the cantonal and *opstina* levels. At the Federation level technical and training support was to be provided. The only real executory assets at the federal level were to be protective services for people and buildings. Operations support (both command and specialty police) was to be provided at the cantonal level, with executory police service concentrated in the *opstina*.

The process also reoriented the responsibilities of uniformed police officers in the *opstina*. The emphasis was placed on responding to requests for service by the public rather than emphasizing state security, a step seen as a key to advancing police democratization.

All members of the Commission ultimately agreed to most of the restructuring proposals. The significant exception remained the border police, a matter hotly disputed between the Commission's Croat and Bosniak Interior Ministry members. The Croat Deputy Interior Minister felt strongly that border control should be reserved to cantonal governments. The Bosniak Interior Minister felt equally strongly that the border police were a Federation police function. Control of these police and, consequently, control over borders was viewed by both of these former adversaries as key to security. Rather than allow this issue to derail the planning process, the IPTF Commissioner deferred the issue of control over these policing assets to a later date.

The Commissioner's Guidance on Restructuring

At the end of May 1996, the IPTF Commissioner issued guidance concerning the restructuring of the Federation police forces. Extensive notes outlining in detail the program for restructuring the Federation police augmented this guidance, encapsulating the restructuring plan and its rationale, and discussing such tangible issues necessary to the creation of new policing structures as the development of training strategies and implementation strategies.

Training Strategies

The issue of training was viewed by the IPTF as critical to successfully democratizing Federation police, and the planning process in this area was greatly facilitated by the efforts of a team of Austrian policing officials who traveled to BiH in late April to conduct a training assessment. The Austrian Training Team (ATT) traveled throughout both the Federation and the RS, interviewing training personnel at the Federation police high school in Bugouno, and the RS police high school in Banja Luka. They also reviewed training curricula in those schools that had been collected by the IPTF.

After collecting the data, the ATT returned to Vienna to formulate recommendations. A meeting between the ATT and the IPTF plans staff followed on May 9th at the IPTF training base near Zagreb, where it was generally decided that the existing training structures and curricula were inadequate to support a democratic policing initiative, and that they would have to be strengthened and the curricula reformatted. It was also concluded that external training resources would be necessary. To this end, the ATT agreed to begin developing programs that they could support with instructors and Austrian training assets, and at the

ATT's invitation a second coordinating session met in Vienna on May 23rd. The agenda there focused on two objectives: determining what training areas and topics would be necessary for the restructuring; and providing a timeline or synchronization matrix for accomplishing those training tasks.

The first task involved identifying those core areas where training was required, and eight areas were singled out: nation building; external relations; new laws and ethics; human rights issues; management issues and police operations; the police mission; equipment and technology; and specialist training. Within each core area, subjects were further identified.

Next, the IPTF and the ATT attempted to identify the priority attached to each particular subject. For planning purposes, training tasks were grouped into near-term (120 days out), mid-term (180 days out), and long-term (more than 180 days out) categories and the assets available to accomplish the tasks were identified.

The near-term tasks were those essential to initial implementation of the restructuring process and to preparing the police to support the fall elections. Training was to be conducted through a general introduction for all police and targeted training for key leaders. Near-term tasks emphasized the need to continue the planning process by developing curricula, training structures, and democratization training programs. Mid-term tasks emphasized strengthening the training infrastructure and adopting new tactics and technologies in policing; for example, by training specific management groups like executives, trainers, and other key personnel. The long-term tasks focused on the traditional requirements of pre-service and in-service training, as well as new equipment and continuing democratization training.

The preliminary observations of the IPTF staff and the ATT were subsequently published by the IPTF Commissioner in a separate guidance on training. That guidance expanded on the initial recommendations, addressing issues such as the development of performance evaluation standards, expanded public information programs, education programs for all governmental officials on democratic principles, establishing university-level police and public safety policy education programs, and opening the education system to outside experiences by creating a Board of Visitors.

Implementation Strategies

The IPTF plans staff also had to consider strategies for implementing its recommendations in light of both political considerations and the availability of resources.

On the political front, the schedule was compressed to complete restructuring before the September elections. However, because the IPTF was still under its authorized strength and lacked sufficient assets to restructure all Federation policing structures at one time, it was decided that restructuring would occur on a canton-by-canton basis, beginning with the larger, more complex Sarajevo Canton. Although starting with this canton taxed available resources, it was felt that the political significance of Sarajevo warranted making it the initial focus of the implementation process.

Political decisions also influenced the way in which the restructuring would be conducted. Under the Commissioner's plan, all members of Federation units were to be demobilized. This total demobilization model with re-vetting of all personnel, rather than partial demobilization of excess personnel, was selected to ensure that the police force was purged of untrained personnel and war criminals in order to foster public confidence in the new police.

The deadlines set in the Agreement proved to be relatively reasonable. Both key-leader training and an information program for local police officers, for example, were already developed and being implemented prior to the issuance of the training guidance in October. The implementation of the actual restructuring, however, proved much more difficult than anticipated and the projected conclusion of implementation by September 1, 1996 proved to be unrealistic. Both competing political priorities and requirements and inadequate resources precluded meeting that schedule. Almost from the start changing political priorities and attendant operational needs shifted attention from the restructuring to other tasks. Given the relatively small authorized strength of the IPTF mission (1,721 monitors) and the fact that it had yet to achieve its authorized strength, there was always tension between the day-to-day operational need for monitors and the need to train monitors for special projects.

Another complication was the pending election in Mostar and the fact that policing there was being supervised by two authorities, the European Union and the IPTF, and the supervision of local policing operations required close coordination between the two. This need for coordination required, in turn, the IPTF to address issues of common policy on freedom of movement, long-barreled weapons, and the restructuring of the Mostar police. Additionally, the IPTF had to coordinate with the OHR, EU policymakers, IFOR, and local and national police and political leaders on policing the Mostar election.

Once those elections were conducted at the end of June, the IPTF's focus shifted to the Federation's September 1996 elections. This focus further drained resources. These constraints, combined with external limitations, pushed the implementation process substantially behind schedule. The need to review each application and conduct background checks on all police applicants for over eleven thousand positions also posed a substantial obstacle to rapid re-vetting.

Moreover, while the requirements of the re-vetting process were the subject of quick agreement at the Zagreb meeting, the rigid standards established in it made the actual process a lengthy one. The Commission agreed to ten minimum criteria for employment as a police officer, including no criminal record, no allegations of human rights violations, and some type of police training at a post-secondary school. Review of this background material in a country whose record-keeping system was in disarray was time-consuming. Police applicants were also required to undergo a psychological examination and take an examination covering the new Federation Constitution, the Principles, and the Code of Conduct.

Delays were also caused by an absence of resources. The relatively simple issue of purchasing and issuing standardized uniforms continued to plague the Federation. While the IPTF hosted a donors conference to solicit $55.2 million in funding for various programs, shortfalls in resources continued.

A final constraint on the pace of implementation was the lack of a legal infrastructure to support the restructured police. The complex internal-affairs laws governing policing operations in the Federation had to be redrafted before the restructuring could be implemented. This task was not accomplished until October 1996, when a model cantonal internal-affairs law consistent with the restructuring program was prepared and the planning for implementation process thus largely completed.

The Information Campaign

The need for a comprehensive information campaign was recognized early in the IPTF planning process; however, the IPTF lacked the internal resources to effectively implement such a program. The only information campaign mounted by the IPTF was thus the one targeted to the Federation police addressing the restructuring of the Federation Police, human rights, international police ethics and principles, the tasks of the police in the election process, and checkpoint policy. The policy was implemented on a Federation-wide basis through a train-the-trainer program, but the desired public education program on the restructuring process was not realized at the time that implementation of the restructuring program commenced.

Conclusions

Although political and resource imperatives slowed the pace of the implementation program, the Federation has subsequently made measured progress in restructuring. Training programs for key leaders and a police information program were begun in the fall of 1996 and continued into 1997. By February 1997, the Sarajevo Canton had been reduced to the prescribed levels and restructured, and officers in Sarajevo had been through an IPTF-designed information program on the restructured Federation police, and issued new uniforms. Five additional cantons were scheduled to complete restructuring by mid-1997.

Hard and fast conclusions about the IPTF's initial efforts at restructuring police in Bosnia and Herzegovina are nonetheless difficult to draw. The IPTF effort to completely redo an existing policing structure was a novel effort. While other UN missions had been tasked with monitoring existing policing operations, no other mission had been given the additional responsibility for redesigning a system in order to democratize it. The success of an undertaking of this nature may thus only be truly measured in the course of decades. However, the *process* applied by the IPTF in developing and implementing its plan provides some useful insights for current and future police democratization missions.

One of the most important of these lessons can be drawn from one of the failures of the IPTF restructuring plan. Efforts with regard to the RS demonstrate that the reform of policing, despite international mandates, is fundamentally a local issue. If local governmental support does not exist, such a structure cannot be imposed. In short, democratic policing cannot create democratic government and cannot survive in the absence of democratic government. The democratization of policing can only serve as a supportive element of an overall process of democratizing a government structure.

As a corollary to that first lesson, the importance of gathering a consensus of key decision-makers in arriving at general principles and the steps to accomplish those principles cannot be overstated. Contrasted with the RS, the process of restructuring in the Federation was much more successful, due to the ability of the IPTF to engage key Federation decision-makers in the process. The Commission proved to be an excellent vehicle for accomplishing this task. It afforded local officials an opportunity to meet and discuss issues, to provide input, and to reach compromise. It permitted decision-makers to understand the reasons for decisions, examine data, and understand the Guidance of the Commissioner before it was issued. It also allowed the IPTF Commissioner to understand more fully local thoughts and sensibilities before making decisions. The Commission made all parties more invested in and supportive of decisions on restructuring.

A second lesson is the need for a general agreement on underlying principles as the foundation for a plan and the need to develop concrete steps to accomplish those principles. The Principles developed by the IPTF and adopted by both the Federation and the RS, as well as the Standards, provide base planning documents which can be used in evaluating and implementing change in any policing organization. These are core statements of the essence of democratic policing. The Principles and Standards were vetted and accepted by trained policing officials from around the world. They are sufficiently broad so as to be applicable in a variety of legal systems, but they contain sufficient measures to enable professionals to determine whether or not any particular system's design is compatible with democratic policing.

In Bosnia and Herzegovina, they provided sufficient general guidance to evaluate existing structures in the Federation and redesign or eliminate them as necessary to achieve a result consistent with the democratization goal. They also revealed where additional functions were required. Through the application of the Principles and Standards, the Commissioner was able to provide guidance as to specific functions to be performed by various structures or elements throughout the organization. While the actual allocations of those functions will vary from organization to organization, the creation of the Commissioner's Guidance and Guidance Notes provides a problem-solving process applicable to any restructuring process.

A third lesson learned is the importance of a dedicated planning staff and planning resources to accomplish a restructuring project. The creation of a dedicated plans staff was a bold move by the IPTF Commissioner and his Deputy. Given the scarce IPTF personnel available in Sarajevo, the dedication of eight monitors to a plans staff constituted a significant commitment to an untested purpose. Had the RS decided to become more actively engaged in the process, an increase in the plans staff would have been necessary.

A final note regarding the IPTF plans staff: there is a need to consider the importance of dedicated planning assets and to incorporate them at the earliest possible time in developing the mission. The IPTF plans section was not formed until almost four months after the initiation of the mission, and then centered on a planner who had been seconded from IFOR for a limited period. Future missions should recognize the need for incorporating trained planning personnel into the design of the mission command structure.

A fourth lesson offered by the IPTF Federation experience is the universally recognized importance of internal information campaigns and training. To a person, every police professional involved in the restructuring process realized its critical importance to the overall success of the restructuring process. Without that training, the implementation of reforms would have been hollow. Moreover, that training must occur at all levels from the chief executive to the officer on the beat. The IPTF plan recognized that training could be derived from a variety of sources in a variety of forums. The plan further recognized the importance of concepts like key leader training and train-the-trainer programs as essential in an environment of limited resources. The training recommendations and plan developed in conjunction with the ATT and later refined in the Commissioner's Training Guidance provide an excellent model for the development of training programs supportive of democratization projects.

Lessons both positive and negative can also be drawn from the IPTF's implementation program. It is clear that its architects underestimated the difficulties of implementation. The process of completely overhauling an organization as large and complex as the Federation police requires months and years to accomplish, not weeks and months. The cross pressures of other political and legal requirements must be more completely taken into account. Resource constraints and the logistic difficulties of the process of vetting itself are also worthy of greater consideration. Nevertheless, the implementation schedules established in the plan, while overly optimistic, still served a valuable purpose in providing accurate road maps toward restructuring and a continuing guide for implementation. While the process may have been delayed from time to time due to an absence of resources or competing priorities, the direction was always clear.

One final lesson to be drawn from the IPTF plan is the importance of an integrated public information campaign. While public information was recognized as essential to overall success in the restructuring program, the IPTF had no real resources to prepare and conduct an information program directed to the Federation public. Implementing such a program would have reinforced and strengthened the democratization process. Unless and until the public understands and accepts the function of police as service providers who are accountable to them, the democratization process will remain tentative.

Notes

1. An earlier and lengthier version of this paper was presented at the *Conference on Pathways in Reconciliation and Global Human Rights*, Sarajevo, Bosnia-Herzegovina, August 17-19, 2005.

2. Donald Zoufal was among the team of U.S. advisors sent to Bosnia-Herzegovina in January 1996 charged with building a professional police force in that country immediately after the conclusion of the Dayton Accord.

Appendix

Standards for Policing in a Democratic State

Consonant with the internationally accepted principles for policing in a democratic state, standards must be articulated to serve as a guideline for the development of police functions and structures. These standards serve as a measure for determining whether a system of policing is properly designed to achieve the internationally accepted principles for policing in a democratic state.

Principle I

Police must be oriented and operate in accord with the principles of democracy. By this statement we mean that police must orient themselves and always operate in a manner which is consistent with the Constitution and the laws of the Federation. It is the law, created by democratically elected representatives of the people, which must guide police action. Arbitrary enforcement of the law is inconsistent with this principle.

Standards

1. Initial and continued training programs for police officers in the Constitution and criminal codes as well as international standards relevant to policing.
2. Policing operations governed by written policies, regulations, and directives.
3. Process for the investigation and punishment of police misconduct.
4. All police officers individually identifiable to the public when performing police functions.

Principle II

Police, as recipients of public trust, are professionals whose conduct must be governed by a professional code of conduct. By this statement we acknowledge that policing is more than just an occupation. The special trust reposed by the public in their police requires that police exercise the highest standards of ethical conduct in the discharge of their duties. A professional code of ethics for Federation police must be developed to guide Federation police officers.

Standards

1. Written code of conduct for law enforcement officials, suitable for carrying

by individual police officers. This code should not be a detailed list of rules, but should express the values that must animate any action by a police officer.
2. Initial and continued training for all police officers in their duties and obligations under the code of conduct.
3. Accredited program of initial and continued professional training for law enforcement personnel.
4. Participation in international professional organizations of police.

Principle III

Police must have as their highest priority the protection of life. By this statement we acknowledge that human life is precious and the right to life is an accepted fundamental human right. While police officers are afforded special privileges and increased responsibilities with regard to force, the application of force should be minimal in all circumstances and deadly force should only be used to protect the life of the police or the lives of other people.

Standards

1. Minimal level of weaponry as necessary for assigned functions.
2. Officers provided with equipment to minimize injury to citizens and the need to use deadly force in the performance of routine police functions.
3. Long-barreled automatic weapons restricted to specialized squads carefully trained in their use.
4. Promulgation of written policies, regulations, or directives regarding protection of life in police operations.
5. Training of all police officers regarding protection of life.
6. Investigation and written documentation of any incident involving death or serious injury to a citizen as a result of police operations.
7. Mandatory reporting and investigation of all discharges of firearms.

Principle IV

Police must serve the community and are accountable to the community they serve. By this statement we acknowledge that the essence of policing is public service. In a democratic society the police are guardians of public safety. They are accountable to the public in the execution of that task. This means the police must act in such a way so that the public knows, understands, and accepts the police measures which are being undertaken to provide for public safety.

Standards

1. Publication and public dissemination of regular reports on crime and police operations.
2. Establishment of mechanisms to facilitate community and individual requests for police service.
3. Establishment of mechanisms to seek and receive community advice and opinion into police planning on crime problems and police response.
4. A system for the external review of the misconduct of police officers.
5. Internal and external system for receiving and investigating complaints against the police in connection with the delivery of police service.

Principle V

Protection of life and property is the primary function of police operations.
By this statement we mean the primary concern of police operations must be directed to the prevention of crime which threatens life and property. While crime detection is unquestionably an important function of police and has great deterrent value, the central focus of police activity must be on measures to prevent crime.

Standards

1. System for data collection and analysis with respect to crime and police response.
2. Educational programs for the community in proactive crime-prevention.

Principle VI

Police must conduct their activities with respect for human dignity and the basic human rights of all persons. By this statement we mean that in the performance of their duties police must show respect for internationally accepted human rights. Torture and other cruel, inhuman, or degrading treatment of either citizens or other detainees are inconsistent with this principle and cannot be practiced or countenanced by police officers.

Standards

1. Police training in the primacy of the protection of human rights.
2. Written policies, regulations, or directives regarding protection of human rights.
3. Mandatory reporting by police officers of all information of known or alleged

violations of human rights.

Principle VII

Police must discharge their duties in a non-discriminatory manner. By this statement we mean that law enforcement, public safety, and protection of human rights must be handled in a manner which is fair and equal for all persons. Discrimination on the basis of race, gender, religion, language, complexion, political opinion, national origin, birth, property, ethnicity, or any other status in the delivery of police services is incompatible with policing in a democratic state.

Standards

1. Written policies, regulations, or directives prohibiting discrimination in the performance of police duties.
2. Capacity to analyze and investigate complaints of discrimination in the delivery of police services.
3. Training of police officers in the fair and equal delivery of police services on a non-discriminatory basis.
4. Monitoring and reporting of the treatment of police personnel with respect to ethnicity and culture in hiring, promotion, and assignment.
5. Special programs for the recruitment of minorities, including women, to the police.

Chapter 24

NGOs, Peace Support Activity, and the UNPREDEP Mission in Macedonia

Daniela Irrera

Since the Cold War, the Balkan region has presented a remarkable security problem to international organizations (IOs). The object of diplomatic and military experiments, the region has also constituted a considerable test for traditional security management tools. Amidst the post-Yugoslav political and military crises, the Macedonia case was the rare one in which the worst consequences of conflict were avoided and inter-ethnic relations, which vividly exploded in neighboring nations, were well monitored and largely controlled.

In examining the Macedonian case of international preventive diplomacy, this essay stresses the broad utility of non-governmental organizations (NGOs) participating in, and sometimes transforming the nature of, humanitarian intervention and multilateral peace operations. The first part of the study is therefore devoted to that topic. The working assumption in the remainder of this chapter is that the intervention of external actors in Macedonia provides an almost unique case of successful intervention in the Balkans. The long-term effects of the intervention are the result of the joint efforts of intergovernmental actors, operating mainly within the mission of the United Nations' Preventive Deployment Force (UNPREDEP), and non-governmental ones. Even though there was no formal, structured relationship between them, the work that both sets of actors did contributed to the conflict's transformation.

Classifying the NGOs and Identifying Their Tasks

The increasing participation of NGOs in relief and peace-building activities reflects the transformation of two important facets of global security: the nature of contemporary civil conflicts (the so-called "new wars"); and the trend towards humanitarian intervention in contemporary world politics. Following the Cold War, the world began to come to terms with the security implications of a growing number of weak states and, in some cases, of their collapse. Institutional weakness, an absence of the rule of law, and economic backwardness became the cause of "new" wars.[1] These wars do not all have the same characteristics, but some common traits distinguish them from traditional wars, the most important of which is the shift from the interstate to intrastate nature of war. This distinction does not, however, imply that the effects of the conflict are contained within a state's borders. On the contrary, conflict normally spreads to neighbouring countries and in the region. Additionally, these wars frequently involve the active presence of non-state actors.

New wars are also fought by a wide range of political and social groups with different identities and alliance relationships. Moreover, the conflicting parties are sometimes inclined to change the latter,[2] and in many cases the states are not the aggressor and have no role in the causes and development of these conflicts.[3] Finally, often the clear distinction between civilians and combatants dramatically fades away as civilians become deliberately chosen as the targets of military action, with a consequent, dramatic increase in the number of casualties. All these conditions make the management of civil wars no longer dependent only on military means. Peacekeeping missions with extensive civilian functions, including economic reconstruction, institutional reform, and election oversight, are needed in order to improve the chance of success in containing violence and building a lasting peace.[4] Collaboration between civil and military actors, therefore, is increasingly important in managing and solving civil conflicts.

The number of NGOs in and near armed conflict zones has, consequently, been steadily increasing. Their priorities are human and civil rights, peace promotion, and environmental and social issues, but their involvement in humanitarian intervention is producing a wider range of new tasks and roles that include providing specialized groups of experts.[5] It is worth noting, however, that their interests are often quite separate from those of the military and officers representing IOs. Moreover, some *agenda-oriented groups* may even embrace radical positions; for example, that the system must be reformed from its roots, or that capitalism and globalization are to blame for fomenting civil conflicts. Not only are these groups often unwilling to cooperate with intergovernmental organizations; they are apt to accuse peace missions of spreading interventionism throughout the world.[6]

Operational- and *agenda-driven* (also known as "campaigning") NGOs take part in peace operations with differing tools and approaches. Operational NGOs participate directly by mobilizing human, financial, and material resources; carrying out projects and programs; and offering expertise and advice. Campaigning NGOs participate indirectly by seeking wider public support for their agendas, and also by fund-raising on a small scale.[7] A better typology of NGOs is nonetheless needed to sort through their differing approaches to conflict management and humanitarian intervention. To this end, a typology is herein offered based on a merger of two NGO attributes: the NGO's identity and basic principles of action; and their approach to conflict management and humanitarian intervention.

Based on identity, Stoddard identifies three types of NGOs: (1) the Wilsonian type named after President Woodrow Wilson, which adheres to the principles of cooperation and multilateralism as practiced by governments and international institutions (CARE International exemplifies this type); (2) the Dunantist type, so named after the Red Cross founder and social activist, Henry Dunant, which adheres to the principles of impartiality, neutrality, and independence (Doctors without Borders [MSF] and Amnesty International are examples here); and (3) faith-based organizations, which act in harmony with religious principles (Christian Aid, and Islamic Relief, for example).[8] These may then be further broken down based on the NGO's approach to conflict resolution, including its willingness to work with local partners and/or international institutions. Thus, four distinct types of NGOs can be discerned in peace and humanitarian operations:

- pragmatist Wilsonian NGOs, which are comfortable playing a role even in highly-politicized missions;
- principle-oriented Dunantist NGOs, whose action is strongly governed by the belief that conflict management should respect humanitarian principles;
- Solidarist NGOs, which see the root causes of conflict as the main problem to be solved, and thus, like Oxfam, focus on the aims and behavior of military and civilian interventionists; and
- faith-based NGOs, for whom charity and compassion are the driving guidelines for their action.

The range of NGO approaches to peace operations matches, to some extent, the range of conflicts and different forms of intervention required to manage humanitarian problems. As Clark remarks, "The economic, informational, and intellectual resources of NGOs have garnered them enough expertise and influence to assume authority in matters that, traditionally, have been solely within the purview of state administration and responsibility."[9]

As far as an NGO's concept of conflict management and humanitarian intervention is concerned, a common, established approach to humanitarian action can be observed. Even where NGOs have been given the right to be consulted on matters where they are able to provide functional resources, they usually prefer to distance themselves from the military and civilian officers that represent International (Governmental) Organizations (IOs). The majority tend to exercise this right and regularly participate in meetings; however, nearly all complain of their lack of involvement in the planning phase of operations and, more importantly, the significant absence of any coordination between their activities and those of the IOs. The tools used by IOs to manage challenges, especially civil conflicts, are generally considered by NGOs to be useful but also sometimes limited or inefficient in practice. In addition, some NGOs (like Oxfam and *Terres des Hommes*) prefer to act as the watchdogs of peace missions, monitoring activity in order to insure mission transparency.

Groups working in the same zones and focusing on the same problems invariably intersect. Generally speaking, there is no formal or structured system for coordinating their activity in either the planning phase or on the ground. However, several channels which can be considered as forums for cooperation or, more frequently, consultation, do exist. Nevertheless, a significant number of NGOs refuse on principle to have any contact with military missions and frequently prefer to work on quite different projects. Meanwhile, for their part international institutions prefer to create a common set of tools and practices for managing the consequences of serious natural and man-made disasters, and consequently have little interest in accommodating the preferences of these non-state actors. The net result has been a widening of the gap between the interests and activity of governmental and non-governmental actors.

The roles that NGOs play in the field shed light on why this gap is increasing. NGOs play multidimensional and long-term roles covering different phases of a crisis. Three of these roles warrant specific consideration: 1) the knowledge-provider role, which involves NGOs assisting in the diffusion of information pertaining to common practices in the area of humanitarian action; 2) the peace-facilitator role, which involves both NGO's support of IO peace missions and their availability for mediation tasks; and 3) the voice-articulator role, which relates to the role of NGOs in amplifying the expectations of local actors in terms of their social, political, and practical needs.

The *Knowledge-Provider Role* is performed by all NGOs, and in doing so all profit from both the studies of experts in the security field and their individual experiences in applying the *newer* approaches to managing security challenges. Traditional security concepts are associated with the nature of the state, the image of the enemy, and the utilization of military power. Changes in arms technologies, the rising importance of non-state actors in international relations, and such changing approaches to managing conflict as the adoption, initially by European countries, of the concept of cooperative and comprehensive security have combined to challenge this view. Analysts now point to three levels of analysis (the individual, the state, and the international system), and to different dimensions (political, economic, and social) of conflict as also relevant to security issues.[10] The Copenhagen School thus stresses the concept of comprehensive security because a wide range of factors (military, environmental, economic, societal, and political) and the different actors concerned with them affect security matters. It has also drawn attention to the importance of public relations specialists in secularizing/domesticating social issues that political manipulators might use to create states of emergency. Efforts have subsequently been made to merge these new concepts into a perspective useful to practitioners.

As W. A. Knight summarized several years ago, terms like comprehensive security, common security, and human security currently "are being utilized to embrace the range of issues that are being placed on a revised security agenda of an emerging global polity."[11] In short, again in Knight's words, the concept of security must change "from an exclusive stress on national security to a much greater focus on people's security, from security through armaments to security through human development, from territorial security to food, employment and environmental security."[12]

NGOs, especially the Wilsonian ones, have been particularly responsive to these suggestions, and have developed their own security management language, processes, and practices. During the same period, Pragmatist and Solidarist NGOs have incorporated a wide range of tools into their security management activities. This process has involved sectors concerned with information, logistics, and the analysis of threats, risks, and vulnerabilities.[13] In turn, Dunantist NGOs have emphasized the importance of rapid, non-partisan, non-bureaucratic, risk-taking intervention. Wilsonian and Dunantist organizations have also been able to supply information useful to regulating conflict and managing peace; for example, effective rule-making procedures, and methods for applying accepted norms and standards.[14] Finally, it is worth mentioning as well under this heading that in recent years, the NGO community as a whole has been particularly keen in championing the responsibility to protect (R2P) principle. Especially the faith-based NGOs have been adamant in arguing in favor of the responsibility to protect principle in challenging the global community's inadequate responses to morally indefensible mass atrocities.

NGOs are able to function effectively as *peace-facilitators* because they are commonly considered independent agents in peace operations rather than a part of the military structure and they strongly desire to protect that independent status. Their personnel do usually work alongside the official, military, and civilian personnel; however, consistent with evolving concepts of peacekeeping, their role is to assist local parties who are promoting human security, strengthening the rule of law, and fostering economic and social development. Peacekeeping was initially conceived as a mechanism to help countries torn by conflict create conditions of peace, but over the years it has changed in terms of aims, methods, and participating actors. This enlargement of the peacekeeping mandate, in particular to include humanitarian and political assistance, has resulted in a massive increase in the number of civilian personnel and non-military activities. Thus, in the organization of complex multifunctional operations with both military duties and civilian tasks, NGOs are now accepted as useful participants in the execution of civilian tasks.

Nor is the value of NGO participation limited to peace and security operations. NGOs can also contribute directly to the political success of humanitarian missions. The Sant Egidio Community, for example, has been an important actor in mediation and diplomatic negotiations, promoting the peace process in conflict zones like Burundi, Mozambique, and Palestine. Similarly, the Centre for Humanitarian Dialogue and the Crisis Management Initiative (CMI) facilitated peace talks in Aceh before the military arrived, and CMI was "called" by the Georgian Government to assist its stabilization efforts. Meanwhile, Dunantist

NGOs like Amnesty International and Oxfam have been successful in creating pressure for humanitarian undertakings, while in still other cases NGOs have helped informally to improve mission performance. Findings of misconduct in their mission evaluations, for example, can lead to a reshaping of mission mandates in such differing areas as the legal basis of the operation and the behavior of military personnel.

At the same time, such criticism can affect the ability of NGOs to cooperate with other personnel in official missions, and may thus hinder an NGO's role as a peace-facilitator. Similarly, the independent and neutral status of many humanitarian NGOs can be a problem in achieving good civil-military cooperation. However, even though some analysts advise NGOs to be less rigid and to take part in coordinated actions, compromising principles is always hard for NGOs working in the field, and is an option they rarely choose.[15] Meanwhile, the NGOs' role as peace-facilitator remains increasingly essential, especially in the area of logistics. There, NGOs manage such tasks as: site selection; the gaining of access to offices, residences, and warehouses; personnel matters such as hiring local workers and attuning them to professional norms; providing vehicles, drivers, and tracking information; and communication in such areas as the broadcasting of daily news and extreme emergency information; and incident reporting. All of these tasks help establish a good relationship between NGO personnel and the local population, and thus better perform the third, *voice articulator*, role of NGOs in peace operations.

Although the military invests significantly in mission preparation, it often remains unaware of the actors in the area where its personnel are deployed. Normally, the military does not participate in coordination meetings, refuses to make information accessible, and has little interest in civil programs. Consequently, peace missions are frequently blamed for neglecting local demands and offers of cooperation. Furthermore, where cooperation programs do exist, they are more likely to reflect the priorities of the military and civilian personnel at the heart of the mission than the needs of the local beneficiaries of the intervention.[16] Conversely, because of the areas left to them, NGOs are able to establish a close working relationship with local individuals and associations.

Wilsonian, Dunantist, and faith-based NGOs, in particular, attach great importance to providing a voice for local civil society. For this reason, they work hard to involve local associations and groups in different phases of a humanitarian intervention undertaking. NGOs like MSF and Oxfam are quite successful in this respect, probably because of their identity and approach to the matter. In many cases, there are established, structural relationships between globally active NGOs; for example, Non Violent Peace Force, Pax Christi International, Interpeace, and *Terres des Hommes,* and their local counterparts or affiliates. The majority of NGOs, however, are very much committed to playing the role of voice-articulator even if they lack such structured ties. Indeed, they must initiate a dialogue with local actors and obtain their confidence because the successful outcome of their mission depends on it.

This objective is normally achieved by NGOs providing assistance and basic goods to the local population. Moreover, the help that NGOs supplied to countries in conflict and to the victims of disasters and emergencies was impressive even during the 1980s and early 1990s. In 1989, for example, European-based NGOs delivered approximately 180,000 tons of food aid to Africa, and two and a half times that amount (450,000 tons) in 1991. By the end of the decade, it was estimated that some 400 to 500 international NGOs were involved in humanitarian actions worldwide, and that NGOs collectively spent an estimated $9-10 billion annually, reaching some 250 million people living in absolute poverty.[17] Those figures have continued to grow.

This solid performance by NGOs tendering emergency relief work allows NGOs to obtain the confidence of local populations which, in turn, facilitates and gives credibility to NGOs as articulators of local opinions even in complex civil conflicts. In other words, the practical assistance that NGOs provide makes them more effective in achieving their objectives in the area of humanitarian intervention, facilitates the building of longer term mutual relationships, and increases the likelihood that the local population will embrace the reconstruction process.

To illustrate the utility of NGOs in this area, let us now turn to an examination of the Macedonian case and the UNPREDEP mission there, which well underscores both the hugely productive potential of NGO-IO cooperation and the practical problems that can result because of the operational gaps often separating their respective activities.

The Conflict in Macedonia

The break-up of Yugoslavia in 1992 contributed to an escalation of the troubles in the adjacent areas pursuing the slow processes of democratization and economic liberalization. These countries were simultaneously undergoing major changes in their institutions of government (including electoral reforms and the introduction of true mechanisms of representation), a thorough transformation of their distribution systems from a centrally planned economy to a market oriented one, and a modernization of civil society life. Overseeing these difficult tasks were government *élites* who were linked to the past and to its old styles of management. Elections took place throughout the region, and new parties and politicians emerged, expressing a public will to embrace democracy and pursue entry into the European Union. In several instances, however, once in office during the early years of the transition process, they evinced a very different attitude. The Southeastern countries, in particular, found it very difficult to escape from their endemic ethnic problems, which led to long and bloody civil wars.

These struggles contributed to a dismantling of the troubled economic situation by creating an illicit black market system in which guerrilla groups, paramilitaries, and sometimes official armies sold and bought weapons. The same networks were used to channel illicit immigration towards Western Europe. External intervention followed, but the diplomatic solutions that the US and EU introduced in their quest to find an acceptable regional geopolitical order (beginning with the Dayton Peace Treaty in 1995) were only partial responses to the situation. Even when they constituted a diplomatic success in ending the wars in the former Yugoslavia, they were not sufficient to help the new countries establish good governing practices. As a consequence, the Balkan region, and in particular its western part, had to face its transition process amidst both old and new problems. Weak institutions and inefficient bureaucracies had to manage depressed economies and inflation, and to accommodate their very dissatisfied peoples.[18]

Background

The Former Yugoslavian Republic of Macedonia (FYROM) was the only union republic of former Yugoslavia that did not suffer from a military conflict when Yugoslavia broke apart, but rather gained its independence in a peaceful manner in 1991. The independence and full diplomatic recognition of the FYROM was strongly supported during the peace talks that produced the Dayton agreement; however, this new country was born with serious endemic and structural problems requiring redress. More specifically, it emerged into independence with weak institutions, a poorly developed economy, and, above all, ingrained lines of ethnic division separating its political leaders as well as its communities. As a consequence, from Macedonia's very beginning, fragmented political parties created an unstable political landscape.[19]

After independence, a census held in June-July 1994 under the supervision of international experts registered approximately 430,000 Albanians or 22.9% of the country's 1,937,000 inhabitants.[20] The Albanians were allowed to organize their own political parties at this time but continued to experience various forms of discrimination. Previously, in order to prevent the wars in Croatia and Bosnia-Herzegovina from spreading to Macedonia, three months after Macedonia's 1991 declaration of independence the United Nations' Security Council passed Resolution 795 authorizing the establishment of a UN Protection Force in the Former Yugoslavia (UNPROFOR). It was this force that was later changed into the UN Preventative Deployment Force (UNPREDEP) when ethnic tensions inside the country became a threat to the country's stability.

Meanwhile, on March 24, 1999, NATO waged war on Yugoslavia in order to stop the Serbian armed attack in Kosovo on that Serbian region's Albanian community. That war had the spill-over effect of destabilizing the Kosovo-Macedonia frontier and acerbating ethnic tensions inside Macedonia. Following NATO's offensive against Yugoslavia, more than half of Kosovo's almost two million population was on the move. The Macedonian government was caught between international expectations that it accommodate the Albanian refugees and protests from Macedonians, many of whom assumed a pro-Serbian and anti-

Kosovo Albanian stance as the proportion of Albanians in Macedonia significantly increased due to the inflow of Kosovo Albanians.[21] Subsequently, fighting erupted between Macedonian Albanian insurgents and Macedonian government security forces, and security conditions in the country rapidly deteriorated. Between February and August 2001, Macedonia edged close to its own civil war as an Albanian insurgency raged in several villages and even in the suburbs of Skopje. Before it ended, the conflict displaced over 170,000 people, including 74,000 internally displaced.

On July 26, 2001, a ceasefire was announced, and on August 13th Macedonian and Albanian leaders signed a political agreement under US and EU pressure. That agreement, the Ohrid Framework Agreement, guaranteed civil rights protection to Albanians on the condition of the Albanian insurgents disarming.

The Power-Sharing Agreement

In September 2002, parliamentary elections paved the way for the signing of a power-sharing arrangement between the Social Democrat-led Macedonian coalition and an Albanian party. That agreement also owed much to the crucial role that international intervention had played in stabilizing Macedonia the previous year.

Preventive diplomacy has been a tool of policy-makers since the Congress of Vienna. As Alice Ackermann notes, since then leading European diplomats have continued to work to promote mutual consultation, collective decision making, confidence building measures, buffer zones, and other means of maintaining a peace.[22] Over the decades, these tools have also been adopted and developed by military alliances and IOs. During his tenure, UN Secretary General Dag Hammarskjold officially included preventive diplomacy in the UN's set of tools for achieving peace, and began the practice of introducing peacekeeping forces into major arenas of conflict as management devices. Such missions have continued to multiply since that time, augmenting such other tools of preventive diplomacy as Good Office Diplomacy and election monitoring. Moreover, since the end of the Cold War these same tools have been widely adopted by a variety of regional organizations, including the Organization for Security and Cooperation in Europe (OSCE), the African Union, and the Orissa Society of the Americas (OSA).[23]

Building on the work of his predecessors, in 1992 UN Secretary General Boutros Boutros-Ghali issued his *Agenda for Peace*, in which the essence of conflict prevention was defined as seeking "to identify at the earliest possible stage situations that could produce conflict, and to try through diplomacy to remove the sources of danger before violence results."[24] Despite all of the precedents, according to Ackermann the case of Macedonia can nonetheless be considered a unique case of conflict prevention because of its buffer role nature, Macedonia's economic fragility at the time, and its highly fragmented, multiethnic society. In somewhat similar contexts, preventive multifaceted diplomacy had been a successful tool in the past, and the presence of the US and UN in the Macedonian action was widely perceived to have been extremely important to the success of the Macedonian mission.[25] So, too, was the presence of NGOs on the ground in the country, sharing the same territory, people, and problems with the military troops, albeit with their own level of activity and under different mandates.

The UNPREDEP Mission

The UNPREDEP mission is now widely seen as the first case of *preventive deployment* by the United Nations involving the stationing of troops between two hostile parties in order to *deter* the onset of violence and war.[26] The mission was initially deployed along the border between Macedonia and Kosovo in southern Serbia in order to prevent the civil wars brewing elsewhere in the former Yugoslavia from spreading to Macedonia after its citizens approved the country's independence in a September 8, 1991 national referendum. More precisely, the deployment was authorized by the Security Council in late 1992, three months after it received an official request from Macedonian President Kiro Gligorov for assistance, and amidst the widespread violence already occurring in Croatia and Bosnia-Herzegovina.[27] In fact, the peacekeepers themselves were initially deployed as part of the UN Protection Force (UNPROFOR), which functioned primarily in Croatia and Bosnia-Herzegovina, and it was not until April, 1995, in response to Croatian and Macedonian requests, that the name of the Macedonian peacekeeping contingent was changed to UNPREDEP, an anagram for United Nations Preventive Deployment. At no point, however, had the Macedonia wing of UNPROFOR approached the size of the units in Croatia and Bosnia-Herzegovina. Quite to the contrary, it began and remained small throughout the 1990s, beginning in 1993 when only 700 or so Norwegian, Finnish, and Swedish troops arrived to set up a monitoring mission, and being only slightly augmented in July of that year when a US contingent of an additional 500 arrived.[28]

The UNPREDEP mission itself consisted of three pillars and phases of operation. The first pillar was the traditional work of peacekeeping missions; namely, the stationing of troops and military observers along Macedonia's borders in order to assist the country's security forces in deterring aggression. The second pillar included the broader political mandate of providing "good offices" in order to maintain peaceful relations among the parties to the potential conflict, and the deployment of a UN police force to prevent human rights violations against minorities. The third pillar was more unique.

Described as the "human dimension" phase, the third pillar focused on strengthening civil institutions in Macedonian society, international aid, and international cooperation. Two of the priority areas of this phase stressed enhancing social development and improving crime-prevention efforts. Thus, according to UN reports, UNPREDEP military personnel conducted more than 160 patrols a week, and during the month of March 1997, those patrols increased to more than 190 per week.[29]

As far as conflict resolution is concerned, missions are generally considered successful when they facilitate or assist in the establishment of power-sharing agreements or in creating the conditions for such agreement. They are partially successful if they only put in place the elements for a peace or power-sharing agreement. By these tests, UNPREDEP can clearly be placed among the successful missions because it fulfilled all of these criteria while also fully containing the conflict.[30]

NGOs in Macedonia

Together with local organizations, several international NGOs have worked in Macedonia since the early 1990s to address the potentially dangerous cleavage separating the country's principal ethnic communities. Among others, Caritas, the Red Cross, the Open Society, and Search for Common Ground have been active in Macedonia in this area.[31]

These and other NGOs in the country have generally sought to help local governmental authorities bring together the ethnic communities that formerly lived in isolation from each other. In particular, international and local NGOs have 1) strongly supported the creation of a social policy and social care think tank; 2) organized the instruction of trainers in developing theoretical and practical skills, and professional ethics; 3) provided home-based childhood education; 4) trained personnel in non-violent conflict resolution and; 5) assisted in the reconstruction of civil society in low-income, multi-ethnic neighborhoods. In addition, during the mid 1990s and again after 2001, Solidarist and faith-based NGOs and university-based research groups labored to get ethnically mixed groups to work together. We will focus here on the activity of one of these groups deeply involved in promoting interethnic dialogue, Search for Common Ground (SFCG).

The SFCG was established in 1982 as a global NGO with headquarters in Washington DC and Brussels. Today, it is the largest NGO participating in peace building activity, focusing broadly on consensus-building in established democracies as well as developing ones (as opposed to just those states specifically affected by conflicts). The organization's primary field activity deals with conflict transformation, based on the assumption that in any situation, conflict is transmitted through public institutions, people, and local organizations. Once the SFCG begins a program in a country, it tends to be active for long periods of time, and that has been true in Macedonia, where it has been promoting programs focused on the media and education, and fostering interethnic dialogue at all levels since 1994.[32]

One of these projects, Bridges for the New Balkans, was established at the regional level to create a common vision for the future of the Balkan area. This project has now entered its second phase, stressing regional interethnic media projects involving the press, television, and radio broadcast stations. *Nashe Maalo* (Our Neighborhood), for example, was the first children's television series in Macedonia. Its programs encourage a mutual respect and understanding among youth of different ethnic groups between ages seven and twelve and, more broadly, aim at integrating members of different ethnic communities into shared reporting endeavors. Accordingly, SFCG engages local journalists and experts in varying fields in its reporting on regional events.

The Mozaik project also deserves mention. It is a unique model of multilingual and multicultural pre-school education initiated in 1998 with "the primary goal of socializing children into a multicultural environment at the earliest possible age, to teach tolerance and respect for the diversity of cultures, and to help different ethnic communities collaborate and communicate with each other." Its long-term aim is to integrate the Macedonian public school system.[33]

As part of its methodology, SFCG personnel regularly evaluate the impact of their programs on local audiences. Thus, during the summer of 2004, SFCG commissioned an evaluation of its work in order to contribute to its understanding of its progress and to test its approach to peace-building.[34] Independent evaluators confirmed that the *Nashe Maalo* show produced by SFCG is widely known, that a large number of children are continually exposed to its influence, and that therefore it contributes to Macedonian society as a whole in terms of outcomes (defined as: audience size, and changes in knowledge, attitudes, and to a certain extent behavior) and impact. As the evaluation confirmed, the SFCG strategy thus has pronounced effects in some priority areas which may in the future reduce the probability of interethnic conflict.[35]

These examples are obviously not exhaustive. Even less do they totally describe all of the activities performed by NGOs in Macedonia. As the SFCG representative told me in Brussels, there are dozens of programs as well as hundreds of organizations working on the ground, all in the hope that their work will someday have an impact that will change and transform the troubles besetting contemporary Macedonia.

Conclusions

Peacekeeping was initially conceived as a mechanism to help countries torn by conflict create the conditions of peace. Over the years, however, it has altered in terms of its aims, methods, and those participating in its activity. The enlargement of the peacekeeping mandate, in particular to include humanitarian and political assistance, resulted in a massive increase in the number of civilian personnel and non-military activities, and in the organization of complex, multifunctional operations with both military and civilian tasks.[36] In this environment, NGOs were accepted as participants supporting the civilian tasks, normally working alongside the official military and civilian personnel of the peace missions while assisting local parties in such fields as the promotion of human security, the strengthening of the rule of law, and economic and social development.

The UNPREDEP mission had several tasks, but its primary goal by the early years of the twenty-first century was to prevent the spread of violence between the country's Macedonian and Albanian communities. From the outset, however, it was organized as a conflict prevention measure with military and civil mandates, including a human dimension. As the UN Secretary General reported, "the civilian component of the mission has also been active in initiating contacts among various segments of the population in order to address a number of underlying socio-economic problems which, if neglected or overlooked, have the potential to exacerbate political tensions." [37]

Within this human dimension, fostering social and interethnic dialogue was a major priority, and here NGOs made a significant contribution. SFCG programs were never directly involved with the peacekeeping mission in the sense that no formal cooperation was either established or required. Indeed, even though NGOs were entitled to be consulted by the UN Peacebuilding Commission on those matters where they could provide functional resources, they usually preferred to maintain their positions separate from those of the military and officers representing the international organizations. This separation also enabled them to serve as watchdogs over the activities of the peace missions, thus insuring mission transparency.[38]

NGOs working in the same areas and on the same problems as the military missions and their IO collaborations, however, invariably results in overlapping activities. Thus, insofar as possible and without compromising their independence, NGOs attempt to promote dialogue among the various political forces and ethnic communities in a country to exert a stabilizing effect on the ground. In terms of the specific roles played by NGOS, the SFCG in Macedonia was most successful as a voice articulator because of its close work with local organizations and partners and its success in attaining the confidence of local actors. Instead of providing basic goods, they worked to attack the lack of understanding that lies at the heart of ethnic conflict. In so doing, they indirectly contributed to UNPREDEP's first aim. Moreover, insofar as they focused their activities on children and young generations, they potentially created the conditions for a more peace-loving future within the country's peoples.

In performing the latter task, the NGOs also performed something of a peace facilitator role because they facilitated the building of mutual confidence among leaders spanning Macedonia's ethnic divides and thus increased the likelihood that the country's peoples would embrace the political and social reconstruction process in Macedonia. This is neither a simple nor automatic outcome of humanitarian intervention, but the work of NGO activists can contribute meaningfully to it.

Finally, the Macedonia case was a unique one, because the conflict that initially prompted the deployment of the troops was linked to the ethnic balance in the country as well as to the wars raging elsewhere in Yugoslavia. This paradoxically made third party intervention both more urgent and more difficult. The conflict was attenuated and a more democratic political process launched because of the international efforts that followed and which have produced long-term and still visible effects. Even though there was no formal and structured relationship between the NGOs and the military, the preventive diplomacy done on the ground by the UNPREDEP mission cannot be considered apart from the local programs promoted by the NGOs. They indirectly and collectively contributed to the Macedonian-Albanian conflict's transformation.

Notes

1. See Kalevi J. Holsti, *The State, War, and the State of War* (Cambridge: Cambridge University Press, 1996).

2. See Mary Kaldor, *New and Old Wars: Organized Violence in a Global Era* (Cambridge: Polity Press, 1999).

3. See C. Monteleone and R. Rossi, "Security and Global Management: A Global Perspective, " in *Security Identity and the Southern Caucasus: the Role of the EU, the US and Russia*, eds. Michael Geistlinger, Francesca Longo, Gocha Lordkipanidze, and Yunis Nasibli (Vienna: Verlag, 2008), 49-80.

4. See Michael Doyle and Nicholas Sambanis, "International Peacebuilding: A Theoretical and Quantitative Analysis, " *American Political Science Review* 94, no. 4 (2000): 779-801.

5. See Dieter Rucht, "Critique of Capitalism in the Era of Globalization – Old Wine in New Bottles?" in *Building a Transnational Civil Society: Global Issues and Global Actors* eds. Ingo Richter, Sabine Berking, and Ralf Muller-Schmid. (London: Palgrave, 2006), 109-134.

6. Rucht, "Critique of Capitalism in the Era of Globalization."

7. See Peter Willetts, "Transnational Actors and International Organizations in Global Politics," in *The Globalization of World Politics*, eds. John B. Baylis and Steve Smith (New York: Oxford University Press, 2001), 356-383.

8. Abby Stoddard, "Humanitarian NGOs: Challenges and Trends," in *Humanitarian Action and the "Global War on Terror": A Review of Trends and Issues,* eds. Joanna Macrae and Adele Harmer (London: HGP Report 14, 2003).

9. Ann Marie Clark, "Non-governmental Organizations and Their Influence on International Society," *Journal of International Affairs* 48, no. 2 (1995): 507-525, 507-8.

10. See Barry Buzan, *People, States, and Fear* (Essex: Pearson, 1991).

11. W. Andy Knight, *Adapting the United Nations to a Postmodern Era: Lessons Learned* (New York: Palgrave, 2001), 14.

12. Knight, *Adapting the United Nations to a Postmodern Era,* 14.

13. See Deborah Avant "NGOs, Corporations and Security Transformation in Africa," *International Relations* 21, no.2 (2007), 143-161.

14. Ulrich Beck, "Reframing Power in a Globalized World," *Organization Studies* 29, no. 5 (2008): 793-804.

15. G. Klose, "The Role of the Military in a Changing World: CIMIC: Military Stepping Stones on the Road to Civil Society," in *Building a Transnational Civil Society: Global Issues and Global Actors*, eds. Ingo K. Richter, Sabine Berking, and Ralk Müller-Schmid (New York: Palgrave MacMillan, 2007), 201-216.

16. See Sebastiaan Rietjens, "Managing Civil-Military Cooperation: Experiences from the Dutch Provincial Reconstruction Team in Afghanistan," *Armed Forces & Society* 34, no. 2 (2008): 173-207.

17. Francis K. Abiew, "Assessing Humanitarian Intervention in the Post-Cold War Period: Sources of Consensus," *International Relations* 14, no. 2 (1998): 61-90.

18. See Daniela Irrera, "The Balkanisation of Politics: Crime and Corruption in Albania," in *International Trade Issues and Perspectives*, ed. P. Satyanarayana Prasad (Hyderabad: Icfai University Press, 2008), 177-212.

19. See Henry Sokalski, *An Ounce of Prevention: Macedonia and the UN Experience in Preventive Diplomacy* (Washington DC: United States Institute of Peace, 2003).

20. The most recent, official population count confirmed that the population of Macedonia remains a mixture of Slavic Macedonians (the majority), Albanians, and small ethnic minorities of Turks, Roma, and Serbs.

21. Mladen Klemencic, "Threats to Macedonia's Stability and Borders," *IBRU Boundary and Security Bulletin,* (Spring 2001): 73-80.

22. Alice Ackermann, *Making Peace Prevail: Preventing Violent Conflict in Macedonia* (Syracuse: Syracuse University Press, 2000), 16.

23. Sokalski, *An Ounce of Prevention.*

24. Boutros Boutros-Ghali, *An Agenda for Peace: Preventive Diplomacy, Peacemaking and Peace-keeping* (New York: United Nations A/47/277 17 June 1992).

25. Ackermann, *Making Peace Prevail*, 162.

26. Paul Diehl, Daniel Druckman, and James Wall, "International Peacekeeping and Conflict Resolution: A Taxonomic Analysis with Implications," *The Journal of Conflict Resolution* 42, no. 1 (1998): 33-55.

27.Klemencic, *Threats to Macedonia's Stability and Borders*, 73-80.

28. More facts about the UNPREDEP mission can be found at the UN DPKO website. See also Daniela Irrera, "NGO's Roles in Humanitarian Interventions and Peace Support Operations," in *Multilateral Security and ESDP Operations*, eds. Fulvio Attinà and Daniela Irrera (London: Ashgate, 2010), 71-85.

29. UN Secretary-General, *Report of the Secretary-General on the United Nations Preventive Deployment Force* (New York: United Nations S/1997/365 12 May 1997).

30. See Sandy Babcock, "The Efficacy of Peacekeeping," in *The Cornwallis Group VIII: Analysis for Governance and Stability* (Ottawa: The Canadian Peacekeeping Press, Lester B. Pearson Canadian International Peacekeeping Training Centre, 14-17 April 2003), 79-99.

31. Ackermann, *Making Peace Prevail.*

32. The author interviewed the SFCG representative in Brussels in November 2009.

33. For more information about SFCG programs see www.sfcg.org.

34. The evaluation can be found on SFCG website www.sfcg.org. It was published on 23 December 2004 by Emery Brusset and Ralf Otto.

35. See Emery Brusset and Ralf Otto, *Evaluation of Nashe Maalo: Design, Implementation, and Outcomes*. Social Transformation through Media (Channel Research, 23 December 2004).

36. See Attinà, and Irrera, *Multilateral Security and ESDP Operations*.

37. UN Secretary-General, *Report of the Secretary-General on the United Nations Preventive Deployment Force.*

38. Alexandru Grigorescu, "Transparency of Intergovernmental Organizations: The Roles of Member States, International Bureaucracies and Nongovernmental Organizations," *International Studies Quarterly* 51 (2007): 625-648.

Part 6

Conclusions

Chapter 25

Conclusions: Third Parties and the Management of Communal Conflict

William J. Lahneman

The preceding chapters have provided both a broad survey of and specific cases involving the diverse set of tools and processes that third parties can use when trying to resolve communal conflicts and rebuild post-conflict states. Individuals in a number of specialized fields, both in and outside of government, wield these tools, the effective employment of which requires careful, interdisciplinary coordination and integration. This is a tall order, since success in each field requires many years of dedicated effort to master its theory and practice. Diplomats spend significant time honing their negotiating skills, military officers concentrate on studying the profession of arms, lawyers practice law, and economists worry about economic matters. As a result, diplomats are not usually also military strategists, military officers are not experts at running NGOs, and international legal scholars are not usually skilled in the application of economic sanctions. Often, political leaders are none of these things, but rather come from backgrounds anchored in domestic social and economic policies rather than security issues.

Yet, if there is one thing that the chapters in this volume have demonstrated again and again, it is the fact that the diplomatic, legal, economic, military, and nation-building aspects of conflict resolution are interrelated and must be treated as such for successful conflict management to occur. It is not so much that practitioners and scholars deny these connections, but rather that their lack of familiarity with the strengths, weaknesses, and vagaries of the other disciplines can lead to misconceptions and missteps, some of which can result in missed opportunities for conflict resolution, or create more problems than they solve.

This volume has sought to improve the practice of conflict resolution by examining each category of conflict resolution mechanism, studying specific cases where these tools have been applied, and attempting to identify pitfalls and best practices in the process. This concluding chapter will draw from this body of knowledge to point out some significant potential misconceptions, make general observations about the conflict resolution process, offer recommendations for improvement, and discuss certain tensions that appear to be inherent features of the third party humanitarian intervention and conflict management processes.

Important Misconceptions?

The volume highlights some aspects of the conflict resolution process that, despite wide acceptance and practice, warrant reexamination because they appear to be misleading.

Stephen Collins asserts that conventional wisdom is incorrect when it holds that economic sanctions are generally ineffective as tools of conflict resolution. He cites evidence indicating that there have been many cases in which economic tools—including both incentives and sanctions—have been used to help diminish or end internal conflicts. He argues that one reason for this misconception is the lack of a dedicated community of stakeholders who advocate for economic measures in the same way that the diplomatic community and military establishments push for negotiated settlements and military solutions respectively.

Matthew Hoddie and Caroline Hartzell argue that the IMF's structural readjustment programs—the standard approach for stabilizing monetary policies to support rebuilding and growing sustainable post-conflict market economies—might do more harm than good in post-conflict situations. Their rigorous argument, based on quantitative analysis, is certainly worth consideration. If correct, at least some current policies are harming rather than enabling the chances for successful nation-building in post-conflict societies.

In the area of military intervention, William Lahneman asserts that, just because the use of military force is considered the last resort, it does not follow that it will succeed in all situations. Not all situations lend themselves to military solutions. One of the benchmarks for determining the efficacy of military intervention should be whether it contributes meaningfully to the achievement of coherent political goals. For example, M.S. Wallace offers reasons why the use of non-violent (i.e., unarmed civilian) peace forces are sometimes superior to using military forces and should play larger roles in stabilization and reconstruction activities in certain circumstances.

With regard to nation building, Joseph Rudolph reminds readers of the incredible difficulty attendant in democratizing multinational populations that have just experienced civil war. He observes that making a post-conflict state into a functioning democracy is a multi-generational project, meaning that the democratization process must continue for many years after intervention has ended. However, as Mohammad Ashraf has detailed, intervening powers' conviction that a top-down, western-designed democratic reconstruction model is the best option is of questionable validity, at least in cases such as Afghanistan.

Among other things, such top-down programs might not stand the test of time after third party pressure, funding, and interest in such endeavors wane.

Meanwhile, Daniela Irrera and other authors point out problems with how governmental entities and nongovernmental organizations typically relate to one another in post-conflict situations. Many of these problems appear to defy lasting solutions because of the disparate goals and interests of these different actors.

Broad Observations

The volume also indicates that several broad generalizations about third parties and internal conflict seem warranted. Some conclusions are more obvious than others, but it is always wise to review basic premises at the beginning of any complex undertaking and keep them in mind as events unfold. First, the range of tools available to third parties interested in intervening in communal conflicts is robust and continues to grow. This is good news, even though many of these advances are the result of past mistakes. While everyone tries to minimize mistakes, the expansion of humanitarian interventions following the Cold War, plus some of the tensions inherent in conducting such operations (discussed below) guaranteed that mistakes would happen. However, it is important to draw the appropriate conclusion from these experiences. It is vitally important to remember that humanitarian third party interventions have been effective at limiting death and destruction over what would have occurred in the absence of intervention. Also, the increasing body of international law on this subject has the potential to clarify future cases of intervention and reduce mistakes in the process.

Second, there is no fixed methodology concerning when and how third parties should apply the different conflict resolution mechanisms. As Stephen Collins notes, "In certain cases, dialogue diplomacy may constitute the optimal approach, with more coercive approaches being unnecessary or counterproductive. In other episodes, robust coercion may be warranted and constitute the only effective strategy." In still other cases, economic sanctions or incentives might work best. Similarly, as Joseph Rudolph notes about nation building, there is no "cookie cutter 'Nation-Building' design. Even when the government is supportive of the efforts and resources exist, strategies must be tailored to the needs and conditions of individual countries, and the process frequently proceeds on a slow, trial-and-error basis."

Third, despite the fact that a particular approach might be the best fit in a given situation, typically a number of different tools used as elements of an integrated strategy will work best. Skillful integration of the different types of conflict resolution tools can produce results that are greater than if each tool were used separately.

Fourth, as Paul McCartney notes, it is useful to distinguish between conflict *resolution* and conflict *cessation*. In addition to lending insight into the negotiating process, this distinction is important at times when it is imperative to prevent a particular event during an internal conflict. For example, in 2011, NATO used air power and a small number of ground forces to intervene in Libya on short notice for the purpose of stopping or defeating Libyan military plans to massacre thousands of civilians in the Libyan city of Benghazi. The goal of intervention was to prevent these imminent mass killings; no one thought that the NATO intervention alone would resolve the underlying factors that were causing the internal conflict. The point is that, while this volume and most of the conflict resolution literature deal with efforts to not only end hostilities but also resolve underlying conflicts and produce functioning, stable, democratic states, there will be times when conflict cessation is urgently necessary. In such circumstances, intervention must occur before comprehensive plans can be developed. One should not expect comprehensive results from such hastily organized and highly focused operations.

Specific Recommendations

The volume offers a number of major, specific lessons that can enhance the conflict resolution process. Paul McCartney stresses that diplomacy is dependent upon "windows of opportunity" if it is to prove effective. Outside these periods, warring parties believe that they can win the conflict and thus lack an incentive to negotiate in good faith, although they might try to use negotiations to gain political or military advantage (e.g., time to rearm and rest their forces). Windows of opportunity usually correspond to situations in which both sides have reached "ripeness" for resolution, i.e., they both have reached a "mutually hurting stalemate" in which they perceive that they can no longer attain their goals through force of arms. Interestingly, Steven Burg asserts that, in Bosnia, western intervening powers induced the necessary state of ripeness by escalating their use of military coercion until the warring parties came to believe that they could not achieve their goals through military force. Is such an induced ripeness something to be used more often to resolve conflicts? Answering this question is outside the scope of this volume, but it is well worth considering.

While diplomacy thus has its limits (as do all of the various conflict management tools), McCartney emphasizes that there are many cases in which third party mediation is *vital* for resolving a conflict. Since each warring faction mistrusts its opponents, the employment of a third party mediator whom both sides perceive to be impartial and have grown to trust can be the essential ingredient for bringing them to the negotiating table and conducting peace negotiations in good faith. This realization argues for continuous diplomatic engagement during an internal conflict even if negotiations are desultory. Such continuous engagement prepares the way for real progress by increasing the odds that trusted third parties will be immediately available when events become ripe for resolution and a window of opportunity opens.

Moving to international law, I. M. Lobo de Souza notes that the development of international law regarding internal conflict "is not an end in itself, but a means to an end. It purports to work alongside complex political processes within the broader international society in order to bring peace, stability, and prosperity to nations that have been plagued by internal armed conflicts." Essentially, the continued development of international law regarding when and how third parties should intervene in internal conflicts—centering around the responsibility to protect doctrine mentioned in several chapters—serves as justification and roadmap for the legitimate use of humanitarian interventions. International law, like all law, clarifies the appropriateness of actions—including third party interventions—by providing rules and benchmarks that have withstood experience and legal scrutiny. As the legitimacy of third party humanitarian interventions becomes increasingly established, rulers who abuse their people's human rights might increasingly weigh the benefit of oppressing their people against the cost of potential intervention. Alternatively, actions by intervening powers that disregard international law will weaken its influence.

In the area of economics, Stephen Collins emphasizes that economic statecraft offers "an intriguing alternate path to conflict resolution, apart from the polar extremes of military intervention or discursive diplomacy." He provides evidence of the successful applications of the different kinds of economic measures for resolving internal conflict, in the process showing how each type of economic sanction and incentive works and validating his claim that the conventional wisdom about the lack of efficacy of sanctions is wrong. How should communities of interest and practice be developed to advocate for the integrated use of economic tools alongside existing military and diplomatic constituencies?

Regarding military aspects of conflict resolution, William Lahneman emphasizes that the very nature of military force makes it a distinctive tool of conflict resolution. Military force is unique among the different categories of conflict resolution tools because it can and usually does arouse strong emotional reactions from both warring parties and associated populations, reactions that can increase violence rather than resolve it. For this reason alone, it is appropriate for military force to be a last resort when other methods have failed. However, Lahneman states that military force often is a *necessary* tool for ending internal conflict, an attitude repeated by several other contributing authors. The flexibility and complexity of the military option is both a blessing and a curse. On the one hand, the varied ways in which military force can be employed means that there almost always is an appropriate type of military option to fit a situation, assuming that an achievable political-military strategy exists. On the other hand, the military tool's complexity makes it difficult to wield without creating unintended consequences.

Joseph Rudolph begins his survey of nation-building efforts by drawing attention to the fact—repeated in many of the volume's chapters—that providing adequate security is the *sine qua non* of any successful nation-building effort. This means, among other things, that all post-conflict reconstruction and nation building efforts will include the need for a policing function. This function is sometimes performed by actual police forces. However, since pre-conflict police forces are usually discredited as corrupt organs of the previous regime, this task usually falls, at least initially, to third party intervening military forces. The result is that, as Rudolph cautions, "The reach of the military in nation-building efforts. . . is limited if extraordinarily important." Third party military forces provide a secure environment until a post-conflict government can field indigenous police and military organizations capable of providing for the population's security. During this period, the secure environment provided by intervening forces also permits the beginning of critical nation-building efforts by civilian political parties, businesses, NGOs, and other elements of civil society.

Rudolph stresses that nation-building efforts are multigenerational. Third parties can help to start and support these efforts for a time, but true nation building can only be legitimately sustained and ultimately accomplished by citizens of the state in question. Accordingly, for nation-building efforts to be successful, they must continue long after intervening forces have left. However, as described below, democratization issues in general and the decision of when to remove intervening military forces in particular are complicated issues.

Rudolph reminds readers of what he calls the "everything at once conundrum" that confronts third parties and post-conflict governments alike as they begin nation-building programs. The greater the degree of state failure preceding the conflict, the more that leaders must *simultaneously* construct viable economic, security, political, social, and cultural structures and processes. In some cases, this involves rehabilitating formerly existing conditions, but more often it involves constructing new political cultures, economic systems, and other similarly enormous undertakings. Rudolph concludes that building domestic constituencies of stake holders who develop a genuine commitment to the new system should be the central goal of democratization efforts because their existence and vitality enable the new state to continue developing along peaceful, democratic lines without the need for occupation by third party military forces.

Inherent Tensions in Third Party Humanitarian Intervention

Even if policy makers were able to avoid misconceptions about third party humanitarian interventions, scrupulously kept the broad dynamics about these enterprises in mind, and carefully applied the specific recommendations described above in unique ways appropriate to each situation (no easy task!), there remain inherent tensions associated with third party humanitarian interventions that portend rough going in the best of cases. These tensions fall under the categories of "too little too late," "mission creep," determining an exit/engagement/stabilization strategy, deciding when to remove intervening military forces, navigating the tensions associated with democratization, and reconciling humanitarian impulses with national interests.

David Laitin has described in detail with respect to Somalia, and William Lahneman has generalized, that the process for authorizing the more intrusive forms of intervention, such as economic sanctions and peace operations, tend to result in interventions that are "too little" in the sense that intervention is performed by military forces with insufficient capabilities to accomplish their mission, and "too late" in the sense that military intervention occurs only after violent internal conflict has been underway for some time and has caused widespread human rights abuses and destruction. These characteristics often render intervening forces inadequate, particularly in the opening phases of military intervention, to reestablish law and order in the wake of internal conflict so that reconstruction can begin.

The result is that the original goals of the intervention are expanded as events indicate that these goals were not realistic. This phenomenon is known as "mission creep." Mission creep should be avoided if possible, but the too little too late dynamics described above make it difficult to avoid. When mission creep occurs, policies and actions that were appropriate early in the intervention prove dysfunctional when the mission expands. Mission creep also adds to the costs of intervention, beyond what would have been the case if an appropriate definition of success and exit strategy had been determined at the outset. Both David Laitin and Steven Burg have detailed how mission creep occurred in Somalia and Bosnia/Kosovo respectively.

The too little too late phenomenon and mission creep contribute to another tension evident in many cases of intervention. This is the problem of determining what different authors have variously called an exit strategy, engagement strategy, or stabilization strategy. While each highlights different priorities, all refer to essentially the same thing. Ideally, formulating an appropriate exit/engagement/stabilization (E/E/S) strategy should occur prior to an intervention and should include the policy objectives or goals for declaring the intervention a success, the means to be employed to achieve these goals, and metrics for measuring both progress toward (or away from) the goals as well as final goal attainment (i.e., "success"). A proper E/E/S strategy enables third parties to weigh the efficacy of different conflict resolution tools, develop a coordinated plan, and provide sufficient resources to achieve policy objectives. In practice, such planning at the beginning of an intervention has been the exception rather than the rule. Rather, devising an E/E/S strategy has been an incremental process conducted while an intervention is in progress. Clearly, the too little too late effect, mission creep, and the dynamic, interactive nature of military operations make some of this unavoidable, but there remains considerable room for improvement.

Deciding when to remove third party military forces is one of the most difficult and important aspects of any E/E/S strategy. If troops are removed "too soon," indigenous security forces might prove incapable of sustaining a stable security environment, the numbers of stakeholders favoring democratization might be insufficient to maintain momentum toward democratization, and dissident factions might still resort to operating outside of the peaceful conflict resolution process that characterizes true democracies. In such cases, the likelihood of backsliding into instability and conflict increases. On the other hand, it becomes problematic if intervening forces stay "too long." The longer that third party military forces remain in a country (at some point "military intervention" becomes "military occupation"), the greater the likelihood that intervening forces will commit unpopular acts that breed resentment and even hatred within a local population. Even if intervening forces behave in exemplary fashion, the presence of foreign troops constitutes an intrusion on sovereignty that irritates a local population over time. Leaving forces too long can create other disadvantages. Minorities can become psychologically dependent on their presence and resist efforts to remove them. The presence of third party military forces can retard the development of indigenous security forces. Why should post-conflict governments saddled with multiple nation-building tasks be in a hurry to produce competent indigenous security forces if intervening forces remain available to provide security? Post-conflict governments might also try to coopt intervening forces for their own agendas, and can come to rely on military assistance and other foreign aid associated with the continued presence of intervening forces.

There is no easy answer to what constitutes "too soon" or "too long" because each situation is unique and exceptions occur. For example, if properly employed in an effective peacekeeping role, third party military forces can remain in place for a very, very long time without provoking much resentment, such as the UN force in Cyprus that has been policing the ceasefire between Greek and Turkish Cypriots since 1964. Of course, in this case, the presence of UN peacekeepers appears to remain a necessary condition for preventing a resurgence of hostilities, meaning that an effective exit strategy continues to be elusive even after almost fifty years!

Some of the issues surrounding democratization have already been discussed. The purpose here is to highlight the tension that sometimes exists between democratization imperatives and E/E/S strategies. The best way to do this might be to restate several of the questions asked by Joseph Rudolph in his introductory chapter to the nation-building section.

> Should elections be held immediately, when the leaders of ethnonationalist parties are far more likely to be elected in the aftermath of an ethnic civil war than coalition parties composed of moderates from different communities? If not, how long, then, can you delay holding elections and claim to be democratizing? How soon should you return refugees to the ethnically cleansed areas from which they were driven, and should you do so even if there will be no jobs for them there? How quickly should you try to change society; for instance, by requiring parties in Muslim states to offer the voters as many women candidates as men? Perhaps above all, how soon should you try to implement unpopular reforms involving the integration of the formerly warring national communities? And how much say should local leaders have in these reforms, and how soon?"

With respect to this last question, Mateja Peter details the ambiguities and conflicting signals associated with using an international administration with authoritarian powers to drive democratization in Bosnia. While use of this method is understandable given the conditions in post-conflict Bosnia, there appear to be limits to how much progress can be achieved in this manner. Peter reaches the same conclusion as Rudolph when she states "the experience from Bosnia also shows that while some reform can be externally directed, international administration cannot substitute for a domestic political process. . . . Structural transformations and revisions of power distribution among different groups need to be rooted in the domestic processes."

A final area of tension associated with third party humanitarian intervention involves the motives for intervening rather than the process of intervention itself. The very fact that this process has been labeled "humanitarian" intervention throughout this volume is testament to the fact that third parties consider that humanitarian motives drive all or most of their reasons for intervention. However, third party interventions are sometimes criticized for being thinly disguised exercises in imperialism. In these narratives, critics assert that intervening powers are really pursuing their own national interests and use humanitarian motives to disguise this fact. To the extent that such charges are perceived to be valid even if false, the influence of the international law and developing norms supporting third party humanitarian intervention is diminished.

William Lahneman has offered an explanation for where third parties perform humanitarian intervention that falls between these two extremes. While acknowledging that states sometimes intervene for humanitarian reasons alone, he notes that the sheer number of potential candidates for intervention at any given time means that states employ other selection criteria as well. His additional reasons include an aversion of third parties to intervene in a large state due to the perceived difficulty in achieving success, the tendency to favor humanitarian interventions that *also* achieve national interests, consideration of the availability of sufficient resources for a new intervention if already involved elsewhere, and reactions to other states' sensitivity about violating sovereignty and other ideological issues. While this list is by no means exhaustive, it makes a case that, rather than arguing that an intervention is based solely on humanitarian purposes when this might not be the case, third parties should acknowledge that a mix of motives have led them to intervene.

In the final analysis, third party humanitarian interventions—including all of their imperfections—will be judged by the humanitarian goals they achieve, and such judgments must ultimately come from the people who have lived through them. If their judgment is positive, then it will not matter that other motives for the intervention besides a humanitarian impulse might have existed. If their judgment is negative, it will not matter if motives were purely humanitarian; the intervention will have failed and the cause of human rights will have suffered a setback. Hopefully the contents of this volume will contribute in some small way to making future judgments about third party humanitarian interventions positive ones.

Bibliography

Abiew, Francis Kofi. "Assessing Humanitarian Intervention in the Post-Cold War Period: Sources of Consensus." *International Relations* 14, no. 2 (1998): 61-90.

Ackermann, Alice. *Making Peace Prevail: Preventing Violent Conflict in Macedonia.* Syracuse, NY: Syracuse University Press, 2000.

Ackerman, Spence. "Afghanistan Human Rights Official Criticizes McChrystal 'Tribes' Initiative," *Washington Independent,* December 1, 2009. http://washingtonindependent.com/69131/afghan-human-rights-official-criticizes-mcchrystal-tribes-initiative (accessed December 15, 2010).

Allard, Kenneth. *Somalia Operations: Lessons Learned.* Washington, D.C.: National Defense University Press, 1995.

Al-Marashi, Ibrahim. "Iraq's Security and Intelligence Network: A Guide and Analysis." *Middle East Review on International Affairs* 6, no. 3 (September 2002). http://meria.idc.ac.il/journal/2002/issue3/jv6n3al.html (accessed September 29, 2011).

Alston, Philip, ed. *The United Nations and Human Rights: A Critical Appraisal.* Oxford: Oxford University Press, 1992.

Alvarez, Michael R., Thad E. Hall, and Susan D. Hyde, eds. *Election Fraud: Detecting Fraud, Deterring Electoral Manipulation.* Washington, D.C.: The Brookings Institution, 2008.

Amnesty International. *Violent Attacks Against Roma in Hungary: Time to Investigate Racial Motivation.* Amnesty International Publications, 2010. http://www.amnesty.org/en/library/ asset/EUR27/001/2010/en/7ee79730-e23f-4f20-834a-deb8deb23464/eur270012010en.pdf (accessed October 22, 2012).

Anderson, Mary, *Do No Harm: How Aid Can Support Peace—or War.* Boulder, CO: Lynne Rienner, 1999.

Andric, Ivo. *The Bridge on the Drina.* Chicago: University of Chicago Press, 1977.

Anglin, Douglas G. "International Election Monitoring: The African Experience." *African Affairs* 97, no. 389 (1998): 471-95.

Aras, Bulent, and Sule Toktas, "Afghanistan's Security: Political Process, State-Building and Narcotics." *Middle East Policy Council* 15, no. 2 (Summer 2007).

Arzt, Donna E. "Views on the Ground: The Local Perception of International Criminal Tribunals in the Former Yugoslavia and Sierra Leone." *Annals of the American Academy of Political and Social Science* 603 (January 2006): 226-39.

Asia Foundation, "Afghanistan in 2010: A Survey of the Afghan People." (2010). http://asiafoundation.org/country/Afghanistan/2010-poll.php (accessed April 05, 2011).

Associated Press, "Text of the Kosovo Peace Plan," *Washington Post*, June 3, 1999. www.washingtonpost.com.

Atashi, Elham, "Challenges to Conflict Transformation from the Streets." In *Conflict Transformation and Peacebuilding: Moving from Violence to Sustainable Peace*, Vol. 5, edited by Bruce W. Dayton and Louis Kreisberg, 45-60. New York: Routledge, 2009.

Atkinson, Carol. "Does Soft Power Matter? A Comparative Analysis of Student Exchange Programs 1980-2006." *Foreign Policy Analysis* 6, no. 1 (January 2010):1-22.

Attinà, Fulvio, and Daniela Irrera, eds. *Multilateral Security and ESDP Operations*. London: Ashgate, 2010.

Auvinen, Juha Y. "IMF Intervention and Political Protest in the Third World: A Conventional Wisdom Redefined." *Third World Quarterly* 17, no. 3 (1996): 377-400.

Avant, Deborah. "NGOs, Corporations and Security Transformation in Africa." *International Relations* 21, no. 2 (2007): 143-61.

Azar, Edward. *The Management of Protracted Social Conflict: Theory and Cases*. Brookfield: Gower Publishing, 1990.

Babcock, Sandy. "The Efficacy of Peacekeeping," In *The Cornwallis Group VIII: Analysis for Governance and Stability*. The Canadian Peacekeeping Press of the Lester B. Pearson Canadian International Peacekeeping Training Centre, 79-99. April 14-17, 2003.

Babst, Dean V. "A Force for Peace." *Industrial Research* 14 (1972): 55-58.

"Baghdad Rescue: Police Chief Escapes Assassination." *Al Sumaria*, May 10, 2011. http://www.alsumaria.tv/en/Iraq-News/1-63889-Baghdad-Rescue-Police-Chief-escapes-assassination.html (accessed October 7, 2011).

Bain, William. *Between Anarchy and Society: Trusteeship and the Obligations of Power*. Oxford: Oxford University Press, 2003.

Bakke, Kristin, Xun Cao, John O'Loughlin, and Michael Ward. "Social Distance in Bosnia-Herzegovina and the North Caucasus Region of Russia: Inter and Intra-Ethnic Attitudes and Identities," *Nations and Nationalism* 15, no. 2 (2009): 227-53.

Baldwin, David. *Economic Statecraft.* Princeton, NJ: Princeton University Press, 1985.

Barany, Zoltan. *The East European Gypsies: Regime Change, Marginality, and Ethnopolitics*. New York: Cambridge University Press, 2002.

Barany, Zoltan, and Robert Moser, eds. *Ethnic Politics After Communism*. Ithaca: Cornell University Press, 2005.

Barbieri, Katherine and Rafael Reuvney. "Economic Globalization and War." *Journal of Politics* 67, no. 4 (2005): 1228-47.

Barnett, Michael. "The New United Nations Politics of Peace: From Juridical Sovereignty to Empirical Sovereignty." *Global Governance* 1, no. 1 (1995): 79–97.

Barnett, Michael, and Martha Finnemore. *Rules for the World: International Organizations in Global Politics.* Ithaca: Cornell, 2004.

Barnett, Michael, Hunjoon Kim, Magdalene O'Donnell, and Laura Sitea. "Peacebuilding: What is in a Name?" *Global Governance* 13, no. 1 (2007):35–58.

Barrie, Janet. "World: Europe Hiding Gypsies Behind a Wall." *BBC*, February 26, 1999. http://news.bbc.co.uk/2/hi/europe/286704.stm (accessed August 21, 2012).

Barro, Robert J. and Jong-Wha Lee. "IMF Programs: Who is Chosen and What are the Effects?" *Journal of Monetary Economics* 52, no. 7 (2005): 1245-69.

Barry, John, and Evan Thomas. "The Kosovo Cover-Up" *Newsweek* 135, no. 20 (May 15, 2000): 22.

Bastian, Sunil. "Politics of Social Exclusion, State Reform and Security in Sri Lanka." *IDS Bulletin* 40, no. 2 (2009): 88-95.

Bauman, Robert, George Gawrych, and Walter Kretchik. *Armed Peacekeepers in Bosnia*. Fort Leavenworth: Combat Studies Institute Press, 2004.

Bayley, David H. *Democratizing the Police Abroad: What to Do and How to Do It*. Washington, D.C.: US Department of Justice, Office of Justice Programs, June 2011.

Beck, Ulrich. "Reframing Power in a Globalized World." *Organization Studies* 29, no. 5 (2008): 793-804.

Bednarikova, Tatiana. "Anti-Roma Wall Through Slovak Village Provokes Outcry," *The Telegraph,* November 25, 2009. http://www.telegraph.co.uk/expat/expatnews/6650958/Anit-Roma-wall-through-Slovak-village-provokes-outcry.html (accessed March 3, 2010).

Beetham, David, ed. *Politics and Human Rights.* Oxford: Blackwell, 1995. Reprinted from *Political Studies*, 43, Special Issue (1995).

Begaj, Behlul. "'Drenica' Homogenization of Albanians," *Helsinki Charter* (March 1998). Reprinted in Helsinki Committee for Human Rights in Serbia, *Helsinki Charter Special English Edition on Kosovo.* Belgrade, January 1999.

Bellamy, Alex. "The 'Next Stage' in Peace Operations Theory?," *International Peacekeeping* 11, no. 1 (2004): 17-38.

Belloni, Roberto. "Civil Society and Peacebuilding in Bosnia and Herzegovina," *Journal of Peace Research* 38, no. 2 (2001): 163-80.

Bendana, Alejandro. "From Peacebuilding to State Building: One Step Forward and Two Steps Back?," *Development* 48, no. 3 (2005): 5-15.

Benjamin, Robert. "Regional Politics: Political Transition and Institution Building." In *Transforming the Balkans: Security, Political Stability and Economic Development.* National Democratic Institute, May 10, 2010. http://www.ndi.org/files/Transforming_the_Balkans_051010.pdf (accessed July 13, 2011).

Bennhold, Katrin, and Stephen Castle. "E.U. Calls France's Roma Expulsions a 'Disgrace,'" *The New York Times*, September 14, 2010. http://www.nytimes.com/2010/09/15/world/europe/15roma.html (accessed October 23, 2012).

Benton, Barbara, ed. *Soldiers for Peace: Fifty Years of United Nations Peacekeeping.* New York: Facts on File, 1996.

Bercovitch, Jacob, and Karl DeRouen, Jr. "Managing Ethnic Civil Wars: Assessing the Determinants of Successful Mediation," *Civil Wars* 7, no.1 (Spring 2005): 98-116.

Berman, Eli, Joseph H. Felter, and Jacob N. Shapiro, "Constructive COIN: How Development Can Fight Radicals," *Foreign Affairs*, June 1, 2010. http://www.foreignaffairs.com/articles/66432/eli-berman-joseph-h-felter-and-jacob-n-shapiro/constructive-coin# (accessed April 8, 2012).

Biden, Joseph R. "Bosnia: Why the United States Should Finish the Job." *SAIS Review* 18, no.2 (Summer 1998): 1-7.

Bienen, Henry S., and Mark Gersovitz. "Economic Stabilization, Conditionality, and Political Stability." *International Organization* 39, no. 4 (1985): 729-54.

Bienen, Henry S., and Robert Gilpin. "Economic Sanctions as a Response to Terrorism," *Journal of Strategic Studies* 3 (1980): 89-98.

Biggar, Nigel, ed. *Burying the Past and Doing Justice After Civil Conflict.* Washington, DC: Georgetown University Press, 2001.

Bildt, Carl. *Peace Journey: The Struggle for Peace in Bosnia*. London: Weidenfeld and Nicolson, 1999.

Bishai, Linda, "Liberal Internationalism and the Law vs. Liberty Paradox," *Journal of International Relations and Development* 15 (2012): 201-23. http://www.palgrave-journals.com/jird/journal/v15/n2/abs/jird201120a.html (accessed October 21, 2011).

Bjornlund, Eric. *Beyond Free and Fair: Monitoring Elections and Building Democracy*. Washington, DC: Woodrow Wilson Center Press, 2004.

Blank, Stephen. *Yugoslavia's Wars.* Carlisle, PA: The U.S. Army War College, 1995.

Bolz Jr, Frank, Kenneth J. Dudonis, and David P. Schulz. *The Counterterrorism Handbook: Tactics, Procedures, and Techniques.* Boca Raton, FL: CRC Press, 2005.

Boot, Max. "The New American Way of War," *The New York Times International*, July 25, 2003. Subsequently published in *Foreign Affairs* 82, no. 4 (July-August, 2003): 41-58.

Boot, Maxwell. *The Savage Wars of Peace: Small Wars and the Rise of American Power.* New York: Basic Books, 2002.

Bose, Sumantra. *Bosnia after Dayton.* London: Hurst, 2002.

Bosnian Institute. http://www.bosnia.org.uk/bosnia/viewMetatype.cfm?metatypeID=25 (accessed July 23, 2011).

Both, Norbert, and Jan Willem Honig. *Srebrenica: Record of a War Crime.* New York: Penguin Books, 1997.

Boutrous-Ghali, Boutros. *An Agenda for Peace: Preventive Diplomacy and Related Matters.* A/RES/47/120, December 18, 1992.

Bowman, Stephen. "Bosnia: U.S. Military Operations." *Congressional Research Service*, July 8, 2003. http://www.au.af.mil/au/awc/awcgate/crs/ib93056.pdf (accessed July 8, 2011).

Breman, Anna, and Carolyn Shelton. "Structural Adjustment Programs and Health." In *Globalization and Health*, edited by Ichiro Kawachi and Sarah Wamala, 219-33. Oxford: Oxford University Press, 2007.

Brewer, John D., "Sectarianism and Racism and their Parallels and Differences," *Ethnic and Racial Studies* 15, no. 3 (1992): 352 -64.

Brigadier General Zehad (Iraqi Police Services). Personal Interviews, October 2010 and May 2011.

Brooks, Risa. "Sanctions and Regime Type: What Works and When?," *Security Studies* 11, no. 4 (Summer 2002): 1-50.

Brown, Keith. "'All They Understand is Force:' Debating Culture in Operation Iraqi Freedom." *American Anthropologist* 110, no. 4 (2008): 443-53.

Brown, Michael, ed., *The International Dimensions of Internal Conflict.* Cambridge: The MIT Press, 1996.

Brownlie, Ian, and Guy S. Goodwin-Gill, ed. *Basic Documents on Human Rights, Fifth Edition.* Oxford: Oxford University Press, 2006.

Brusset, Emery, and Ralf Otto. "Evaluation of Nashe Malo: Design, Implementation, and Outcomes. Social Transformation through Media." *Channel Research*, December 23, 2004.

Brysk, Alison, and Gershon Shafir, eds. *National Insecurity and Human Rights: Democracies Debate Counterterrorism.* Berkeley: University of California Press, 2007.

Buergenthal Thomas. "The Evolving International Human Rights System," *American Journal of International Law* 100, no. 4 (October 2006): 783-95.

Bull, Hedley. *The Anarchical Society: A Study of Order in World Politics.* New York: Columbia University Press, 2002.

Burg, Steven L. "The Failure of Early Warning in Kosovo." In *The Application of Prevention Report of the Center for Preventive Action's Fifth Annual Conference.* New York: Council on Foreign Relations, December 11, 1998.

———. "Nationalism and Democratization in Yugoslavia," *The Washington Quarterly* 14, no. 4 (Autumn 1991): 5–19.

———. *War or Peace? Nationalism, Democracy, and American Foreign Policy in Post-Communist Europe.* New York: New York University Press, 1996.

Burg, Steven L., and Michael L. Berbaum. "Community, Integration, and Stability in

Multinational Yugoslavia," *The American Political Science Review* 83, no. 2 (1989): 535-54.

Burg, Steven L. and Paul S. Shoup. *The War in Bosnia-Herzegovina: Ethnic Conflict and International Intervention.* Armonk, NY: M. E. Sharpe, 1999.

Burnell, Peter, ed. *Democracy Assistance: International Co-operation for Democratization.* London: Frank Cass, 2000.

Bussman, Margit, Gerald Schneider, and Nina Wiesenhomeier. "Foreign Economic Liberalization and Peace: The Case of Sub-Saharan Africa." *European Journal of International Relations* 11, no. 4 (2005): 551-79.

Buzan, Barry. *People, States, and Fear.* Essex: Pearson, 1991.

Byrne, Sean J. "The Roles of External Ethnoguarantors and Primary Mediators in Cyprus and Northern Ireland," *Conflict Resolution Quarterly* 24, no. 2 (Winter 2006): 149-72.

Byrne, Sean, Chuck Thiessen, and Eyob Fissuh. "Economic Assistance and Peacebuilding in Northern Ireland," *The Canadian Journal of Peace and Conflict Studies* 39, no. 1-2 (2007): 7-22.

Call, Charles T., and Susan E. Cook. "On Democratization and Peace-building," *Global Governance* 9, no.2 (April-June 2003): 233-46.

Callwell, Charles E. *Small Wars: Their Principles and Practice, Third Edition.* London: Harrison and Sons, 1906.

Caplan, Richard D. *A New Trusteeship? The International Administration of War-torn Territories, Adelphi Paper Number 341.* London: Routledge, 2002.

———. *International Governance of War-torn Territories: Rule and Reconstruction.* Oxford: Oxford University Press, 2005.

Carbetta, Renata. "Determinants of Third Parties' Intervention and Alignment Choices in Ongoing Conflicts, 1945-2001." *Foreign Policy Analysis* 8, no. 1 (January 2010): 61-85.

Cardenas, Sonia. *Conflict and Compliance: State Responses to International Human Rights Pressures.* Philadelphia: Penn Press, 2007.

Cardoso, Eliana, and Ann Helwege. *Latin America's Economy: Diversity, Trends, and Conflicts.* Cambridge, MA: The MIT Press, 2003.

Carnegie Commission on Preventing Deadly Conflicts. *Preventing Deadly Conflict: Final Report with Executive Summary.* New York: Carnegie Corporation, 1997.

Carothers, Thomas. *Aiding Democracy Abroad: The Learning Curve.* Washington, D.C.: Carnegie Endowment for International Peace, 1999.

———. "Democracy Assistance: Political vs. Developmental?" *Journal of Democracy* 20, no. 1 (January 2009): 5-19.

———. "Promoting Democracy and Fighting Terror." *Foreign Affairs* 82, no. 1 (January/February 2003): 84-97.

———. "The Rise of Election Monitoring: The Observers Observed." *Journal of Democracy* 8, no. 3 (1997): 17-31.

Carpenter, Ted Galen. *Delusions of Grandeur: the United Nations and Global Intervention.* Washington, D.C.: CATO Institute, 1997.

———. *"The Domino Theory Reborn: Clinton's Bosnia Intervention and the "Wider War" Thesis."* CATO Foreign Policy Briefing 42, (August 1996). http://www.cato.org/pubs/fpbriefs/fpb-042.html (accessed July 7, 2011).

Cassese, Antonio, ed. *The New Humanitarian Law of Armed Conflict.* Napoli: Editoriale Scientifica, 1979.

Castle, Stephen, "Serbia's E.U. Aspirations Face Long Road Ahead," *New York Times*, October 28, 2010.

CBC News, "Canadian Sanctions Working in Burma, Sui Kyi Says," February 29, 2012. http://www.cbc.ca/news/politics/story/2012/02/29/pol-cp-aung-san-suu-kyi.html (accessed July 29, 2012).

Celador, Gemma Collantes. " Police Reform: Peacebuilding through 'Democratic Policing?,'" *International Peacekeeping* 12, no. 3 (2005): 364–76.

Chandler, David. *Bosnia: Faking Democracy after Dayton.* London: Pluto Press, 2002.

———. *Empire in Denial: The Politics of State-building*. London: Pluto Press, 2006.

Chandrasekaran, Rajiv. *Imperial Life in the Emerald City: Inside Iraq's Green Zone.* New York: Alfred A. Knopf, 2006.

Chesterman, Simon. *You, the People: the United Nations, Transitional Administration, and State-building*. Oxford: Oxford University Press, 2005.

Christopher, Warren. *Face the Nation.* Interview with Bob Schieffer. October 22, 1995. http://dosfan.lib.uic.edu/ERC/briefing/dossec/1995/9510/951022dossec (accessed July 23, 2011).

———. "Send Troops to Bosnia," *USA Today*, October 18, 1995.

———. "Statement at the Opening of the Balkan Peace Talks, Wright Patterson Air Force Base, Dayton Ohio. November 1, 1995." In *In the Stream of History: Shaping U.S. Foreign Policy for a New Era,*360-63. Stanford; Stanford University Press, 1998.

Cic, Milan. "About the Constitution and Constitutionalism." In *Constitutionalism & Politics*, edited by Irena Grudzinska Gross. Bratislava: Slovak Committee of the European Cultural Foundation, 1994.

Clark, Ann Marie. "Non-governmental Organizations and their Influence on International Society." *Journal of International Affairs* 48, no. 2 (1995): 507-25.

Cochrane, Feargal. *Unionist Politics and the Politics of Unionism Since the Anglo Irish Agreement.* Ireland: Cork University Press, 2001.

Cockburn, Patrick. "Sadr's Militia May Live to Fight Again," *The Independent,* July 14, 2008. http://www.independent.co.uk/news/world/middle-east/sadrs-militia-may-live-to-fight-again-8668866.html (accessed October 1, 2011).

Cohen, Eliot. "Change and Transformation in Military Affairs." *The Journal of Strategic Studies* 27, no. 3 (Spring 2004): 395-407.

Collier, Paul and AnkeHoeffler. *Greed and Grievance in Civil War.* Washington, D.C.: World Bank, 2001. http://econ.worldbank.org/programs/conflict/library/doc?id =12205 (accessed March 25, 2012).

Collins, Stephen D. "Can America Finance Freedom?: Assessing U.S. Democracy Promotion Via Economic Statecraft." *Foreign Policy Analysis* 5, no. 2 (October 2009): 367-89.

———. "Democracy Sanctions: An Assessment of Economic Sanctions as an Instrument of Democracy Promotion." *Taiwan Journal of Democracy* 5, no. 2 (December 2009): 81-83.

———. "The Efficacy of Economic Sanctions: Economic Sanctions and American Foreign Policy in the Unipolar Era." *New England Journal of Political Science* 3, no. 2 (November 2009): 235-63.

———. "Regional Trade Agreements and Democracy Promotion: Measuring the Influence of Democracy Requirements in Regional Trade Agreements." *Politics & Policy* 38, No. 4 (August 2010): 751-52.

Colonel A (Iraqi Police Services). Personal Interview, November 9, 2010.

Comras, Victor. "Economic Sanctions and US Foreign Policy," *Statements to the Open Forum*, February 25, 2002. http://www.state.gov/s/p/of/proc/tr/9128pf.htm (accessed August 12, 2009).

Connolly, Michael, and John Loughlin. "Reflections on the Anglo-Irish Agreement." *Government and Opposition* 21, no. 2 (April 1986): 146-60.
Connor, Walker. "The Politics of Ethnonationalism." *Journal of International Affairs* 27, no. 1 (1973): 1-22.
Coogan, Tim P. *The Troubles: Ireland's Ordeal 1966-1996 and the Search for Peace.* Boulder, CO: Roberts Rinehart, 1996.
Cookson, John. "How Much Does the Libya Intervention Cost the U.S.?," August 23, 2011, http://globalpublicsquare.blogs.cnn.com/2011/08/23/question-how-much-does-the-intervention-in-libya-cost-the-u-s/ (accessed March 12, 2012).
Cordesman, Anthony H., and Jose Ramos. *Sadr and the Mahdi Army: Evolution, Capabilities, and a New Direction.* Washington, D.C.: Center for Strategic & International Studies, 2008.
Cot, Jean-Pierre and Alain Pellet. *La Charte des Nations Unies.* Paris: Economica, 1985.
Coulon, Jocelyn (Phyllis Aronoff and Howard Scott, translators). *Soldiers of Diplomacy: the United Nations Peacekeeping and the New World Order.* Toronto: University of Toronto Press, 1998.
Cousens, Elizabeth M., Chetan Kumar, and Karin Wermester. *Peacebuilding as Politics: Cultivating Peace in Fragile Societies.* Boulder, CO: Lynne Rienner, 2000.
Cox, Harvey. "Managing Northern Ireland Intergovernmentally: An Appraisal of the Anglo Irish Agreement." *Parliamentary Affairs* 40, no.1 (*1987*): 80-97.
Cox, Michael, "Bringing in the International: The IRA Ceasefire and the End of the Cold War." *International Affairs, Royal Institute of International Affairs 1944* 73, no. 4 (October, 1997): 671-93.
Coy, Patrick. "Cooperative Accompaniment and Peace Brigades International in Sri Lanka." In *Transnational Social Movements and Global Politics: Solidarity Beyond the State*, edited by Jackie Smith, Charles Chatfield, and Ron Pagnucco, 81-100. Syracuse: Syracuse University Press, 1997.
Coyne, Christopher J. "Reconstructing Weak and Failed States." *The Journal of Social, Political and Economic Studies* 31, no.2 (2006):143-62.
Crawford, Gordon. *Foreign Aid and Political Reform.* New York: Palgrave Macmillan, 2001.
Crawford, James. *The Creation of States in International Law.* Oxford: Clarendon Press Oxford, 1979.
Crawford, Neta. *Argument and Change in World Politics: Ethics, Decolonization, and Humanitarian Intervention.* Cambridge: Cambridge University Press, 2002.
Crocker, Chester. "Lessons of Somalia." *Foreign Affairs* 74, no. 3 (1995): 2-8.
"Czech Government to Leave Smelly Pig Farm on the Lety Holocaust Site," *Romea.cz*, August 10, 2010. http://www.romea.cz/english/index.php?id=detail&detail=2007_1949 (accessed October 23, 2012).
Daalder, Ivo H. *Getting to Dayton: the Making of America's Bosnia Policy.* Washington D.C.: Brookings Institute Press, 2000.
Daalder, Ivo H., and Michael E. O'Hanlon. *Winning Ugly: NATO's War to Save Kosovo.* Washington, D.C.: Brookings, 2000.
Dahlman, Carl, and Gearoid O Tuathail. "The Legacy of Ethnic Cleansing: The International Community and the Returns Process in Post-Dayton Bosnia–Herzegovina." *Political Geography* 24, no. 5 (2005): 569–99.
Daley, Suzanne. "Fiscal Crisis Takes Toll On Health Of Greeks," *New York Times*, December 27,2011, 4(A).
Darby, John. *The Effects of Violence on Peace Processes.* Washington D.C.: The United States Institute of Peace Press, 2001.

Davis, A.C. "In Iraq, Assassinations are a Nightly Event." *Washington Post*, May 3, 2011. http://www.wasingtonpost.com/world/middle-east/in-iraq-assassinations-are-a-nightly-event/2011/04/26/AFEWfVgF_story.html (accessed October 1, 2011).

Daxecker, Ursula E. "International Election Monitoring, Fraud, and Post Election Violence." Paper Presented at the annual meeting of the International Studies Association, Montreal, Canada, March 15-19, 2011.

Dayton Peace Accords. Wright Patterson Air Force Base. November 21, 1995. http://www.state.gov/www/regions/eur/bosnia/bosagree.html (accessed July 23, 2011).

de Jonge Oudraat, Chantel. "Intervention in Internal Conflicts: Legal and Political Conundrums." *Global Policy Program for the Carnegie Endowment for International Peace,* no. 15 (August 2000).

———. "Making Economic Sanctions Work." *Survival: The IISS Quarterly* 42, no. 3, (Autumn 2000): 105-27.

de Soto, Alvaro and Graciana del Castillo. "Obstacles to Peacebuilding." *Foreign Policy* 94, Spring (1994): 69-83.

de Soysa, Indra and John R. O'Neal. "Boon or Bane? Reassessing the Productivity of Foreign Direct Investment." *American Sociological Review* 64, no. 5: (1999): 766-82.

Del Ponte, Carla, and Chuck Sudetic. *Madame Prosecutor: Confrontation with Humanity's Worst Criminals and the Culture of Impunity.* New York: Other Press, 2009.

Delbruck, Josh. "A Fresh Look at Humanitarian Intervention Under the Authority of the United Nations." *Indiana Law Journal* 67, no. 1 (1992): 887-901.

"Department of Defense Directive 3000.5." Washington D.C., November 28, 2005. http://www.dtic.mil/whs/directives/corres/pdf/300005p.pdf (accessed March 20, 2011).

"Department of Defense Special Study on Irregular Warfare." *U.S. Joint Forces Command.* http://www.smallwars.quantico.usmc.mil/search/Papers/Irreg%20War fare %20Special%20Study.pdf (accessed March 10, 2011).

Detter, Ingrid. *The Law of War.* Cambridge: Cambridge University Press, 2000.

Deutsch, Karl, and William J. Foltz, eds. *Nation Building.* New York: Atherton Press, 1963.

Diamond, Larry, Marc F. Plattner, Yun-han Chu, and Hung-mao Tien, eds. *Consolidating the Third Wave Democracies.* Baltimore, MD: The Johns Hopkins University Press, 1997.

Dickinson, Laura. "The Promise of Hybrid Courts." *The American Journal of International Law* 97, no. 2 (April 2003): 295-310.

Diehl, Paul, Daniel Druckman, and James Wall. "International Peacekeeping and Conflict Resolution: A Taxonomic Analysis with Implications." *Journal of Conflict Resolution* 42, no. 1 (1998): 33-55.

Divjak. B., and M. Pugh. "The Political Economy of Corruption in Bosnia and Herzegovina." *International Peacekeeping* 15, no. 3 (2008): 373-86.

Doherty, Paul, and Michael A. Poole. "Ethnic Residential Segregation in Belfast, Northern Ireland, 1971-1991." *Geographical Review* 87, no. 4 (October, 1997): 520-36.

Domin, Thierry. "History of Bosnia and Herzegovina: From the Origins to 1992." *SFOR Informer* 117, July 11, 2000. http://www.nato.int/SFOR/indexinf/117/p03a/ chapter1.htm (accessed August 19, 2011).

Donia, Robert J., and John A. Fine. *Bosnia and Hercegovina: A Tradition Betrayed.* New York: Columbia University Press, 1994.

Donnelly, Jack. "Human Rights at the United Nations 1955-1985: The Question of Bias." *International Studies Quarterly* 32, no. 4 (1988): 275-303.

———. *Universal Human Rights in Theory and Practice, Second Edition*. Ithaca, NY: Cornell University Press, 2003.

Dorff, Robert. "Failed States After 9/11: What Did We Know and What Have We Learned?" *International Studies Perspectives* 6, no. 1 (January 2005): 20-34.

Dougherty, Beth K. "Right-Sizing International Criminal Justice: The Hybrid Experiment at the Special Court for Sierra Leone." *International Affairs* 80, no. 2 (March 2004): 311-28.

Doyle, Michael W. "Liberalism and World Politics." *American Political Science Review* 80, no. 4 (1986): 1151-69.

Doyle, Michael W., and Nicholas Sambanis. "International Peacebuilding: A Theoretical and Quantitative Analysis." *American Political Science Review* 94, no. 4 (2000): 779–801.

Drezner, Daniel. "Conflict Expectations and the Paradox of Economic Coercion." *International Studies Quarterly* 42, no. 4 (December 1998): 709–31.

Duffield, Mark. *Global Governance and the New Wars: The Merging of Development and Security*. London: Zed Books, 2001.

Eastmond, Marita. "Transnational Returns and Reconstruction in Post-war Bosnia and Herzegovina." *International Migration* 44, no. 3 (2006): 141–66.

Echevarria, Antulio. "Toward an American Way of War." *Strategic Studies Institute of the U.S. Army War College* (2004). http://www.strategicstudiesinstitute.army.mil/pubs/display.cfm?pubID=374 (accessed October 14, 2011).

Eck, Kristine. "A Beginner's Guide to Conflict Data: Finding and Using the Right Dataset." *Uppsala Conflict Data Program Paper No. 1* (December, 2005).

Eilasson, Jan. "Humanitarian Action and Peacekeeping." In *Peacemaking and Peacekeeping for the New Century,* edited by Olara A. Otunnu and Michael W. Doyle, 203-213. Lanham, MD: Rowman & Littlefield, 1998.

Ellis-Jones, Mark. *States of Unrest III: Resistance to IMF and World Bank Policies in Poor Countries.* London: World Development Movement, 2001.

Emerson, Rupert. *From Empire to Nation: the Rise of Self-Assertion of African and Asian Peoples.* Cambridge: Harvard University Press, 1960.

Encarnacion, Omar G. "The Follies of Democratic Imperialism." *World Policy Journal* 22, no. 1 (2005): 47-60.

Eriksen, Erik O. *The Unfinished Democratization of Europe*. New York: Oxford University Press, 2009.

European Commission. "Employment, Social Affairs and Inclusion." http://ec.europa.eu/social/main.jsp?catId=518&langId=en (accessed September 25, 2010).

European Commission. *Enlargement Strategy and Progress Reports 2010: Serbia.* 2010.

European Council. "Presidency Conclusion: Copenhagen European Council, 21-22 June 1993." http://www.europarl.europa.eu/enlargement/ec/pdf/cop_en.pdf (accessed August 21, 2012).

European Union at the UN. "EU Council Conclusions on the Western Balkans." September 15, 2006. http://www.europa-eu-un.org/articles/en/article_6252_en.htm (accessed 13 December 2010).

European Union at the UN. "EU External Relations Council Conclusions on the Western Balkans." February 27, 2006. http://www.eu-un.europa.eu/articles/fr/article_5739_fr.htm (accessed 13 December 2010).

European Union at the UN. "EU Presidency Statement—United Nations General Assembly: Reports of the ICTY and ICTR." October 15, 2007. http://www.eu-un.europa.eu/articles/en/article_7419_en.htm (accessed 13 December 2010).

European Union at the UN. "'EU Western Balkans Relations'—Speech by EU Commissioner Rehn." February 12, 2007. http://www.eu-un.europa.eu/articles/fr/article_6770_fr.htm (accessed 13 December 2010).

European Union at the UN. "Introductory Remarks on Western Balkans by EU Commissioner Rehn." March 21, 2007. http://www.europa-eu-un.org/articles/en/article_6881_en.htm (accessed 13 December 2010).

European Union at the UN. "'Serbia's European Road'—Speech by EU Commissioner Rehn."October 24, 2007. http://www.eu-un.europa.eu/articles/en/article_7432_en.htm (accessed 13 December 2010).

European Union at the UN. "Speech by Commissioner Olli Rehn: Commission Declaration on the Balkans 10 Years after Srebrenica." July 6, 2005. http://www.eu-un.europa.eu/articles/en/article_4866_en.htm (accessed 13 December 2010).

European Union at the UN. "Speech by Commissioner Olli Rehn on 'Progress in the Western Balkans.'" April 13, 2005. http://www.eu-un.europa.eu/articles/fr/article_4561_fr.htm (accessed 13 December 2010).

European Union at the UN. "Speech by Commissioner Olli Rehn on 'The Next Steps towards Europe.'" Lecture at Belgrade University, April 18, 2005. http://www.europa-eu-un.org/articles/en/article_4582_en.htm (accessed 13 December 2010).

Evans, Tony. *US Hegemony and the Project of Universal Human Rights*. London: Macmillan, 1996.

Fairbanks, Charles H. "Georgia's Rose Revolution." *Journal of Democracy* 15, no. 2 (2004): 110-24.

Farer, Tom. *Beyond Sovereignty: Collectively Defending Democracy in the Americas*. Baltimore, MD: Johns Hopkins University Press, 1996.

Farrell, Michael. *The Orange State*. London: Pluto Press, 1976.

Fawn, Rick. "Czech Attitudes Towards the Roma: Expecting More of Havel's Country." *Europe-Asia Studies* 53, no. 8 (2001): 1193-1219.

Fearon, James D. and David D. Laitin. "Ethnicity, Insurgency, and Civil War."*American Political Science Review* 97, no. 1 (2003): 75-90.

Featherstone, Kevin, and Claudio Radaelli, eds. *The Politics of Europeanization*. Oxford: Oxford University Press, 2003.

Ferguson, Neil, and Ed Cairns. "Political Violence and Moral Maturity in Northern Ireland." *Political Psychology* 17, no. 4 (December, 1996): 713-25.

Fierke, Karin M. *Diplomatic Interventions: Conflict and Change in a Globalizing World*. Basingstoke, UK: Palgrave MacMillan, 2005.

Findlay, Trevor. *The Use of Force in UN Peace Operations*. Oxford: SIPRI and Oxford University Press, 2002.

Fisk, Robert. "What will the Northern Alliance do in our Name Now? I dread to Think." *The Independent (UK)*, November 14, 2001. http://www.independent.co.uk/opinion/commentators/fisk/robert-fisk--what-will-the-northern-alliance-do-in-our-name-now-i-dread-to-think-616866.html (accessed December 13, 2010).

Fitzduff, Mari. *Beyond Violence: Conflict Resolution Process in Northern Ireland.* Tokyo: United Nations University Press, 2002.

Fleitz, Frederick. *Peacekeeping Fiascoes of the 1990s: Causes, Solutions, and U.S. Interests*. New York: Praeger Publishing, 2002.

Folch, Abel Escriba. "Economic Sanctions and the Duration of Civil Conflicts." *Journal*

of Peace Research 47, no. 2 (March 2010):129-41.
Fonseca, Isabel. *Bury Me Standing: The Gypsies and their Journey.* New York: Random House, 1996.
Foreign & Commonwealth Office. *Edited Transcript of a Press Conference by the Foreign Secretary, Mr. Robin Cook, Ljubljana, Slovenia,* November 23, 1998. www.fco.uk/news.
Forest, James L., and Russell D. Howard, eds. *Weapons of Mass Destruction and Terrorism, Second Edition.* New York: McGraw Hill, 2013.
Forsythe, David P., ed. *Encyclopedia of Human Rights.* New York: Oxford University Press, 2009.
———. *Human Rights in International Relations, Second Edition.* Cambridge: Cambridge University Press, 2006.
———. "The United Nations and Human Rights, 1945-1985." *Political Science Quarterly* 100, no. 3 (Summer 1985): 249-69.
———. "UN Peacekeeping and Domestic Instability." *Orbis* 15, no. 4 (Winter, 1972): 1064-84.
Fortna, Virginia Page, and Lise Morje Howard. "Pitfalls and Prospects in the Peacekeeping Literature." *Annual Review of Political Science* 11, no. 1 (2008): 283–301.
Franks, Tommy, Stephen Biddle, Peter Charles Choharis, John M. Owens, Daniel Pipes, Gary Rosen, and Dov Zakheim. "Is this Victory?" *The National Interest*, November 10, 2006. http://www.nationalinterest.org/Article.aspx?id=12988 (accessed July 14, 2011).
Freedom House. *Freedom in the World – 2000-2001.* Washington, DC: Freedom House, 2001.
Freeman, Will. "The Accuracy of China's 'Mass Incidents.'" *Financial Times*, March 2, 2010. http://www.ft.com/intl/cms/s/0/9ee6fa64-25b5-11df-9bd300144feab49a.html #axzz1tFVEUJ2A.(accessed April 27, 2012).
Friedman, Francine. *Bosnia and Herzegovina: A Polity on the Brink.* New York, Routledge, 2004.
Friedrich, Carl J. *Constitutional Government and Democracy: Theory and Practice in Europe and America.* Boston: Ginn and Company, 1946.
Fukuyama, Francis. *The End of History and the Last Man.* New York: Free Press, 1992.
———. "The Future of History: Can Liberal Democracy Survive the Decline of the Middle Class." *Foreign Affairs* 90, no. 1 (January-February 2012): 53-61.
———. "Iran, Islam and the Rule of Law," *Wall Street Journal*, July 27, 2009. http://online.wsj.com/article/SB10001424052970203946904574300374086282670.html (accessed October 23, 2012).
———. *State-Building, Governance and World Order in the 21st Century.* Ithaca, NY: Cornell University Press, 2004.
Gagnon, Valére. *The Myth of Ethnic War: Serbia and Croatia in the 1990s.* Ithaca, NY: Cornell University Press, 2004.
Gallagher, Mary E. "Reform and Openness: Why China's Economic Reforms Have Delayed Democracy." *World Politics* 54, no. 3 (2002): 338-72.
Galtung, Johann. "On the Effects of International Economic Sanctions: With Examples from the Case of Rhodesia." *World Politics* 19, no. 3 (April 1967): 378-416.
Geer, John G., ed. *Encyclopedia of Public Opinion.* Santa Barbara, CA: ABC-Clio Press, 2004.
George, Alexander L. *Forceful Persuasion: Coercive Diplomacy as an Alternative to War.* Washington, D.C.: United States Institute for Peace Press, 1991.

Gibney. Mark. *Political Terror Scales Dataset 1980-2005*. Asheville, NC: University of North Carolina, 2006.

Glasius, Marlies. "Human Security from Paradigm Shift to Operationalization: Job Description for a Human Security Worker." *Security Dialogue* 39, no. 1 (2008): 31-54.

Gleditsch, Nils Petter, Peter Wallensteen, Mikael Eriksson, Margareta Sollenberg, and Havard Strand. "Armed Conflict 1965-2011: A New Dataset." *Journal of Peace Research* 39, no. 5 (2002): 615-37.

Glendon, Mary Ann. *A World Made New: Eleanor Roosevelt and the Universal Declaration of Human Rights*. New York: Random House, 2001.

Glenny, Misha. *The Balkans: Nationalism, War, and the Great Powers, 1804-1999*. New York: Viking, 1999.

Goldston, James A. "Role of the OSCE in Bosnia: Lessons from the First Year." *The Helsinki Monitor* 8 no. 3 (1997): 6-36.

Goodhand, Jonathan, and Oliver Walton. "The Limits of Liberal Peacebuilding? International Engagement in the Sri Lankan Peace Process." *Journal of Intervention and Statebuilding* 3 no. 3 (2009): 303-23.

Gordon, Ruth. "United Nations Intervention in Internal Conflicts: Iraq, Somalia, and Beyond." *Michigan Journal of International Law* 15 (Winter 1994): 519-46.

Gottlieb, Gidon. "Nations Without States." *Foreign Affairs* 73, no. 3 (May-June 1994): 100-112.

Government of Yugoslavia. "Public Opinion Survey on the Federal Executive Council's Social and Economic Reform." *Yugoslav Survey* 31, no. 3 (1990): 3-26.

Gow, James. *Triumph of the Lack of Will: International Diplomacy and the Yugoslav War*. London: Hurst, 1997.

Gowing, Nik. *Real-Time Television Coverage of Armed Conflicts and Diplomatic Crises: Does It Pressure or Distort Foreign Policy Decisions?* Working Paper 94-1, The Joan Shorenstein Barone Center on the Press, Politics and Public Policy. Cambridge: Harvard University, 1994.

Graham, Brian. "The Past in the Present: The Shaping of Identity in Loyalist Ulster." *Terrorism and Political Violence* 16, no. 3 (2004): 483-500.

Gray, Christine. *International Law and the Use of Force: Foundations of Public International Law*. Oxford: Oxford University Press, 2000.

Gray, Colin. "The American Way of War: Critique and Implications" in *Rethinking the Principles of War*, edited by Anthony McIvor, opening essay. Annapolis: Naval Institute Press, 2005.

Greenhill, Kelly M. "People Pressure: The Coercive Use of Refugees in the Kosovo Conflict." (unpublished paper).

Greenwood, Justin, and Mark Aspinwall, eds. *Collective Action in the European Union: Interest and the New Politics of Associability*. New York: Routledge, 1998.

Grieg, J. Michael, and Patrick M. Regan. "When Do They Say Yes? An Analysis of the Willingness to Offer and Accept Mediation in Civil Wars." *International Studies Quarterly* 52 (2008): 759-81.

Grigorescu, Alexandru. "Transparency of Intergovernmental Organizations: The Roles of Member States, International Bureaucracies and Nongovernmental Organizations." *International Studies Quarterly* 51 (2007): 625-48.

Gromes, Thorsten. "Federalism as a Means of Peacebuilding: the Case of Postwar Bosnia and Herzegovina." *Nationalism and Ethnic Politics* 16, no. 3/4 (2010): 354-74.

Gross, Eva, and Ana Juncos, eds. *EU Conflict Prevention and Crisis Management: Roles, Institutions and Policies*. London: Routledge, 2011.

Guelke, Adrian. "The United States, Irish Americans and the Northern Ireland Peace Process." *International Affairs* 72, no. 3 (July 1996): 521-36.
Gurr, Ted R. "Containing Internal War in the Twenty-First Century." In *From Reaction to Conflict Prevention: Opportunities for the UN System,* edited by Fen Osler Hampson, and David M. Malone, 41-62. Boulder, CO: Lynne Rienner Publishers, 2002.
Gurses, Mehmet, Nicolas Rost, and Patrick McLeod. "Mediating Civil War Settlements and the Duration of Peace." *International Transactions* 34 (2008): 132-33.
Gutierrez-Solana, Ander. "From Kuwait to Myanmar: New Challenges for Humanitarian Intervention." Paper presented at the Convention of the International Studies Association, February 15, 2009.
Guy, Will, ed, *Between Past and Future: the Roma of Central and Eastern Europe*. Hertfordshire, UK: University of Hertfordshire Press, 2001.
Hadar, Leon and Christopher Preble. "U.S. Policy in the Middle East." In *Cato Handbook for Policymakers Seventh Edition*. The Cato Institute. www.cato.org/pubs/handbook/hb111/hb111-52.pdf (accessed October 25, 2011).
Hafner-Burton, Emilie, Susan D. Hyde, and Ryan Jablonski. "Terrorizing Freedom: When Governments Use Repression to Manipulate Elections." Paper Presented at the annual meeting of the International Studies Association, New Orleans, Louisiana, February 17, 2010.
Haig, Alexander M., Jr. "The Question of Humanitarian Intervention." *Foreign Policy Research Institute Wire* 9, no. 3 (February, 2001). http://www.fpri.org/fpriwire0902.haig.humanitarianintervention.html (accessed November 12, 2011).
Halkett, Kimberly. "U.S. Combats Afghan Aid Corruption." *Al Jazeera News* (2009). http://english.aljazeera.net/news/americas/2009/12/2009123042621747107.html (accessed February 27, 2011).
Halperin, Morton H., and Kristen Lomasney. "Guaranteeing Democracy." *Journal of Democracy* 9, no. 2 (April 1998): 134-47.
Halperin, Morton H., David J. Scheffer, and Patricia L. Small. *Self-Determination in the New World Order*. Washington, D.C.: Brookings Institute Press, 1992.
Hancock, Ian. *We are the Romani People*. Hertfordshire, UK: University of Hertfordshire Press, 2005.
Hansch, Steven, et al. *Excess Mortality and the Impact of Health Interventions in the Somalia Humanitarian Emergency*. Washington, D.C.: Refugee Policy Group and Centers for Disease Control and Prevention, August 12, 1994.
Hartmann, Michael E. "International Judges and Prosecutors in Kosovo: A New Model for Post-Conflict Peacekeeping." *USIP Special Report* no. 112. Washington, D.C.: October 2003.
Hartzell, Caroline A., and Matthew Hoddie. *Crafting Peace: Power-Sharing Arrangements and the Negotiated Settlement of Civil Wars.* University Park, PA: Pennsylvania State University Press, 2007.
Hartzell, Caroline A., Matthew Hoddie, and Molly Bauer. "Economic Liberalization via IMF Structural Adjustment: Sowing the Seeds of Civil War?" *International Organization* 64, no. 2 (2010): 339-56.
Harzl, Benedikt C. "Conflicting Perceptions: Russia, the West and Kosovo." *Review of Central and East European Law* 33 (2008): 491-518.
Haas, Ernest B. *When Knowledge Is Power: Three Models of Change in International Organizations*. Berkeley: University of California Press, 1990.
Hawley, Leonard, and Dennis Skocz. "Advance Political Military Planning." In *The Quest for Viable Peace: International Intervention and Strategies for Conflict Ter-*

mination, edited by Jock Covey, Michael Dziedzic, and Leonard Hawley, 37-76. Washington, D.C.: United States Institute of Peace Press, 2005.

Headrick, Daniel R. *The Tools of Empire: Technology and European Imperialism in the Nineteenth Century.* New York: Oxford University Press, 1981.

Heidelberg Institute for International Conflict Research. *Conflict Barometer 2008: Crises—Wars—Coups d'Etats—Negotiations—Mediations—Peace Settlements, 17th Annual Conflict Analysis*. http://hiik.de/en/konfliktbarometer/pdf/ConflictBarometer _2008.pdf (accessed November 9, 2011).

Hegre, Håvard, Ranveig Gissinger, and Nils Petter Gleditsch. "Globalization and Internal Conflict." In *Globalization and Armed Conflict*, edited by Gerald Schneider, Katherine Barbieri, and Nils Petter Gleditsch, 251-75. Lanham, MD: Rowman & Littlefield, 2003.

Helmke, Gretchen and Steven Levitsky. "Informal Institutions and Comparative Politics: A Research Agenda." *Perspectives on Politics* 2, no. 4 (December 2004): 725-40.

Henkin, Louis. *How Nations Behave*. New York: Columbia University Press, 1979.

———. "International Law: Politics and Values." *Recueil des Cours* 216 (1989).

Hepburn, Anthony C. *A Past Apart: Studies in the History of Catholic Belfast 1850-1950.* Belfast: Ulster Historical Foundation, 1996.

Hettne, Bjorn, and Frederik Soderbaum. "Intervening in Complex Humanitarian Emergencies: The Role of Regional Cooperation." *The European Journal of Development Research* 7, no.3 (2005): 452.

Hills, Alice, "The Inherent Limits of Military Forces in Policing Peace Operations," *International Peacekeeping* 8, no. 23 (2001): 70-98.

Hodson, Randy, Dusko Sekulic, and Garth Massey. "National Intolerance in the Former Yugoslavia," *American Journal of Sociology* 99, no. 6 (1994): 1534-58.

Hoge, Warren. "U.N. Rejects Belarus for Seat on Its Rights Panel," *New York Times*, May 18, 2007, A6.

Holbrooke, Richard. "Rebuilding Nations. . . ," *The Washington Post*, April 1, 2002.

———. *To End a War: Sarajevo to Dayton: An Inside Story*. New York: Random House, 1999.

Holsti, Kalevi. *The State, War, and the State of War.* Cambridge, UK: Cambridge University Press, 1996.

Howard, Michael and Peter Paret, editors. *Carl von Clausewitz: On War*. Princeton, NJ: Princeton University Press, 1976.

Hufbauer, Gary Clyde, Jeffery J. Schott, and Kimberly Ann Elliot. *Economic Sanctions Reconsidered: History and Current Policy, Second Edition*. Washington, D.C.: Institute of International Economics, 1990.

Human Rights Watch. *A Week of Terror in Drenica*. New York: Human Rights Watch, 1999.

———. "Blood-Stained Hands Past Atrocities in Kabul and Afghanistan's Legacy of Impunity." (2005).

———. *Failure to Protect: Anti-Minority Violence in Kosovo, March 2004*. July 26, 2004, D1606. http://www.unhcr.org/refworld/docid/421eec8b4.html (accessed September 4, 2012).

———. "Recurring Nightmare: State Responsibility for 'Disappearances' and Abductions in Sri Lanka," *Human Rights Watch Report*. March 5, 2008.

———. "Sri Lanka: End Harassment, Attacks on Journalists: Post-Election Crackdown Feared," *Human Rights Watch Press Release*, January 29, 2010.

Huntington, Samuel P. *The Third Wave: Democratization in the Late Twentieth Century.* Norman, OK: Oklahoma University Press, 1991.

Hyde, Susan D. "The Observer Effect in International Politics: Evidence from a Natural Experiment." *World Politics* 60, no. 1 (2007): 37-63.

———. *The Pseudo-Democrat's Dilemma: Why Election Observation Became an International Norm.* Ithaca, NY: Cornell University Press, 2011.

Hyde, Susan D., and Judith G. Kelley. "The Limits of Election Monitoring: What Independent Observers Can (and Can't) Do." *Foreign Affairs.* Forthcoming. Snapshot at Susan D. Hyde's web-page, http://hyde.research.yeale.edu/CV-Susan_D_Hyde.pdf. (accessed September 22, 2011).

Hyde, Susan D., and Angela O'Mahoney. "International Scrutiny and Pre-election Fiscal Manipulation in Developing Countries." *Journal of Politics* 72, no. 3 (2010): 690-704.

Ignatieff, Michael. *The Lesser Evil: Political Ethics in an Age of Terror.* Princeton, NJ: Princeton University Press, 2004.

Ingrao, Charles, and Thomas A. Emmert, eds. *Confronting the Yugoslav Controversies: A Scholars' Initiative.* West Lafayette, IN: Purdue University Press, 2009.

International Center for Transitional Justice. *The Sierra Leone Truth and Reconciliation Commission: Reviewing the First Year.* New York, NY: The International Center for Transitional Justice, 2004.

———. *The Special Court for Sierra Leone: The First Eighteen Months.* New York, NY: The International Center for Transitional Justice, 2004.

———. *The Special Court for Sierra Leone under Scrutiny.* New York, NY: The International Center for Transitional Justice, 2006.

———. *The War Crimes Chamber in Bosnia and Herzegovina: From Hybrid to Domestic Court.* New York. NY: The International Center for Transitional Justice, 2008.

International Commission on the Balkans. *Unfinished Peace: Report of the International Commission on the Balkans.* Washington, D.C.: The Brookings Institution Press, for the Aspen Institute and the Carnegie Endowment for International Peace, 1996.

International Council on Human Rights Policy. "When Legal Worlds Overlap Human Rights, State and Non-State Law." (2009). http://www.ichrp.org/ (accessed March 30, 2011).

International Council on Security and Development. "Struggle for Kabul: The Taliban Advance," *Afghanistan Reports* (December 2008). http://www.icosgroup.net/report/report-afgh/page/2/ (accessed December 20, 2011).

International Crisis Group. "Belgrade's Lagging Reform: Cause for International Concern," *Europe Report No. 126* (March 7, 2002). http://www.crisisgroup.org.

———. "Bosnia's Stalled Police Reform: No Progress, No EU," *European Report No. 164* (6 September 2005).

———. "Handing Back Responsibility to Timor-Leste's Police," *Asian Report No. 180* (3 December 2009).

———. "Kosovo's Fragile Transition." *Europe Report #196* (September 2008).

———. "Milosevic in The Hague: What It Means for Yugoslavia and the Region," *Europe Briefing No. 19* (July 6, 2012). http://www.crisisgroup.org.

———. "Policing in Afghanistan: Still Searching for a Strategy," *Asian Briefing No. 85* (December 18, 2008).

———. "Reforming Afghanistan's Police," *Asian Report No. 138* (August 30, 2007).

———. "Trial by Fire: The Politics of the Special Tribunal for Lebanon," *Middle East Report No. 100* (2 December 2010). http://www.crisisgroup.org.

———. "Why the Bosnian Elections Must be Postponed." *Europe Report No. 14* (1996).

Irrera, Daniela. "The Balkanisation of Politics: Crime and Corruption in Albania." In *Crimes in International Trade. Issues and Perspectives*, edited by P. Satyanarayana Prasad, 177-212. Hyderabad, India: Icfai University Press, 2008.

———. "NGO's Roles in the Humanitarian Interventions and Pace Support Operations in Multilateral Security and ESDP Operations." In *Multilateral Security and ESDP Operations*, edited by Fulvio Attinà and Daniela Irrera, 71-85. Catania, Italy: University of Catania, 2010.

Ish-Shalom, Piki. "Theory as a Hermeneutical Mechanism: The Democratic-Peace Thesis and the Politics of Democratization." *European Journal of International Relations* 12, no. 4 (2006): 565–98.

Ismail, Qadri. *Abiding by Sri Lanka: On Peace, Place, and Postcoloniality*. Minneapolis, MN: University of Minnesota Press, 2005.

Ito, Ayaki. "Politicisation of Minority Return in Bosnia and Herzegovina: The First Five Years Examined." *International Journal of Refugee Law* 13, no. 1-2 (2001): 98–122.

Jacobs, Andrew. "Farmers in China's South Riot Over Seizure of Land," *New York Times*, September 24, 2011, 5(A).

Jakobsen, Peter Viggo. *Western Use of Coercive Diplomacy After the Cold War: A Challenge for Theory and Practice*. New York: St. Martin's Press, 1998.

Johns, Michael. "'Do as I Say, Not as I Do: The European Union, Eastern Europe and Minority Rights." *East European Politics and Societies* 17, no. 4 (November 2003): 682-99.

Joint Doctrine for Military Operations Other Than War. Joint Publication 3-07. Washington, D.C.: J-7 Operational Plans and Interoperability Directorate, Joint Chiefs of Staff, U.S. Department of Defense, June 16, 1995.

Joint Operations. Joint Publication 3.0. Washington D.C.: J-7 Operational Plans and Interoperability Directorate, Joint Chiefs of Staff, U.S. Department of Defense, September 17, 2006. ahttp://www.fas.org/irp/doddir/dod/jp3_0.pdf (accessed September 1, 2011).

Judah, Tim. "At Last, Good News from the Balkans," *New York Review of Books*, March 11, 2010.

Jukic, Elvira M. "Bosnia Vows to End Ethnically Divided Schools," *IEWS*, August 31, 2012. http://www.balkaninsight.com/en/article/bosnia-plans-uniting-divided-schools (accessed September 6, 2012).

Kakar, M. Hassan. *Afghanistan: The Soviet Invasion and the Afghan Response, 1979-1982*. Irvine, CA: University of California Press, 1997.

Kaldor, Mary. *New and Old Wars: Organized Violence in a Global Era.* Cambridge: Polity Press, 1999.

Kalyvas, Stathias N. "'New' and 'Old' Civil Wars: A Valid Distinction?" *World Politics* 54, no. 1 (2001): 99–118.

Kaplan, Robert. *Balkan Ghosts: A Journey through History.* New York: St. Martin's Press, 1993.

Katz, Lee Michael. "Afghanistan's President is Ousted," *USA Today,* April 17, 1992.

Katzman, Kenneth. "Iraq: Post Saddam Governance and Security," *CRS Report RL31339*, May 9, 2008, 33.

Kaufmann, Chaim. "Intervention in Ethnic and Ideological Civil Wars." In *The Use of Force: Military Power and International Politics*, edited by Robert J. Art and Kenneth N. Waltz, 406-26. Lanham: Rowman and Littlefield, 2009.

Keen, David. "Liberalization and Conflict." *International Political Science Review* 26, no. 1 (2005):73-89.

———. "War and Peace: What's the Difference?" *International Peacekeeping* 7, no. 4 (2000): 1–22.

Kelley, Judith. "Assessing the Complex Evolution of Norms: The Rise of International Election Monitoring." *International Organization* 62, no. 2 (2008): 221-55.

———. "D-Elections: The Politics and Norms of International Election Observation." *International Organization* 63, no. 2 (2009): 765-87.

Kennedy, David. *The Dark Sides of Virtue: Reassessing International Humanitarianism*. Princeton, NJ: Princeton University Press, 2004.

Kille, Kent, ed. *The UN Secretaries-General and Moral Authority: Religion and Ethics in International Leadership*. Washington: Georgetown University Press, 2007.

Klemencic, Matjaz. "Threats to Macedonia's Stability and Borders." *IBRU Boundary and Security Bulletin* (Spring, 2001): 73-80.

Klose, Gerhard. "The Role of the Military in a Changing World—CIMIC: Military Stepping Stones on the Road to Civil Society." In *Building a Transnational Civil Society: Global Issues and Global Actors*, edited by I. Richter, S. Berking, and R. Schmid, 201-216. London: Palgrave, 2006.

Knight, W. Andy. *Adapting the United Nations to a Postmodern Era: Lessons Learned.* New York: Palgrave, 2001.

Knock, Thomas J. *To End All Wars: Woodrow Wilson and the Quest for a New World Order*. Princeton, NJ: Princeton University Press, 1992.

Knudsen, Tonny Brems, and Carsten Bagge Laustsen, eds. *Kosovo between War and Peace: Nationalism, Peacebuilding and International Trusteeship*. London: Routledge, 2006.

Kohler-Koch, Beate, and Rainer Eising, eds. T*he Transformation of Governance in the European Union*. London: Routledge, 1999.

Kostovicova, Denisa, ed. *The European Union and Transitional Justice: From Retributive to Restorative Justice in the Western Balkans*. Belgrade: Humanitarian Law Center, 2009.

Kraus, Gerald and Felix Martin. "Travails of the European Raj." *Journal of Democracy* 14, no. 3 (2003):60-74.

Krause, Keith, and Jennifer Milliken. "Introduction: The Challenge of Non-State Armed Groups." *Contemporary Security Policy* 30, no. 2 (2009): 202-220.

Kristoff, Nicholas, and Sheryl WuDunn. *Half the Sky: Turning Oppression into Opportunity for Women Worldwide*. New York: Knopf, 2009.

Kron, Josh. "Recruits for Police in Sudan are Abused," *The New York Times*, February 25, 2011.

Kumar, Krishna, ed. *Rebuilding Societies After Civil Wars: Critical Roles for International Assistance.* Boulder, CO: Lynne Rienner Press, 1997.

Kunovich, Robert, and Randy Hodson. "Ethnic Diversity, Segregation, and Inequality: A Structural Model of Ethnic Prejudice in Bosnia and Croatia." *Sociological Quarterly* 43 no. 2 (2002): 185-212.

Kuntz, Philipp, and Mark R. Thompson. "More than Just the Final Straw: Stolen Elections as Revolutionary Triggers." *Comparative Politics* 41, no. 3 (2009): 253-73.

Lahneman, William J. "Explaining Post-Cold War Humanitarian Military Intervention: Theory and Practice." Paper presented at the 28th Political Studies Students'

Conference—Twenty Years of Western Military Intervention: Protecting Whose Rights? Winnipeg, Canada, February 1, 2012.

———. *Keeping U.S. Intelligence Effective: The Need for a Revolution in Intelligence Affairs*. Lanham, MD: Scarecrow Press, 2011.

———, ed. *Military Intervention: Cases in Context for the Twenty-First Century*. Lanham, MD: Rowman and Littlefield, 2004.

———. "The Nation Building Strategy of the Roman Empire: Lessons for Today." Paper presented at the Annual Convention of the International Studies Association, New Orleans, Louisiana, February 17, 2010.

Lancaster, Carol. "Redesigning Foreign Aid," *Foreign Affairs* 79, no. 5 (September/October 2000).

Lau, Lawrence, Yingyi Qian, and Gérald Roland. "Reform without Losers: An Interpretation of China's Dual-Track Approach to Transition." *Journal of Political Economy* 108, no. 1 (2000):120-43.

Lauren, Paul Gordon. "'To Preserve and Build on its Achievements and to Redress its Shortcomings': The Journey from the Commission on Human Rights to the Human Rights Council." *Human Rights Quarterly* 29, no. 2 (May 2007): 307-45.

Lebovic, James H., and Erik Voeten. "The Politics of Shame: The Condemnation of Country Human Rights Practices in the UNCHR." *International Studies Quarterly* 50, no. 4 (December 2006): 861-88.

Lee, Matthew. "Clinton arrives in South Pacific to begin six-nation Asian Tour," *The Washington Post*, September 1, 2012.

Leland, John. "Iraq Prime Minister Visits Egypt and Iran," *New York Times*, October 20, 2010. www.nytimes.com/2010/10/21/world/middleeast/12iraq.html (accessed October 5, 2011).

Lempinen, Miko. *Challenges Facing the System of Special Procedures of the United Nations Commission on Human Rights.* Abo, Finland: Institute for Human Rights, Abo Akademi University, 2001.

———. *The United Nations Commission on Human Rights and the Different Treatment of Governments*. Abo, Finland: Abo Akademi University Press, 2005.

Levi, Michael A. and Henry C. Kelly. "Weapons of Mass Disruption." *Scientific American* (November 2002): 77-81.

Levitsky, Steven, and Lucan Way. "Elections without Democracy: the Rise of Competitive Authoritarianism." *Journal of Democracy* 8, no. 2 (2002): 51-65.

Levy, Jack S. "Domestic Politics and War." In *The Origin and Prevention of Major Wars*, edited by Robert I. Rotberg and Theodore K. Rabb, 79-100. New York: Cambridge University Press, 1989.

Licklider, Roy. "Obstacles to Peace Settlement." In *Turbulent Peace,* edited by Chester Crocker, Pamela Aall, and Fen Osler Hampsen, 697-718. Washington, D.C.: United States Institute of Peace, 2001.

———, ed. *Stopping the Killing: How Civil Wars End.* New York: New York University Press, 1993.

Lieberthal, Kenneth. *Governing China: From Revolution to Reform*. New York: W.W. Norton and Company, 2004.

Lijphart, Arend. *Democracy in Plural Societies: A Comparative Explanation*. New Haven, CT: Yale University Press, 1977.

Lind, Michael. "In Defense of Liberal Nationalism." *Foreign Affairs* 73, no. 3 (May-June, 1994): 87-99.

Lindberg, Staffan I., ed. *Democratization by Elections: A New Mode of Transition*. Baltimore, MD: The Johns Hopkins University Press, 2009.

Lipson, Michael. "Peacekeeping: Organized Hypocrisy?" *European Journal of International Relations* 13, no. 1 (2007): 5-34.

Losman, Donald. *International Economic Sanctions: The Cases of Cuba, Israel, and Rhodesia*. Albuquerque: University of New Mexico Press, 1979.

Lotta, Harbom, and Peter Wallensteen. "Armed Conflict, 1989-2006." *Journal of Peace Research* 44, no. 5 (Sep. 2007): 523-634.

Luttwak, Edward. "Religion and International Affairs." In *Religion, the Missing Dimension of Statecraft*, edited by Douglas Johnston and Cynthia Sampson, 17-18. New York: Oxford University Press, 1994.

Lynch, Timothy J. "The Gerry Adams Visa in Anglo-American Relations." *Irish Studies in International Affairs* 14 (2003): 33-44.

Lyon, Peter. "The Rise and Fall and Possible Revival of International Trusteeship." *Journal of Commonwealth & Comparative Politics* 31, no. 1 (1993): 96–110.

Lyons, Terrence, and Ahmed I. Samatar. *Somalia: State Collapse, Multilateral Intervention and Strategies for Political Reconstruction*. Washington D.C.: Brookings, 1995.

MacFarlane, S. Neil. "Humanitarian Action and Conflict." *International Journal* 54, no. 4 (1999): 537–61.

MacGinty, Roger. "American Influences on the Northern Ireland Peace Process." *The Journal of Conflict Studies* 17 no. 2 (Fall, 1997): 31-43.

MacGinty, Roger, and John Darby. *Guns and Government, the Management of the Northern Ireland Peace Process*. New York: Palgrave, 2002.

Mackinlay, John, and Jarat Chopra. *A Draft Concept of Second Generation Multinational Operations*. Providence, RI: Thomas J. Watson Jr. Institute for International Studies, Brown University, 1993.

Mackintosh, Kate. "The Development of the International Criminal Court." *Humanitarian Exchange Magazine* 32 (December, 2005). http://www.odihpn.org.report.asp?id2767> (accessed January 15, 2012).

Mahony, Liam. *Proactive Presence: Field Strategies for Civilian Protection*. Geneva: Centre for Humanitarian Dialogue, 2006.

Mahony, Liam, and Luis Enrique Eguren. *Unarmed Bodyguards: International Accompaniment for the Protection of Human Rights*. West Hartford, CT: Kumarian Press, 1997.

Maitra, Ramtanu. "The Party's Over for Afghan NGOs," *Asia Times Online*, April 21, 2005. http://www.atimes.com/atimes/Central_Asia/GD21Ag01.html (accessed February 27, 2011).

Malcolm, Noel. *Bosnia: A Short History*. New York: New York University Press, 1994.

"Maliki restructures Interior Ministry rendering it more loyal," *Al-Hurriyaa News-Report 2*, May 5, 2011. http://alhurriyya.com/en/permalink/3617.html (accessed October 1, 2011).

Mamdani, Mahmood. "The Politics of Naming: Genocide, Civil War, Insurgency." *London Review of Books*, March 8, 2007.

"Mandate of the OHR." *UN Office of the High Representative to Bosnia Herzegovina*. http://www.ohr.int/ohr-info/gen-info/default.asp?content_id=38612 (accessed July 8, 2011).

Mandelbaum, Michael. "Foreign Policy as Social Work." *Foreign Affairs* 75, no. 1 (1995): 16-32.

———. *The Ideas that Conquered the World: Peace, Democracy, and Free Markets in the Twenty-first Century*. New York: Public Affairs, 2002.

Maney, Gregory M., Ibtisam Ibrahim, Gareth I. Higgins, and Hanna Herzog. "The Past's Promise: Lessons from Peace Processes in Northern Ireland and the Middle East." *Journal of Peace Research* 43, no. 2 (March, 2006): 181-200.

Mansfield, Edward L., and Jack Snyder. "Democratization and the Danger of War." *International Security* 20, no. 1 (1995): 5-38.

Mansfield, Edward L., and Jack Snyder. *Electing to Fight: Why Emerging Democracies Go to War*. Cambridge: MIT Press, 2005.

Maoz, Zeev and Bruce Russett. "Normative and Structural Causes of the Democratic Peace." *American Political Science Review* 87, no. 3 (1993): 624-38.

Maren, Michael. *The Road to Hell: The Ravaging Effects of Foreign Aid and International Charity*. New York: Free Press, 1997.

Marie, Jean Bernard. *La Commission des droits de l'homme de l'Onu*. Paris: Pedone, 1975.

Marshall, Monty G., and Ted Gurr. *Peace and Conflict, 2005: A Global Survey of Armed Conflicts, Self Determination Movements and Democracy*. College Park, MD: Center for International Development, University of Maryland, 2005.

Masood, Salman. "Deadly Bombings Strike Pakistani Police." *New York Times,* February 1, 2011.

Massey, Garth, Randy Hodson, and Dusko Sekulic. "Ethnic Enclaves and Intolerance: The Case of Yugoslavia." *Social Forces* 78, no. 2 (1999): 669-91.

McAllister, Ian. "The Armalite and the Ballot Box: Sinn Fein's Electoral Strategy in Northern Ireland." *Electoral Studies* 3, no. 1 (March, 2004): 123-42.

McCrummen, Stephanie. "Iraqi PM Maliki pledges reform after 'Day of Rage,'" *The Washington Post*, February 27, 2011. http://www.washingtonpost.com/wp-dyn/content/article/2011/02/27/AR2011022700985.html (accessed September 28, 2011).

McKiernan, Eoin. "IRA Deserves Credit for Progress in Talks," *National Catholic Reporter*, December 12, 1997.

McMahon, Patrice. "Rebuilding Bosnia: A Model to Emulate or to Avoid?" *Political Science Quarterly* 119, no. 4 (2004): 569-94.

McMahon, Patrice C., and David P. Forsythe. "The ICTY's Impact on Serbia: Judicial Romanticism Meets Network Politics." *Human Rights Quarterly* 30, no. 2 (2008): 412-35.

McMahon, Patrice, and Jon Western. "The Death of Dayton: How to Stop Bosnia from Falling Apart." *Foreign Affairs* 88:5 (2009): 69-83.

"The Medieval Era: Nation Building—Holy Roman Empire." http://themedievalera.wikispaces.com/Nation%20Building%20-%20Holy%20Roman%20Empire (accessed September 13, 2012).

Mégret, Frédéric. "Beyond the 'Salvation' Paradigm: Responsibility To Protect (Others) vs. the Power of Protecting Oneself." *Security Dialogue* 40, no. 6 (2009): 575-95.

"Mihailovich: Yugoslavia's Unconquered," *Time,* May 25, 1942.

Moghalu, Kingsley. *Global Justice: the Politics of War Crimes Trials*. Stanford, CA: Stanford University Press, 2008.

Mojsilović, Juliana. "We Don't Know Where War Criminals Are, Dacic," *Balkan Insight,* November 4, 2008. http://www.birn.eu.com.

Monaghan, Rachel. "The Return of Captain Moonlight: Informal Justice in Northern Ireland." *Studies in Conflict and Terrorism* 25, no.1 (2002): 41-56.

Monteleone, C., and R. Rossi. "Security and Global Management: A Global Perspective." In *Security Identity and the Southern Caucasus*, edited by M. Geistlinger, F. Longo, G. Lordkipanidze, and Y. Nasibli, 49-80. Wien: Verlag, 2008.

Morgenthau, Hans J. *Politics Among Nations: The Struggle for Power and Peace, brief edition*, revised by Kenneth W. Thompson. New York: McGraw-Hill, 1993.

Morsink, Johannes. *The Universal Declaration of Human Rights: Origins, Drafting & Intent*. Philadelphia: University of Pennsylvania Press, 1999.

Mortimer, Edward. "International Administration of War-Torn Societies." *Global Governance* 10, no. 1 (2004): 7–15.

Moser-Puangsuwan, Yeshua, and Thomas Weber, eds. *Nonviolent Intervention Across Borders: A Recurrent Vision*. Honolulu, HI: Spark M. Matsunaga Institute for Peace, 2000.

Muehlmann, Thomas. "Police Restructuring in Bosnia-Herzegovina: Problems of Internationally-led Security Sector Reform." *Journal of Intervention and Statebuilding* 2, no. 1 (2008): 1–22.

Mueller, John. "The Banality of 'Ethnic War.'" *International Security* 25, no. 1 (2000): 42-70.

Murray, Megan, and Gary King. "The Effects of International Monetary Fund Loans on Health Outcomes." *PLoS Medicine* 5, no. 7 (2008): 1011-13.

Nan, Susan Allen, Daniel Druckman, and Jana El Horr. "Unofficial International Conflict Resolution: Is There a Track 1½? Are There Best Practices?" *Conflict Resolution Quarterly*, 27, no.1 (2009): 77.

Narayan, Jayaprakash. *Three Basic Problems of Free India*. Bombay: Asian Publishing House, 1946.

Nation, Craig. *War in the Balkans, 1991-2002*. Carlisle, PA: U.S. Army War College, 2003.

"MP calls on parliament to vote on Maliki's candidates for security ministries," *National Iraqi News Agency*, May 5, 2011. http://www.ninanews.com/english/News_Details.asp?ar95_VQ=FGIELG (accessed October 6, 2011).

National Security Strategy. Washington, DC: The White House, May 2010.

Nigeria—Report of the Commission Appointed to Enquire into the Fears of Minorities and the Means of Allaying Them. London: H.M.S.O., 1958.

Nonviolent Peaceforce (NP). *Living Peacework: The Faces of Nonviolent Peaceforce, Annual Report 2008*. http://nonviolentpeaceforce.advantagelabs.com/sites/nonviolentpeaceforce.advantagelabs.com/files/AR2008_0.pdf (accessed December 17, 2009).

Nooruddin, Irfan and Joel W. Simmons. "The Politics of Hard Choices: IMF Programs and Government Spending." *International Organization* 60, no. 4 (2006): 1001-33.

O'Day, Allan. *Political Violence in Northern Ireland, Conflict and Conflict Resolution*. Westport, CT: Praeger, 1997.

Office of the High Representative (OHR). "High Representative Acts to Ensure that Military in BiH are under Effective Civilian Control." *Press Release*, April 2, 2003.

———. "High Representative Outlines Required Action Following 'Orao' Scandal," *Press Release*, October 28, 2002.

———. *Office of the High Representative Bulletin No. 8*, 23 June, 1996.

Office of the Press Secretary. "Remarks by the President in Address to the Nation on the Way Forward in Afghanistan and Pakistan," *The White House*, December 1, 2009. http://www.whitehouse.gov/the-press-office/remarks-president-address-nation-way-forward-afghanistan-and-pakistan (accessed December 28, 2010).

O'Grady, Joseph. "An Irish Policy Born in the U.S.A.: Clinton's Break with the Past." *Journal of Foreign Affairs* 75, no. 3 (May-June, 1996): 2-7.

O'Keefe, Ed, and Aziz Alwan. "Iraqi police, soldiers targeted in wave of attacks," *The Washington Post*, July 5, 2011.

Olsen, Gorm Rae. "Civil-Military Cooperation in Crisis Management in Africa: American and European Union Policies Compared." *Journal of International Relations and Development* 14, no. 5 (July 2011): 333-53.

O'Neal, John, and Bruce Russett. "The Kantian Peace: The Pacific Benefits of Democracy, Interdependence, and International Organizations, 1885-1992." *World Politics* 52, no. 1 (1999): 1-37.

Orentlicher, Diane F. *Shrinking the Space for Denial: The Impact of the ICTY in Serbia.* New York: Open Society Institute, 2008.

Orford, Anne. *Reading Humanitarian Intervention: Human Rights and the Use of Force in International Law*. Cambridge: Cambridge University Press, 2003.

Organization for Security and Cooperation in Europe/ Office for Democratic Institutions and Human Rights (OSCE/ODIHR). *Election Observation Handbook*. Vienna: OSCE, 2011.

Orjuela, Camilla. "Dilemmas of Civil Society Aid: Donors, NGOs and the Quest for Peace in Sri Lanka." *Peace and Democracy in South Asia* 1, no. 1 (2005): 1-12.

———. "The Bullet in the Living Room: Linking Security and Development in a Colombo Neighborhood." *Security Dialogue* 41, no. 1 (2010): 99-120.

Ottaway, Marina. "Promoting Democracy After Conflict: The Difficult Choices." *International Studies Perspectives* 4 (2003): 314-22.

Otto, D. "Nongovernmental Organizations in the United Nations System: the Emerging Role of International Civil Society." *Human Rights Quarterly* 18, no. 1 (1996): 107-141.

Owen, Col. Robert C., USAF. "The Balkans Air Campaign Study, Part II." *Airpower Journal* 11, no. 3 (Fall 1997): 6-27.

Owen, David. *Balkan Odyssey*. New York: Harcourt Brace and Company, 1995.

Paris, Roland. *At War's End: Building Peace after Civil Conflict*. Cambridge: Cambridge University Press, 2004.

Paris, Roland, and Timothy D. Sisk, eds. *The Dilemmas of Statebuilding: Confronting the Contradictions of Postwar Peace Operations*. New York: Routledge, 2009.

Parish, Matthew. "Depressed West Averts Gaze from Bosnia's Demise," *Balkan Independent Reporting Network (BIRN)*, available through Balkan Insight Premium Weekly, August 15, 2012.

Partlow, Joshua, and Sayed Salahuddin. "Afghan Police targeted in attack," *The Washington Post*, May 23, 2011.

The Paul Nitze School of Advanced International Studies, Johns Hopkins University. "The Power of Elections?" *SAISPHERE* (2007).

Peabody, John W. "Economic Reform and Health Sector Policy: Lessons from Structural Adjustment Programs." *Social Science and Medicine* 43, no. 5 (1996): 823-35.

Peacebuild: the Canadian Peacebuilding Network. "Emerging Issues: Government, Democratization, and Violent Conflict." Summary of Dialogue on Topic, Website of Ursula Daxecker, http://www.colostate.edu/dept/PoliSci/faculty/daxecker.html (accessed September 12, 2011).

Peacekeeping Operations. Joint Publication 3-07.3. Washington, D.C.: J-7 Operational Plans and Interoperability Directorate, Joint Chiefs of Staff, U.S. Department of Defense, October 17, 2007. http://www.fas.org/irp/doddir/dod/jp3-07-3.pdf (accessed September 1, 2011).

Peck, Connie. *Sustainable Peace: the Role of the UN and Regional Organizations in Preventing Conflict*. New York: Rowman & Littlefield Publishers, 1998,

Pei, Minxin. "The Dark Side of China's Rise." *Foreign Policy* 153 (February 2006): 32-40.

Pei, Minxin, and Sara Kasper. "Lessons from the Past: The American Record on Nation Building." *Carnegie Endowment for International Peace,* Policy Brief 24 (2003): 1-8.

Perito, Robert M. "United States Institute of Peace—Special Report 'The Iraq Federal Police U.S. Police Building under Fire.'" *United States Institute of Peace* (October 2011). http://www.usip/org/files/resources/SR291_The_Iraq_Federal_Police.pdf (accessed October 20, 2011).

Perlez, Jane. "Usti nad Labem Journal; A Wall Not Yet Built Casts the Shadow of Racism," *New York Times,* July 2, 1998. http://www.nytimes.com/1998/07/02/world/usti-nad-labem-journal-a-wall-not-yet-built-casts-the-shadow-of-racism.html (accessed October 23, 2012).

Perriello, Tom, and Marieke Wierda. *Lessons from the Deployment of International Judges and Prosecutors in Kosovo*. New York: International Center for Transitional Justice, 2006.

Peskin, Victor. *International Justice in Rwanda and the Balkans: Virtual Trials and the Struggle for State Cooperation*. New York, NY: Cambridge University Press, 2008.

Peskin, Victor, and Mieczysław P. Boduszyński. "International Justice and Domestic Politics: Post-Tudjman Croatia and the International Criminal Tribunal for the Former Yugoslavia." *Europe-Asia Studies* 55, no. 7 (2003): 1117-42.

Philpott, Charles. "Though the Dog is Dead, the Pig Must be Killed: Finishing with Property Restitution to Bosnia–Herzegovina's IDPs and Refugees." *Journal of Refugee Studies* 18, no. 1 (2005): 1–24.

Pickering, Paula. "Generating Social Capital for Bridging Ethnic Divisions in the Balkans: Case Studies of Two Bosniak Cities." *Ethnic and Racial Studies* 29, no. 1 (2006): 79-103.

Pictet, Jean, ed. *Commentary to the III Geneva Convention Relative to the Treatment of Prisoners of War*. Geneva: ICRC, 1960.

Pitts, Joe W., III and David Weissbrodt. "Major Developments at the UN Commission on Human Rights in 1992." *Human Rights Quarterly* 15, no. 1 (February 1993): 122-96).

Pogány, Istvan. T*he Roma Café: Human Rights and the Plight of the Romani People.* London: Pluto Press, 2004.

Pridham, Geoffrey, Eric Herring, and George Sandord, eds. *Building Democracy? The International Dimension of Democratisation in Eastern Europe*. New York: St. Martin's Press, 1994.

Pye, Lucien. *Aspects of Political Development*. Boston, MA: Little, Brown and Company, 1966.

Qian, Yingyi."How Reform Worked in China." In *In Search of Prosperity: Analytic Narratives on Economic Growth*, edited by Dani Rodrik. Princeton, NJ: Princeton University Press, 2003.

Racioppi, Linda, and Katherine O'Sullivan. "Grassroots Peacebuilding and Third-party Intervention: The European Union's Special Support Programme for Peace and Reconciliation in Northern Ireland." *Peace and Change* 23, no. 3 (July 2007): 361-90.

Rawski, Thomas G. "Implications of China's Reform Experience." *The China Quarterly* 144 (1995): 1150-73.

Regan, Patrick, M., and Aysegul Aydin. "Diplomacy and Other Forms of Intervention in Civil Wars." *Journal of Conflict Resolution* 50 (2006): 751.

Reiding, Hilde. *The Netherlands and the Development of International Human Rights Instruments*. Antwerp, Belgium: Intersentia, 2007.

Reno, William. *Corruption and State Politics in Sierra Leone*. New York: Cambridge University Press, 1995.

Report on the Palestine Disturbances of August, 1929. London: His Majesty's Stationery

Office, 1930.

The Responsibility to Protect: Report of the International Commission on Intervention and State Sovereignty. Ottawa, Canada: The International Development Research Center, 2001.

Reychler, Luc, and Thania Paffenholz, eds. *Peacebuilding: A Field Guide*. Boulder, CO: Lynne Rienner, 2001.

Rhodes, R.A.W. "The New Governance: Governing without Government." *Political Studies* 44 (1996): 652-67.

Richmond, Oliver P. "Becoming Liberal, Unbecoming Liberalism: Liberal-Local Hybridity via the Everyday as a Response to the Paradoxes of Liberal Peacebuilding." *Journal of Intervention and Statebuilding* 3, no. 3 (November 2009): 324-44.

———. "Emancipatory Forms of Human Security and Liberal Peacebuilding." *International Journal* 62, no. 3 (2007): 459-72.

———. "Liberal Peace Transitions Need Urgent Rethink," *OpenDemocracy*, November 20, 2009. http://opendemocracy.net/oliver-p-richmond/liberal-peace-transitions-rethink-is-urgent (accessed October 23, 2012).

———. "UN Peace Operations and the Dilemmas of the Peacebuilding Consensus." *International Peacekeeping* 11, no. 1 (2004): 83–101.

Richmond, Oliver P. and Jason Franks. *Liberal Peace Transitions: Between Statebuilding and Peacebuilding.* Edinburgh, Scotland: Edinburgh University Press, 2011.

Rietjens, Sebastiaan. "Managing Civil-Military Cooperation." *Armed Forces & Society* 34, no. 2 (2008): 173-207.

Ringold, Den, Mitchell A. Orenstein, and Erika Wilkens. *Roma in an Expanding Europe: Breaking the Poverty Cycle*. Washington, D.C.: The World Bank Press, 2005.

Risse, Thomas, Stephen C. Ropp, and Kathryn Sikkink, eds. *The Power of Human Rights: International Norms and Domestic Change*. Cambridge: Cambridge University Press, 1999.

Ritchie, Cyril. "Collaboration Among Entities of the UN System and of Civil Society. Notably NGOs." *Transnational Associations* 55, no. 4 (2003): 207-11.

Roberts, Adam, and Benedict Kingsbury, eds. *United Nations, Divided World, Second Edition.* Oxford: Oxford University Press, 1993.

Rodrick, Dani. "Goodbye Washington Consensus, Hello Washington Confusion? A Review of the World Bank's Economic Growth in the 1990s: Learning from a Decade of Reform." *Journal of Economic Literature* 44 (2006): 973-87.

———. "Introduction: What Do We Learn from Country Narratives?" In *In Search of Prosperity: Analytic Narratives on Economic Growth,* edited by Dani Rodrik. Princeton, NJ: Princeton University Press, 2003.

Rogers, Elizabeth. "Economic Sanctions and Internal Conflict." In *The International Dimensions of Internal Conflict*, edited by Michael Brown. Cambridge: MIT Press, 1996.

———. "Using Economic Sanctions to Control Regional Conflicts," *Security Studies* 5, no. 4 (Summer 1996): 43-72.

Roper, Stephen D., and Lillian A. Barria. "Gatekeeping versus Allocating in Foreign Assistance: Donor Motivations and Contributions to War Crimes Tribunals." *The Journal of Conflict Resolution* 51, no. 2 (April 2007): 285-304.

Rosegrant, Susan. "A 'Seamless' Transition: United States and United Nations Operations in Somalia: 1992—1993." *Case Program (Part A),* CO9-96-1324.0. Cambridge: John F. Kennedy School of Government, Harvard University, 1996.

Rotberg, Robert I., ed. *Vigilance and Vengeance: NGOs Preventing Ethnic Conflict in Divided Societies*. Washington, DC: Brookings Institution Press, 1996.

Rourke, John T. *International Politics on the World Stage, Eleventh Edition*. New York: McGraw-Hill, 2006.
CPT Rousseau, D (USA). Personal Interview, October 4, 2011.
Ruane, Joseph, and Jennifer Todd. *The Dynamics of Conflict in Northern Ireland: Power, Conflict and Emancipation*. Cambridge: Cambridge University Press, 1996.
Rubin, Barnett. "Peace Building and State-Building in Afghanistan: Constructing Sovereignty for Whose Security?" *Third World Quarterly* 27, no. 1 (2006):177-85.
———, ed. *Toward Comprehensive Peace in Southeast Europe: Report of the South Balkans Working Group of the Council on Foreign Relations Center for Preventive Action*. New York: Twentieth Century Fund Press, 1996.
Rucht, Dieter. "Critique of Capitalism in the Era of Globalization—Old Wine in New Bottles?" In *Building a Transnational Civil Society. Global Issues and Global Actors*, edited by Ingo K Richter, Sabine Berking, and Ralf Muller-Schmid, 109-34. New York: Macmillan/Palgrave Press, 2006.
Rudolph, Joseph R., Jr. *Ethnoterritorial Politics, Policy, and the Western World*. Boulder, CO: Lynne Rienner, 1989.
———. "Intervention in Communal Conflict." *Orbis* 39, no. 2 (Spring, 1995): 259-273.
———. *Politics and Ethnicity A Comparative Study*. New York: Macmillan/Palgrave Press, 2006.
Rudolph, Joseph R., Jr., and Robert J. Thompson. "Ethnonational Movements and the Policy Process: Accommodating Nationalist Demands in the Developed World." *Comparative Politics* 17 (April, 1985): 291-311.
Sahnoun, Mohamed. *Somalia: The Missed Opportunities*. Washington, D.C.: United States Institute of Peace Press, 1994.
Sapone, Montgomery. "Ceasefire: The Impact of Republican Political Culture in the Ceasefire Process in Northern Ireland." *Peace and Conflict Studies* 7, no. 1 (May, 2000): 21-47.
Saunders, Harold, H. *Public Peace Process: Sustained Dialogue to Transform Racial and Ethnic Conflicts*. New York: St. Martin's Press, 1999.
Schedler, Andreas, ed. *Electoral Authoritarianism: The Dynamics of Unfree Competition*. Boulder, CO: Lynne Rienner Pulishers, 2006.
Schiff, Amira. "'Quasi Track-One' Diplomacy: An Analysis of the Geneva Process in the Israeli-Palestinian Conflict." *International Studies Perspectives* 11 (2010): 93-111.
Schimmelfennig, Frank, Engert Stefan, and Heiko Knobel. "Costs, Commitments, and Compliance: The Impact of EU Democratic Conditionality on Latvia, Slovakia, and Turkey." *Journal of Common Market Studies* 41, no. 3 (2003): 495-517.
Schirch, Lisa. *Civilian Peacekeeping: Preventing Violence and Making Space for Democracy*. Uppsala, Sweden: Life & Peace Institute, 2006.
Schraeder, Peter J., ed. *Intervention in the 1990s: US Foreign Policy in the Third World*. Boulder: Lynne Rienner, 1992.
Schreiber, Anna. "Economic Coercion as an Instrument of Foreign Policy: US Economic Measures against Cuba and the Dominican Republic." *World Politics* 25, no. 3 (April 1973): 387-413.
Schlesinger, Stephen C. *Act of Creation: The Founding of the United Nations*. Boulder: Westview, 2003.
Sekulic, Dusko, Garth Massey, and Randy Hodson. "Who were the Yugoslavs? Failed Sources of a Common Identity in the Former Yugoslavia." *American Sociological Review* 59, no. 1 (1994): 83-97.
Shahrbanou Tadjbakhsh. "Liberal Peace is Dead? Not so Fast," *OpenDemocracy*, November 27, 2009. http://www.opendemocracy.net.

Shams, Shamsul Hadi. "Assessing the Role of DDR in Afghanistan: Internal Security Revision and External Environment." In *Toward Bringing Stability in Afghanistan: A Review of the Peacebuilding Strategy*, edited by Yuji Uesugi. Hiroshima: Institute for Peace, Hiroshima University, 2010. http://home.hiroshima-u.ac.jp/heiwa/Pub/E24/yujiuesugied.pdf (accessed February 25, 2011).

Shapiro, Ian, and Stephen Macedo, eds. *Designing Democratic Institutions.* New York: New York University Press, 2000.

Shaw, Martin. "The Contemporary Mode of Warfare? Mary Kaldor's Theory of New Wars." *Review of International Political Economy* 7, no. 1 (2000): 171–80.

Shultz, Richard and Andrea Dew. *Insurgents Terrorists and Militias: The Warriors of Contemporary Combat.* New York: Columbia University Press, 2006.

Sidell, Scott R. *The IMF and Third-World Political Instability: Is There a Connection?* New York: St. Martin's Press, 1988.

Singh, Harkirat. *Intervention in Sri Lanka: The IPKF Experience Retold.* Colombo, Sri Lanka: Vijitha Yapa Publications, 2006.

Smith, Austin. "The Implications of Segregation for Transport within Northern Ireland." *Community Relations Council for Northern Ireland Report* 2 (June 2000).

Smith, B. C. *Understanding Third World Politics: Theories of Political Change and Development.* Bloomington: Indiana University Press, 2003.

Smith, Rupert. *The Utility of Force: The Art of War in the Modern World.* New York: Alfred A Knopf, 2007.

Snider, Lewis W. "The Political Performance of Governments, External Debt Service, and Domestic Political Violence." *International Political Science Review* 11, no. 4 (1990): 403-22.

Snyder, Jack. *From Voting to Violence: Democratization and Nationalist Conflict.* New York: W.W. Norton and Company, 2000.

Sokalski, Henryk. *An Ounce of Prevention: Macedonia and the UN Experience in Preventive Diplomacy.* Washington: United States Institute of Peace, 2003.

Solis, Gary. *The Law of Armed Conflict: International Humanitarian Law in War.* Cambridge: Cambridge University Press, 2010.

Sommer, John G. *Hope Restored? Humanitarian Aid in Somalia 1990-1994.* Washington, D.C.: Refugee Policy Group, Center for Policy Analysis and Research on Refugee Issues, 1994.

Soudriette, Richard W., and Andrew Ellis. "Election Systems Today: A Global Snapshot." *Journal of Democracy* 17, no. 2 (2006): 78-88.

Soudriette, Richard W., and Juliana Geran Pilon, eds. *Every Vote Counts: The Role of Elections in Building Democracy.* Boulder, CO: University Press of America, 2007.

"Special Support Programme for Peace and Reconciliation in Northern Ireland and the Border Counties of Ireland (1995-1999)." *Commission of the European Communities Communication.* Brussels, 26.11.1997. COM (97)642.

Special Inspector General for Afghanistan Reconstruction. "US Combats Afghan Aid Corruption," Al Jazeera, 2010. http://english.aljazeera.net/news/americas/2009/12/2009123042621747107.html (accessed February 26, 2011).

Sriram, Chandra Lekha, and Karin Wermester, eds., *From Promise to Practice: Strengthening UN Capacities for the Prevention of Violent Conflict.* Boulder, CO, Lynne Rienner, 2003.

Stahn, Carsten. *The Law and Practice of International Territorial Administration: Versailles to Iraq and Beyond.* Cambridge: Cambridge University Press, 2008.

———. "Responsibility to Protect: Political Rhetoric or Emerging Legal Norm?" *The American Journal of International Law* 101, no. 1 (2007): 99-120.

Stanvocic, Vojislav. "Problems and Options in Institutionalizing Ethnic Relations." *International Political Science Review* 13, no. 4 (1992), 359-79.

Stavenhagen, Rodolfo. *Ethnic Conflicts and the Nation-State*. New York: St. Martin's Press, 1996.

Stedman, Stephen J. "Spoiler Problems in Peace Processes." *International Security* 22, no. 2 (1997): 5-53.

Steiner, Henry J., and Philip Alston. *International Human Rights in Context: Law, Politics, Morals, Third Edition*. Oxford: Oxford University Press, 2007.

Stevenson, Jonathan. "Peace in Northern Ireland: Why Now?" *Foreign Policy* no. 112 (Autumn 1998): 41-54.

Stiglitz, Joseph E. *Globalization and Its Discontents.* New York: W.W. Norton and Company, 2002.

Stoddard, Abby. "Humanitarian NGOs: Challenges and Trends." In *Humanitarian Action and the 'Global War on Terror': A Review of Trends and Issues* edited by Joanna Macrae, and Adele Harmer. London: HGP Report 14, 2003.

Stover, Eric, and Harvey M. Weinstein, eds. *My Neighbor, My Enemy: Justice and Community in the Aftermath of Mass Atrocity*. Cambridge: Cambridge University Press, 2004.

Stuckler, David, Lawrence P. King, and Sanjay Basu. "International Monetary Fund Programs and Tuberculosis Outcomes in Post-Communist Countries." *PLoS Medicine* 5, no. 7 (2008): 1079-90.

Subotić, Jelena. "The Paradox of International Justice Compliance." *International Journal of Transitional Justice* 3, no. 3 (2009): 362-83.

Svensson, Isak. "Who Brings Peace?: Neutral versus Biased Mediation and Institutional Peace Arrangements in Civil Wars." *Journal of Conflict Resolution* 53 (2009): 446-69.

Tanner, Murray Scot. "China Rethinks Unrest." *The Washington Quarterly* 27, no. 3 (2004): 137-56.

Taras, Raymond C., and Rajat Ganguly. *Understanding Ethnic Conflict: The International Dimension*. New York: Longman, 2002.

Tawfeeq, Mohammed. "At Least 65 Die in Attack at Recruitment Center in Northern Iraq." *CNN World*, January 18, 2011. http://articles.cnn.com/2011-01-18/world/iraq.violence_1_recruitment-center-tikrit-residents-sunni-muslim-city?_s=PM:WORLD (accessed September 29, 2011).

Terlingen, Yvonne. "The Human Rights Council: A new Era in UN Human Rights Work?" *Ethics & International Affairs* 21, no. 2 (Summer 2007): 167-78.

Terrill, W.Andrew. *Regional Spillover Effects of the Iraq War*. Carlisle, PA: The Strategic Studies Institute, 2008.

Thakur, Ramesh. "From Peacekeeping to Peace Enforcement: the U.N. Operation in Somalia." *Journal of Modern African Studies* 32, no. 3 (1994): 387-410.

Therese, Fay M., Mike Morrissey, and Marie Smyth. *Northern Ireland's Troubles: The Human Costs*. London: Pluto Press, 1999.

Thomas, Ann, and A. Thomas. *Non-Intervention: the Law and Its Import in the Americas*. Dallas: Southern Methodist University Press, 1956.

Thursby, Gene R. *Hindu-Muslem Relations in British India*. London: E. J. Brill, 1975.

Tilly, Charles, and Sidney Tarrow. *Contentious Politics*. Boulder CO: Paradigm Publishers 2007.

Toka, Gabor. *An Inventory of Political Attitude & Behavior Surveys in East Central Europe & the Former Soviet Union (1989-1997)*. Bergisch Gladbach, Germany: Erwin Ferger, 2000.

Tolley, Howard Jr. *The U.N. Commission on Human Rights*. Boulder, CO: Westview, 1987.

Tolley, Howard, Miko Lempinen, and Philip Alston. "Reconceiving The UN Human Rights Regime: Challenges Confronting the New UN Human Rights Council." *Melbourne Journal of International Law* 7, no. 2 (2006): 185-224.

Tonge, Jonathon. *Northern Ireland.* Cambridge: Polity Press, 2006.

Touval, Sadia, and I. William Zartman, eds. *International Mediation in Theory and Practice*. Boulder, CO: Westview Press, 1985.

Transparency International. "Global Perception Index 2010." (2010). http://www.transparency.org/policy_research/surveys_indices/cpi/2010/results (accessed April 05, 2011).

Trindade, A. A. Cancado. "International Law for Humankind: Towards a New Jus Gentium." *Recueil des cours* 316 (2005).

United Nations. "Agreement on Provisional Arrangements in Afghanistan Pending the Re-Establishment of Permanent Government Institutions." (2001). http://www.un.org/News/dh/latest/afghan/afghan-agree.htm (accessed January 10, 2011).

———. "Supplement to an Agenda for Peace: Position Paper of the Secretary-General on the Occasion of the Fiftieth Anniversary of the United Nations." A/50/60–S/1995/1, January 3, 1995. http://www.un.org/Docs/SG/agsupp.html.

United Nations Economic and Social Council. *Consultative Relationship between the United Nations and Non-Governmental Organisations* 31 (1996).

United Nations General Assembly. *Resolution on Human Rights Council*. A/RES/60/251, April 3, 2006.

United Nations Office of the High Commissioner for Human Rights. "Human Rights Dimension of Poverty in Afghanistan," March 31, 2010. http://www.humansecuritygateway.com/documents/OHCHR_HumanRightsDimensionOfPovertyInAfghanistan.pdf (accessed February 25, 2011).

United Nations Office of the Secretary General. "Secretary-General Calls for Unconditional Respect for Human Rights of Kosovo Citizens, in Statement to North Atlantic Treaty Organization: Kofi Annan Stresses Peaceful Negotiation Only Way to Resolve Kosovo Conflict," *United Nations Press Release* SG/SM/6878, January 28, 1999.

United Nations Peace-building Commission. *Provisional guidelines for the participation of civil society in meetings of the Peacebuilding Commission, submitted by the Chairperson on the basis of informal consultations*. PBC/1/OC/12, 2007.

United Nations Secretary-General. *An Agenda for Peace. Preventive Diplomacy, Peacemaking and Peace-keeping.* A/47/277, June 17, 1992.

———. *Report of the Secretary-General on the United Nations Preventive Deployment Force,* S/1997/365, May 12, 1997.

———. "UN Millennium Development Goals Report," *UN Department of Public Information*, 2000.

United States. "Administration Policy on Reforming Multilateral Peace Operations, May 1994." *Presidential Decision Directive 25*. http://www.kentlaw.edu/academics/courses/admin-perritt/pdd-25.html (accessed December 2, 2011).

United States Department of State, Bureau of Diplomatic Security-OSAC. *Iraq 2011 Crime and Safety Report: Baghdad*. https://www.osac.gov/Pages/ContentReportDetails.aspx?cid=10884 (accessed October 1, 2011).

United States Institute of Peace and U.S. Army Peacekeeping and Stability Operations Institute. *Guiding Principles for Peace Operations*. 2009.

http://www.usip.org/resources/guiding-principles-stabilization-and-reconstruction. (accessed October 23, 2012).

United States Policy on Multilateral Peacekeeping Operations. *Presidential Decision Directive 25*, May 6, 1994. http://www.fas.org/irp/offdocs/pdd25.htm (accessed July 8, 2011).

United States Senate, Armed Services Committee. *Hearing on Operation Allied Force and Relief Operations in Kosovo*, November 3, 1999. As published by Federal Document Clearing House, Inc. on CIS Congressional Universe (Lexis-Nexis).

Uyangoda, Jayadeva. "Review Essay: Reinterpreting Tamil and Sinhala Nationalisms." *South Asia Bulletin* 7 (1987): 39-46.

Vankovska-Cvetkovska, Biljana. "UNPREDEP in Macedonia: Achievements and Limits of Preventive Diplomacy." *Online Journal of Peace and Conflict Resolution* 2, no.1 (March 1999). http://www.scribd.com/doc/70423632/CROSSROADS-The-Macedonian-foreign-policy-journal-January-August-2011 (accessed October 23, 2012).

Velikonja, Mitja. *Religious Separation and Political Intolerance in Bosnia-Herzegovina*. College Station: Texas A&M University Press, 2003.

Vermeersch, Peter. *The Romani Movement: Minority Politics and Ethnic Mobilization in Contemporary Central Europe*. New York: Berghahn Books, 2007.

Vogt, Heidi, and Kay Johnson. "NATO Troops Targeted Again: U.S. Ambassador Calls Fifth Attack by Afghan Police 'Troubling,'" *The Washington Post*, August 14, 2012.

Von Hippel, Karen. *Democracy by Force: U.S. Military Intervention in the Post-Cold War World*. Cambridge: Cambridge University Press, 2000.

Walder, Andrew. "China's Transitional Democracy: Interpreting Its Significance." *The China Quarterly* 144 (1995): 963-79.

Wallace, Molly. "Confronting Wrongs, Creating Wrongs: Official Discourses and the Legitimation of Violence in Sri Lanka." Paper presented at the annual meeting of the International Studies Association, New Orleans, Louisiana, February 17, 2010.

Wallis, Tim, and Claudia Samayoa. "Civilian Peacekeepers: Creating a Safe Environment for Peacebuilding." In *People Building Peace II: Successful Stories of Civil Society*, edited by Paul van Tongeren, Malin Brenk, Marte Hellema, and Juliette Verhoeven, 263-68. Boulder, CO: Lynne Rienner, 2005.

Walter, Barbara F. *Committing to Peace: The Successful Settlement of Civil Wars*. Princeton, NJ: Princeton University Press, 2002.

Walter, Barbara, and Jack Snyder, eds. *Civil Wars, Insecurity, and Intervention*. New York: Columbia University Press, 1999.

Walton, John and David Seddon. *Free Markets and Food Riots: The Politics of Global Adjustment*. Cambridge: Blackwell Publishing, 1994.

Walzenbach, Gunter P.E., ed., *European Governance: Policy Making between Politicization and Control*. Franham, UK: Ashgate, 2006.

Wardak, Ali, Daud Saba, and Halima Kazem. "Afghanistan Human Development Report 2007." *Center for Policy and Human Development* (2007). http://hdr.undp.org/en/reports/nationalreports/asiathepacific/afghanistan/nhdr2007.pdf (accessed February 26, 2011).

Wardak, Ali. "Building a Post-war Justice System in Afghanistan." *Crime, Law & Social Change* 41 (2004): 319–41.

———. "The Tribal and Ethnic Composition of Afghan Society." In *Afghanistan: Essential Field Guides to Humanitarian and Conflict Zones, Second Edition*, edited by Edward Girardet, and Jonathan Walter. Geneva: Crosslines Ltd, 2003.

Wasserstein, Bernard. *The British in Palestine: The Mandatory Government and the Ar-*

ab-Jewish Conflict 1917-1929. London: Royal Historical Society, 1978.
Weber, Thomas. *Gandhi's Peace Army: The Shanti Sena and Unarmed Peacekeeping*. Syracuse: Syracuse University Press, 1996.
Weiss, Thomas G., David P. Forsythe, Roger A. Coate, and Kelly-Kate Pease. *The United Nations and Changing World Politics, Fifth Edition*. Boulder, CO: Westview Press, 2007.
Weller, Marc. "The Rambouillet Conference on Kosovo." *International Affairs* 75, 2 (1999): 211-51.
Welsh, William A. ed. *Survey Research and Public Attitudes in Eastern Europe and the Soviet Union*. New York: Pergamon Press, 1981.
White, Robert. "From Peaceful Protest to Guerrilla War: Micro-mobilization of the Provisional Irish Republican Army." *The American Journal of Sociology* 94, no. 6 (May 1989): 1277-1302.
Whitworth, Sandra. *Men, Militarism and UN Peacekeeping: A Gendered Analysis*. Boulder: Lynne Rienner Publishers, 2004.
Whitt, Sam. "Institutions and Ethnic Trust: Evidence from Bosnia." *Europe-Asia Studies* 62, no. 2 (2010): 271-92.
Whitt, Sam, and Rick Wilson. "The Dictator Game, Fairness and Ethnicity in Postwar Bosnia." *American Journal of Political Science* 51, no. 3 (2007): 655-68.
Wierda, Marieke, Priscilla Hayner, and Paul van Zyl. *Exploring the Relationship between the Special Court and the Truth and Reconciliation Commission of Sierra Leone*. New York, NY: The International Center for Transitional Justice, 2002.
Wilde, Ralph. *The Administration of Territory by International Organizations*. Oxford: Oxford University Press, 2005.
———. *Report of the Panel on United Nations Peace Operations*. A/55/305–S/2000/809, August, 2000. http://www.un.org/peace/reports/peace_operations/ (accessed October 23, 2012).
———. "Taxonomies of International Peacekeeping: An Alternative Narrative. ILSA." *Journal of International and Comparative Law* 9 (2002): 391–408.
Willetts, Peter. "Transnational Actors and International Organizations in Global Politics." In *The Globalization of World Politics*, edited by John B. Baylis and Steve Smith, 356-83. Oxford and New York: Oxford University Press, 2001.
Williams, Ian. "UN Report: As Europeans Stall Bosnia Action, UN Mission Harassed by Serbs." *The Washington Report on Middle East Affairs* 12, no. 1 (July 1993).
Williamson, Arthur, Scott Duncan, and Peter Halfpenny. "Rebuilding Civil Society in Northern Ireland: the Community and Voluntary Sector's Contribution to the European Union's Peace and Reconciliation District Partnership Program." *Policy & Politics* 28, no. 1 (January 2000): 49-66.
Williamson, John. "What Washington Means by Policy Reform." In *Latin American Readjustment: How Much Has Happened?* edited by John Williamson, 7-20. Washington, DC: Institute for International Economics, 1989.
Wilson, Andrew J. "Doing the Business: Aspects of the Clinton Administration's Economic Support for the Northern Ireland Peace Process, 1994-2000." *Journal of Conflict Studies* 23, no 1 (2003).
———. "From the Beltway to Belfast: The Clinton Administration, Sinn Fein, and the Northern Ireland Peace Process." *New Hibernia Review* 1, no. 3 (Autumn 1997): 23-39.
Winner, Andrew. "You and What Army? Coalitions and Coercive Diplomacy." *Ph.D Dissertation*. College Park, MD: University of Maryland, 2002.

Wimmer, Andreas and Conrod Schetter. "Putting State-Formation First: Some Recommendations for Reconstruction and Peace-Making in Afghanistan." *Journal of International Development* 15 (2003): 525-39.

Woodward, Bob. *The Choice*. New York: Simon and Schuster, 1996.

Woodward, Susan. *Balkan Tragedy: Chaos and Dissolution after the Cold War.* Washington, DC: The Brookings Institution, 1995.

World Bank. "Afghanistan Development Forum 2007." *World Bank* (2007). http://www.worldbank.org.af/WBSITE/EXTERNAL/COUNTRIES/SOUTHASIAEXT/AFGHANISTANEXTN/0,,contentMDK:21314955~pagePK:141137~piPK:141127~theSitePK:305985,00.html (accessed January 17, 2011).

World Summit Outcome Document. High Level Plenary Meeting of the United Nations General Assembly, September 2005.

Wright, Joanne, "PIRA Propaganda: The Construction of Legitimacy." *Conflict Quarterly* (Summer 1990): 24-41.

Youngs, Tim. *Kosovo: The Diplomatic and Military Options*. Research Paper 98/93. London: House of Commons Library, 1998.

Zahar, Marie-Joelle. "Norm Transmission in Peace- and State-building: Lessons from Democracy Promotion in Sudan and Labanon." *Global Governance: A Review of Multilateralism and International Organizations* 18, no. 1 (2012): 73-88.

Žarković, Dragoljub. "Mala Nočna Straža" (A Little Night Guard Duty), *Politika Online*, September 19, 2008. http://www.politika.co.yu.

Zartman, I. William, and Maureen Berman. *The Practical Negotiator.* New Haven: Yale University Press, 1983.

Zartman, I. William, ed. *Peacemaking in International Conflict*. Washington, DC: United States Institutes of Peace, 1997.

———. *Ripe for Resolution: Conflict and Intervention in Africa, Second Edition.* New York: Oxford, 1989.

Zimmerman, Warren. *Origins of a Catastrophe: Yugoslavia and its Destroyers—America's Last Ambassador Tells What Happened and Why.* New York: Random House, 1996.

Index

abduction, 322, 336, 337, 338, 340
Adams, Gerry, 40-44, 47
Adenaur, Konrad, 360
Afghanistan, 369, 378, 382; defense and security in, 376; ethnic conflict in, 372-74; nation building in, 371; warlords in, 372-76
African Charter on Human and Peoples Rights, 116
African Union, 100, 249, 471
al Qaeda, 321, 370-71, 375
Albania, 138-39
Albright, Madeleine, 284, 289, 290, 291, 292
amnesty, 28, 129, 130, 132
Amnesty International, 225
Anglo Irish Agreement, 38, 39
Anglo Irish Treaty, 35
Annan, Kofi, 99, 102, 269
anti-Taliban groups, 372
antiziganism, 214, 215
Arab Spring, 325
armed conflicts, 84-86, 88, 90, 153
assassination, 320, 321, 323, 324, 325, 328, 376

Badr Brigade, 322, 328
Baghdad Police Professional College, 318, 322-23
Baldwin, David, 146-48
Balkans, 189, 191, 463
bin Laden, Osama, 370
biological weapons, 243
Blair, Tony, 42, 47
Bloody Sunday, 37
Bolton, John, 264
Bonn Agreement, 370, 372, 373, 381, 382
Bosnia, 127, 132-33, 135-37, 140, 152, 278, 304; coercive diplomacy in, 285-89, 303-13; distrust of politicians in, 399-400; ethnic conflict in, 391-98; High Representative, 425-31, 439-40; interest in European integration, 405-406; policing, 446-47, 449-51; public opinion in, 390-91; restructuring of, 449-51; war in, 279-91, 441
Bosniaks, 307, 310, 358, 391, 392, 293, 294, 295-405, 425, 436n33, 441
Buergenthal, Thomas, 105, 107
Bush administration (George H.W.), 258, 259, 265
Bush administration (George W.), 364

Cambodia, 127, 130, 131, 138, 139, 141n2
campaigning NGOs, 464
Carothers, Thomas, 78, 161, 355
Carter administration, 40
Carter Center, 23, 71, 72
Charter of Fundamental Rights of the European Union, 213, 215
chemical weapons, 243
child soldiers, 337, 338
Christmas Warning, 276
Christopher, Warren, 304, 307
Clausewitz, Carl von, 236, 237, 238, 248, 251
Clinton administration, 40, 259, 266, 286, 304, 306, 341, 357; cruise missile strikes and, 241
Clinton, William, 289, 292, 303, 305, 309, 427; as mediator, 41, 43, 47
Cold War, 8, 33, 44, 72, 152, 239, 259, 420, 463

Commission on Human Rights (CHR), 100-105, 115-17
Commission Information Network (CIN), 340, 342, 343
Commission on Security and Cooperation in Europe (CSCE), 224-25
Comprehensive Anti-Apartheid Act (1986), 152
Concert of Europe, 7
Conference on Yugoslavia, 275
Conflict Barometer, 2
conflict, 6-7, 25-26; armed, 84-86, 88, 90, 92-93; management, 3, 5-7, 158; resolution, 57, 145-58, 163; suspension, 28, 29
Convention on Forced Disappearances, 106
Council of Europe, 8, 100, 224
covert action, 241
crimes against humanity, 60, 127, 129, 130, 132, 138, 192
criminal apprehension, 137-38
Criminal Defense Resource Center (CDRC), 139
Croat-Muslim Federation, 364
Croatia, 4, 11, 275-77
Czechoslovakia, 2, 6
Czech Republic, 200, 215, 217, 219

Darfur, 60, 62, 91, 113, 119, 195
Dayton Peace Accord, 13, 72, 76, 132-33, 137, 140n1, 152, 240; basis for, 284, 287; detailed, 426; implementation of, 303, 309-10, 427, 428-29; incentives of, 159; monitoring of, 406; multi-ethnic framework of, 395
Del Ponte, Carla, 193, 198, 199, 205
democracy assistance funds, 160-61
Democratic League of Kosovo, 281-82, 283
democratic peace, 356, 422
democratic reconstruction model, 371, 384
Democratic Unionist Party, 38, 49, 56
democratization, 69, 71, 72, 161, 218, 262, 355, 356, 363-64, 369; of policing, 448, 451; problems with, 74-75, 173-74
deportation, 211, 212
Dindic, Zoran, 131, 194
diplomacy, preventive, 75, 77, 78, 342, 463, 471, 476
dirty bombs, 244
Disarmament, Demobilization and Reintegration (DDR), 374-76, 381
displaced people, 283, 308, 339, 430, 471
doctrine of implied powers, 93, 97n44
Downing Street Declaration, 40
drug trafficking, 376
Dunandist NGOs, 465

East Timor, 127, 131, 132, 134, 136, 138, 140
economic development, 42, 45, 62, 159-62; benefits of, 158-59; defined, 147; incentives for, 145-46
economic hardship, 175
economic liberalization, 171, 172, 179-81, 185n22, 422-23
economic reform, 56, 174, 179, 180, 181, 183, 190
economic statecraft, 145, 146-48, 164-65
Eisenhower administration, action plan of, 115, 124n58
elections, 75, 121, 393, 427; assistance, 160-61; ethnicity in, 390, 407n5, 408n11; monitors, 69-78, 471; transitioning states in, 76; and violence, 63-65
ethnic, 361; cleansing, 72, 76, 89, 136, 239, 285, 304, 307, 363, 430, 411; cleansing in Bosnia, 391, 394, 395; conflict, 13, 213, 215; groups, 389-405; identity, 22, 390-92; tolerance, 392-93; violence, 396
European Union (EU), 6, 11, 163, 190, 195, 213, 219; directive violations, 211; election monitors, 70, 72; leverage of, 194, 195, 200; and mediation, 214; NATO and, 192-93; policies of, 190, 191, 192, 197, 204, 212; reform incentives of, 163, 165; strategy alterations, 198-99; threats of, 13
European Commission, 202, 211-12, 213, 214, 222
European Constitutional Treaty, 222

European Convention on Human Rights, 8, 45, 224
European governance, 222-23
European integration of Bosnia, 404-05
European Roma Rights Centre, 211
Europeanization, 223, 227n8
explosive weapons, 244
extortion, 376

faith-based NGOs, 465
Federation of Bosnia-Herzegovina, 440
financial incentives or sanctions, 147, 150
forced disappearances, 106, 121n13
foreign aid, 159
Former Yugoslavian Republic of Macedonia (FYROM), 470
Franks, Jason, 56, 59
free market reform, 422, 23
Friedrich, Carl, 69

Gates, Robert, 371
Gelbard, Richard, 277, 282
General Framework Agreement for Peace (GFAP), 439-40
Geneva Convention, 85, 86, 90
genocide, 127, 128, 129, 130, 132m 239, 287
Genocide Convention, 198, 205
global accountability, 128-29, 140
global economy, 172
global frameworks, 57
global peace building, 56, 59. *See also* peace building
global security, 463
global terrorism, 101
global trade, 151, 152, 173
globalism, 151, 336, 464
Good Friday Agreement, 6, 34, 45, 46, 47-50
Gornji Obrinje massacre, 283
Government of Iraq (GoI), 317, 320
Gulf War, 9, 10
gypsies. *See* Roma

Hadzic, Goran, 189, 203
Hague Convention (1907), 85
Hairi, Rafiq, 130, 141n6
health and education issues, 175-77
Hiedelberg's Institute for International Conflict Resolution, 2
High Representative, 427, 430
Hillsborough Declaration, 47
Holbrooke, Richard, 283, 287, 288, 359
hostage taking, 280, 281
human rights, 56, 90, 118, 135, 189, 190, 213, 376; issues of, 89, 101, 115; law, 86, 93; NGOs, 119; obligations, 104-05; protections, 72, 105, 251; violations, 8, 84, 87, 96n22, 103, 137-40, 153, 239
Human Rights Council, 86, 87, 99, 110, 119
Human Rights Watch, 113, 363
humanitarian conditions, 259, 283, 326
humanitarian intervention, 60, 259, 463, 464
humanitarian law, 91
humanitarian relief, 257, 259, 260-61, 263-65, 370
hunger strikes, 39
Hussein, Saddam, 317, 318, 319
hybrid tribunals, 128-33, 137, 139, 140

Implementation Force (IFOR), 312, 426, 427, 428, 440, 453
implied powers, 93, 97n44
improvised explosive devices (IEDs), 243, 322
incentives, 160, 275; trade and economic, 147, 157-58, 162, 163
incremental liberalization, 172, 179-80, 183,
Indian Peace-Keeping Forces (IPKF), 344
indirect aggression, 88
Indo-Lankan Accord, 344
inequality, as role in conflict, 159
international administration, 419-20, 423-25, 425-29
International Body on Decommissioning of Weapons, 42
International Committee of the Red Cross (ICRC), 106, 338
International Conference on the former Yugoslavia (IFY), 277, 279, 286
International Council on Security and Development, 384

International Court of Justice, 88, 93, 95n7, 119, 198
International Covenant on Civil and Political Rights (ICCPR), 87, 103, 109
International Covenant on Economic, Social, and Cultural Rights, 103, 107
International Criminal Court (ICC), 8, 60, 94, 127, 128, 135-35
International Criminal Tribunal for Rwanda (ICTR), 131, 135, 137
International Criminal Tribunal for the former Yugoslavia (ICTY), 42, 128, 131, 134, 137, 138, 189, 190, 192, 193, 194, 198
international customs, 84, 95n7
International Displaced Person camp (IDP), 339
international financial institutions (IFIs), 171, 174, 180
International Foundation for Elections Assistance, 71
International Fund for Ireland, 43
International Government Organizations (IGOs), 23, 465-69
international human rights organizations, 200, 219
international humanitarian law, 85, 105-06, 132
international intervention, 257, 389, 419
international judicial personnel, 134
international justice, 119, 135, 136, 191, 195, 204, 205
international law, 83, 84, 86, 92, 93, 189; social structure of, 102, 121n8; training, 139
International Monetary Fund (IMF), 9, 171, 174, 175, 178, 183
International Police Task Force, 439-56
international preventative diplomacy, 463
international society, 83-84, 94
international tribunal, 193, 203, 204
Internationally Accepted Principles for Policing a Democratic State, 446-47
intervention; in Bosnia, 278, 279; direct, 281; international, 419; non-coercive, 212; non-violent, 334, 344
intrastate conflict, 21, 25, 84, 149, 153, 154, 157-58, 464
Iran, 2, 318, 319, 321, 322, 323, 324, 325
Iranian Revolutionary Guard, 322
Iraq, 2, 9, 10; army of, 324; assassinations in, 321, 323, 324, 325
Iraqi Islamist National Movement, 321
Iraqi Ministry of Interior, 317, 319, 322, 323, 327
Iraqi Police Service, 317, 318-320, 326, 327
Iraqi Security Forces, 328, 322
Ireland, 4
Irish Free State, 35
Irish Northern Aid Committee, 43
Irish Republican Army (IRA), 34, 35, 37-38, 40-43, 47, 49

Jaysh al-Mahdi, 321, 322, 323
judicial reform, 127, 138, 139
just war, 238-39. *See also* Responsibility to Protect
justice, barriers to, 136-138

Karadzic, Radovan, 131, 196, 198, 201
Karzai government, 380
Key Leadership Engagement, 323
Khmer Rouge, 130, 131, 133, 138
kidnapping, 322, 326, 336, 337, 338, 340, 376
Kosovo, 4, 9, 10, 11, 127, 133, 137, 139, 141n4, 192; coercion and, 289-94; compared to Bosnia, 294-97, 363; declaration of independence, 200; diplomatic observer mission, 284; liberation army of, 273, 281, 282, 283, 285, 291, 292; war in, 280-85
Kosovo Chamber of Advocates, 139
Kostunica, Vojislav, 131, 192, 193, 194-95, 197, 198
Kurds, 319, 321

language as barrier to justice, 134
League of Human Rights, 217, 225
LeBovic, James, 108, 109, 110, 113, 119
legal protection, Roma, 211
Legal System Monitoring Section, 139

liberal economics, 172, 173
Liberal Peace, 55-60
liberalization, 173-74, 178, 179-82, 422
Liberation Tigers of Tamil Eelan, 333, 336, 341, 344
Lome Peace Agreement, 132, 136

Macedonia, 4, 13, 463-76
Magnetically Attached Improvised Exploding Devices, 324
marginalization, 217, 223, 224, 226
massacre, 112, 155, 156, 267, 373; Gonji Obrinje, 283; Hargeisa, 262; Racak, 290; Srebrenica, 196, 304, 307
mediation, 23, 25, 27, 34, 40, 262. *See also* third party mediation
military operations other than war, 245-47, 251
military action, 236, 237, 241, 242, 243; just cause of war, 238; just conduct of war, 238-39; exit strategies, 249-50; personal motivation, 290-91; traditional use of, 239-41
military intervention, 8, 235-41, 250, 252, 303, 334, 369
Milosevic, Slobodan, 131, 134, 152, 162, 192-93, 196, 281; and Yeltsin, 284; negotiation with United States, 286-87
minority rights and demands, 5, 218
Mitchell, George, 42, 43, 47
Mladic, Ratko 131, 189, 196, 197, 198, 201, 202, 203
Mogadishu, 258
Mujahedeen, 369, 375
multilateral peace operations of NGOs, 463
Multilateral Peacekeeping Operations, 308
multinational army, 260

nation building 250, 273, 371; in Afghanistan 369-371; defined, 381; history of, 376-80, 382; problems of, 361-62, 376; third party, 355-66; top down approach to, 371-80, 383
Nationalists in Northern Ireland, 35, 36, 38, 42
Nikolic, Tomislav, 198, 199, 202
Non-Government Organizations, (NGOs), 9, 10, 117, 465-66; in Macedonia, 473-74; as peace facilitators, 467-69; problems with, 376-80
Nonviolent Peaceforce (NP), 333-48
North American Free Trade Agreement (NAFTA), 154
North Atlantic Treaty Organization (NATO), 8, 192, 220, 303, 305, 312; air strikes, 159, 280; in Kosovo, 11, 270
The Northern Alliance, 372, 373
Northern Ireland, 33-43; as successful peace process 44-50
Northern Ireland Human Rights Commission, 45

Office for Democratic Institutions and Human Rights, 70, 71, 72
Office of Internal Oversight Services, 137
Office of the High Representative, 9, 74, 139, 423, 26, 428, 430, 433, 440, 453. *See also* High Representative
Office of the UN High Commission for Human Rights, 115-16
Ohrid Framework Agreement, 471
Operation Deliberate Force, 303, 304, 307, 314n27
Operation Horseshoe, 285
Operation Iraqi Freedom, 317
Orange parades, 35, 47
Orange Revolution, 76
Organization for African Unity, 20, 70, 226
Organization Council for Peace and Coexistence, 340, 342, 343
Organization for Security and Cooperation in Europe, OSCE), 9, 70, 72, 73, 75, 76, 139, 214, 216, 220, 224, 284, 426, 427, 430, 471
organizations providing humanitarian relief, 260-61
Orrisa Society of the Americas, 471

Peace Brigade International, 334
peace building, 160, 162, 330, 420, 421-22; problems, 62, 66

Peace Implementation Council, 423, 429-30
peacemaking, 40-41, 274, 277
peace money, 44
peace operations, 246-47, 255n20
peace over justice, 131
peace process, 21, 33, 38, 43, 45, 130, 133, 161
peace settlement, 28
peace walls, 37. See also walls
peacekeeping, 72, 92, 179, 246, 274, 279, 308, 474; defined, 355; dilemmas in, 265-71; failures of, 7, 10; functions of, 464-65
People's Republic of China, 180-82
Phare program, 226, 230n52
Plantation Plan, 34-35
Platform for Roma Inclusion, 214
police organizations, restructuring of, 443, 445, 449-51, 452-54
Police Service of Northern Ireland, 45, 49, 50
policing in a democratic state, 458-61
policy change, sanctions and incentives, 148, 154
policy makers, 273, 290
political instability, 179, 182
political process for peace, 48-49, 355
political terror scale (PTS), 108, 109, 110, 111
positive reciprocity, 157
Presidential Decision Directive 25 (PDD25), 308
preventive diplomacy, 75, 77, 78, 342, 463, 471, 476
preventive deployment of troops, 472
privatization of public corporations, 177
Property Law Implementation Plan, 430
Provisional IRA, 37-38

racism, 215
radiological weapons, 244
Rambouillet Accord, 291, 292
Reagan administration, 40
reconciliation commissions, 132
reconstruction, post-conflict, 28, 424
Reding, Viviane, 211, 212
refugees, 308, 369. *See also* displaced peoples
regional trade agreement, 162-63
relationship building, 342
Republic of Ireland, 39
Republika Srpska, 76, 276, 287, 431, 440
responsibility to protect (R2P), 89-90, 96n30, 97n33, 239, 249, 252, 334, 467
Revolutionary United Front, 270
Richmond, Oliver, 56, 57, 58, 59
riots, 182, 195, 262, 363, 367n13
Rogers, Elizabeth, 148, 150
Roma, 211-220; and EU, 220-27; in Holocaust, 216, 223-24; integration, 213-14, 218; sterilization of women, 216-17, 224, 225
Rose Revolution, 76
Royal Ulster Constabulary, 36, 37, 45
Rugova, Ibrahim, 281-82, 360
Rwanda, 128, 134, 136, 137

Sahnoun, Mohammed, 258, 263
sanctions, 91, 150, 151, 157-58, 163-64, 278, 319; against human rights violations, 57, 103, 109; economic, 118, 145, 146, 149, 150, 152-53; trade, 147, 153-55, 162, 164-65
Sarajevo, 278, 279, 425, 448
Sarkozy, Nicolas, 211, 212
Search for Common Ground, 473-74
segregation, 36, 37, 43, 219-20, 223, 224, 364
self-determination, 85-86, 96n17
Serbia, 4, 11, 76, 77, 134, 152-53, 189-99, 275, 307
Serbian Radical Party, 134, 198-99
Shi'a, 321, 322
Shiite Supreme Court of the Islamic Revolution of Iraq, 328
shurta, 318, 319, 320, 324
Sierra Leone, 127, 130, 132, 133, 134, 140, 141n5, 151, 172, 193-94
Sinn Fein, 35, 39, 40, 42, 46, 47, 49-50
Slovakia, 8, 163
Social, Democratic and Labor Party, 40
soft law, 119
soft power, 357
Somalia, 10, 258, 262

South Africa, 152
Soviet Union, 2, 72, 148, 369, 370
Special Court for Sierra Leone, 132
Special Tribunal for Lebanon, 141n6
Srebrenica massacre, 196, 304, 307
Sri Lanka, 333, 334, 341, 342, 348
Stabilization and Association Agreement (SAA), 194, 195, 196, 199, 200, 201, 432
Stabilization Force, 312, 365, 394, 428
State Court of Bosnia and Herzegovina, 134, 139
state-owned enterprises, 180-82
sterilization of women, 216-17, 224, 225
Stormont, 36, 37, 50
structural adjustment programs, 171, 174-76, 177, 178
Sudan, 55, 59-64
suicide bombers, 324, 325, 366
Sunni Arab Triangle, 318

Tadic, Boris, 199, 200, 201, 203
Taliban, 370, 383
Tamil Makkal Viduthalai Pulikal, 337, 339, 342, 346, 348n2
Tamil Tigers. *See* Liberation Tigers of Tamil Eedam
Taylor, Charles, 132, 133, 138, 140
terrorists, 243, 282
third party intervention, 1, 7, 12, 38, 40, 44, 164, 213, 223, 239; military, 235, 245, 246-51, 253
third party mediation, 20,21, 27-29, 44
third party nation building, 355-66
threats of force from US, 279, 280
trade incentives and sanctions, 147, 153-55, 162, 163
traditional justice, 127-39, 140, 205
transitioning states, 73, 76, 79n19, 178
tribunals, 128-33, 135, 190, 193, 204
Trimble, David, 44, 47
truth and reconciliation commissions, 127, 132, 135

Ulster, 4, 6, 34, 35, 37, 38, 41
United Nations (UN), 7, 11, 23, 25-26
UN Charter, 84, 89, 239
UN General Assembly, 92, 99, 116
UN High Commissioner for Refugees, 426, 430
UN Interim Administration in Kosovo, 424
UN Economic and Social Council, 100
UN Emergency Force, 93
UN Mission in Bosnia-Herzegovina, 426, 430
UN Mission in Kosovo, 9, 74, 134
UN Mission in Sierra Leone, 270
UN Operation in the Congo, 93
UN Operation in Somalia (UNSOM I), 258, 265, 266, 267
UN Operation in Somalia (UNSOM II), 259, 264, 266, 268
UN peacekeeping forces, 8, 10, 60, 259, 266, 344
UN Peacekeeping Operations, 267, 269
UN Protective Force in the former Yugoslavia, 426, 470, 472
UN Security Council, 87, 89, 91, 118, 239, 249, 252, 257; Resolution 713, 295; Resolution 757, 278; Resolution 795, 470; Resolution 1160, 282; Resolution 1199, 283, 284; Resolution 1244, 294
UN Transitional Authority in Cambodia, 425
UN Transitional Administration in East Timor, 424
United Somali Congress, 258
United States Agency for International Development, 70, 220
United States Army Peacekeeping and Stability Operations Institute, 57
United States foreign policy, 40
United States Institute for Peace, 56, 60, 61, 62, 63, 64
United States Navy Sea, Air, Land Units (SEALs), 241
United States State Department Human Rights Country Report, 104, 122n30
United Task Force, 259, 263, 264, 265, 266, 268
Universal Declaration of Human Rights, 87, 105

vehicle born IEDs, 325

walls, 37, 219-20, 223, 226, 229n29

war crimes, 84, 127, 129, 132, 136, 190, 203
War Crimes Chamber, 134, 137
warfare, 1, 2, 242-43
warlords, 258
wealth, as deterrent to conflict, 172, 173
weapon procurement, Iraq, 319
weapons, 243-45, 322, 337-38
Weapons of Mass Destruction (WMD) 241-42, 244, 317
Wilson, Woodrow, 19, 422, 425
Wilsonian NGOs, 465
World Bank, 175, 178, 179
World Development Movement, 175

xenophobia, 215, 226

Yeltsin, Boris, 284
Yugoslavia, 10, 128, 152, 275

About the Contributors

Mohammad Ashraf is an independent consultant. His research interests are in the agricultural, political, and socio-cultural development of Afghanistan. He can be reached at m.ashraf.naimi@gmail.com.

Elham Atashi is an Assistant Professor of peace studies at Goucher College. Her research interests primarily center on post war reconstruction and peace building, peace processes, and transitional justice. She has published on issues relating to transforming armed groups into political parties, bottom-up approaches to peace building, and the role of civil society in reconciliation and conflict transformation, and has worked extensively as a practitioner focusing on peace building on the ground, consulting with various international organizations, and providing training programs and workshops focusing on Northern Ireland, the Middle East, the Balkans, Afghanistan, and South and Central Asia.

Linda S. Bishai is senior program officer in the Academy for International Conflict Management and Peacebuilding at the United States Institute of Peace, where she specializes in higher education and conflict management training in conflict contexts. She has focused on Sudan, but has also worked in Pakistan, Afghanistan, Iraq, and Rwanda. Before coming to the Institute, she was at Towson University, where she taught courses in International Relations, International Law, the Use of Force, and Human Rights. During 2003-2004, she served as a Supreme Court Fellow at the Federal Judicial Center where she worked on an introduction to international human rights law for the Federal Judiciary.

Mieczysław P. Boduszyński is a Foreign Service Officer with the U.S. Department of State. He has served in Albania, Kosovo, Japan, Egypt, and, most recently, Libya. He received his doctorate from the University of California, Berkeley, and is the author of *Regime Change in the Yugoslav Successor States: Divergent Paths toward a New Europe* (Johns Hopkins University Press 2010). DISCLAIMER: The views expressed in his article are those of the author, and do not necessarily reflect those of the United States Department of State or the United States Government.

Steven L. Burg is Adlai E. Stevenson Professor of International Politics, Brandeis University. He is co-author of *The War in Bosnia-Herzegovina: Ethnic Conflict and International Intervention* (M.E.Sharpe, 1999), awarded the 2000 Ralph J. Bunche Prize of the American Political Science Association for "the best scholarly work in political science which explores the phenomenon of ethnic and cultural pluralism." His more recent publications focus on identities and nationalisms in Spain. He served as principal consultant to the project on the South Balkans of the Council on Foreign Relations in New York's Center for Preventive Action, and worked with the Princeton-based international NGO, Project on Ethnic Relations, before becoming Chairman of the Board of Directors of the Council for Inclusive Governance, an international NGO based in New York that works with governments to secure minority inclusion in the Balkans.

Stephen D. Collins is associate professor of Political Science and International Affairs at Kennesaw State University. He earned his PhD in Political Science from the Johns Hopkins University in 2004. Dr. Collins' research and publications focus on the practice of economic statecraft in international politics, especially in the areas of international and internal conflict, democracy and human rights, terrorism, and nuclear proliferation.

Neil Cruickshank is assistant professor of Political Science in the Department of Law and Politics at Algoma University, Canada. A PhD in International Relations from the University of St Andrews, Scotland, he is currently researching Roma nationalism, democracy, and democratization in Eastern Europe, and ethno-politics in Europe and North America. He has an article forthcoming in *Journal of Studies on European Integration and Federalism,* and a chapter, "Judging Europe: Drawing Lessons from the European Court of Human Rights," in a volume on Canadian Supreme Court appointments (McGill—Queen's University Press).

David P. Forsythe is University Professor and Charles J. Mach Distinguished Professor of Political Science, Emeritus, at the University of Nebraska-Lincoln. A Princeton PhD, he has held postdoctoral fellowships at Princeton and Yale, and visiting professorships at universities in Denmark, Ireland, the Netherlands, and Switzerland. He has been a consultant to the International Red Cross and Red Crescent Movement, and to the U.N. Office of the High Commissioner for Refugees. His more than 100 publications include *The Humanitarians: The International Committee of the Red Cross* (Cambridge University Press, 2005); *Human Rights in International Relations* (Cambridge University Press, 2000, translated into Chinese, Turkish, Korean, and Bulgarian; 3rd edition 2012); and *The Politics of Prisoner Abuse: US Policy toward Enemy Prisoners after 9/11* (Cambridge University Press, 2011). He is the General Editor of *The Encyclopedia of Human Rights* (Oxford University Press, 2009, 5 volumes), winner of the Dartmouth Medal for the best reference publication in that year by the American Library Association. A recipient of the Mid-West Section of the International Studies Association's Quincy Wright Distinguished Scholar Award in honor of his lifetime professional achievements, he is widely regarded as having been among the first to help establish the study of human rights and humanitarian affairs in the disciplines of political science and international relations. For this and other roles, the Human Rights Section of the American Political Science Association named him a Distinguished Scholar in 2007, and in 2008 he was awarded the Senior Fulbright Distinguished Research Chair for Human Rights and International Studies at the Danish Institute for International Studies.

Caroline A. Hartzell is a professor of Political Science at Gettysburg College. Her research, which focuses on the effects the terms of civil war settlements have on the post-conflict peace, has been published in the *American Journal of Political Science*, *Conflict Management and Peace Science*, *International Organization*, the *Journal of Conflict Resolution*, and the *Journal of Peace Research*. She is the co-author, with Matthew Hoddie, of *Crafting Peace: Power-Sharing Institutions and the Negotiated Settlement of Civil Wars* (Pennsylvania State University Press, 2008).

Matthew Hoddie is associate professor of political science at Towson University. His work focuses on ethnic politics and post-civil war conflict management. He is co-author of *Crafting Peace: Power-Sharing Institutions and the Negotiated Settlement of Civil Wars* and co-editor of *Strengthening Peace in Post-Civil War States: Transforming Spoilers into Stakeholders* (University of Chicago Press, 2010). His recent articles have appeared in *International Organization* and *International Studies Quarterly*.

Daniela Irrera is assistant professor of Political Science and International Relations at the University of Catania. A PhD recipient in International Relations at the University of Catania, she has been a Research Assistant at Stony Brook University, New York, and a Visiting Fellow at the Clinton Institute for American Studies at the University College, Dublin, Ireland. A member of the executive committee of the Standing Group on Organised Crime, European Consortium for Political Research, she has published two books, two edited books, and several articles in the areas of International Relations and EU politics, global terrorism, trans-national organised crime, civil society, and humanitarian action.

DiJon Jones is the President and CEO of Frontline Homeland Security (FHS), Inc., which specializes in service delivery at the intersection of Defense, Homeland Security, and Public Safety, and provides practitioner-based public safety and homeland security solutions to national security, criminal justice, and corporate agencies. A former Senior International Police Advisor/Criminal Investigations Expert assigned to support the Iraq Training and Advisory Mission, he has served in local and federal law enforcement and is considered an expert in police operations and executive management by the U.S. Department of State, the U.S. Army, and the U.S. National Institute of Justice.

William J. Lahneman is an associate professor of Political Science at Towson University, and a Senior Research Scholar at the Center for International and Security Studies at Maryland (CISSM) at the University of Maryland's School of Public Policy. He holds a PhD in International Relations from the Johns Hopkins University's School of Advanced International Studies, an M.A. in National Security Affairs from the Naval Postgraduate School, and a B.S. from the U. S. Naval Academy. He has held academic positions as Associate Director for Programs at CISSM and as Associate Chair of the Political Science Department at the U.S. Naval Academy. A former U.S. Navy Commander, his publications include *Military Intervention: Cases in Context for the Twenty-first Century* (ed., 2004) and *Keeping U.S. Intelligence Effective: The Need for a Revolution in Intelligence Affairs* (2011).

David D. Laitin is the James T. Watkins, IV and Elise V. Watkins Professor of Political Science at Stanford University. Following his service as a Peace Corps Volunteer in Somalia and Grenada, he received his PhD from the University of California, Berkeley. Over his career he has conducted field research in Somalia, Nigeria, Spain, France, and Estonia focusing on issues of language and religion. A recipient of fellowships from the Howard Foundation, the Rockefeller Foundation, the Guggenheim Foundation, and the Russell Sage Foundation, he has authored numerous books and articles, and over the past decade, mostly in collaboration with James Fearon, his work has also included several papers on ethnicity, ethnic cooperation, the sources of civil war, and on policies that work to settle civil wars.

I. M. Lobo de Souza is a Research Fellow at the Centre for Defence and Security Studies and Lecturer at the Department of Political Studies at the University of Manitoba. He has LL.B. and M.A. degrees from the University of Brasilia and a PhD in International Law from the University of London. A former Chevening Scholar (FCO, UK), he was a Researcher in the Chair for UNESCO on Human Rights and Violence, and co-chaired the research line "Globalization and Human Rights" within the GEDIM–Globalization and Economic Rights in Mercosul (MOST-UNESCO) Program. His research interests include legal responses to the use of force by non-state actors, human rights and humanitarian law, and international peace and security.

Paul T. McCartney is an associate professor at Towson University. He is the author of *Power and Progress: American Nationalism, the War of 1898, and the Rise of American Imperialism* (Louisiana State University Press, 2006) and various articles and chapters on U.S. foreign policy. In addition to his teaching responsibilities, he currently directs the *Towson Journal of International Affairs*, a nationally distributed journal publishing undergraduate and graduate student papers in the field of international and comparative politics.

CAPT Brigid Myers Pavilonis, U.S. Coast Guard, is an associate professor of International Relations at the United States Coast Guard Academy (USCGA), New London, Connecticut. Her research interests include security studies, conflict resolution, and irregular warfare and armed groups. She is a graduate of the U.S. Coast Guard Academy and earned her Masters in Law and Diplomacy and PhD in International Relations from the Fletcher School of Law and Diplomacy at Tufts University.

Victor Peskin is currently an associate professor in the School of Politics and Global Studies at Arizona State University. He received his doctorate in political science from the University of California, Berkeley, and specializes in the politics of international war crimes tribunals and transitional justice. In addition to his journal articles in the field of human rights, he is the author of *International Justice in Rwanda and the Balkans: Virtual Trials and the Struggle for State Cooperation* (Cambridge University Press, 2008).

Mateja Peter is currently a Transatlantic Post-doctoral Fellow at the German Institute for International and Security Affairs in Berlin, following her recent internship at the United States Institute of Peace. She pursued her PhD studies at the University of Cambridge on the topic "Constructing international authority: the international administration of Bosnia and Herzegovina." Her interests lie in peace and state-building, and the politics of military intervention. Her current work explores sustained third-party engagements, the politics of peace-building, and exit strategies for state-building operations.

James DeShaw Rae is an associate professor of Government at California State University, Sacramento. A former intern at the United States Institute of Peace and a Fulbright Scholar in China during 2011-12, his most recent book is *Peacebuilding and Transitional Justice in East Timor* (Lynne Rienner, 2009).

Joseph R. Rudolph, Jr., received his Ph.D. from the University of Virginia, is currently a professor of Political Science at Towson University, has served as a Fulbright appointee to Czechoslovakia (1991-2) and Kosovo (2011-2), and has published in the field of ethnic and nationalist politics for more than 30 years. He has also frequently been a part of the democratization operations of the Organization for Security and Cooperation in Europe (OSCE) in areas of the former Yugoslavia since 1997. His more recent work includes *The Encyclopedia of Modern Ethnic Conflicts* (ed., 2003), *Politics and Ethnicity: A Comparative Study* (2006), and *Hotspots in North America and Europe* (2008).

M. S. Wallace is Hood House Lecturer in International Affairs at the University of New Hampshire, where she teaches courses on war and political violence, nonviolent action, the ethics of war and peace, and global politics. She taught previously at Brown University after earning her PhD in Political Science at Brown, and has conducted research in Sri Lanka and Rwanda on NGOs working in the areas of civilian peacekeeping and peace-building.

Samuel Whitt is currently an assistant professor of Political Science at High Point University. A Fulbright Scholar in Kosovo in 2010-11, he worked in the United States Department of State before joining the faculty at High Point. DISCLAIMER: The views expressed in his article are those of the author, and do not necessarily reflect those of the United States Department of State or the United States Government.

Donald R. Zoufal is currently a Safety and Security Industry executive with System Development Integration, LLC. He has held a series of high-level public sector safety and security posts, including First Deputy for the City of Chicago's Office of Emergency Management and Communications and Deputy Commissioner for Safety and Security for the City of Chicago's Department of Aviation. He is a retired Colonel in the US Army Reserve. Mr. Zoufal received two graduate degrees from the University of Illinois in law and public administration. He also has obtained a Master of Arts in Security Studies from the U.S. Department of Homeland Security sponsored Center for Homeland Defense and Security at the Naval Postgraduate School in Monterey, California, with a focus on emerging security technologies.